IMAGES OF AMERICAN LIVING

*Four Centuries
of Architecture and Furniture
as Cultural Expression*

BY ALAN GOWANS

ICON EDITIONS

HARPER & ROW, PUBLISHERS

NEW YORK, HAGERSTOWN, SAN FRANCISCO, LONDON

To My American Children

PETER and JANE, born in New Jersey
JOHN, born in Vermont
ABIGAIL, born in Delaware

A hardcover edition of this book was published by J. B. Lippincott Company. It is here reprinted by arrangement.

First Icon Edition published in 1976.

ISBN: 0-06-730072-2

76 77 10 9 8 7 6 5 4 3 2 1

Acknowledgments

THIS BOOK was begun in 1958 on a Summer Faculty Fellowship
from the University of Delaware Research Council; it was completed
during the summer of 1962. Over this period I have had the assistance of all kinds of correspondents in all kinds of ways; I wish it
were possible to thank each of them personally, and I hope my letters
have expressed something of my gratitude. In particular I want to
express my appreciation to Charles F. Montgomery, former director
of the Henry Francis du pont Winterthur Museum, for his early
encouragement; to Dr. John M. Dawson, Director of the University
of Delaware Libraries; to John Maass of Philadelphia for so gener-
ously providing me with some of the illustrations from his *Gingerbread Age*; to Dean A. Fales of the Essex Institute and Joseph T.
Butler of Sleepy Hollow Restorations; and not least to my wife,
so patient and so cheerful a "paper widow" for so long.

A. G.

Newark, Delaware
August 13, 1962

Contents

CONTENTS

VICTORIAN AMERICA: THE 19TH CENTURY

CONTENTS

20TH-CENTURY MAN and 20TH-CENTURY ART IN THE UNITED STATES

Preface

THERE are many ways of looking at architecture and furniture, past and present, in the United States.

One is the antiquarian's, the way of people fascinated with old things as such—Mrs. Louisa Caroline Huggins Tuthill, first historian of American architecture, going "in 'search of the picturesque' through the beautiful villages of New England" more than a century ago; John Fanning Watson, even earlier than that, eagerly and lovingly collecting relics tangible and legendary of "famous men and our fathers who begat us" for his *Annals of Philadelphia*; the modern housewife poking around a junk yard for some "conversation piece" redolent of the past. Another is the way of all those diverse artists, from elegant eclectics like McKim, Mead, and White, and the compilers of the *White Pine Series* to the lowliest speculative "developer" and purveyor of "unpainted early American furniture" who, however shallowly or deeply, mine the heritage of the past for present purposes. A third is the cultural historian's—the way of Lewis Mumford and Thomas Jefferson Wertenbaker and the rest, who study and interpret what earlier generations built and made and left behind in terms of all those forces—economic, political, religious, technological—that shaped the lives of societies and the individuals in them. Then there is the way of the research scholar—hunting out documents and data, compiling lists of furniture labels and comparative motifs in ornament, checking local legend against deeds in the county courthouse and traditional assumptions against ascertainable fact. And finally there are the people who just like to look at architecture because they find it pretty, or impressive, or picturesque, or whatever.

All these are valid approaches.

The antiquarian's indiscriminate passion for snuff boxes and statues, for the porticos of Monticello and umbrella stands made from the feet of elephants shot by Teddy Roosevelt, may seem amusing or ridiculous at times, but only a barren spirit could find such instincts contemptible or such activities negligible: "That man is little to be envied," as Dr. Johnson once said, "whose patriotism would not gain force upon the plain of Marathon, or whose piety would not grow warmer among the ruins of Iona"; and without the loving collections of early antiquarians, how much would be left for cultural historian or artist to study? If we must condemn the Colonial Revivalists, then let us condemn their lack of imagination, not their drawing on the past as such, which Frank Lloyd Wright also did. Though cultural historians' generalizations may sometimes seem too sweeping, suited better to lemmings than men, yet their shrewd insights and illuminating analogies can rescue appreciation from degenerating into an esoteric affair of cabrioles and cabochons and comparative cornice mouldings, bring life into art history, and art history to life. As for the scholar, if he is pedantic he is also indispensable; on his patient fact-finding collectors, connoisseurs, and cultural historians ultimately depend.

For a complete historical picture of architecture and furniture in the United States we need something of all these diverse approaches; and we need the complete historical picture now as never before. For never before has interest in American history been so vital and urgent. People everywhere—in Europe, in Asia, in Africa—have a new interest in learning something of the background and character of this nation which, after centuries of standing more or less alone, so suddenly emerged as leader of the Western community; Americans themselves, no less aware of the dramatic change in their national image and role, have begun to study their own origins, ends, and purposes with a new intensity, and above all a new comprehensiveness. They have begun to realize the complexity of American history as earlier generations rarely did—how many and how diverse the threads woven into its still far from set pattern. And they have realized as never before, too, how much that history is embodied in American architecture and furniture—by nature arts which represent the collective efforts and ideals of a civilization. Affected by economic conditions, social structure, climate, technology, religious beliefs, and tides of fashionable taste to a degree rare in more individualistic arts like painting or sculpture, architecture and furniture are history in its most tangible form.

To understand American—or any—architecture and furniture you must see them as a whole. You have to circle round the subject, approach it from many points of view. You have to consider examples individually, as they express the taste and outlook of the particular people who made and used them. You have to consider them collectively, as revealing in their common characteristics the national origins and fundamental ways of life in diverse states and regions. Above all, you need to see the broad patterns in their over-all historical development; for it is as they express the evolution of civilization as a whole that American architecture and furniture are most significant.

Until quite recent times, most of the forms of American architecture and furniture were obviously borrowed from elsewhere. Neither have

there been until fairly recently any really great or seminal figures on that scene—no Berninis or Wrens or Gibbses, not even a Chippendale or an Adam or a Pugin. To be sure, there has always been a certain quality we might call an "American spirit"—put all the derivative elements together, and the result has been something more than the sum of borrowed parts, something recognizably American; but it has been undeniably vague, elusive, almost indefinable. From the beginning, however, there have been patterns of development in American architecture and furniture that at once grow from and express the fundamental character, aspirations, and moods of historic American civilization.

In architecture and furniture has been manifest a pattern of basic traditions, evolving with the centuries, which reflects the evolving relationship of America to Europe. First the "medieval mind" of the 17th century, transported here by the diverse peoples who first settled the Atlantic coast from Massachusetts Bay to Florida, each of whose arts has a history of its own. Then the "classical mind" of the 18th century, embodied in architecture and furniture evidencing those principles of precision, self-containment, and measured control of environment which were at once vehicle for and expression of the urge for unity which transformed scattered colonies and provinces into united states. Next, the three successive phases of that characteristic "literary" concept of art as a set of forms to be read, of "styles" taken as symbols for ideas, which we call Victorian—a cultural rather than a chronological epoch, beginning early in the 19th century, and persisting well into the 20th, in the course of which is reflected the growth of a nation from Arcadian simplicity to cosmopolitan world power. (In 1832 Mrs. Trollope felt about the United States Capitol as Johnson about a dog's walking erect—amazed not so much that the thing was done well, as that it was done in America at all; a century later the *New Yorker* was publishing cartoons of American tourists in

France equally amazed to find, "You have Burgundy here too?") Finally, the three phases, or more exactly generations, of "modern" architecture in the United States—from the time of the "pioneers of the modern movement" in the 1890s and early 1900s who overlapped into the Late Victorian period and shared many of its qualities, through the violent anti-Victorian reaction represented by the "International Style" of the 1920s and 30s, to the new developments after World War II—collectively marking emergence of the nation from isolationism to a position of leadership in the Western world.

The pattern of progressive conquest over nature can also be seen, from the time men first faced this wilderness with primitive iron tools to the age of jet travel and electronic computers. There is the pattern of social change, from homestead and self-contained plantation to megalopolis. There is the pattern of changing concepts of the nature of art and architecture, from the idea that the artist's proper concern is with beauty (however that may be defined) to the dogma that he ought to express the reality of himself and his work (whatever *that* may be). Finally, the history of architecture and furniture reflects a pattern of evolving democracy, political and economic—both the ideal of raising the whole cultural level of a population en masse, to create a society like none seen in the world before, a nation without peasants or hereditary aristocrats, whose every citizen would be a responsible and contributing member; and something of the cost in folly, perversity, and vulgarity the pursuit of life,

liberty, and happiness by the "common man" has often entailed.

It is with patterns like these that we will be primarily concerned here. Limited in size as it is, this book is not intended to be anything like an encyclopaedia of American buildings and furnishings. What it tries to do is no more than suggest the broad patterns of development in American architecture and furniture, how selected monuments fit into them, and how in that setting they may be read as a living and tangible record of the course of American civilization. And perhaps this is justification enough.

For in its patterns is the key to history. Outside their context, individual facts—whether documents or buildings or furnishings—float like objects in interstellar space, with no means of our determining what is up or down. Only as we see them within broader patterns can we begin to understand what we see; and only as we understand what we are seeing can we learn history. Knowing the patterns, we know history. "Who controls the past controls the present; who controls the present controls the future"—we may not want to control the future in the sense meant by the rulers of *Nineteen Eighty-Four*, but knowledge of history is a great protection against those who might. And above all, to know history is to know ourselves: "Humanity," as C. S. Lewis once wrote, "does not pass through phases as a train passes through stations. . . . Whatever we have been, in some sort we are still." *

---

* *Allegory of Love*, Chap. I.

CHANGING PATTERNS OF AMERICAN LIVING

ABOVE:

This white frame Greek Revival house on the Plymouth Road east of Ann Arbor, Michigan, is a representative symbol of the Republic of the late 1840's when it was built—small, absolutely and in relative scale, as the nation still was in relation to the great European powers; simple, in forms and materials, as the rural economy its builders knew. In this distinctive regional "basilica" variant of Greek Revival house, with "nave" and "side aisles," the characteristic independence of spirit in that age is manifested; in the self-contained classical outline and plan, its characteristic self-sufficiency of personal life and national isolation from Great-Power entanglements.

FACING PAGE:

A very different kind of American living is imaged in the complex of buildings that makes up Rockefeller Center, thrusting up from the maze of steel and glass and masonry that is mid-Manhattan. All that can be seen of the old America are the towers of St. Patrick's on Fifth Avenue which were designed in the 1850's to dominate the New York skyline but now seem shrunken and swallowed up by the soaring embodiments of international economic, social, and technological power that surround them on every side—the International Building directly opposite, with its flanking companions the Palazzo d'Italia, the British Empire Building, and La Maison Française; the RCA building (center); the General Dynamics Building (extreme left, at 48th Street) and the Sinclair Oil Building next it; the Eastern Airlines Building and the U.S. Rubber Company Building on the Avenue of the Americas (left background); the Esso Building (far right); the Time & Life Building (upper right background).

MEDIEVAL AMERICA:
THE 17th CENTURY

THE 17TH CENTURY in America was above all an age of diversity. It was the age when the various peoples of Western Europe—French, Dutch, English, and the rest—were most actively transplanting their national cultures across the Atlantic. With them was transplanted, too, something of the whole successive historical experience of the Old World—the primeval struggle with nature, the improving technology of an Iron Age, immemorial folkways, the feudal society of lords and serfs, authoritarian rule by divine hereditary right, capitalism of small city-states, Reformation mysticism and religious autarchy, the rise of representative parliamentary government. Running through all this diversity, however, was a common thread, a medieval tradition which all these cultures shared. To a greater or lesser degree, all of them represented not the modern Europe that was emerging in the 17th century, but an older, medieval world that lived on in the strata of society which had largely settled the new colonies; hence, "medieval America."

By the end of the century, other national traditions were rapidly being subsumed under the dominant English, and their common medieval heritage overlaid by the very different principles of a nascent classical age. The culture whose foundations had then been established was more than English; deriving something from many sources, it was yet distinct from all; it was already American. And like an unseen star deflecting planets from their courses, its underlying medieval foundation long continued to affect the later evolution of civilization in America. A predilection for standardization; faith in mass education; a cult of the out-of-doors and a cult of vulgarity; churches as social instruments; a mystic "organic" attitude to nature; noble idealism and a streak of foolish gullibility—how much these and other characteristics of 20th-century American life may owe to 17th-century beginnings could hardly be proven. Certain it is, however, that we shall see something like them first developing and finding tangible expression in the architecture and furniture of this early, medieval America.

1. BACKGROUND:
Arts of Survival on Stone and Iron Age Frontiers

ARCHITECTURE, furniture, and civilization begin in America—as they begin everywhere else, at all times—with men facing raw nature, trying to find shelter, comfort, security. Wherever and whenever there is a frontier, it is the same. Massachusetts pioneers having to "burrow themselves in the Earth for their first shelter under some Hillside" at Salem, "casting the Earth aloft upon Timber" to make their "poore Wigwames" in 1626. Kansas pioneers two and a half centuries later, throwing together houses of prairie sod. The founders of Jamestown, whose "walls were rales of wood, our seats unhewed trees," whose church was a "homely thing like a barne set upon Cratchets [crotched poles] covered with rafts, sedge, and earth." "Those Adventurous Men whose ambition is to make a home . . . and fortune in any location and with whatever means nature may supply," for whom C. P. Dwyer's *Immigrant Builder* of 1872 explained "how to plan and construct dwellings in the bush, on the prairie, or elsewhere . . . in Wood, Earth, and Gravel," make table legs from "the perfectly straight limbs of any tree" and chairs from "sticks of ash . . . the pieces should be an inch and a half or two inches thick, and should have the bark peeled off. . . ." Philadelphia's first settlers, sheltering in caves along the Delaware riverbank. Hunters in forest clearings of Kentucky and Ohio hastily assembling crude cabins

1. STONE AND IRON AGE BUILDING

(A) Chapel built for the Indians by French Jesuit missionaries at Vincennes, Indiana, early 18th century. Employing poteaux *construction (= upright logs set together for walls), with smoke from a central fire escaping through a* hole in the bark roof, this crude 18th-century building closely resembles an Indian long house in forms, plan, and materials. Wherever men met raw North American wilderness without the tools of civilization, they had to begin on the Stone Age cultural level, with rude shelters like this.*

against the winter. Alaskan miners squatting in frail shacks of poles and blankets. Everywhere civilization in America begins with a brief, embryonic recapitulation of architectural history. Always, moving on to new frontier places meant moving back in time to earlier, more primitive worlds.

The frontier meant first returning to a kind of Stone Age, facing nature unprepared, with a few crude tools, as the Indians had. It meant building as they did, not "architecture" in the proper sense of man organizing and controlling an environment to suit his material and psychological needs, but more like birds piecing a nest together, or beavers piling up dams; caves and huts and wigwams taking form far less from human will or pleasure than at the raw dictates of nature—bark and poles in the forest, hides and sod on the plains, desert rock and adobe. It meant reliving, however briefly, those long ages

of prehistory when nature, not man, was in command.

To Stone succeeds an Age of Iron. Now men learn the proper tools to meet forest and desert; with axes, hammers, saws, they shape trees into timber, mould bricks from clay, chip fieldstone foundations and fireplaces. This is the age (depending on place and time) of plank and shingle, of "half-timber" construction, of the log cabin, of "balloon" framing with two-by-fours and nails. In it the raw materials of nature, though still very much in evidence, are increasingly brought under man's control. But technology is still elementary. The Iron Age knows few specialists; any man, with no special training, can perform all the simple operations necessary to build cabins of logs, wattle-and-daub cottages, or plank benches. When specialists—carpenters, thatchers, joiners, masons—do appear, when some kind of choice can be exercised over arrangement, proportion, and shapes of elements, the buildings of an Iron Age melt immediately, imperceptibly, into folk architecture; faint yet distinct outlines of diverse national tastes and traditions come into evidence; the history of American art proper begins. In any given place, the whole process takes but an instant of history. It is over almost before it has begun.

Yet in another, wider sense, the Stone and Iron Ages never end. A century after the last bark-and-log and wattle-and-daub shelter on the coast has rotted into ruin, their like reappears in rude forts on the foothills of the Appalachians, *poteaux* construction in the Mississippi Valley; a century after that, in the log cabins of the old North-West Territory, then in sod houses on the Great Plains; even today, among hunters in the woods and small boys playing in backyard huts and tree-forts, the Stone and Iron Ages in architecture live on.

In furniture, their survival is more tangible still. By the 1680s, when John Ward built his house in Salem, the old wigwams were long gone from Massachusetts Bay; pioneer days were a fading memory for the craftsmen who framed the hall and parlor and family chambers of the Ward house, and the furniture in them, with a conscious eye to traditional style and taste. But the forms of those early epochs still lived on in the obscurity of kitchen, servants' quarters, and other out-of-the-way places, where, following a cycle operating from times immemorial to our own, whatever older furnishings the family had come to possess were relegated. Stools like the slabs of wood standing on three or four rough-hewn sticks around this servants' table might well have been made by the wigwam builders. Wood and rushes are shaped almost as directly to their use in these simple ladder-back chairs as in woven baskets or thatched half-timber and plank houses. The crude shelves hanging from these rafters, even manufactured items like pewter and earthenware and iron utensils, all take almost the same line of least resistance to utility

as their precedents in Jamestown or Plymouth.

Move on now to the log cabin in New Salem, Illinois. Logs and clay chinking instead of studs and plank, a few evidences of early American industrialization like the Connecticut-type clock on the fireplace, tell us it is a century and a half later, a thousand miles and five new states to the westward; but essentially, it is the same timeless thing. The youth who visited and studied in this cabin went on to be sixteenth president of a Union not even imagined when the kitchen of the Ward house first took form, yet the same spirit informs the furnishings of both. Here are chairs built in the same straightforward way of rushes and slats and poles, beds and spinning wheel with the same bulbous turnings of vaguely Elizabethan or Jacobean suggestion, plain earthenware and simple utensils of tin and iron. On again to the stove, lamps, toilet set, crib, chairs, table of the Kansas sod house in the 1880s. The United States is now on the way to becoming one

---

(1 B) A house at Jamestown, Virginia, c.1620. In its straightforward use of materials— thatch, rough-hewn timbers, chimney of wood and wattle smeared with clay—this structure still vividly recalls the primitive Stone Age shelters Captain John Smith described from Jamestown's early days. But quite as clearly it belongs to a later Iron Age, when men have tools—still simple, but adequate—better to shape nature to their will; and it already looks forward to the succeeding age of folk architecture.

of the world's great industrial nations, and these are "store-boughten," not handmade, pieces. But still the rush-bottomed chair stands in the corner; still, as we look beyond superficial surfaces, we can recognize everywhere the same plain timeless utilitarian quality of "country" furniture —furnishings, that is to say, with no style as such, belonging to no particular tradition and no precise time, like the plastic dishes and "everyday silver" you still find in 20th-century kitchen cupboards. In this timeless, universal expression of the lowest common denominator of American taste the Stone and Iron Ages have lasted for centuries. And not alone in forms; even more,

we find them throughout American history subtly influencing what we think of as characteristic ends, means, and attitudes in American art.

They affected first the very concept of what art is. The Stone and Iron Ages were the childhood of American civilization, that indefinable time of life when accents and attitudes are established which no amount of later refinement disguises, which come out in unexpected moments of stress, which go on coloring value judgments throughout life, on which depend the ultimate success or failure of cartoonists and commentators, of politicians and "hidden persuaders." And these ages, persisting on the moving frontier,

2. FRONTIER SHRINES

(A) Lincoln homestead, near Springfield, Kentucky. In essence, the log cabin is a very simple version of "half-timber" technique—the structural members in this case being more roughly shaped and notched, set horizontally only, and the fill between them less visually obvious. Considered as cultural expression, then, it is beside the point whether (as Harold R. Shurtleff maintained in his 1938 Log Cabin Myth*) English settlers learned log-cabin building only*

from the Swedes on the Delaware, or (as those believe who find it incredible no Englishman, in a land covered with trees, ever thought of laying one log on another) they invented the form independently. The significant thing is that by the time this cabin was built log construction was the normal and universal frontier type in forest areas; that it is the best expression of America's Iron Age, being fashioned entirely with one sharp tool, the axe; and that it has long been the cult object of one of America's great myths, symbol of rugged Americanism.

impressed on successive generations of Americans an unconscious conviction that waste motion—activity serving no obvious practical ends—was folly, if not actual wickedness; that "art" was this kind of activity—an extraneous indulgence to be reserved for easy times and luxurious people; that, in short, "art" was one thing and "life" another.

At first, when the frontier was new, this attitude was weak and soon overlain by older traditions transplanted from Europe. From Governor Bradford's time to the days of Washington and Jefferson it could still be taken for granted in America that acquaintance with the arts was a normal part of a full life. But with the Revolution came a formal break with Old World habits of mind, followed at once by a mass migration—not, like the original one that peopled the seaboard, in boats that could carry the physical setting of culture like furniture or glass or pottery and even bricks and window frames with it, but overland, across the mountains, in wagons whose cultural baggage (to all intents and purposes) was limited to books. The result, inevitably, was to bring the frontier attitude to art closer to the surface. By the 1850s you can see it very well in the comparison between a man like Lincoln and his Virginian predecessors. Their equal in command of language and the basic ideas of Western civilization, in moral stature, in native intelligence, he may well have been; but of their concern for architecture, for furniture, for gardening, for music as integral parts of life, he has next to nothing. Even at the busiest times of their lives Washington and Jefferson are always sending home directions for furnishing and embellishing their homes, storing away ideas for future decorating reference: Lincoln, when he comes back from a circuit to find his little wooden house in Springfield remodeled, does no more than stare in mock astonishment, and wonder quizzically, who lives here in such magnificence? And how could it be otherwise? In his formative years at New Salem, he could stock his mind from the Bible, from Blackstone, from Burns, but for his eye and ear there had been little or nothing; all that side of

(2 B) Main street of Virginia City, Montana, as reconstructed from 1946 on. Despite all the color and remembrance of crimes past that intrigue modern visitors to what Collier's Magazine, *in a burst of malapropism, once called the "Williamsburg of the West," the city's original settlers had no sooner passed beyond Stone Age prospectors' tents and huts to the plain frame and log structures of an Iron Age, than they wanted to "add" the beauties of civilization back east; this they did, quite literally, by constructing false fronts with cornices, pseudo-Palladian windows, and even classical porticos.*

culture had been left behind as impedimenta.

It is no accident that (as we shall see) the most genuinely "popular" art America has ever known is what we technically call Victorian. The theory of Victorian art, essentially, is that their decoration makes architecture and furniture "beautiful," hence that "utilitarian" objects without decoration (like factories or machines) cannot be art; that this decoration need have no integral connection, structural or otherwise, with the thing it "beautifies," hence that art is something you can put on or leave off at will. By the mid-19th century this was a concept enthusiastically accepted by the great mass of people everywhere in America as no other has been before or since. The "false front" is a typical architectural example. When you think of a Midwest main street or a Far West mining town, even today, what comes first to mind is a row of rectangular boxes, each sporting a great flat façade like a stage backdrop, which has no relation to the structure behind, and is obviously added for effect, at equally obvious pains and expense. This was not a regional expression, however; the Western builders were only trying, like new settlers everywhere, to imitate main streets in the cities "back East." And it would be absurd to pretend that as universal an expression as the false front—or the Victorian "merchants' blocks" with their attached cornices and window framings that still make up the core of most American towns, or for that matter the earlier American enthusiasm for wrapping unpretentious structures in envelopes of extraneous Doric colonnades or Gothic lacework—proceeded from consciously held "Victorian" theories. Then as now, few Americans held any conscious theories about any kind of art whatever. It was simply that to the great mass of 19th-century Americans the "Victorian" concept of art had come to seem self-evidently right. It corresponded precisely to the attitude towards art as something "extra," something apart from utility, instilled by the continuing frontier experience.

Now the frontier and the Victorian age proper both are gone. But we could hardly say either is forgotten. Think of the corner grocer who sincerely believes he can make his shoebox of a store into a thing of beauty and a joy forever by spraying its walls with imitation stonework from an air gun. Think of the stubborn resistance there has always been in this country to acceptance of functional expression in its own right—the insistence on making steel-and-concrete structures "beautiful" by wrapping them in tiers of ornamental columns, Gothic spires and

buttresses, or (more recently) elegantly abstract, decorative screens. Think further—and this is the most dismally pertinent example—for how many Americans "culture" still means something you "get" by attending plays, concerts, art exhibitions, and the like; to how few the thought occurs that it might be the other way round, that liking for paintings and books and intellectual adventure generally might be the manifestation of a good mind, not its peripheral embellishment. It seems, according to W. H. Whyte's *Organization Man*, that in the personality test given prospective employees by a great American corporation in the 1950s, not only was 0 an entirely acceptable percentile in the "aesthetic values" category, but a score higher than 10, which might indicate the acceptance of "artistic beauty and taste as a fundamental standard of life," was highly suspect. It was not so much that these unfortunates might be maladjusted socially, as simply that "cultural considerations are not important to Sears executives, and there is evidence that such interests are detrimental to success." And where was this evidence? Ultimately, it originates in the American Stone Age. It comes from the old frontier experience of art as a useless and dangerous distraction, an extraneous ornament not growing naturally out of life, but artificially added to it.

Just as subtly and continuously as it affected American ideas of what art is, the frontier influenced what kind of art Americans would characteristically produce.

"It was near a whole year," wrote 'Robinson Crusoe', "before I had entirely finished my little pale or surrounded habitation . . . , raised rafters from it leading to the rock, and thatched or covered it with boughs of trees and such things as I could to keep out the rain. . . . And now I began to apply myself to make such necessary things as I found I most wanted, as particularly a chair and table. . . . I had never handled a tool in my life, yet in time by labor, application, and contrivance I found at last that I wanted nothing but I could have made it. . . ."

3. Kitchen of the John Ward house, Salem, Massachusetts, c.1684. By the time this pretentious manor-type house was built, older American communities like Salem had long passed out of their Stone and Iron Ages. But in the unselfconscious obscurity of attics, cellars, and kitchens, older forms lingered on; the interior of the 1620 Jamestown house (1 B) might well have looked much like this.

Robinson Crusoe is, among other things, an allegory. It is an allegory of man's ancient dream of starting life wholly afresh in an entirely new and unspoiled world, the more vivid because when Defoe was writing there were men still living whose grandfathers had done precisely that, who had come to a completely raw wilderness with only the sparsest tools of civilization, had broken its power, and made a new and successful life for themselves in it. By the time Defoe was writing, that first phase was over, and daring men could imagine even more wonderful things. For years Crusoe kept watching for ships from the Old World, in hopes they would end his predicament, but when at last they came it was he and not they who did the rescuing, he who set their affairs to rights; just so, perhaps, it was now possible to conceive a day when the Old World might depend on the New. . . . But their frontier experience would go on affecting the way Americans worked for centuries to come.

Among the earliest migrants to New England and Virginia, as among the earliest settlers in Kansas, Utah, and California, there was certainly a fair proportion of men specially and thoroughly trained in particular crafts like chairmaking or glazing or bricklaying, as there were men bred up to law and theology and belles-

9

4. *Interior of the Jack Kelso cabin, in the re-constructed village of New Salem, Illinois, as it was in the 1830s. When Lincoln came to New Salem, in 1831, the settlement was only three years old, and by the time he left in 1839 to practice law in Springfield, it was already mori-* *bund; with the county seat being established at Petersburg in 1841, it was practically abandoned. After the site had been acquired by the State of Illinois in 1906, restoration of its thirteen cabins and miscellaneous buildings (tavern, school, stores, etc.) was begun in 1932.*

lettres. But on each successive New World frontier it took many decades for labor to become plentiful enough for anyone to confine himself to any one specialty. Like Crusoe on his island, everybody in these new communities had to do a bit of everything. Lawyers had to prepare account books as well as briefs; poetesses had to keep house; ministers had to farm; artisans had to be jacks-of-all-trades. The man who made tables had also to make rafters and looms and sledges; the blacksmith had to turn out hinges and ornamental ironwork as well as nails and

gun barrels. One result was that no matter how well he knew his job, no craftsman had the time for sophisticated finishing touches. All the subtler graces of life dropped away; and once lost, they are not easily or entirely recovered. Even when New World populations and leisure progressed to the point where finer elaboration was possible again, a tendency to straightforwardness and plainness persisted. It was not so much that versatility had been demanded and rewarded too long, as that Old World systems of apprenticeship simply could not be carried on. You could not hold young men to the six or seven years' training maintained in Europe. Why should they spend two or three more years mastering fine points they might never use, when it was so easy to set up a thriving business for themselves simply by moving to the next town or the next colony? Society did not exactly condone the practice; until well past the Revolution American newspapers were full of advertisements demanding the return of apprentices run away before their time. But as long as the labor shortage continued —as long, that is, as there was a frontier to absorb surplus population—society could do little about it.

Three related tendencies followed, which to a greater or lesser extent have characterized American civilization ever since. One encouraged a certain inventive improvisation ("I found at last I wanted nothing but I could have made it"), a penchant for labor-saving devices of one sort or another. A second encouraged a general simplification that distinguished American-made arts from their European counterparts; it may well have contributed to a curious conviction, long held in Europe, that the American environment somehow had a deleterious effect on everything. But the most important result, at least for American art, was the encouragement of standardization. From very early times training and circumstance led American craftsmen to reduce the variants and differences among their inherited European models to a few common denominators. In consequence, American art history often shows a curious reversal of what might seem its

---

5. Interior of a sod house of the 1880s at Colby, Kansas, as reconstructed in the Kansas State Historical Museum, Topeka. True sod houses like this, where even the roof consisted of sod blocks, are more characteristic of the second pioneer generation of the 1870s and 80s than of the first wave on the Great Plains. Like log cabins, sod houses were intended to last a number of years (six or seven was the average) and had furnishings which, while still sternly utilitarian, were often manufactured.

normal or predictable pattern of evolution.

Thinking (as our century habitually does) in "scientific" terms, we tend to assume that the one-celled buildings and uncomplicated furnishings of America's Stone and Iron Ages were like those simple organisms from which, in biological evolution, later and more complicated types developed by a natural process of accretion and growth. But in fact nothing "grows" from them in this way. Their forms and function remain constant over generations and centuries. What actually happens is quite the opposite. First-generation immigrants from the Old World brought with them from the complex and highly developed societies they had left a rich variety of building types and art forms. For example, in the *Description of the Province of New Albion* which Sir Edmund Plowden published in 1648 as a promotional pamphlet for the colony he had been trying to establish in New Jersey since 1634, six distinct building types are listed which, he says, were commonly used by new settlers in all the English colonies; they range all the way from Stone Age shelters ("an 'Arbour' of poles and bark boards") to such advanced types as "a brick house or square tower three stories high," and include—significantly enough in view of the current dogma that log cabins were unknown to the English—"a log house of young trees, 30. foot square notched in at corners." Second-generation Americans did not carry on such diversity, however. Instead of expanding and developing these types, they eliminated and simplified them, so much so that of all the many early varieties of architecture and furniture introduced in the first half of the 17th century, only a very few were perpetuated into the second. And it was the same for generations to come. Not really until the last third of the 19th century, when the United States began to attain full intellectual, social, and economic equality with the older nations of Europe, did American artists begin to produce their own new types and variants of architecture and furniture, as distinct from simplified and standardized versions of inherited

models. Until then, what was distinctively American about architecture and furniture in America was primarily that treatment and use made of borrowings from Europe which go back to the Stone and Iron Age beginnings of American history.

Finally, it is from that early subworld of wigwam and plank, cabin and kitchen, that there comes much of that elusive quality we call the "spirit" of American art and life. We today, living in a society where nature is so largely a servant, can hardly imagine what nature as a master might be like. We are only intermittently aware of nature's ceaseless hostility to man, and it more annoys than frightens us to think how she combats our works—how relentlessly the pipes rust, the grass grows, the bugs multiply, the paint peels, wood rots, and concrete crumbles. But if we have only a dim idea how our ancestors felt facing raw nature directly and inadequately prepared, so too we can only dimly share the thrill they felt in personally conquering her. However much we may admire the pioneers' fortitude and appreciate their sufferings, we have to envy them, too. For theirs was a unique opportunity. How seldom in the history of the world does it fall to men to see civilization literally take shape before their eyes, by the work of their own hands! Few frontiersmen were much given to contemplation—they would hardly have lasted on the frontier if they were; but surely as they looked around a new forest clearing, over freshly plowed prairie land or a Far West boom town, men felt a deep, unique satisfaction at the thought of their conquest of nature. Certainly those who immediately followed them expressed it often enough: "The Progressive Improvements . . . of the British Settlements in North America" is *the* great theme of early American writing. "Let them produce any colonie or commonwealth in the world where more hath beene done in 16 yeares," boasted the magistrates of Massachusetts Bay in 1646. A century later, in his *Travels through the Middle Settlements in North America,* Andrew Burnaby contemplated the site of Philadelphia, so recently a "wild and uncultivated desert, inhabited by nothing but ravenous beasts, and a savage people," and reflected, "Can the mind have a greater pleasure than . . . in perceiving a rich and opulent state arising out of a small settlement or colony. This pleasure everyone must feel who considers Pennsylvania." Theodore Roosevelt felt it when he wrote *The Winning of the West* in the 1880s: "The spread of the English-speaking peoples over the world's waste space," he thought, was "the most striking feature of the world's history." This spirit of pride, of confidence and optimism engendered on the frontier, was never

lost. As we shall see, it predisposed Americans in favor of the confident order of classical forms throughout the 18th century; it burst out in 19th-century Victorian exuberance; it informs much of the 20th-century American attempt to raise the entire cultural level of a nation en masse. Historically, the Stone and Iron Ages were no more than a brief introduction, a prelude to the development of architecture and furniture in the United States. But they were an essential beginning, a prelude in which may be detected themes from every subsequent age in American civilization.

NOTES

Notes here and following other chapters are not intended to provide a full bibliography, but simply to give sources of quotations and references, and suggestions for further reading. Place of publication is New York, unless otherwise indicated. *JSAH: Journal of the Society of Architectural Historians.*

Quotations on early Salem from Edward Johnson, *History of New-England from the English planting in the Yeere 1628 untill the Yeere 1652* (London, 1653–1654); on Jamestown, from John Smith, *Advertisements for the unexperienced Planters of New England, or anywhere* (London, 1631). The revealing *Description of the Province of New Albion* by Sir Edmund Plowden, which deserves to be better known, is summarized in *JSAH*, XV, 3, 1956, p. 2.

Charles P. Dwyer's *Immigrant Builder, or, Practical Hints to Handy-Men* was published in Philadelphia in 1872, and went through ten editions. Dwyer was typical of those many obscure architectural writers whose influence on ordinary American 19th-century building was literally incalculable. It would be impossible to say how much the vogue for cobblestone architecture in Upper New York was influenced by his description of the technique in *The Economic Cottage Builder* (Buffalo, 1855, 1856), or whether Utah pioneers learned how to build in adobe from this same book (they could have; the method is carefully described there); but certainly his works and others like them were used all over the country.

On the earliest American frontier, see John L. Cotter and J. Paul Hudson, *New Discoveries at Jamestown* (Washington, 1957); on the 18th-century and post-Revolutionary frontier, Rexford Newcomb, *Architecture of the Old North-West Territory* (Chicago, 1950); on settlement of the Great Plains, Everett Dick, *The Sod-House Frontier* (1938); on the Far West, Harold Kirker, *California's Architectural Frontier* (San Marino, 1960); on the general question, Louis B. Wright, *Culture on the Moving Frontier* (Bloomington, Ind., 1955).

A good example of early jack-of-all-tradesmanship is the record of John Alden of the *Mayflower*, sometime governor of the Plymouth colony, making chests and cupboards with Kenelm Winslow. Lack of specialization produced the same traditional tendency to straightforward plainness in literature as in the visual arts; it is well presented in G. F. Whicher's study *Emily Dickinson*, (1939) e.g., Chap. IX.

Kenneth Umbreit describes early European ideas regarding the inevitable degeneration of everything in America in *The Founding Fathers* (1941), pp. 37ff. The opposite belief, in the inevitability of progress, which colonial success engendered, is described by Daniel J. Boorstin, *The Americans* (1958), from which references to Burnaby and the Massachusetts Bay magistrates are taken.

2. HOMESTEAD AND FORT:
National Traditions in Folk Forms

WELL INTO THE 19TH CENTURY, travelers through older-settled regions of the United States were struck by their differing characteristics. From one region to the next, changes in the shapes of fields and fences, the kinds of crops grown and trees planted, were plain. Even more obvious were differences in types of buildings—barns and forts, churches, houses, and the furniture in them; for it is in what he builds that man always has put his most distinctive stamp on the landscape.

And still today, despite all that development builders and urban renewalists have done to wipe out old landmarks, plenty of survivors from the colonial epoch and descendants in their traditions remain. You can find them everywhere: in the shadow of superhighways and skyscrapers; on the back streets of villages and ancient farms; buried deep in slums. And you can find them in every kind of condition; as no more than gaunt walls and chimney stacks rising out of a tumble of foundation stones, honeysuckle, briar roses and wild apple trees; as conglomerates of the additions and remodelings of half a dozen generations; as meticulous period restorations serving as museums of furniture. Through them, much of the American landscape is still colored today by the diversity of early American civilization.

Colonial America was a land of diverse peoples, all trying, in the manner of migrants from time immemorial, to perpetuate in their New World their culture from the Old; and their buildings showed it. Distinctive and consistent preferences for certain materials and dispositions; for characteristic proportions of height to width, roof to wall, solid to void; for peculiar structural and decorative details—all unmistakably reveal the various parts of the Old World from which their original builders had come. Originally, these differences were great enough—

not merely as between New Spain and New Netherlands, but even between New England and Virginia—that the various New World colonies seemed to be quite distinct, with separate lives and histories; and historically they still are, to the extent that we can hardly understand 17th-century American art without considering it in terms of nationalistic cultural expression, as we shall in chapters following.

But at the same time we can see in retrospect that all these peoples responded to their new surroundings in a fundamentally similar way. However great their differences in building or furniture detail may be, in retrospect it seems clear that essentially the same principles appear throughout—principles which, surpassing national traditions, manifest in common the characteristics of that universal phase in social evolution we call folk art.

After the pioneer's cabin and plank bench, built for a day's shelter or a year's convenience, come the family homestead, the local church, the community fort—folk architecture, with folk furniture in them, made by local craftsmen to last generations. They mark that stage in the growth of civilization when a land has been explored and claimed, and society begins to settle into more stable and organized patterns of life. Still anonymous products of community life, their straightforward construction and direct use of materials still reminiscent of earlier bitter struggles with raw nature, they have much in common with Stone and Iron Age forms. But essentially they are very different. In them is expressed a new and much more favorable relationship between man and nature. The primitive builder was dominated by the materials he used, and the axeman still left them raw; but these are the work of men with enough time and resources and experience behind them to develop specialized skills in masonry, carpentry, joinery, to be

6. *Birthplace of Daniel Webster, Franklin, New Hampshire. Since Daniel Webster was born on this stony farm in 1782, the house probably dates from the 1770s. But houses essentially like this could have been built any time during the first three centuries of New England history. This is folk architecture—no temporary shelter from the elements, but a permanent home. The tradition is not yet a local one; our association of architecture like this with New England is largely a historical accident. This contiguous plan (the right section added later, in the 19th century), this "natural" use of wood in shingle and clapboard, this undisguised frame construction and fieldstone foundation, these doors and windows unplanned in spacing and location, are all features derived ultimately from a medieval heritage common to settlers everywhere, of all nationalities, in early America—a heritage which, in forts and barns and corncribs as well as simple homesteads like this, was perpetuated far into the 19th century.*

perfectly familiar with their materials and manage them with ease. And now too more specialized kinds of buildings and furniture can appear; no longer having to worship in houses, use chests for chairs or churches for forts, settlements can begin to provide themselves with something like the precise forms they want. Now builders are able to go beyond mere stability or convenience and begin to make their work suit their tastes; in a word, to consider matters of fitness, design, or beauty.

It will not be, as yet, a personal expression. We hardly ever know these artisans by name, and as far as appreciation of their work is concerned have no need to. For the folk artisan's knowledge of what his materials can do is based, not on personal experiment or scientific theory, but on generations of practical trial and error; and this inevitably inhibits him from trying anything new and daring, or indulging any personal whims. Unself-consciousness is the basic quality in folk art. The folk artisan works not so much functionally as adaptably; that is, not so much consciously thinking out solutions to particular problems of light or structure or use (like modern designers), as embodying in his houses and furniture inherited generations of experience with, and adjustment to, local climate, materials, and social customs. And if he expresses materials frankly, it is not from any conscious convictions about architectural honesty or the virtues of handicraft (he will not hesitate to cover the handsomest stonework with plaster or whitewash if experience shows this will give protection from frost, or paint over the finest-grained wood if custom favors it), but simply because, having only local materials to work with, and neither time nor resources to spare, he must proceed to work in the simplest and most direct way he can.

In all this we may be reminded of the modern formula: Form Follows Function. But, of course, no such conscious theorizing produced the kind of unadorned simplicity that connoisseurs of homesteads and folk furniture find so appealing today, or the plain geometric shapes—pyramids, cones, octagons, cubes—that make old forts reminiscent of "International Style" architecture. The functional problems of homesteads were worked out in a roundabout way, by the gradual adaptation of building forms to general conditions of climate and customs and materials over generations; the military builder's straightforward use of materials was dictated not by aesthetic considerations but by the practical needs of withstanding arrows or artillery and keeping a garrison in good health and spirits within the limits of given conditions, and with something like a definite budget in mind. Whatever taste or broad principles the folk artisan's work expresses will never be his own invention,

but always those of the community and national tradition in which he was trained.

In sum, folk art marks a Great Divide in history. On the one side, it belongs to a universal phase of culture that all civilizations have gone through. The churches and homesteads and forts of early America are counterparts of those that appeared in those misty centuries when Celt and Teuton and Roman were first clearing the Neolithic forests of Europe; behind palisaded walls and crude towers like those we see in Plymouth and Jamestown, Tennessee and Oregon, the infant civilization of Europe was sheltered from Viking raids in Carolingian and Anglo-Saxon times, an orderly framework for civilized life, learning, and commerce was established and protected. American folk art collectively embodies a medieval tradition which formed the first common stratum of civilization in America. But on the other side, this folk art belongs, too, to the particular histories of the differing national cultures transplanted from the Old to the New World. It has, as Stone and Iron Age art never can, particular associative values. It calls to mind images of the Pilgrims at Plymouth and wagon trains on the Great Plains, forgotten squatters and famous statesmen and battles long ago—all those lost instants of time and space whose interwoven pattern makes up the fabric of American history. And these associations are genuine. Unlike Victorian "revival" architecture and furniture, for which a spurious air of antiquity was contrived by loading on lavish copyings of ornament from earlier styles, folk art recalls the storied past not primarily by reason of any great historic events connected with it, but simply because by its nature it more properly belongs to the past than to the present. Just because these old forts and homesteads were built and furnished so "functionally," to serve the needs of a particular phase of evolution, they have become useless as times and needs have changed; in them, the past lives literally on into the present. And being so genuine, they are the most cogent of witnesses to the

7. *Holy Trinity ("Old Swedes") Church, Wilmington, Delaware. Begun 1698 for Swedish pastor Eric Bjork by Philadelphia masons named Yard; arched south porch added 1750 to prevent walls spreading; brick tower and belfry, 1802. The jerkin-headed roof (possibly influenced by Swedish example) and the curious iron letters by "one of our own people," Matthias Foss, give Holy Trinity the most Teutonic flavor of the three churches built around 1700 by descendants of the old New Sweden colony (the others: Gloria Dei, Philadelphia, begun in 1698 and still standing; Swedesboro, New Jersey, begun 1704, replaced 1763). But its predominant characteristics—the direct expression of construction and materials, and additive composition, derive less from Swedish Lutheran (or any other) national tradition than from universal principles of folk art everywhere.*

collective outlook, values, and aspirations of the diverse peoples who made up 17th-century America. They are at once documents of particular history and general sociological evolution; and it is in this double aspect that we shall be considering them in the chapters that follow.

3. LORDS AND SERFS:
Feudal Traditions in New Spain

FIRST OF EUROPEAN PEOPLES on the North American scene were the Spaniards. By the 1550s, it seemed only a matter of time before the whole New World would be Spanish; secure in the possession of all South America (except Brazil), Mexico, and most of the Caribbean Islands, the Spaniards began to push northwards in a steadily lengthening chain of forts and missions that reached into Florida by the 1560s, New Mexico by the 1590s, Texas by the 1680s, Arizona and California during the 18th century. Nowadays, we take the collapse of this empire for granted. But when Ambassador Zúñiga reported to Philip III from London on the first English settlement of Virginia, sent a plan of James Fort supplied by an Irish spy, and added, "I hope that you will give orders to have these insolent people quickly annihilated," it was no empty threat; Spain was then the New World's greatest power. A century and more later, the Spaniards were still threatening enough for Oglethorpe to lay out his new city of Savannah along the lines of a military encampment, to guard against them. Even then it would have taken a perceptive prophet to guess how swiftly, how easily the Spanish colonies would go down to defeat and disintegration before the advancing English settlements. Only in retrospect is it obvious how hollow was Spanish power, why it crumbled so fast, why English colonization swept over and reduced it so easily to a string of tourist attractions. Yet the causes of Spanish weakness were always plain to see. Still today we can read them in the record built into the furniture, churches, forts, and houses that embodied the old civilization of New Spain.

They are all evident in a typical chest (8).* That chests were still, in the middle of the 18th century, the commonest single article of furniture in the Spanish missions of the Southwest, when

* See Illustration 8. Figures in italics refer to illustration numbers.

elsewhere they had long been regarded as obsolescent medieval survivals, betokens a backward society, a kind of fossil in this remote desert of a way of life the rest of the Western world had largely left behind. The poor quality of its wood —coarse Western yellow pine, soft and easily worked, with a smooth-wearing surface, but so weak and easily split that angle irons have to reinforce the corners, and deep or detailed carving is impossible: here is the record of a culture paralyzed and made permanently dependent by poverty of natural resources. Whereas the very first ship leaving Jamestown for England carried a load of barrel staves from Virginia's rich forests; whereas almost at once, that is to say, English colonists could begin paying off their debt to their homeland and put themselves in a "bargaining position" whence independence of spirit and culture could grow, the Spanish settlements of the Southwest, in a land offering little but coarse and knotty woods like piñon, cottonwood, and juniper, and a limited supply of red spruce, remained almost entirely dependent on the mother country. Compare with the characteristic waste and squandering of lavish natural resources that went on in the English colonies the state of affairs in New Mexico implied in Fray Francisco Atanasio Domínguez' reports on his visitations there in 1776: commending the settlement at one place because "the usable lumber that was in the old church and friary has been kept. It consists of a door . . . the balustrade of the choir loft and its small beams, along with the little balustrade of the high altar . . . an ordinary table, three small chairs, three doors, and four windows . . ."; at another, because they have preserved "a saw. A lever. Two crowbars so worn out that they are no longer useful. A plane. (All came from the King.) Adze, chisel, but Father Fernández did not find this for they say it is lost. . . ." From first to last the barren Spanish settlements had to

8. *Chest from a Spanish mission in northern New Mexico. Known and explored before 1550, New Mexico was first settled by Spaniards at the end of the century, but Spanish population never grew large; by 1630 it was estimated at no more than 250, and an Indian rebellion in 1680 drove all Spaniards out of the territory for twelve years. Gradually, in the course of the 18th century, Spanish control was re-established through a string of missions. This little chest (about five feet long, two feet high, and two feet wide) was made, probably by Indian workmen, for a mission about the middle of the 18th century; the form, and especially the characteristic but inconvenient chest stand in two parts, persisted well into the 1800s.*

be artificially nurtured—orangeries in the wilderness, surviving only through constant transfusions from remote sources.

Most of all the basic weakness of New Spain is evident in the kind of carving characteristic of chests like these. For it is more than crude; it is degenerate. It reflects not so much a failure of technique as a failure in comprehension, a misinterpretation and misapplication of the art forms employed. The motifs—naturalistic floral forms of Renaissance origin, and the rampant lion of Castile—and the basically heraldic composition are Spanish, descended from the medieval and *mudéjar* heritage of Spain established in the New World centuries before. But the treatment of them is not. For while most Spanish settlements in the Southwest had a few Spanish artisans, or priests with at least a smattering of training in design—and sometimes a good deal more than that—from the first the Spanish had begun to train Indians in woodworking, and as time went on Indian craftsmen

were employed more and more extensively. From visitation reports we know that Indians were entirely responsible for altar screens in such churches as San Miguel in Santa Fe, San Esteban del Rey in Acoma, and many other places; that they built more than one mission in its entirety; in all probability they were responsible for the chest here. And in Indian hands, the principles and forms of Spanish arts and architecture subtly and inevitably began to change into something different—something primitive, more Indian than Spanish in fact and spirit.

To be meaningful and comprehensible, any kind of visual art—and especially two-dimensional representational forms—has to be "translated." What we call a "picture of a lion" (or anything else) is in fact never anything more than a collection of lines, shapes, and colors; for it to put us in mind of a four-footed flesh-and-blood beast, we need to have been trained to recognize such a particular arrangement of lines and colors as a symbol of one. If we happen not to have had such a training, lines and colors they will remain, just as what will be a succession of meaningless noises to one man may be another's intelligible speech, depending on what combination of sounds he learned to associate with images and ideas in childhood. So here; what to European eyes suggested ideas of lions or leaves, to the Indian remained lines and colors, which he modified in the direction of those geometric patterns his people had been accustomed to see and create for countless generations past. In fact, here in the Southwest was being repeated on a small scale in the 18th cen-

tury what had happened ages before when barbarous Celts and Teutons overran the Roman provinces, took over the sophisticated forms of Graeco-Roman art, and interpreted them in terms of their own visual experience, their own traditions of flat linear pattern. Not that such a development is necessarily a disaster; far from it. Coming upon the worn-out forms of Roman art with a fresh eye—like the man who found Times Square at night an exquisitely beautiful sight because he couldn't read—the Celto-Teutonic way of seeing eventually resulted in a revitalization of ancient art, in the fresh and vigorous creations of the Middle Ages; and something like that might well have happened, given the same length of time, in the Southwest. But there was no time. By the end of the 18th century, the civilization of New Spain was still based on not much more than an uneasy balance of power between rulers and ruled. As the decoration on this little chest—still neither good Spanish ornament, nor good Indian design—shows, Spanish colonial art rarely got much past a stage comparable to the Merovingian or Visigothic era in Europe. Its two components were not yet in process of fusion; instead, they tended to cancel each other out. In this art is the record of a society still composed of two fundamentally incompatible elements; a society which, once the unifying force of Spanish military power weakened and the divisive pressures of "Anglo" penetration began, was bound to fall apart, to be an easy conquest. And we will find the same story, writ small in Spanish colonial furniture like this, spelled out large in all the "major" arts of New Spain as well.

---

9. High altar and retable, Church of San Xavier del Bac, Tucson, Arizona. The first church of San Xavier was built by Jesuits, who established a mission there in 1700; Franciscans replaced them after 1767, and built the present church 1783–97. Two "architects," the Gaona brothers, are traditionally credited with the design; the workmen were mainly Subaipari—and later

Papago—Indians. Except for the foundations, San Xavier was constructed entirely of kiln-baked clay brick, covered with a white lime plaster; the altar is of the same material. The life-like santo represents St. Francis Xavier. The Franciscans left the mission in 1822, but returned in 1911; this is the only one of the seven or eight Arizona missions to remain in reasonably good condition.

It is plain, for instance, in such architectural sculpture as the high altar of San Xavier del Bac. This heaped-up mass of fantastically indented columns and flying cherubim, volutes, sprays, baldachins, cornucopia, flowers and fruit, saints and crucifixes, looming up so suddenly in the flickering glitter of candlelight at the end of a cavernous nave, making such a dramatic contrast with the plain adobe walls and simple square pillars around it, is a concept that derives immediately from the churrigueresque churches of Mexico, and behind that from the Baroque churches of the Counter-Reformation in Europe. Ultimately, however, the idea goes back to those first centuries when the Catholic Church was spreading over the Mediterranean world. The priests of the San Xavier mission, like many of their predecessors, found that for simple peoples, accustomed to understand power in terms of stature, strength, and tangible possessions, magnificently rich architectural display was the most effective presentation of the awful majesty of God, King of Kings, Lord of Lords. In their small way they tried to overawe their Indian congregations, as soaring Gothic spires and ponderous Romanesque vaults had overawed the peasants and tamed the barbarian nobles of the Middle Ages. They wanted to achieve something of the same effect as Justinian's great church of Holy Wisdom in Constantinople, where once (we read) an envoy from one of the rude nations of the north was so overcome by the splendor of the mighty dome that he fell in a stupor to the floor; they hoped to capture something of the magnificence of those basilicas Constantine built to impress the new faithful with the glory and majesty of his chosen Church. And in their small way, they succeeded.

Furthermore, they succeeded, as in early medieval Europe, by setting their newly won flock to work for them. An altar piece like this was not always the work of mission Indians, to be sure; at least one or two Spanish artisans might often be employed on it as well. But Indian craftsmen probably carved the bulk of the detail; and it is

here, just as on the chest, that they have left their mark. These motifs are by no means as abstract, of course; but they reveal the same "barbarization." These naïve, stubby, stiff cherubim are not the work of men who really understand the anatomy of a human body. No awareness of Renaissance laws of proportion or classical sophistication went into these clumsy sprays, ill-proportioned volutes, lumpy columns, this harsh and heavy color. Through all the diverse forms of true Spanish churrigueresque there can always be sensed subtle yet strong principles of design that unify the whole; they are missing here. Jumbled and cramped together, the details are assembled piece by piece, building up a whole that is no more than the sum of its parts. Where the churrigueresque designer worked in the Renaissance tradition, seeing all his details in relationship to the whole, the carvers here add details together like "primitive" painters, like children making a human figure—head, plus two arms, plus body, and so on. The result is again a whole which lacks both the comprehensive unity of Spanish design and the patterned discipline of Indian work. Like the decoration on the chest, it is the manifestation of two irreconcilable traditions each canceling out the other's excellences.

No "modern" society of upper, middle, and lower classes (such as, for example, the English colonies were developing) would have produced work like this; this is the product of an infinitely older kind of social structure—priests and rulers on the one hand, planning this lavish, ambitious ensemble, and Indian workmen (serfs would be the better word, probably) on the other, clumsily and naïvely carrying out their orders in detail. Here in this remote corner of the New World the old feudal society of medieval Europe has survived, a society of masters and slaves. Such an altarpiece is hardly conceived as a thing of beauty, nor does it serve purely religious ends; essentially, it has a political function. Through it the savage Indian, like the Teutonic churl and the Mediterranean peasant before him, was brought to an awareness not only of the power of

10. Mission Church of San José, San Antonio, Texas. *Although exploration began early, serious Spanish occupation of Texas only began under the stimulus of French competition, in 1681. In the course of time, however, there developed an impressive chain of presidios (= military stations, fortified areas within which were contained troop quarters, dwellings, and a church), pueblos (= "free towns," consisting of allotted home sites, pasturage, orchards, etc.), and missions (each with its adjoining cloister and patio, domestic living quarters, granaries, storehouses, water supply, etc.). One of the most notable was this, the mission of San José y San Miguel de Aguayo, established 1720. The present church was begun 1768; though restored several times, it has not been substantially altered. Most mission churches were based on either a simple basilican or cruciform plan, with twin towers (one or the other often left unbuilt) planned to flank the façade, and a pierced belfry above it.*

God but, with at least equal forcefulness, of the social and cultural superiority of his rulers. In the process of making such an altarpiece the Indian was being civilized, to be sure; but his work was also an effective means of keeping him "in his place." This we will realize most fully, however, when we consider the Spanish mission church as a whole.

"Half church of God, half fortress . . ." What was said of medieval Durham cathedral applied quite as aptly to the Spanish mission churches of the Southwest. Churches built for and often largely by the Indians, to bring them to a knowledge of God, they were also the physical bastions of Spanish imperial power. Indian in their abstract geometric simplicity and often in

23

their materials as well, Spanish in plan and over-all design—Spanish Baroque monasteries in fact, complete with characteristic contrasts of intricately massed decorative sculpture set off against plain wall surfaces—they proclaim in full-scale architectural language the same record of a feudal civilization of lords and serfs that furniture and altarpieces reveal in subtler, smaller ways. The Indian they enveloped in the majesty of Spanish culture and the splendor of the Spanish church; the Spaniard they supported both psychologically and, on occasion, physically, even to the extent of enabling him to withstand sieges by rebellious populations. In spirit, they recall the monasteries of the early Middle Ages; like St.-Gall, Mont-St.-Michel, Iona, Monte Cassino, they were small islands of civilization in a barbarous wilderness as well as fortresses to protect that civilization. But unlike them, they rarely functioned as bases from which to extend civiliza-

tion over the surrounding countryside. They were too self-contained, too precarious economically, ever to sustain strong roots; they were shells, not seeds. If anything happened in them from generation to generation, it was less the spread of Spanish culture out from them over the Southwest than the slow barbarization of Indians and Spaniards alike; the farther away in space and time these missions are from their Mexican bases, the more surely apparent becomes the failure of the Spanish effort to colonize and civilize the Southwest from them. That was not the fault of the dedicated men who served in them, of course. It was the inherent weakness, built into Spanish colonial policy from the beginning, that is to be read in every work of Spanish colonial culture.

Even more dramatically than in the mission churches you see this fatal characteristic in a great fort like the Castillo de San Marcos in St. Augustine. At once the protection and the prison of its inhabitants, sustained by continuous direction from far-distant bases in Mexico and Spain, such an establishment is even more of a dependency than the mission churches. Of necessity the missions had to be built largely of local materials; here, almost everything—from massive cut stones to doorframes and window latches—came from the mother country. Where the first forts of the English colonies were built by the settlers themselves from native resources, Florida contributed practically nothing but coquina for retaining walls to the Castillo. Into this fortress went three million dollars' worth of Spanish labor, materials, and planning; the result could hardly be considered a product of Florida or New Spain. It belonged entirely to Old Spain —a wholly artificial planting. From it nothing indigenous could grow—and worse, by its very existence, it smothered any possible native shoots that might have appeared. There it sat, century after century, stagnating, until another civilization, rooted in American soil, pushed in to overwhelm it. How heavy, how crushing was the inert weight of Spanish imperial power on the

11. CASTILLO DE SAN MARCOS, ST. AUGUSTINE, FLORIDA

(A) Air view. Begun 1672 as a great statement of Spanish power and claims in the Floridas in reaction to the founding of Charleston, South Carolina (1670), the Castillo was a fort completely European in style, with star-shaped bastions in regular ashlar stonework, surrounded by a moat. The huge retaining walls (thirty feet high, and up to twelve feet thick) were of coquina—a soft whitish stone, abundant in the region, composed of crushed shells and coral cemented together.

growth of Spanish colonial life is evident from the fact that to all intents and purposes it was only after that weight was lifted, when the Castillo had been abandoned and Spanish rulers expelled from Florida and elsewhere, that anything like a genuine Spanish-American house type began to develop.

"The Spanish colonial house" brings to mind the agreeable image of a type almost perfectly suited to the climate, resources, and mode of life in the Southwest. We think, for instance, of some admirable combination of indigenous forms and materials with ultimately Mediterranean traditions like the Governors' Palace at Santa Fe—adobe walls, projecting beam ends, and simple geometric shapes derived from the native terraced Pueblo houses of New Mexico; an arrangement of rooms contiguously around and facing in on an open square, and a *portal* (covered walk) developed for just such a climate as this in the cities of the Imperial Roman world. Or we think of what Professor Kirker calls "the architectural legend of Spanish California . . . given classic statement in Helen Hunt Jackson's novel *Ramona* [Boston, 1884] . . . a pastel-tinted hacienda with tile roofs, carved woodwork, cantilevered balconies, and glazed galleries opening onto brick-paved verandahs and walled gardens." And it has been the fashion to damn the English-speaking settler in the Southwest for his chauvinistic failure to realize how immeasurably superior this house type was to his own building traditions. He is pictured as an insensitive clod who never understood how exquisitely Spanish houses had been adapted to just such environments as this over many centuries; who ignored the advantages of native materials, of cool balconies and porches; who took over the covered

(11 B) Courtyard of the Castillo. For roofs and other parts requiring tensile strength, the builders used "tabby," or tapia, a kind of cement made from the copious Indian shell deposits along the Florida and Carolina coasts, poured in three layers varying from ten to twenty inches in thickness depending on the curve of the arches below. Often besieged but never taken, the Castillo was turned over to Britain in 1763, reoccupied by Spain 1783–1821, used as an American military prison (Fort Marion) through the rest of the 19th century, before being made a national monument in 1921.

12. *Palace of the Governors, Santa Fe, New Mexico. Street front, as restored in the 20th century. Originally founded 1609, rebuilt after the Indian insurrection of 1680, the Palace by the* late 19th century was dilapidated and disfigured. Restoration began with the portales, or covered walk, in 1914; subsequently the patio was restored at the rear of the block seen here, and other parts of the building surrounding it.

sidewalk for his Western mining towns not because but in spite of Spanish precedent; who (as one writer put it) "stubbornly and painfully set about improving much less efficient or suitable substitutes of his own for these obvious models."

Even if all this were true, however, the attitude of the "Yankee" would be quite understandable. What charmed his descendants, the bungalow dwellers of West Hollywood and Coral Gables, had no appeal for him. He found nothing romantic about Spanish colonial building, because by definition "the romantic" implies something remote from everyday experience, something lent charm by distance in space and time—which Spanish culture certainly was not, for him. Just as it was the 18th-century philosophers of Europe and the 19th-century novelists of the civilized Eastern states—not the frontiersmen of Massachusetts or Pennsylvania or pioneers trekking the Great Plains—who waxed ecstatic about "the noble red man," so it took late 19th-century litterateurs and 20th-century television scriptwriters

to find glamor and romance in Zorro, the Cisco Kid, and the Old Spanish Southwest. Neither was the Yankee enchanted by the textural qualities of Spanish colonial building, by the play of shadows and light over simple forms of white adobe, creamy "tabby," or rudely carved natural wood. Only in the later 19th century, when heavy industry began to encase the world in gleaming steel and synthetics and concrete, would people develop much aesthetic enthusiasm for "arts and crafts." The most a Yankee settler would notice about Spanish colonial materials and building forms was that they were unfamiliar—which, given his traditional and instinctive attitude of superiority towards all other cultures, was hardly a recommendation.

But it is not true either that Spanish colonial houses were what romantics claimed them to be, or that the Yankees learned nothing from them. This Professor Kirker has made clear in his admirable study, *California's Architectural Frontier*. Rejecting the conventional image as "based upon unreliable contemporary testimony and an

13. "SPANISH COLONIAL" HOUSE TYPES

(A) "Ramona's Marriage Place," San Diego, California, as it was c.1916. In the foreground, a monument to the first raising of the American flag. Lovers of romance were fond of making the kind of contrast between "Spanish" and "Yankee" California suggested by the two buildings here—on the right, a low, cool, tiled, casemented house built around a patio, recalling the atmosphere of Helen Hunt Jackson's 1884 novel, Ramona; on the left, an ungainly box surrounded by an ill-proportioned two-story porch. In sober fact, however, both seem to represent fusions of the two cultures—the one being an imaginative reconstruction of a culture that existed only in legend, made possible by the wealth Yankee enterprise piled up in later-19th-century California; the other, a distant relative of the distinctive adaptation of a New England house type to California climate and materials made in Monterey during the 1830s.

(13 B) Thomas Larkin house, Monterey, California. Begun 1835 and completed 1837, this house and others like it were monuments to a brief moment of balance between the culture of Americans coming into California during the 1820s and 30s, and the culture established there by the Spaniards who founded the province in 1769 and the Mexicans who ruled it after the revolution of 1821. Though intending to reproduce the kind of New England merchant's house he had known at home in Boston, Larkin was forced to use adobe brick in place of scarce timber for his walls, and to protect them with a double porch; the result was a distinctive local fusion of folk traditions that has been called "Monterey colonial." By the 1840s, the balance was shattered; as Americans took control of the province in 1846 during the Mexican War and then, after the Gold Rush, made California a state in 1850, such houses increasingly conformed to American standards, and by the 1860s California architecture was hardly distinguishable from High Victorian building elsewhere.

inaccurate interpretation of the much-reconstructed remains of several extant adobes," he declares:

> When Spanish rule ended in 1822 there was apparently only one planked floor in the entire province, and that was in the governor's house at Monterey. The columns, fanlighted doorways, small-paned windows, brick chimneys, and balconies that . . . later romantics found so endearing are not representative of the Spanish period at all but were introduced into California by New England merchants and belong only to the decade immediately preceding American annexation.

According to him, it was the house begun by Thomas Larkin at Monterey in 1835 which first introduced what has come to be thought of as the typical Spanish colonial house type. Earlier, that type had been, far from any storied hacienda, a sort of one-room box like the Casa de Soto at Monterey (c.1820), with walls of adobe, floors of hard-packed dirt, windows without glass, and a flat roof of pebble-sprinkled asphalt—a product of poor materials and inadequate tools like the chest with which we began this chapter. Larkin, a Boston merchant settled in the provincial capital, whose retail store and American child were both firsts in the colony, had no wish or incentive to imitate it. Like immigrants everywhere, he wanted to build the kind of house he had known at home—a framed, clapboard, New England homestead. And in plan, structure, hipped shingled roof, and symmetrical fenestration, he did. It was shortage of milled lumber that made him use adobe brick for his walls, and it was to protect the adobe from weather that he built double porches all around. What resulted was "a unique instance in California of an important compromise between competing colonial cultures," useful enough to be adopted by both Americans and Spanish-Mexicans in the region, constituting in effect a style of its own—Monterey colonial.

It may be that the similar Spanish colonial houses of Florida in the period c.1760–1810, like the Fatio or Llambias houses in St. Augustine, will turn out on examination to have comparably late dates and Yankee inspiration. There is no reason why Spanish culture in Florida should have been any less sterile than in California. Everywhere, in everything from the furniture of New Mexico missions to the evolution of Monterey colonial houses, the same record of an obsolescent feudal society is there to read. For all its initial advantages, New Spain was destined in the end to provide no more than a background footnote to the history of the United States; and all its arts are a commentary on that fact.

NOTES

Quotations on Spanish spying and threats on Jamestown, from H. C. Forman, *Jamestown and St. Mary's* (Baltimore, 1938), pp. 12, 37–8; on resources in New Mexico missions, from Fray Domínguez in E. B. Adams and Fray A. Chávez (ed. and trans.), *The Missions of New Mexico in 1776* (Albuquerque, 1956); on Spanish colonial house types in California, from Harold Kirker, *California's Architectural Frontier* (San Marino, 1960), Chap I.

On the planning of Savannah, Georgia, along the lines of a military encampment to meet Spanish threats, see Turpin C. Bannister, "Oglethorpe's Sources for the Savannah Plan (*JSAH*, XX, 1961, 2, pp. 47–62). On New Mexico missions, useful recent studies are those by George Kubler, *The Religious Architecture of New Mexico* (Colorado Springs, 1940), and Richard E. Ahlborn, *Spanish-Colonial Woodcarving in New Mexico* (unpublished M.A. thesis, University of Delaware, 1958). Valuable background material and general survey are provided by George Kubler, *Art and Architecture in Spain and Portugal and Their Spanish Dominions* (Baltimore, 1959). Hugh Morrison, *Early American Architecture* (1952) is here as for other fields a standard reference work. Of earlier studies, Rexford Newcomb's *Spanish-American Architecture in the United States* (1937) is still a useful source of illustrations and general survey, though in some respects it now needs revision. An earlier version of this chapter was published in *Delaware Notes*, 32nd series, 1959, pp. 16–32.

4. PRINCE AND PEASANT:
Authoritarian Traditions in New France

14. "FRENCH COLONIAL" HOUSE TYPES IN QUEBEC
(A) Henri Parent house, Giffard. A typical French-Canadian home-
stead like this, with eave flaring over a porch, and elevated first floor,
could have been built on the St. Lawrence any time from the late 1600s
to the early 20th century.

NATURE made the St. Lawrence Valley one of the most picturesque parts of North America, and the men who first settled the region did little to spoil it. Still today in many places along the valley you can see the *ancien régime* farmsteads stretching back in long ribbons from the river into the hills, each with its narrow strip of river frontage; still today you can find in the old villages plenty of houses, either from the *ancien régime* or from the "population explosion" and consequent boom in building that followed the Cession of 1763—houses whose distinctive combination of thick fieldstone walls, high-pitched roofs nearly two-thirds the total height of the building, brightly painted woodwork, and tall vertical casements identifies them as belonging to the folk tradition brought here in the 17th century by peasantry from Maine, Anjou, and Normandy. These houses present certain variants and problems, to be sure. There is a Quebec City

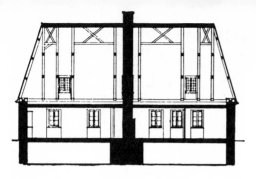

(14 B) Longitudinal section, Villeneuve house, Charlesbourg, c.1690. Ground floor a single room, divided only by the central fireplace. In the majority of cases, especially nearer Montreal, fireplace is in side walls, ground floor area unbroken.

---

type, oblong in shape, with flared eaves (presumably the legacy of the Norman craftsmen whom Bishop Laval imported to settle his seigniorial parishes), and usually, though not always, a great central fireplace and chimney; and there is a Montreal type which presumably owes its distinctive features—generally squarer and heavier proportions, chimneys set in massive end walls—to practices forced on early Montreal builders, who, on a site far more exposed than Quebec City's, had at once to guard against Indian attack by putting their houses close together, and against fire by thickening the common side walls into protective firebreaks. And in both regions there is a problem as to when and how such features as verandahs and elevated first floors were introduced.* But, essentially, the "French colonial" house type is so simple that such problems are more or less irrelevant. What is indubitable, and significant, is that these forms were evolved, not designed—the product of generations of family living in both Old and New Worlds. This is peasant building.

This peasant character is obvious in both plans and furnishings. Characteristically, houses had three floors, each essentially one large room, and each with its space disposed according to family needs; in the high basement, domestic industry (anything from harness repairing to

* See notes to this chapter.

furniture making; in the Villeneuve house, e.g., half of the basement was a sheep pen); the first floor given over to living and eating, oriented around a fireplace (and later, stove), subdivided by the location of furniture rather than formal partitions; the attic, given light and air by small gable or dormer windows, for sleeping. And the kind of folk furniture that originally went into these houses perfectly complemented and paralleled their architecture. The buffet illustrated is typical. Its forms originated deep in the Middle Ages—basically, this is an old Gothic type of dole cupboard, preserved far into the 18th century and long after it had evolved into a court cupboard and thence to obsolescence

15. "HABITANT" AND "TOWN" STYLES IN QUÉBECOIS FURNITURE

(A) Typifying the sturdy, utilitarian, medieval, naïvely folk character of the habitant style is this pine buffet in the Museum of the Province of Quebec, Quebec City.

---

elsewhere. Although New France was too far north for oak to grow well, so that the *Québecois* folk craftsman had to substitute for the traditional medieval material local woods like pine (as here), soft walnut, wild cherry, or basswood, still this late he perpetuates the large bosses and folds natural to oak carving, in preference to the more delicate forms he might have achieved in the lighter, more malleable woods he was using.

His habitant style perfectly exemplifies those principles of work and attitudes to life we think of as typical of folk art—additive composition, gay childlike painting in solid colors or patterns, sturdy expression of materials and structure.

Mixed in with this medieval folk furniture there is, however, a very different kind, usually and loosely called the "town style." It consists of *retardataire* imitations of reigning French styles —Louis Treize Renaissance, Louis Quatorze Baroque, Louis Quinze Rococo, Louis Seize classical—and it represents quite another side of the culture of New France. Its origin was in furnishings made by local craftsmen to the order of the old administrative class in the colony. To all intents and purposes that class disappeared after the British Conquest; but already by the middle of the 18th century town furniture was beginning to drift down to habitant homesteads, where its forms persisted, often with an extraordinary cultural lag, well into the 19th century—as late

(15 B) Typifying the town style are the Louis Quatorze forms of this commode in the Montreal Museum of Fine Arts. Introduced to Quebec by the upper classes under the ancien régime, *such recognizably French 18th-century furniture styles were perpetuated long after the Cession, and long after they had disappeared in France, by local artisans who frequently added a few touches of their own—like the incongruously naïve French military boots serving for feet on this example (see detail). Artisans generally continued, also, to paint or stain their wood in folk fashion rather than polishing or graining it.*

as 1800 you occasionally find even Louis Treize styles in degenerate form. Often enough, too, recognizably 18th-century styles are mixed up with naïve folk principles in the same piece— in the Provincial Museum at Quebec you can see chairs of vaguely Rococo form with seats woven in the manner of snowshoes, for instance; or the reasonably recognizable Louis Quatorze commode, with its incongruous termination in a great set of French military boots. But generally speaking, town furniture, with its details (Rococo ornament, cabriole legs, imported brasses) more or less consciously borrowed from specific styles, and materials handled to simulate walnut or mahogany rather than painted in flat colors or directly revealed, properly belongs more to the consciously classical tradition of the 17th and 18th centuries than to the realm of folk art. But, historically, it is important as a reminder that the founders of New France had no intention of creating any quaint reservoir of medieval folk tradition in the New World. The men who commissioned these "royal" styles saw the St. Lawrence Valley as the seat of an empire stretching from Nova Scotia to New Orleans. And so once it was. Here and there, in the form of French colonial homesteads scattered from

16. "FRENCH COLONIAL" HOUSE TYPES ON THE MISSISSIPPI

(A) Louis Bolduc house, Ste. Genevieve, Missouri. Most important of a group of 18th-century houses in this early (c.1750) settlement of Canadians in the Mississippi Valley, the Bolduc house was built c.1770, somewhat remodeled c.1845. Its most distinctive feature is the galerie around all four sides, in one corner of which was built a stone kitchen c.1820; like typical Québecois houses in plan, it differed from them in materials—frame instead of stone, and preserving in parts the old construction de pieux (= upright logs set together) which was a hundred years out of date in Canada. Restored 1956–7, including garden, orchard, and eight-foot fence of cedar logs, by the National Society of Colonial Dames of America under the direction of Ernest Allen Connally.

(16 B) Parlange Plantation house, New Roads (Pointe Coupée Parish), Louisiana, c.1750. Typical of the more pretentious house types of the lower Louisiana parishes in its raised first floor; ground-story walls and floor of brick, upper of timber with clay and moss interstices; galerie encircling house, carried on classical columns of brick below, wooden colonnettes above.

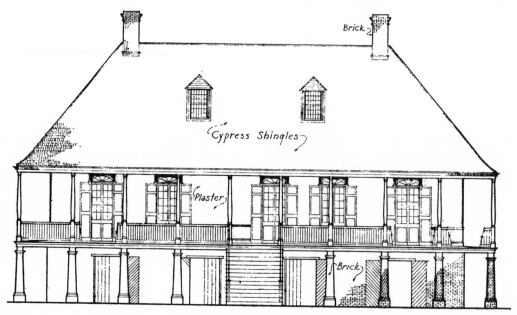

the Great Lakes to the Gulf, the remains of that empire are still to be seen. But outside Quebec, they represent only a handful of accidental or modern preservations—a few houses in New Orleans, a few more at Ste. Genevieve in Missouri, one or two in odd places like Kaskaskia and Mackinac Island and New Paltz; that is about all. In that fact is the measure, and in the arts of New France generally the record, of French failure in the New World.

By all the laws of probability, most of North America ought to speak French, not English, today. Seventeenth-century France was beyond question the strongest state in Europe; and New France was equally beyond question the most potentially powerful state in the New World. The founding of Louisbourg in 1714 at one end, and New Orleans in 1718 at the other, completed

a chain of forts and settlements that dominated both main waterways into the continent; had this strategic arc of territory been filled in with anything like the population of the English colonies, the latter would have been neatly penned in by it against the Atlantic seaboard, and French mastery of North America assured. But, of course, things did not work out that way. Within fifty years it was New France, not the English colonies, that had been wiped off the map in what seems retrospectively the unbelievably sudden, easy, and total defeat of a great power. Whatever happened?

One of the most obvious reasons for French failure in the New World is suggested by the architectural remains of French Protestant building in the English colonies. Consider, as one

(16 C) Mayor Girod house, New Orleans, Louisiana, built 1814. A standard sort of 18th-century French town house, with vaguely Louis Seize or Adamesque–Federal detail, typical of the relatively few buildings that give the French Quarter of New Orleans its claim to "Frenchness." Photo taken in 1934.

typical example, the Jean Hasbrouck house at New Paltz, New York. How did such a typical north-of-France peasant house, with thick stone walls, two-to-one proportion of roof to wall, and general fortresslike appearance so unmistakably similar to contemporaries in the Montreal area of New France, come to be built here in the Hudson Valley? Because New Paltz was a French settlement, founded in 1660 by a group of French Protestants coming to New York from a temporary refuge in the Palatinate (hence the name); Jean Hasbrouck, who built this house in 1712, was a native of Calais. And how did he and thousands like him come to settle here, give their talents and their future to the English colonies instead of to New France? Ultimately because they were driven there by deliberate French policy, by the "absolute will and pleasure" of Louis XIV, King of France. France was ruled, and New France's destiny was determined, by a rigidly authoritarian principle; and ultimately this kind of government always defeats its own ends. That is a platitude, of course. But then, like all platitudes, it happens to be true. And if the scanty architectural remains of New France have any lasting significance for American history, it is surely in this —that they are above all a commentary on the theory, practice, and results of absolute government.

"Why, Sir," Samuel Johnson once remarked, "absolute princes seldom do any harm. But they who are governed by them are governed by chance. There is no security for good government." Precisely. Absolutism anywhere, any time, in practice means government by whim. And government by whim not only makes successful long-term planning impossible, it makes disastrous mistakes inevitable. Human judgment being what it is, first thoughts are all too usually fallible; it is, then, no discredit to any man if the sparkling ideas he had at midnight look sick in the plain light of day. But when the man is an absolute ruler, first thoughts rule his life. His midnight enthusiasms are law by morning;

last night's whim may be felt for generations. Such a whim, for instance, was the decision of Louis XIV to repeal the Edict of Nantes, and make French Protestants conform to his notions on religion. "To people Canada it would be necessary to depopulate France"—this had been the Sun King's excuse for the slow growth of his colony; yet this revocation, combined with the earlier decree of 1628 prohibiting Protestant settlement in New France (which also seems to have been largely a whim of Mazarin's), turned what had been a trickle of Huguenot immigration to English colonies into "a great flood" of some 15,000 settlers before 1750, at least as many Frenchmen as ever were induced to come to New France, and probably more. South Carolina ("in Charleston whole streets were built by Huguenots . . . ," Howard Mumford Jones wrote in *America and French Culture*, Chapel Hill, 1947), Massachusetts (which received such families as the Reveres, Bowdoins, and Faneuils), and New York (in 1688 a quarter of the population of New York City was Huguenot) benefited most from Louis's fatuous munificence; but every colony had its useful contingent of Huguenots. And they were valuable settlers indeed. Professor Jones concluded that "no single body of aliens (i.e., non-English-speaking people) have contributed more to American life."

Of course there are not many Huguenot buildings extant today—the New Paltz houses, the Demarest house in North Hackensack, others here and there. However, architectural remains for New France as a whole (outside Quebec) are notoriously scanty, too. But, while Huguenot remains are scanty largely because so many of the places they settled grew, with their help, into large and prosperous communities which soon (in what is unfortunately the usual American manner) tore down and built over their earliest architecture, French remains elsewhere are scanty for quite a different reason. New France had few buildings because it had so few people. And this is significant indeed.

17. "FRENCH COLONIAL" HOUSE TYPES OUTSIDE NEW FRANCE

(A) Jean Hasbrouck house, New Paltz, New York, c.1712. Huguenot building in the English colonies.

(17 B) Beaumont house, Mackinac Island, Michigan, c.1800. Built by French-Canadian employees of John Ogilvie, a Scottish fur trader operating out of Montreal; after 1816 a retail store for John Jacob Astor's American Fur Company. Restored 1953–5 as a memorial to William Beaumont, the young American doctor who in 1822 put a window in the stomach of voyageur *Alexis St. Martin to observe the healing of a wound suffered in this store, and thereby made medical history.*

France in the 17th century had every advantage over England in peopling colonies—better strategic position, more stable government (England, after all, had two revolutions and a civil war in this period), a population three times as large. There was only one reason why New France should not have been populated early and thickly—deliberate policy. While the one thing New France needed above all was people, the kings of France insisted on providing everything but. They subsidized troops of missionaries to make Christian settlers out of the Indians. They poured money into great fortresses to hold their territories. They provided legions of administrators and soldiers. But people they would not send. Almost every Frenchman who ever spent more than a few years in North America came to the conclusion that New France could not survive without steady and abundant immigration. But the kings never "heard" them. They listened instead to people who knew about Indians from philosophers' textbooks on the "noble savage" rather than to those who had actually fought them and knew how many generations it would take to make "civilians" of them; they listened to court generals who managed their European armies and knew about occupying territories in Flanders or the Rhine-

land, rather than those who knew what wilderness conditions did to the morale of regular army troops far from home. So the Indian schemes collapsed, and Louisbourg was taken by raw militia from New England fighting for their homeland; and so in the end a few thousand Frenchmen were left to face half a million English settlers in the final battles of the Seven Years' War: the result was inevitable.

But it had always been inevitable. For the absolute ruler can never, in the nature of things, have the kind of advice which he—again in the nature of things—more than any other kind of administrator, must have. By definition he reserves all authority to himself; he delegates only responsibility (and blame, needless to say). He of all people, therefore, most needs to know exactly what the factors in any given situation are, if he is to avoid making decisions on non-existent grounds, or giving orders that cannot be carried out. But this is precisely the sort of information that he, being who he is, will never get—first, because there are always too many problems coming before him to concentrate properly on any one; but, even more fundamentally, because he has no "loyal opposition" to give him the kind of advice and criticism he needs, regardless of how unpleasant it may be. Instead, he will be surrounded by a crowd of sycophants who tell him not what he ought to know, but what they think he wants to hear; who spend their energies not in discovering facts, or weighing considerations, but in guessing what the king—or president, or chairman, or whoever it may be in this universal situation—is going to think about before he thinks it, so that they can flatter him with corroboration. These people are certainly not the sort to go off to a wild place like New France, or to tell him what it really needs even in the unlikely event they do. The courtiers who surrounded the King of France in his colony's crucial years were men who correctly guessed that his head was filled with illusions of glory, who adroitly praised him for sending men to battlefields all over Europe instead of peopling the empty wastes of snow of New France. And because they had the King's ear, empty wastes of snow New France remained. When things finally changed, and a new regime came to power with intentions of actively promoting New France, it was too late; authoritarian ways had become so habitual that every plan and program, however well conceived, was frustrated and crippled in execution. Of this, Louisiana is the great example.

"Two hundred people have been sent here to build a city, and are encamped on the great river, where their only thought has been to protect themselves from the elements while waiting for someone to draw up a plan and build houses for them. M. de Pauger has just shown me his idea of a plan; it is indeed handsome, and most orderly, but it will not be as easy to execute as it was to trace on paper." Father Charlevoix, who so described the state of New Orleans in 1718, was not always fair in describing what he saw in New France; and at first reading this picture—people sitting around waiting for someone to tell them where and how to build—does seem an astonishing contrast with the way English colonies were settled. But it conforms well enough with other pictures we have of the way things were done under the absolutist regimes of France. Of the aging Louis XIV directing armies in Flanders from his couch at Versailles, for instance. Or of Intendant Jean Talon in the 1670s obediently trying to move his colonists away from the detached riverside homesteads demanded by the geography of Quebec onto regular model townsites north of the city, because the King felt his colonists should be living in neat villages, as in Europe. And in particular it conforms with what we know of the physical appearance of the early cities of New France. Compare an early-18th-century view of Quebec with one of Boston, say, or Philadelphia, or New York. In these English cities, we have rows of private houses with only here and there a small church spire; waterfronts bristling with masts; crowds of wharves and warehouses— these cities have grown up naturally, spontaneously, as commercial and cultural centers for large, populous, prosperous areas of settlement roundabout. But Quebec mainly consists of a cluster of spires marking out great official buildings—churches, palaces for intendants and bishops and governors, hospitals, barracks, college —all of them built with funds supplied by the kings and religious orders of France. On the river are only a few small boats and a French warship or two; what you could call the settlement proper is nothing more than a poor line of houses straggling along the waterfront. Indeed, this is not a "settlement" in the real sense at all; it is hardly more than an administrative headquarters. Quebec's appearance speaks for itself; we need hardly be told that since 1663 New France had "enjoyed" the status of a French province, with a complete paraphernalia of governor, intendant, sovereign council, deputy governors, deputy intendants, bishops, the full complicated French legal code. However starved New France may have been for settlers, it never lacked administrators, and its architecture proved the fact.

Half a century later a French captain of marines, Vaugine de Muisement, records much the same impression of New Orleans, in his *Journal* of 1752. The first thing he, like most visitors, notices about the city is its regular plan—"laid out on a square, its streets 36 feet wide, and all *tirées au cordeau*." So far, so fine. But, then, again like most visitors, he remarks that ". . . it is not as well peopled as it should be—diverse accidents one after another having handicapped its development." On the cause of this propensity for "accidents" he does not speculate. But he hints at it unwittingly, perhaps, when he comes to describe the general character of the town. He finds that "only lately" have "a few good and commodious houses" been built of brick (*au défaut de pierre*, as he carefully explains, the only good available stone being two hundred miles away) to replace the first makeshift *chaumières*. Only lately!—think of Philadelphia, say, with its rows of brick houses standing only ten years after the city's founding! And, he goes on, "the most remarkable buildings are two barracks, which face each other, and surround a magnificent *place d'arme* located on the river shore. The Ursuline convent, which was restored after 1752 [*sic*] might pass for attractive. . . ." How like the picture of Quebec that is! Furthermore, despite the small population, "the garrison of the place is ordinarily 24 regular companies and four of militia, a governor, intendant, royal lieutenant, *procureur général, major, aide-major, commissaire contrôleur, notary Royal*, treasurer, *grand voyer*, and a grand-vicar dependent on the Bishopric of Quebec." Again how, like the picture, this speaks for itself! Perhaps that is why Vaugine de Muisement drew no conclusions from what he observed. He hardly needed to; the conclusion was obvious.

For all their show of imposing buildings, for all their hierarchical panoply of administra-

tors and regiments, both New Orleans and Quebec were feeble settlements. Yet they did have that characteristic superficial glitter of authoritarian enterprises everywhere then as now—that certain masterful aura hovering about the Leader and his works, whether you find him in marbled Baroque palaces or pine-paneled broadloomed administrative offices; that majestic promise of purposeful, untrammeled, concentrated action that untidier forms of administration can never hope to match. When Louis XIV personally "takes over" the government of New France in 1663, for instance, he can reorganize the whole colony in one fell spate of commands. He can promise hordes of settlers and even produce a few (before he changes his mind). He can erect great new buildings, and found whole new industries, simply by signing pieces of paper. And all this he can do with such a grand air of calm command that thoughtful citizens in the patchwork English colonies to the south must despair—how can their people, so chronically and cantankerously resistant to authority, hope to withstand the kind of unified, disciplined, single-minded society marching to its preannounced goal that the acts of Louis promise to create? As late as 1719, Jean Law's grandiose plans can still make the Atlantic seaboard uneasy; surely, with all the concentrated resources of absolute government behind them, the French may yet fill the Mississippi Valley with hostile settlements, encircle the English, choke them in behind the Appalachians. But when the fanfare dies away, when the frantic dust of bustling officials subsides, it turns out that nothing much has changed. Every passing year the English colonies grow stronger; New France goes on stagnating.

That the habit of waiting for top-level decisions will destroy self-reliance is obvious, of course. Occasions there are, no doubt, when societies require a considerable degree of obedience and docility to survive or prosper; but first settlement in a New World is not one of them. New France went on paying for this lack of initiative throughout history. The people Charlevoix saw sitting on the riverbank "waiting for someone to draw up a plan for them" fathered those who submitted, with only a spark of protest, to the top-level decision handing Louisiana over to Spain. (It is interesting to speculate on the reaction had Britain in 1763, say, ceded her American colonies to France.) And the people who let the Spaniards rebuild their city fathered in their turn what Americans coming to Louisiana after its cession to the United States in 1803 so commonly described as "slovenly," "lazy," "slow-moving" Creoles. Throughout history these people seemd to be content, figuratively speaking, to

18. QUÉBECOIS *PARISH CHURCH ARCHI-TECTURE AS CULTURAL EXPRESSION*

(A) Church of St. Laurent, Île d'Orléans, begun 1695, façade 1708, destroyed 1864; a combination of craft and Baroque elements representing perhaps the first distinctively Canadian expression, a result of early independence of spirit in Québecois parishes.

sit on the bank and let administrators build their city for them. Look at the traditional center of the "French Quarter," the old Place d'Armes, and what do we find? A town hall—the Cabildo—and a *presbytère* built by Spaniards in their 18th-century manner (begun after the fire of 1788, remodeled with mansard roofs in 1847). A cathedral begun at the urging of a Spanish governor (in 1789–94, under Don Andrés Almonster y Roxas), its tower added by an American architect (B. H. Latrobe, in 1820), the whole completely reconstructed in 1849 by an academician from France (Jacques N. B. de Pouilly, 1805–1875, who also built the Old St. Louis Hotel with its dome of earthenware pots, and St. Augustine Church). The statue of an American general from Tennessee. Even the famous iron balconies of New Orleans were mostly made in New York. As for the famous Quarter, it—to quote Professor Jones again—"is not French . . . the standard type of architecture is mainly Spanish-American." And for all this there is one main reason—the legacy of absolute government to French America.

The heart of New France was not in Louisiana, however; it was in the parishes of the St. Lawrence. And, here again, if French culture survived the 18th century with any real vitality, it was in spite and not because of official policies. Unlike the more concentrated settlement of New Orleans, Canada consisted of a 150-mile-long string of parishes along both banks of the river whose local curés, seigneurs, and habitants were able to exert a kind of passive resistance to the central power rather like their counterparts in the *Pays d'État* in France. *Ancien régime* administrators were always complaining about "communications" being "difficult," by which they meant, after the manner of their kind, that they were never able to control the settlers there to their liking. They tried hard enough, to be sure; they were always passing edicts and mandates to regulate the number of horses habitants should have, and how they were to be used; what kind of clothes ought to be worn and what sort of

(18 B) Church at Cap Santé, begun 1754 on designs of Jean Maillou, Royal Architect of New France (a Canadian, b.1668, d.1753), *completed by local artisans after the Cession; its ostentation manifests the great vitality of parish life.*

19. THE LEGACY OF ABSOLUTE GOVERN-MENT IN NEW FRANCE

(A) Main Street, L'Île-aux-Coudres, Quebec, as it was c.1948. Probably no house is *earlier than the 19th century, and the church was built c.1880; but in the one instance traditional craft forms are preserved, in the other a traditional social function from the Middle Ages in France.*

entertainments indulged in; how people should feel about local and international events, and so on. But they were never able to enforce them "properly." Their failure was signalized in 1722, when Laval's successor, St.-Vallier, was forced to split the Bishop of Quebec's once monolithic and private mission field into eighty-two independent parishes, thus giving up attempts at autocratic control of religious—and by extension, social—life in the colony. These parishes at once became, and remained well into the 20th century, the basic units of *Québecois* society. And it is no coincidence that only in them was any significantly independent spirit ever displayed in New France.

In them the first distinctively Canadian architectural form developed—a unique fusion of upper-class Baroque principles, promoted by the intendants and bishops who initiated church building, with medieval craft traditions perpetuated by the artisans who did the construction; it begins in the parish churches of Laval's seigniories on the Island of Orleans and culminates in the more independent mid-18th-century parishes. In them too there developed, after the 1722 Act of Delimitation, whatever of democracy New France may be said to have had. This was not political democracy, to be sure; the parishes had only one representative official, the *capitaine de milice*, and he was selected, not elected. But it was social democracy of a kind—a corporate consciousness, manifesting itself again best in competition among parishes to erect what were for the time and resources enormous church buildings. A good two dozen of these were built in the twenty years after 1730, including Ste.-Famille (1743) and St.-François (1734–6) on the island of Orleans, and culminating in the clumsily monumental church of Cap Santé (begun 1756, completed after the Cession), all of them providing impressive evidence of the energy and vitality even this minimum of independence was able to generate.

Whatever independence of spirit there was in *Québecois* parishes grew out of medieval roots, not 18th-century concepts of freedom, however. This was a fact that became obvious once the Bourbon bureaucrats had been driven out at the Conquest. The "state of nature" into which the villages then relapsed was a medieval, not a democratic, condition; they became, that is to say, simply communities of peasants, living off the surrounding land; commerce and manufacture were confined to essentials as in Europe during the Middle Ages, and the Church, with all competitors removed, reoccupied its old medieval seat of unchallenged authority.

The Quebec landscape reflected the change

(19 B) Jackson Square (Place d'Armes), New Orleans, Louisiana. "Look at the traditional center of the 'French Quarter,' and what do we find? A town hall—the Cabildo—and a Presbytère built by Spaniards in their 18th-century manner. A cathedral begun at the urging of a Spanish governor, then rebuilt by an academician from France. The statue of an American general from Tennessee. Even the famous iron balconies were mostly made in New York. . . . This is the legacy of absolute government to French America."

at once. Whatever small evidences of the Baroque world there had been—city squares with royal statues, regular town plans (however abortive)—all vanished; the Quebec countryside began increasingly to resemble the backgrounds of 14th- and 15th-century illuminations: neat strips of cultivated field alternating with woodland, with here and there brightly colored groups of houses on hill or riverside, clustered around the village church spire. Even today it retains much of the same character. Only as you come closer, and pick out classical and Victorian details in the church, and the tin, tar paper, and Coca-Cola signs along the main street, does the modern world intrude on that medieval pattern which so decidedly broke through again at the end of the *ancien régime.* And this is as it should be. The Quebec village looked medieval because it was medieval. The church dominated the village visually because it did in fact. This was a medieval peasant community, transplanted directly from Old France.

Exactly the same growth in independent spirit and social democracy, accompanied by the emergence of basically medieval patterns of life, was apparent in the old Louisiana Territory. Here, of course, it was not so much the result of official classes being driven out as of these small settlements being too remote for any effective authoritarian control to be exercised. Places like Cahokia, Kaskaskia, St. Charles, St. Louis, and Ste. Genevieve were settled in such a haphazard manner, indeed, that the dates of settlement are uncertain; and, in any case, people who drifted away from the parishes along the St. Lawrence to take up land around the Indian villages by the Mississippi must have had considerable independence of spirit to begin with. This much is obvious from ecclesiastical records alone. In 1768, for instance, the Bishop of Quebec learned that as soon as the old North-West Territory passed out of French control, one Jean-Baptiste Beauvais bought the church property of Kaskaskia and proceeded to appropriate the sacred vessels for his personal domestic use.

Another report had it that one-fourth of the library of Auguste Chouteau, one of the founders of St. Louis, consisted of books on the Index; still another—Bishop Flaget's of 1814—that in Ste. Genevieve there were families who had received no sacraments for twenty, forty, and even fifty years; and so on. And this freedom from directive authority resulted, as in Quebec, in the emergence of strikingly medieval patterns of peasant life.

Ward Allison Dorrance described Ste. Genevieve, for instance, as "a colony of peasants who grouped their cottages after some feudal memory. There were no inns, shops as we know shops, not even streets as we know streets. Each house was a farm-house, with the ample grounds, the gardens, orchards, and outhouses pertaining to such an establishment anywhere. . . . Each property (or two or three properties) made up a kind of town square or 'block,' placing 'streets' at right angles. One difference was noted regularly by the Anglo-American traveller to whom 'street' meant the wide thoroughfare of New England . . . the Creole lane was narrow. The settlement was huddled elbow to elbow as if, to make the picture complete, a beetling castle should rise from some eminence in its midst."

In Quebec, of course, the picture *was* complete, with a "beetling castle" of a church rising in the center of the village, its size and magnificence in contrast to the houses still astonishing visitors in the mid-20th century.

But in both Quebec and Louisiana, it was in the individual house, the peasant's dwelling, that the medieval character of New France appeared most clearly. Everywhere the French settled, there appeared the same extraordinarily timeless, styleless kind of folk building. That is hardly surprising, after all, for this is the sort of cultural expression we should expect to find above all from the subjects of an authoritarian regime. What is surprising, and particularly significant, is to find the same architectural expression in an example like the Beaumont house on Mackinac Island in Michigan, built c. 1800 by descendants of those French Canadians who had first come to Mackinac in connection with the fur trade of New France, and carried on their language and traditions under British employers and rulers after 1763 (17B).

The peculiar importance of houses like these as historical records comes not so much from local associations, as from their reminding us of a facet of the culture of New France we may all too easily forget—that alongside the docile habitant there grew up the untrammeled *voyageur*, the reckless and lawless *coureur de bois*. And he too survived the political extinction of New France; until well into the 19th century he remained the backbone of the fur trade, providing its folklore and its terminology. The local agents or chief traders were

bourgeois; under them worked clerks or *commis*; under them again, *voyageurs* or *engagés*—*mangeurs de lard* (pork eaters, unaccustomed to nomad fare) if first-year men, *hivernants* if they had spent a season in the woods, and so on. And where did these rough and tough *voyageurs* come from? From the same St. Lawrence parishes that produced the plodding, patient, orthodox peasant.

From earliest times we have two distinct images of the French Canadian—the meek and orthodox peasant who lives in the quiet St. Lawrence parishes content to conform with every dictate of his betters; and the wild woodsman who ventures off into the untamed Missouri country and the old North-West Territory, who has the wilful nature of a savage, who fathers the

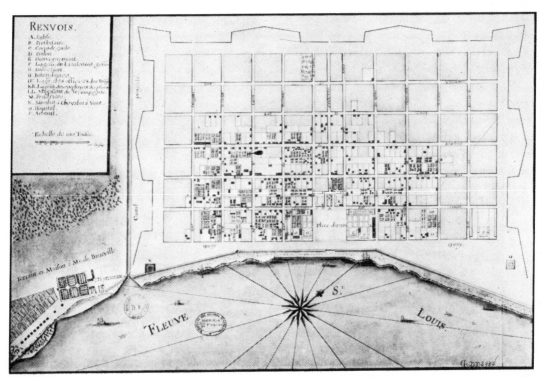

(19 C) "Plan de la . . . Nouvelle Orléans en . . . 1725." This plan was discovered by Samuel Wilson in the archives of the Ministry of Foreign Affairs in Paris. Though the specified fortifications were never in fact executed, their very presence on the plan is significant—an indication that New Orleans was conceived, like the Castillo in St. Augustine, not as a seed from which a thickly settled countryside might grow, but as a shell, a garrison-fortress inherently limited in size, intended to guard the natural resources of an unsettled hinterland.

rebellious half-breed Métis and confounds all constituted authority with his combination of Indian cunning and white man's calculation. At first the two images seem entirely contradictory. But in fact they are complementary. Both are inevitable products of the theory and practice of absolute government.

It is the practice of authoritarian regimes always, everywhere, to centralize authority and delegate responsibility. This means in effect that they maintain a heads-we-win-tails-you-lose position—if official policies succeed, the regime gets all the credit; if they fail, whoever carried them out gets all the blame. It follows that for people living under this kind of administration there are only three sensible courses of action. You may contrive to become a minor official yourself— affiliate with what in Orwell's *Nineteen Eighty-Four* was called the Outer Party—in which case you may be able to identify with the ruler's successes and avoid his censures (in plain language, this is the "if you can't lick 'em, join 'em" attitude). Few native-born Canadians or Louisiana French managed this, however. Most of them found the second course easier—to make a habit of avoiding responsibility by becoming or pretending to be unambitious drones, capable of doing no more and no less than exactly what they were told. But in every generation there are always some who find it temperamentally impos-

sible to be either sycophants or peasants. In this group are ne'er-do-wells, delinquents, social misfits of all sorts, of course; but also vital, intelligent, creative and imaginative people, whose views and insights could do the state great service. In New France there was no way to express any views contrary to official policies and programs. Absolute governments by definition provide for no "loyal opposition"; opposition by definition implies disloyalty. For the "contrary-minded" there was only one alternative—to go beyond or outside the law. In well-settled communities this means peasant revolts, *Jacqueries*; in New France, as in the earlier Europe of Robin Hood or William Tell, it meant taking to the woods. To lose so many of its potentially best citizens from every generation was, of course, a drain on human resources New France simply could not stand; houses buried in the wildernesses of Michigan or Missouri are as surely manifestations of the futility of absolute government as are the ancestral peasant habitations still being perpetuated along the St. Lawrence in the burgeoning world of the 19th century. Truly, as Professor Lower wrote in *Canadians in the Making*, "the defeat of the French was written in every aspect of their institutions"—and nowhere more inexorably than in the architectural remains of New France.

NOTES

It is common dogma that extension of roof eaves into a spreading porch or *galerie* originated in the French West Indies, presumably to provide a place to catch cool breezes in a hot climate; that it was adopted by French settlers in Louisiana; and that it spread up the Mississippi to appear ultimately in Canada. Certainly *galeries* seem to have been extensively developed in the Louisiana Territory; they were often used on all sides of houses, giving the distinctive "umbrella" roof line, and on occasion even churches (apparently) had *galeries*. Yet there are some serious objections to this theory:

(1) The dating of porches. This is notoriously difficult to establish, but what evidence there is does nothing to support the theory that use of porches spread from south to north. The famous *galerie* on the Louis Bolduc house at Ste. Genevieve seems to date c.1770, whereas according to Rexford Newcomb (*Architecture of the Old North-West Territory*, [1950] Chap. III), the Cass house in Detroit had deep *galeries* on three sides as early as c.1700. Furthermore, the numerous examples of galerie-like porches on *Québecois* houses are given 19th-century dates largely by a convention based on the very the-

ory they are supposed to prove. Finally, houses like Lafitte's Blacksmith Shop in New Orleans were being built without *galeries* as late as 1772–91.

(2) It was clearly established by Ward Allison Dorrance ("The Survival of French in the Old District of Ste. Genevieve," *University of Missouri Studies*, X, 2, [pp. 1–133] April 1935) that settlers there and elsewhere along the Mississippi came down from Canada, not up from Louisiana, bringing their *Canadien* accent in speech and other customs with them; why and how use of porches should have spread in the opposite direction is not apparent.

(3) If porches were devised for comfort in hot climates, why were they so common in Quebec and in the Hudson Valley? Furthermore, who could use a porch in comfort without screens to keep out the insects, which abound in such warm climates as the West Indies or Louisiana? Yet, according to an article in "American Notes" (*JSAH*, X, 2, May 1951), screens were first mentioned in English colonies c.1732, and only by the 1770s did "skreens" of "brass wire" become common, so that one could hardly expect them earlier in technologically backward New France. Finally, folk architecture by definition only very slowly adapts traditional building types to new climatic situations; for all these reasons, a West Indian origin and early Louisiana development of porches seems suspect.

In sum, the origin of the *galerie* is to be sought, I think, not in some particular region or situation, but rather in those habits of folk building which were common to early architecture all over the New World. On similar grounds, we may suspect the theory that elevated first floors were invented to cope with low ground in Louisiana, and thence spread to Canada. There is no real evidence that this feature was any less common, or arose any later, in Canada than in Louisiana; it too is found in the Hudson Valley; and it too can best be explained in terms of a common North European folk building tradition.

Vaugine de Muisement was captain of marines in Louisiana; quotations from his *Journal* of 1752 are given in *France et Louisiane* (René Cruchet, ed., Baton Rouge, 1939), pp. 53ff. His statement about the Ursuline convent is in error; the building completed c.1752 was not a restoration of the 1727 convent but a completely different structure on a different site, designed by Broutin in 1745; surviving the fires of 1788 and 1794, it still stands, somewhat altered and repaired.

Further on medieval and Baroque traditions in New France, and architecture in Quebec generally, see my *Looking at Architecture in Canada* (Toronto, 1958) and *Church Architecture in New France* (Toronto, 1955); also Gérard Morisset, *L'Architecture en Nouvelle-France* (Quebec, 1948), and Ramsay Traquair, *The Old Architecture of Quebec* (Toronto, 1947). The researches of Samuel Wilson, Jr., Charles E. Peterson, Buford L. Pickens, and others on French architecture in Louisiana and the Mississippi Valley are summarized in Hugh Morrison's *Early American Architecture* (1952). Other useful works on New Orleans by Samuel Wilson, Jr., acknowledged authority on the subject, include *B. H. Latrobe, Impressions Respecting New Orleans* (ed., 1951), *A Guide to Architecture in New Orleans* (1951), *The Capuchin School in New Orleans* (New Orleans, 1961; with comment on the city plan and Ursuline convent). I am grateful to Mr. Wilson for his criticisms of an earlier draft of this chapter, which appeared in *The Tamarack Review* in 1960 and was republished in *The First Five Years: A Selection from . . . Tamarack* (Oxford, Toronto, 1962).

5. PATROONS AND PAUPERS:
Mercantile Traditions in New Netherlands

A FEW MILES UPRIVER from the Bear Mountain Bridge, in a little backwater eddy off the main line of modern traffic, is the hamlet of West Coxsackie, New York, one of a few remaining places where something of the original Dutch character of the Hudson Valley survives. Nearby stand two old "Dutch colonial" houses, both built by members of that Bronck family after whom The Bronx is named. They are very different types, however. One of them, built by Leendert Bronck c.1738, is a large structure of brick, two and a half stories high, with an elegant gable edged in distinctive "mouse-tooth" brickwork. It is reminiscent of, and may well have been copied from, Fort Crailo, seat of the eastern branch of a vast "patroonship" granted Kiliaen van Rensselaer by the Dutch West India Company, and begun in 1642 with tile and brick sent out from the van Rensselaer estate in Holland. (Fort Crailo may still be seen—as remodeled in the 1740s and restored in modern times—in Rensselaer, New York.) Being in the country, both Fort Crailo and Leendert Bronck's house have their entrances in the long side; otherwise, however,

20. *Bronck houses, West Coxsackie, New York. Stone house built by Pieter Bronck c.1663, left;* brick, *by Leendert Bronck c.1738, right. Maintained by the Greene County Historical Society.*

21. NEW NETHERLANDS URBAN HOUSE
TYPES, AS THEY WERE

   (A) Drawing by George Holland of Upper
Broad Street, New York, c.1797, showing the new
Federal Hall (center), the furniture establishment of Duncan Phyfe (left), and two survivors
of old Dutch New York (right). The one dated
by its ornamental beam anchors "1689" was
built for John Hendricks de Bruyn and demolished c.1830.

both are clearly variants of the distinctive kind
of houses you can find in old descriptions and
pictures of New York, Albany, and Schenectady
as they were in the 17th and 18th centuries—
houses of salmon, yellow, red, and purple brick
set off by glazed tiles and headers laid in geometric patterns, with tall narrow gables fronting
the street, edged in steps or mouse-tooth designs,
decorated with iron "beam anchors" wrought
into ornamental patterns, numbers, or letters, and
finials in the form of balls, urns, and weather
vanes. This is, in short, a distinctly urban house
type, traceable directly to origins in the mercantile cities of Holland.

   The other Bronck house, built by Leendert's
ancestor Pieter in the 1660s, is very different. It
is quite as clearly a variant of a type which,
from its still numerous representatives in the

countryside and out-of-the-way villages today, we
may recognize as a rural house type, characterized by fieldstone walls (occasionally, and perhaps once invariably, whitewashed), a long
front (three contiguous rooms in the most characteristic plan), one low story high and one
room deep, giving a horizontal, ground-hugging
effect reminiscent of nothing so much as rustic
cottages in Scotland or Ireland or Flanders. Here
together, then, built on the same land by the
same family, are two entirely divergent types of
house. Yet both are typical of New Netherlands.
The origins of both go back to the time when
the United Provinces, through their agent the
Dutch West India Company, laid claim to the
whole vast territory between the Hudson and
the Delaware by virtue of Henry Hudson's discovery of the "North" and "South" rivers in

(21 B) Detail from the famous water-color drawing by William Strickland and/or Robert Mills in connection with B. H. Latrobe's survey of New Castle, Delaware, 1804–5, representing Front Street (now the Strand). Founded by the Dutch as Fort Kasimir c.1646, briefly held by the Swedes 1653–5, taken over and named by the English in 1664, New Castle was for a few decades the leading port on the Delaware. But following the rise of Philadelphia it sank into provincial insignificance, and the architecture here summarizes this history. John Boyer, who built the Tile House (second from right) c.1687, was the son of a Dutch or Huguenot settler of 1651; his house was typical of the urban New Netherlands house type (demolished 1884). By c.1722 the old Read house (far left) was already based on early Philadelphia house types, however; and by c.1803, when the present Read house was built beside it, New Castle had long been a cultural backwater—this is essentially a Philadelphia type of the 1770s, only a certain fineness of detail suggesting its later date.

1609. To understand the difference between them is to understand much of the history of Dutch settlement in the New World, and the power of those cultural traditions the West India Company merchants established here.

In all probability, examples of the rural house type always did outnumber those of the urban in New Netherlands; certainly they do now. Rows of stepped-gable brick houses that appear in old drawings of New Amsterdam and Albany, even odd examples that survived elsewhere like the Tile House in New Castle on the Delaware, have all disappeared. The Burgis view of New York early in the 18th century shows that while the newer city was all English Georgian, the lower end of Manhattan Island was still dominated by Dutch houses; the great fire of 1776 destroyed most of them there, however, and in subsequent decades the survivors in New York and elsewhere disappeared through acts of God and man, one by one. By the time interest in preserving architectural heritages had developed, in the early 20th century, they were all gone; their only representatives were variants originally built in the country (and hence somewhat untypical) like Fort Crailo and the Leendert Bronck house. Of the rural-type houses, on the other hand, there are still plenty of extant examples. You can find them scattered all over the old territory of New Netherlands, incluling that part of it along the Delaware founded by a rival Swedish trading company and known in its brief life as New Sweden. Undoubtedly that is why, when we think of a Dutch colonial house, it is the low stone cottage that comes first, and often exclusively, to mind. As early as 1877 a writer in the American Architect was praising the "Dutch Farmhouses of New Jersey" as epitomizing the virtues of solid Dutch colonial settlers: "The Dutch houses are broad (seldom lofty)," wrote J. Cleveland Cady; "horizontal lines predominate; their roof masses are simple, expressive, and often graceful. The houses never seem ambitious or pretentious; the big chimneys, broad, well-lighted doorways, and spreading roofs suggest hospitality and good cheer. . . . The color of these houses was usually quiet; the first story being of brownstone, the gable-ends and carpentry painted an olive or drab. Very often, however, this woodwork was in white, but there was so little of it that it was not glaring." Later generations admired their stonework, their low lines, their homey qualities, even more; with the result that still today Dutch colonial in thousands of suburban houses means the rural house type of New Netherlands, while the urban type is ignored and forgotten.

In early New Netherlands, and well into the 18th century, the situation was quite the reverse. Then the urban house type was considered not only superior functionally to the rural type, but a distinct symbol of upper-class status. This we can deduce from much evidence. From cases where both were used on the same building: we naturally think of stone as a more expensive and aristocratic material than brick, but not so in New Netherlands, where "it is amusing," as Professor Morrison has written, "that [stone] was considered the humbler material, while brick— the Dutchman's true love—was boasted on front and end walls." From the consistent use of brick by the ruling classes of New Netherlands, both

22. "Fort Crailo," Rensselaer, New York. Except for its entrance being in the long side instead of in the stepped-gable end (presumably because in its original country setting there was no such need to conserve street frontage as in the crowded cities of Holland), a characteristic example (and practically the only one extant) of the urban house type identifiable with the patroons of the Hudson Valley and the merchant classes of New Amsterdam and Albany. Traditionally begun 1642 by Kiliaen van Rensselaer, rebuilt to an undetermined extent in the 18th century; rear wing probably added 1762. Extensively restored by the State of New York after 1924.

23. NEW NETHERLANDS RURAL HOUSE TYPES

(A) The "Dutch colonial" rural house type at an early period: "Senate House," Kingston, New York, begun last quarter 17th century as the home of Wessel Wesselse ten Broek, gutted 1777, while serving as temporary headquarters of the state government (hence the name), reroofed shortly thereafter. One-story stone walls, three contiguous rooms on plan, but otherwise lacking most distinctively "Dutch colonial" features.

patroons like Kiliaen van Rensselaer and the wealthy merchants of the towns. And from examples like the Bronck houses: if the house Leendert Bronck built in the 1730s was so different from the one his ancestor Pieter built on land acquired as wilderness from the Indians three-quarters of a century before, it was not because brick was, or in the course of time had become, easier to obtain or use than stone, but because by Leendert's time the Bronck family had come up in the world. Pieter Bronck's house, of fieldstone rather than the flimsy frame structures poorer settlers on Hudson Valley lands so often had to start with, had been for its time and place ambitious enough; but for Leendert it would not do. It was not a question of regional preference, obviously. Neither was it a matter of materials, for already in Pieter's day bricks had been available; kilns were operating in New Amsterdam by 1628, and Kiliaen van Rensselaer had built one for his patroonship in 1630;

further, by the 1640s brick was being exported from Albany to the South (Delaware) River, so that bringing it to the site was no problem. Nor yet did it concern changing styles, for rural stone house types like Pieter's were still being built along the Hudson into the 19th century. This was a matter of prestige. Stone houses were the mark of lower-class and lower-middle-class living, the kind of dwelling proper for smaller farmers. By the 1730s, the Bronck family wealth had increased; Leendert wanted a house to express his aspirations towards the status of larger landowners. Still at that time he felt only the elegant brick gables of the urban house type would do it. And it remained so, as long as the original culture patterns of New Netherlands still held in the Hudson Valley.

You could once see the distinction between upper and lower social classes symbolized with equally deliberate clarity in furnishings. Early inventories dramatize how different the furnish-

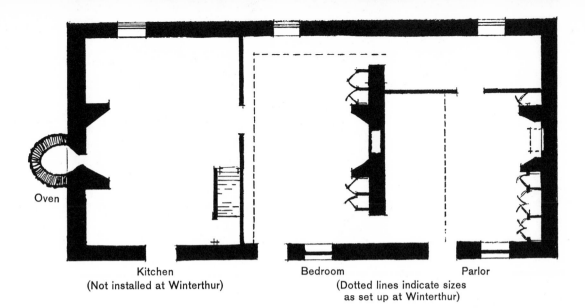

Oven

Kitchen
(Not installed at Winterthur)

Bedroom
(Dotted lines indicate sizes
as set up at Winterthur)

Parlor

(23 B) "Standard plan" of the rural New Netherlands house type: three contiguous rooms make up the Hardenbergh house, near Kerhonkson (Ulster County), New York, as built for Johannes G. Hardenbergh (1731–1812) in 1762. Parts of two of the rooms, acquired by Mr. Henry Francis du Pont when the house was demolished in 1938, are restored in the Winterthur Museum, Delaware.

---

ings of the urban house type must once have been from those of a rural cottage. In the one case, furniture, china, pictures (often in astonishing numbers), appointments of all kinds imported from all over the world, in the latest fashion, with a provenance as definite as the origins of the urban house type itself; in the other, simple handmade articles practically indistinguishable from folk art anywhere. But in the course of the 18th century, with the gradual assimilation of the old Dutch ruling class into English society, the distinction dissolved, beginning at the top and working down. The Philipse mansion at Yonkers (c.1720) and the Van Cortlandt town house in New York (1748–9) were early evidences of it—the abandonment of older conventions in favor of the current standards of English taste, which prescribed Palladian forms and stone as the proper building material for gentlemen. By the 1760s Colonel Johannes Hardenbergh, though belonging to an old established family whose patent to extensive lands had been confirmed by Queen Anne, evidently felt no great prejudice against building a typical rural house type for himself near Kerhonkson, New York; certainly the two rooms from his house restored in the Winterthur Museum have the typical exposed transverse and summer beams, "Dutch door," and lintel stone inscribed with family monogram and date, of Hudson Valley farmsteads. Yet the furnishings still show that no ordinary farmer lived there. Delft garniture from Holland; delft bottles, barber bowl, yellowware and "scratch-blue" white salt-glaze stoneware from England; other ceramics from New York, New England, Pennsylvania, New Hampshire, Long Island; artifacts of brass, iron, and copper from Holland, red-and-green gilt-crested clock from Friesland; works by Netherlands goldsmiths and silversmiths—such a variety of imported articles originally was proper not to a rural cottage but to the merchants' houses of New York and Albany. As for the metalwork and furniture by local artisans— the broadly proportioned Queen Anne chairs with heart-shaped splats and the great poplar *kas*

51

made locally c.1710, with its *trompe l'oeil* decoration in grisaille, clumsy ball feet and bold projections—these represent a parallel to the *Québecois* town style, work whose derivation from specific styles (in this case, Dutch Baroque furniture), at however great a remove, still manifests an upper-class heritage.

After the Revolution, the disappearance of the old Dutch ruling classes as such proceeded apace; and out with them went their characteristic house type. By the time the last vestiges of the old patroon system were formally abolished by act of the New York State Legislature in 1846, stepped-gable brick houses had practically vanished from the landscape, to general approbation; in 1853 a writer for *Putnam's Magazine* still recalled with satisfaction how one of the last survivors of Dutch New York, John Hendrick de Bruyn's house on upper Broad Street, had been demolished twenty years before: "We never waste a tear," he exulted, "over the death of an old Fogy, especially a Dutch one, which . . . must be admitted to surpass in desolation all the other varieties of conservatism extant." And that was symbolic; for, as this writer perhaps dimly realized in his democratic enthusiasm, the urban house type had been the peculiar vehicle and expression of a kind and degree of class consciousness uniquely characteristic of New Netherlands among the American colonies.

The great Dutch trading companies responsible for first claiming, governing, and peopling New Netherlands established there an essentially new kind of society. Nothing quite like it had existed before. Spain had preserved and transplanted to the New World the old feudal society, where rank was determined by birth and conquest. Position in French society, in both Old and New Worlds, depended on a hierarchy of family connections and court influence. But in the mercantile capitalist society developed in the late-medieval bourgs of Flanders and perfected in early-17th-century Holland, rank and position came essentially not from heredity or land or influence, but from wealth, commercial enterprise, and financial speculation. Though here as anywhere else the right cradle never hurt a career, still it was possible to move from one class to another, up or down, with a new and unheard-of freedom. With such fluidity came a new problem, however. Like all people who have risen in the world, the Dutch mercantile classes needed to satisfy themselves by outward signs that they had indeed reached comparable upper-class status to the old feudal lords of Europe. Lacking castles and imposing family trees or royal titles like those Louis XIV distributed so munificently, they had to seek other means of expressing their wealth and social position. In clothes, in furniture, in paintings, above all in buildings—and especially the distinctive gabled brick mansions of Amsterdam and Haarlem and Dordrecht—they found them.

The burghers who had created Holland's mercantile empire did not invent the Dutch urban house type. Its characteristic features and plan—main entrance in the narrow gable end, long dimension running back into the lot—were common to north European cities from late medieval times on; the London house type later brought to Philadelphia had the same origins, for instance. But these burghers had perfected the type and made it their peculiar social symbol. In an alluvial country, lacking forests and stone, they had developed the most skilful brickwork in Europe, distinctive in size ("Holland brick" was a standard in both Old and New Worlds), bond, and variety. In cramped cities where land was too valuable to waste on warehouses, they had developed the gable end into a remarkable combination of beauty and utility. The winch and pulley by which the merchant owner's goods could be lifted directly from street or canal into his top-floor attic for storage became an ornamental device, complementing the decorative patterns of iron beam-ends, which in turn were set off by richly textured brickwork, stepped gable edges, and finials. And the new kind of city they had created in Holland gave these houses a distinctive symbolism. Medieval towns had here-

24. FOLK VARIANTS IN THE NEW NETHERLANDS RURAL HOUSE TYPE

(A) "Van Cortlandt Manor," Croton, New York. Actually a farmhouse, begun even before 1683, when Stephanus van Cortlandt (1643–1700) began to acquire the extensive properties along the Hudson he patented in 1697 as the Van Cortlandt manor. Steep roof, elevated first floor, and what would be called in the Louisiana territory a galerie combine to give the manor a French appearance, but all seem part of the original design, or added by the mid-18th century, when the family first took up year-round residence; in 1770 George Whitefield preached from this verandah.

tofore been communities of feudal peasants, who went out in the morning to work surrounding fields, returning to the protection of walls at night. But the Dutch city was created by merchants, middlemen whose homes and places of business were one and the same (hence the winch and pulley for loading goods into the attic which, significantly enough, were specified by the Dutch West India Company for the first houses in New Amsterdam), who took raw materials from the country and transshipped them either directly or as finished products of some kind, controlling in this way the wealth of the country and so becoming its ruling class. In situation and function these houses were different from those of farmers, or of the "working class"; and the difference in appearance soon became symbolic of class status as well. This was the type of society, city, and house the merchants

of the West India Company transplanted to the New World.

The origin of the New Netherlands urban house type, and its association with upper-class pretensions, are thus obvious. But where did the rural house type come from? That is quite another and still largely unresolved matter. The basic problem is that it is hardly a "type" in the same sense at all. For, while the general and collective image seems plain enough, in detail it dissolves into a mass of contradictions. In any typical selection of examples, we will find that some have flaring eaves and some have not; some have flat dormers and some have none; some have gambrel roofs and some straight gables; some have a raised first story and some not; some have stone walls and others (on Long Island particularly) clapboarded frame; some

(24 B) "Flemish colonial" variant of the rural house type: Zabriskie-von Steuben house, begun 1737 by miller John Zabriskie, confiscated and presented to Baron von Steuben after the Revolution, bought back by the Zabriskie family 1797, now the headquarters of the Bergen County Historical Society. In its present form, with three contiguous rooms, wide flaring eaves forming a porch, gambrel roof and long low walls of red sandstone, it seems the very paradigm of the distinctive house type developed in Northern New Jersey by settlers from New Netherlands pushing into this region after the English conquest of 1664; but appearances are deceptive. As originally built by Zabriskie, it consisted of a single-room house of brownstone with a straight-gabled roof; in 1752 his sons John and Peter added a second room to the south, and another to the north thirty-odd years later, also increasing its depth to the rear. Only then did the gambrel roof and flaring eave tie the whole into the single dwelling we see in North Hackensack, New Jersey.

have three contiguous rooms on the same level and some do not; one has almost "French" *galeries* and another no porch at all, and so on. Partly in consequence, it seems impossible to point to any one part of Europe as the source of the rural New Netherlands house type. All its characteristic details can be found in one place or another; but, despite the most vigorous ransackings of the Low Countries, no generally satisfactory explanation has been forthcoming as to why "Dutch" farmhouses on Long Island or in New Jersey, say, appeared when and with the distinctive combination of features they did.

These circumstances made some observers think that this rural house type must have developed locally in the Hudson Valley. Very early it was noted that the flaring eave, perhaps its most distinctive single feature, seems to appear most frequently on later examples, suggesting some sort of evolution from slight or no projections to flaring extensive enough to form a porch roof. On such grounds some scholars—notably Rosalie Fellows Baily in her 1936 study, *Prerevolutionary Dutch Houses . . . in Northern New Jersey and Southern New York* (areas where flaring eaves are particularly conspicuous)—argued that the 18th-century Dutch colonial was in fact "a native style that had no prototype in Europe."

Others persisted in looking for a European origin, however. Thomas Jefferson Wertenbaker's theory in *The Middle Colonies* (1938) was perhaps the most ingenious. Noting that "houses duplicating in almost every detail the 'colonial Dutch' farmhouse . . . are to be found in Canada," he proposed that the origin of the rural house type "must be sought in some part of Europe which sent emigrants to both Quebec and to southern New York and northern New Jersey. This leads us directly to the maritime sections of Flanders. . . ." Whence he deduced that "if one sees a cottage with the roof lines curving out over the front and rear walls, he may assume that the original owner came from the clay house region of Flanders; if the roof lines are straight and the projection is lacking, that it belonged to a settler from the sandy plains or some other district where the farmers built solidly of brick."

In the intellectual climate of the 1930s, when claims for unusual originality or independence in American life were fashionably derided as naïve and provincial survivals of 19th-century chauvinism, and the opposite principle—that colonies, so far from initiating new forms, tend instead to preserve old ones longer even than their homelands—was scoring some of its most brillant successes, the theory of a "Flemish colonial" style rapidly took precedence. Yet it presents at least as much difficulty as the "native genius" concept. To believe it, you must assume that settlers of Flemish descent not only went on reproducing their national house types exactly to the third and fourth generations, but that they reproduced them more accurately as time went on—for the more pronounced its flared eave, the later a Flemish colonial house is likely to be. You must forget that in Quebec the flared eave is also found most frequently on later houses; and that in the earlier examples it is associated with Normans, not Flemings. Furthermore, you must assume that Flemish emigration to Quebec was extensive enough to account for the house types developed there, an assumption not borne out by *Québecois* statistics, and inherently dubious, since it would be strange indeed to find in

Quebec, whose immigration (especially in the 17th century) was so notoriously restricted to the most orthodox Catholics, settlers from the same regions as those that peopled Protestant New Netherlands. That there are similarities between *Québecois* and Hudson Valley house types is incontestable, and significant; but I think they must be explained on grounds broader than local or national origins. For the first fact about the rural population of New Netherlands is that it was drawn, like the details of the rural house type, from no obvious single place in Europe; both are explicable, like the urban house type, in terms of the peculiar mercantile capitalist society established in New Netherlands.

25. Bedroom of the Hardenbergh House, from Kerhonkson, New York, as restored in the H. F. du Pont Winterthur Museum to the period c.1763.

Any history book will confirm that the Dutch West India Company was never much interested in national colonization as such. Its 1621 charter did not even mention a claim to the territory of New Netherlands, and not until 1664 did the States General finally declare that the charter "was not to be construed as directed only to trade, but . . . implied the right to establish colonies. . . ." Trade was what interested the founders of New Netherlands; people they looked on as an incidental and even annoying necessity for securing maximum profits on their New World investment. They had to have people manning their colonies for the same reason they needed men to man their armies; and they went about obtaining them the same way. Just as European historians describe the Dutch armies as "recruited from every Protestant country in Europe," so we learn that "Rensselaerswick, the great patroonship on the Hudson, recruited its leaseholders from among the Norwegians, Danes, Germans, Scots, and Irish as well as Hollanders." From this, two conclusions follow—aside from the merchant and patroon class, the first settlers of New Netherlands must have been (1) unusually heterogeneous; and (2) unusually poor.

For their heterogeneity we have plenty of evidence: the well-known remark of Father Jogues, in 1644, about hearing eighteen different languages spoken in Manhattan; records of Walloons and French in Albany, of twenty-three Jews come to New Amsterdam from Brazil; Peter Stuyvesant's description of New Netherlands as "peopled by the scrapings of nationalities," and so on. Their poverty we can infer; for who but the most destitute could have been induced to come to live in a wilderness under a government that "looked upon its colony as a source of dividends . . . bound the settlers by contracts that prohibited trade, change of residence, and transfer of property . . . imposed heavy taxes, including taxes on imports . . . discouraged enterprise . . . and shirked all obliga-

tions of a social character . . ."? Only people with no prospects at all, surely—miscellaneous drifters, social derelicts of one sort or another, peasants from the very bottom of the heap. That is to say, New Netherlands from the first differed significantly from early New England and Virginia in having what was, and was intended to remain, a genuine lower class in its population.

What kind of architectural traditions could we expect from a class like this? We get some idea, perhaps, from the famous early description of lower-class habitations in New Amsterdam, where people "huddled rather than dwelt"; something more, surely, from the fact that "when there was an important building to be built [in New Amsterdam]," as the late R. G. Vail pointed out, "the contract generally showed that the builder, if he was either a mason or a carpenter, was an Englishman. The first Dutchmen who came over were in the fur trade—they weren't mechanics." The upper class was in the fur trade, that is. The class below them—the people who supplied carpenters and masons for early New England or Virginia—here supplied none, because their social stratum was too low for such specialized trades. The kind of building they were used to was too primitive to require such craftsmen. It was also too primitive to survive long. Only by inference from writings, and from evidence provided by the simpler extant early buildings in New Netherlands territory, like the two end sections of the Morton homestead at Essington or the "old Dutch house" in New Castle, can we get some idea what the prototypes of the New Netherlands rural house must have been.

They have been called "pens," and must have been much like the "Irish house of posts walled and devided with close watlle hedges, and thin turfed above" of Plowden's 1646 *Description of the Province of New Albion*. Even so, they were probably better housing than people of this class had known in Europe. "Rightly to imagine the home of a Scots farmer in Queen

26. EVOLUTION OF NEW NETHERLANDS RURAL HOUSE TYPES

(A) Morton homestead, Essington, Pennsylvania. In 1654 the first log section of this house was built by a great-grandfather of John Morton (1724–1777; member of the Continental Congress and only signer of the Declaration of Independence of Swedish descent), one of those settlers brought to the Delaware Valley by the New Sweden Company in defiance of Dutch claims to the territory. Morton's grandfather built a second house near it in 1698, and in 1806 the two houses were joined by a center section of stone to create the effect of a three-room house with separate doors.

Anne's reign," wrote Trevelyan, "we must forget the fine stone farms of a later date, and think of something more like the cabins of western Ireland. It consisted almost always of one story, and often of one room. The style and material of building and the degree of poverty varied in different regions, but walls of turf or unmortared stone, stopped with grass or straw, were very common; chimneys and glass windows were rare; the floor was the bare ground; in many places the cattle lived at one end of the room, the people at the other, with no partition between. The family often sat on stones or heaps of turf around the fire of peat, whence the smoke made a partial escape through a hole in the thatch overhead. . . ."

And if this was true of Scotland, what must conditions in war-wracked northern Europe have been? It has been supposed that the people Peter Minuit found in New Amsterdam in 1628 who "would dig several feet into the ground and line the space with planks and bark, then roof it over with beams covered with bark or sod" were merely putting up temporary habitations; it may well be they were really at the later stage of trying to reproduce the kind of folk building they had known at home!

But despite every handicap of misgovernment and exploitation, the country had resources enough, and inhabitants well enough proportioned to them, so that the standard of living soon began to rise, rapidly and for everyone. Soon even the poorest tenant was able to think of providing himself with a more permanent house of timber, and eventually stone. First appeared simple one-story structures like those of the Morton homestead; with further prosperity, other, larger units might be built next to it, resulting in the appearance of types like the Branford–Van Horne house at Wyckoff or the Dyckman house in New York.

Now, many times before, in many different civilizations, a rise in living standards resulted

in the replacement of primitive habitations of mud or sticks or grass by more permanent structures in wood and stone. And wherever it has happened, what we can call the primitive principle of mimesis has always come into operation. This is the principle whereby forms invented in simpler media tend to be reproduced in later, more complex, and more permanent ones, no matter how difficult or inappropriate that reproduction may be. By the principle of mimesis, ceramic vessels cast on the potters' wheel preserved for centuries the shapes and decorations of the clay-smeared baskets that were their ancestors; by the principle of mimesis, Egyptian temples preserved the archaic forms of ancestral chiefs' houses built of mud and reeds thousands of years earlier. By the principle of mime-

(26 B) Branford–Van Horne house, Wyckoff, New Jersey. A manifestation of the steady growth in prosperity of successive generations of farmers in the old territory of New Netherlands was the practice of adding successively larger units to the original house, relegating the latter to the status of a "back kitchen," or perhaps slave quarters. Typical is this house with its three sections dating from 1747, 1760, and 1800, each slightly different in proportions and roof treatment. Restored in 1957.

sis, Greek builders created in stone architectural orders deriving from the wooden forms of archaic temples. By the principle of mimesis—the simple psychological fact that people find familiar forms "look better" even if new materials have made them pointless and obsolete—the steel bodies of mass-produced 20th-century station wagons were made to imitate the appearance of their wooden-paneled custom-built forerunners. In the "patroon painting" of the Hudson Valley, primitive principles are everywhere apparent. And if found there, in the most individualistic of the arts, how much more should we expect to see architecture, the most collective of the arts, influenced by them?

Like the huts of European peasantry everywhere, the first ordinary houses in New Netherlands had roofs of thatch or straw; that was mentioned in the company's early instructions to its agents, and Wassenaer's 1626 report on New Amsterdam notes that even "the counting house [general store] there is kept in a stone building thatched with reed." A thatched roof normally has an overhang; that is an integral part of the technique. What is more natural than that people as primitive as the New Netherlands lower class would, in replacing their first dwellings in wood, be governed by the principle of mimesis and reproduce this familiar feature, with a result something like the "old Dutch house" in New Castle? Or that they would continue to do so for as many generations as they remained unsophisticated and unconscious of style, going on elaborating the overhang until it developed into an elegant flare, much as archaic Greek art became richer and richer without abandoning primitive principles, or as automobile fenders sprouted purely ornamental fins, and automobile bodies purely ornamental strips of chrome? Wherever the progression from primitive thatched dwellings to larger and more permanent constructions went on, we might expect to find the principle of mimesis at work—and it, rather than common national origins, can most conveniently explain why we find flared eaves sporadically yet so

universally in Quebec, on Long Island, in New Jersey, in Maryland (e.g., "Susquehanna," c.1654, now in the Ford Museum, Dearborn), in New England (e.g., the Hart house, Guilford, Connecticut)—indeed, everywhere.

And it may be that the workings of primitive principles help explain other problems in colonial and provincial American art as well. The practice of raising first floors considerably above ground level, for instance. This too is a characteristic of houses both in New Netherlands and Quebec; it also is evident in Louisiana. There, it is explained as an ingenious adaptation to environment—raising houses off damp or flooded ground. But that explanation has never been very useful when it comes to houses built on rocky bluffs high above the St. Lawrence, or on the well-drained plains of the Hudson Valley. Might it not be, perhaps, that at least one root of this form is the reproduction in permanent materials of the appearance of simpler, more perishable predecessors? That, like the developed flare of 18th-century eaves, the raised basement at least in part originated in imitation of the appearance of those early frame houses erected on top of the first bark or sod dugouts?

Certainly it is the primitive principle of additive composition that can most simply explain the characteristic Dutch colonial floor plan of three contiguous rooms, with separate entrances. In structures like the Branford–Van Horne house, an obvious origin for this kind of composition is suggested; here the whole is simply the sum of three parts, each quite distinct from the other two, like the additive compositions of a Hudson Valley "patroon painter." If it should happen that the several parts of such a house had the same size and proportions, their addition would result in something like the floor plan we find for the 17th-century Senate House at Kingston, or the 18th-century Zabriskie–von Steuben house at North Hackensack. How this plan could develop as an accidental and unconsidered outgrowth of the primitive additive principle is evident from examples like the Morton home-

27. NEW NETHERLANDS PUBLIC BUILD-INGS

(A) New Amsterdam waterfront as it was c.1660. Model based on the Costello plan of New York, showing the commercial district. Largest building is the City Tavern built 1641–2 to accommodate visiting merchants. Rented to the town in 1654 for use as a Stadthuys *(town hall) and also on occasion as a jail and law court; torn down, 1699. Contemporary documentation and views of it differ; here we see a large two-story house, with roomy loft and basement, but basically unpretentious, befitting its mercantile origin.*

stead, where the two end rooms were not merely unconnected until the 19th century, but actually had a road running between them.

So considered, the rural house type of New Netherlands is a distinctive and significant cultural expression. But it was not, like the urban type, an expression of Dutch (or Flemish, or any other) national traditions transplanted to the New World. Materially and culturally destitute to a degree unparalleled in New England or Virginia or even New France, the lower classes of New Netherlands developed an architecture based on the universal principles of primitive art; whatever of national tradition appeared in it was diverse, vestigial, incidental. That is the truth behind the theory that this was an indigenous American creation. It was perhaps the first expression of that process of fusing many diverse national types into a new creation, borrowing something from all but distinctive of none but itself, which in the world's mind has been one of the most characteristic features of the civilization of America in general, and of New York in particular.

Besides the two distinctive house types, mercantile capitalist cultural patterns also help explain much about public architecture in New Netherlands. We often assume that because modern nationalism began to develop at the same time as mercantile capitalism, both are products of the same impulse. But the fact is—and New Netherlands affords an excellent demonstration—that they not only are unrelated but often antipathetic. Nationalism emphasizes the differences between one group of people and another. Its tendency is to bring together people of similar race, language, customs, and religion and exclude others. Capitalism, on the contrary, depends for its growth on needs for goods and services common to men everywhere; the capitalist's instinct is always to include more and more people in his operations, regardless of such irrelevancies as national origins or culture—"Money talks a universal language." If, in order to secure investments and expand markets, some kind of political control seems necessary, the capitalist may undertake "imperialist" policies; but they are much more in the nature of beating the competition—"business continued by other means"—than of nationalist wars for "glory" or power for its own sake. War means risking a disastrous and perhaps irremediable interruption of normal mercantile operations; all things being equal, the capitalist would much rather conduct business peacefully, even to the extent of overwhelming his own culture with hordes of foreigners. It is this fundamentally antinationalist bias of capitalism that the history of New Netherlands records; forts, public buildings, churches, all make it manifest.

Because the spirit established in New Netherlands by the capitalist burghers who founded it was so set against "imperialist expansion," the "miserable little fort" that a visitor to Albany saw in 1643 was still more like "a pound to impound cattle" than a military post when Governor Bellomont inspected it in 1699; not until 1702 was Fort Orange even provided with a stone wall. The fort at New Amsterdam was little better; people frequently complained that it was hardly in condition to withstand rootings by pigs and foragers after firewood, let alone hostile forces. On the Delaware, where commercial interests were threatened by Swedish competition, the Dutch built more energetically

—Fort Kasimir at New Castle seems to have been quite respectable. But even here, the contrast of these lightly garrisoned and niggardly

(27 B) First Dutch Reformed church, Bergen, New Jersey, constructed by builder Willem Day in 1680, demolished c.1773. Aside from the twin-gabled and belfried stone church built at New Amsterdam in 1642 by two Englishmen from Stamford, Connecticut, the earliest Dutch church in New Netherlands was one on the Rensselaer lands near Albany c.1656, evidently based on a "wooden model" Kiliaen van Rensselaer is recorded as sending out in 1640, "the shape being mostly that of an eight-cornered mill." This octagonal or hexagonal form, with steep "candle-snuffer" roof, interior with white plastered walls and exposed roof timbering, and pulpit facing the entrance, seems to have been a distinctively Dutch Reformed creation. Its precedent is known to have been followed, both in form and small size, at Hackensack and New Brunswick as well as Bergen in New Jersey, and on Long Island at Brooklyn, Bushwick, Jamaica, and New Utrecht.

maintained establishments makes a striking contrast with the elaborate bases of Spanish or French power in the New World.

The Dutch had the same attitude to public buildings. Combining the functions of commercial tavern and civic administration in New Amsterdam's first town hall (built as a tavern, 1641–2, rented to the town as the Stadthuys, 1653) was an economical gesture, no doubt; but hardly one suggesting a community with the degree of public spirit enduring New World colonies demanded. As for schools and churches, the contrast with other colonies was even more painful. Even the Swedish government, long after it had lost its short-lived colony, gave more generous support to the churches planted there than did the burghers of the Dutch West India Company, who, according to Mr. Vail, only built a church in New Amsterdam after Governor Kieft got them to subscribe for one while they were drunk in a tavern: likewise the patroons "shirked all obligations of a social character, throwing on the Dutch Reformed Church the burden of education and the care of the poor." Tiny churches, distinctive in appearance but hardly beginning to serve the needs of more than a fraction of the settlers, makeshift schools of which Ichabod Crane was to seem a representative symbol, were the immediate result. The ultimate result was English conquest and assimilation of New Netherlands.

For the most obvious thing about the public

buildings of New Netherlands was their inadequacy (if not, for all intents and purposes, their nonexistence). And this, like everything else about the colony's architecture and decorative arts, was an expression of the mercantile spirit that pervaded New Netherlands. Maintaining schools, churches, and government buildings was, in mercantilist terms, "unprofitable." In the short run, their absence was not felt. But in the long run, it meant the inevitable extinction of Dutch culture. Churches, schools, and public institutions are the essential agencies for transmitting a national heritage from one generation to another; without them, only folk culture can survive long. The mercantile spirit was set against providing them. So it was that while mercantile capitalism was a much better foundation for colonization than New Spain's decadent feudalism or the absolute government of New France, it was not enough. It was a large factor in the success of the English colonies, to be sure; and it left a large impress on New York for all time. But, to survive, colonies need something more. There has to be some overriding sense of purpose, of national destiny, some enthusiastic commitment to principle, to bring colonists from settled civilized homelands into the wilderness in numbers large enough to establish a new civilization permanently there. This the mercantile spirit alone could not provide; so it was that the future in the New World belonged to others than the Dutch.

NOTES

Quotations from J. Cleveland Cady, "Some Features of the Dutch Farmhouses of New Jersey" (*American Architect*, 2, 1877, pp. 401–2), given by Vincent Scully, *The Shingle Style* (New Haven, 1955), pp. 48–9; from Hugh Morrison, *Early American Architecture* (1952), p. 116, referring to houses in Dutchess County, New York; from *Putnam's Magazine* in John Kuwenhoven, *The Columbia Historical Portrait of New York* (1953), p. 138; on the Dutch West India Company's attitude to colonization and nonsupport of churches and schools from S. G. Nissenson, *The Patroon's Domain* (1937), and the Federal Writer's Project, *New York: A Guide to the Empire State* (1940). R. G. Vail's remarks on early building in New Amsterdam, given at the annual meeting of the Society of Architectural Historians in January 1952, were published as "The Beginnings of Manhattan" (*JSAH*, XI, 2, 1952, pp. 19–22). On inventories of early furnishings, see especially Esther Singleton, *Dutch New York* (1909).

Further on the derivation of the New Netherlands rural house type from universal principles rather than national tradition, it is worth noting that the same growth by successive additions obtains commonly everywhere in early America—from Maine farmhouses to Philadelphia-inspired house types of the Delaware Valley like the Dickinson mansion near Dover, Delaware, or the Willian Hancock house at Hancock's Bridge, New Jersey; ultimately, it derives from the medieval attitude to building. See further Chap. 9.

New Sweden was a far smaller and feebler colony than New Netherlands, on whose claimed territory it briefly encroached (founded 1638 on similar mercantilist lines by a rival trading company, it was conquered by the Dutch in 1655). It contributed little more than peripheral coloring to the main fabric of civilization in America—Swedes are credited by some writers with introducing log-cabin construction; a distinctive type of gambrel roof; possibly the corner fireplace in early Philadelphia houses (e.g., Letitia Street house, Fairmount Park). But the consistent support they afforded their church makes an interesting contrast with the state of New Netherlands. Pastor Nicholas Collin, writing his *Brief Account of the Swedish Mission* at the end of the 18th century, described the mission as

> composed of three distinct rectorships, viz., Wicaco [=Philadelphia] with Kingsessing and Upper Merion; Christina [=Wilmington] in Delaware; and Racoon [=Swedesboro] with Penns Neck in West Jersey. The clergy consisted of three respective rectors, and in later times a minister extraordinary, or common assistant. One of the ordinary pastors was also provost, or commissary, having a degree of superintending authority over the whole mission. The minister extraordinary had from Sweden a yearly salary of £33 1/3 sterling, the commissary office . . . £50. The crown gave to every coming missionary £50 sterling to defray the expense of the voyage, and an equal sum returning. . . .

The remarkable fact that the Swedish crown continued to support Swedish churches in America until 1789—that is, almost a century and a half after losing all political control over its colonists—goes far to explain how the Swedes, despite their very small numbers, maintained their cultural identity almost as long as if not longer than the Dutch.

6. CULT AND CIRCUMSTANCE:
The Puritan Tradition in New England

"THE PARTY which in November 1620 set foot on the shore of New England where the town of Plymouth now stands was not by any means an ideal unit for purposes of colonization; and it is one of the miracles of history that so small a company was able to determine the ultimate destiny of a great nation." So the English writer Martin Briggs introduced his 1932 book, *The Homes of the Pilgrim Fathers in England and America*—as if here at least were a statement no one could question, that everyone took for granted. And so, by and large, it is still. If there is one idea about early American history firmly fixed in most people's heads, it is the primacy of New England. The very name calls to mind an image of grave and pious men, dressed in black, dwelling in austerest surroundings on their own and other people's sins—but exceedingly practical and progressive withal, in whose colleges American learning began, in whose homely workshops American industrial inventiveness first found expression, in whose town meetings lay the seeds of American democracy. It is a noble image, one that Yankees from Governor Bradford to John Adams to Calvin Coolidge never tired of confirming and embellishing. Not until quite modern times, however, was it often confirmed by anyone else. And in the record of 17th-century New England architecture and furniture, it is more often than not flatly contradicted.

Is a room like this (*28A*), or any other typical 17th-century New England interior, remarkable for evidences of a progressive spirit? Hardly. To be sure, represented in this furniture are both what would be called in New France a "town style" and in New Netherlands the "urban type"—pieces evidently imitating at greater or lesser remove tides of Elizabethan and Jacobean taste—and a folk tradition. But the pre-dominant forms and principles are those of medieval folk art. The same direct expression of construction that appears in the great summer beams and rafters of the architecture is evident in the sturdy strutting and pinning of joint stool and bed, and in the elaborately turned court cupboard. Everywhere the stiff angularity and additive composition of medieval heritage prevails—in stretcher and trestle tables, in all the various New England chair types, whether "Brewster" with its spindles beneath the arms and sometimes under the seat; "Carver" with spindles in back only; ostentatiously Tudor "Harvard"; or simple slat-backs with rush seats; even later "Windsors."

Or is this furniture remarkable for plainness? Even less; indeed, quite the opposite. Color and pattern and ornament run riot everywhere. The only difference here between more elaborate and self-consciously styled pieces like the court cupboard and the simplest chair is one of degree. Typical of early New England furniture is such ornament as applied "jewels" made of half-spindles and bosses painted black; inset patterns of different-colored woods; chip-carved geometric panels; paintings in flat solid colors of sunflowers, initials, dates, vines, and so on. More than anything else, the furniture has what we think of as a "Pennsylvania Dutch" lavishness of decoration. Even the exposed oak corner posts and plaster wall-filling between creates a decorative pattern. Cumulatively, 17th-century New England interiors give an overwhelming impression of rural folk traditions, medieval survivals, and above all exuberant ornament. Far from being the image of the dour Puritan, they confirm that, in C. S. Lewis's words, "the doctrines of early Protestantism . . . were at first doctrines not of terror but of joy and hope. . . ."

It follows that nearly every association which now clings to the word Puritan has to be elim-

28. NEW ENGLAND INTERIORS

(A) Room from the house of tanner Thomas Hart of Ipswich, Massachusetts, presumably built c.1650, as restored in the H. F. du Pont Winterthur Museum. The room has been furnished as a typical rather than a specific example of New England furnishings in the third quarter of the 17th century.

---

inated when we are thinking of the early Protestants. Whatever they were, they were not sour, gloomy, or severe; nor did their enemies ever bring such charge against them. For More . . . Protestantism was not too grim, but too glad, to be true: "I could for my part be verie wel content that sin and pain all were as shortlye gone as Tyndale telleth us" (*Confutation*). Even in Calvin himself we shall find an explicit rejection of "that uncivile and froward philosophy" which "alloweth us in no use of the creatures save that which is needful, and going about as it were in envie to take from us the lawful enjoyment of God's blessings. . . ."

Protestantism springs directly out of a highly specialized religious experience . . . a catastrophic conversion. The man who has passed through it feels like one who has waked from nightmare into ecstasy. Like an accepted lover, he feels that he has done nothing, and never could have done anything, to deserve such astonishing happiness. All the initiative has been on God's side; all has been free, unbounded grace. . . . It is faith alone that has saved him; faith bestowed by sheer gift. From this buoyant humility, this farewell to the self with all its good resolutions, anxiety, scruples, and motive-scratchings, all the Protestant doctrines originally sprang.

This "buoyant humility," this joy, is everywhere expressed in the New England interior, in gay and intricately decorated furniture, richly patterned carpets, rows of colorful dishes, glowing pewter. Whatever the "Puritan plain style" may

(28 B) Interior of "Old Ship" Meeting House, Hingham, Massachusetts. Originally built 1681, successively enlarged 1730 and 1755, altered in detail during the 19th century. In con-trast to the profusion of decorative detail on the furniture of the Hart Room at Winterthur is the "plain style" of the interior here, with an ex-posed structure in the medieval tradition.

be, it must be something very different from this. To find it, we have to go outside the Puritan's home, to his 17th-century meeting house.

"Forthright and severe, like the Puritan divines who preached within it, this high, square church has a quaint and prim propriety"—so Professor Morrison described Old Ship at Hingham, sole survivor of the old meeting-house type. Now this is more like it! This is what we mean by the "Puritan style"! But what about the Puritans themselves—is this what they thought of as their "natural expression"? Not exactly. Like Christian in Bunyan's *Pilgrim's Progress*, Puritans were people acutely aware of being sojourners in a strange and hostile world.

This meant that their every public act was more liable to scrutiny and judgment than ordinary people's: "For we must consider," as John Winthrop preached aboard the *Arabella*, "that we shall be as a city upon a hill, the eyes of all people are upon us." It also meant that they had special problems to face on the road to the Celestial City. One of the worst of them was what Bunyan called "Vanity Fair." Vanity Fair, as he described it, was "no new erected business, but a thing of ancient standing," and it seems odd at first that in Bunyan's allegory the Pilgrims come upon it so well along in their journey. Why had they not met its attractions—"houses, lands, trades, places, preferments, honours, titles . . . "—at the outset, when they were still in the City of Destruction? Because, says Bunyan —and here he speaks the Puritan mind—Vanity Fair stands for temptations of a subtle and spiritual, not a gross and carnal, sort:

> As in other fairs of less moment, there are several rows and streets . . . where such and such wares are vended; so here, likewise, is the Britain-row, the French-row, the Italian-row, the Spanish-row, the German-row, where several sorts of vanities are to be sold. But as in other fairs some one commodity is the chief of all the fair; so the ware of Rome and her merchandise is greatly promoted in this fair. . . .

The temptation, that is to say, is of pomp and worldly circumstance attaching to the Church— especially the established "national" churches, but even to the most "purified" and reformed bodies as well—as a human institution. The sin is spiritual pride. That is why it attacks Christians well along the way, not at the beginning of their journey, and why Bunyan shows it to be one of their deadliest perils. Against it no precautions are too extravagant. Nothing of possible spiritual pride must be expressed in, or incited by, the architecture of church buildings, or any other public expression of the Christian commonwealth. Seductive attractions of stained-glass windows, of tracery, of towers and pinnacled buttresses and polished pews—all such must be sternly suppressed. Out of this conviction came the Puritan plain style.

The plain style, then, was not a natural expression of Puritan culture. It was the public face Puritanism showed the world, an assumed manner, as consciously and deliberately put on as the sober black and white and grey costume or the nasal gravity of speech. Not that there was anything necessarily hypocritical about the Puritans' expressing one mood in private houses and another in town and meeting houses, any more than there is in one man's being able to deliver a Gettysburg Address and also tell droll stories. Between the private ornateness of Pilgrim furniture and the public Puritan plain style

there is no necessary contradiction; both are complementary manifestations of a coherent, consistent attitude to life. For while the one belongs to an artistic tradition, the other is not a matter of aesthetics at all. The plain style is not a style; it is a declaration of principle and belief.

Except for doctrinaire "Separatists" like the Pilgrims who founded Plymouth, most Puritans were nominally still members of the Church of England, still Englishmen who shared the instinct of colonists everywhere to reproduce the civilization whence they came. But in one respect they differed; they had no intention of reproducing the religious structure of English society. As their name implies, the "Puritans" (i.e., "purifyers") wanted a Church not merely nominally, or organizationally, or legally Christian, but one that would be integrally Christian— something like Heaven, made up all of sheep, with no goats and no hybrids. Theirs was to be a church of the "elect." It seemed plain to them that God, for some reason inscrutable to men, had elected some people for salvation—some were naturally good, others just as naturally bad and, apparently, damned—and society should be built around that fact. Not that this doctrine of predestination or election was something the Puritans invented to justify themselves, of course; as in all enduring theology, the fact came first and the theory later. Predestination was simply something thoughtful people observed (and still can observe—our disciplinary schools and prisons are full of cases of people who for no discernible psychological, environmental, or any other reason will not or cannot "go straight"). They deduced the theology from observation; if it gave the saved (as even the Anglican prayer book judiciously conceded) "unspeakable comfort" to think of their election, that was an effect and not a cause of the doctrine. And it was from this doctrine that the basic differences between parish church and meeting house, in forms and in function, all derived.

The parish church was intended to accommodate the entire population of a town or countryside; the meeting house, only the elect. It followed that meeting houses were smaller, in proportion to the population, than parish churches; one writer has calculated that in 1700 the meeting houses of New England could have accommodated no more than a quarter of the total population on Sundays. Even had the English government not dumped all sorts of convicts and others of what it considered its "surplus population" in the colonies, this would have been so; heredity being what it is, the elect were soon a minority even in very early New England. It followed further that meeting houses could never be churches in the Roman or Anglican sense of houses where God is more available than in other buildings. To "purify" the Church of what they considered a distorted and pernicious medieval distinction between the religious and the secular life was one of the great aims of all Reformers, and especially of the Puritans. Preaching the "priesthood of all believers," they emphasized that the way to Heaven lay not in any special spiritual vocation or religious works, but simply through the spirit in which one did the work of everyday; not the kind of work it was, but how one did it, was what counted. They felt it then a kind of blasphemy for a man to claim that by putting on robes of some sort he could become something more than a man, or that one particular day—like Christmas or Easter—could be more sacred than the rest. They felt it blasphemous to presume that a piece of bread by having words read over it could become something other than a piece of bread. In the same way they felt it blasphemous to imagine that a building could by statues or exquisite proportions or "glorious" ornament or special ceremonies ever become anything more than a building: "No place is capable of any holiness under Pretence of whatsoever Dedication or Consecration," as the Westminster Confession put it. They objected, in short, to "consecration" —of men, of wafers, or of buildings. It followed, finally, that whatever form their place of worship should take, it should above all not look like

a church. It was on these premises that the distinctive form of the New England meeting house was worked out.

29. NEW ENGLAND MEETING HOUSES, EARLY AND LATE

(A) First Meeting House, West Springfield, Massachusetts, built 1702, as it was before demolition c.1870. With a squarish ground plan, pyramidal roof, and medieval verticality, a characteristic example of the "plain style" Puritan meeting house as it developed in the course of the 17th century. Treatment of roof details varied considerably—sometimes the pyramid ended in a flat deck, or directly in a cupola (as at "Old Ship," Hingham); use of dormers or "lucombs" (= lucarnes) instead of the steep medieval gable is specified in some contracts.

In Old England, the Puritans worshiped in houses. In New England, they did not; from the first—as the Plymouth meeting house–fort shows —they began to develop, and in the course of the century worked out, a type of their own, distinctive in form and function. Squarish in plan, usually two stories high, it had seats oriented

(29 B) Third Ohio State Capitol, Columbus, in use 1816–52. Long after being superseded for public worship by towered, spired, and generally more "churchy" types of buildings, the 17th-century New England meeting house remained a standard type for schools, courthouses, and capitols. Buildings like this—and its predecessors in Chillicothe and Zanesville, which were of the same type—clearly evidenced the strength of ancestral cultural patterns brought from New England by early settlers in Ohio.

around a pulpit set in one of the walls opposite the entrance; often there was a gallery running around the walls, and the whole was covered with a pyramidal hipped roof, variously terminated. The combination of fort and meeting house at Plymouth (now restored in the "Plimouth Plantation") was early abandoned as unnecessary, but not so the idea of more than one function; characteristically, the meeting house served

for both divine worship and town business, often as schoolhouse as well.

Where this type originated has long been debated. Neither a tenuous connection with Calvinist churches in Holland nor resemblances with hall-markets in English country towns are particularly meaningful. The probability is, indeed, that here, as in the case of the New Netherlands rural house type, no European antecedents can be found because none really existed, because the New England meeting house was created in New England. That need not be surprising. It was, in fact, almost inevitable. No Old World type could usefully serve as a model for meeting houses in the New, because the Puritans' social status had so radically changed. There, they had been a dissenting minority, dramatizing the completeness of their separation from the City of Destruction by house-churches conspicuously different from those of the dominant majority. But here, they were themselves the dominant element in society, themselves determined its cultural patterns; the old symbolism was meaningless. Living no longer as sheep among goats, but in a very citadel of the elect, they had no incentive to reproduce anything of their older houses of worship, every incentive to devise a type of their own. The surprising thing is, in view of our image of New England as the cradle of progressive ideas, what a fundamentally backward and medieval type it was, and how long the Puritans maintained it.

Medieval it was—no doubt about that. In concept and forms the New England meeting house grew from folk traditions rooted deep in the English Middle Ages; traditions of mixed functions, as in chairs that doubled as benches or chests in the great halls of medieval manors, or as in the halls themselves, serving in turn for dining rooms, parlors, bedrooms; of pervasive verticality, in proportions and steep gables; of construction and materials starkly expressed. And the meeting house remained a basically medieval folk expression right into the early 18th century, despite what the first Puritans would have considered such needlessly luxurious and churchy features as the great expanses of

30. The "manorial" New England house type: Ironmaster's house, Saugus, Massachusetts, as restored to its original state c.1636–42. Domestic industries, serving local needs, were appropriately housed in domestic settings; as late as 1798, when the Slater Mill was built in Pawtucket, Rhode Island, American industrial establishments still looked like villages. No harbinger of the Industrial Revolution this, but rather a survivor of the Middle Ages, when domestic industry provided local community goods and services. Its forms, too, are medieval—steeply vertical proportions, sharp peaks and gables, overhangs, all are far closer to the immediately Elizabethan and medieval past than to the Jacobean present or classical future.

window, lofty timberwork roof, and neatly whitewashed walls of Old Ship, or the belfry-like roof termination of the West Springfield meeting house. As late as 1755 enlargement of Old Ship introduced little more than a veneer of classical mouldings. Only gradually, too, did the old medieval plurality of function break down; only by the end of the 18th century had the square building type become distinctively associated with schools or town halls (in which capacity it was carried westwards in the great early-19th-century New England emigrations), and places of worship as such become commonly distinguished by towers, liturgical seating arrangements, and neat plaster vaults. Such extraordinarily tenacious folk traditions can be explained only partly in terms of any deliberately perpetuated plain style. Essentially, this is another manifestation of a pattern common to all aspects of New England culture—a pattern established at the very foundation of the colony.

The early leaders of New England—unlike,

say, the founders of Virginia—were not "ordinary" Englishmen. Whole areas of contemporary English culture were either outside their interest or anathema to them. With the intellectual ferment of Shakespeare's London, with the world-wide expansion of English trade and commerce, with the aesthetic and literary life of the early Stuart courts, they had little or no sympathy. What they wanted to see reproduced in Massachusetts Bay and the Connecticut River valley was a purified version of the world they had known in East Anglia, the rural society of country squires, substantial yeomen, and small crofters from which Puritanism originally drew its strength. And these were the classes of people they brought with them to New England—rural classes, in whom medieval folk traditions were still strong and vital. By such people and their traditions the forms and decoration of New England colonial furniture were determined; from them the basic character of the New England meeting house derived. You can see their qualities best of all, perhaps, in the 17th-century New England colonial house type.

One of the best ways to get the "feel" of New England is to see the change in architectural landscape as you strike into its hinterland across the ranges of Green, White, and Blue mountains. The change appears first perhaps in barns (which, like kitchens, usually preserve older forms longer than houses). You begin to see barns in frame and shingle, often with rear rooflines running down lower than the front to produce a distinctive "salt-box" outline; then running together in connected chains with sheds and ells into the houses themselves. Most of the buildings we see in this region are comparatively recent, not more than a century old, usually; only here and there have a few older ones been preserved as historical monuments, like the Webster homestead (6). To find the classic examples of which northern New England building preserves the essence and background, we have to go further, into the old heartland of the region around Massachusetts Bay, in the Connecticut

Valley and the Providence Plantations. There, along the coast generally, we will see in examples like the Jethro Coffin house (Nantucket, c.1685), the rural English cottage types with hall, parlor, and central chimney brought across the Atlantic by artisans and small farmers when New England was first founded, from which these homesteads in the hinterland are descended; there too we can see their close relative the "Cape Cod cottage," later product of the urge towards simplification and standardization so characteristic of American civilization.

The most distinctive buildings of old New England, however, are not so much cottages like these as the great gaunt clapboarded houses two or more stories high built by the middle- and upper-middle classes of early Puritan society. Some of them, like the Ironmaster's house at Saugus (c.1636–42), the House of Seven Gables or the John Ward house at Salem (c.1684), are quite ostentatious—small Elizabethan manors, whose rambling expansiveness in plan and broad peaked gables make a striking contrast with the simplicity of lower-class dwellings. But, in most cases, what Professor Garvan says of Connecticut is true of all the old New England regions:

> One style, neither too large nor too small, came to represent the architectural ideal of the Connecticut colonist. In views, maps, and present-day remains the clapboard lean-to house directly descended from the yeoman post-enclosure farmhouse of eastern England crowded out all the other styles and laid the foundation for later architectural development in the colony. Architectural uniformity recalled the high per-capita land wealth of the colony, its equitable land division—all conditions which led to stable society and aversion to architectural novelty.

Plenty of these "classic" New England colonial houses survive in old Massachusetts Bay towns—the Scotch–Boardman house at Saugus (c.1650) and the Parson Capen house at Topsfield (c.1680) spring readily to mind. But it is in the Connecticut Valley, preserved by isolation from the newer ideas and population pressures brought to bear elsewhere by waves of later immigration, that we can see them best, perhaps. The Stanley–Whitman house in Farmington is typical—a stark two-story oblong box of sturdy oak timbers squared with a broadaxe and fitted together with notches and pins; nogging of straw, clay, or brick between the vertical studs; the whole covered with riven oak clapboards or shingles. Most striking and characteristic of its features is the "overhang" of one story above another (commonly the second over the first, on the front wall, but frequently varied), and below it carved ornaments or "drops" of various kinds pendant from the crossbeams. Single, double, occasionally even triple windows pierce the walls at irregular intervals; some are casement, and some fixed. Doors usually come more or less in the center, facing a narrow enclosed staircase which winds around a great central fireplace. On one side of the fireplace is the "hall," on the other the "parlor"; upstairs are bedrooms. If, as is common, the house has a lean-to providing extra rooms at the back of the first floor, they will usually be the "buttery" and the "borning room."

Local variations of these basic features are numerous. Some houses have overhangs on several sides; on others there are no more than vestigial overhangs; still others have none at all. Chimneys may be brick or stone, clustered or T-shaped, occasionally in side walls (e.g., the Rhode Island "stone enders," and the Paul Revere house in Boston, c.1677). The salt-box shape is sometimes built in, sometimes the accidental result of adding a lean-to (as in the Whitman house). Certainly there is no uniformity about additions—witness the rambling collection of units that makes up New England's earliest house, the Fairbanks homestead at Dedham (c.1638); in this example, too, we can see how common and how early a variant of the straight gable is the gambrel roof. But basically it is clear that, for all the variants, we are dealing with the same common core of medieval folk

tradition in the colonial house type of New England as in its furniture or meeting houses.

That tradition was even more pronounced in the original New England town as a whole. Boston's medieval village lanes of the 1640s, winding through the allotted holdings of husbandmen; the medieval type of garrison settlement around fortified "bawns" which, as Professor Garvan has convincingly proposed, was once a normal pattern for New England foundations and of which the Whitfield house at Guilford, Connecticut (c.1639), is a representative survivor; the Elizabethan type of manor house which served for the 1636 and 1676 Harvard College buildings at Cambridge—all these details and many more fit into the same picture, tell the same story of a determination by New England's founders to perpetuate the immemorial rural patterns of an old medieval folk world. That any of their settlements should grow into a city was the furthest thing from their minds. Whenever a settlement showed signs of growing, a small new community was at once split off from it—as Charleston and Dedham (among others) were split from Boston, Woburn and Medfield in turn from them, and so on. Had the ideals of its early leaders been realized, New England would have consisted forever of a chain of small townships rather like that of the Spanish presidios and pueblos in the Southwest—differing somewhat in their relationship to the Indians, to be sure (though the idea of Indian serfs was not entirely unheard of), but essentially manifesting the same feudal concept of society. Had the founders remained in control, New England would have been kept a land of small, largely self-sufficient country villages; a society patterned ultimately on the later Middle Ages, with its focus in small market towns at most. It would have had little economic development, still less of democracy, for general political and religious freedom was no part of its founders' creed. They came to America not to perfect whatever of religious toleration and parliamentary government was developing under

31. Paradigm of the "classic" New England house type, neither cottage nor manor, as it developed in an environment of social and aesthetic egalitarianism: the Stanley–Whitman house, Farmington, Connecticut, begun by Samuel Whitman c.1660; lean-to added c.1760, modern museum wing at the time of its restoration, 1935.

Elizabeth and the first James, but to get away from it. Their idea of the church as a polity restricted only to professors of a particular kind of religious experience looked not to some broadening future, but narrowly to the past, to what they thought the "primitive church" had been. If their town meeting was a "seedbed of American democracy"—a fact by no means certain— only expediency made it so. Whatever of change, growth in prosperity, rising living standards there were in early New England came about not merely without their efforts or approbation, but in spite of their misgivings and often in the face of their opposition.

But the first leaders of New England did not remain in control. Almost at once their plans went awry. Too many settlers found all too soon how much easier it was to take to sea and be-come a merchant or carrier than to till the stony hills and swamps of the Promised Land; how salable in other English colonies, in the West Indies, all sorts of places, were the diverse articles—from rum to salt fish to furniture— that the poverty of their land had from the first forced them to begin making for themselves. Rapidly, irresistibly, settlements around good harbors—Boston chief among them—began to grow into port towns, and their people into a ruling class of merchants. Already by the 1650s this merchant class was important enough to erect Boston's most imposing building, the first Town House; by the 1680s it was visibly displacing the older ministerial oligarchy and making New England's destinies its own.

You might think such a change would necessarily have resulted in more progressive social attitudes and the end of medieval folk traditions. Not at all. These new leaders were in fact hardly more forward-looking than the old. Boston under them was much larger than it had been under the ministers in the 1640s, but scarcely less medieval: the evidence is everywhere. Though an ordinance requiring all town houses to be built in brick with tile roofs had been passed following the great fire of 1679, hardly anyone had complied with it; houses like the extant "Paul Revere" house of the 1670s were still typical of Boston in 1700—framed, clapboarded,

with overhangs, as in a rural village. True, as early as 1676, immigrant English merchant Peter Sergeant had built an imposing brick mansion on his great tract between Washington and Tremont streets; but Sergeant's house was so much the exception that fifty years later it was still thought magnificent enough to house a royal governor. As for the Town House, which stood as symbol and proud creation of the mercantile community facing the open-air market place at the old center of Boston, it was no more advanced in style than the monuments of

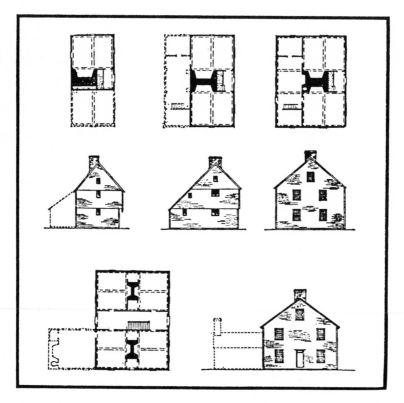

32. *The evolutionary theory of New England house types, as proposed in the works of J. Frederick Kelly (e.g.,* Early Domestic Architecture of Connecticut, *New Haven, 1924). Kelly's thesis was that the colonial house in Connecticut (and by inference elsewhere) evolved from early and simple types to late and complex ones, on the analogy of biological evolution. Later studies, notably Anthony N. B. Garvan's* Architecture *and Town Planning in Colonial Connecticut (New Haven, 1951, from which this plate is taken), while acknowledging their debt to Kelly's work generally, made it evident that in this particular instance he was mistaken. The reverse was in fact true; early colonists introduced all sorts of types, from single-room cots to multistoried manor houses, and their successors steadily reduced the complexity to a few simple standard types.*

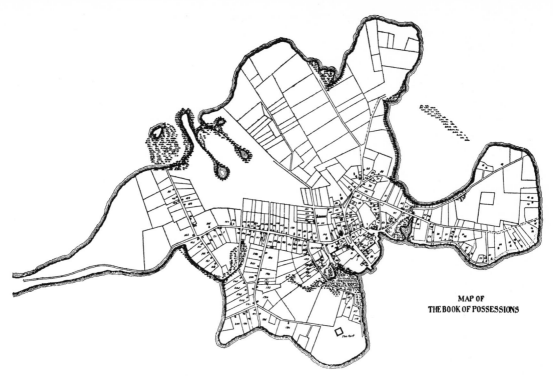

MAP OF
THE BOOK OF POSSESSIONS

*33. THE NEW ENGLAND COLONIAL TOWN
(A) Map of Boston in the 1640s. The Massachusetts Bay Company planted its settlers in 1630 on the Shawmut Peninsula, a narrow neck of land dominated by three hills. As the original site was never chosen with a future large city in mind, settlers had to begin filling in various marshes and coves almost at once, with earth cut out of the hills. The first recorded major project was the filling of Town Cove in 1641; the largest, filling of the Back Bay, was begun in 1858. As a result of this process, modern Boston occupies a peninsula more than twice the size of the 17th-century one; but in many cases, outlines of the winding lanes that gave early Boston its distinctively medieval character have been preserved.*

the old ministerial ruling class next to it—Governor Winthrop's mansion with its great Tudor gable and half-timber walls, or the square and steep-roofed First Meeting House. For all that it was the large and busy center of New England's trade with Old England, the West Indies, and Spain, the Town House was in form the open-walled market, in function the moot hall traditional in country villages of medieval England, its first story given over to stalls, the others to rooms for local courts and elders and "the Ancient and Honorable Artillery Company of Massachusetts," which was, of course, the hoary village institution of trainbands. Only a ". . . walk upon the Top 14 or 15 foot wide, with two turrets & turned Balasters and railes around

the Walkes . . ." suggested something more.

In the beginning, when Puritan elders ruled New England, the lack of proper public buildings was quite understandable. The elders were chronically suspicious of government in general (as a tool of the Church of England); they were satisfied with education directed to practical domestic needs—chiefly more ministers; and their meeting houses served any other local civic needs adequately enough. The merchants' failure to do better, in larger towns where need for public buildings proper could not reasonably be ignored, demands another explanation, however. Fundamentally, it was a matter of class outlook. To begin with, New England merchants primarily represented the small bourgeoisie, a class which had grown up in obscurity in English towns from the end of the Middle Ages onward. In the nature of things this class had experienced government largely as something that interfered or persecuted; consequently, it lacked a vital tradition of public service and tended to see everything in terms of individual success. The community existed for it primarily as an instrument for making individual success (whether in this world or the next) possible. Except when occasional crises, like King Philip's Indian War, forced communal responsibilities on them, these merchants shirked such responsibilities as consistently as their counterparts, the burghers and patroons of New Netherlands, neglecting public buildings in the same way and for the same reasons. Furthermore, merchants as a class, unlike traditional hereditary landed aristocrats whose wealth means leisure, have neither time nor inclination to weigh questions of taste or dare departures of style in the arts. They will think of buildings and furnishings, whether their own or the community's, essentially as public demonstrations of private success, rewards for long labors in countinghouse or exchange, for self-denying accumulations of capital. Experience makes them habitually cautious; they have learned the hard way the risks of making poor investments. Not for them the advance-guard house or the latest thing in furniture; what if house or chair never "caught on," went out of fashion, and had to be replaced in ten years' time? Prudent speculators, they will invest only after the "market trend" is reasonably sure. They will stodgily imitate, that is to say, the progression of upper-class styles at a safe distance. And they will go on doing it throughout the next century.

So a pattern is set. Small traders and craftsmen will follow the lead of New England's big merchants and manufacturers. Both will eschew extremes of luxury and of taste. Nature and habit will keep both to a conservative middle ground. "The New-England men that trade into this Province," wrote a Marylander about 1660,

had rather have fat Pork for their Goods, then Tobacco or Furrs. . . . Madera-Wines, Sugars, Salt, Wickar-Chairs, and Tin Candlesticks is the most of the Commodities they bring in: They arrive in Maryland about September, being most of them Ketches and Barkes and such small Vessels, and those dispersing themselves into several small Creeks of this Province, to sell and dispose of their Commodities, where they know the Market is most fit for their small Adventures. . . .

You may be sure those "Wickar-Chairs" were hardly the latest style. They were, as the middleman's wares have been from the time of the small Yankee peddler to that of the modern development-builder, geared to the lowest common denominator of taste.

It was not from "small Adventures" like these that the planters of Virginia and Maryland furnished their mansions; whatever furniture prosperous Southerners bought from them went into second-best rooms, into kitchens and attics and slave quarters. Neither would the big merchants have much to offer Southerners; their parlors were furnished direct from London. Already in the 17th century the leaders of Virginia were aspiring to be pacemakers of artistic taste in America—and this was a role the cautious merchants of New England long left them.

While colonial Virginians built classical courthouses and capitols, Boston remained content with a "merchants' exchange" and a fifty-year-old governor's mansion, frugally made over. When the Revolution came, it began in Boston with a riot, and was pursued there in the spirit of medieval burghers defending their town charter against some feudal lord; it was from Virginia that there came those reasoned statements of the rights of citizens against a crown, those declarations of principle and analyses of the nature of government in the spirit of classical Enlightenment, which made rebellion into the creative force behind a new nation. And when the new nation first took shape, New England was hardest to fit into it. Just as the Massachusetts Bay stockholders had taken their charter across the Atlantic with them and stubbornly refused to surrender it, so did their village-minded descendants of the first post-Revolutionary generation rebel against federal taxes, and the small bourgeoisie of the next try to secede from the new United States at Hartford in 1814. People living in those times would have found incomprehensible the 20th-century writers who talked about a small company of Pilgrims having been "able to determine the ultimate destiny of a great nation"; the development of any such idea is itself one of the "great miracles of history." How and why that idea grew is outside the scope of this present chapter; certainly it never came from studying architecture and furniture in 17th- or 18th-century New England.

BOSTON'S FIRST TOWN-HOUSE
1657~1711

(33 B) First Town House, Boston. Conjectural restoration by Charles A. Lawrence on the basis of specifications made in the contract of August 1, 1657, for Thomas Joy and Bartholomew Bernad to erect, at the bequest of London merchant Robert Keayne, "a very substantiall and comely building . . . 66 foot in Length and 36 foot in Breadth from outside to outside, the wholl Building to Jetty over three foot without the Pillers everie way." Destroyed by fire, 1711.

NOTES

Of lavish medieval folk decoration in New England furniture, the so-called Hadley chests of the Connecticut Valley (where folk traditions survived remarkably long in architecture as well) are spectacular examples; cf. C. F. Luther, *The Hadley Chest* (Hartford, 1935). As late as c.1700–15, furniture like the Hannah Barnard press cupboard in the Henry Ford Museum at Dearborn was being lavishly decorated in polychrome with the owners' names, and hearts, flowers, and geometric designs.

Quotations on the nature of Puritanism, from the general discussion of the Reformation and culture—the whole very useful in this connection—in "New Learning and New Ignorance," Chap. I of C. S. Lewis, *English Literature in the Sixteenth Century* (Oxford, 1955): on New England house types, from the illuminating treatment of the subject by Anthony N. P. Garvan, *Architecture and Town Planning in Colonial Connecticut* (New Haven, 1955), p. 130, and Chap. IV *passim*.

A useful presentation of the problem of Puritan-meeting-house origins is found in Donald Drew Egbert's chapter "Religious Expression in American Architecture" in *Religious Perspectives in American Culture* (Princeton, 1961). As early as 1883 the transformation of the old "four-square" meeting house into a church proper was described by Noah Porter in the *New Englander*, for May of that year. An extensive analysis of the process is made by T. J. Wertenbaker, *The Puritan Oligarchy* (1947), pp. 109ff. In the main, he accepts Porter's scheme: the simple square or rectangular building remaining common until c.1730, the years 1730–90 distinguished by a rectangular building with tower attached being more and more used exclusively for worship, after c.1790 a "regular" church with integral tower, portico, etc. Professor Wertenbaker sees the process as paralleling and expressing dissolution of the original Puritan polity as commercial interests became dominant.

Theories on the purpose and significance of overhangs are varied. An old and persistent one, that they were intended for defense against Indians (on analogy with blockhouses), may be dismissed out of hand, for the requisite trap doors or openings to make them useful for such a purpose are absent. Professor Garvan thought (*op. cit.*, p. 91 *et al.*) that the overhang was originally a device to protect wall fillings from rain, which "because it gave additional space in the upper story . . . had been found very useful in crowded London. With the general increase in demand for two-story yeoman houses in country districts at the end of the 16th century the overhang became a symbol of its owner's London contacts and also served the function of protecting the interstices of the frame." A simpler, and, in New England circumstances, more obvious, explanation is that it was a technical device developed by medieval folk builders. It is so described by Hugh Braun, *The Restoration of Old Houses* (London, 1954), as follows:

> . . . Even the most important buildings in medieval England . . . did not waste stone and masoncraft on building unloaded partition walls. Partitions were in the nature of wooden screens, formed of vertical boarding set between head and sill-piece. An alternative was to use studs instead of boarding and fill the panels with wattle-and-daub; from this form of construction was developed the framed house of the late-medieval period with its screen-walls set between posts planted at intervals upon sturdy ground-sills. The addition of another storey was effected by laying the upper floor and adding another set of screen walls, *supporting these on the projecting ends of the floor-joists in order to convert these into cantilevers and thus make them more rigid.** This is the "jettied" type of frame house.

Overhangs for this purpose survived long in hinterland areas.

Revealing inferences about the character of late-17th-century Boston can be drawn from "Boston Building Ordinances, 1631–1714" (*JSAH*, XX, 1961, 2, pp. 90–93). That medieval overhangs were still common at the end of the century is suggested, for example, by one of "severall Rules, Orders, and By-laws" adopted May 12, 1701, which ordered that "no person shall Erect or set up any Pentice, jetty, or Pendal over any of the Streets, lanes, or highways of this Town, of less than eight foot in hight from the ground." Quotation from an account of his stay as an indentured servant in Maryland between 1658 and 1662 by George Alsop, *A Character of the Province of Maryland* (Cleveland, 1902), pp. 71–2, extract reprinted by John N. Pearce in the *Winterthur Newsletter*, November 28, 1958.

* Author's italics.

7. INSPIRED EXPERIMENTS:
Traditions of Independence in Pennsylvania

WILLIAM PENN was many things to many men, and so was the colony he founded. Pennsbury, his country manor twenty-five miles up the Delaware River from Philadelphia, was the image of both. During the time Penn was in England, 1684–99, he was continually sending instructions for its completion to his agent James Logan ("I would have the back door a two-leaved one and the front made from tip to bottom. . . . I would have a rail and bannisters before both fronts. . . . I desire that a pair of handsome steps be made at the landing. . . . The partition between the best parlour and the great room . . . should be wainscoted, with double-leaved doors. . . . I will send this fall divers seeds and plants . . . etc."); and certainly, had you come upon Pennsbury in the days its owner lived there, you could have been sure of one thing— however much Penn longed for the world to come, he did not neglect the one here. Well-kept terraces, set off by choice trees, sloped up from the riverside, where the Proprietor's elegant six-oared barge ("above all dead things, my barge, I hope no body uses it on any account") was wharved; as for the house itself, for a moment it was almost as if you were boating along the Thames past one of the elegant new mansions then beginning to rise in a fashionable London suburb like Twickenham. Penn's manor was plainer than some, perhaps, but there was no mistaking the fashionable modernity of its façade. It had some medieval casements, to be sure; but compared to, say, contemporary houses in New England with their clumsy triangular gables, overhangs, and windows haphazardly located here and there, Pennsbury's hipped roof, symmetrically disposed doors, rows of windows and dormers, and formal grounds marked off its river façade as belonging to a new and different world, the classical 18th-century world coming to birth in England. And had we

entered Pennsbury then, our external impression of up-to-date elegance would have been at first confirmed. Records show that Pennsbury was well, even elaborately, furnished with such rare and costly items as damask cloths and napkins, "a suite of Tunbridge ware," silver forks, and furniture that in some cases was not merely up-to-date but even somewhat advance-guard.

As might be expected from a man for whom the highest concerns of life were hardly questions of fashionable taste, however, Penn introduced no consistent style of furniture to Pennsylvania. Besides very advanced pieces, he and the settlers who came with him on the *Welcome* also brought furniture almost as *retardataire* and medieval as anything in New England. Pennsbury had another side, too. Go around to the back, land side, and classical symmetry abruptly vanishes. Here we are back in the medieval world of clapboard, of haphazard fenestration, of additive composition; it is as if they were two different buildings altogether. Pennsbury, in short, embodies something of that same contradiction, that conflict of interest, which the Founder himself—by turns pacificist to the Indians and plotter against William of Orange. Quaker martyr and court favorite, statesman of liberty in America and supporter of Jacobite claims to medieval kingship at home—manifested so markedly. In this sense it is an admirable introduction to the arts of early Pennsylvania; this fundamental contradiction is perhaps their most common characteristic.

When the young Benjamin Franklin made his famous trip from Boston to Philadelphia in 1723, the contrast between the two cities must have been extraordinary. Where Boston had grown along the cramped, twisting, haphazard streets of a medieval village, Philadelphia was laid out on a uniform grid, with spacious lots, focal intersections, and formal parks devised by

34. Pennsbury, near Bristol, Pennsylvania. Above: *River*, and Below: *Land façades*. The center of an eight-thousand-acre estate reserved for the Proprietor before his arrival in America in 1682, this country manor was begun c.1682–3 and completed over a period of years thereafter. Following Penn's second and final departure for England at the end of 1701, Pennsbury was maintained for some years—his son William Penn, Jr., lived there briefly in 1704—but already by 1707 Logan was writing Penn, Sr., about its empty and "decaying" condition. Upon Penn's death in 1718 it was abandoned and gradually fell into ruin; by 1803 the property had been sold and a frame farmhouse built on part of the manor-house foundations, and by 1867 all trace of Pennsbury above ground had vanished. In 1932 the site was presented to the Commonwealth of Pennsylvania, excavation and research initiated, and the present reconstruction (completed 1938–9 under direction of R. Brognard Okie) undertaken.

Penn and his surveyor, Thomas Holme, in 1683. Even more striking was the contrast of their house types. True, Penn's original concept, a spacious "greene country town," was already fast disappearing. He had envisaged houses built (for speed and economy) on standard plans like those of Restoration London, but each house set in its own lot surrounded by gardens, and freely varied in size, number of stories, and rooms according to its owner's means or station. Unfortunately, however, just as speculative builders like Nicholas Barbon had ruined the more visionary hopes of a dramatically spacious and orderly London rising on its burnt medieval

35. ENGLISH FURNITURE USED BY WILLIAM PENN

Heterogeneous, but all "of the best sort," these pieces, connected with Penn by long tradition and now in the collections of the Historical Society of Pennsylvania, embody the same sort of dichotomy apparent in the contrast between river and land façades of Pennsbury. The chest still belongs stylistically to the medieval tradition in form and geometric paneled oak ornament; but its ball feet, drawers above and below indicate that it is well along in the evolution from chest to lowboy and highboy. The chair is in the full William and Mary style of the 1690s, its spacious proportions already looking forward to the coming Queen Anne era, to which the desk, with its slim cabriole legs and refined proportions already belongs.

ruins, so Philadelphia's phenomenal growth had all too soon raised real estate to the point where it was too valuable to "waste" on trees and flowers; already Philadelphia was on the way to becoming the city of close-packed houses, wall-to-wall and front-to-sidewalk, that the next three centuries would know. That row houses were no part of Penn's original plan is clear; for the earliest ones—Budd's Long Row, built c.1691—were of old, folk, half-timber construction, rather than the official brick mode, and the planned row proper (i.e., whole streets designed at one time, individual units subordinated to total effect) did not appear much before the end

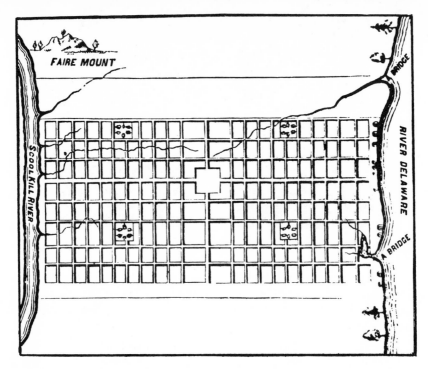

36. URBAN PATTERNS IN PHILADELPHIA
(A) The Holme Plan of Philadelphia, 1682. This orderly grid, with parks at regular intervals and systematically named streets (east–west named after native trees—Mulberry, Spruce, Walnut etc.; north–south numbered) may instructively be compared with the unplanned growth of Boston (33A).

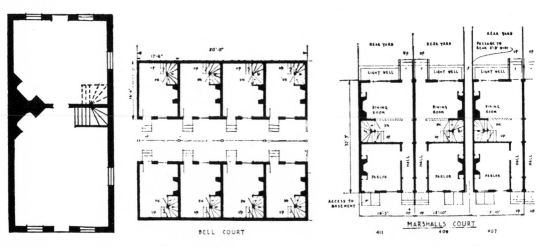

BELL COURT

MARSHALLS COURT

(36 B) Characteristic Philadelphia house plans. Left: first-floor plan of the Letitia Street house, now in Fairmount Park, c.1715. A typical early lower-middle-class house, designed for simplicity, economy, and speedy construction. Its characteristic features are easily adaptable to row-house building: blank side wall; corner chimney; in plan, twice as deep as it is wide. Center: "bandbox" type: two or three stories high; one room on each floor; one door and window in façade; stairwell in corner; often in groups designed around a court. Right: "London" type: a rectangle two rooms deep; entrance hall at side; stair in middle of long wall.

of the 18th century. No matter; their economic advantages soon made variants of "bandbox" and "London type" row houses predominant in the city. Only a minority of wealthy families were able to retain their original spacious lots, where the neat brick cubes could be seen with crisp white woodwork set off by pleasant flowers and foliage as Penn intended (and as we can still see them in outlying Philadelphia regions, either in the brick of southwestern New Jersey and northern Delaware, or the stone of southeastern Pennsylvania). But to an early visitor, come from the stark wooden boxes of New England and the low stone peasant cottages of the Hudson Valley, Philadelphia's orderly rows made the city all the more remarkable.

Philadelphia's early houses were not without certain folk elements, of course. There was something medieval about their generally tall and narrow proportions, the way their red brick walls were often set with blue-glazed headers to form checkerboard or zigzag patterns and even initials or dates as on folk furniture, particularly in the country builders' habit of stringing one, two, or even three contiguous additions beside their house, and otherwise varying elements to suit family circumstances. Even the London prototype had folk characteristics. Its plan, standardized to enable the great city to be rebuilt quickly from its ashes, was not so much a product of conscious style or taste as a combination of concessions to tradition, experience, and exigency. Brick walls and slate roofs conformed to the prohibition of inflammable exterior materials enforced with the

(36 C) The Restoration London house type, taken by Penn as model for his new city, seen here in a detail from Hogarth's print "Morning." The effect of twin-gabled roofs with a valley between was produced by setting two of these "standard" houses back-to-back; it was occasionally reproduced in Philadelphia. This flexibility is characteristic of the type; it essentially consisted of simple basic units which might be executed in wood or stone as well as brick, as well horizontally as vertically, or developed into contiguous row houses, depending on resources and circumstances.

37. "PHILADELPHIA COLONIAL" HOUSE TYPES

(A) William Hancock house, Hancock's Bridge, Salem County, New Jersey. Built (as initials and date in blue glazed headers set in brick side wall indicate) by Quakers William and Sarah Hancock in 1734. Though settled earlier, Salem County came immediately under the cultural domination of Philadelphia, and remained so, as the main house here clearly shows —plan, blank side walls, façade with symmetri- *cal fenestration and pent eave all evidentally representing the common vertically composed version of the basic Philadelphia urban house type. In these more isolated and rural circumstances, however, medieval folk traditions are more prominently in evidence than in the city: characteristic is the addition of contiguous buildings, and particularly the elaborate zigzag patterning of the brickwork, presumably deriving from an English folk predilection for dynamic line pattern which can be traced back to Anglo-Saxon times.*

great fire of 1666 fresh in mind. Blank side walls permitted not only great flexibility in adapting buildings to irregular medieval plots but also the survival of an Old English folk-liking for flat dynamic line pattern that went back in many media to Anglo-Saxon times. The pent eave provided protection for passers-by on the sidewalk directly in front and also, if carried around the sides, could be connected with one on a house adjoining to provide a covered passageway into the back yard; but besides these practical advantages, the eave also satisfied the mimetic demand

for something to carry on the effect of old medieval overhangs. Basing plans on a few stock units allowed city builders to take full advantage of varying sites and clients; it also provided a useful psychological bridge between the older medieval concept of rambling organic design and a classical concept of rigidly predetermined overall planning for which the English public was not yet generally ready. All these characteristics the Philadelphia house type took over and, particularly as reproduced in the countryside around, developed into a full-fledged folk expression.

(37 B) Collins Mansion, West Chester, Pennsylvania. The vertically composed Philadelphia house type rendered in stone—façade in the distinctive green serpentine of the locality, *regularly dressed; sides of fieldstone. Begun for Quakers Joseph and Mary Collins in 1727, north wing added 1758–60 by Nathaniel Moore. For an example of the horizontally composed house type, cf. the Old Read house, New Castle (21B).*

At the same time these houses also had, like Pennsbury, elements basically new and strikingly "modern." They manifested a new sense of order. Windows and doors arranged with planned balance; little flights of purposefully placed wooden steps leading up to first floors; a new, coherent system of proportions in the basic units of which houses are composed; floors neatly marked off and exterior design articulated by spacings of elements and particularly by pent eaves (often enough neatly coved in wood or plaster) running across house fronts and frequently sides as well, divided into measurable parts by precisely centered triangular pediments —all these are marks of a new spirit, an urban, geometric, controlled approach to architectural design. As at Pennsbury, so in the Philadelphia house type—from the first it represented a dis- tinctive combination (often similarly evident in the contrast of front with side and back façades) of surviving elements from medieval folk tradition with others presaging the ordered world of 18th-century, classical America, worthy of the town that in only twenty years was already "astonished at its own strength and greatness."

This same combination and contrast appeared in the furniture that went into these houses. It had folk elements, which certainly were developed and elaborated by furniture makers working in the countryside around Philadelphia just as they were by housewrights of this region. But it also and equally looked forward to the coming classical era. There was no furniture entirely "folk" in early Philadelphia—little of oak, or painted chests, or court cupboards. From the first the prevailing material was walnut, which, as it happened, grew plentifully in the Delaware Valley; from the first the style was basically informed by those lighter, more co-ordinated, more unified principles we call William and Mary. Philadelphia itself, then, almost from its beginnings was moving steadily forward into the second great era, the classical age of American civilization.

Once go beyond the bounds of the city, however; once go past the limits of grants to Quakers and Welshmen, once reach communities and counties settled by the great early-18th-century waves of German immigration, and the scene is very different. For here we have, not merely folk-inspired variants of Philadelphia types, but a different art entirely—different in national origin, and above all different in fundamentals. The Middle Ages lived on in German Pennsylvania as perhaps nowhere else in colonial America. And so the basic contrast of medieval survivals with classical anticipations embodied in the art of the Philadelphia region was repeated, on a broader scale, in the general contrast of English with German Pennsylvania.

"Pennsylvania Dutch" is a vague term, with all sorts of vague associations clinging to it. "Quaintness" is the common denominator, perhaps; what comes to mind is a composite image of eccentric costumes and customs and sects, amusing turns of speech in a fractured mixture of English and German, big barns covered with hex signs, a charmingly crude and childish style of decorating dishes, chests, baptismal certificates. Needless to say, this popular image hardly corresponds to fact, if only because the Germans who pushed out from their first settlement at Germantown in wave after wave into a great arc from Lancaster to Allentown and further on again came from so many parts of Germany, represented so many different classes and religious ideas. Nevertheless, it is not entirely a creation of 20th-century tourist bureaus. The idea that Germans were quaint and different goes back to the first general impression they made on their English-speaking neighbors. No doubt the

sober Lutheran congregations who summoned Heinrich Melchior Mühlenberg from a theological chair in Hanover to organize churches at New Hanover, New Providence, and elsewhere felt little in common with the Society of the Solitary or the Order of Spiritual Virgins at Ephrata; but to eyes accustomed to the measured order of Georgian Philadelphia there seemed little to choose between Mühlenberg's Trappe Church (1743), with its rough stone walls and hand-hewn timbers, its folk decoration of cut-out hearts and crude "capitals" and clumsily patterned hand-forged ironware, and the rude boards, steep-pitched roofs and tiers of straight-roofed dormers of Johann Conrad Beissel's Saal and Sharon at Ephrata. And while in Pennsylvania German house interiors you might see anything from the most primitive details to quite elaborate German Baroque and even Rococo designs, collectively they belonged in a different world from the houses that lined Arch, Sassafras, Mulberry, and Vine streets. Far into the 18th century, Philadelphia German culture was still permeated with a medieval spirit that had long been obsolete in the capital, and among English-speaking Pennsylvanians generally; to them, it all seemed old-fashioned, quaint, and "different" —as what remains of it does to this day.

Had an upper-class Quaker from Philadelphia chanced to visit Georg Müller's house in Millbach, for instance, he must have thought, when he compared it with the kind of interiors he and his friends were furnishing in the 1750s, that he had stepped off some kind of time machine back into the world of his remote ancestors. Müller was prosperous enough himself, to be sure, but everything about his house smacked of another era, of the lost Middle Ages—its great twin summer beams and rafters unself-consciously displayed and painted, its plain plastered walls so thick that the small windows are set in deep splayed reveals, the clumsy luxuriance of carving on cupboards and chair and *schrank*, the bright naïve painting on chests and pottery. And this was one of the more up-to-date

Pennsylvania German houses! How much more incomprehensibly ancient must have seemed the log barns, or the half-timbered houses (one of which, the Moravian Meeting House in Oley Valley, c.1743–5, still stood well into the 20th century)! How curious were the Ephrata community buildings—great *bauernhäuser* such as Pieter Breughel painted in the 16th century, where walls were hung with long rolls of *fraktur* as medieval castles had been hung with tapestry, depicting in spiky Gothic word and picture visions of the Three Heavens, of the Narrow and Crooked Way. Why did these people cover barns and chests and cradles with whole repertoires of half-symbolic, half-decorative motifs—tulips and phoenixes, roses and rosettes—whose purpose and meaning were already long distorted by vast passages of time? How, such a solid citizen

38. *Kitchen from the house of Georg Müller, Lebanon County, Pennsylvania, reconstructed in the Philadelphia Museum of Art. The house, as built in 1752, was a famous and rare example of a notably German type, with a gambrel roof featuring a bell-cast at the eaves, and fieldstone walls—unusual for the time and place, most German contemporaries being log or half-timber* —set off by dressed brownstone quoins. The interior was likewise more conscious of style than was usual among Pennsylvania Germans—the balusters of the stair, for example, have definite German Baroque characteristics, however awkwardly reproduced. But the general character of house and furnishings is, like practically all 18th-century Pennsylvania German art, predominantly and even overwhelmingly medieval.*

39. "CHURCH COMMUNITIES" IN PENN-SYLVANIA

(A) Greater (Quaker) Meeting House and Town Hall, Second and High streets, Philadelphia, painted c.1830 by W. L. Breton. The Greater Meeting House was built c.1755 to replace the first Great Meeting House of Philadelphia (1696). "Except possibly for their larger size and the simplicity of their architectural lines," writes G. B. Tatum in Penn's Great Town (Philadelphia, 1961, p. 24), "there was little to distinguish a Quaker meeting house from any of the more substantial private residences of the day."

(39 B) Guinston (Presbyterian) Church, near Muddy Creek Forks, York County, Pennsylvania. Built 1774, probably the third church erected by Presbyterian congregations in Chanceford Township. By this time the characteristic stark simplicity of earlier Presbyterian churches —though still evident in the plain boxlike plan and rugged fieldstone walls—was being relieved by classical detail in doors and windows.

might well have asked himself, did these Old World relics ever get to the New? And, what is more to the point, what could they possibly have in common with the rest of this province?

By the 1750s the ruling classes of Pennsylvania were full of such misgivings. Theirs was a province like no other in the New World. On the one hand, there was the capital city of Philadelphia—growing into the second-largest city in the British Empire, elegant center of worldly fashion, wealth, fine furniture, and cultivated society on the best London models. On the other, there was German Pennsylvania—uncompromisingly rural, medieval to a degree unparalleled anywhere. Then, as if to compound confusion, there was a third element, the Scotch-Irish, which differed from both. The Scotch-Irish people came in great waves from Ulster after their quitrent leases expired in 1718, and in whole villages from Scotland once the 1701 Act of Union opened the Empire to them. Bringing with them fierce traditions of Covenanters and bitter Irish wars, they took up land everywhere—sometimes

(39 C) "The Cloisters," Ephrata. In 1720 Johann Conrad Beissel was driven from Germany by religious persecution; after much wandering around Pennsylvania, he and his followers established a celibate community on the site of Ephrata in 1735. For the men a Saal (House of Prayer, left) was built in 1741; for the women, the Sharon (Sisters' House, right) in 1743; and a number of other buildings. In general outline and in many details these structures had a decidedly Germanic character, reminiscent especially of the large multifamily dwellings of South Germany. When the Ephrata community was formally dissolved in 1934, its buildings were acquired and restored by the Pennsylvania Historical Commission.

legally and sometimes not—founded schools and colleges, filled them with their sons, pushed aggressively upwards to positions of leadership. To Penn's successors it must have seemed as if his colonizing agents had shown such lack of discrimination that his colony was taking a form almost as heterogeneous and unmanageable as the New Netherlands his commission had been given to supplant. Fortunately, events proved otherwise. For while among the Quakers, Scotch-Irish, and Germans who founded Pennsylvania there was indeed no common body of national tradition as in older English colonies, they did share a particular kind of religious attitude to life. And it was on this plane that Pennsylvania's destiny as the keystone colony was to be fulfilled.

When he described his proposed colony as a "holy experiment," when he expounded on the love he as a Quaker professed for all mankind, Penn was acting the cultural prophet as well as the saint. The appeal of his agents was not indiscriminate; Pennsylvania did not attract everybody, but primarily "all those oppressed in any way, in mind, body, or estate." That was what drew English, Welsh, and Irish Quakers who felt discriminated against in religion; Presbyterians from Ulster anxious to escape economic exploitation; Scots who remembered the grim days of the Covenanters and starving times under Queen

Anne; Protestants from the Palatinate and Moravia who had never known the time when a change of princelings might not return some of the horrors of persecution and the Thirty Years' War. And from this common spiritual and religious background there developed, not a uniform style in art or architecture, but a common attitude to culture—what it is, what its ultimate values are—evident in the arts of Quakers, Scots, and Germans alike, and through them transmitted into the mainstream of American life.

This attitude appears most characteristically perhaps in their places of worship. Externally, structures like those illustrated (*39 A, B, C*) could hardly be more diverse. The Quaker meeting house shares with courthouse or private dwellings forms derived from Restoration London building. A plain style stark and barren as any Puritan's is characteristic of early Presbyterian kirks. The forms of German buildings—whether of the Moravians at Bethlehem, the Lutherans at Trappe, or extreme Pietists at Ephrata—are permeated by folk principles rooted in the Middle Ages. But the same spirit, the same concept of what "religious building" is, informs them all. None of them makes any real distinction between what we would call the "religious" and the "secular" life. Whether in the microcosm of the house, or the macrocosm of towns like Bethlehem, church and community are considered coterminous, manifesting the same common ideal. When we speak of religious art, we generally mean paintings with "sacred" subjects, or objects connected with some sort of liturgy. When we speak of religious architecture, we mean buildings designated as churches or synagogues, looking different from others. This was not a distinction recognized by any of these people. Like Puritans, Quakers used the same building for both sacred and secular functions (the "meeting" to settle community affairs, as well as for periods of meditative waiting on the Holy Spirit), had the same aversion to any suggestions of "churchiness" in architecture or decoration that might distract souls from their

Maker; but they went even further. Since for them nonconformity was not merely a by-product of emphasis on individual conviction, but the positive mark of a "peculiar people," it followed that Quaker meeting houses, though functioning like the Puritans' as public buildings from the first in the New World, were much more consciously and deliberately kept domestic in appearance and scale. Similarly, given a premise like the one expressed in Bishop Spangenberg's 1757 letter to his patron, Count Zinzendorf, that "the farmyard becomes a temple of grace, full of priestly activity," it is not surprising to find no "church" as such in Moravian Bethlehem for sixty years; every part of the community was considered no more and no less essential to its religious life than any other—from the *Gottesaker* where its dead were laid to rest, to the mill that ground its flour, and the houses for its Sisters and "choirs" of Single Brethren. So too the Presbyterian kirk was no consecrated building, no temple set apart for liturgy or sacrament, but the Scotch-Irish community's "shelter 'gainst the stormy blast," its "eternal home," where words of life proceeded from the high pulpit towards which all seats were turned, giving strength and guidance to meet common problems and frailties of every day. All these people in their several ways saw all work, all art, all architecture as "religious," provided only that the spirit in which they were undertaken and carried out was "religious."

Of course this was a doctrine as old as Protestantism itself. It informed Luther's insistence on the priesthood of all believers, as it did Mistress Anne Bradstreet's *Meditations* ("There is no object that we see, no action that we doe, no good that we injoy, no evill that we feele or fear, but we may make some spiritual advantage of it all") in early New England; from it grew the distinctive half-Puritan half-Quaker culture of the Shaker colonies.* But circumstances gave it a special force in Pennsylvania.

* See notes following this chapter.

90

None of the major groups who settled Pennsylvania had the same close ties to and affection for their homeland that influenced, say, the early Virginians, or even the bulk of Puritans. For all their differences with English polity, most Puritans had no hesitation professing loyalty to their sovereign lord Charles I as they neared Massachusetts Bay; they came to the New World quite as much to show friends and enemies alike how Old England ought to be governed—"We shall be as a city upon a hill"—as to escape from or abandon it. But Scotch-Irish and Germans and Quakers had mostly bitter memories of their homeland; they had no hope of seeing it reformed; they set all their hopes and put all their treasure into building a truly new society. That is why they set no store by national traditions as such—why what "Scottish" architecture you find in Pennsylvania is not a distinct style, but a general influence, a tendency to build in rugged stone that appears wherever Scotch masons and quarries existed together; why there is nothing like a widespread "German" architecture or furniture style in Pennsylvania comparable to, say, New England architecture in Connecticut; and why within fifty years German characteristics are abandoned even in as self-contained a community as Bethlehem; and why Quakers never developed a distinctive and specific plain style for meeting houses comparable to New England's, but instead were content with something "plain, but of the best sort" in whatever style might be current.

Of all New World foundations, then, Pennsylvania was the one most saturated with the ideal of a transformed society, the hope of a genuinely new start. And with what result? Superficially, if we consider Pennsylvania today, or even as it was in 1800, we might be tempted to say none; the only result was that these people conformed to the world all the more easily and quickly. Quakers, for instance, though still building meeting houses instead of churches with spires and central aisles and altars, insisted on internal fittings of exquisite taste and refined proportions quite belying their ostensible "plainness." Presbyterians early set out on the same road; by the middle of the 18th century even churches like Old Drawyers in Odessa or Guinston in York County, while still spireless preaching boxes, have an elegance of finish and detail very far removed indeed from the primitive simplicity of conventicles two or three generations before. As for the Germans, the Pennsylvania German countryside was early and long famous for lush prosperity, with travelers from far and wide marveling at the rich crops and fat herds, gaping at what one in the 1830s described as the German farmer's "piggery of a residence [comparatively speaking] and his palace of a barn." Only among eccentrics like the Amish or the Shakers did the old ideals seem to survive, and then only by figurative and indeed literal acts of social suicide. It would be easy to end the story here, to see the history of Penn's "holy experiment" as nothing but one more example of the principle that for Churches Militant nothing fails like success. It would be easy; it would also miss the point.

When most people think of Pennsylvania, they think first not of Quakers or German sectaries or London house types; they think of Independence Hall, of the Continental Congress, of the Declaration of Independence, and the Constitution of the United States; they think, in other words, of the founding of a new kind of nation, something never seen in the world before. And this is appropriate; for while the choice of Philadelphia as the scene for these events was a matter of convenience—a central location, largest city in English America, neutral meeting ground between New England and the South—it was also symbolic. More than any other American city, Philadelphia was identified with determination to disavow the past, with the ideal of building a new society whatever the cost.

Historians from John Adams on have recognized that American revolution and independence were not the beginning but the culmination of a vision that took shape long before. The idea of creating a new nation was not generated by the Continental Congress; what happened there was that the old religious ideal of a New World, a new society where Old World corruptions would be purged and a life of new spiritual freedom possible, was transformed, given a new shape and direction. Without that ideal, there would have been no new nation. Something of that ideal had been implanted in Jamestown and St. Mary's City, something more in Plymouth and Boston and Salem; but where it was fresh-est in memory and in fact was in Pennsylvania. It was in Pennsylvania that the vision of society transformed, of a community life on new principles and dedicated to new values, was most endemic. It was here that the concept of a *Novus Ordo Seclorum* had always seemed most tangible. The success of Penn's "holy experiment" took a form he could hardly have anticipated or approved, but that in this sense it was a success, who can doubt? *Si monumentum requiris, circumspice.*

NOTES

Penn's instructions regarding details of Pennsbury quoted from Catherine Owens Peare, "William Penn's Dream House" (*Bucks County Traveler,* May 1957), and *Remember William Penn, A Tercentenary Memorial* (Harrisburg, Pa., 1945), p. 13. Quotation from Bishop Spangenberg in K. G. Hamilton, *Church Street in Old Bethlehem* (Bethlehem, Pa., 1942), where many other instances of the spiritualization of work will be found—William Smalling's account book is particularly remarkable. Comment on Pennsylvania German barns by Tyrone Power (ancestor of the Hollywood figure) in *Impressions of America: During the Years 1833, 1834, and 1835* (Philadelphia, 1836), quoted in Alfred L. Shoemaker, ed., *The Pennsylvania Barn* (Lancaster, Pa., 1955), p. 15.

T. J. Wertenbaker, in *The Middle Colonies* (1938), provides a good introduction to Pennsylvania house types. It was he who made the famous observation that if you draw a line from Princeton, New Jersey, through Wilmington, Delaware, colonial buildings north and west of it are almost invariably of stone, south and east of it, of brick. The explanation is in part geologic: this line also corresponds to a belt running from New York to Washington where some of the best potters' clay in the East was deposited (cf. John N. Pearce, "The Early Baltimore Potters and their Wares, 1763–1850," unpublished M.A. thesis, University of Delaware). It also has to do, however, with patterns of settlement. Brick building tends to appear in English settlements (e.g., Salem County, New Jersey, settled by English Quak-ers seven years before Philadelphia was founded), stone building in regions settled by Welsh and Irish Quakers, and Scotch-Irish; when Germans outgrew the half-timber or log traditions native to most of them, they turned to their neighbors for bricklayers or stonemasons. Perhaps the most elaborate extant examples of brickwork patterns are to be found in Salem County, New Jersey; they are illustrated in Joseph S. Sickler, *Old Houses of Salem County* (Salem, N. J., 1949).

The Shakers, whose first, celibate colony was established in Upper New York soon after "Mother" Ann Lee came to America with a small band of followers in 1774, never literally formed part of the Pennsylvania scene or culture; yet they belong to it more than any other, both in spirit and through their close affinity to original Quaker doctrines. Each of the fifty-odd Shaker colonies that flourished when the movement was at its height (c.1840) had workshops wherein individuals worked out their salvation and incidentally manufactured merchandise whose sale permitted the Shakers to "import" necessities. Furniture was a particular specialty, and in this Shaker furniture we can recognize the final distillation, the purest and most conscious expression of the old ideal of a "peculiar people" shaping their environment to a new and godly pattern.

Shaker furniture has lately become one of the great 20th-century cults of connoisseurship. In the stark simplicity of its lines people profess to see premonitions of Scandinavian design; the community workshops that produced it suggest the later ideals of William Morris or the Bauhaus; and there seems a curious anticipation of International Style precepts in such Shaker doctrines as "Beauty rests on utility," "All beauty that has not a foundation in use soon grows distasteful and needs continual replacement with something new," and "That which has in itself the highest use possesses the greatest beauty." Undeniable though resemblances may be, the fact is, however, that between what motivates Shaker and contemporary arts there could hardly be a greater gulf.

Shaker art knew nothing of 20th-century glorification of individual, personal expression. That was discouraged to the point where craftsmen were forbidden to identify their work in even the smallest way; and, more, the very concept of individual inspiration was denied. "The Shakers believe," a mid-19th-century visitor to the Niskeyuna (Watervliet, New York) community wrote, "that their furniture was originally designed in heaven, and that the patterns have been transmitted to them by angels." Since Ann Lee, the foundress, could not read or write at the time of her marriage, direct connections between ideas like these and Plato's doctrine of archetypal forms are, to say the least, doubtful. Nevertheless, when Shakers talked about "the beautiful," they had in mind much the same absolute concept—the "morally good," the "virtuous," the "conducive to salvation." About pleasing the eye they had little concern and much suspicion. Whatever "modern" beauties Shaker furniture may have are, then, accidental. In much Shaker work, indeed, we can hardly escape the impression that the gawkiness of proportion is deliberate, that a Protestant plain style has been consciously pushed to a point of unpleasant barrenness, that here in sum is the culminating expression of that medieval insistence on letting nature take its course which produced the harsh proportions and awkward fenestrations of colonial New England house types. I have discussed this question in "Spiritual Functionalism in Shaker Furniture" (*Dansk Kunsthaandvaerk*, IX, 9, 1960, pp. 192–7). Standard works on Shaker art and culture are by Edward Deming Andrews—*Shaker Furniture* (with Faith Andrews, New Haven and London, 1937), *The People Called Shakers* (1953), *The Hancock Shakers* (Hancock, Mass., 1961).

8. PLANTERS OF URBANITY:
Traditions of Leadership in the Old South

FOR MOST PEOPLE TODAY, "early America" means "New England." Most Americans—and, for that matter, almost everyone else—take it more or less for granted that New England was the great cradle of early American culture, the source of all those democratic liberties, representative institutions, moral values, and plain "know-how" that made the United States a great nation.

Yet it was by no means always so. Nobody in the 17th century thought of Massachusetts, Rhode Island, and Connecticut as the most important English colonies in America. Still less did anyone in the 18th century, when the mansions of Virginia were the wonders of the continent and the men who came from them guided the Revolution, formulated the principles, and framed most of the Constitution for the new nation. Nor yet in the early republic, when four of the first five Presidents were Virginians. Only with the slow 19th-century shift of political power from an agrarian to an industrial base did the idea begin to develop; and only in the course of the Civil War did it really take root. What triumphed at Appomattox was, among other things, a New England version of American history. Henceforth, the nation's image of its ideals and origins would be a Puritan one. Henceforth, generations of schoolchildren would be taught a catechism that held all virtues to spring from Plymouth Rock, traced all democracy to town meetings in Salem and Roxbury and Bethel Center, and taught that America had always looked to Massachusetts for leadership just as in '61. This was an article of faith born of a distracted nation's need for assurance that its enemies were not and never had been of real account, and fostered by the nostalgia of a gilded age longing for consoling symbols of lost simplicities. Never based on any measured view of American history, every detail often attacked

and most demolished, still the "cult of New England" persists; its influence is still felt, especially in cultural history, to this day. From the Independence Centennial of 1876 in Philadelphia, where log cabins and Cape Cod houses showed "how our forefathers lived," until well into the 1930s, the cult of New England overwhelmingly dominated most writing about American art. Architects of every persuasion, from proud Frank Lloyd Wright to the humblest speculative development builder, took for granted that "Americanism" was most surely expressed in clapboards and overhangs, central fireplaces, "quaint and rambling" (or alternatively, "spaciously simple") plans, inspired by classic 17th-century New England house types. Tacitly or explicitly, an assumption that new ideas appeared first in New England colored the thinking of one writer after another on American cultural history in general, and on the evolution of American architecture and furniture in particular. Yet evidence to the contrary there has always been— evidence that everywhere points not to New England but to Virginia as the cultural leader of pre-Revolutionary America.

St. Luke's Church, near Smithfield, Virginia, is a good place to begin reconsideration. Now proved the oldest extant church building in North America, there is no better example of the distorting influence of the cult of New England than the stubborn reluctance to admit its early date. And nowhere is the fundamental difference between Anglican and Puritan culture more apparent than in the contrast of such a church with Puritan meeting houses.

In contrast to the Puritan conviction that salvation lay in escape from the world and separation from the community, the belief of the Church of England, best expressed by its great spokesman Richard Hooker, was that for Church and State to function as they should, in this

40. ST. LUKE'S (EPISCOPAL) CHURCH, SMITHFIELD, VIRGINIA

(A) Exterior. Except for the upper section of the tower, added later in the 17th century, the church now stands very much as built in 1632.

Verification of this date, rather than the 1682 date accepted by earlier scholars on the basis of a mutilated inscription, was an outstanding contribution to American cultural history by the committee headed by Dr. James G. Van Derpool which restored St. Luke's in the 1950s.

---

world or the next, they must be interdependent. Anglican teaching maintained that the Church belonged to all the people of England, and all the people of England belonged to it. Because the Church's body of revealed truth is necessarily the foundation and the justification for every law of the realm, the State must be the supporter and defender of the Church, and cannot exist apart from it; without the Church, the State is a frail tissue of temporary agreements imposed by transitory needs. To be English means, then, to be Anglican; to be Anglican means to inherit the whole history and tradition and outlook of

England. This inheritance included, as a matter of course, the church buildings of medieval England. They are the creation of the English people in history; the only change Anglican, rather than Papist, proprietorship of them will make is to remove the few things that suggest "superstitious"—i.e., un-Biblical—guarantees of salvation: sacramental roods, relics, and the like. In their place went, entirely logically, symbols of the communal function of the Church: royal arms; the Ten Commandments, on which the royal and civil powers rest; a common table instead of a privileged priestly altar, to which all

(40 B) Interior. Furnished in Jacobean rather than Gothic forms, on the basis of discovery of an original baluster with bulbous Jacobean turnings, from which the others were reproduced. Interior arrangements were determined partly by reference to Newport Chapel on the Isle of Wight, England, whence so many settlers of Isle of Wight County in Virginia came, but more on documentary indications of contemporary Anglican usage in the period between Elizabethan custom and Laudian High Church reforms.

the people of England are entitled to draw near. When Anglicans need to build new churches, they will naturally use whatever forms are current at the place and time—from medieval survivals in rural areas early in the 17th century to borrowings from the Baroque architecture of Italy or the new classical scholarship in later London. Just such an example of Anglican church building as an expression of the continuing historical life of a community is what we have in St. Luke's.

As early as 1617 King James was requesting financial aid to be sent twice yearly from every English parish to that part of the Church of England which was in the "Virginia plantations." Donations of plate and appointments from Anglicans in England to Anglicans in Virginia are recorded as early as 1618. By 1632, when St. Luke's was begun, the Established Church of England had been firmly planted across the ocean, complete with tithes and pastoral letters from London. The architecture of St. Luke's showed it. Nothing suggested that this parish stood on the edge of three thousand miles of wilderness. In plan, it was a small unaisled medieval parish church, with chancel unexpressed on plan, of a type common in England and then common in Virginia too (e.g., Jamestown, 1639, only tower surviving; second Bruton parish church, Williamsburg, 1682, known through old drawings and archaeology; etc.). Its forms likewise as they developed faithfully mirrored the mainstream of English life everywhere. The 1632 building followed prevalent Late Gothic traditions of building in Eastern England—windows with pointed tracery, buttresses, square tower (probably capped originally with crenelations at the second story) with open porch below, stepped gable of a type introduced to England in the late Middle Ages by Flemish immigrants, steep tie-beam timber-truss roof structure open to the collar beam. Interior fittings, completed over the next twenty-five years or so, were in the succeeding Jacobean manner. And when the third story of the tower was added c.1685, the builder's attempt to suggest in his treatment of the corners an effect of pilaster strips above a rusticated base (i.e., the quoins of the lower two stories) provides one of the first intimations of the coming classical age.

This is the great significance of establishing the proper 1632 date for St. Luke's. That date means not merely that St. Luke's is a major monument much older than anything in New England, but that it was extremely up-to-date architecturally. To have been building such a Gothic church in 1682 would have been backward indeed; it would—and for many earlier scholars, did—confirm the conventional image of an old-fashioned and rural South, preserving architectural forms as perfunctory as the religion they housed. Existing half a century earlier, and continuously developing and changing, these forms express a very different kind of society— one far closer to the central stream of English life and thought, far more "modern," than anywhere else in America. And what modern research has found here has been repeated everywhere; the more evidence is uncovered, the plainer it becomes that it is to Virginia that we must look for the first introduction of new ideas and trends throughout the colonial period.

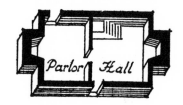

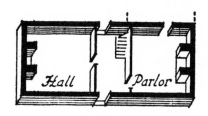

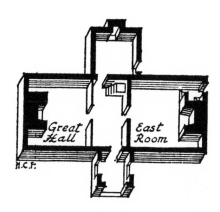

41. Seventeenth-century Virginia rural house plans. Such characteristics are common to English houses in the medieval tradition everywhere in America, and are abundantly paralleled in New England. As in New England, these types should not be thought of as developing in an evolutionary sequence, but as all appearing simultaneously in the first decades of settlement.

When serious scholarly interest in Virginia and the South first began to develop, a major concern, naturally enough, was to find some "Southern colonial" house type of Old World origin to set beside those distinctive of New England, New Netherlands, and the rest. And there was little difficulty finding one. The Adam Thoroughgood house represents an early version of it, Smith's Fort Plantation the later, more "standard" form. Such houses have most, if not all, of the common features of medieval folk tradition found elsewhere. Their plans are variants of the familiar hall-and-parlor arrangement. Construction and materials are expressed and exposed directly, inside and out, in features like the great side chimneys piling up to clustered stacks, and in the tendency to pattern brickwork.

Everywhere the familiar additive principle is evidenced. Lean-tos at the back give rise to a salt-box shape called in the South a "cat-slide roof"; the John Blair house at Williamsburg (c.1710) is an example. Strung-out elevations of the sort common in New England and New Netherlands are also found; the addition of a western unit with separate door produced this effect in the Blair house c.1765, for instance, while an even better example is Susquehanna from St. Mary's County, Maryland, now in Dearborn, dating from the 1660s—its contiguous three-room plan and flared-eave porch closely resemble Hudson Valley types. Often, too, wings were added to form an L or half-H plan, as in the Brush–Everard house at Williamsburg (c.1717–19) or the Carroll the Barrister house at Annapolis

---

42. "SOUTHERN COLONIAL" HOUSE TYPES
(A) Adam Thoroughgood house, Princess Anne County, Virginia. Built c.1640, restored in the late 1920s. It is significant, possibly, that this rural house type was built by a man who, while he rose in fifteen years to be a member of the House of Burgesses and substantial plantation owner, had begun his Virginia life in 1621 as an indentured servant.

(42 B) "Smith's Fort Plantation," Surry County, Virginia. By tradition, built in 1652 on property inherited by Thomas Rolfe from his mother, Pocahontas, who acquired it from Chief Powhatan on her marriage to John Rolfe; but many details (larger dormers, inside chimneys, etc.) suggest an early-18th-century date. It is in any event a good example of what has been called the "Southern colonial" house type.

(c. 1720). Southern colonial houses show, too, a flexibility comparable to Philadelphia house plans; they can be composed both vertically as well as horizontally. Gambrel roofs occur (e.g., Christopher Hohne house, Annapolis, c.1720), and many kinds of dormers (hipped, hooded, pedimental). There are diamond-paned leaded casement windows, T-shaped chimney stacks, summer beams, and so on through the roster of medievalisms. Besides brick, there was plenty of frame and clapboard, and occasionally a cottage in stone (e.g., Poe house, Richmond, c.1686).

The South, then, could also be shown to have a characteristic medieval house type. But it was not quite the same as other such types.

First, it was not as common. In New England, simple but unmistakable variants of the distinctive regional type (like the Webster homestead) were ubiquitous in the hinterland almost into modern times. Of the South, however, with the exception of a few towns like Williamsburg or Annapolis, and great plantation houses, what Jefferson remarked in his *Notes on Virginia* remained broadly true up to twenty or thirty years ago:

The private buildings are very rarely constructed of stone or brick, much the greatest portion being of scantling and boards, plastered with lime. It is impossible to devise things more ugly, uncomfortable, and happily more perishable. There are two or three plans, on one of which, according to its size, most of the houses in this state are built. . . .

Second, the Southern house type lacked a certain quality you could only call "distinctiveness"; it had neither the "picturesqueness" of the Hudson Valley nor the "starkness" of New England. And culturally, these two characteristics are very significant.

The Southern colonial house is duller—if that is the word—than, say, the clapboarded overhang house of New England, for the same reason that St. Luke's, Smithfield, is "dull" compared to Old Ship Meeting House at Hingham. Both represent, not the picturesque, eccentric, "distinctive" periphery of 17th-century English culture, but its norm. In the two generations after 1570, England, rural England in particular, experienced an unprecedented wave of prosperity and a great increase in population. One manifestation of it was the settlement of Ulster, the West Indies, and Virginia—the result not of religious zeal or discontent but of normal national expansion. The other was a great building boom that largely replaced the old one-room cots of a medieval peasantry with the modern farm cottages of substantial yeomen, solidly built of stone or rubble or brick as the region allowed, with two or three rooms (hall, parlor, and sometimes passageway) and sleeping quarters above, all warmed by chimneys in the end walls. As soon as Virginia and Maryland had passed the first primitive stages of settlement, this was the house type introduced. It remained common into the early decades of the 18th century. But then great plantation owners like the Carters, the Shirleys, and the Pages began to pyramid their holdings, forcing the independent small farmers whose expression this "Southern brick cottage" essentially was into the position of poor tenants, or off the land altogether. Virginia and the Old Tidewater South generally became the land of great style-conscious plantation manors on the one hand, and frame dwellings of poor white trash (or something like it) on the

other, that Jefferson knew, and that we—except for the mansions Civil War and neglect wiped off the landscape, and the buildings recent prosperity has put there—know still.

By the same token, however, the Southern house type was more advanced than its Northern contemporaries. This is apparent even in as early an example as the Thoroughgood house. Compared with the Whitman house in Farmington (*31*), say, its façade is more symmetrical, its fenestration more regular, its exposed framing smaller and finer, its plastering evener. Both buildings speak an architectural language of medieval folk tradition common all over 17th-century America; but here in Virginia the accent is somehow more refined, as if betraying more elevated origins. What these origins were, it remained for the archaeologists of Jamestown to discover.

Describing *New Discoveries at Jamestown* in 1957, J. L. Cotter and J. P. Hudson wrote that although "a half-million individual artifacts at the Jamestown museum represent the largest collection from any 17th-century colonial site in North America . . . the highlight of archaeological discoveries at Jamestown is undoubtedly the long-forgotten buildings themselves, ranging from mansions to cottages." It is indeed. And perhaps the most significant of them, culturally speaking, were the row houses. It is not so much that there were many of them—Jamestown had apparently no more than a few dozen houses of any description standing at any one time throughout the 17th century—as that they existed at all, and continued to be built so late. For they are dramatic evidence of a fact long obscured and ignored—that Virginia was not founded as a land of plantations but as an expansion of the commercial empire of London merchants. From the beginning, the founders of Jamestown envisaged the city as a second London, a great emporium for the New World. The James was to be as crowded with shipping as the Thames. Both primary and secondary industries were to

43. URBAN FOUNDATIONS IN THE SOUTHERN COLONIES

(A) Conjectural restoration of row houses in Jamestown, Virginia, based on excavated foundations. Until archaeological work began in the summer of 1934, Jamestown was no more than a ruined church tower and a legend; the capital of Virginia, and the main currents of American life, had shifted elsewhere centuries before. But the 140-odd structures of all sorts whose traces have been unearthed reveal much of the formative pattern of Southern culture. It was not so much that brick houses were common as that the contiguous row house—i.e., a distinctly urban type—appeared from the first. Besides this one of c.1630, at least two others—one of five houses in 1675, another of four in 1680—are known.

be established: ironworks, potteries, glassworks, carpenters' shops, wine presses, dry docks. And its buildings were prescribed accordingly. As a capital, Jamestown would of course have a seat of government; not some medieval structure of timber doubling for church meetings or business transactions, but a proper legislative building, reserved for the purpose, suitably adorned with fine furniture and with the coat of arms of England proudly displayed for all to see; pieces of it were still there for excavators to find. And this statehouse—in each of its successive embodiments, apparently—was located in the most important building unit of the town, the row house.

Obviously it was impossible for Jamestown's London sponsors to prescribe in detail how each settler would house himself; this was a settlement of Elizabethan Englishmen, not the sort of docile peasants brought to Quebec or New Orleans. Most built on what they knew, that is, the traditional English hall-and-parlor plan. But the official housing model, the one which it was hoped would eventually set the pattern for the growing city, was not this rural type; it was based on the kind of close-packed row house we see in contemporary views of London. Jamestown, in short, was built on an urban model. It represented, indeed, not merely the contemporary trends of London but something even in advance of them. In place of medieval half-timber and overhanging gables which might (and in 1666, did) all go up in one great con-flagration, Jamestown's houses were to have been those of a modern fireproof city—brick-walled, roofed with tiles made on the spot or slate im-ported from England. Virginia was founded, in short, on an entirely different pattern from the one brought to New England; the ideal in this colony was not to perpetuate a rural society of the late Middle Ages, but to reproduce the con-temporary, increasingly urban-centered society of 17th-century England. And this, though in ways hardly foreseen by its founders or often recognized by those who came later, it always did.

For nothing in American history is quite so paradoxical, perhaps, as the way New England and Virginia both departed in unexpected and mutually contradictory ways from the ideals of their founders. New England, conceived as a kind of perpetual paradise of rural townships, was by the end of the 17th century obviously becoming a land of towns and tradesmen. Quite as obviously, Virginia was developing in an opposite direction. Authorities dreaming of a bustling metropolis on the James were always urging Virginians to stay and build "James Citty" up to its name; nothing could make them do it. It took no time at all for the first Virgin-ians to realize that the way to prosperity in this country lay not in trade but in the cash crops, especially tobacco, that its incomparably rich soil and genial climate would produce. The more you raised, the more land you could buy; the more land you bought, the more you could raise; there was no end to the process and its prospects, particularly once Negro slaves became available. From the first, Virginia planters shunned cities and lived near their fields, where operations could best be supervised. More to the point, they had no need of a local center for trade; their market was England, and any of the dozens of inlets on Virginia rivers was as convenient for

getting their produce to market as the harbor at Jamestown. Already by the 1650s the Virginia landscape was beginning to diverge as far from what the London merchant companies who founded Jamestown had envisaged as the bur-geoning towns of shopkeepers and merchants had diverged from what had been visualized by Ply-mouth Pilgrims—a land of broad plantations, fields broken only by forests and the occasional crossroads hamlet with a church, courthouse, and inn.

By the 1680s or so, the two patterns were well formed. They made a contrast as remarkable as it was deceptive. Compared to the Massachu-setts Bay capital, Jamestown and St. Mary's were tiny, decaying places; Charleston was barely established. While New Englanders were crowd-ing into Boston to make their fortunes as ship-owners, merchants, and manufacturers, Virgin-ians with equal eagerness were spreading all over the countryside, setting up manorial estates that were to all intents and purposes self-con-tained communities. Any observer might well have concluded that New England must be by far the more cosmopolitan and urbane society; after all, "civilization" means life in a "civis," and in the South no cities were to be seen.

But appearances were deceptive; even in the tiny capitals of later-17th-century Virginia and Maryland, and in the plan of Charleston, there were evidences that all was not as it superficially seemed. These were cities laid out on systematic plans, with all the appurtenances of grand capi-tals which Boston so conspicuously lacked. Tiny though they were, they had public buildings— the St. Mary's State House is a good example— compared to which the old-fashioned exposed beams and medieval clapboard of the Boston Town House belonged in another world. Indeed, their symmetrical cross plans, arches, and gen-eral spaciousness did already look forward to the new classical age that was just beginning to achieve a broad base in contemporary England.

More significantly, the reason Jamestown and St. Mary's remained small was not that the

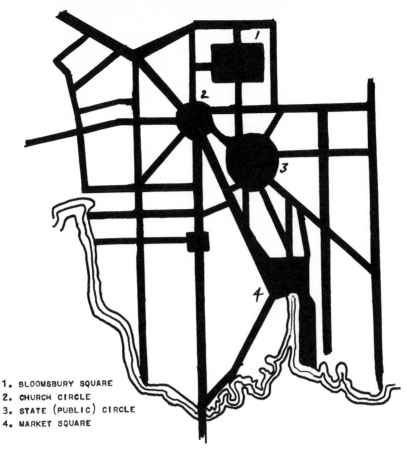

1. BLOOMSBURY SQUARE
2. CHURCH CIRCLE
3. STATE (PUBLIC) CIRCLE
4. MARKET SQUARE

(43 B) Plan of Annapolis, Maryland, 1694. Devised by Governor Sir Francis Nicholson when he moved the Maryland capital from St. Mary's City to the village of Anne Arundel Town and renamed it Annapolis. Though always a much smaller place than Philadelphia or Boston, Annapolis from the first had a more basically urban atmosphere—as this plan with nothing of the "greene country town" *or medieval village about it shows. Nicholson took inspiration from late-17th-century Baroque city plans, with streets radiating from foci (one the church, another the Capitol, a third the Public Square) to offer diverse vistas in the manner of Wren's plan for London. Life in Annapolis was correspondingly more cosmopolitan, with theatres, horse racing, dances, etc.*

leaders of Virginia were country folk. It was because the competition was too great. The Virginia planters developed no metropolis on this side of the Atlantic, because they already had one. Already in 1686, Durand de Dauphiné noted in his *Description of Virginia* how "they barter with tobacco as though it were specie. With it they buy land, they rent it, they buy cattle, & as they can get anything they need in exchange for this commodity, they become so lazy that *they send to England* for clothes, linen, hats, women's dresses, shoes, iron tools, nails, & even wooden furniture, although their own wood is very fine. . . ." Virginians, that is, lived on a cash economy, buying what they needed in town instead of making it themselves. And that town was London—which, in days of wretched roads and cumbersome wagons, was almost as close to the planters of Virginia as to lords in the farther shires of England itself. London was the metropolis of Virginia. And this meant that the leaders of Virginia were far from rural squires or cautious New England merchants in outlook. Bartering their tobacco for finished goods directly from England—from wharves on the James and the Rappahannock to slips in London—the planters of Virginia were able to keep abreast, as the Puritan merchants and divines of New England neither could nor would, of every shifting tide in English taste and opinion. To make a fair comparison between New England and the South in the 17th century, we need to remember that the mark of a successful man in Virginia or Maryland or the Carolinas was not a great merchants' town house, like Peter Sergeant's in Boston, but a plantation owner's mansion set in the midst of tobacco or rice fields. We need to look, not at the tiny capital cities which were the nominal centers of Southern culture, but at the real heart of that society, the great plantations where its wealth and ambition were concentrated. Then the comparison will be plain enough. Though Bacon's Castle, for instance, was far from a palace by modern standards, it was far in advance, stylistically, of anything standing in New England in the 1650s. And there is reason to suppose it was not unique, that other, later, 17th-century mansions continued to keep pace with the taste of the times. For already in the second half of the century an aristocracy was taking shape in Virginia, and elsewhere in the South. It produced little in the way of books or paintings or furniture comparable to what was being done in the same period in New England; but we should not be misled into imagining that the reason was some lack of cultural interests. The reason was that there was no need to produce them here. In the mainstream of English culture as they were, these emerging gentry had nothing like the dissenting Puritans' incentive to write books for their own edification; they could use, and had the means to buy, what was being written and published in England. Why should they have portraits painted by itinerant colonial

limners and inn-decorators, when they could command the services of professionals in London? And why make their own furniture, when they could buy up-to-date work direct from the source for their mansions, and supply the needs of their tenants from itinerant peddlers? The only thing they could not buy and import, obviously, was their houses. That is the peculiar significance of the plantation house from, say, 1650 to the Revolution; it is the one certain and constant indicator of the taste of the leaders of Virginia. To be sure, these great plantation houses expressed a two-class system of great landowners on the one hand, tenant farmers and slaves on the other, repugnant to modern concepts of the good life. But the time when that system would develop to the point of vitiating and strangling Southern culture was still far in the future. In the 17th and 18th centuries, the system represented no more than the kind of concentration and inequality of wealth which had always been the historic price of advancing civilization. Because men like Adam Thoroughgood had the luck and persistence to amass more lands, slaves, and goods than their neighbors, their sons and grandsons owned lands as extensive as any English lord's. And with such ever-growing resources behind them, their progeny in turn could be educated at the Inns of Court, have wives dressed in the latest London fashions and houses built by imported English craftsmen, learn the ideals of Free Trade and responsible government and latitudinarian religion that drove Catholic James off the throne, and bring in the new age of classical Reason to America. One day the lords of Virginia would apply these lessons nearer home, and drive another English king off his American throne:

It is hard to bring ourselves to believe that the great Virginia fathers of the Republic were nourished in the soil of aristocracy, slavery, and an established church. Modern American democracy, we are told, must have had its roots in some 18th-century "democracy," so

44. *Bacon's Castle, Surry County, Virginia. Reconstruction of original appearance from a drawing in* Leslie's Weekly, *by Henry Chandlee Forman (above). Built c.1655 by Arthur Allen, a successful immigrant come to Virginia twenty-odd years before. Its name refers to followers of Nathaniel Bacon who used it during their rebellion against the Governor of Virginia in 1676. Medieval folk traditions survive in many ways—triple chimney stacks set diagonally; frame kitchen and "curtain wing" since demolished; enclosed porch and stair tower; leaded casements with mullions and transoms; first-floor windows arched; great summer beams. But this builder, like those who built St. Luke's, Smithfield, tried to keep abreast of current English taste, incorporating Jacobean features like the great curved Flemish gables at each end, and framing around the second-story windows. And in details like the triangular pediment of moulded brick above the vestibule doorway, in general spaciousness, and in protosymmetry, typical large cross-plan Virginia houses like this (see present floor plan, below) pointed, however clumsily, towards the coming classical age.*

we have looked for its seeds in the New England town meeting (supposed to be a microcosm of democracy) rather than in the Virginia tobacco aristocracy. But the ways of history are obscure and even self-contradictory. May not the proudly independent spirit of the Virginia planting aristocrats have been rooted in their vast plantations, in their sense of aristocratic responsibility? May not the value they placed on their individual liberties have been increased by the sharp contrast with the slavery they saw about them? May not their aristocratic habit of mind—their "habit of command" and their belief that they could make judgments on behalf of their community—have

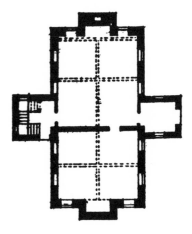

helped make them leaders of an American Revolution? . . . Perhaps a reliable toleration has its roots in the quiet catholicity of a not-too-passionate established church, rather than in the explicit liberalism of rationalists and anti-religionists.

So writes Professor Boorstin, in *The Americans.* So belated, so curiously apologetic, are modern historians in stating the case. Yet the record has always been there. Implicitly in the 17th century, unmistakably in the 18th century, churches, courthouses, and mansions in Virginia and elsewhere in the South reveal in their developing classical forms that attitude of mind from which the institutions of a new nation would grow. Already in the 17th century it was plain that Southern planters, not Pennsylvania farmers or New England merchants, would lead American civilization into its next, classical, phase.

Dr. James G. Van Derpool, "The Restoration of St. Luke's, Smithfield" (*JSAH*, XVII, 1958, pp. 12–18), gives an authoritative account of the history of the controversy over dating this church. On the spread of the Southern house type, and the survival of buildings like those in Jefferson's description, a good commentary is provided by Elliot A. P. Evans, "The East Texas House" (*JSAH*, XI, 4, 1952, pp. 1–7). The "renaissance" of English cottage building which formed a background for Southern colonial house types is discussed by W. G. Hoskins, "The Great Rebuilding" (*Past and Present*, IV, [pp. 44–57] November 1953). The classic account of how a Southern aristocracy was formed is by W. J. Cash, *The Mind of the South* (1941). Quotations from Durand de Dauphiné, in *A Huguenot Exile in Virginia* (G. Chinard, ed., 1934), p. 112; from D. J. Boorstin, *The Americans* (1958), pp. 139–41. For a selected bibliography of earlier writings on 17th-century Virginia, see the National Park Service publication by J. P. Hudson and J. L. Cotter, *New Discoveries at Jamestown* (Washington, 1957), pp. 98–9.

The Jamestown Tercentennial of 1907 symbolized, in the architecture of its pavilions, prevalent concepts of Southern culture since the Civil War and for long afterwards—an ill-digested potpourri of "plantation porticos" with little attempt being made to discover what architecture in Jamestown or anywhere else had really been like. Curiously enough, it was on this occasion that Frank Lloyd Wright made his first appearance on the East Coast:

> . . . The Larkin Company . . . had acquired space at the . . . Tercentennial . . . and called upon Wright to follow through with the necessary architectural display. . . . Wright's low, severely geometrical little building looked lost and out of place, although a carnival note was struck by a lot of Japanese-looking vertical banners on poles. It seems to have attracted little attention. [Grant Manson, *Frank Lloyd Wright to 1910*, 1958, p. 154]

Once restoration of Williamsburg and excavations at Jamestown were under way in the 1930s, however, serious re-evaluation of the relative states of culture in early New England and Virginia was inevitable; but fuller implications were only slowly drawn. For example: as great a scholar as Henry Chandlee Forman, on whose books so much of our knowledge of the Old South generally depends (*Early Manor and Plantation Houses of Maryland*, Easton, 1934; *Jamestown and St. Mary's*, 1938; *Tidewater Maryland Architecture and Gardens*, 1956), was still enough influenced by the cult of New England to feel somehow obliged to "defend" Virginia and Maryland by dwelling on medieval elements in their early buildings, as if to prove that they were just as "good"—in the sense of embodying and expressing a great historical past—as anything in Massachusetts or Connecticut; his major work, *The Architecture of the Old South* (Cambridge, 1948), carries the subtitle *The Medieval Style, 1585–1850*. That they were "better," in the sense of being more modern, looking forward to the classical era, is a fact revealed conclusively in his researches but commented on almost incidentally. With the publication of Thomas T. Waterman's studies of the great plantation houses (*Domestic Colonial Architecture of Tidewater Virginia*, 1932; *The Mansions of Virginia*, Chapel Hill, 1948), all doubt of Virginian leadership in introducing new architectural ideas was effectively removed; but even Waterman retained something of the old attitude in an evident preference for earlier over later 18th-century examples, shown in his appreciations and his restoration interests. Likewise T. J. Wertenbaker seemed torn between the premises of the cult of New England and evidences to the contrary he piled up on every page of *The Old South* (1942). And still in 1950 Professor Carl Bridenbaugh felt it necessary to offer on the first page of his *Seat of Empire* (Williamsburg, 1950) an explanation of the title for possibly skeptical readers:

> In 1750 . . . Virginia could lay valid claim to a princely domain of 359,480 square miles —a territory three times the size of King George's British Isles. As it existed at the close of the War of Independence, the Commonwealth was still larger than all of New England with Delaware tossed in for good measure.
>
> In population as well as size Virginia led all the colonies. It contained nearly twice as many inhabitants in 1776 as Massachusetts, or Pennsylvania, or Maryland, or North Carolina. . . .
>
> By the standards of the 18th century this oldest, largest, and most populous colony was properly regarded by Britons as the prime link in the great chain of empire. . . .

9. MEDIEVAL SPIRIT IN FOLK FORMS:
The Tradition of 17th-century American Art

WHAT IS A TRADITION in architecture or furniture? Essentially, like most human creations, it is made up of two elements—form and spirit. By form, I mean that buildings, tables, chairs, etc. within a tradition will show certain distinctive combinations of shapes, materials, proportions, and ornament which can be recognized as characteristic of them as a group and not of others. By spirit, I mean that men working within it will share certain inner beliefs about the nature of beauty, and what art is—indeed, what life is—that make them prefer some particular forms over others, consistently, over years and generations. It is through outward forms that we recognize a given tradition, but we understand it only as we know its spirit. Just as a sacrament by definition is the outward and visible symbol of an inward and spiritual grace, so the outward forms of architecture or furniture have lasting significance only when we understand them as expressions of cultural spirit, of forces intangibly shaping history. This is particularly true in 17th-century America.

In form, 17th-century American architecture and furniture are, as we have seen, as diverse as the national colonies that produced them, the record of many different and indeed conflicting patterns of culture. In form, too, they are remote from us. Technologically, sociologically, functionally—in every way these overhangs and drops, court cupboards and casements, joint stools and clustered chimney stacks, open fireplaces and linen-fold ornament, lozenge patterns, diamond panes, jetties, and the rest belong in another, older, vanished world. But the spirit in which these forms were used is another matter. "Someone said of the old poets," T. S. Eliot once wrote, "that they are remote from us, because we know so much more. Yes; and they are that which we know." It is the same with 17th-century American art. Not the differing

forms, but a spirit common to craftsmen in every early colony, is what has ultimate meaning for us.

That spirit is embodied in many ways. In a consistently additive principle of composition and plan, apparent in everything from contiguous lean-tos and successive running extensions of buildings to haphazard arrangements of windows and doors and artless combinations of furniture elements. In an undisguised use of natural materials—gaunt boarding or half-timber or adobe work with marks of axes or froes or smoothing hands plain on them; ornamental brickwork, patterned independently of structure; furniture unpainted and unpolished. In structural elements directly revealed—exposed summer beams, furniture pins, gable ends and overhangs and struts. Far into the 18th century, long after outward forms have disappeared, this characteristic spirit persists in plan and ornament and structure, albeit in lower and lower strata of society; the High Victorian concept of "picturesqueness" revives and makes it a dominant characteristic of mid-19th-century American art; thence it carries over into the 20th-century movement towards an organic architecture and furniture to match. In this sense it has never died—and with good reason. For unlike the forms of 17th-century folk art, this spirit was only incidentally related to 17th-century technology or social organization. What it expressed was an attitude to life which, though often denied in other, later circumstances, and superseded by other later, differing philosophies, never ceased to be meaningful to the American people generally. That spirit, that attitude grew out of a particular concept of the relationship between man and nature which was essentially an inheritance from the Middle Ages. And so it was as a vehicle for transplanting the medieval spirit and tradition to America that 17th-century architecture and furniture made their most lasting contribution to the development of an American civilization.

At first sight, such a claim seems exaggerated and tenuous. What, we may well ask, can the rough buildings and simple furnishings of 17th-century America have to do with the glorious art of the Middle Ages? What do these low heavy ceilings, these crudely hewn beams and rafters, these tiny casements with as often as not oiled paper instead of glass, these chests and chairs chipped and sawn from heavy boards, have to do with the soaring vaults of Lincoln and Laon, the rich sculpture of Amiens and Santiago? How can these paltry-proportioned plans, with doors and windows and ells and lean-tos aimlessly added here and there, be related to subtle Aristotelian theories of a golden section, or metaphysical speculations on divine geometry? That is the normal reaction of our age, and it is an entirely intelligible one; for, more than we realize, we have been brought up on a general idea of the Middle Ages created in the enchanting prose of Chateaubriand, Ruskin, and William Morris a century ago. Taught by them to see the medieval world as a golden age of faith and beauty, we forget that they wrote better polemics than history; that they were out to destroy the older Renaissance concept of a Middle Age of dirt, darkness, squalor, and superstition; that their image was quite as one-sided and blind to inconvenient facts as the one they attacked. The fact is, there were two "Middle Ages." More truly than in our own age we can talk about a coexistence of "two cultures" then. There was one medieval world that produced great cathedrals and illuminated manuscripts, esoteric treatises on divine geometry and the cosmic nature of beauty. And there was another—a feudal world of brutally ignorant serfs and armor-plated barbarians ruling them, for whom all these things were largely meaningless abstractions, whose art was a much simpler, more direct, more elementary response to their human condition. Forget this, and we misunderstand early American art; for it was from this other side of

the Middle Ages, for good or ill, that the medieval tradition in America largely derived.

The culture of the cathedrals—if we may call it that—was a thin veneer of civilization imposed on what was essentially still a half-barbaric population. It never penetrated the lower strata very far. The men who read Aristotle and talked about Plato's theories and pondered the mighty harmonies of God were never numerous, probably no more than a few thousand people, even in the High Middle Ages. By the time America was being founded, this culture had almost entirely disappeared; the upper classes of Europe generally, and of England in particular, were in violent transition from the Middle Ages to the modern world. Theories of monarchy by divine right were jostling embryonic forms of parliamentary government, mercantile wealth was challenging the old privileges of landed aristocracy, the principles and practice of "cathedral" art were being ousted by newer ideas from Renaissance Italy. But for some decades yet all this ferment remained little more than a veneer confined, like the cathedral culture before it, to an upper intellectual and social crust of society. The crust was getting steadily deeper, to be sure, but it still had not penetrated very far. Just as Shakespeare, however Renaissance his concepts and staging, still had to provide broad veins of pure medieval buffoonery to tickle the ears of "groundlings" who made up the bulk of his audiences, so, except for a very few isolated men and monuments, Renaissance principles in the visual arts remained long after his death still little more than a foreign accent affecting more or less —generally less—the ordinary man's native medieval idiom. Not until the end of the 17th century would the Renaissance begin to stand on anything like a broad mass base in England. Consequently, to most of the earlier settlers in America it was of no concern whatsoever. They belonged—in the nature of things, inevitably— to the middle and lower classes; and what they established in the New World was a medieval tradition deriving from that earlier, older, lower stratum of the culture of the Middle Ages.

That culture knew little of the "cathedral artist," the subtle creator of ineffable beauty. Its art was the utilitarian creation of artisans building peasants' homes and sheds, pegging boards together to make tables and pallets. But the same impulses moved both. The cathedral artist expressed construction directly in soaring rib vaults and flying buttresses; the artisans, in gaunt summer beams and crude struts. Where the cathedral artist followed the additive principle to multiply bays and embellish monasteries with chapter houses, the artisans revealed it in lean-tos and bench backs and enlargements to early homesteads. Instead of cut stone and rich tapestry, the materials they left naturally exposed were clapboard and patterned brick and oak plank. True cathedral art depended on conscious theories of cosmic geometry, whereas theirs had nothing to do with aesthetics as such. But whether premeditated or spontaneous, the same attitude to life was expressed by both artisan and cathedral artist; both held the same assumptions about man's proper place in this world.

In the characteristic handling of materials and construction something of medieval Europe's long push into new frontiers was expressed, certainly—generations of hard and uncertain struggles with nature, against harsh rulers, through hostilities and difficulties of all kinds. But this was no Stone or Iron Age. The art of an age which could build cathedrals and castles and manor houses like those the Middle Ages left us can hardly be explained as wholly or even largely determined by straitened resources or technological inadequacies. You cannot say that medieval man had not mastered his environment; for practical purposes, he had. Rather it was that he took no satisfaction from his mastery. For him there was none of that reveling in man's control over nature which characterized the Renaissance. Medieval man's general attitude was that nature existed for his use, not his enjoyment; it should be interfered with no more than necessary. Even in the 20th century vestiges

of this attitude survive in the opposition to birth control by inheritors of medieval traditions. In the Middle Ages it went much further. Then there was (logically enough, indeed) some diffidence about death control as well—a certain reluctance to dabble much in medicine beyond making sufferers comfortable, a feeling that nature ought to be allowed to take its course. You prayed that its course might be towards recovery; if it was not, then you co-operated with the inevitable. And in art there was much the same feeling expressed. You ought not to force materials to behave unnaturally; you should work in the nature of the material. Houses or chairs that observed these principles were "good" houses and chairs, as craftsmen (or anyone else) who observed them were good men.

"In the nature of materials"—that familiar phrase we should understand here not in the pantheistic, naturalistic, applied-scientific context of the 20th century, but within the metaphysical pattern of thought that is the key to the medieval mind. The medieval attitude to nature was based on a feeling that men must not take destiny into their own hands, that all things work together for good for them that love God, hence man should beware of deliberately pitting himself against the natural order of things. What we would call maximum exploitation of natural resources they would count as the kind of classical or Faustian *hubris*—men's attempts to dominate the world through their own efforts—which could lead only to ruin. And this is the medieval spirit that consistently informs furniture and architecture throughout 17th-century America.

It was in this spirit that planks and beams and shingles were left unmoulded and unpainted in New England and Texas, South Jersey and the Hudson Valley; that patterns were made in the brickwork of walls; that the sweeping of freshly strewn sand on hall floors became an arranger's art. It was in this spirit that doors and windows were inserted where they came most naturally; that so little attempt was made to impose pleasing proportions or much formal order of any kind; that lean-tos, sheds, wings, additions of all kinds were put together with no thought for over-all effect, to produce what the Victorians so aptly called the "picturesque piles" of medieval building; this spirit made furniture in the medieval tradition much more a matter of assembled units than co-ordinated design—backs put to benches to make chairs, lids to boxes to make chests, trestles under boards to make tables. These early American folk artisans worked as medieval peasants had, as the primitive peoples of antiquity made sculpture, as children and savages draw a human form today, on the additive principle, conceiving the whole as no more than the sum of agglomerated parts.

It was in this spirit too that structural elements, inside and out, were left plainly in view—second-story balconies on houses in Monterey and St. Augustine, summer beams on Hudson Valley homesteads, spindles on New England chairs; that adobe was smoothed and brick patterned, beams rough-hewn and clapboard left to weather—for all these are in essence ways of letting nature take its course. So these rough farmhouses and simple furniture perpetuated in the New World the spirit of those hovels and the cathedral towers soaring above them that together represented the mind of the Middle Ages; and through them they passed into the mainstream of American civilization. If in the 18th century Americans generally seemed content with plainer and simpler versions of European models than their labor conditions dictated, it was perhaps because there survived, under all the classical delight in human powers of order typical of that century, much of the earlier medieval suspicion of a life too elegantly appointed—an inherited reluctance to put too much treasure into this world, a vague feeling that life ought not to be too comfortable. To this medieval inheritance was due much of the favorable reception of Andrew Jackson Downing's ideas on "natural" landscape gardening a century afterwards, and the characteristic American exuberance of the Picturesque Eclecticism that followed him; from that source Richardson drew inspiration for his natural expression of materials, Sullivan his insistence on letting structures find their natural form, Wright his confidence that "organic" principles of building and community planning were self-evidently best. Soon enough the folk forms and medieval spirit of 17th-century America were overlaid by later forms and concepts, as they had superseded Stone and Iron Age art before them; but in these and other ways the collective spirit of that century lived on, a vital thread in the growing pattern of a new and distinctively American civilization.

CLASSICAL AMERICA: THE 18th CENTURY

1. FROM COLONIES TO NATION:
The Classical Spirit

AT THE BEGINNING of the 18th century, English America was a thin line of more or less well-established settlements strung along the Atlantic coast from the Maine country to Carolina, various in social structure, heterogeneous in race and language, diverse in economic basis, architecturally ranging from the wooden boxes of New England, firmly rooted in medieval tradition, to Virginian imitations of the great brick mansions, courthouses, and elegant public buildings of upper-class England. At the end of the century, these scattered colonies had become a great new nation, whose regional peculiarities seemed to survive only as interesting variations within a basic cultural unity. In place of medieval homesteads dotting the 1700 landscape, buildings and furniture new in principle and different in form had appeared. And in the new forms and principles was revealed, better than anywhere else perhaps, the agent which more than any other had effected this transformation —those premises, concepts, and philosophy of life which collectively we can best call the "classical mind."

In practically every one of the original states an "old capitol," sometimes still so used, sometimes not, has been preserved from the 18th century. This is no accident. For in this type more than any other, the spirit of that age was most fully embodied, as the four capitols (*45A, B, C, D*) illustrate admirably.

We can see them first as symbols of a dramatic change in status wrought over these hundred years. The old Williamsburg Capitol was the seat of a colony—a settlement stronger and more self-sufficient than the others, but still dependent on the mother country for economic and emotional essentials. By the time the old capitols of Pennsylvania and Maryland were building, these and most other colonies had become provinces, dependent still to a degree, but already stable

and self-sufficient enough to have distinct cultural character of their own; their people have ceased to think of themselves as Londoners or Swedes or Scots living away from home, have begun to acquire characteristics and outlook in common, differing from any of their heritages. And when Massachusetts finally acquired a capitol proper, it was as an independent state, freely joined in a Federal Union. All of these capitols, by contrast with their predecessors, are true civic buildings, created by and for a *civis*; as such they manifest a dramatic transformation of pioneer autarchy into complex community life. But most dramatic of all is their change in form. It is a change not simply in composition and detail from one quarter of the century to the next— though as we shall see, this is far from insignificant—but in the common spirit pervading them all, a spirit informed by premises and principles that clearly identify these capitols as belonging to a new and very different cultural tradition.

Where 17th-century buildings had a rambling spontaneity of composition, these are self-contained. Casual addition of ells, another story, or extra wings would be more than superfluous, it would destroy carefully calculated effects of over-all symmetry and balance; even when changes are made generations apart, each is done with a definable relationship to other parts, and to the whole, in mind. A new sense of discipline ends the old haphazard irregularity of miscellaneously massed gables, lean-tos, overhangs, pent eaves; it crisply defines and precisely co-ordinates details and total design. A new sense of proportion finds intolerable windows and doors stuck in here and there and everywhere; it spaces them, arranges them by predetermined design, and indeed takes precedence over structure; if need be, structure is concealed under veneers of paneling or brick facing or stonework designed to simulate a system of co-ordinated

45. PHASES OF CLASSICAL DEVELOPMENT IN FOUR 18th-CENTURY CAPITOLS

(A) The Capitol, Williamsburg, Virginia. First American legislative building to bear such a distinctively Roman title, this capitol as begun in 1701 by Governor Francis Nicholson and supervisor Henry Cary was a monument to the transition from medieval to classical traditions in America. Though in it was preserved the late-medieval and Elizabethan E-type plan, the ar-rangement of burgesses' hall and clerk's office in one wing, general court and Secretary of State's office in the other, already suggested in embryo that classical separation of powers which later Virginians would write into the Constitution of the United States. Gutted in 1747, rebuilt 1751 as the "light and airy structure" with a two-story portico that Jefferson knew, abandoned after 1779 and burned 1832, the Capitol was restored to its original 1701–5 form in the early 1930s.

parts artificially where none in fact exists. Increasingly, as the century goes on, doors and windows as well as eaves, porches, and corners are framed with elements copied from Graeco-Roman or Renaissance building: pediments, pilasters, cornices, quoins, entablatures.

More than a change of "style" or detail is involved here; this is a change in basic tradition.

Like folk buildings earlier, these structures grow out of a way of life, a new and different concept of the relationship between man and nature. Gone is the medieval "acceptance" of nature taking its course, along with the unworked materials, exposed construction, and additive composition that expressed it. This design is informed by very different convictions: that the

(45 B) Independence Hall, Philadelphia, as it stands today is the product of so many major and minor alterations that it has been described as "a veritable jungle, archaeologically speaking." No archaeologist is needed to see, however, that the tower on the south front completed to house the Liberty Bell c.1749 is not well integrated with the main block lawyer Andrew Hamilton and master carpenter Edmund Woolley planned and began to construct in 1732; or that Philosophical and Congress halls flanking it date from much later—1787 and 1789; or that the paneling and painting of its interiors were done at many different times. Yet it is the mark of 18th-century architecture generally, and particularly of the period 1725–1750 to which most of Independence Hall belongs, that the building as a whole has an over-all unity deriving from common principles of composition and a proportional system pervading all its diverse parts. State House of Pennsylvania until 1799, the building is now part of the large Independence National Historical Park restoration program of the National Park Service.

world has a basic immutable order; that men by powers of reason can discover what that order is; and that, discovering it, they can control environment as they will. This is architecture embodying the old classical principle of Aristotle that "a work of art should have a beginning, a middle, and an end"—should be composed, that is to say, so as to be immediately and self-evidently comprehensible to the individual human mind. No endless trailings off of additions in all directions here; no accidental effects of weathering; no tolerance of independent flat patterns in half-timber or brick. This is the creation of men who scale and co-ordinate

(45 C) The Maryland State House at Annapolis, as originally begun in 1772 on the plans of local Annapolis architect Joseph Horatio Anderson, represented the new mature dignity of classical architecture in the third quarter of the 18th century; though still essentially domestic in concept, its exterior was given monumental solidity and its exterior a grand spaciousness of effect by a great dome (originally lower than now, it was raised by local builder Joseph Clark in 1785–93).

Later alterations made the building an extraordinary witness at once to the vicissitudes of later classical taste and the persistent strength of classical tradition in American architecture. In the interior as rebuilt 1876–8 by George A. Frederick of Baltimore we may see the lavish and bombastic classical detail favored by High Victorian taste; in the large west annex and heavier, tripled version of the original east-front portico added 1902–5, the cold and stiff academic classicism of the early 20th century; and in the old Senate Chamber, as restored by J. Appleton Wilson of Baltimore in 1904 in conformity with Annapolis decorative forms of the 1770s, one of the first attempts at accurate archaeological restoration of an 18th-century American building. (Data from brochure prepared for Historic Annapolis, Inc., by Wilbur H. Hunter, Jr.)

(45 D) The Massachusetts State House in Boston, as designed by Charles Bulfinch in 1795 and completed 1798, was a lordly pile indeed compared with even the Annapolis capitol begun a mere twenty years before. Everything about it proclaims the new dignity and pretensions of independent statehood. But still Bulfinch works within the same classical tradition of balanced, proportioned, co-ordinated interrelationships of elements that guided Nicholson and Cary at the Williamsburg capitol a century before.

the world to their own measure. This is an expression of what the 18th century called Reason in philosophy, Enlightenment in religion, and the Classical in art. It is the monument to a great mood in American history—the self-confidence and elation of that century when, though Indians and Frenchmen and hard frontiers might persist, the ultimate success of English America was sure; when, in the widening space between shore and wilderness, wealth and leisure were accumulating so that more and more men had time to stop doing and start thinking, writing, creating in spiritual and artistic and political realms; when two or three generations had the unique privilege of seeing a new civilization take shape as they chose.

2. FOUR PHASES OF THE CLASSICAL MIND:
18th-century Furniture as Historical Expression

WHAT we call the "classical mind" of 18th-century America was hardly new to history, and only incidentally American. Two millennia and more ago, its characteristic forms and spirit had developed in Greece and, as taken over by the Romans and perpetuated in many variations, remained in evidence until the ancient world collapsed in the fourth century after Christ. A thousand years later, they were brought to a "rebirth" or "Renaissance" in Italy; it was then that the term "classical" came into general use. "Classical" in theory meant art that was "classic" or "standard," in contrast to the "barbarous" or "Gothic" art of the Middle Ages. In practice, "classical" meant art with some basic relationship to Greece or Rome—sometimes directly reproducing Graeco-Roman forms; sometimes only applying what were considered the Graeco-Roman principles of proportioning buildings to human scale, designing with clear rational organization of elements, and so forth; or any combination of these characteristics. What appeared in 18th-century England and America was a third recurrence of the classical mind, differing in circumstantial detail, but the same in spirit and basic forms; and in it the same pattern of evolution that had marked the other two was repeated.

In the two preceding classical epochs, it is easy to recognize four more or less well-defined phases of development. They follow a kind of cycle, not, of course, because they obey some German mystique of history or immutable biological law, but simply because by its nature classical art is a creation of the human mind, and the human mind works within predictable limits. First comes an age of transition from a previous era when art was not oriented in terms of individual human perception. In antiquity, this is the transitional period from c.500 to

c.475 B.C.; in the Italian Renaissance, the early 15th century, the age of innovating genius, of Ghiberti, Masaccio, Brunellesco, Donatello; an age of intuitive creation when, by a combination of circumstances, men almost accidentally realize the possibility of ordering the world in terms of their own experience, capabilities, and scale, and are preoccupied with the practical problems of finding forms to embody and express this new frame of reference. Next comes a generation consciously aware of the new orientation, whose task it becomes to formulate the possibilities into a definite system—to write a creed for the new faith. In this second phase (c.475–c.450; the mid-15th century), the new techniques are rationalized and the new principle of organic unity made consistently manifest, as in the Temple of Zeus at Olympia, or the work of theoreticians like Alberti and Piero della Francesca; it is a phase of idealism, when men write and theorize not about art as it is but of art and life as they might and ought to be. Their work prepares the way for "Great Masters" of the third, "golden age," of maturity— the age of Pheidias and the Parthenon, of Leonardo, early Michelangelo, and Raphael in the High Renaissance. They perfect in form what was implied by the theory, put the ideals into practice, embody them in "definitive" forms. But inevitably disillusionment follows. The golden age cannot be maintained; perfection is not attainable in this world; the vision fades. There follows a final, long-drawn-out phase, when although the confidence in man's control of the world that nurtured them has faded, although their rationale has decayed, classical forms persist as a "style," maintained by habit, inertia, or the veneration of long usage. They become ends in themselves, to be played with, refined, polished for the delectation of the connoisseurs and specialists whose appearance characterizes this final classical age, the age to which the little temple of Nike Apteros, the Erechtheon, the Altar of Pity, and the Hellenistic "schools" belong in antiquity, and in the Renaissance those Mannerists and Baroque artists who so skilfully use classical forms to express nonclassical ideas.

That we do not immediately recognize comparable phases in 18th-century American art is perhaps because we are so conditioned to look first for them in what we think of as the "major arts," where they were evident in earlier classical cycles. But in the nature of things painting and sculpture were not major arts in 18th-century America, and architecture—certainly in the first half of the century—hardly more so. Only one art did the times and circumstances permit of full development. That was furniture. Possibly this seems too extravagant a claim? The most cursory study of American art will confirm it. At a time when the best architecture in America was still being designed by itinerant carpenters and bookish gentlemen, when most American painting consisted of fumbling imitations of mezzotints after Kneller or Lely, when American sculpture was a matter of figureheads and tombstones, there were professional craftsmen in consistent and competent command of their medium turning out American furniture that, if not altogether the equal of its British prototypes, certainly bore a comparison with them that none of the other American arts could. In later generations, while young Americans who wanted careers in sculpture and painting were still finding it best to study and practice in England or France or Italy, fine furniture makers like Seymour, Phyfe, and Lannuier were coming to America to live. Even now furnishings are a generally surer indication of taste and background than architecture, furniture being within most people's means to choose as architecture is not. Two hundred years ago it was even more so; it is no accident that next to public buildings furniture comes most readily to mind in the

18th century, for this was the great, the "classic" as well as "classical," era of furniture in America.

Circumstances conspired to make furniture the great mirror of this age. The "spirit of the times" generally favored it: in Europe even more than America the intellectual climate was one disposed at once to broad frameworks of general principle and practicality in detail, so favoring arts like furniture which must be concerned with both abstract design and physical function; the same insistence on order and reasoned principle that frustrated the peculiar genius of epic poets or religious painters encouraged the best in furniture and interior decoration of all sorts. And American conditions in particular favored it even more: a lingering frontier mentality which discouraged nonutilitarian arts; availability of imported models to furniture makers when architects had to work from poor guidebooks without ever seeing a first-rate building; patrons (except for the richest Southern planters) whose means allowed fine furniture but no baronial mansions. For all these reasons, furniture earliest and best embodied the classical mind of 18th-century America. And there, where historical evidence is least distorted (you may store old chairs or tables in a garage, their upholstery may fade and their legs chip, but you are not as likely to rebuild or add to them as you are to remodel your house), the characteristic phases of classical development are still most plainly revealed.

Within the general framework of classical principles, four distinct "styles" have long been recognized in American furniture. Like all historical phenomena, they cannot be precisely defined in form and time; but substantially, they are quite distinct, and form a consistent evolutionary sequence, each dominating a successive quarter of the century, lagging in time some years behind their corresponding English prototypes. Traditionally they are designated as William and Mary (in England c.1685–c.1700; in

America c.1700–c.1725); Queen Anne (in England—including Early Georgian—c.1700–c.1740; in America c.1725–c.1750); Chippendale (in England c.1740–c.1765; in America c.1750–c.1785); and classical—English styles like Adam, Sheraton, Heppelwhite (c.1765–c.1810), in America the Adamesque–Federal (c.1785–c.1820). By convention they are called "styles"; analyze their characteristics and the rationale behind them, however, and it becomes apparent that here are no whims of fashion varying from year to year like "styles" in women's shoes or bathing suits. This is a pattern of development, as consistent as the one evident in the classical art of the Greece in the 5th century B.C. or of Renaissance Italy. These are, in fact, the four phases of appearance, growth, maturity, and decline characteristic of the classical mind in history everywhere. And in them is a key to understanding the classical art of 18th-century America as a whole.

Once recognize the four styles of 18th-century American furniture for what they are, analyze their characteristics, and you will find corresponding characteristics and the same four phases in 18th-century American architecture and, to a lesser extent, painting as well. Furthermore, these arts will in turn illuminate the history of furniture. For while furniture as an index to 18th-century cultural history has the advantage of showing its four phases most clearly, it also has peculiar disadvantages. Not only is it unusually complicated by cultural lag (as we shall see), but its problems of provenance and dating are much greater. Very few pieces of early furniture are labeled, and some of the labels we do have may be spurious. Furthermore, where account books of cabinetmakers have been found, it is seldom certain—at the very least—to what known pieces entries may refer. By contrast, the history of architecture presents an opposite set of problems. Here precise data are known oftener than not; here some kinds of records—deeds, wills, letters, and so forth—are

usually available, requiring only research to yield original dates of building and alterations. As for provenance, we need only know where we are. Stylistic development is what plagues the architectural historian with uncertainties; in analyzing buildings he has to take into account all sorts of "outside" factors that as a rule have little or easily determinable effect on design in furniture—climate, geography, size of families, changing social status, available materials, accessibility of site—and consequently has tended to treat American architecture primarily by region, only secondarily in terms of an evolving style. Take 18th-century American architecture and furniture together, as complementary studies, however, and each helps solve the other's problems: stylistic patterns in architecture can be seen by analogy with furniture, provenance of furniture by analogy with regional characteristics in building. That is how we propose to treat the two here. In the sections that follow we shall consider first the common characteristics of furniture and architecture in each of the four phases, and how they may be seen as cultural expression, by analyzing a comparable interior and exterior. We use Southern examples, for reasons that will become apparent in the second section, which compares how the classical mind evolved in different regions of the country. Finally, in a third section, we consider how the four-phase pattern is expressed in, and can be used to better understand the significance of, the changing status and role in society of the individuals who created the buildings and furniture of classical America.

In a work of this length, exhaustive treatment is out of the question; our purpose is only to suggest the general lines of approach, and through them the breadth in scope of American architecture and furniture as cultural expression. For they become fully significant only when we see them as more than isolated objects to be admired by connoisseurs, or as lists of buildings with more or less archaeologically correct "Georgian" features to be identified, or even as provincial variants of English taste with prototypes to be found; we need to see them in the perspective of broad patterns stretching back far and deep into space and time, as particular aspects of one of the great universal expressions of the human mind and spirit in history. Only then, perhaps, can we fully understand what classical art meant to American history—how it was a vehicle originally for expressing America's first great coming of age, then for helping to transform its diverse colonies into provinces sharing a common outlook and aspirations, finally for moulding the mind of a new united nation.

3. AN AGE OF TRANSITION:
The William and Mary Period, 1700–1750

EVEN MORE than other American furniture styles, William and Mary is difficult to date or define with precision. In America, it actually represents a coalescence of several late-17th-century English modes, in forms ranging all the way from near-medieval stiffness and angularity to bold robust curves presaging the subsequent style we call "Queen Anne." But its general principles and characteristics are evident enough. They embody a transition to an age when individual human experience is the primary measure of life and art, from one where it was not. As such, William and Mary is far from unique. The transition from archaic to classical in Greece, from medieval to Renaissance in Italy, were much more spectacular examples of the same sort of sweeping change; and to put the American development into historical perspective it will be helpful—if somewhat presumptuous, perhaps—to begin by recalling briefly what happened then.

Once the classical mind appears, it develops fast. Only a decade or two separates the "Dying Warrior" of the west pediment on the Temple of Aphaia at Aegina, executed when the temple was originally built c.500 B.C., from its counterpart on the east, executed as part of a restoration c.475, following Persian occupation and sack of the island; only a decade or two separates the first and last panels of the "Paradise Doors" of the Baptistry in Florence, executed by Lorenzo Ghiberti in the years 1425–52. Yet between each pair there is—to borrow an appropriate cliché—all the difference in the world. Primitive principles still inform the Aegina west pediment; conceived frontally and assembled additively, this warrior is a collection of parts each represented in its most characteristic aspect—legs and arms in side view, body and head full front. Expressionless face, mechanical posture, the obvious gesture of extracting a spearhead, all com-

bine to suggest not a man dying, but a symbol of death. This is an art concerned not with persons but with things, with abstract concepts; this is a manifestation of that primitive mind which dominates the early civilizations of Egypt, of Mesopotamia, of China, of archaic Greece. And so, essentially, is Ghiberti's first panel. For all its introduction of details borrowed from Greek and Roman prototypes—Venus figures used for Eve, and the like—this is still a creation of the Middle Ages. It represents the Garden of Eden story not as human minds could have perceived it, as a sequence of events each taking place at one specific time and seen from one specific place, but all at once, in a divine cosmic present. Past, present, and future events (the creation of Adam, then of Eve, the Fall and subsequent Expulsion) all occur simultaneously, as the Creator of Time and He alone could see them; this composition is a collection of episodes, added together almost as arbitrarily as the parts of the west-pediment warrior.

But now in the space of a few short years comes a great and fundamental change. All of a sudden the old formulas revealed so long ago, and for so long accepted, lose their power. They do not yet disappear—primitive principles and forms remain in evidence throughout this transitional classical stage everywhere—but they are subordinated to new controlling concepts of unity and humanly imposed order. Where the old Aegina warrior was simply placed in the triangular corner of the pediment like another gift added to the shrine, the new one is obviously designed to fit there, a visually integrated part of a larger whole. Where the old figure was an assemblage, the new one is an organic unit. It is because a man is dying that this head droops, that this body pulls down on this shielded arm as it does; every detail, that is—muscles, sinews, toes, etc.—is disposed in relation to what is hap-

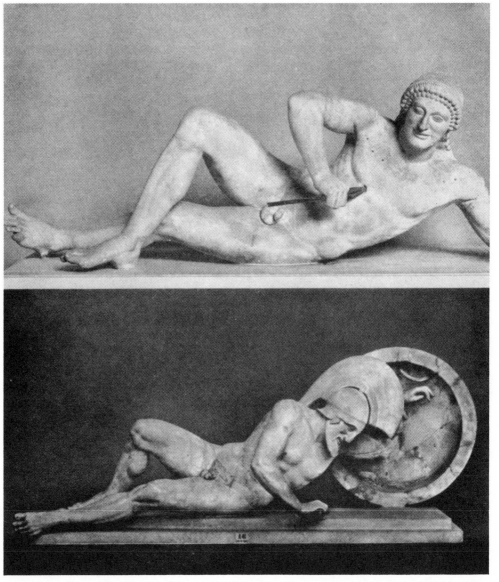

46. *TRANSITIONAL CLASSICAL ART IN*
ANTIQUITY AND THE RENAISSANCE
Parallels to the William and Mary style.
    (A) "Dying Warriors" from the west
(above) and east (below) pediments of the Tem-
ple of Aphaia, Aegina, restored by Thorwaldsen
in the early 19th century. Glyptothek, Copen-
hagen.

---

pening to a particular figure at a particular moment in time. And, in the same way, Ghiberti in his last panel depicts the marriage of Solomon and Sheba as a single event, seen from a single individual's point of view. Except for the size of the two main figures—larger than the rest, in deference to the medieval (and primitive) convention of the "bigger" (in terms of divine and anecdotal importance) "the better"—everything is now in human perspective, each part visually and psychologically organized in terms of human experience.

No simple shift of taste or passage of time accounts for what has happened here; this

(46 B) First panel of the "Paradise Doors" of the Baptistry in Florence executed by Ghiberti c.1425–c.1452, representing the creation of Adam, creation of Eve, Original Sin, and expulsion from Eden.

change is fundamental. It is the whole framework of reference that is different. Mythopoeic thought or received theology no longer determine how the artist represents the world; instead, he organizes it on the basis of his own (and therefore the individual spectator's) personal perceptions and experience. As a result, we can identify with and "comprehend" these later works as we never could the earlier. The east-pediment warrior is undergoing an experience that we can understand personally, because it is a possible human experience; he exists, as we do, in a particular moment in time. Similarly, the marriage of

Solomon and Sheba takes place in "our" time, in a world ordered and controlled as we know it. And in this organization of experience in human terms we recognize the beginnings of the classical mind in art.

Exactly how and why the change occurs when it does is hard to say. Certainly external events have something to do with it. There must have been an enormous surge of self-confidence among the small Greek states who so successfully withstood the Persian invasions, for instance; and certainly economic factors like the spurt in wealth and commercial importance experienced by Florence and other Italian city-states at the beginning of the 15th century played a part. But there have been many other times in history when similar conditions seem to have been present without any corresponding appearance of a classical mind in art. All we can really say is that every now and then some *Zeitgeist* develops —and this is a proper occasion to use that vague but cogent term—which encourages men to put the world into human perspective; something in the "spirit of the time" gives them incentive and confidence to relate their environment to themselves and their personal experiences, and in the process create a "classical art." The early 5th century before Christ was one of those times. The Renaissance of the 15th century A.D. was another. And at the end of the 17th century there came a third. Its first expression in the Anglo-American world was the William and Mary style. The "Flock" Room from Morattico Hall at Win-

terthur, and the restored Governors' Palace at Williamsburg, are typical American examples.

As in those earlier transitional epochs, so now—vestiges of older forms persist everywhere in William and Mary furniture. The stiff and stark chest-with-back-attached of the Middle Ages, as much symbol of rank as article of use, is not long out of the minds of men who make the characteristic stiff, high-backed, vertically proportioned William and Mary chairs. For all their new lightness and bold turnings, William and Mary tables still perpetuate much of the additive composition and awkward angularity of their medieval ancestors. However elegant the gilded

---

47. "Flock Room" from Morattico Hall, Richmond County, Virginia, as restored and reconstructed in the H. F. du Pont Winterthur Museum. As originally built by Charles Grymes, probably before 1717, Morattico Hall was basically the "Southern colonial" house type—one and a half stories high with a hall and parlor on each floor, with an inside chimney. The paneling was a re-

markable feature—high wainscot around three walls, end wall paneled completely with a fireplace framed by bolection mouldings containing three painted panels representing exotic birds and an elaborate country seat. That it was the fireplace wall which was fully paneled suggests visual articulation more than insulation as the primary motivation.

or japanned decoration of a William and Mary chest of drawers, it still seems almost as flat and two-dimensional in conception as the painted sides of medieval chests or the chip-carved backs of medieval chairs; in the drops ornamenting its lower edges, we can find reminiscences of those decorating the overhangs of medieval buildings. Direct expression of structure persists in the stretchers which reinforce the legs of William and Mary furniture as consistently, if not so sturdily, as ever. And medieval reminiscences are equally evident everywhere in William and Mary rooms as a whole—in the flock wallpaper, descended from the medieval tradition of tapestry-covered walls; in the pronounced verticality of paneling; most of all in the total effect of a heterogeneous collection, assembled on the additive principle—some pieces (like the table) still strongly medieval, others in the newer, lighter woods and manner.

But in every case the spirit is different. There is a new emphasis on control of the material, evidenced in a new lightness, a new deftness of touch. Furniture dimensions generally become thinner, materials finer; caning, upholstery, finer-grained and more easily worked walnut displace the ponderous solidity of oak. On interiors, summer beams and rafters are covered by plaster, thick walls and cavernous fireplaces go out of fashion; the whole looks tidier and lighter, with axes and saws less in evidence, planes and rulers more. Spools, spindles, and the like are turned with a new conscious ostentation. All these characteristics express the same fundamental delight in man's ability to manipulate materials and bend nature to his will typical of the classical mind; in them are the first great manifestations of a new age. And everywhere we can sense, too, the beginnings of a new insistence on unity, both formal and organic, beneath superficial medieval incoherence. Symmetry and balance are emphasized as never before in the disposition of carved decoration on furniture, the articulation of wall paneling, the spacing and organization of architectural elements.

A pervasive system of mathematical relationships appears—a practice of making all ma-

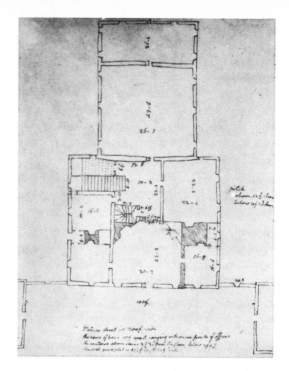

48. THE GOVERNORS' PALACE, WILLIAMS-BURG, VIRGINIA
    (A) Plan drawn by Thomas Jefferson when he was Governor of Virginia.

jor dimensions in both buildings and furniture divisible by a common integer (5 or 6, usually) —which creates an organic unity all the more effective because it is so subtle. Most significant of all, shapes and proportions of individual details are changed to conform with designs as a whole. This we can see most strikingly in the treatment of furniture legs. Suddenly the medieval concept of stocks and boards to raise pieces off the floor, still perceptible in 17th-century furniture, passes away. Legs of chairs and tables and chests begin to function as columns do in classical architecture—they become key elements, determining proportions, scale, and general character for the whole. Just as capitals, shafts, and entablatures are shaped and proportioned to express varying relationships of load and support in the classical orders, so now at the bottom of the furniture leg a foot develops—first a fat ball, then a real foot with "toes"

(48 B) Reconstruction, based on Jefferson's plan, excavated foundations, and a plate in the Bodleian Library at Oxford, begun December 1931 and completed April 1934.

As begun by Henry Cary in 1706, the Palace was essentially a provincial version of the naïve Renaissance sort of "double pile" sporadically introduced into England in the mid-17th century. Governor Alexander Spotswood, who arrived in 1710, had other ideas, however; it was he who framed the act of 1710 authorizing "a Court-Yard of dimensions proportionable to the said house . . . encompassed with a brick wall," division of Cary's medieval-like "great hall" into entrance hall and southeast room, a garden with long vistas, and heightening of the brick wall from four to six feet—in short, the kind of subtle changes that related the building to palaces in the 16th- and 17th-century Baroque tradition. Repaired in 1749–52 and again 1768–70, with ballrooms and supper rooms added c.1754–5, the Palace was destroyed by fire December 1781; its flanking buildings, however, survived until the Civil War.

curved as if to carry weight—not simply the last of a string of parts, but designed in terms of the whole. In this, more than anything else, we see how William and Mary cabinetmakers, like classical artists in antiquity and the Renaissance before them, have begun to think of their work in terms of personal experience, to conceive of furniture legs as things living like their own, bearing the weight of what is above them, and to be shaped accordingly. They have begun the process of relating their art to man, the process that manifests the classical mind.

It is the same in architecture. Here the great monuments are in Williamsburg, made capital of Virginia in 1699; any early building there will show a combination of lingering medievalisms and new classical spirit comparable to contemporary William and Mary furniture. Perhaps the best example is the "palace" Francis Nicholson began for himself and future governors in 1706, in size and magnificence dramatically proclaiming the degree of confident prosperity and prestige England's oldest American colony had attained in only a century. In a way, the Governors' Palace symbolizes the whole classical era in American civilization. It marked the first really consistent appearance of the classical mind in American art; its destruction by fire, during the Yorktown campaign of 1781, was the beginning of the end. For with Thomas Jefferson, last Virginia governor to occupy it, describing the Williamsburg buildings as "rude misshapen piles which, but they have roofs, would be taken for brick kilns," there was no incentive to rebuild, even had the capital not been removed to Richmond. Soon, all traces of the building above ground had disappeared as completely as the classical mind was submerged in the proto-Victorian literary symbolism and pedantic formal correctness of American architecture in Jefferson's generation. Thanks to the Williamsburg restoration, however, we are able to see it again, and with rather different eyes, as a historical record—in the same language as the new furniture being imported to the flourishing plantations around it, but on a larger, monumental, architectural scale—of the moment of transition from medieval to classical America.

Here in William and Mary architecture, as in furniture, vestiges of medieval tradition persist abundantly, in whole and in detail. These flanking buildings which, like furniture in attics and kitchens, always and everywhere tend to be less consciously designed and so preserve older forms longer, are here still based on the old Southern colonial house type of medieval inspiration, comparable to Smith's Fort Plantation. The same surviving medieval verticality that characterizes William and Mary furniture still dominates the Palace's proportions; its essential dimensions are all much higher than wide, and the towered cupola visually functions like a spire to pull eyes rapidly upward. These building planes are as entirely flat and two-dimensional, as basically lacking spatial sense in either composition or decoration, as they are in William and Mary furniture. Nor—for all that Governor Nicholson evidently had precedents from classical antiquity in mind when he laid out the town and named its capitol—are there any more specifically Greek or Roman forms here than on William and Mary chairs or chests. The classical mind here, as in furniture, is a matter of spirit, of new emphasis on control of the material and organization of the whole.

Compared to Jacobean houses preceding it —Bacon's Castle, for instance—or to the ponderous furniture in them, everything about the new palace, from window muntins to cupola, was proportionately lighter. These were no longer medieval builders, traditional artisans working in the nature of materials, but men feeling pride and a new confidence in their abilities to impose their will on an environment, to create measured human order in clay and wood and iron. Details like sash windows—first in the colonies—express this new architectural spirit: providing panes set in measured ratios instead of limitless diamond patterns and ventilation regulated precisely as never before, they represent a new degree of technological and psychological control over nature, a literal and figurative command of air and light. Even more is it evident in the complex as a whole. What in earlier buildings like the St. Mary's City State House was only an inherent unity has now found explicit expression. Nothing of the old rambling quality of medieval building here, no casual assembling of elements; this is a co-ordinated design, governed by a master plan. Each part of it has a clearly determinable relationship to the next; all conform to the whole. For all its medieval reminiscences, this is something basically new on the American scene. This is a classical building, a manifestation of the classical mind.

It is far from a perfect manifestation. These transitional artists speak the classical language like children. As yet they know very few words; it is a telling characteristic of the American William and Mary style that direct copying of Graeco-Roman or Renaissance detail is so rare. And the words the artists do know they often mispronounce, as in the decoration of crestings and stretchers, or the odd dormers that perch so precariously and so unclassically on the steep-pitched roofs of William and Mary buildings. Sometimes it even seems as if they have forgotten what they once knew, for the ambitious builders of Elizabethan and Jacobean houses used more classical details than they. But there is a great difference. Those earlier English builders were adults speaking a foreign language; their native tongue was medieval. But these William and Mary designers speak the classical language naturally. They instinctively use its balanced grammar and orderly syntax; they have the "feel" of the language, because the classical idiom is what naturally expresses their new, humanly oriented attitude to life. Soon enough they will develop a proper vocabulary of cornices and capitals and pilasters; and when they do, they will know how to use it organically, and not simply as applied decoration, for they are making the classical mind their own.

That this should have happened first in Williamsburg, the old "Middle Plantation" renamed for William of Orange, was entirely appropriate, for it was William who effected the real transition from medieval to modern times in England. The Glorious Revolution of 1688 that put William III on an English throne was a turning point in British history, politics, and culture. Out for good and all went the Stuart kings with their quaint medieval ideas of divine monarchy and inquisitorial torture, their papistry, their subservience to France and Spain. In came a dynamic ruler from the most progressive nation in Europe, to introduce constitutional monarchy in the modern sense, systematic national financing, government by cabinet, freedom of the press and religious toleration (in spirit if not yet fully in law), all the basic features of a modern nation-state. In his reign England triumphantly re-entered European power politics. If William did not live to see Marlborough's brilliant victories, still it was he who set the stage for them, he who, in Macaulay's famous words, "made England once again the England of Elizabeth and Cromwell"—but this time for good, with a population and economic base grown broad enough to support her new powers and prestige indefinitely. It was thanks to William's policies that England after 1689 enjoyed the unbroken string of successes that made a small and relatively poor 17th-century island the heart of the world's greatest empire in the space of a single lifetime. Only the most foolhardy had dared predict that North America might one day be English, a century before; now, with Dutch and Swedish rivals long gone, Indian resistance broken in King Philip's War, and peasants along the St. Lawrence learning to chant "Malbrouk s'en va t'en guerre," only the timidest doubted still. Everywhere, in every way—from the first paper money being printed to take care of New England's increasing volumes of trade abroad, to the hundreds of slaves being imported to make great plantations vaster and great planters richer in Virginia and the Carolinas—the provinces were visibly growing in wealth and strength. And now the resultant wave of pride and self-confidence demanded a sudden and fundamental change of artistic expression, made the Anglo-American world turn to rediscover and borrow from those classical forms created under similar circumstances in antiquity and the Renaissance, centuries and ages before.

By the 18th century the classical spirit was long derelict in Italy. Italians had long since discovered, like the Greeks and Romans before them, that they did not in fact control their environment, nor could ever be independent of it; that man in the last analysis cannot control his own body, let alone anything else. They had discovered that it is only the rare moment in history when such a pretense can be managed, that the kind of art which sustains it never seems real for long. But the 18th century was just that rare moment of success for England, and even more for America. The self-sufficient and imperious spirit of classical art corresponded perfectly to the mood of confident security engendered in England by the Glorious Revolution, exactly suited the mood of provinces boasting great mercantile cities, fertile farmlands, and prosperous plantations where all had been trees and rocks and swamp a few decades before. All at once, it seemed, the medieval attitude to nature, the sense of men being controlled by some destiny higher than themselves, began to fade into unreality. The fact was, or so it seemed to many, that man was quite capable of looking after his own destiny. He need not "co-operate with the inevitable" in the medieval sense; to men who could reason out the principles of nature, nothing was inevitable, anything could be ordered to their will. All at once medieval forms and traditions in art seemed somehow crude and pointless. All at once, the controlled forms of classical art, the principle of organizing and arranging environments in relation to themselves seemed so self-evidently right that Englishmen and Americans—at least those benefiting most from the new power and prosperity—could hardly endure any others. Another of those brief peaks rising out of the long level plains of history was at hand, when men were encouraged to try and build a world to their own specifications, put a world in perspective to themselves. As in ancient Greece, as in Renaissance Italy, so now in the Anglo-American world of the 18th century there was established and came to dominance that attitude of mind called long ago the "classical" view of experience. So began a third classical age, introduced in England and America by the William and Mary style.

These are the spiritual origins of this first phase of the classical mind. Where its forms came from is harder to determine. Obviously, they were not the invention of individual genius in America; America at the beginning of the 18th century was not the kind of place where geniuses were likely to be found. Marcus Whiffen has made the attractive suggestion that Francis Nicholson could see himself in the role of that Marcus Hostilius, described by Vitruvius, who moved Old Salpia in Etruria from its original marshy site to a newer and healthier one some four miles away and laid it out in orderly fashion on two cardinal axes (as the Virginia capital was moved from Jamestown and laid out along Duke of Gloucester and England streets); his act of 1699 naming the proposed new statehouse a "Capitoll" and assigning five acres for its grounds may well have been inspired by the account in Basil Kennett's *Roman Antiquities* of the four-acre site of the Capitol or Temple of Jupiter Capitolinus. But this is very far from saying that Nicholson, or Cary, or Governor Spotswood was a seminal figure like Ghiberti or Brunellesco in the Renaissance, or the Master of Aegina in antiquity, creative spirits through, in, and around whom new principles and forms crystallized. The new classical architecture of early America was no more their creation than the imported furniture they put in it. That they borrowed its forms is clear; where they borrowed them from, not at all.

Traditionally, the great source is supposed to be Sir Christopher Wren, dominant figure in English architecture during the last quarter of the 17th century; and Williamsburg buildings like the Governors' Palace, the Capitol, and the College of William and Mary do have many details generally characteristic of the Wren manner. But specific parallels are hard to prove. The problem is that Wren worked for a sophisticated upper class—kings, an established high church, great noblemen—which did not yet exist in America, even in Virginia; the plans and forms he took direct from Versailles and Rome were at once too subtle and too grand to have any direct application at this stage in the New World. Parallels at all convincing exist only with simpler and smaller works of late-17th-century England—works that might be quite as well attributed to anyone else as the master. So, too, in furniture; American William and Mary forms seem to be derived less from a single source than from a simplification and standardization of several modes current somewhat earlier in upper-middle-class England. In both architecture and furniture, that is to say, William and Mary forms have the same general and diffuse origins as the new classical spirit. That is why you find real parallels to the architecture of Williamsburg only in country houses of run-of-the-mill country gentlemen, designed by anonymous or obscure people, of the sort seen (for one instance) in Kip's *Britannia Illustrata* of 1707. And that too is why if one influence was more decisive on them than others it was not Wren but the builders and craftsmen who came over from Holland in such numbers after William of Orange became king—cabinetmakers like the Huguenot Daniel Marot (1663–1752), whose mastery of the Louis Quatorze style was put in William's service after revocation of the Edict of Nantes in 1685, and thence brought to England; or the many decorators who worked under William's direction to refurbish Hampton Court and Kensington Palaces in simulation of the great country house he had designed at Loo. They brought to England the new taste for walnut and Baroque decorative motifs in cabinetmaking; they brought sash windows to replace casements; they brought centuries of experience in skilled brickmaking. Most important, they brought to England Italian

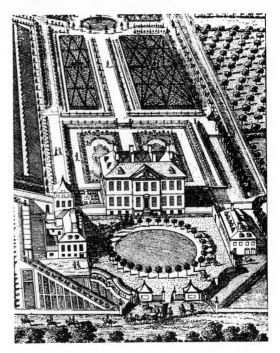

49. BACKGROUND OF THE WILLIAM AND MARY STYLE

(A) New Park, Surrey, from J. Kip, Britannia Illustrata (1707). An "Anglo-Dutch" country house of the late 17th century. Anticipating the Governors' Palace at Williamsburg are such features as the "double-pile" plan; formal entrance gates and courtyard; clipped gardens behind; dependencies forming an entrance court. These features in turn are anticipated in earlier Netherlands buildings. A telling detail is the roof treatment of the little entrance pavilions; comparable structures are common in Holland. Ultimately, the general scheme can be traced back, like the basic features of William and Mary furniture, to 16th-century Italy; compare, e.g., 49B.

Renaissance forms in precisely the way and at precisely the time England was ready to accept them. The result was what has aptly been called an "Anglo-Dutch" style—counterpart in art to the joint reign of Dutch William and English Mary—which perfectly suited the needs of the Anglo-American world for a classical cultural expression.

Renaissance forms were by no means new

in late-17th-century England, of course. But never before had they gained general acceptance. Always they had been either in the nature of exotic upper-class "conceits," as in the Elizabethan age, or associated with foreign or papist ideas, as in the case of Inigo Jones under Charles I. Now it was different; what the English would not take from Spain or France or Rome they were willing to accept from Protestant Holland in the course of a national patriotic revolution, and precisely modified in the course of the preceding half-century to suit English traditions and needs.

Already by the mid-17th century Holland had become the wealthiest and most progressive nation in Europe. Long before classical art affected Englishmen generally, the Dutch had felt the special appeal it always has in such circumstances; they had looked to France and even more to Italy, still center of the European art world, for forms to express it. What they had found to satisfy them was not the mature classical expression of the High Renaissance—no art for beginners to understand or appreciate—but the later development of it known to art history as the Baroque. Here the classical doctrine of man controlling his environment could be seen at its most obvious and most dramatic. That it was also paradoxical—that Baroque artists used classical forms and principles for nonclassical ends—could be overlooked; what appealed was the way mid-16th-century Italian cabinetmakers ostentatiously dramatized control over materials by great carved crestings and front stretchers, the way Baroque architects constructed great stages on which men could experience their own greatness. Ultimately, Michelangelo's Capitol Square in Rome was the great inspiration; and there we can still see those principles that became the basis of the William and Mary style.

The experience begins with a long ramp, difficult to climb, progressively narrower, hemmed in at the top by heavy statuary. Once through it, however, you are suddenly released into the great open space of the piazza. But then constriction begins again; the piazza rises to a mound at the center, with a statue atop it and a pavement design radiating outwards, so that you are forced to walk around its perimeter, and, as you do, the flanking buildings begin to hem you in, for they are not parallel to each other but inclining inwards towards the central capitol. Slowly, deliberately, you make the long circuit, then find yourself released again in the free space in front of the Capitol. Then comes a third constriction; the convex foundation and the reversed steps force you to climb a long way round to gain the doorway, which, like the entrance to the piazza, is heavily framed and narrow. Only after all this do you finally gain the spacious halls of the interior. The whole experience is calculated; in each of these successive constrictions and releases men can experience the elation of overcoming difficulties and emerging into a grand and ordered space. This is man's control of the world dramatized, insisted upon, repeated over and over until no one can escape it. Here on a grand scale is what we have seen in small in the proliferating, bombastic turnings of William and Mary furniture.

For the Dutch it was too grand. They were not princes or potentates but Protestant bourgeois merchants; and they simplified accordingly. The result was architecture like Peter Post's Ten Bosch house in The Hague—which preserved the essential elements and spirit of its Italian models, but with all forms simpler and all dimensions smaller. And it was this kind of architecture that the Dutch brought to England, in the persons of builders and craftsmen, and in the form of design books by Vingbooms and his successors—an architecture perfectly suited to English needs. Small and simple enough to be feasible, precise and balanced enough to satisfy the developing classical mind of England, it was not too rigidly or eruditely classical to be understood; indeed, the very departures from doctrinaire classicism involved in the Baroque style —its verticality, the way the building reaches out to encompass its environment—made it all the more acceptable at a time and place where medieval traditions were far from extinct.

And this Anglo-Dutch architecture was if anything even more suited to American cultural conditions. So it was that forms and principles once designed to impress the world with the grandeur of papal Rome came across the North Sea and the Atlantic to impress colonists in Virginia with the present greatness of England and the future promise of America. So it is that we can experience, however remotely, the Governors' Palace in Williamsburg in the same way that we can experience the Campidoglio in Rome, like a play in a succession of acts—circling the drive, constricted at the gate with its brick piers, released into the forecourt, constricted again at the doorway to the Palace, released finally into the entrance hall. So it is we can understand the arrangement of the windows and dormers of the main façade—their spacing narrowed towards the center to produce an effect of constriction at the entrance, as the elements of the façade of Michelangelo's Capitol, of Il Gesù, of countless buildings in the Baroque tradition before them, are squeezed together, and for the same reason. So it is that the plan of the Governors' Palace is based on 16th-century Italian sources (Serlio, Rubens's *Palazzi di Genova*, and others)—a double-pile type, a compact block two rooms deep—and not on the older Elizabethan–Jacobean tradition. The Williamsburg buildings mean many things to many people. To some, they mean wealth, the wealth of early Virginia that built them, the wealth of 20th-century America that restored them. To others, they mean a style to copy. But their greatest significance remains historical. They are the first deliberate dramatizations in America of men's power to organize their environment meaningfully; they are the first works of and for men consciously delighting to feel themselves in command of the world they inhabit. No accident, then, that it should be Virginia where this kind of building first appears; for Virginia was first of the American provinces to feel the new confidence in human powers and potentialities requisite for real appreciation of the measured and controlled principles of classical art. Here are manifested the beginnings of that spirit which two generations later inspired the Declaration of Independence, the Bill of Rights, and the Constitution of the United States.

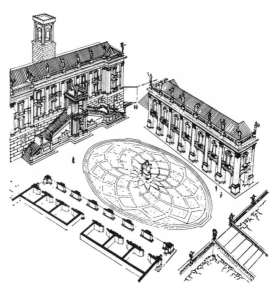

(49 B) Michelangelo's Project for the Capitoline Hill, Rome, c.1550.

NOTES

Marcus Whiffen's writings have been since their appearance the classic sources on Williamsburg. References in this chapter are to *The Public Buildings of Williamsburg* (Williamsburg, 1958).

The paragraph concluding Chap. XXII of Macaulay's *History of England,* describing the country's mood at the conclusion of the Treaty of Ryswick in 1697, sums up the spirit that informed the William and Mary style:

> There was indeed reason for joy and thankfulness. England had passed through severe trials, and had come forth renewed in health and vigour. Ten years before, it had seemed that both her liberty and her independence were no more. Her liberty she had vindicated by a just and necessary revolution. Her independence she had reconquered by a not less just and necessary war. She had successfully defended the order of things established by her Bill of Rights against the mighty monarch of France, against the aboriginal population of Ireland, against the avowed hostility of the nonjurors, against the more dangerous hostility of traitors who were ready to take any oath, and whom no oath could bind. . . . But those dangers were over. There was peace abroad and at home. The kingdom, after many years of ignominious vassalage, had resumed its ancient place in the first rank of European powers. Many signs justified the hope that the Revolution of 1688 would be our last Revolution. The ancient constitution was adapting itself, by a natural, a gradual, a peaceful development, to the wants of a modern society. Already freedom of conscience and freedom of discussion existed to an extent unknown in any preceding age. The currency had been restored. Public credit had been reestablished. Trade had revived. The Exchequer was overflowing. There was a sense of relief everywhere, from the Royal Exchange to the most secluded hamlets among the mountains of Wales and the fens of Lincolnshire. The ploughmen, the shepherds, the miners of the Northumbrian coalpits, the artisans who toiled at the looms of Norwich and the anvils of Birmingham, felt the change, without understanding it; and the cheerful bustle in every seaport and every market town indicated, not obscurely, the commencement of a happier age.

An admirable and well-known presentation of the comparable Renaissance change from medieval to classical spirit in architecture is by Nikolaus Pevsner, *Outline of European Architecture* (Baltimore, 1943), Chap. V.

On the origins of the William and Mary style. see particularly the presentations of "Architecture" by Dr. Margaret Whinney and "Furniture" by Ralph Fastnedge in the Connoisseur Period Guide to *The Stuart Period* (London, 1957). On the specific role in formulating the new style played by Daniel Marot (son of Parisian architect and engraver Jean Marot, pupil of Jean Lepautre and Charles-André Boulle), see the biography by M. D. Ozinga (Amsterdam, 1938), reviewed by N. Pevsner in *Burlington Magazine* (LXXIII, September 1938, pp. 134–5). That Marot was more than Ozinga's *De Schepper van den Hollandschen Lodewijk XIV-stijl*, and had a distinctive style of his own, is suggested by Arthur Lane, "Daniel Marot: Designer of Delft Vases and of Gardens at Hampton Court" (*Connoisseur,* CXXIII, March 1949, pp. 19–24). Lane establishes that Marot worked in England c.1694–7. Certainly Marot's engravings of architecture and furnishings (fireplaces, garden designs, etc.) suggest more the William and Mary than an academic Louis Quatorze manner. But certain it is, too, that Dutch modifications of Renaissance ideas came to England as a pervasive wave, rather than through any one agency:

> The construction and workmanship of walnut furniture from the beginning of the walnut period to the reign of Queen Anne was strongly influenced by the Dutch. . . . At this period the craft of furniture-making in England was undoubtedly, to a large extent, in the hands of Dutchmen. . . . Gerreit Johnson, a Dutchman . . . supplied china cabinets to Queen Mary. . . . Grinling Gibbon . . . was of Dutch origin. Dutch immigrants adapted the design of the furniture they produced to suit the taste and needs of the English market. . . . [R. W. Symonds and T. H. Ormsbee, *Antique Furniture of the Walnut Period,* 1947, p. 9]

4. FORMULATION OF THE CLASSICAL MIND:
American Queen Anne, 1725—1750

AFTER THE GENERATION of innovators, a generation of formulators. New forms and new combinations of old forms have been found to express the transition from otherworldly or primitive states of mind to one that makes man the measure of experience; now it is time to digest, codify, work out rational theories. This is the generation that built the Temple of Zeus at Olympia in the quarter-century 475–450 B.C., the generation of Alberti, Filarete, Mantegna, Piero della Francesca, and the young Leonardo, whose rationalizing and theoretical cast of mind dominates Renaissance Italy in the mid-15th century. In both ages, the overriding concern of this generation is similar—to discover what common guiding principles underlie all the diverse possibilities opened up by this new classical view of the world, and use them to create an art expressing, above all, human powers of organizing disparate experience into meaningful activity. Self-conscious emphasis on unity, bold overstated forms typical of men displaying to others an accomplishment only just mastered by themselves—these are the characteristic qualities of this second classical phase everywhere.

Both these qualities are evident in the sculptures of the Temple of Zeus at Olympia. So plain, so robust are these forms that older admirers of mature classical art often found them painful; Percy Gardner, for example, wrote in *New Chapters in Greek History* (1892) that "the heads have a heaviness which sometimes seems to amount to brutality, and are repellent, if not absolutely repulsive." At the same time, the concern to demonstrate and develop all kinds and expressions of unity is so obvious and so pervasive throughout the monument as a whole as to suggest that the Master of Olympia could hardly have been a carver. Surely it took some kind of trained intellect—a dramatist, perhaps—to dis-

cover all the subtle kinds of unity demonstrated in the twelve metopes, let alone the great gables, of this temple. Here is formal unity—balanced relationships of horizontal and vertical forms within each metope, repetitions of their compositional lines in surrounding architectural elements and thence in the building as a whole. Here is psychological unity, with each figure of a group in meaningful interaction with others; whereas a primitive carver would have conceived the "Stymphalian Birds" subject as an assemblage of symbolic figures set side by side, each a separate contribution to the idea, like the words in children's sentences or Egyptian hieroglyphs ("lady sit, man bring birds"), the Olympia Master's figures are so disposed that each makes sense only in relation to the rest, is what it is and does what it does only because of a common interest (in this case, the bunch of birds, now disappeared—in metal to bring out their focal importance—once held in Herakles' outstretched fist). Here, finally, is total intellectual unity in human space and time. Earlier art had depicted the labors of Herakles as essentially independent episodes—the hero's infant prodigies, his miscellaneous conquests of demigods and monsters at home and in lands of myth, each existing out of context with the others in a timeless vacuum of folk legend. But the Olympia Master organizes them into a humanly believable sequence of events, coherent in geographic space. They begin with local episodes, as here, and proceed in later ones further and further afield—and in historical time, making both main figures look older in later episodes; gods, heroes, and men are put into human perspective, made parts of a whole unified in terms of human perception.

Such too were the dominant qualities of work and writing in mid-15th-century Renais-

50. SECOND–GENERATION CLASSICAL ART IN ANTIQUITY AND THE RENAISSANCE
Parallels to the Queen Anne style.

(A) Section through the Temple of Zeus at Olympia (c.460 B.C.) as conjecturally restored, showing frieze of the inner temple-house with six of the metopes depicting the labors of Herakles in comprehensible chronological and geographic sequence.

(50 B) "Ideal Piazza for an Italian City" attributed to Luciano da Laurana, c.1440. Painting in the Walters Art Gallery, Baltimore.

(50 C) "Herakles presenting Athena with the Stymphalian Birds," metope from the Temple of Zeus, Olympia, in the Louvre.

sance Italy. How ostentatiously a designer like Laurana articulates the buildings in his ideal city square, how studiously he relates them to each other through a single focal point! Where innovators of the first classical generation like Brunellesco were content simply to consolidate the vertical and additively composed elements of medieval Italian palace types into a single solid block, the generation that follows him must go further, must insist on a formal and visual unity of interrelated parts, artificially create the effect of articulated wholes by applying ranges of pilasters and cornices as independently of structural function as entablatures on Greek temples. This generation dreams of city squares and paintings and furniture all organized into one dramatic and unmistakable unity; the definition of principles on which such unity can be based is an obsession. And when, three centuries later, England and America enter a comparable phase in their classical evolution, these are the concerns created and everywhere manifest in what we call the "Queen Anne style."

At first sight the Queen Anne style in America seems to mark a great and decisive break with the past. All the more obvious survivals and reminiscences of medieval tradition that characterized the preceding William and Mary period have disappeared. The additive principle becomes obsolete. Organic relationships, only suggested in the expression of load and support in the William and Mary "Spanish foot," are now fully and pervasively realized. Where William and Mary cabinetmakers added turning to turning, square to cylinder, to compose a furniture leg, their Queen Anne successors see the leg as one curved form; they develop a "pad" or "slipper" foot which is no longer composite, but a single simple unit, flowing as smoothly into the leg and thence into the knee and body of the whole as if it were a living limb. This leg, in turn, they relate to the total design, varying its shape according to function (short and stubby to support a heavy chest of drawers, tall and slender for light tea tables, and so on), making

it structurally and visually an integral part of the whole, no longer "attached" to what it supports, but curved to repeat and reinforce the major outlines. And as in individual pieces all elements are integrally related, so too rooms as a whole no longer consist of agglomerations of disparate objects, but are conceived as subtle variations of a single theme—curves in chairs picked up and echoed in the lines of desks, beds, curtains, textile designs, silverware; reinforced by doorjambs and mantels and paneling in comparably bold high relief. This new inherent interior unity is matched by exterior design. Where all elements of the Governors' Palace façade were given approximately equal emphasis, so that the total effect was one of individual parts assembled in a pattern, the façades of Westover in the next generation have a deliberate focal point. The main doorways, decisively framed with pilasters and entablature, interrupting the first-story belt course, at once dominate and co-ordinate all other elements, giving visual meaning to the irregular fenestration inherited from the Governors' Palace, producing a whole which is unmistakably based on the greatest of fundamental classical principles: that good art, art controllable by the human mind, should have a definable and perceptible beginning, middle, and end.

Direct expression of construction becomes obsolete, too. Queen Anne cabinetmakers try to make each work a single visual unit, no matter how complex its parts; they design bold curves to sweep over every join and angle, hide pins and notches under skirts, stain, and polish. In such a context, exposed supporting stretchers look intolerable; they disappear, except in the work of conservative or rural artisans who thereby reveal to what extent they misunderstand the principles and demands of the classical spirit. Equally painful to the maturing classical eye are wide floorboards of oak and pine exposed in the medieval tradition; they too vanish beneath narrow matched and patterned hardwoods which make floors visually self-contained

51. *Parlor from Readbourne, Queen Anne's County, Maryland. Restored to the period of building, c.1733, in the H. F. du Pont Winterthur Museum. Furniture generally from Philadelphia, made in the 1740s and 50s. The visual unity among all objects in the room, characteristic of* the Queen Anne period, is carried out even in the portrait of Experience Johnston Gouverneur above the fireplace, with its markedly vertical mannerisms, sharp angles, and blue gown repeating the color of velvet window hangings and Ispahan carpet.

units. As Renaissance architects in this phase articulated palace walls, so Queen Anne carpenters panel interiors with anything from symmetrically arranged insets to complete orders of pilasters, entablatures, and cornice; so builders compose façades independently of the disposition of rooms behind—if a given belt course that establishes a horizontal relationship of elements happens to coincide with an actual floor line on the second story, well and good, but if not, it goes where the formal design requires, regardless. Not structure, but visual proportion and geometrical ratio, are what architecture and furniture design expresses now.

Obsolete, again, is direct expression of materials. Cane and nail-studded leather disappear; walnut becomes ever smoother and darker, and soon will be replaced by marble-like mahogany. No longer do shapes conform naturally to the material of which they are made; visual unity in whole and detail demands that the same bold curves and projections appear in wood, in brick, in stone, in plaster—and they do. Moulding and shaping of brick become common, as in the water table at Westover and the segmental arch heads over its windows. Even the finest-grained wood paneling is painted oftener than not; exterior wood and bricks too may be painted, or plas-

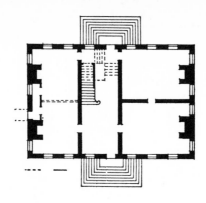

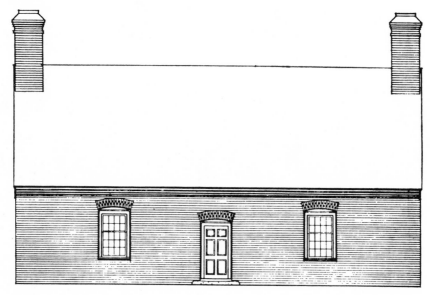

52. WESTOVER, CHARLES CITY COUNTY, VIRGINIA

(A) Plan, and measured drawing of the north front of Westover and restored east dependency, as originally built for William Byrd II, c.1729–35.

tered and scored to resemble stone. Westover's bricks were painted red and its belt courses—unmoulded gauged brick laid in Flemish bond—white; neighboring Nomini Hall, built at the same time for Robert Carter, was described in Philip Fithian's diary as having its brick walls "covered with strong lime mortar, so that the building is now perfectly white." In this same

spirit Peter Harrison would be admired, twenty years or so later, for treating the wooden walls of his Redwood Library in Newport to look like masonry; for this second phase of the classical mind is a generation that delights to parade man's full control over the materials he works.

In architecture, and to some extent in Queen Anne furniture too, more or less obvious borrowings from classical sources begin to appear—scrolls, acanthus-like leaves, entablatures, cornices, pilasters. They are seldom used with what a later age would call "correctness"; characteristically, they are more robust, more bulging, more "broken," more vigorously handled, than strict classical rules would allow. For the mo-

ment it does not matter; the important thing is that they evidence a new conscious awareness of classical art as such.

Dominating, directing, ordering all these other qualities is a new pervasive insistence on unity of design; on furniture proportioned, scaled, co-ordinated by ratio; on correspondences among the outlines and proportions of furniture and interior architectural settings, between interior and exterior forms. As the same tendency to concentrate decoration in a few robust patches is evident in chair crestings and entrance porticos, so simple ceiling cornices are repeated on a larger scale under outside eaves, pediments on roof dormers recall those over inside doorways. In so fitting every element—furniture, façades, ornament, fenestration—into a single comprehensive framework, the Queen Anne designer expresses and embodies the classical concept of man organizing his environment within set and absolute principles to a degree far beyond the capacities of his William and Mary predecessors.

But appearances are deceptive; the classical mind is not yet entirely in command. Much medieval spirit survives, however vestigially, in the Queen Anne period. Something of the old steep medieval verticality persists in the proportions of height to width of Queen Anne chair backs, in the height of legs in relation to width

143

of seat, and in the relative height and thinness of paneling compared to what follows in Chippendale–Georgian art. It persists, too, for all the strength of horizontal belt courses, in the rising tiers of windows and dormers and the over-all proportions of façade and roof together at Westover. Nor is Queen Anne art entirely emancipated from medieval concepts of flat two-dimensional design. However robust the mouldings of Queen Anne decorative details, however bold the curving of chair backs and legs, they remain confined essentially to their own plane. You can see this particularly well in the treatment of splats; intricate though their piercings often are, they remain characteristically conceived as holes in a flat surface, protruding no more into surrounding space than William and Mary spindles. You can see it too in the handling of doorways and window frames on the façade of Westover; however sculptural by comparison with the Governors' Palace, they are still kept within the plane of the wall almost as consistently. This again is characteristic of the second phase of classicism; neither in the Master of Olympia's generation, nor yet by the mid-15th century in Renaissance Italy, was full three-dimensionality realized. Then again, vestiges of the old additive principle are still perceptible. However far from those strings of spools and bulbs that composed as well as ornamented William and Mary work, the nicely placed crestings and shellwork decoration of Queen Anne furniture still seem not entirely integral to the design as a whole; one could imagine adding or removing them at will, like the pious Quakers who reputedly sawed decorative shells off their fine furniture in the interests of proper "plainness." Of the elaborate doorways on such façades as Westover, much the same could be said. And, finally, in the very robustness and elaborately bold breaking curves of Queen Anne detail generally, more than a reminiscence survives of that naïvely ostentatious manipulation of materials which in the first classical phase implied an incomplete transition from medieval "naturalness"

to fully confident control.

In short, while the Queen Anne age brought the classical mind to obvious dominance, it did not bring a complete rejection of or revolution against the past, of the kind that created, say, "modern" art. Like most great creative ages in history, it was a building upon, a development out of, a transformation of the old. Quite the opposite of revolutionary, its instinct was to reconcile opposites; to comprehend, not to exclude; to unify diverse elements into some new and greater whole. In every aspect of American culture in the quarter-century from 1725 to 1750, we can recognize this unifying principle at work. Queen Anne furniture is a small and tangible example of it—not rejecting the bold crestings and ornamental turnings of the William and Mary style but subtly modifying and co-ordinating them so that they make a single integrated whole. Westover is an example on architectural scale, building upon, improving, incorporating the best features of its model from the preceding period. Political life embodies it on a greater scale still—the attempt to reconcile British sovereignty and colonial aspirations at the Albany Congress of 1754 is its product. But its broadest manifestations are in religious life and aesthetic theory—in this age not as far apart as one might suppose.

In this age the Church of England flourished in America as never before (or indeed, since), precisely because it of all denominations was the most tolerantly comprehensive. Within its Low or High Church wings there was a place for all but the most doctrinaire—Calvinist Huguenots in South Carolina, Lutheran Swedes in the Delaware Valley, Quakers in Newport, these and so many others moved into its orbit that by 1769 Governor Wentworth thought that even in New England, "if a governor's chaplain . . . were to be sent over to New Hampshire, he could . . . within two years have a parish of 500 people." As daily Anglican prayers offered for the welfare of the British monarchy provided a common spiritual and patriotic bond among men of Eng-

lish derivation in every part of the globe, so Anglican church architecture became the norm during this period in every American province. Liturgically oriented and towered structures displaced old square meeting houses on the New England landscape; judicious proportion, classical balance, and symmetry "of the best sort" graced the plainness of Quaker meetings; the systematic proportions, calculated correspondences, and bold robust mouldings of the great Anglican churches by Gibbs and Wren were adopted from Boston to the Carolinas. And even men like Jonathan Edwards, who were acutely aware of the contradiction between classical and Christian premises, who saw how assumption of

human powers to organize experience into meaningful order could not ultimately be reconciled with entire dependence on grace, showed the spirit of this age in attempts to reconcile both in one comprehensive unity; like those builders who saw nothing incongruous in lucidly composed classical temples to the Creator of human reason, Edwards used classical language to urge a return to the Christian traditions of America's 17th-century past, proclaiming in balanced periods and nicely interacting phrases man's helpless confusion before an angry God.

Calvinist preachers and Anglican priests, Virginia planters and Philadelphia Quakers, builders and craftsmen—all of them are finding the measured forms of classical art a self-evidently right vehicle of expression. And as it was in earlier cycles, so now—the deeper the classical spirit permeates society, the more pervasive is preoccupation with theory, the greater the demand for treatises which will codify, formulate, explain the new principles so that artists and patrons everywhere, insofar as their comprehension allows, can embody the principles and reproduce the forms of the classical mind as developed in this, its second phase. Men as disparate in temperament as courtly philosopher Bishop Berkeley and printmaker William Hogarth feel impelled to write treatises on aesthetic principles and analyses of beauty. Of more practical significance in the American provinces is an unprecedented outpouring of guides for builders and craftsmen—twenty-three published between 1725 and 1735 alone, considerably more than the total number available in England from all the centuries before. Salmon's *Palladio Londinensis* (1734), Ware's *Designs of Inigo Jones* (1735), Batty Langley's *Workman's Treasury of Designs* (1740), voluminous works by William Halfpenny like the *Modern Builder's Assistant* (1742), Abraham Swan's *British Architect* (1745); these and many more helped shape American classical expression in the Queen Anne period. But most helpful, most used, most famous, first in the field were the works of James Gibbs (1682–1754); on his *Book of Architecture* (1728) and *Rules for Drawing the Several Orders* (1732), more than on any other foundations, American Queen Anne architecture was built. For this there was good reason. Gibbs not only first explained the principles, he demonstrated the practice. When he presented an elevation, he inserted the plan along with it, so that the relationship of each part to the whole could be unmistakably seen, the total unity demonstrated. He provided all kinds of alternative plans and details, among which builders could choose what might best suit their different economic and geographic and social circumstances. Books such as Salmon's *Palladio Londinensis*

or Francis Price's 1733 *British Carpenter*, which discussed practical problems like building roofs and staircases or considered theoretical questions like determining "just proportions" and modules, without illustrating plans and only rarely with specific forms, had not nearly the same usefulness for provincial builders. To an age which no longer admired and adapted classical forms intuitively or haphazardly but knew at least in part consciously why it liked them, which recognized that the forms of classical art implied a considerable departure from medieval presuppositions about the ends and means of life, Gibbs gave practical and satisfying demonstration that the rules of classical art were neither whimsical nor vacillating, but proceeded logically from given intellectual premises. Above all, he drew his inspiration and chose his forms from prototypes precisely calculated to appeal to the particular stage of comprehension the classical mind had reached by the Queen Anne period in America—High Baroque art in Italy.

In Italy at the beginning of the 18th century, Gibbs had studied with followers of Bernini and Borromini; and it was of their High Baroque style—the style that grew out of that Late Renaissance or Early Baroque art which was the ultimate inspiration for William and Mary—that he was basically thinking when he designed his great London churches: St. Mary-le-Strand (1714–17), the steeple of St. Clement Danes (1719), St. Martin's-in-the-Fields (1722–6), as well as the Radcliffe Library at Oxford (1737–49), and his country mansions. The High Baroque use of full robust curving forms, its ostentatious manipulation of materials in small detail and great mass within a powerful controlling over-all framework, admirably suited the mood of a generation just mastering the full implications of classical expression, a generation already too mature to be satisfied with the naïve bombast of William and Mary turnings, at once too self-consciously erudite and too unsophisticated to accept Michelangelesque "distortions," but not yet sure enough in its classicism to ap-

53. *Elevation and plan of the Church of St. Martin's-in-the-Fields, London, from James Gibbs,* Book of Architecture *(1728). Gibbs's volume was entirely characteristic of the second generation of the classical cycle, in that it formulated theory after the creation of art, rather* than before *(as has occurred in the "modern" era). Coming at just the right psychological time culturally, it proved to be the greatest single influence on American architecture in the quarter-century 1725–1750, and was still popular in the 1770s.*

preciate and employ the restrained and subtle refinements of the High Renaissance. This is the expression of a generation less basically concerned with the end result of art—with perfecting all the subtleties and refinements of the work itself—than with means. What fascinates these men is the formulation in theory and demonstration in practice of broad comprehensive principles covering all the arts—absolute principles, good at all times and places. It is this preoccupation that explains why men like Gibbs and Hogarth, Lord Burlington and Thornhill, as well as Americans like Washington, Jefferson, and Peter Harrison, were such ardent Freemasons; they were attracted to this organization (which grew so fast, and had such a great and still not fully understood or appreciated influence on the culture of this age) not by its religious pretensions but because of its claims to have preserved through all the ages the secrets of perfect, ideal proportion. And that, too, is why they were as yet little affected by Freemasonry's teachings about the literary symbolism of classical forms. This was an age when the traditional idea that artists should express themselves in wood and paint and stone rather than in words still prevailed. Books and treatises are still means to an end—the expression through broadly unified forms of a new, humanly oriented, and integrated concept of life. This is the phase of classical development dominant when Queen Anne ruled England, when the new Virginia aristocrats like William Byrd II were being sent to London to study; and as soon as they reached maturity, it began to appear in America.

As it marks the decisive break with medieval tradition, so the Queen Anne period in America marks the great break from colonial beginnings into a new era of self-reliance and prosperity. In it is expressed a society that has reached a new level of intellectual and economic maturity. That level was highest in Virginia, where

by 1730 . . . the vast extent of an old Virginia plantation could barely be imagined by the contented English squire who never came over to get one for himself. Such an area conceived as fixed productive property rather than negotiable wealth brings no image whatever to the modern urban mind which thinks, not in space but in time, for Time is Money. The Washingtons owned several counties . . . the immigrant ancestor of Colonel Fielding Lewis had entailed upon his descendants a tract of 33,000 acres, besides large holdings elsewhere. The founder of the Carter family owned so much land that local history calls him King Carter. In between the large estates small landowners . . . had got a foothold. They were either independent farmers or tenantry to the squires; negro slavery was not much developed before the Revolution. But by the middle of the 18th century most of the small plantations of a few hundred or thousand acres were taken up. Most of the owners were respectable minor gentry. Others had sunk to the squalor they have not got out of to this day. They were the poor white. . . . [Allen Tate, *Stonewall Jackson*, 1928, Chap. II]

That a private citizen's house like Westover should deliberately imitate, and indeed surpass, the seat of the English Governor of Virginia is significant of the status the aristocrats of the South were already claiming for themselves. Nowhere else had wealth developed quite so far; but everywhere—in Philadelphia, in New York, in Newport on Rhode Island, in Boston—aristocracy of a kind was beginning to appear, or at least men with means and leisure enough to affect some cultivation of the arts, to have some conscious and educated interest in "style." All over the provinces there were men no longer satisfied with whatever artisans working in the inherited local traditions of their time and place could provide, who were beginning to seek out the kind of workmen whose advertisements now start to appear with increasing frequency in journals and newspapers, "trained in the latest mode," "newly arrived from London"—or, failing that, men who could at least pretend to follow the builders' guides and design books coming out in such numbers. That classical forms and spirit were not equally well understood everywhere we shall demonstrate in a later section; for now, the important thing is that to the extent they were understood they acted as a powerful impetus towards a unity of outlook among educated men in all the provinces.

In the Queen Anne period regional characteristics still perist: wood is still the normal building material of New England, as brick is in Philadelphia and the South or stone in rural Pennsylvania and New York. But just as brick, wood, and fieldstone are being plastered and painted to look like classically precise cut masonry, so now local differences are increasingly being subordinated to a common set of stylistic standards, the same universal principles of design being accepted and applied in all regions. Everywhere American architecture and furniture in the second quarter of the 18th century begin to manifest a culture held in common by wide segments of society—educated upper class and artisans alike—throughout every province.

There is as yet little sense of active unity among these people or provinces. Like spokes joined at a hub but without a rim, they are united only in a common dependence on English sources. But this is no longer the simple mimesis of colonial times, the instinctive reproduction of forms nostalgically remembered from home. This is a conscious imitation of what are considered to be universally correct standards; standards, furthermore, to which Americans can begin to contribute their own distinctive embodiments. This is the beginning of a distinctive culture. Just as for England the age of Queen Anne was the age of Blenheim and Ramillies, the age when the nation first became aware of its potentialities, when it stepped from the periphery of European affairs to become a major power, when the First Empire took shape, so for America it was now possible to see that this country would not always be a distant outpost, a perennial frontier, a refuge for rejects from the mainstream of Western civilization. As security brought wealth and leisure, and wealth and leisure brought proud reflections on present accomplishments and future greatness, so in this age Americans first began to speculate, almost in spite of themselves, on the possibility that America might one day be a larger, wealthier, more populous nation than England. The same confidence that made the colonists certain of their ability to manage their own affairs and govern their own destiny, and made the controlled and measured forms of classical art seem self-evidently right, inevitably would make a subservient political role seem self-evidently wrong. Acceptance of common standards for rooms and chairs and churches and gardens everywhere from New Hampshire to the Carolinas would prepare minds to accept common standards in philosophy, in manners, in literature, in political theory as well. And just as these common standards absorbed rather than overcame regional traditions in architecture and furniture, so now it was possible to imagine a political unity achieved not by conquest or by the dominance of one region over another but by the gradual approximation of all regions to a common set of cultural standards and political ideals. So the classical art which came to dominate in America's Queen Anne age can be seen both as the expression and the vehicle of the future unity of the nation. Men born in this generation will be the first to think of themselves more as "Americans" than as Virginians or Pennsylvanians or New Englanders; the common attitudes and values taking root in this period and expressed in its architecture and furniture they will all grow up to share, and, sharing them, they will be able to transform the disparate American colonies of the late 17th century into a new unified nation.

NOTES

Quotations from the diary of Philip Fithian in T. T. Waterman, *The Mansions of Virginia* (Chapel Hill, 1946), pp. 139–41, from which documentation on Westover has generally been taken. Helen Parks, "A List of Architectural Books Available in America Before the Revolution" (*JSAH*, XX, 3, 1961, pp. 115–30), is a most useful article on which I have drawn several times in this chapter. On Gibbs, see Bryan Little, *The Life and Work of James Gibbs* (London, 1957). Some further implications of the classical collaboration between artisan and intellectual are discussed in my article "The Master of Olympia" (*Delaware Notes*, XXX Series, pp. 35–46, 1957).

Further on Freemasonry as an influence on classical development, see my "Freemasonry and the Neoclassic Style in America" (*Antiques*, LXXVII, 2, 1960, pp. 171–5). On Peter Harrison's connection with Freemasonry, see Carl Bridenbaugh, "Peter Harrison Addendum" (*JSAH*, XVIII, 4, 1959, pp. 158–9), referring to records in St. John's Lodge, Newport, for 1759–60, of Harrison's designing plans for a Masonic lodge hall there.

5. CLASSICAL MATURITY:
The Chippendale-Georgian Period, 1750–1775

FIRST THE INNOVATORS, then the formulators; now, the principles of classical expression having been realized and forms to embody them worked out, the mature phase of classical art can begin—in antiquity, the "Golden Age" of Greece; in its rebirth, the High Renaissance at the turn of the 16th century; in America, what we call here the Chippendale–Georgian period. Now it is no more a question of making discoveries or theorizing, but of perfecting what has been done, of embodying the classical mind in art as completely as means and matter will allow. Now is the time for great masters to appear, "geniuses" in the true sense of the word, who will give final form to the new art, provide definitive solutions to all the problems earlier developments have raised. This is the age of Pheidias and the Parthenon, of Raphael, Leonardo's "Last Supper" and Michelangelo's "Pietà," Bramante's Tempietto and St. Peter's. To us, the preceding phase of classical art often seems more interesting; we rather prefer its unfinished, tentative exuberance to the smooth polished perfection that succeeds it. But that may be only the measure of our own cultural inadequacies. Living in an age when little seems sure, we instinctively resent the self-assurance implicit in classical maturity. Men so much masters of their world as to feel no need of flaunting their control of nature, refinements of form so subtle as to remain undetected for centuries, techniques so sure that we hardly recognize the difficulties overcome, proportional systems so complex and so perfectly scaled to human measure as to be entirely unobtrusive, make us feel inadequate somehow. When we consider the perfect balance of human and divine, of "structural" and "decorative" elements, of color and of compositional forms in the world created by Raphael or Michelangelo or Bramante in this age, we become all the more uneasily aware of the instability

of our own. And the whole ethos of our culture inhibits us from escaping from our world into theirs. We have the technical tools to more than match the accomplishments of the Renaissance, of Pheidian Greece, of Chippendale–Georgian America—but we lack the will and the circumstances to enjoy them. This third classical generation had both; for them, the step from Olympia to the Parthenon, from Alberti to Michelangelo, from Queen Anne to Chippendale was logical, inevitable, entirely satisfying.

"Without an acquaintance with this science [architectural geometry] and some knowledge of the rules of perspective, the cabinetmaker cannot make the designs of his work intelligible, nor shew, in a little compass, the whole conduct and effect of the piece. . . ." So Thomas Chippendale introduced his *Gentleman and Cabinet Maker's Director* in 1754; and in such a passage is the essence of classical maturity. To "shew, in a little compass, the whole conduct and effect of the piece" had been the theoretical ideal of Queen Anne designers. Now their successors have the technical skill to realize it in practice. This is the theme of the golden age of classical maturity in furniture, when technical skill fully matches inspiration.

Now the last lingering vestiges of medieval verticality vanish. Chair backs become almost square, the proportionate height of legs is lowered, all proportions are subtly altered and adjusted to precisely the point where furniture neither squats nor soars, but achieves just that effect of balanced stability which is the essence of what we call the "monumental." Now all semblance of additive composition is lost. Ornament, neither confused with structure nor concentrated in a few obvious places, is so uniformly distributed that each motif balances the next and all contribute to the whole. A genuine sculptural quality replaces that naïve robustness which in

54. *Classical maturity in antiquity: replica of the Parthenon, Centennial Park, Nashville, Tennessee. To illustrate such a monument by this replica made in plaster for the Tennessee Centennial of 1897 and permanently modeled in concrete during the 1920s may seem presumptuous. Yet the illustration serves as a reminder not only of the Parthenon's familiar features, on which so much Greek Revival architecture in America depended, but also of the remarkable persistence of classical influences in American culture.*

Queen Anne forms still perpetuated something of William and Mary naïveté; now designers have a plastic confidence that needs no such bombastic reassurance. Chair splats, conceived no longer as solids pierced by holes, become compositions of tangible forms overlapping in three-dimensional space, intersecting in true spatial voids. Combinations of forms composed in three dimensions replace the bold simple shapes of earlier feet—the claw gripping a ball is most familiar and representative. Edges are scalloped, gadrooned, and otherwise made to move into surrounding space as never before. And with this scuptural concept comes a change in material; just as finer-grained walnut replaced oak at the beginning of the classical era, so now it in turn is superseded by mahogany— a material in which designers can express a command of their medium unparalleled before, which they can handle with the precision and spatial intricacy of moulded clay or poured metal, polish like classical bronze or oiled marble.

Now subtle variations appear. Thoroughly understanding basic classical principles, Chippendale designers can extend their range of expression like mature writers breaking the rules of grammar, as the great masters of antiquity and the High Renaissance rang changes on entasis or pictorial structure. Novelty is no longer to be feared as a challenge or a distraction; fashionable whims like "Gothick" or *chinoiserie* are welcomed as chances to demonstrate how everything in nature can be comprehended within the framework of universal classical principles. And with this development come new opportunities for personal expression; this is the age, as we shall see, when artists with recognizable "styles" of their own first appear. Finally this is an art, as was Pheidias's and Raphael's and Michelangelo's, based on subtle syntheses of many earlier forms and ideas. This is an art

55. GUNSTON HALL, LORTON, VIRGINIA

(A) Parlor. Executed by William Buckland, "citizen and joiner of London," who arrived in Virginia bound apprentice to George Mason, builder of Gunston Hall and later author of the Virginia Bill of Rights, in August 1755. Brought to Gunston Hall primarily to do the interior decoration, Buckland executed it in the newest fashion. He introduced smooth walls instead of the now old-fashioned paneled wainscot and, in the drawing room, the very advanced treatment of damask hangings over pine boarding; in the woodwork, he exhibited a combination of Rococo lavishness contained within strictly classical geometrical systems very much in the spirit of Chippendale's Director (which he owned). Gunston Hall was restored in the 1950s by a committee headed by Mrs. Lammot du Pont Copeland.

whose complex origins reveal it as fully the creation of its own age and spirit.

Certainly Thomas Chippendale was far from being the creator of the style that bears his name. "Chippendale" is in fact a generic term to describe a particular approach to and concept of design exemplified by many masters more skilful and prolific than he. Not only did Chippendale himself apparently never use such a distinctive "Chippendale" feature as the claw-and-ball foot but there is some evidence that even the plates in his book were drawn and engraved by others. Chippendale's essential accomplishment was the hardly extraordinary recipe for success of listening to what other people were saying and repeating it, in his Director, in a louder voice. He was a creation of his age, not the other way round. But in that role his place in art history is not entirely undeserved. His was the first book to be published by a cabinetmaker on a scale comparable to earlier presentations of architecture and ornament. Furthermore, both by the device of

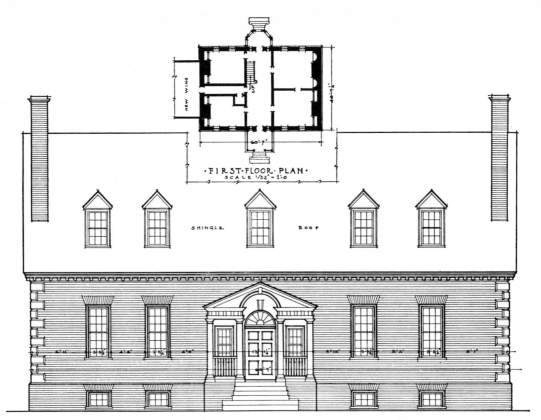

(55 B) Land front elevation and plan of Gunston Hall, measured drawing from the White Pine Monograph Series, *XVI, 3, p. 203. The original intent of this series (like the articles appearing from 1898 on in* The American Architect, *which W. R. Ware collected and published as* The Georgian Period *in 1923), begun in 1915, was to provide motifs and ideas eclectic architects could* use in composing "colonial Georgian" buildings. *Now that this kind of archaeological architecture is waning in appeal, such drawings have become increasingly interesting as historical records, particularly since they record a good many monuments lost by the time the* Historic American Buildings Survey *(which they helped stimulate) was begun in the 1930s.*

appealing (as the title implies) at once to those who commissioned and those who made furniture, and by his insistence on the importance of furniture ("Of all the Arts which are either improved or ornamented by Architecture, that of CABINET-MAKING is . . . the most useful and ornamental," he wrote in the Preface), he in his way did for the social status of furniture in England what Reynolds in the same generation did for painting; he made it a respected and respectable major art. But it was as a complex synthesis of diverse forms and influences that "Chippendale" was most comparable, on however narrower a stage, to the great works of the Golden Age of Greece and the High Renaissance.

As English classicism in the 1720s, and American in the 1740s, moved towards maturity, two distinct and opposite influences were at work. The first was that trend towards delicate, light, decorative forms we call the Rococo, the final phase of an alternating Renaissance–Mannerist, Baroque–Rococo cycle in progress since the early 15th century. At the time that cycle began, Italy had been the center of European cultural developments, and England a far outpost hardly affected by it at all. But now, in the early 18th century, France was the cultural center of Europe, and England moving in to contest her place; already in Queen Anne's time England was borrowing ideas from the Baroque art of Louis Quatorze, and it was inevitable that the shift from it to the Rococo of Louis Quinze would be followed under the early Georges. It is this Rococo trend that is manifested in the increasing intricacy and delicacy of shellwork ornament on furniture and the elaborate plasterwork ceilings (Kenmore near Fredericksburg is a good Virginia example) that begins to appear in America from the 1750s on. It is this trend, too, that explains how and why "Gothick" and

chinoiserie were introduced to American interiors —not because increased trade had brought any great appreciation or understanding of Chinese culture, or historical research made the mind of the age any more sympathetic to medieval awesomeness and infinity, but simply because developing Rococo taste made the delicate, fragile, intricate forms of medieval and Ming–Ching art seem interesting as they could never have been before.

But Rococo could never wholly satisfy the psychological needs of the great Whig noblemen

---

56. Two chairs designed by Thomas Chippendale. From A Gentleman and Cabinet Maker's Director. *Thomas Chippendale was born near Otley, Yorkshire, in 1718, into a family of carpenters and joiners. Moving to London sometime in the 1740s, he published a first edition of the* Director *in 1754, a second in 1755, and a third and expanded edition in 1764. He died in 1779.*

In his hands, the "Chippendale" style had much more of Rococo fragility in structure and decoration than in the adaptations of it common in America; nevertheless these chairs reveal that firm containment of Rococo ornament within a geometric discipline which made the Chippendale style so admirably expressive of the classical mind in its age.

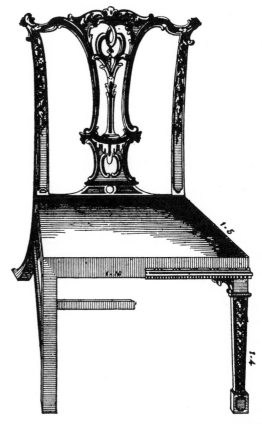

of the 1720s in England, or the emerging upper classes of mid-18th-century America. For them, classical art was much more than a matter of taste, of following fashions set elsewhere; it was an attitude to life, with an ethos of its own. The French may have had their fill of *gloire* with Louis le Grand; they had not. With every new decade successes multiplied—military, economic, political; before their eyes, England was building the greatest empire known since Rome. Indeed, in many ways these lords felt themselves not only the equals but the superiors of those ancient patricians. No light, frivolous, airy art could satisfy aspirations like theirs; what they wanted and needed was some stronger, severer expression, something more definitely Roman, not less. To satisfy them, all sorts of books on the architecture of antiquity, drawings by visitors to Athens and Rome and the Near East and the Balkans, now began to appear, in a spirit best summed up in the Preface to one of the earliest of them, Colin Campbell's *Vitruvius Britannicus* (1715), which lamented that

> . . . the *Italians* can no more now relish the Antique Simplicity, but are entirely employed in capricious Ornaments, which must at last end in the *Gothick*. . . . How affected and licentious are the Works of *Bernini*. . . . Parts without Proportion, Solids without their true Bearing, Heaps of Materials without Strength, excessive Ornament without Grace, and the whole without Symmetry. . . .

It was because Andrea Palladio seemed so admirably to meet their need for authoritatively Roman art that this (by the standards of his own age) relatively obscure 16th-century architectural theorist became the mentor of mid-18th-century classicism, his *Four Books* more famous and influential than they had ever been in his lifetime. They provided, as no other source quite did, the kind of exact information—or what was believed to be exact information—Lord Burlington and his circle of aristocratic aesthetes wanted. Palladio purported to explain, not in generalities but specifically, how the Romans designed houses and laid out cities, how their orders were proportioned and properly used, what Roman public buildings looked like. That Palladio's—and all other writers'—information was inaccurate did not for the moment matter. What the age did not know, it, like Palladio, was quite content to guess at; the mere conjecture of their use by Romans was enough to make house fronts adorned with temple porticos or furniture legs terminating in "Roman" claw-and-ball feet eminently satisfactory and desirable.

Yet Palladianism alone could no more fully satisfy the mind of this age than Rococo refinement alone. For all but the most dedicated doctrinaires it was too erudite, too cold—in both the psychological and the physical senses. What this age needed was some combination of Palladian rules to embody its passion for reasoned order with luxuriant, exotic, imaginative Rococo ornament to express its equally strong sense of abounding wealth and widening intellectual, geographic, and historical horizons. And this combination it was the genius and lasting accomplishment of Thomas Chippendale—or, more exactly, of the generation of designers for whom his *Director* is a representative symbol—to provide. In "Chippendale" art, the two great mid-18th-century trends are combined. Imaginatively free ornament and disciplined geometrical principle are united in one distinctive style.

No matter how intricate the forms of Rococo ornament, no matter how exotic the motifs of *chinoiserie*, how limitless the "Gothick" patterns Chippendale designers may employ, they are always set within a controlling geometric framework. Decoration, literally, has to be "within reason." A Chippendale room may be papered with a Chinese design conceived as an over-all pattern, expanding without inherent boundaries, limited only by the physical extent of the available space; it is framed in neat sections with precise mouldings and cornice. The "Chinese" or "Gothick" taste in furniture may mean employing lattices or brackets or repeated arches that by nature meander and multiply themselves

57. EXOTIC ELEMENTS IN CHIPPENDALE-GEORGIAN

(A) "Gothick" porch, Gunston Hall. George Mason had already begun building his house along the basic lines of an old Southern colonial house type when Buckland appeared on the scene. Buckland's exterior work was thus largely limited to three wooden porches—one on the east, long vanished and only conjecturally restored; the formal main entrance, a Palladian motif of central arch with flanking rectangular openings; and, to balance this formal dignity (in typical high classical fashion), the more intimately scaled and delicately detailed engaged octagon with ogee arches on the river front, seen here.

indefinitely; Chippendale cabinetmakers discipline them within a precisely moulded and proportioned framework.

Gothic Architecture Improved by Rules and Proportion—this title of Batty Langley's famous builders' guide sums up the whole rationale of what we could best call the Chippendale–Georgian style in both architecture and furniture. Or, as Robert Morris put it in his *Lectures on Architecture* published as early as 1734–6 and known in Virginia at least by 1751: "In delineating the Plan or Elevation of a Building, the Out-line is to be first form'd . . . it is from thence the internal parts, as well as the *ornamenting* and *disposing* the proper Voids, and Decoration of the Front, are to be regulated."

Between the Chippendale and Queen Anne styles there was nothing like the striking change in forms that distinguished Queen Anne from William and Mary, or the change in fundamentals dividing William and Mary from its still medieval antecedents. The development here was not so much in invention or formulation as in mastery and maturity. As this made for an art more complex and subtle than anything in earlier phases of the cycle, so it meant that the style had no dramatic introduction on the American scene; you cannot point with anything like the same confidence to a particular place or time when it originated. At Drayton Hall near Charleston you can find a two-story free-standing portico of the Palladian type in South Carolina as early as c.1738; the Palladian temple-house appears on Rhode Island in the late 1740s and in Maryland in the 1760s; Rococo lavishness in plaster ceilings and chimney pieces appear sporadically here and there from the 1750s on. But it was in Virginia that the major characteristics of the third classical phase were first assembled and co-ordinated, as it were; and Gunston Hall, in the mid-1750s, was perhaps the best example of it.

At Gunston Hall you can find a three-dimensional concept of form consistently as never before. It is particularly apparent in the two porticos. Queen Anne doorways, for all their robust detail, seldom projected far from the plane of the wall, always conserved something of the medieval feeling for flat pattern; and even such a technically advanced Palladian motif as the façade of Harrison's Redwood Library was still drawn, conceived, and executed with the same basic frontality. But here, on the land front, the Palladian motif is understood in its full three-dimensionality; this portico, like the one on the water front with its vaguely "Gothick" ogee arches, is conceived not so much as a projection from the wall as a tunnel through it, enveloping exterior space and uniting it with the space within. Like the backs of the new Chippendale chairs, they represent a kind of composition of solids and voids rarely seen in American plastic arts before, common afterwards. Had Buckland been in charge of Gunston Hall from the first, the new design concepts apparent in its interior woodwork would no doubt have been evident on the exterior as well—the sort of

deliberate sequence of advancing and receding planes created at Buckland's Hammond house in Annapolis by projecting the central section of the main block and relating flanking buildings to it in various subtle spatial relationships; as it is, this handling of elevations (with or without full porticos) only becomes characteristic of advanced American architecture by the 1760s. But already the porticos and interiors of Gunston Hall show the characteristics of mature classicism well established—spacious but not attenuated, graceful but not fragile, they have the essence of true monumentality.

At Gunston Hall too we can see perhaps the first consistent appearance of the new concept of ornament characteristic of Chippendale–Georgian. There is more of it; as in the furniture, it is no longer spotted or concentrated in a few places, but provides an almost even balance between plain and ornamented surfaces. It is at once more delicately and more deeply cut than in the Queen Anne period; beside the easy, unaffected mastery of material it displays, the robust bursts of Queen Anne decoration seem almost as crude, bombastic, and naïve as William and Mary decoration seemed earlier. It is more correct—not because Palladian or other motifs are easily traceable to specifically classical sources (T. T. Waterman, on whose studies reconstruction of Gunston Hall was largely based, thought that the river-front portico came from a Roman coin representing the Temple of Tyche at Eumenia, a source which, even if provable, would have been obscure enough), but because of that obviously greater emphasis on precision in detail, proportion, and spacing of elements which the age accepted as classical Roman discipline. Yet it is at the same time more lavish; in these ogee arches, in the increasing lightness and delicacy that permits a luxurance of detail rare before, we recognize the Rococo element always present in the Chippendale style. But most of all, the ornament of Gunston Hall marks the maturity of the classical mind in America in the way all elements (Palladian and Rococo alike)

(57 B) Chinoiserie in the Entrance Hall from Port Royal, built at Frankford, Pennsylvania, c.1764 and re-erected in the H. F. du Pont Winterthur Museum. The precise source of motifs for 18th-century chinoiserie or "Gothick" has been much discussed, to no great profit. Essentially, such exotic ornament represents no real attempt to revive or understand nonclassical styles; like "beauty patches" on the faces of 18th-century women, it was frankly intended to provide an exotic and playful contrast with "serious" art, a foil to enhance the effect of classical order.

are permeated, controlled, guided by a framework of systematic geometric proportions. Freedom within order, this is the informing principle not only of furniture and architectural design but of every aspect of life in this age; we recognize it everywhere.

Consider, for example, the following eyewitness account of Patrick Henry's oratory:

When he said "Is life so dear, or peace so sweet, as to be purchased at the price of chains and slavery?" he stood in the attitude of a condemned galley slave, awaiting his doom. His form was bowed; his wrists were crossed; his manacles were almost visible as he stood like an embodiment of helplessness and agony. After a solemn pause, he raised his eyes and chained hands towards Heaven, and prayed, in words and tones which thrilled every heart, "Forbid it, Almighty God!" He then turned toward the timid loyalists of the House . . . and he slowly bent his form yet nearer to the earth, and said, "I know not what course others may take," and he accompanied the words with his hands still crossed, while he appeared to be weighed down with additional chains. . . . After remaining in this posture of humiliation long enough to impress the imagination with the condition of the colony under the iron heel of military despotism, he arose proudly and exclaimed, "but as for me"—and the words hissed through his clenched teeth, while his body was thrown back and . . . he looked for a moment like Laocoön in a death struggle with coiling serpents; then the loud, clear, triumphant tones "give me liberty" electrified the assembly. . . . And, as each syllable of the word "liberty" echoed through the building, his fetters were shivered . . . he spoke the word "liberty" with an emphasis never given it before . . . while the sound of his voice and the sublimity of his attitude made him appear a magnificent incarnation of Freedom. . . . After a momentary pause, only long enough to permit the echo of the word "liberty" to cease, he let his left hand fall powerless to his side, and clenched his right hand firmly, as if holding a dagger with the point aimed at his breast. . . . As he closed with the solemn words "or give me death" . . . he suited the action to the word by a blow upon the left breast with the right hand which seemed to drive the dagger into . . . his heart.

Here is the same characteristic combination —luxuriant freedom of illustrative imagery set in a basic framework of rigidly disciplined thought. To contemporaries, it represented the true classical ideal reborn. "Patrick Henry," Thomas Jefferson once declared, "appeared to me to speak as Homer wrote." And they were right. If today the description of such a speech sounds to us (at least as far as the delivery, with its interminable pauses and melodramatic gestures, is concerned) more like comic opera than high drama, that only proves how great, for all the popularity of modern "Georgian" gymnasiums and housing developments and mail-order furniture, is the gulf separating our world from that of the 18th century. For the fact is, the classical mind was different from ours; and people who possessed it were different from us, and thought and acted differently.

In the short time that has elapsed between the 18th and the 20th century, a physiological change has taken place in the human body. It has not only grown bigger, but it also moves itself faster—not merely by mechanical means, but of itself. It changes its positions faster—

no "studied gestures"—runs faster—as one can see by looking at athletic records—boxes faster—for the endless rounds of an 18th-century match often had only one blow really delivered—speaks faster, reads faster, and even eats faster. The 18th century managed to eat so much more than we do because it ate more slowly. It could drink more, by drinking all night. Old Lady Dorothy Nevill, who was born in the reign of George IV, survived to complain in 1910 because "everything is served at such a lightning speed that it is as much as one can do to swallow the few mouthfuls called dinner before one's plate has been snatched away. . . ." It would be interesting to find out whether the pulse rate has gone up.

This observation, by T. H. White in *The Age of Scandal*, could be amplified over and over. Certainly it is true of art; the 18th century not merely liked to look at classical forms or found classical principles congenial, it *was* classical, in a most basic sense.

By our standards, the knowledge these men had of life in the city-states of Greece of the 5th century B.C. or the independent self-governing communities of Renaissance Italy was vague, and often enough wildly inaccurate. But they had an instinctive understanding of the kind of classical art created there, because they lived in the same mental and social atmosphere. The forms of classical design presuppose a world moulded and controlled by the human mind, a world whose proportions are determined by human standards, a world that excludes everything suggestive of infinity, the impermanence of life, or human limitations. Only when a man feels fully in command of his environment can the classical spirit really flourish; and he can really feel this way only in a small and substantially independent community. Nowadays, a man may have some hope of keeping his personal affairs in reasonable order, and perhaps influencing local conditions; but in larger national or international affairs he is practically helpless. Great events like wars or depressions, which can change or ruin his life, simply happen to him. They result from decisions taken at levels where he has at most one voice among millions; all he can do is accept them.

In the small self-contained communities of 18th-century America, however, things were very different. There—on Virginia plantations, microcosmic societies sufficient to themselves; in compact little cities like Philadelphia or Charleston or Annapolis; even on frontier farms, especially after the vaguely menacing cloud of French power lifted so suddenly and finally in 1760—a man could really feel he knew what was going on, and could do something about it. He lived off his own land, or at least felt he could if he had to; he made his own decisions about joining the militia or educating his children; and if he felt oppressed and frustrated where he was he could always move on in hopes of escaping a lifetime of drudgery. And because he had this feeling of confident control, the ordered forms of classical art were not "a" style, they were "the" style; measured precision was not a matter of adopting "rules" taught in some treatise or guide, it was *the* rule, part of the very stuff of life, implicit in everything he did:

A gentleman in Walpole's period [writes White] was judged not only by his accent but also by his deportment, as if he were a ballet. It is literally true that a gentleman had to move in a stylized way. George III complained that Lord Liverpool's "motions were never very graceful." . . . Books like The Dancing Master mentioned by M. Delahaute provided "the Rules required for walking, saluting, and making bows in all kinds of company" with a chapter entitled "How to take off your Hat and replace it." Frenill took "a month's course of instruction from the celebrated Petit, at 12 francs a lesson, in order to learn how to introduce himself to a "circle."

To us, "natural" behavior means the untaught, the unaffected, the spontaneous, the untrammeled. It means public figures delivering speeches with hands in pocket, relaxed in armchairs; it means singers slouched over tables, comedians talking in easy slang. That these performances may follow as rigid a code, take fully

as much practice to perfect, as any 18th-century dancing master demanded, is beside the point. The 20th century cultivates this kind of "natural" behavior, and thinks it good, in the same way and on the same premises it has professed to believe that only artificially imposed restrictions and standards prevent men from expressing their "natural" honesty and loving-kindness in perfect systems of government, or developing their "natural" genius into ever-higher flights of artistic creation—that is, on the assumption that most men are basically good and most restrictions on them basically bad. But that was not at all what "naturalness" meant to the 18th century. The men who spoke its majority mind believed that "natural" men in our sense were licentious social parasites, that "originality" in our sense of freedom from all rules would be a horrible barbarism. Of Rousseau Dr. Johnson said succinctly, "Sir, he should be sent to the plantations."

Men in this age thought it highly *un*natural to live without rules. Disciplined order in mind and habits was not only what distinguished men from animals, but on it all true growth, all real progress, depended. Observation of nature amply confirmed what their religion inculcated—that the "natural" state of man was nasty, brutish, and short. In politics, the "natural" man is avaricious, cruel, greedy for power; good government is one that puts abundant checks on all its officials. In society, the "natural" man is self-centered, sensual, crude; good society is one where agreed standards of moral behavior are supplemented by an established religion, "civil intercourse" encouraged by rigorous codes of manners. Man has no "natural" sense of fitness or beauty; good art depends on absolute rules being understood and accepted to control and channel personal whims of patron and artisan alike. It follows that artistic freedom means, not that the artist may do anything he pleases, but that he should have liberty to take advantage of earlier discoveries and build upon them, attaining a giant's vision by standing on the shoulders of giants. That was what "progress" meant in the classical cycle of antiquity; that is what happened in the Renaissance; and now likewise in mid-18th-century America men took it for granted that future advances must grow out of past achievement.

These men would have thought it just as unnatural to let decoration run away with form. That is the great difference between 18th-century Rococo ornament and the High Victorian art of the 1860s and 70s which superficially so much resembles it. Where in Victorian design decoration takes command and determines the outline of the whole, in Chippendale–Georgian it is always held within a controlling geometrical framework. Exteriors like Gunston Hall, mantelpieces, Chippendale chair backs, Mozart sonatas, and Johnsonian prose all express this fundamental "natural" rule of reason which governed the mind of the 18th century.

It was the Virginia gentleman of this age who embodied the classical idea best. Few writers have described the parallel as brilliantly as Marcus Cunliffe in his study *George Washington, Man and Monument:*

> The English gentleman of the 18th century, at home or in a colony like Virginia, held what we might call a dual citizenship. He was an Englishman; he was also an honorary Roman. He even looked like one; the firm, beardless but masculine faces of 18th-century portraits often bear a striking resemblance to Roman portrait busts. . . .
>
> Consciously or unconsciously, the gentleman of Washington's day drew much of his metaphor and his code of values from Rome. . . . It is no accident that he [Washington] frequently quoted from Addison's *Cato* . . . one of the century's favorite plays. It may well have been in the mind of the young Connecticut hero, Nathan Hale. . . . "I only regret that I have but one life to give for my country" echoes Addison's
>
>> "What pity is it
>> That we can die but once to save
>> our country."
>
> And *virtus* was one of the famous Roman vir-

tues (and, in practice, a Virginian one). *Gravitas, pietas, simplicitas, integritas* and *gloria* were other valued Roman qualities.

> . . . Rome was a martial civilization, always aware of the unrest along the frontiers, the bringer of law and imposer of order. Roman culture was a trifle hard and unsubtle, or at any rate rooted in reality rather than raptly poetic; religious feeling was moderate in tone, excess being deplored. Rome was a slave-holding society in which (outside the capital and the provincial centers) the unit of neighborhood was a farm estate. It was a society that relied upon the family as a cohesive force. Affection, respect, loyalty spread outward from the family, which was thus the state in microcosm. . . . Such are the implications of words like *gravitas* (seriousness), *pietas* (regard for discipline and authority), *simplicitas* (lucidity).
>
> For "Rome" here, may we not read "Virginia"? And were Washington's old-style biographers, or the admirers of his own generation, so wildly wrong when they said that he was set in the antique mould, Cincinnatus reborn? . . . It would be idle to pretend that Washington's Virginia simply repeated the modes and experiences of the ancient world, or that all his contemporaries were as markedly "classical" in temperament. The point is that his age differed profoundly from ours; that in certain ways he is better understood within a classical framework than as a man of modern times; and that his planter Virginia was in a way more truly "Roman" than the mother country.

And the architecture and furnishings with which such men surrounded themselves were equally the product and expression of an intrinsically classical way of life. In them is manifest a society whose outlook on the world sprang from the same disciplined self-confidence, the same assurance in absolute rules of life and art, that motivated the great classical eras of the past. American art in the Chippendale–Georgian era was the expression of a nation grown to mature self-sufficiency. It was not yet entirely aware of the fact, perhaps; but the realization could not long be delayed. Men who naturally create and live with art forms like these cannot long be content to have their ultimate affairs dictated by others. Looking at Chippendale–Georgian architecture and furniture, we understand graphically what John Adams meant when he said that "the American Revolution began in the hearts and minds of the people."

NOTES

Quotations of Patrick Henry's speech from K. Umbreit, *The Founding Fathers* (1941), pp. 218–19; from T. H. White, *The Age of Scandal* (1950), pp. 44–5 and 49; from Marcus Cunliffe, *George Washington: Man and Monument* (1958), Sec. V, "The Classical Code."

Restoration of Gunston Hall is authoritatively described by Fiske Kimball, "Gunston Hall" (*JSAH*, XIII, 2, 1954, pp. 3–8). Already in 1933 R. T. Halsey recognized how advance-guard the Rococo elements in Gunston Hall were: its "front parlor," he wrote, "must have been the last word in America in the new style of architecture over which fashionable England was going wild. . . . Probably no early American room has such a profusion of ornament" (*Great Georgian Houses of America*, I, p. 14).

Classical porches as introduced in the Chippendale–Georgian period should be distinguished from survivals of the medieval tradition of porches created by extensions of eaves. The latter, of course, were perpetuated in lower strata of society throughout the 18th century, whereas the classical porch as a conscious spatial element in design only becomes common in the South c.1755 and (following the regional pattern) progressively later farther north. Common in Philadelphia by the 1770s, it was still unusual in Boston at that time, when J. S. Copley has to describe a "peazer" to Pelham in a letter of 1771 (published by C. Bridenbaugh, *The Colonial Craftsman*, 1950, p. 158 and fn. p. 202); and unusual in Connecticut still in the 1780s: the Cowles house at Farmington was considered by Frederick Kelly to have the oldest classical porch in the state.

6. CLASSICAL DECADENCE:
Adamesque-Federal, c.1780—c.1820

Let us suppose that a traditional form has been employed with success in the past, that important things have been said and works of value produced in that form. Writers and artists then continue to write, paint, and compose in this form, when they have no content of importance to put into it. They produce poems, tracts, essays, or sermons, not because they are impelled by a consuming desire to say something which seems to them to be convincingly right, but because it seems right for them to say something. As a result, the form and style of the work, which, rightly regarded, are only the vehicles in which the artist or writer brings his wares to the market to offer them to the public, become themselves the wares.

THIS, SAYS C. E. M. JOAD in his study *Decadence*, is how the disappearance of external values, the "dropping of the object" which for him marks the decadent society, is most commonly manifested in literature and music. Certainly it is so in architecture and furniture. And at the end of the 5th century B.C. in Greece, early in 16th-century Italy, now again at the end of the 18th century in America, the process is evident—classical forms no longer express self-evidently good and unquestioningly accepted principles of life, but become ends in themselves.

Of course the change is never complete or sudden. Three generations have made classical forms a familiar language, a lingua franca that will persist in use for many decades more. But the accent, the content, are different; forms are used for different ends and in another spirit. Those invented to embody confidence in the powers of individual men to control and order their world now are used to dramatize individual futility; what was once the spontaneous expression of a way of life becomes a play on senses designed for the satisfaction of connoisseurs. In antiquity, the spontaneous and intuitive

classicism of the golden age fades off into exhibitions of exquisite refinement in the late 5th century; then, in the 4th, come flamboyant personalities with self-conscious "styles": Praxiteles with his smooth sensuous Venuses and Apollos, Scopas and his "wild style," Zeuxis and Apelles with their "magic realism" and "bohemian" liberties; thence to the extravagances of "ancient Baroque," the schools of Rhodes and Pergamon with their Laocoöns and Dirkes and Dying Gauls that ring changes on the theme of human futility in the face of mindless chance, the "revivals" of the 2nd century and Roman times, the "imperial" styles, and so on. Renaissance art follows the same pattern: after the Sistine Ceiling and the Camera della Segnatura, come Raphael's proto-mannerism and Michelangelo's exposures of the vanity of human wishes in the cramped and twisted classical forms of his Medici Chapel and Ricetto at San Lorenzo; where earlier generations ransacked mythology and Biblical history for Judiths and Davids and Pallases to allegorize individual powers over nature, men of the later 16th century find Danaës, Bathshebas, daughters of Leucippus and Europas who present the futility of resistance to supernatural destiny, or Daphnes and Ariadnes who show that resistance means transformation into something less or more than human. Again the great eccentric personalities appear; again artists become men who, instead of giving fame, work to get it. And now once more the process is repeated in the Anglo-American cycle at the end of the 18th century. Once more art becomes a matter of styles and personalities rather than a product of motivating belief. And as in earlier 18th-century America, furniture and architecture show the change first and best.

Chippendale—Georgian forms, so admirable an expression of the spirit that made the American Revolution, were not soon or everywhere

58. The Banquet Hall, Mount Vernon, Fairfax County, Virginia. Though most of Mount Vernon was built before the Revolution (mainly in the years 1757–8 and 1773–9) and is generally Chippendale–Georgian in architectural character, Washington had to postpone completion of his two-story banquet hall until his return from the war, so that this hall differs in style from the other interiors. As decorated by John Rawlins and Richard Thorpe (or Tharpe) between April 1786 and July 1787, it was a monument to the appearance in America of the fourth, Adamesque–Federal phase of the classical mind.

given up after the Revolution was won. For another quarter-century at least they remained popular among conservative elements of society; workmen's row houses and factories, old-fashioned cabinetmakers and their patrons, mass-circulated builders' guides and the raw new cities burgeoning westwards perpetuated them in various garbled ways well into the early decades of the 19th century. Probably for the majority of people today "early American" still brings this "post-Georgian" style to mind, for in number of examples produced it far exceeded later rivals

over many decades. Nevertheless, the same forces that won the Revolution inevitably and inexorably changed the character of American civilization; and as it changed, so did the forms that seemed self-evidently right to the taste-making upper strata of society.

The history of George Washington's successive building programs at Mount Vernon illustrates very well how taste changed after the Revolution. When acquired from Lawrence Washington's widow in 1754, Mount Vernon had been an unpretentious farmhouse. In the years 1757–8

Washington rebuilt it as the typical Chippendale–Georgian mansion of a gentleman planter of Virginia, raising it from one and a half to two stories, covering the exterior with channeled boarding sanded to imitate stone, choosing motifs from Swan's *British Architect*, Langley's *Ancient Masonry*, and other recent builders' guides in designing the entrance hall, dining room, and west parlor. Then in 1773 he projected further enlargements in the same manner—a library with master bedroom above, and a great banquet hall suitable to his now more public station as burgess, Truro parish vestryman and Pohick church warden, justice of the peace, and soon delegate to the first Virginia Provincial Convention and the First Continental Congress. By 1776, however, the banquet hall had been no more than framed and roofed; its Palladian window taken from one of Batty Langley's books was in place, but the interior was otherwise unfinished. And when in 1783 Washington returned from the Revolutionary War his tastes had begun to change; he determined to finish the room in the new fashion, employing plaster and cast ornament, to which he had been introduced by such friends as Samuel Vaughan, fashionable merchant and builder newly come to Philadelphia from London. "I want to finish in stucco," he wrote; "it is my intention to do it in a plain neat style; which, independently of its being the present taste (as I am informed) is my choice." For the purpose he needed English-trained decorators; after some searching, he engaged John Rawlins, who had come from London to Maryland in 1771 and worked as an ornamental plasterer in Annapolis and Baltimore. The result was a "new room," completed in 1787, quite different from the others, painted in "buff—of the lightest kind, inclining to white," with delicate plaster swags and tendrils "picked out" by small paintbrushes, and green-ground wallpaper with classical borders outlining the openings. At this time too Washington added to Mount Vernon the famous two-story porch fronting the Potomac; equally novel in its free handling of space, with

equally little precedent (indeed, its precise model has never been identified; perhaps it was the General's own invention). With these developments the new style was established, for, as Washington [Cunliffe remarks] "was well aware," he was a "factor on the national scene; whatever he did tended to have national repercussions."

Ascendancy of the new style was confirmed by the outcome of the national competition to design the President's house in Washington. Most of the submissions represented variants of Chippendale–Georgian forms and principles still; but the winning design, by Irish-trained James Hoban of Charleston, on which construction was begun in 1792 was in this same new manner which we can best call, from the English designer who most extensively popularized it and the epoch in American history when it most flourished, the Adamesque–Federal. In it Washington and the competition commissioners recognized the most appropriate expression of a new epoch; and, as we consider the principles and practice of this architecture and the comparable "classical" style of furniture, it becomes plain how right they were.

Perhaps the simplest way to describe the Adamesque–Federal phase of the classical mind is to say that it embodies all the classical qualities of the preceding three, to self-conscious excess. Lightness is perhaps its most obvious characteristic. Materials, colors, shapes—all are lighter. Cabinetmakers begin to introduce woods lighter in weight, color, and texture—satinwood, holly, tulipwood, curly maple, pine—cut in thin strips and used as veneers and inlays to relieve the solidity of mahogany. Carvers make extensive use of plaster in ever more delicate detail, not alone on ceilings but for cornices, fireplaces, even case pieces; often it is hard to tell by sight whether a given piece is carved in wood or moulded in plaster. Wallpaper, designed in patterns of intricate delicacy, replaces paneling to the point where little more than a baseboard remains. Heavy stonework walls are superseded

59. THE WHITE HOUSE, WASHINGTON, D.C.
(A) North front, from a photo c.1900.

*(59 B) South front of the White House in the 1960s. This first public building in the new United States capital was begun October 1792 on the plans of James Hoban. After it was gutted during the British occupation of Washington in 1814, rebuilding was begun under Hoban in 1815 on plans amended (including the porticos and terraces) by B. H. Latrobe and President Jeffer-*son in 1807, and completed 1817 with the exception of the south portico (completed 1824), East Room and north portico (completed 1829). Among the more notable subsequent developments were the reconstruction of main floor and redecoration in 1902, rebuilding of roof and third floor in 1927, reconstruction and restoration of walls and interiors 1948–52, and the systematic program of historic furnishing undertaken by Mrs. John F. Kennedy and a committee headed by Henry Francis du Pont from 1960 on.

in fashion by brick and stucco. White becomes the predominant color for decorative details, from porticos to fireplaces; characteristically, these are set off against pastel walls so that whole buildings, outside and in, resemble in effect contemporaneous Wedgwood china. White also becomes popular for outside walls—the White House being the most obvious example. Furniture too is frequently painted in white, gold, or pastel shades; where it is not, the dark marble-like quality of Chippendale mahogany is set off, if not entirely replaced, by straw- and orange-colored inlays and veneering, grained to produce a characteristic "tortoise-shell" effect. Applied gilt ornament becomes common, its glitter helping to break up solid lines and produce a quality of insubstantiality. Drawer pulls, handles, upholstery nails are made thinner, more deliberately decorative. Shapes are lighter in whole and detail; everything, from chair legs and backs to window muntins and portico colonnettes, is attenuated to a point that makes Chippendale–Georgian seem heavy, Queen Anne almost grotesque, William and Mary primitive. Ironwork, appearing more and more frequently throughout the century (Westover already had a fine pair of iron gates), becomes a major element in architectural design now that taste calls for balcony and stair railings so thin as to be impractical in wood. Similarly, because of its exceeding fineness more and more ornament is moulded in plaster. Structure too is lighter; the delicate tambours, sliding panels, legs tapering to needle-like slenderness characteristic of this age seem so fragile that we marvel at their preservation; porticos are supported and doorways framed by reedy colonnettes and pilasters; airy curving ceiling vaults and flying staircases seem to float in space.

Horizontality of proportion and effect is now predominant. Legs shorter in proportion to seat widths give chairs a low-slung appearance; the characteristic "advance-guard" chair back is at least slightly wider than it is high. Tables, sofas, cupboards are markedly enough wider

than they are high to give rooms predominantly horizontal lines, despite the spindliness of individual forms and generally higher ceilings; these lines are accentuated by the increasing practice of bringing windows down to floor level, so that interiors have a new low center of gravity. Whenever function allows it, buildings as a whole are made wider than they are high or deep, with roofs as flat as possible and balustrades running along the eaves to conceal what pitch there is. Sideboards, desks, and chests of drawers tend to lose their upper sections so that they become as horizontally oriented as chairs and tables.

There is a new spatial sophistication. Voids become as positive an element in total design as solids; designers play with them, in everything from chair backs that are practically all void to ground plans calling for complicated combinations of convex and concave forms— niches, curving balconies, oval central sections set off by straight side wings—advancing and receding as if propelled by the pressures of surrounding space. Walls become complicated exercises in successive planes—cornice, pilasters, wall planes, arches within the wall, windows within them (the Boston State House (45D) is a good example). Stairways float in high-ceilinged rooms of new spaciousness; balconies, their details picked out in delicate ironwork, hang as if congealed in frozen islets of space; porticos seem rather to leap than project from the plane of the wall. Space-embracing ovoid forms dominate the outlines and details in furniture, architectural plans, and elevations alike.

Ostentatious and self-conscious sculptural effects are attempted. Details are moulded not merely to manifest command of materials, but as sculpture in their own right—chair legs becoming little colonettes, backs shaped like lyres or urns, swags and sheaves of wheat and bunches of grapes conceived as practically independent still lifes. Panels are ornamented with landscapes or figural scenes in low relief, wallpaper is designed with elaborate three-dimensional illusion. Actual statuary becomes common; you see it in niches and atop pediments of buildings, as finials on furniture. Sometimes, indeed, whole buildings or pieces of furniture seem conceived more as works of sculpture to be looked at than as functional objects. Related to this sculptural quality is a much more deliberate and pedantic emphasis on archaeological correctness. As yet it is largely confined to details—vases, details of entablature, lyres, brackets, acanthus leaves, figures in classical costume. Buildings and furniture as a whole still allude to rather than directly copy Roman or Renaissance prototypes, like the tortoise-shell inlay which recalls in a general way the color scheme of Greek vases, or the white walls and portico of the President's house, which no more than suggest to those who can read the language that here lives a Roman patrician, a Cincinnatus chosen by his peers to leave the plow and lead the nation in four years of public service. Direct imitation on a large scale will come soon enough, however; indeed, in such works as the new State Capitol at Richmond it has already appeared on the scene, and with it a new attitude to art entirely.

Like Chippendale–Georgian, the Adamesque–Federal period takes its name from an individual, a generic figure who seems to sum up its complex origins, characteristics, and spirit. This was the Scottish architect and decorator Robert Adam (1728–1792), whose *Ruins of the Emperor Diocletian's Palace at Spalatro* (1764) introduced, and whose *Works in Architecture* (published in collaboration with his brother James from 1773 on) summed up, this fourth phase of the classical mind, as Chippendale's *Director* had the third. In these books was embodied and manifested the outlook of a generation which had inherited a fully developed classical tradition. Adam's contemporaries could never experience that excitement at discovering new means of expression which had gripped men at the beginning of the 18th century, nor yet the satisfaction in formulating and perfecting them characteristic of the middle years of the century. But as masters of both principles and practice from the beginning, they had an easy command of classical forms their predecessors

60. *"Interior of the Temple of Jupiter," plate from* The Ruins of the Palace of Diocletian at Spalatro, *by Robert Adam, 1764. Robert Adam and several companions, most notably the French archaeologist Clérisseau (later friend of Jefferson), visited this imperial palace (2nd century* A.D.*) in the summer of 1757. Like travelers in all ages, they saw there what their background and taste inclined them to see—in this case, an apparently "purer Roman" style than Palladio's, one that emphasized bold departures from "Palladian" rules of proportion and order, spatial intricacies in vaulting and successive wall planes, elegantly refined decorative motifs; on his observations here and elsewhere (most notably the excavations of Nero's Golden House in Rome), Adam developed a new style of architecture and furniture that came to bear his name.*

never knew. Having neither to learn classical rules nor perfect classical forms, they had a new freedom to break, bend, play with these forms in new combinations and for varied effects. Adam's books made no claim to discoveries of purer classicism, of better embodiments of classical principles than those known before. That would have been difficult to maintain, even had he so wished, for obviously the examples presented of both his own and ancient work were almost torturously playful and ornate; in them almost every earlier accepted canon of classical perfection was broken. Adam spoke to and for a generation more concerned with technicalities than fundamentals, caring more for novelty than correctness, demanding specialized data instead of broad principles, a generation for whom classical principles were not so much self-evidently right as self-evidently convenient points of departure in search of varied effects. "The great masters of antiquity," he wrote in the Preface to Part I of the *Works*, "were not so rigidly scrupulous, they varied the proportions as the general spirit of their composition required." In the Preface to Part II he gave more specific examples: the proportion of columns, he maintained, "depends upon the situation of these columns, whether they make parts of outside, or inside decoration, whether they stand insulated, or engaged, whether raised much above the eye, or level with it"; and, speaking "of freedom in the use of entablatures," "a latitude in this respect, under the hand of an ingenious and able artist, is often productive of great novelty, variety, and beauty."

Adam's forms were the expression of a subtle but basic shift in understanding of classical principles in that generation. Where horizontality had been a spontaneous expression of the classical urge to stability, Adam made it a stylistic cliché, negating its psychological effect by using excessively thin shapes and fragile structure. He affected lightness to the point of frustrating utility. He cultivated three-dimensionality for its own sake, at the expense of over-all unity of design. He supplanted the older unaffected admiration for Graeco-Roman and Renaissance art, which had been spontaneously generated by a comparable attitude to life, with a sophisticated and scholarly cultivation of classical "motifs." He introduced a new kind of conscious and literary symbolism, urging imitation of Imperial Roman forms on grounds that their associations made them peculiarly suitable

in the even greater empire ruled by George III:

> I Beg Leave to lay before your Majesty the Ruins of Spalatro, once the favourite Residence of a great Emperor, who, by his Munificence and Example, revived the Study of Architecture. . . .

> At this happy Period, when Great Britain enjoys in Peace the Reputation and Power she has acquired by Arms, Your Majesty's singular attention to the Arts of Elegance, promises an Age of Perfection that will compleat the Glories of your Reign, and fix an Aera no less remarkable than that of Pericles, Augustus, or the Medicis.

Post-Revolutionary Americans could hardly follow that particular line of argument; but they could readily enough develop the principle on their own. Thomas Jefferson, indeed, already has developed what he calls an "American" architecture, a full-fledged vocabulary of symbolic meanings attachable to Roman forms; soon enough, with the Empire style in furniture and the neoclassical movement in architecture, artists will begin to copy Greek and Roman art wholesale, and the end of the classical mind in American civilization will be in sight. That, however, is another story; as yet, in the Adamesque–Federal style, the old framework of forms and principles may be shaky, but it is still intact.

Chair legs may be treated like little columns, and chair backs like lyres or urns, but there is still a sense of controlling order; the details, however sculptural, are still parts of the whole. The rooms of the White House may be individualized, on a basis vaguely symbolic of their different functions, so that they contrast with each other as rooms did not, say, in a typical Chippendale–Georgian house; but the Gold Room, the Blue Room, the Red Room, and the rest all have an immediately intelligible relation to one another in terms of the total plan. Decorative details may be entities in their own right as they were not before, but they are still contained within, and contribute to, a common pattern. There may be deliberate symbolism in the White House, but it is not yet of the explicit, limited, or personal kind being introduced by advance-guard figures like Thomas Jefferson (whose anonymous submissions to the competition were rejected, significantly enough). Belonging to no one province or state, its design is as much a matter for all English America to debate and decide as is the location of the national capital; this vital common concern is thrown open to everyone, in a democratic competition, and the resulting building expresses in general rather than specific terms the character of the new nation. Finally, though more self-conscious than in earlier phases, classical forms in Adamesque–Federal still spring spontaneously from at least one particular way of life. In them we recognize the natural expression of that rising class of capitalists and merchants whom collectively we call "Hamiltonians" (after their early spokesman and representative leader, Alexander Hamilton) or, from their stand in favor of strong central government by a limited electorate of propertied leaders, "Federalists." In the refined luxuriance of Adamesque–Federal ornament were manifested the same pretensions to becoming the new republic's permanent aristocracy that motivated the Federalists' policies of protective tariffs, private banks, and free speculation in land; and in its obvious English origins, the same advocacy of close commercial and social ties with England which in the time of the War of 1812 earned them a derisive title of "the English party."

Yet, given the new freedom, the new self-consciousness, it became plain that disintegration could not long be delayed. What happened to the classical tradition in this Adamesque–Federal phase is in fact strikingly parallel to the fate of that Virginia aristocracy in which the classical mind had found its best American embodiment. In Professor Boorstin's words:

> The Revolution which the Virginia aristocracy did so much to make and "win" was in fact the suicide of the Virginia aristocracy.

. . . The Federal Constitution was a national road on which there was no return. The leadership of Virginians in Federal life continued only so long as the national government was an aristocratic camaraderie like that of Virginia. When the United States ceased to be a greater Virginia, Virginians ceased to govern the United States. The virtues of 18th-century Virginia, when writ large, would seem to be vices. Localism would become sectionalism; the special interests of where a man lived would come to seem petty and disruptive.

Just so, the classical mind in becoming an American national expression lost its spontaneity and its savor. As forms nurtured in the small city-states of Greece lost their spirit and survived as empty shells in the sprawling Hellenistic and Roman empires, as the art created in the local states of 15th-century Italy changed its character when it became the basis for international Mannerism and the Baroque, so now in losing its local roots the classical tradition in America also lost its self-evident justification, its basis in absolute rules unthinkingly accepted. It became a "proper style" for Americans to use, a matter of good taste. And whereas the old absolute framework admitted only internal variations, "good taste," as a matter of general agreement, can change overnight. Sometimes, indeed, it can change completely within artists' lifetimes, as we will see in the work of McIntire, of Duncan Phyfe, of Thomas Jefferson himself. The ordered stability of the patrician world of the 18th century which was the foundation of the classical mind and the Virginia aristocracy dissolves into an ever more complicated welter of conflicting "tastes" and "styles," a jungle of struggling capitalist industrial enterprises, in which the old classical principles and the old plantation system are hopelessly outmoded, distorted, and buried. As William and Mary marked the beginning, so Adamesque–Federal marks the end, of the classical mind proper; as then classical principles gradually supplanted medieval vestiges, so now these principles in turn are supplanted by the new neoclassical concept that heralds the Victorian age. The cycle is complete; the classical era in American civilization is ended, and Victorian America begins to take form.

NOTES

Quotations from C. E. M. Joad, *Decadence* (London, 1948), p. 57; from Daniel J. Boorstin, *The Americans* (1958), p. 143. On Robert Adam and the Adamesque, see particularly James Lees-Milne, *The Age of Adam* (London, 1947).

An authoritative account of the banquet hall is by Worth Bailey, "General Washington's New Room" (*JSAH*, X, 2, 1951, pp. 16–18). Rawlins was assisted by Richard Thorpe, an Irish stuccoworker who (coincidentally, it would seem) had been recommended to Washington earlier when he had written to Sir Edward Newenham in Dublin inquiring about possible decorators for the hall a year previously. Rawlins died in 1786. On the painting of the White House, see "White for the White House" ("American Notes," *JSAH*, X, 2, 1951, p. 22).

7. DIVERSITY WITHIN UNITY:
The Classical Mind as Regional and Class Expression

IN THE FOREGOING CHAPTERS we have seen how the distinctive characteristics of the four traditional "styles" of furniture in the four quarters of the 18th century are paralleled in architecture, how each represents a progressive stage in American cultural evolution, and how these stages are comparable to the historic four-phase evolution of the classical mind in earlier cycles during antiquity and the Renaissance. But when it comes to the whole great body of architecture and furniture made between 1700 and 1800 from Maine to Georgia, this pattern seems to break down. Only by arbitrarily choosing examples that fit it, and ignoring the many that do not—Queen Anne chairs occasionally being made as late as the 1780s, essentially William and Mary pieces imported as early as the 1680s, good Chippendale–Georgian houses still being built in 1820, and so on—can we do more, apparently, than maintain some broad distinction of "early" from "late" within a generally "Georgian" manner. Yet this difficulty is more apparent than real, I think. If we remember that classical art in 18th-century America was not so much a style as a state of mind; if we look not for details or individual buildings that represent the first or last appearance of this or that characteristic, but for the progressive embodiment and expression of a characteristic attitude and outlook on life in architecture and furniture broadly considered, then we shall find a pattern of evolution that is very consistent indeed. Systematically throughout the century we can trace the development of six basic principles, each manifesting a particular aspect of the classical mind growing to maturity. In order of appearance (and not so incidentally) from the more general to the more specific, they are:

(1) *A progressive change from predominantly vertical to predominantly horizontal proportions*, apparent in total dimensions (total height to total width of buildings; total height to total width of furniture) as well as in detail (dimensions of windows and doors; dimensions of wings and center sections of buildings; heights of chair seats above floor versus their widths; pitch and shape of roofs, etc.). Expressing an instinct for stability, for scaling things down to human level, horizontality develops in contrast and reaction to that medieval impulse towards verticality which is so obviously evident in everything belonging to the preceding tradition, from the soaring vaults of Gothic cathedrals to the spiky crockets of altar pieces and the paneling of bench backs. As it develops, the still strongly vertical cast of William and Mary proportions becomes vestigial in Queen Anne, and is superseded in Chippendale–Georgian architecture and furniture by characteristic balance of horizontal and vertical elements; by the Adamesque–Federal period horizontal accents predominate.

(2) *Progressively more "correct"*—archaeologically, i.e.—*classical detail.* Conscious awareness of the classical mind as such, growing throughout the century, makes for increasingly literal copying of individual details from recognized Greek and Roman inspiration or models. Where men in the William and Mary period drew on Greek and Roman forms more by coincidence of instinct than deliberate intent, by the Queen Anne period they know what they want and where to find it, and details obviously drawn from Greek and Roman sources begin to appear. Only in the Chippendale period, however, do much conscious selection and rejection among specific alternatives from earlier art begin; an ever wider range of models is evidenced by variations in detail—porches, fireplaces, decorative motifs—within the same building or the work of a given cabinetmaker. This aware-

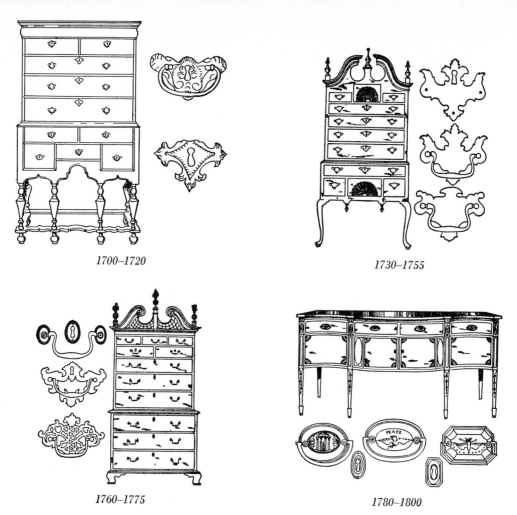

1700–1720

1730–1755

1760–1775

1780–1800

61. *Case pieces from four quarters of the 18th century, illustrating the consistency of classical evolution in whole and detail in each of its four successive phases. Drawings from Moreton Marsh,* The Easy Expert.

ness of specific prototypes so spurs archaeological investigations, however, that new and more scholarly information about ancient and Renaissance art accumulates speedily. It is put to extensive use in the Adamesque–Federal period, which is characterized by copious and direct copying of details from Greek, Renaissance, and especially Roman sources—vases, colonnettes, balusters, ornament; men at the end of the century know actual monuments, not simply descriptions of them in books. Now that art is motivated more by cultivated aesthetic sensibilities than by any deep commitment to the classical view of life, archaeology begins to dominate creative design. This, of course, is a sign of the coming disintegration of classical art, of a transition from spontaneous manifestations of the traditional classical mind to the self-conscious and romantic reproduction of entire models—temples, Roman chairs, and so on—which introduces the Victorian attitude in American art.

(3) *A progressively increasing sculptural, tactile, or three-dimensional sense.* To touch and hold a thing is the first, the most immediate and direct means of controlling it, and symbolic of all the others (to "comprehend" something is to "grasp" it). That insistence on controlling the world which the classical mind above all looks for and tries to realize in art is thus expressed in details by an increasingly sculptural emphasis, and in plans and elevations by increasing spatial complexity. In the William and Mary period this characteristic is evident in details—elaborate spools, spindles, and crestings on furniture, finials on roofs and gateposts— but there is little or no three-dimensionality in compositions as a whole; the spindles are arranged in flat planes parallel with each other, the basic building planes are bald and flat, there is little projection of doorframes and window frames, little overhang of eaves. In the Queen Anne phase the rather naïve and bombastic character of William and Mary decoration persists in a characteristic robustness of form— doorways with great broken cornices, massive shells ornamenting furniture. So does a basically two-dimensional composition; for all their greater sculptural sense in detail, Queen Anne architecture and furniture are still basically composed in one plane, as may easily be seen in the treatment of façades or chair backs. True three-dimensional concepts appear commonly in Chippendale–Georgian details; here are found chair backs composed of forms interpenetrating in space, buildings with projecting porticos of free-standing columns. But fully three-dimensional concepts *in toto* generally belong to the Adamesque–Federal period, with its liking for large oval forms breaking boldly through flat planes into surrounding space, or receding into concavities; niches, airy balconies, free-standing staircases; furniture in which voids and solids combine as comparable and integral parts of the whole design.

(4) *An increasing unity in composition,* manifested in progressively greater precision and self-containment. This outward expression of an inward, felt conviction that the world is basically orderly, that it is governed by principles and laws which man can understand by reason and, understanding, can use to his advantage, has a necessarily somewhat different embodiment in architecture than in furniture.

Unity in architectural design essentially means self-containment of the whole, co-ordination of details, and precision in both. The classical mind likes to think of a world in man's control; the idea of vagueness and infinity—of things beyond the reach of human understanding or physical capabilities—is abhorrent. Therefore in architecture the supreme example of the classical mind is the central-type building, wherein all parts are clearly and comprehensibly related to a central point or element, and the building as a whole is precisely cut off from its surrounding environment and horizon, as were the buildings on the Acropolis, for instance (someone has described them as arranged like pots on an untidy shelf, without any apparent orientation towards one another or to the site as a whole), or the domical buildings designed by Brunellesco, Leonardo, and Bramante. In American architecture this means, instead of trailing strings of connected ells and outbuildings added one to another without logical termination as in the medieval tradition, buildings increasingly conceived as unified blocks deliberately set off from their environment, their outlines more and more precisely defined, less and less broken by projecting gables, finials, or extraneous ornament. It means details—window frames, ornament, cornices—increasingly conceived as at once complete in themselves and co-ordinated in a total design, set in a coherent, systematic, and self-evidently perceptible relationship to one another and to a whole.

In furniture design, however, unity is expressed first as a consistent elimination of small units by integrating them in a single organic whole. In the William and Mary style a multitude of spools, balls, spindles, and crestings detract from any precise conception of the whole, and break up smooth outlines by their visual irregularity. Queen Anne designers eliminate most of the smaller units, but vigorous curves and sharp decorative projections keep the outline visually irregular. In Chippendale furniture, though ornamental projections persist and indeed are generally more elaborate, they no longer determine the outline, but instead are contained within a framework of geometric ratios, visually established. By the Adamesque–Federal period, smooth and continuous outlines are the rule; inlay and veneered ornament permit complete integration of structure and decoration. It is in the treatment of legs and feet that organic unity is best revealed in furniture, however. Like the column and capital in classical architecture, they become determinants of proportion and formal relationships for the whole. So the "Spanish foot" of the William and Mary period shows designers first beginning to think of details in terms of the whole, shaping them, like capitals in architecture, to express an organic relationship of load to support. So the transformation of legs from collections of balls and turnings into single simple forms running in unbroken lines from foot to crest marks the moment when Queen Anne designers decisively realize the implications of classical unity. So in Chippendale–Georgian furniture the essence of classical maturity is expressed in feet and legs that are lighter, lower, more sculptural, derived from more "classical" sources (eagle grasping orb, e.g.), whose ornament is at once more elaborate and more visually integrated with the whole. And the final fragmentation of the classical mind is nowhere better manifested than in the Adamesque–Federal tendency to treat legs like actual classical columns, visually dissociated from the whole.

Unity in furniture design is further expressed in an increasing precision of function. In the medieval tradition of letting nature take its course which persisted into the late-17th-century Jacobean era, pieces of furniture rarely had a single specific function. Chairs doubled as chests or benches, beds doubled as day couches, the same type of cupboard might be used alternately to store food or clothes. The appearance of new furniture types, with specific functions, in the William and Mary period, is a telling mark of the emerging classical mind with its insistence on precise means and ends. And throughout the 18th century types continue to multiply as times and circumstances demand, culminating in the immense variety of chairs, tables, cupboards, and so on devised for each and every occasion by Adamesque–Federal cabinetmakers. (To a lesser extent the same principle is apparent in architecture; from the medieval house with its hall, parlor, and sleeping chambers that serve all manner of function we progress to specific types of buildings—the Williamsburg Capitol, for instance, is already a public building as the Jamestown State House was not—and finally by the end of the century to houses with rooms specifically designated for sleeping, cooking, bathing, entertainment, dining, music, etc.; in large Southern plantation houses kitchens and washhouses develop into separate structures, though other, social considerations played as much a part in the process as the classical mind, undoubtedly).

(5) *An increasing lightness of form.* This expression of delight in man's control over nature by manipulating and forcing materials into "unnatural" shapes and uses (in contrast and reaction to medieval "naturalness") is necessarily best expressed in the handling of details. Its appearance in the William and Mary period, when elaborately turned walnut and intricate caning make such an ostentatious contrast with the solid, lumpy oak forms of medieval tradition, is one of the most obvious marks of the

emerging classical mind. But the great balls and turnings of the transitional phase seem almost medieval when contrasted with the boldly simple command over natural materials expressed in Queen Anne furniture, and the increasingly crisp and incisive treatment of Chippendale–Georgian mahogany. By the end of the century lightness culminates and indeed reaches a point of exaggeration in the tenuous colonnettes, delicate ironwork, pastel colors, and reedy legs of Adamesque–Federal furniture and architecture.

(6) *Progressively greater and subtler balance.* In contrast to lightness, this quality is primarily embodied in total composition. Expressing the most fundamental of classical concepts, which Aristotle summed up in his requirement that a good work of art should have "a beginning, a middle, and an end"—i.e., should be complete within itself, represent a total co-ordination of all parts within the whole—this balance is inherent in, and the consummation of, all other classical characteristics: lightness, three-dimensionality, horizontality (balance of vertical and horizontal elements), unity. Where it is most readily apparent, however, is in the distribution of ornament over furniture and architecture as a whole—from the clumps and bunches of ornament on William and Mary, and the characteristic spotting of decoration in a few places in Queen Anne work (e.g., doorways, cresting of chairs) to the visual balance created by subtle repetitions and respondences of Chippendale–Georgian ornamental forms, culminating in the Adamesque–Federal concept of ornament as so integral a part of the composition as to be indistinguishable from structure (e.g., treatment of chair legs as colonnettes, balconies and ironwork used both structurally and decoratively, etc.).

It is possible to trace the evolution of the classical mind in 18th-century America almost mechanically, by analyzing the degree of development of these six basic principles in given classical buildings or pieces of furniture. Suppose we allot points on the following basis:

10 for *horizontality:* assuming 1 = decided and consistent emphasis on verticality, 5 = decided and consistent emphasis on horizontality, allot 1–5 points according to the degree of horizontality of proportion in details, 1–5 for over-all proportions.

10 for *archaeological correctness:* assuming 1 = evidence of general classical principles only, 5 = obvious copyings of specific Graeco-Roman or Renaissance prototypes, allot 1–5 points for "correctness" of detail, 1–5 for "correctness" in the larger elements of building as a whole (porticos, etc.).

10 for *three-dimensional conception:* assuming 1 = composition and/or ornament basically conceived in two dimensions, confined to a single plane, 5 = evidence of true spatial concepts, with voids an integral part of the composition, allot 1–5 points for handling of details, 1–5 for over-all plan and elevation.

10 for *unity of design:* assuming 1 = evidently additive concepts, indefinite outline, fenestration, and other features dictated by circumstances and structure rather than by co-ordinated visual plan, 5 = self-containment, precise outline, total co-ordination of details in the whole, allot 1–5 points for details, 1–5 for over-all composition.

5 for *lightness:* assuming 1 = heavy, lumpy forms, 5 = fragile, delicate ornament, allot 1–5 points for the handling of media in details.

5 for *balance:* assuming 1 = concentration of ornament in a few odd places, 5 = ornament evenly distributed, made an integral part of total design, allot 1–5 points for balanced relationship of decorative to structural features.

It then appears that "scores" of 10–20 points correspond roughly to what is conventionally defined as the William and Mary, 20–30 the Queen Anne, 30–40 the Chippendale–Georgian, and 40–50 the Adamesque–Federal phases of classical evolution. But when we come to correlate the "scores" of given buildings with the traditionally accepted chronological limits of these four phases as accepted in furniture—roughly, the four quarters of the 18th century—an interesting and significant complication appears. It turns out that while advance-guard architecture in the South generally corresponds—i.e., great plantation houses and official buildings "scoring" 20–30 points in Virginia, South Carolina, and Maryland will usually be found to date in fact c.1725–50, and so on—dates must be pushed on both the lower in the social scale and the farther north we go. Thus while scores of 20–30 generally indicate a date of c.1725–50 in aristocratic Southern architecture, corresponding buildings in upper-class Philadelphia usually are datable c.1735–60; if products of the mercantile society of New York, Newport, or Boston, c.1740–60; buildings of middle-class origin anywhere, urban or rural, c.1750–75.

A similar complication is evident on analyzing comparable examples of furniture from different regions. The three Queen Anne chairs illustrated here (62 A, B, C), all are attributed to 1730–50; the three Chippendale (63 A, B, C), to c.1740–60. Yet in both phases those from Philadelphia "score" significantly higher than those from Newport or New York, and they in turn show classical principles more developed than the Massachusetts pieces.

The picture of 18th-century American culture such an analysis suggests is rather different from the usual one; it implies new ideas and principles being introduced consistently earlier in the South than the North, and the great Southern planters being consistently more "progressive" in this sense than the Northern merchants. Yet on reflection it is only what we might expect. What is involved here is the familiar and universal phenomenon of cultural lag—i.e., the lag between inception of ideas by (to borrow the Toynbeean phrase) a "creative minority," and their general acceptance in broad segments of society. Assuming that for all practical purposes in this case the source of ideas—of classical

forms and spirit—is London, the time of their appearance and acceptance in America will be conditioned by the availability of knowledge about those ideas and the degree of receptivity to them in any given region. And economic basis, social structure, and religious background all would tend to make Southern plantation society more favorably disposed to the classical mind than any other class or region. The classical tradition being essentially a state of mind rather than a matter of taste, its development involves more than mere visual acquaintance with classical forms in some guidebook; it takes intellectual understanding of the rationale behind them. Builders who do not realize how classical forms are determined by intelligible relationships to one another and to the whole will betray it in their work, just as patrons who merely want furniture that is up-to-date, without the rightness of classical forms being self-evident to them, will surely betray that in their willingness to accept perpetuations of the additive principle, verticality, structural directness, and so on. Proper comprehension of classical principles demands a degree of leisure, travel, and resources much commoner in aristocratic plantation society than among the busy merchants of Northern ports, and to all intents and purposes out of reach of the middle classes generally. With these considerations in mind, it is not surprising to find in the 18th-century architecture and furniture of classical America six more or less distinct cultural strata represented, in each of which classical principles are realized predictably later in practice. Taking examples necessarily restricted in number and arbitrary in selection, we find a pattern roughly as follows:

(1) *Southern Plantation Society.* Almost from the beginning, we find Southern planters, and the upper class of Charleston and Annapolis who move in their orbit, furnishing houses with silver, china, plate, glass, rugs, and furniture bought direct by agents handling their shipments of tobacco and rice in the port of London, or

A

B

C

62. THREE QUEEN ANNE CHAIRS
Henry Ford Museum, Dearborn, Michigan.

(A) From Philadelphia, attributed to 1740–60; (B) from Rhode Island, attributed to 1740–60; (C) from New England (Massachusetts), attributed to 1730–50.

When the comparative evolution of basic classical principles in such examples is analyzed, it becomes apparent that on almost all counts the Philadelphia chair is most advanced—visually unified through correspondence of curves in stiles, splat, legs, seat; already employing mahogany for more precise sculptural effects, including claw-and-ball foot (the other two chairs are walnut still), proportions squarer. The Massachusetts chair, with William and Mary stiffness and verticality still apparent in its back, and the additive principle persisting in its stretchers (evidenced both by their continued presence and by their forms), is most retardataire; the Newport example in between.

179

A

B

63. THREE CHIPPENDALE CHAIRS
Henry Ford Museum, Dearborn, Michigan.

(A) From Philadelphia, attributed to 1760–80; (B) from New York City, attributed to 1760–80; (C) from Salem, Massachusetts, attributed to 1760–80. It is probable that the first two were made before the Revolution, the last after it. Again classical principles appear most highly evolved in the Philadelphia piece—more balanced distribution of ornament, three-dimensional conception of the splat as composed of forms overlapping in space, contrasted with the essentially uniplanar concept evident in the other two; claw-and-ball organically realized with sculptural precision, in contrast to claws essentially resting on a flattened ball characteristic of Massachusetts; horizontal accent provided by flaring corners of back cresting, making the back visually a square (even though actual ratio of height to width of all these chair backs is about the same. In total height-to-width Philadelphia example is slightly more vertical—41½″ x 22½″ vs. 38″ x 21⅞″. The New York example we could call, like the New York architecture of the time, "more an ostentatious tour de force than a spontaneous manifestation of the classical mind."

C

through factors and merchants coming direct from London to them. By the time George Washington sent his well-known order to London in 1755 for "a Mahogany bedstead with carved and fluted pillars . . . six mahogany chairs with gothic arched backs . . . a fine neat, mahogany serpentine dressing table with mirrors and brass trimmings . . ." the practice was commonplace. Almost from the beginning, too, we find records of English-born and English-trained cabinet-makers settling and working in the South alongside such famous English-born or English-trained architects and builders as John Ariss, Ezra Waite, William Buckland, and John Hawks; P. H. Burroughs compiled an impressive list of them in *Southern Antiques*. As a result, Southern plantation architecture and furniture followed the pace of classical evolution in England at a consistently close interval of time throughout most of the first two centuries of American history.

Any sequence of great Southern houses will show the pattern very well. Making a William and Mary transition from medieval to classical traditions comparable to that seen in the official buildings at Williamsburg is Mulberry plantation house at Moncks Corner, South Carolina (c.1714), for instance; or Stratford in Westmoreland County, seat of the Lees of Virginia (c.1725). Mulberry represents a provincial but unmistakable variant of Baroque planning, with side "wings" coalesced and simplified into projecting corner pavilions that in principle at least encompass a court and so express controlled command of environment; curiously shaped pavilions like these can be seen in the gatehouses and garden buildings of many a late-17th-century mansion in England. Stratford's plan echoes these same mansions with their wide forecourts and flanking wings, and like them, goes back to palaces of mid-16th-century Italy; its forms have heavy projections comparable to the bulbous spools and turnings on William and Mary furniture; its doorways embody in a provincial yet significant way the basic staged Baroque principle of constriction and release; its chimneys are no longer additive clusters of stacks in the medieval tradition, but distinct forms, each treated in the manner of classical columns with bases, shafts, and terminal caps set in a co-ordinated relationship to the rest by balanced brick arches; and it has characteristic medieval vestiges, too, like the vertically proportioned windows and brickwork patterned independently of the total design.

In the Queen Anne period there is in Virginia alone a whole galaxy of houses so comparable to Westover that it sometimes seems one architect might have designed them all—Nelson Hall in Yorktown (c.1740), Cleve (c.1750), Wilton (1753), and, greatest of all, Carter's Grove (1750–53). And, of course, the Chippendale–Georgian forms of Gunston Hall were imitated, rivaled, surpassed in every province; architecturally, this was the South's great hour. In South Carolina they appeared as early as c.1738 in a two-story portico of superimposed Doric and Ionic columns projecting from the recessed center section of Drayton Hall on the Ashley; by 1765–9, when Ezra Waite, "Civil Architect, House-builder in general, and carver from London," built Miles Brewton's town house with hipped roof and comparable two-story portico, they were commonplace. You could see an elegant display of them in the palace at New Bern which North Carolina Governor Tryon brought John Hawks (1751–1790) from England to construct for him; the command of three-dimensional concepts evident in its colonnades, projecting pedimented central section, and free-standing portico, and the awareness of newer stylistic trends revealed in the horizontality of its pronounced belt coursing and low-hipped roof, made Tryon's Palace one of the most advanced pieces of design in the country. In rural Maryland Governor Sharpe had the very advance-guard Whitehall built for him by Horatio Anderson in 1764, with giant portico extending the full height of the building and a plan based on Palladio's "Roman Country

64. COMPARATIVE CLASSICAL EVOLUTION IN TWO DOORWAYS

(A) Gilead, Connecticut, c.1750; (B) 61 Beacon Street, Boston. In rural Connecticut clas-sical principles are still largely misunderstood at mid-century—verticality is predominant, Queen Anne robustness represented in bolection mould-ings and broken cornice, but in naïve misinter-

pretations; *classical capitals are rendered as almost medieval flat patterns; the whole composition clings to the plane of the wall. Compare with this the Adamesque–Federal style fifty years later—three-dimensional space-embracing composition, delicacy of detail (colonnettes, iron railing, low-relief ornament), predominantly horizontal emphasis.*

House"; in Annapolis, William Buckland and his followers built a whole series of elegant Chippendale–Georgian town houses, of which the Hammond House is most famous. And in Virginia there was one great mansion after another—Fielding Lewis's Kenmore at Fredericksburg; George Washington's Mount Vernon; John Tayloe's Mount Airy, designed by Virginia-born and English-trained John Ariss (c.1725–1799), who drew his ideas from Gibbs's *Book of Architecture* and William Adam's 1750 *Vitruvius Scotticus*, but significantly picked out and emphasized precisely those three-dimensional concepts in Gibbs that earlier American Queen Anne designers had not yet been prepared to recognize and appreciate.

No sooner had Mount Airy been completed (1758–62), however, than Thomas Jefferson's first designs, for Brandon (c.1765), made it almost obsolete. Anticipating Adamesque–Federal horizontality, Brandon pointed up what a curious persistence of vertical effect resulted from Ariss's apparently slight and inconsequential departures from his model in the relative size and number of windows, and the grouping of chimneys in the center; the lightness of Brandon's forms showed how much of Queen Anne robustness Mount Airy retained, for all the three-dimensionality of its open-porched façades. In Virginia development was so smooth, so sure, so fast, that the third and fourth phases of the classical mind were beginning to overlap, the more as the cultural lag between England and the Old Dominion steadily lessened. Nor did the Revolution end the process. To be sure, it marked the beginning of the decline of the plantation system, so that post-Revolutionary Southern mansions were more and more representative of the interest and taste of a rising mercantile class; inevitably, too, the South was more affected by the break with England than other regions less closely following the cycle of English taste. But still in architecure like Manigault's in Charleston or the houses Jefferson designed for his friends and neighbors, the South continued

to pace classical standards for at least a generation more.

Or we might consider a sequence of Southern churches. In the first quarter of the 18th century, a South Carolina church as small as St. James's at Goose Creek (1711) or one as large as St. Philip's, Charleston (begun 1710, completed c.1721, demolished 1835), reveals, in symmetrically balanced façades, precisely self-contained elements, and systematic correspondence of design, a spirit that justifies the claim of either to be the "first Georgian church in the colonies," and typifies the William and Mary phase of classical evolution. As early as 1732 Christ Church in Lancaster County, Virginia, is a perfect monument to the second, Queen Anne phase. Its builder, "King" Carter, attempted to emulate the chapels of ease of great English lords not only by stipulating a special family pew and burial places in the chancel forever (his body was buried there, under a great marble tomb, in the English fashion), but by making it a demonstration of up-to-date art patronage: an almost perfectly symmetrical central-type building, its every part integrated in one self-contained whole by systematic proportion and visual correspondences in flared eaves, convex steps, cut-stone sills, paneled walnut doors, rubbed brick dressings. In short, the classical ideal of a world ordered in precise, measurable human terms made manifest, a church glorifying God by showing forth the divine powers of Reason with which He has endowed His creatures.

Then there are Chippendale–Georgian churches like St. James's, Santee, South Carolina (1768), with low-hipped and finely proportioned block and balancing porticos front and back. Or Pohick at Lorton, Virginia (1769–74), traditionally attributed to vestryman George Washington, though latterly by some to John Ariss— a perfect expression of the balance and clarity of the mature classical mind in its simple and almost square plan, its ornament at once elegant and sober, its insistence on precision and perfection extending, according to the vestry book

65. TRANSITIONS FROM MEDIEVAL TO CLASSICAL, IN VIRGINIA AND NEW ENGLAND

(A) Stratford, Westmoreland County, Virginia, ancestral home of the Lees of Virginia, built c.1725. A basically classical structure, with some medieval survivals in detail.

(65 B) Foster–Hutchinson house, Boston, begun c.1688 by Colonel John Foster from Buckinghamshire; occupied by Thomas Hutchinson as lieutenant governor and governor of Massachusetts on grounds that it was more magnificent than his official residence; severely damaged in Stamp Act riot of 1765; demolished 1833. In this view published 1836, only the façade represents the original structure, in all probability, and it is characteristic—a basically medieval conception, with classical detail added in an unorganic and misunderstood way.

66. COMPARATIVE QUEEN ANNE DOMES-TIC INTERIORS

(A) Carter's Grove, James City County, Virginia, built for Carter Burwell, c.1750–53. An extant account book records payments to David Minitree of Williamsburg and Richard Bayliss, supposedly a woodworker brought from England. Last of a series of great houses built by and for members of the Carter connection, it is very similar to the interiors of Westover. Seen here is the replica made for Thorne Miniature Rooms on exhibit at the Art Institute of Chicago. Such reconstructions, while lacking the authenticity only originals can provide, have at least one advantage: they permit, as originals do not, a visualization of the actual appearance of interiors as they were when new, with fresh paint, bright upholstery, unworn edges, and unscarred surfaces.

for July 8, 1778, even to the "stone coins" being thought "coarse grained and rather too soft" and so ordered to "be painted with white lead and oyle, which they think will make them sufficient . . . also . . . the rub'd bricks at the return of the windows ought to be painted as near as possible the same colour with the arches, and the director is desired to do the same accordingly." And if for obvious reasons there are no good examples of Adamesque–Federal Anglican churches from the plantation country, yet the Southern sequence may be considered completed by such a church as St. John's in Washington, which showed, in what Talbot Hamlin called its "superb and commanding unity" and "detail . . . of elegant simplicity," the taste of its Southern parishioners. As originally designed by B. H. Latrobe in 1815–16 (later alterations include addition of a Doric portico c.1820 and Gothic chantry by James Renwick, 1883), it was "definitely a unit, with the congregation the chief factor to be considered . . . humanist rather than mystical and as such . . . a perfect expression of its time"—and of the continuing advance-guard

(66 B) "Queen Anne Dining Room," Henry Francis du Pont Winterthur Museum. Thirty years after Queen Anne maturity in Virginia, the paneling of this room from the vicinity of Derry, New Hampshire, in the 1760s still shows vestiges of William and Mary thinness, verticality, naïveté in handling classical detail. More advanced, but still retardataire by Southern aristocratic standards, are the New York chairs, whose eccentric curves show a typically ostentatious exaggeration of classical forms at the expense of basic classical principles.

taste still maintained by Southerners throughout the Federal period.

(2) *Upper-class Philadelphia.* From Penn's example, as well as from their own continuing close relations with London—of which Jefferson was thinking when he called them "Protestant Jesuits . . . acting with one mind, and that directed by the mother society in England"—upper-class Quakers in Philadelphia soon developed and long maintained a tradition of cultivated taste modeled on English precedent. At the same time, their city's rapid growth into a populous cosmopolitan seaport soon brought to it a large number of Anglicans with cultural pretensions—British officials, wealthy merchants. Together, these people constituted an upper class which resembled the Southern landed and hereditary aristocracy in that ownership of land and trading facilities gave them ultimate control of the wealth of a lush and rapidly developing hinterland, and consequently something at least of the same kind of leisure to cultivate the arts and pursue questions of taste. But whereas Southern planters produced goods readily salable in Europe, and so dealt directly with London, Pennsylvania's wheat and leather had to be sold elsewhere, by carrying merchants; the Philadelphia aristocracy's dealings with London were at second hand, and more of their wealth stayed

at home. The result was a school of local craftsmen encouraged to work to highest standards and specifications, which by the mid-18th century had made Philadelphia the most advanced center of American-made arts. Inevitably, however, it was always—generally speaking—a little behind the pace set by English-trained artisans and imported art in the South.

Even in the William and Mary period, when Philadelphia was very new, this character was apparent in the contrast between buildings of comparable function and symbolic importance like the Virginia Governors' Palace and the Pennsylvania Proprietor's mansion-home on the Delaware. Given its earlier date, Pennsbury's river front was at least equally as advanced, if not more so, in incorporation of the new classical principles, but on closer examination it is evident that the incorporation is superficial; even on the river façade, diamond-paned upper window panels are a disturbing medievalism, while the land

67. CHIPPENDALE–GEORGIAN PUBLIC BUILDINGS IN NORTH CAROLINA

(A) Governor Tryon's Palace, New Bern. Built 1767–9 on the plans of English-trained John Hawks; destroyed 1798; seen here in 1958, under reconstruction, with the free-standing front portico not yet added.

(67 B) *Chowan County Courthouse, Edenton. Built 1767, possibly by a builder from Williamsburg.*

North Carolina before the Revolution was one of the poorest and most sparsely populated of the Southern provinces. Yet in Tryon's Palace it had one of the largest, most elegant, and stylistically most advanced houses in America; and in the Edenton courthouse, an example of mature Chippendale–Georgian design remarkable for unity, balance, co-ordination, and proportion.

front has relapsed entirely into the clapboarded and haphazardly fenestrated world of medieval tradition.

The same kind of comparison can be made between Westover and Stenton, the home James Logan (1674–1751) was building in Germantown about the same time (1728–34). Logan's position in Pennsylvania (wealthy lawyer, Penn's agent during any absences, Chief Justice, Secretary of the Province, etc.) was comparable to Byrd's in Virginia as regards social prestige and responsibility, but hardly in aristocratic pretensions, and Stenton shows it. Superficially, Stenton anticipates Westover in many respects. Its two-story façade with basement and attic, its proportion of height to width, and the pitch of its roof all are roughly the same, and represent the same degree of advance over an earlier type like Pennsbury that Westover shows over the Governors' Palace. In Stenton too evidences of the distinctive preferences of the new style can be recognized—curving front steps; the beginnings of brick pilasters articulating the façade; wider windows; solider dormers. But again, closer

68. COMPARATIVE QUEEN ANNE CHURCH EXTERIORS

(A) Christ Church, Lancaster County, Virginia. A subtle exercise in pure classical form, deceptive in its simplicity.

analysis shows much weaker grasp of fundamental classical principles. It is not so much that specifically classical detail is so conspicuously absent—no pilasters or entablature framing the doorway (it may originally have had a hood), unshaped blocks instead of proper modillions for the roof cornice; Quaker principles are enough to explain this simplicity. Not simplicity, but basically confused and feeble expression of the fundamental principles of classical design, is what puts this house stylistically so far behind those in Virginia. Flanking the door are two narrow windows, physically functioning as side lights for the entrance hall, but visually so reminiscent of medieval forms as to negate the classical impression of the fenestration as a whole. Because they are in effect windows, and not side lights, they do not in fact carry out the designer's

(68 B) Christ Church, Philadelphia, Pennsylvania. Begun 1727 as an enlargement of the first (1695, enlarged 1710–11) Anglican church in Philadelphia, it was built mainly during the 1730s, finally completed 1744, the tower added 1751–4. Records indicate that Dr. John Kearsley superintended the construction, whether of his own or some other design is uncertain. One "Mr. Harrison" designed the spire—196 feet high, one of the tallest in the British colonies— which was constructed by carpenters Robert Smith and John Armstrong; repaired by Smith in 1771, it was rebuilt after a fire in 1908. The wooden urns ordered by Dr. Kearsley from England and put in place 1736 are now replaced by cast-iron replicas. An ostentatious but more clumsily robust, fussier, and less essentially classical version of James Gibbs's London church architecture.

(68 C) First Baptist Meeting House, Providence, Rhode Island. Designed 1775 by Joseph Brown, following plates in James Gibbs's Book of Architecture; *the spire, executed by master carpenter James Sumner of Boston, is an almost exact copy of one of the alternate designs for St. Martin's-in-the-Fields. Here, however, for a congregation conservative by religious background and mercantile outlook, the style is roughly thirty-five years out of date, by comparison with upper-class Philadelphia.*

69. QUEEN ANNE CHURCH INTERIORS,
SOUTH AND NORTH

(A) Christ Church, Lancaster County, Virginia, built for "King" Carter, c.1732. Though hardly a single specifically classical detail is here in evidence, the furnishings and structure are so imbued with basic classical principles that the visual and conceptual unity of this church, effected through repetition of motifs, balance of accents, and systematic proportion, is apparent in any random view.

(69 B) Trinity Church, Newport, Rhode Island, built 1725-6, basically on the model of Old North, Boston (1722-3) by master carpen- ter Richard Munday; enlarged two bays, 1762. In details more classical than Christ Church, Lancaster County; in basic understanding of classical principles of structure and unity, less.

(69 C) Christ Church, Philadelphia, interior. Largely built in the 1730s, with some changes by Thomas U. Walter in 1834. The wineglass pulpit made in 1769 by John Folwell, whom W. M. Hornor (The Blue Book, Philadelphia Furniture, 1935) called "the Thomas Chippendale of America" because of his proposal in 1775 to publish an American version of Chippendale's work, to be called "The Gentleman and Cabinet-Maker's Assistant."

apparent intention of balancing the windows above them; instead, the symmetrical relationship between first- and second-story openings is frustrated. Finally, the lack of any effective horizontal belt coursing means that the over-all patterned effect of the brickwork dominates the façade visually, destroying whatever articulation it may have.

Or again, we could compare "King" Carter's Christ Church in Virginia with Christ Church, Philadelphia, begun 1727 and built mainly during the 1730s; i.e., at about the same time. Larger and far more lavish than its Virginia namesake, the Philadelphia church is a more striking demonstration, too, of the way the Anglican church kept American civilization in the mainstream of English culture, for here, in the Friends' very citadel, is introduced all the "pomp" and "worldliness" of fashionable St. Martin's-in-the-Fields in London. Comparison of the two soon makes it apparent, however, that the classical idiom is not yet as natural a speech to upper-class Philadelphians as to the planters of the South. Christ Church, Philadelphia, did

70. QUEEN ANNE MANSIONS OF NEW HAMPSHIRE

(A) The McPhedris–Warner house, Portsmouth, built for Captain Archibald McPhedris, 1718–23; roof remodeled later, possibly 1762. The original façade design may have come direct from England; McPhedris was a Scot who came to the province as an adult, made a fortune in the fur trade, became a member of Governor John Wentworth's council and married the Governor's daughter Sarah. House and man both give dramatic evidence of the change in New England's social structure, as its economy turned from land to sea and its leadership passed from Puritan elder to merchant and trader.

indeed manifest throughout a consistent robustness of relief and fondness for bold curves characteristic of Queen Anne principles; but on the exterior particularly the mastery of classical co-ordination evident in the Virginia church was lacking; visual unity is established mainly by sheer profuse repetition of pilasters, Palladian windows, urns, and other ornamental detail. Essentially this design is a collection of elements picked out of Gibbs's *Book of Architecture* rather than an organic whole, assembled by expedient agreement rather than according to any controlling proportional system. The tower looks like the afterthought that it is. Even the urns along the roof line, which Dr. Kearsley evidently conceived as a particularly elegant classical touch, in fact function to the opposite effect—they destroy precisely that clear definition of outline which is one of the hallmarks of the classical mind.

Brilliant though Philadelphia's great galaxy of Chippendale–Georgian cabinetmakers was, you can tell from dates alone that their work must always have been somewhat behind current

(70 B) John Paul Jones house, Portsmouth. Built c.1758 by Gregory Purcell, sea captain and merchant, who in 1759 married the niece of Governor Benning Wentworth, it shows McPhedris's example translated into the local architectural vernacular, a quarter-century later.

197

71. COMPARATIVE QUEEN ANNE FAÇADES
(A) Stenton, home of James Logan (1674–1751), wealthy lawyer and Penn's agent in Pennsylvania during the Proprietor's absences, built in Germantown 1728–34. An early example of what soon became the common practice of substantial Philadelphians—building mansion houses in the country north and west of the nascent metropolis.

(71 B) East façade, Isaac Royall house, Medford, Massachusetts. Added by Isaac Royall to a 17th-century brick house, 1733–7. In the years 1747–50 Isaac Royall, Jr., added a west façade, and thus painfully completed the "classicization" of the family mansion.

English fashions being imported direct to the South. Thomas Affleck (d. 1795) arrived from Scotland in 1763, at which time Benjamin Randolph (c.1735–c.1800), James Gillingham (1736–1781), Jonathan Gostelowe (1745–1795), and Thomas Tufft (c.1740–1788) were only in their twenties. Others, like Quaker William Savery (1721–1788), were often *retardataire* for sociological reasons; Chippendale–Georgian furniture continued fashionable in some Philadelphia circles, indeed, well past the Revolution. And the Chippendale–Georgian mansions of Philadelphia were their counterparts in style.

Not until the 1770s do examples comparable to Southern houses of the 1750s and 60s begin to appear in the Delaware Valley. Lansdowne, built for William Penn's grandson John when he was governor of Pennsylvania (c.1773, destroyed 1854), was typical, with its proto-Adamesque three-sided wing, and two-story portico still rather heavy in proportions and still not spatially related to the wall behind. As for such famous houses as Mount Pleasant in Fair-

mount Park (1761–2), Port Royal in Frankford (1764), or the Corbit House in Odessa, Delaware (c.1773), they represent not so much the cultural level of the proprietary and official class as the growing influence of merchants in Philadelphia. Mount Pleasant, built for Scottish trader John Macpherson, ostentatiously imitated the "grand mansion manner" of the South with a composition of main block and flanking dependencies; it was stuccoed and quoined to produce a Palladian stone effect, and displayed what was even then considered a rather vulgarly *nouveau-riche* luxuriance of ornamental detail. Yet the façade that seemed so grand in Philadelphia, with its projecting center section dominated by a great Palladian window, was in comparable Southern mansions relegated to the garden; it is very similar to the rear façade of the Miles Brewton house in Charleston, for instance. And so throughout; despite its show of advanced detail, Mount Pleasant is *retardataire* in all basic respects—relative proportions of block and details more vertical; entrance set in

72. MERCANTILE PALLADIAN ELEGANCE

(Left) *Detail of main entrance, Mount Pleasant, Fairmount Park, Philadelphia, built for Captain John Macpherson, 1761–2. Palladian window and other detail treated with Queen Anne robustness, largely confined to the plane of the wall.*

(Above) *Drawing by Eugène Pierre du Simitière (1768) of the Redwood Library in Newport, Rhode Island, as originally built on the designs of Peter Harrison in 1748, to house the books purchased through Abraham Redwood's gift to the city of £500. Essentially an assemblage of Palladian motifs, drawn by Harrison plate by plate out of books he owned—Edward Hoppus's* Palladio, *Isaac Ware's* Designs of Inigo Jones and Others, *Kent's* Designs of Inigo Jones.

the plane of the wall, not moulded in space; even entrance steps no more than faintly suggesting mature spatial complexities; all sculptural elements heavier and reminiscent of Queen Anne robustness. Full realization of Chippendale–Georgian principles was similarly limited in the house Robert May of Philadelphia built for Quaker tanner and merchant William Corbit in Odessa. Its proportions are appropriately horizontal; its ornamental detail—"Chinese Chippendale" roof railing, dormer frames, and the like—appropriately light and "correct." Its façade elements were carefully balanced, even to the shutters being black above and white below (a local characteristic), to serve both a decorative and a functional purpose. Originally, before connecting passages were added, the Corbit

house was a self-contained block achieving that nice separation of building from surroundings so characteristic of the mature classical mind. But full three-dimensionality is not achieved. This façade is essentially conceived in two dimensions, its details kept within a single plane. And this *retardataire* concept is attributable, again, not so much to William Corbit's "Quaker simplicity" precluding any such ostentatious feature as a free-standing portico, as to the basic conservatism that almost always and almost everywhere characterizes the architecture and furniture of the mercantile class to which he belonged.

(3) *Mercantile Society.* Already in 17th-century New England we have seen how the rising merchant class tended to be conservative by

temperament and circumstance, content to follow at a safe distance whatever trends of taste were set by hereditary and landed aristocracy, whether in England or the provinces. And it remained so throughout the following century, a century during which the merchant class grew steadily in power and influence everywhere except the South, and after the Revolution aspired to become an aristocracy itself, even in Charleston, Norfolk, and Savannah.

You can see early examples of this conservatism in the Governors' Houses of Massachusetts: the Foster–Hutchinson house, begun c.1688; and Peter Sargeant's mansion of the late 1670s, remodeled in 1728 as Province House, the official Royal Governors' residence. In 19th-century drawings they look at first, and have often been called, surprisingly advanced in design. Yet appearances are deceptive, and when we come to analyze what is known of these vanished houses, most of their advanced features begin to melt away. We discover that so far from being transformed from a Jacobean manor to a Georgian mansion by one grand gesture in 1728, Province House was remodeled in several stages, in none of which a portico is mentioned; after the Revolution the house was used by the state and for private business in various ways, so that the "advance-guard" portico may well belong to the 19th century, as what we can judge of its proportions in fact suggest. Province House in the 1730s must in fact have presented a primitively naïve appearance; there was little resemblance to the disciplined co-ordination of the Williamsburg Palace, let alone anything later in Virginia, in its façade composed of rows of different-sized windows, its third story obviously squeezed in later under the eaves, with a jumble of minuscule dormers and outsize cupola above it, and the whole capped by Shem Drowne's grotesque glass-eyed, pot-bellied, mighty-bowed Indian weather vane.

As for the Foster–Hutchinson house, its roof was at least damaged by fire in 1748, and rioters protesting the Stamp Act in 1765 destroyed it

completely; one eyewitness reported how "the Governor . . . saw crow-bars and axes busy on the roof of his magnificent dwelling" and how "down fell the magnificent cupola, crushed to a thousand atoms." Presumption is strong, then, that the astonishingly low-pitched roof and balustrade above the eave, supposedly so far ahead of their time, were in fact replacements made just before or more probably somewhat after the Revolution, precisely in the Adamesque–Federal period when they could be expected. And in terms of basic classical principles, this was an even more primitive building than Province House, its giant stone pilasters and other "classical details" notwithstanding. For designers who understand how the form of classical capitals is determined by their effecting a transition from load to support do not terminate pilasters with quaint ornamental swags and garlands like these, or so render the entablature above them as to make it seem the shaft grows through instead of culminates in them. Neither do they set pilasters in from the edge of a building so that instead of defining its outline and making it self-contained they seem merely attached to the wall; nor again do they tie windows together in bundles of three, making them seem to float like flotsam on water. There is classical detail here, in short, but not classical principles; applied decoration, not articulated order. This is still medieval language spoken with an affected classical accent, not the other way round. As such, it is the real expression of New England culture in the age of William and Mary.

Advance-guard detail that turns out to be superficial or added later, basically *retardataire* principles—this is the architectural expression of mercantile society throughout classical America. New England, as might be expected, has particularly striking examples of it.

The McPhedris–Warner house in Portsmouth, New Hampshire, for instance. As it stands now, it looks to be in advance of contemporary Queen Anne designs like Westover or Stenton—well-balanced façade, unified by repetition of curved motifs in doorway pediment, relieving arches of the windows, and dormer pediments alternating with triangular pediments in the newest Palladian fashion; brick belt courses for horizontal effect; low-pitched gambrel roof with balustrade and cupola. But on closer analysis, we find that as originally built in 1718–23 the house was roofed like Restoration London house types, by parallel gables with a deep valley between which produced a decidedly vertical and vestigially medieval effect; that it still has a clapboarded north wall and attached ell in the 17th-century New England tradition; that whatever advanced classical principles its façade embodies came not from local artisans, but from the background of its builder, Scottish sea captain Archibald McPhedris, who came to the province as an adult. Where we find the characteristic expression of the state of New England culture in the Queen Anne period is not in this product of accidental circumstance, but in regional statements of the universal classical idiom as understood by local builders and patrons, like its neighbors the John Paul Jones or Wentworth–Gardner houses in Portsmouth. They repeat the general proportions and more obvious classical motifs of the McPhedris house—alternating Palladian dormers, window pediments. But they repeat them with crude naïveté, and in the traditional material of the region, wood; they ignore niceties like articulating belt courses and balanced fenestration—the windows are paired and pushed up under gables as the windows of 17th-century New England houses were before them; and they achieve such regional adaptations of the Queen Anne style forty years later—in the 1750s.

Or the Hancock house, in Boston. Thomas Hancock, who built it between 1737 and 1740, was an importer of what earlier, more Puritan generations in New England would have called "luxury goods"; he had something like the Virginia planters' freedom of intercourse with England, and, like them, drew heavily on English imports in furnishing his house, from window glass and Dutch tile to yew trees for his garden; his successor, John Hancock, was the nearest thing to an aristocrat in the Virginia sense in New England. Here at least, we might suppose, is one merchant's house comparable to the mansions of Virginia. Yet for all that its details were correct enough—properly robust Queen Anne broken cornice with scrolls, attached columns with strong projecting brackets, boldly terminating railings—the way they were handled was characteristically *retardataire*. The turned balusters and knobs of the railing, for instance, curiously recall the sort of crude naïveté shown in the Foster–Hutchinson house sixty or seventy years before; they are William and Mary or even, considering how the ornament seems piled on, Jacobean in feeling. Furthermore, the artisans who assembled these details—master mason Joshua Blanchard, joiner William More, and the rest—were not British imports as they might have been in contemporary Virginia, but products of local tradition who seem hardly to have been aware of classical principles of composition at all. They pushed windows so far up under the eaves that classical façade balance was ruined; they spaced dormers so widely that all visual contact among them was lost; one pediment—if we may trust the pictures—was a half-circle rather than elliptical in form, the others almost equilateral triangles.

Or the Royall house at Medford. What could be a more complete misunderstanding of classical principles than this east façade of 1733–7, with its miscellaneous assemblage of more or less classical motifs all piled up together in an almost Jacobean way, its three stories of windows added one above the other to create a completely vertical accent run right up to the eaves, its door looking as if someone stuck it in as an afterthought, and nowhere any sense of balance or spacing? Nor is the west façade of 1747–50 much better. Still the proportions of the whole are vertical; still the third-story windows hang down from the eaves; still the designer shows almost no understanding of the function

"one of six Queen-Anne chairs by Job Townsend [1699–1765]," its cabriole legs and slipper feet were combined with turned and serpentine stretchers of William and Mary or even earlier character, while its stiles rose with almost medieval steepness and narrowness, then suddenly bulged out at the cresting in an awkward Queen Anne half-circular curve.

Or consider again, in the next generation, the curiously *retardataire* way Peter Harrison handled motifs borrowed from Gibbs and Palladio. Possibly the local artisans who executed Harrison's work were responsible for the marked survival of Queen Anne qualities in so much of it—the kind of robustness, strongly marked projections and angles, and heaviness generally evident in everything he designed. But they can hardly be held accountable for his consistent failure to grasp the three-dimensional implications and principles of co-ordination inherent in the models he followed. Harrison's ingenious

and much-admired adaptation of a Palladian scheme of intersecting pediments for the façade of the Redwood Library (1749–50) is a good case in point. When Palladio used it on Venetian churches, he made the first pediment so shallow, and the receding planes established by the second so complex, that both could be seen together from any angle of approach; i.e., he conceived them in a spatial relationship. Harrison, however, copied the motif so cold from a book that his intersecting pediments are visually effective only from directly in front; from any other angle the second pediment and the little wings built to establish it appear as functionally and visually meaningless excrescences. King's Chapel in Boston (1749–54) is another example. Only an a priori assumption that Harrison was a great and advanced designer could justify seeing much in this design beyond a misunderstood adaptation of some Gibbsian church like St. Martin's-in-the-Fields—a collection of motifs up-

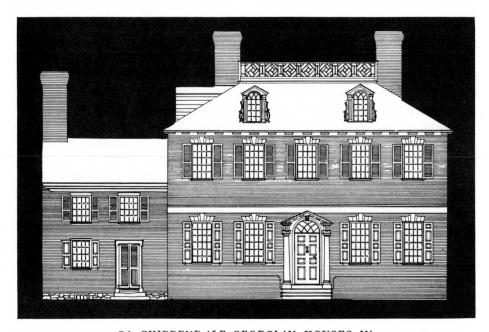

74. CHIPPENDALE–GEORGIAN HOUSES IN
THE DELAWARE AND HUDSON VALLEYS
(A) William Corbit house, Odessa, Delaware, built c.1773 by Robert May of Philadelphia. Maintained by the Winterthur Corporation.

to-date enough in themselves, but added together without perception of their integral relationships, almost as Munday added tower to church body at Trinity in Newport. It is the same characteristic that distinguishes Chippendale furniture in Newport—advanced details, handled in a *retardataire* and naïve way. As you can compare Harrison's architecture with Philadelphia work by, say, Robert Smith in the years 1750–75, so you can compare Goddard–Townsend furniture of the same period with comparable Philadelphia pieces, and find in each case relatively heavier forms, more vertical proportions, ornament less evenly distributed, details less classically correct.

New York, too, developed a distinctive mercantile aristocracy. Based on intermarriages of old Dutch landowning families with English officials and merchants, it only began to mature in the Chippendale—Georgian period, when crude versions of the Queen Anne style like Philipse Manor at Yonkers (its several parts belonging variously to the 1730s, 40s, and 50s) or the Van Cortlandt house in New York (1748–9) were superseded by houses with such advanced architectural detail as the elegant Chinese lattice rail running around the eaves of Philip Schuyler's house in Albany (c.1761–2); the giant portico on the house Major Robert Morris and his wife, Mary Philipse, built in New York in 1765; or the two-story recessed entrance porch framed by Ionic pilasters, full entablature, and pediment that appeared on the Apthorpe house in New York c.1767. Remarkable though such features were, however, they could not disguise the characteristic conservatism of mercantile society. For along with these advanced details went others incongruously crude; they formed part of generally *retardataire* architectural compositions, in which persistence of Queen Anne fondness for heavy, robust forms was combined with misunderstanding of the full subtleties of Chippen-

(74 B) Apthorp house, New York, New York. Built c.1767, demolished c.1910.

dale–Georgian principles of proportion and total co-ordination of all elements in the design. They represented more an ostentatious tour de force than any spontaneous manifestation of the mature classical mind. And New York furniture, as represented by typical examples like the sets of chairs made for Sir William Johnson (two in Winterthur, one in the Garvan collection, Yale) and the Van Rensselaer family (Metropolitan Museum, New York), presumably by Gilbert Ash (1717–1785), has much the same character— ostentatiously elaborate Chippendale–Georgian carving on knees and back, along with rounded seats and other reminiscences of the Queen Anne phase.

Then came the Revolution, driving into exile much of the old aristocratic possessing class, upsetting the economic base of the rest, especially in the South, leaving the mercantile class in a position of at least temporarily unchallenged predominance in the country. The rise of that class was marked by wholesale shifts in economic, political, social, and cultural patterns. New England, earliest and most wholeheartedly mercantile stronghold, grew rapidly in importance, especially relative to the South; mercantile Baltimore, at the expense of aristocratic Philadelphia and Annapolis. Industrialization of Rhode Island and southern Massachusetts meant that Newport was displaced by Providence as economic and soon political capital of the region. Merchant-speculators opening up the Hudson and Mohawk valleys, and lands to the west, capitalized on New York's location at the entrance to the continent to make it the new nation's largest city. New political parties crystallized around support or opposition to mercantile-class interests. A new upper class began to form, filling the social vacuum left by Tories languishing in London, New Brunswick, or Upper Canada; in this age were founded the fortunes of the Proper Bostonians, the Astors and Vanderbilts of New York, the Biddles of Philadelphia, the du Ponts of Wilmington. As yet they were hardly the equals of their predecessors, however; in-

deed, as a result of the simultaneous collapse of the old direct tie with England and of the class which had maintained it, the cultural lag between America and Europe suddenly lengthened, so that at the beginning of the 19th century America was, in general, culturally more provincial than it had been fifty years before.

Postwar America, in short, was all in flux; and its arts reflected the prevailing confusion. Where before the war there had been, to all intents and purposes, a single homogeneous classical tradition, three divergent trends came in evidence after it. These we can best designate, perhaps, as the Adamesque–Federal proper, classical revival, and post-Georgian styles. One of them, the conscious revival of Graeco-Roman architecture for symbolic purposes, was so advance-guard as to be fundamentally outside the classical tradition altogether; its history forms a prelude to Victorian America. Post-Georgian art was correspondingly *retardataire*; it represented a perpetuation of Chippendale–Georgian forms well into the 19th century by what was left of the old possessing classes, and the more conservative element of the mercantile class. You can find post-Georgian architecture sporadically wherever older aristocratic families survived— in New Castle on the Delaware, for example, where George Read, Jr., built a house in 1803–4 which, except for a certain Adamesque–Federal delicacy of detail, might as well have been built in 1775; or in Jefferson County, West Virginia, where houses like Samuel Washington's Harewood (c.1803), in form not unlike Gunston Hall half a century earlier, recall how members of the Washington family tried to transplant the plantation system to the frontier, failed, and, as one writer delicately put it, "went peacefully to seed." As might be expected, however, the post-Georgian style was commonest among the merchant class of New England. Joseph Brown's work in Providence is one good example of it— his First Baptist Meeting House (1774–5), already half a century out-of-date as compared with, say, Christ Church in Philadelphia; his

75. POST–GEORGIAN MANSIONS

*(A) Joseph Nightingale house, Providence,
Rhode Island, c.1792. Based on a house built by
Joseph Brown for his brother John, 1786
(though possibly built by Caleb Ormsbee).*

*Joseph Brown, professor of philosophy at Rhode
Island College (later Brown University), was
essentially a mathematician and astronomer; he
belonged to the leading family in the mercantile
aristocracy of Providence, whose retardataire
taste Brown's work illustrates remarkably well.*

Joseph Nightingale house (1790s); his John
Brown house (1786), which John Quincy Adams, significantly enough, called "the most
magnificent and elegant mansion that I have
ever seen on this continent." The work attributed
to William Spratt in Connecticut is another; his
mansions for the social leaders of Farmington
(e.g., Samuel Cowles house, 1780) and Litchfield (e.g., The Lindens, 1790) are comparable
to up-to-date Philadelphia houses thirty years

(75 B) Harewood, built by Samuel Washington, brother of the President, near Charles
Town, West Virginia, c.1800. Despite some Adamesque–Federal features (doubled porch columns, and especially the drawing-room mantel),
in stylistic essentials the house is not too different from Gunston Hall, half a century before.

before. Post-Georgian furniture was common in
New England, too. Chippendale forms were perpetuated in Boston by John Cogswell, for example (active by 1769, d. 1818); in Connecticut
by Elijah Booth of Southbury (1754–1825) and
Eliphalet Chapin of East Windsor (1741–1807);
in New Hampshire (in an even more eccentri-
cally *retardataire* way) by the Dunlaps of Sal-
isbury. But even in New England, the majority
among the new mercantile aristocracy adopted
Adamesque–Federal classicism in the course of
the 1780s and 90s, and they made it a great and
enduring expression of their ascendancy during
the early Republic.

It is in New England, in fact, that Adamesque–Federal architecture can still be seen at
its best. This is the age when Charles Bulfinch
and his followers built the Adamesque–Federal

façades, with their contrasts of straight and
curved surfaces, lacy iron balconies, delicate
colonnettes and play of decorative elements in
low white relief against rosy brick walls that
still give distinction to the old streets on Beacon
Hill in Boston; when Samuel McIntire built and
furnished his elegant mansions for the merchant
princes of Salem; when the Boston–Salem school
of "classical" cabinetmakers flourished; when
the English-trained John Seymour (c.1738–
c.1820), and his son Thomas (1771–1848),
helped such local men as Stephen Badlam
(1751–1815), William Hook (1777–1867), Elijah Sanderson (1752–1825) and his brother
Jacob (c.1758–1810), William Lemon (d. 1827)
and Nehemiah Adams (1769–1840) to rise above
the traditional conservatism of their region and
eliminate the old cultural lag between New Eng-

land and the rest of the country. And for New England seaports generally, this was their finest architectural hour. Later Greek Revival growth rivaled but never surpassed the work of Russell Warren (1783–1860) in Bristol, John Holden Greene (1777–1850) in Providence, anonymous local builders in Newburyport and Kennebunk and Portsmouth—low oblong clapboarded mansions, their delicate white relief ornament set off against pastel yellows and greys, witnessing to the prosperity and spirit of the New England merchant class which organized the Hartford Convention. Country estates, too, survive, recalling Federalist mercantile pretensions to the status of English country gentlemen; only in particulars—like the strange absence of specifically Greek or Roman detail at Gore Place near Waltham, Massachusetts (c.1805), or the old habit of imitating stone in wood at Montpelier, near Thomaston, Maine (original c.1795, now reconstructed)—do they betray the fact that New England's new upper class was still not quite as sophisticated as it wished to be.

Adamesque–Federal art was by no means a regional affair, however. Wherever the merchant class flourished, its chosen Adamesque–Federal expression appeared; and merchants flourished everywhere. The mercantile wealth of this age built mansions on the outskirts of every great city. We get some idea of them from survivors like Gracie Mansion, now on East End Avenue at 88th Street in New York (c.1799); Lemon Hill and The Woodlands in Philadelphia (both substantially dating from the 1780s or 90s); Homewood in Baltimore (1801–2); The Octagon (designed by William Thornton for John Tayloe, Virginia aristocrat "engaged in the manufacture of iron, in ship-building, and in various other enterprises," and a violent Federalist in politics, 1798–1800), and Tudor Place (begun 1794 by Thornton for shipping merchant Francis Lowndes, completed 1815 for Thomas Peter and his wife, Martha Parke Custis) in Washington; Gabriel Manigault's architecture in Charleston; William Jay's in Savannah. Mercantile wealth largely patronized cabinetmakers like Henry Connelly (1770–1826) in Philadelphia, Duncan Phyfe (1768–1854) in New York, and many more. As this mercantile aristocracy of the early republic was the first truly national social class, and their Federalist party the first truly national political group to develop, so the Adamesque–Federal was America's first truly national style.

(4) *Middle Class.* In the 18th century, as in any other, only a small proportion of the total building done consisted of mansions, great public buildings, or fine furniture whose style was a matter of deliberate choice. Then as now, the great bulk of what was built was intended for people of humbler means and aspirations—what we can loosely call the "middle" and "lower" classes of society. By "middle class" architecture we mean here primarily the simpler, basically unpretentious buildings of tradesmen, artisans, and farmers substantial enough to own property and have a recognized place in the social scale, but content in matters of style to follow the lead of their "betters" at a considerable remove, to embody classical principles in simpler, broader, more general ways and forms. Most of the "old architecture" people see around them in the older parts of the United States belongs in this category; Illustration 80 shows a few typical examples. Usually all of the six basic classical principles are evidenced in one way or another, but in blurred form, often mixed up with vestigial survivals of medieval tradition, so that on stylistic analysis they "score" low in terms of their actual building dates—i.e., they may be as much as thirty, forty, even fifty years behind the most advanced level of taste in their times.

Perhaps the best example of "middle class" taste in furniture was the "Windsor" chair. As first introduced c.1725 in Philadelphia (for some decades the type was widely known as "the Philadelphia chair"), Windsors represented a precise parallel to middle-class Delaware Valley architecture, standardized for economy like the rows of houses built on the Restoration London

76. ADAMESQUE–FEDERAL IN SOUTH CAROLINA

(A) Gabriel Manigault house, Charleston, c.1790–1800.

plan; embodying in their directly expressed materials and construction the same sort of vestigial survival of familiar medieval tradition as the pent eave, diaper-patterned brickwork, and general verticality of, say, the William Hancock house at Hancock's Bridge (*37A*). In following decades, the pervasive classical mind of 18th-century America modified proportions and moulded legs and spindles into reasonably intelligible expressions of relationships between load and support. By the time delegates assembled for the First Continental Congress in Carpenters' Hall in 1774, and for the Second in Independence Hall a year later, Windsor chairs were provided for them which could be considered classical in principle, but half a century behind

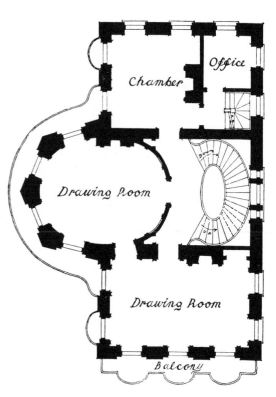

(76 B, C) Nathaniel Russell house, Charleston, street façade and second-floor plan, c.1803. Characteristic Adamesque–Federal play on spatial planes—in the recessed arches of the façade windows; in the oval drawing room; in the fly- *ing staircase. Despite the traditionally high Charleston house type, horizontality is emphasized by the use of balustrade, string courses, cornices, and by the equalization of the height of first and third stories.*

77. ADAMESQUE–FEDERAL IN THE MIDDLE ATLANTIC STATES

(A) Montebello, Baltimore, drawn by William Birch, c.1820. Samuel Smith, son of a wealthy Irish-born merchant who traveled in Europe 1772–5 and rose to the rank of brigadier general in the Revolutionary War, built Montebello after his own designs 1799–1800, naming it, following the pro-French fashion of the moment, after a French victory over the Austrians in 1800. With its three oval rooms, formal hall, and delicately thin decorative forms, it was the most advanced architecture in Baltimore when built. Demolished 1909.

(77 B) Du Pont Dining Room, H. F. du Pont Winterthur Museum. Winterthur was begun in 1827 as the home of James Antoine and Evelina Gabrielle du Pont Bidermann, named for Bidermann's ancestral city in Switzerland. Upon inheriting it in 1927 Henry Francis du Pont began to install there the examples of American craftsmanship he had been collecting since 1923. Winterthur continued to grow, eventually comprising over eighty rooms when made a public museum in 1950. In this room, however, are to be seen some of the original furnishings acquired by the family in its early American years, notably the dozen square-back Sheraton chairs. Remarkable also is the harmony of color in sideboard, table, chairs, and cabinets—a combination of reddish-orange, browns, and blacks deliberately reminiscent of Grecian vases.

78. BULFINCH'S BOSTON

(A) Beacon Street, showing a succession of façades with characteristic Adamesque–Federal alternating flat and curving planes, ironwork, delicate ornament. For a detail, see 64B.

(78 B) Faneuil Hall, a rebuilding and enlargement by Charles Bulfinch in 1805 of the 1762 building, which in turn was a rebuilding of the 1742 structure. With market stalls on the first floor, assembly hall and headquarters of the Ancient and Honorable Artillery Company above, it was successor in function to the Town House of 1657 (33B). In the background, the tower of the United States Customs House, a typical example of Beaux-Arts skyscraper design by the Late Victorian firm of Peabody & Stearns, 1913–15.

79. McINTIRE'S SALEM

(A) Pingree house, built on the designs of Samuel McIntire, 1804. Compare the very elementary play of spatial forms here with the sophistication of the Russell house in Charleston, built at the same time (76. B and C).

(79 B) Endicott Memorial Rooms, Pingree house, maintained by the Essex Institute. Furniture from the McIntire circle.

80. CLASSICAL EVOLUTION IN MIDDLE-CLASS ARCHITECTURE

(A) Jerusalem (Lutheran) Church, near Springfield, Georgia. Built 1767–9 by a congregation from Salzburg invited to Georgia by Governor Oglethorpe in 1734. With only general symmetry and balance suggesting the classical mind, and in broad outline reminiscent of Austrian village churches whence its builders' fathers had come, such a building suggests more the transition from medieval to classical traditions characteristic of the William and Mary phase of classical evolution than anything of the "high" Chippendale–Georgian style of its chronological time.

FACING PAGE:

(80 B) "Washington's Headquarters," Valley Forge, Pennsylvania. Built as the ironmaster's residence at Mount Joy (later Valley) Forge; at the time Washington stayed here (1777–8), owned by one John Potts. Though built c.1770, it is very similar to the Philadelphia house type of forty years and more before (compare the Collins Mansion in West Chester, 37B). Only the more advanced pedimental treatment of the side wall suggests its later date.

214

the times in style; analyze the kind of chairs advertised by Thomas Ash of New York in 1770, or John Kelso of Philadelphia in 1774, and you find that Windsors of the 1770s and 80s represent approximately the level of classical development achieved in upper-class furniture at the beginning of the Queen Anne phase.

(5) *Lower Class.* One of the striking characteristics of 18th-century American society is the absence of a genuine lower class in the European sense. Broadly speaking, and excepting the slave population, it was not until the 19th century—and not really until after the great post-Civil War European immigrations—that there was in the United States anything very comparable to a *lumpenproletariat,* a permanently submerged bottom stratum of society. "Lower class" in the 18th century means, then,

(80 C) Pierce homestead, Hillsborough, New Hampshire. Built c.1800 by Benjamin Pierce (1757–1839). Coming to Hillsborough to farm in 1786 after serving in the Revolutionary War, Pierce soon rose to wealth and influence, becoming twice governor of New Hampshire (1827–8 and 1829–30). Except for its low roof line and squarish plan (resembling the large and almost square two-and-a-half and three-story houses popular among New England merchants and shipowners in the Federal period), the house reflects—insofar as it has conscious "style"—the stage of evolution reached in aristocratic Southern or Pennsylvania architecture fifty years before.

(80 D) Alna Church and Meeting House, Maine. The woodwork of pulpit and balconies is classically proportioned, but the exposed framing timbers and treatment of spindles are curi- *ously reminiscent of medieval tradition; indeed, though built c.1804, this rural meeting house is not entirely different from 17th-century Old Ship Church in Hingham.*

either an urban poor whose living quarters may be shabby enough but hardly what we would call slums, or the "rural poor" of all descriptions—homesteaders eking out livings in the stony backwoods of New England, German and Scottish immigrants settling central Pennsylvania and the foothills of the Appalachians, Southern tenantry, early pioneers across the mountains. In their "country" furniture and their architecture—New England farmhouses like the Webster Homestead (6), the "Dutch" houses of the Hudson Valley, the homes of poor whites in the South—there can be no question of "style," classical or

any other. Even if they knew anything about it, temperament and circumstance alike would keep them building in the framework of inherited folk tradition. Not until the early 19th century do vaguely classical principles of proportion and a few classical details begin to appear, and then they linger on to the Civil War period and beyond, long after disappearing in higher social strata. And never at any time is there what could be considered a consistent development in them.

(6) *Western Frontier Society.* Architecture and furniture from the new territories and states

81. VESTIGIAL CLASSICISM IN THE 19th CENTURY

(A) "The Old Hitchcock Chair Factory on the Farmington River."

(81 B) "Hitchcock Rush Seat Side Chair."
The factory built c.1826 to house large-scale production of chairs by Lambert Hitchcock (1795–1852) at Riverton (originally Hitchcocksville), Connecticut, embodies the same sort of vaguely classical proportions and simplified classical forms as the chairs Hitchcock so successfully designed for a middle- and lower-middle-class market. This sort of post-Georgian classicism was common in early factory building.

being settled in the West in the decades after the Revolution can rarely be judged in terms of any systematic scheme of classical evolution, either. Much that is produced, obviously, is a lower-class expression; but even the more pretentious churches, courthouses, and homes of the emerging upper class generally show a confused mixture of post-Georgian, Adamesque–Federal, and later-neoclassical-revival principles. The three examples illustrated (83A, B, C) are typical. All of them ostensibly belong to the Adamesque–Federal phase of classical evolution, and display many of its characteristic principles—oval forms, delicate detail, and so on. But in all of them, too, there are inconsistencies which reveal that here on the frontier there could never be the degree of stability necessary to support a mature classical tradition. So in the Vermont church we are disconcerted to find columns, capitals, entablatures, and window frames of Gibbsian form and Queen Anne robustness next to an airy and spacious oval ceiling ringed with delicate mould-

82. *Clinton Inn, restored in Greenfield Village, Dearborn. Built 1831–2 as the first overnight stop on the Detroit–Chicago stagecoach, this inn was furnished with a variety of descendants of the 18th-century classical tradition, lingering on here among the lower classes—the sideboard, the fireplace, the clock, most of all the chairs. As late as 1835 farmers were still occasionally making Windsor-type chairs in their homes, and* chair shops and factories went on turning them out for decades more. These last-gasp Windsors often reverted to the low-backed form of their early ancestors, though with heavy-handed mouldings owing something to persistent Empire taste. Sometimes, too, they approximated the forms of "fancy" chairs, and were painted, decorated, or striped. They remained in use for ordinary offices, barber shops, hotel lobbies, and the like almost into the 1880s.

ing. In Samuel Polk's Columbia house, elegant French windows and finely detailed doorway are set in an ill-proportioned white brick box devoid of all but the most elementary pretentions to composition in space. The furniture of Thomas Worthington's Adena included not only elegant Adamesque–Federal pieces appropriate to the Virginia society of Berkeley County, whence he had come to Ohio in 1798, but also family heirlooms in Chippendale and Queen Anne, and the work of local artisans. And by the time a social and economic basis stable enough to permit spontaneous manifestation of the classical mind had developed in the West, self-conscious Victorian eclecticism had already set in; this is apparent even in such an overtly pure Adamesque–Federal example as the Taft house in Cincinnati (c.1820–21).

83. *CLASSICAL TRADITIONS ON THE WESTERN FRONTIER*

(A) First Congregational Church, Ben- *nington, Vermont. Built 1806 by Lavius Fill-* *more, using Pl. 33 of* The Country Builder's Assistant, *published by Asher Benjamin in 1797.*

(83 B) Samuel Polk house, Columbia, Tennessee. Early home of President James K. Polk, it was built by his father in 1816.

(83 C) Adena, Chillicothe, Ohio. Built for Thomas Worthington, first governor of Ohio, possibly on plans drawn for him by B. H. Latrobe; completed 1807. The sofa by Duncan Phyfe of New York, chairs attributed to Henry Connelly of Philadelphia; French wallpaper with delicate ornament and spatial illusion characteristic of Adamesque–Federal taste may have been part of the original furnishings of this room.

221

Of the six cultural strata in classical America, then, two fall outside any consistent pattern of evolution. But within the other four, the development is remarkably consistent. It is possible, in fact, to compose a table roughly correlating points of stylistic development with dates and regions somewhat as follows:

Points	Southern plantation society	Philadelphia upper-class society	Mercantile society (New York, Newport, Boston etc.)	Middle class, urban and rural
10–20	c.1700–1725	c.1715–1735	c.1720–1740	c.1725–1750
20–30	c.1725–1750	c.1735–1760	c.1740–1760	c.1750–1775
30–40	c.1750–1775	c.1760–1785	c.1760–1785	c.1775–1800
40–50	c.1775–1800	c.1780–1810	c.1785–1815	c.1790–1825

With some reservations—taking for granted that Southern plantation society is represented by imported English furniture, and remembering that furniture allows more scope for individual taste and expression and a much easier deviation from community norms than architecture—some such scheme could be applied to furniture also. Not that it is my intent to provide some kind of infallible scheme for dating 18th-century American art forms, of course. Far from it; exceptions and compromises are much too numerous and obvious. What is significant is that the American classical tradition develops consistently enough for any such pattern to be apparent at all. That we can so systematically trace the evolution of the classical mind in this remote outpost of Western civilization is the most striking evidence possible of that mind's depth, pervasiveness, and power. When Americans at the end of the 18th century looked back over their history and at the new nation they had created, and declared that in it the Roman Republic had come to rebirth, they were not acting out some romantic literary conceit; they were only expressing a truth that to them seemed self-evident. The proof of it was in the buildings and furniture they had all around them. The classical mind had shaped their world; the four phases of its evolution expressed four great stages in the growth of American civilization to maturity. And if we turn now from art to artists, from chairs and churches to the men who made them, we will find the same four phases again, expressing the evolution from artisans to individual artistic personalities in classical America.

NOTES

Quotations from P. H. Burroughs, *Southern Antiques* (Richmond, 1931). A good idea of the number, varied origins, and quality of cabinetmakers working in the Old South is gained from the references to them Burroughs published. For example, the 1768 advertisement in the *South Carolina Gazette* by Abraham Pearce, "cabinetmaker and carver from London," that "orders from the Country or any of the Northern provinces will be punctually dealt with." (Pearce later did carving for Thomas Elfe, apparently leaving Charleston with the British forces in 1782). Or again,

So much was foreign training taken as a matter of course, that Isaac Johns [who in 1796 was a cabinetmaker in Baltimore] according to the *Maryland Journal* felt called upon to explain that although he "cannot boast of a European education" he had "served his apprenticeship to William Moore in this town. . . ." [p. 10]

That Negro slaves made some of the "native" furniture in the South is unquestionable; but in most shops they probably functioned as more or less well-trained assistants rather than the actual designers or makers. For example, Ethel Hall Bjerkoe in *The Cabinetmakers of America* (1957), p. 88, cites the will of English-trained Thomas Elfe, leading cabinetmaker of Charleston (b. c.1719 in London, in Charleston by 1747, d. 1755), leaving his son Thomas Elfe, Jr. (1759–1825), his father's tools, workbench "and three negro fellows brought up to my Business named Joe, Jack, and Paul"—the implication being that they are merely additional pieces of equipment.

On the Quaker aristocracy, their close ties with England, and their "satisfying their hunger for esthetic pleasure as well as their desire for the conspicuous display of wealth appropriate to their station in the world" by "fine materials . . . sound workmanship . . . harmonious proportions," see particularly Frederick B. Tolles, "The Quaker Esthetic," *Quakers and the Atlantic Culture* (1960), Chap. V. On the New York mercantile aristocracy, see Anson Phelps Stokes, *Memorial History of New York*, quoted by Dixon Wecter, *The Saga of American Society* (1937), and Cleveland Amory, *Who Killed Society?* (1960):

The Bayards, Van Cortlandts, Roosevelts, Livingstons, Schuylers, and Rhinelanders were in the sugar-refining business. . . . Barclays, Rutgers and Lispenards were brewers. General traders and shippers were Verplancks, Whites, Murrays, Baches, and Franklins, while Beekmans, Van Zandts, Clarksons, Setons and Buchanans were importers or dealers in dry-goods. . . .

The Washingtons' settlement in West Virginia is described by T. J. Wertenbaker, *The Old South* (1942), p. 214.

Quotations on St. John's church from T. F. Hamlin, *Benjamin Henry Latrobe* (1955), p. 462–3; on the Washingtons in West Virginia from a syndicated article in the "Journeys to Great Homes" series by Louise Hubbard, October 1956. Harrison's *retardataire* dependence on motifs from Gibbs's *Book of Architecture* and *Rules for Drawing* is admirably illustrated in plates from Carl Bridenbaugh, *Peter Harrison* (Chapel Hill, 1949); on Palladio's command of spatial composition, see the discussion by R. Wittkower, *Architectural Principles in the Age of Humanism* (London, 1952). For a different interpretation of King's Chapel in Boston, see Priscilla Metcalf, "Boston before Bulfinch: Harrison's King's Chapel" (*JSAH*, XIII, 1, pp. 11–14, 1954).

On Windsor chairs, see especially T. H. Ormsbee, *Early American Furniture Makers*, pp. 105–13, and Carl W. Drepperd, *Handbook of Antique Chairs* (1948), Chap. IV, "American Windsor Chairs." It is worth noting, perhaps, that the first cathedra in Christ Church, Philadelphia, was a Windsor; it is illustrated on p. 39 of *The Story of Christ Church, Philadelphia* (Philadelphia, 1959), as is its successor, the elegant cathedra in Sheraton style executed by Ephriam Haines (or Haimes, 1775–c.1815).

Perpetuation of older classical forms in lower levels of society was made possible by, and in turn fostered, the extraordinarily long professional "lives" of such works as *The Builder's Pocket Treasure* of William Pain (c.1730–c.1790), first published 1763 in London, appearing in America in 1794, and used twenty or thirty years thereafter; most famous of them was *The Carpenter's New Guide* by Peter Nicholson (1765–1844), which first appeared in London in 1792 and went through sixteen American editions, the last as late as 1867!

8. ARTISAN TO ARTIST:
The Classical Mind as Personal Expression

MORE AND MORE the 18th century seems to us, in retrospect, an age of great creative personalities. By contrast with our own, it has for us the same kind of appeal that has led to the great 20th-century revival of Shakespearean theatre. As we turn with relief from the spectacle of little people fumbling with little woes enacted on our stage to grand Renaissance dramas of men born to greatness coming to grips with mighty problems of mind and spirit, so it seems that two hundred years ago America bred a race of giants, resolute in war, wise in peace, fertile in invention. Such a race, we argue, must have produced great men of art, too. Yet when we come to ask who exactly was responsible for the buildings and furniture of classical America, only vague references are forthcoming—a shadowy parade of miscellaneous carpenters, lawyers, merchants, and planters of whose artistic accomplishments their own age took so little notice that most of them were quite forgotten until restored to history by scholarship in ours. It seems odd; but the reason is not hard to discover. In the two centuries that separate the 18th century from us, the whole concept of individual freedom and creative expression in art has changed.

By individual freedom, we primarily mean freedom from restrictions—the right of artists to do what they want, when they want, as they choose. But when the 18th century talked about artistic freedom, it meant freedom to work within certain defined limits towards certain definite goals. Key to the classical mind is its concept of an orderly world—a world governed by law, art governed by accepted rules. In this orderly world everything had its proper place and function. The object of art, as well as the proper business of artists, was beauty. Beauty might mean many things. It might mean natural appearances ordered into more meaningful and visually pleasing patterns. Or it might mean

noble thoughts put before the mind. But whatever it meant, one thing was clear—the artist was not expected to invent or create beauty; beauty was something he discovered and revealed. Nor was he left to his own devices of representing it. What kinds of composition, proportion, and associative ideas could be called "beautiful" were among those truths this age held to be self-evident. Born into every man was the ability to distinguish between good proportions and bad, between beautiful objects and ugly—an innate faculty, part of every human being's inherited mental furniture, one of the attributes, like speech and reason, distinguishing men from beasts. Balance is preferable to instability, harmony to dissonance, the sweet to the sour, not by personal or community agreement, but simply because that is how things are. "Rules" are not imposed on the artist; they grow out of the natural workings of his mind. They are absolutes, to be learned, not questioned. If we discuss or differ about them, it is because, just as some human beings have a better musical ear or more muscular co-ordination than others, so are there different degrees of ability to recognize the beautiful. But all have some; and to all, the same rules apply. Break them, and the result is chaos and license. Understand and follow them, and you enjoy not only ordered beauty but true freedom as well.

By "absolute," the classical mind did not understand something static, or immutable rules to be applied indiscriminately in all times and places. As Bishop Berkeley put it in *Alciphron*:

The ancients, who from a thorough consideration of the grounds and principles of art, formed their idea of beauty, did not always confine themselves strictly to the same rules and proportions; but whenever the particular distance, position, elevation, or dimension of the fabric and its parts seemed to require it, made no scruple to depart from them, without deserting the original principles of beauty, which governed whatever deviations they made.

Precisely. The ordered beauty of classical art, like the truths of Berkeley's religion, could not change; but means of expressing and modes of apprehending it did. The sophisticated spatial proportions of Adamesque–Federal designers were very far indeed from the naïvely simple mathematical ratios that determined the main dimensions of early public buildings in Williamsburg—multiples of 5 in the Capitol, of 6 in the Governors' Palace, the Golden Section in the College of William and Mary, and Bruton Church. But because all of them embody the basic principle of parts being systematically related to the whole according to a recognized scheme, they all unmistakably belong to the same classical tradition, express the same basic classical impulse to order and control environment in the same intellectual rather than obviously visual way. So in ornament; as long as consistent balance and proportion in total design are observed, artists may employ much or little, be robust or delicate, Roman or "Gothick" or Chinese, all within classical rules. Nowhere more than in the classical tradition, the letter killeth and the spirit giveth life—the moment artists begin to depend on inflexible formulas and immutable models, the classical mind proper will die.

The 18th-century concept of creative expression was different from ours, too. We think of artists basing their work on personal experience, of manifesting through "honest" use of materials, or integrity of style, or whatever, the realities and spirit of their age, as they themselves experience it. Not then; whatever of reality the 18th-century artist presented to his world was only incidental. Then as now, life had its seamy and desperate side; impressed seamen, starving beggars, dispossessed tenants, plague-stricken towns would have been surprised indeed to find posterity considering theirs an optimistic, secure, self-confident age. Certainly few artists thought these realities any business of theirs. Their function in society, as they saw it, was to make the world in the broadest sense a better, a "more beautiful" place to live in. You went to their plays not primarily to be instructed in the facts of life but to enjoy yourself, whether in the diversions of a bawdy farce or in some tragedy that made life seem, for all its pathos and distress, worth living still. Their music transformed the chaotic discordant realities of natural sound into disciplined harmonies and rhythms and chords, which the mind could respond to with comprehension, and anticipate with pleasure. So with the visual arts. The proper business of architects—by comparison with mere shelter builders—was to adorn the community, to make of houses and churches, kitchens and courthouses things of beauty and joys forever, imbuing them with harmonious proportions and balanced symmetries. Cabinetmakers and woodworkers tried to do the same for chairs and chests and cornices. Theirs were not personal creations; neither was there much difference between them. It follows that the reason great artistic geniuses cannot be found in 18th-century America is not alone because the country was too small and provincial to support them; even more it is because the genius in our sense—the man who at once invents great ideas and gives them great tangible expression—did not belong in this age.

As in most great creative ages in the past, the men of the 18th century doubted that those gifted at expressing themselves tangibly, through the work of their hands in clay and wood and stone, were likely to be equally gifted at expressing themselves verbally, or be at home in the realm of abstract ideas. In the Golden Age of Greece no one expected the men who carved the sculptures of the Temple of Zeus at Olympia or the Parthenon to work out all the complicated historical and mythological implications the occasion demanded; this was left for intellectuals—poets, dramatists, and the like—to provide. In the Cathedral Age no one expected the theologians who worked out the sculptural programs of Chartres or Amiens or Rheims to do the carving as well. Neither had laymen like Michelangelo or Raphael, great artists though they were, been entrusted with determining what concepts were to be presented to the world on the Sistine Ceiling or in the Stanze of the Vatican; for all their increased individualism, Renaissance and Baroque patrons here and in every other major monument left scholars and theologians to devise their artists' subject matter. In 18th-century America, similar collaboration between artisans and designers— between men who designed and men who executed —was the almost invariable rule for buildings of any size or consequence. It follows that controversy as to whether we should call Governor Nicholson or Henry Cary architect of the Williamsburg Capitol; whether Cary or Governor Spotswood was responsible for the Palace; whether William Price or Richard Munday was ultimately responsible for the design of Trinity Church, Newport; whether Independence Hall should be attributed to Andrew Hamilton or Edmund Woolley; whether George Washington or John Ariss should be "credited" with the enlargement of Mount Vernon, and so on, is essentially pointless. The age itself did not distinguish among them; why should we? It did not look for dynamic and original artistic personalities spreading themselves large over the pages of history. It took for granted that just as understanding of English common law was widespread enough that every educated man might be in some degree a lawyer, so classical principles were self-evident enough that it was no more remarkable for an educated gentleman to draw up competent classical plans for a courthouse or mansion than for a trained artist to embody them in proper classical forms. Furthermore, collaboration between the two was considered so normal, so natural, so inevitable that trying to determine which was the "real" architect was like trying to decide which scissor blade does most. Even in England, as Professor Jenkins has shown in *Architect and Patron*, the architectural profession was hardly specialized before 1750; how much less would we expect pro-

fessional "architects" in the provinces! We have seen how the evolution of classical principles is a manifestation of broad cultural levels; how much more were builders, cabinetmakers, patrons the creations rather than the creators of the spirit of their age! It follows that the artists of classical America are best considered not as individual personalities but as representatives of four phases in the evolution of the classical mind.

First comes the William and Mary phase of transition from medieval to classical practice. At the beginning of the century, medieval practice prevails everywhere. When Pastor Bjork undertakes to build his Holy Trinity Church for the Swedish congregation at Wilmington, when Governor Keith decides to have a country house for himself at Horsham, when Penn lays out his mansion house on the Delaware, each gives only general directions to the masons and carpenters he employs, and the workmen carry it out in the folk traditions in which they have been trained, with the result that buildings often have a more medieval appearance than the patron might have wished. Even in England, this could happen. For example, Professor Whiffen has described how Sir Christopher Wren's style

was so much purer than that generally current in England at that time that when they [his designs] got into the hands of any except his chosen craftsmen the results were apt to be quite different from what he intended. . . . In 1693 Wren supplied a design for Sir John Moore's school, to be built at Appleby in Leicestershire. Thomas Woodstock, one of his favourite carpenters, was to supervise the work. But Woodstock died before things had progressed far, and a Midland mason, Sir William Wilson, took over. The school, as completed by Wilson in 1697, and Wren's design for it both exist. That there is any connection between them is not, at first glance, obvious.

Something similar certainly happened at Pennsbury and Graeme Park, and probably at Holy Trinity too.

The same practice obtained in the first buildings at Williamsburg. When Governor Nicholson gets authorization to build a capitol at Williamsburg, he has a general idea of what he wants ("I doe recommend to you to have such a Pile of Buildings Erected so soon as possible as may be not only larger, but more conveniently serve the publick Uses than that which was unfortunately burnt the last ffall" (i.e., the fourth statehouse at Jamestown) and then looks for workmen to carry it out. As representing the Building Committee, he advertises that he is "ready to receive the proposal of any person concerning what of the sd building he is willing to undertake either in the quality of an Undertaker, Overseer, or Workman. . . ." Response is received from a native Virginian, one Henry Cary, born in 1650, son of a 1646 immigrant named Miles Cary, who is duly appointed overseer. This man has done some building before—a jail and the platform of a fort at Yorktown, among other things—presumably in the traditional manner; like the master masons of the Middle Ages, he has considerable standing in the community, owning a six-hundred-acre tract of land in Warwick County, where his brother Miles is an official. Under his supervision, the capitol takes shape as "a visual equivalent of the good plain English in which the doings of those who met in it were written down"; whatever classical style it has probably originated with Governor Nicholson, whose plans for Williamsburg and Annapolis display considerable awareness of the new spirit, and the three bricklayers and three carpenters brought from England to work on it. The building was satisfactory enough, and when in 1705 legislation was passed to build a governors' palace, the same procedure was followed. Nicholson's successor, Governor Edward Nott, had little interest in matters architectural (or Virginian, either); when the Burgesses requested him "to cause a draught of such a house as by him shall be thought most convenient to be laid before the House," he replied, "I leave it wholly to you to give such directions therein as you think proper," and by an act of 1706 Henry Cary is again made overseer, to build the house

of brick, fifty-four foot in length, and forty-eight foot in breadth, from inside to inside, two story high, with convenient cellars underneath, and one vault, sash windows, of sash, glass, and a covering of stone slate, and that in all other respects the said house be built and finished according to the discretion of the overseer, which shall be employed by virtue of this act to take care of the same. . . .

When Governor Alexander Spotswood arrived in the colony in 1710, however, things changed. Spotswood was a man of the new classical age; "well acquainted with Figures," Sir William Keith wrote of him in his *History of the British Plantations in America* (1738), "and so good a Mathematician, that his skill in Architecture, and in the laying out of Ground to the best Advantage is yet to be seen in Virginia . . . in the considerable Improvements which he made to the Governor's House and Gardens." One of his first "Improvements" was to secure Cary's dismissal the next year. Only the structural shell of the Palace was as yet complete, and evidently Spotswood had no intention of seeing it "medievalized," like Wren's country designs, by some builder finishing it in traditional fashion. He had no use for the old medieval practice of leaving important buildings to the "discretion" of men like Cary. On medieval precedent, such people might claim to have rights in the matter: " 'Tis usual," Joseph Moxon's *Mechanick Exercises* (London, 1700), proclaimed, "and also very convenient, for any person before he begins to erect a building, to have Designs or Draughts made upon Paper or Vellum. The drawing of Draughts is most commonly the work of a Surveyor, but there be many Master Workmen that will contrive a building and draw the Designs thereof"; Spotswood would have none of them. He would have agreed entirely with what the Duchess of Marlborough said in 1732 about these medieval "overseers" and their pretensions to be "architects":

I know of none that are not mad or ridiculous, and I really believe that anybody that has sense with the best workmen of all sorts could make a better house without an architect, than any has been built these many years. I know two gentlemen of this country who have great estates and who have built their houses without an architect, by able workmen that would do as they directed which no architect will, though you pay for it.

He held, in short, the classical Renaissance view that architectural design was an intellectual operation, no business for craftsmen; that the proper function of artisans was to carry out the ideas of educated persons like himself. By 1713 he succeeded in putting this idea into practice, recommending in his message to the House of Burgesses in December of that year the dismissal of Cary's successor as overseer and undertaking to direct completion of the Palace himself: "What now remains to be finished may, in my opinion, be either let out, or performed by so few workmen, as the Country needs no longer be at the Expense of an Overseer; for I will take care of the work. . . ." Hiring his own workmen "that would do as . . . directed," Spotswood carried the Palace to substantial completion on his own. As it embodied the transition from medieval to classical in style, then, so the Palace embodied the transition from medieval to classical in building practice—from folk building to the kind of collaborative enterprise between the "intellectual" who devises plans and artisans who carry them out. It remains to see how the nature of this relationship changes through the three phases of classical evolution which follow.

In the first, William and Mary phase, the patron-designer is everything, the workman nothing. We have no idea who those workmen were that carried out Spotswood's plans for completing the Palace, nor would it matter, for his criterion presumably was that they have no minds of their own. Representative of the next, Queen Anne phase, is the relationship between William Price and Richard Munday at Trinity Church, Newport; Edmund Woolley and Andrew Hamil-

ton at Independence Hall; the "Master of Christ Church" and "King" Carter. Here again the "intellectual" dominates the collaboration. While Munday, Woolley, and the "Master of Christ Church" are almost entirely creations of modern research and inductive scholarship, tradition and history have preserved the names of William Price, Boston bookseller who supplied (presumably from prints of Wren's churches) the basic plans for both Trinity, Newport, and Old North, Boston (and be it remembered, booksellers in those days were often more like librarians and scholars than stallkeepers—Samuel Johnson largely educated himself in his father's bookshop); of Andrew Hamilton, lawyer and speaker of the Pennsylvania colonial legislature, who in 1732 "produced a Draught of the State-house, containing the Plan and Elevation of that Building," and of Dr. John Kearsley and Thomas Lawrence, who worked on the building committee with him; of "King" Carter and his family, who commissioned Christ Church and the series of mansions related to it. But the artisans who worked for them are no longer entirely anonymous; though personally they remain shadows, we can know them now through the styles of their work.

As individual personalities, these artisans remain vague at best. Of the three, only Munday is more than a name. And the few records concerning Munday that have been discovered—of his marriage in Newport in 1713; of his keeping an inn on occasion; of his death in 1739; of his working as a carpenter on Trinity Church, the Daniel Ayraut and half a dozen other houses, and the new legislative building, Old Colony House, begun 1739 and completed 1741—confuse more than clarify his position. For all that he evidently was paid £25 "for draughting a plan" of Old Colony House, it still seems strange that states as populous and important as Rhode Island by 1740 would entrust sole responsibility for the planning of a great public building to some innkeeper and house carpenter who otherwise took no evident part in public affairs. Only the fact that Old Colony House is *retardataire* in concept makes it at all credible. For it is through their "stylistic personalities" that we really know these artisans as people; and even had Richard Munday not died two years before Old Colony House was completed, we could doubt that he was its "architect" in the modern sense of the word because of the fundamental differences in conception between it and, say, Trinity Church. In the legislative building as a whole there is manifest an understanding of Queen Anne principles simply not evident in the church—façades with central focusing accent created by door and balcony, systems of repeating curved forms in balcony, dormers, window frames and stairway to create visual unity, repetition of the same pediment motif front and side to unify the building as a whole. And whereas it is a strong vestigial survival of William and Mary flat two-dimensionality that characterizes the detail of Trinity Church, the exterior detail of Old Colony House departs from Queen Anne standards in the opposite direction, towards a naïve and clumsy overemphasis on essential robustness. That the same person could have made two such totally different interpretations of basic Queen Anne principles is improbable, to say the least. But at the same time the basic similarity in handling—and a common difference in the handling of exterior detail—between the square Doric pillars each with their pedestal and inserted piece of entablature standing in the center of the large first-floor space of Old Colony House, and the comparable forms on the interior of Trinity Church, suggest that the same person executed these details. And if we add to this the comparison between the handling of the Trinity interior with Old North, Boston, that Morrison has made in *Early American Architecture*—"added depth to the gallery fronts, which have fine raised panels framed by bolection mouldings, gives a more dignified architectural effect, and the projection of the arched vaults over the gallery bays into the nave to form a kind of groined vaulting contributes to a more monumental interior unity"—we can

begin to know Munday (whose work all this presumably is) as a personality in a way we can never know, say, Henry Cary, or the traditional artisans of Holy Trinity in Wilmington, or Graeme Park.

Edmund Woolley of Philadelphia we know in the same way. Woolley may well have been the man who made the famous "parchment drawing" of the north front of Independence Hall traditionally assumed to be the one Andrew Hamilton presented for the Assembly's approval. Charles E. Peterson, among others, assumed that this was the plan referred to in a bill from Woolley of £5, receipted by John Penn, "to drawing the Elevation of the Frount. . . . Allso the Plans of the first and Second floors of the State House . . ."; on this basis he proposed that "Edmund Woolley should have the title of *Architect*, because he was paid for the drawings from which the structure was erected." Almost certainly Woolley was responsible for the tower as built 1750–52; it was the kind of thing a master carpenter would do, and a detailed bill of particulars submitted by Woolley for work on the tower exists, from which it appears that the legislature allotted him a lump sum for labor and let him pay subordinate workmen out of it. But Woolley was not, of course, responsible for the decision to add a tower to the statehouse; and it was only in its conception (an attempt to transform the building from a domestic to a civic scale) that the tower was a significant manifestation of the classical mind. The very concept of "civic," like the word, is truly classical; but the forms of the tower themselves were not. A rather naïve and clumsy pile of pilasters, pediments, Palladian window and other details with little sense of any larger whole, they are precisely what we might expect of someone starting life as an artisan, working with details rather than accustomed to think in theoretical terms of broad principles. Woolley's work reveals a man of whom we could say, with Hazlitt, that "persons without education certainly do not want either acuteness or strength of mind in what concerns themselves, or in things immediately within their observation; but they have no power of abstraction—they see their objects always near, never in the horizon."

As for the "Master of Christ Church," his style is all we know about him; as Professor Morrison has remarked (*Early American Architecture*, p. 350):

> The similarity of certain details in the church and in the early group of Carter houses ["King" Carter's own mansion, Corotoman, c.1715–20; his son-in-law's, Rosewell, 1726–30; Landon Carter's Sabine Hall, c.1730; Robert Carter II's Nomini Hall, c.1730] . . . leads us again to the hypothesis—and it is purely an hypothesis—that some architect as yet unknown to us, a man of English architectural training and high repute in the colony, designed some of its most notable buildings in the early 18th century. Perhaps some day his name will be discovered, just as patient study of the ruined remnants . . . has recovered for us some conception of the vanished splendours of these great houses.

That style suggests, however, that here we have a more advanced figure. For what distinguishes the unknown "Master of Christ Church," like the unknown "Master of Olympia" in antiquity, is not so much technical mastery of detail as command of basic classical principles, the way he unifies details into a total design. In this respect, T. T. Waterman's suggestion of Richard Taliaferro or Toliver (1705–1779) as the man in question may not have been entirely wrong after all. Professor Whiffen has shown that the supposed reference to Taliaferro as "our most skillful architect" in connection with repairs to the Palace at Williamsburg in 1749 was a misreading of the text, and that "until some tangible proof of his skill as a designer turns up it is fair to picture him as a substantial planter whose capital and credit were important qualifications for such an undertaking as the repair of the Palace." The reasons for disqualifying Taliaferro as the "Master of Christ Church" are not that he was a planter instead of an artisan, however,

but because his dates are a little too early to be credibly associated with the Carter houses and church, and that the buildings which were associated with him (including Westover and Carter's Grove) have a different set of characteristics from those typical of Christ Church. When the "Master of Christ Church" is identified, he may well turn out to be no artisan, but a man of education and substance like Taliaferro, a kind of early Thomas Jefferson, anticipating in the usual advanced Southern pattern the developments of later classical phases.

Be that as it may, certainly all these examples—Christ Church, Independence Hall, Trinity Church in Newport (and there are others)—represent a step forward in the evolution of the classical artist. Still dependent on and subservient to the "intellectual" who provides the broad framework of principles within which they work, Munday, Woolley, and the Christ Church master are yet personalities in a way the old medieval artisans could never be. Rather than as collections of dates and records pasted together, or as emanations of folk tradition, we can begin to visualize them as individuals with characteristic techniques and minds of their own. The classical mind, beginning in this second phase to be diffused through lower strata of society, is encouraging individuals to put the world into meaningful relationship to themselves. Now that classical principles are being consciously formulated, and guidebooks to disseminate them becoming widely available, a framework is being provided within which individual creative personalities can express themselves; artisans have a chance actively to influence the final form of buildings on which they work, as they could not before. With the third phase of classical maturity, they will take their place as equal collaborators, working "with" rather than "under" men of leisured education and taste, and for the first time we will meet something like "architects" in the modern sense of the word.

Now, in the Chippendale–Georgian period, designers and builders with distinct personalities appear. Peter Harrison of Newport, Robert Smith of Philadelphia, John Ariss in Virginia, John Hawks in North Carolina, William Buckland of Gunston Hall and Annapolis—these are people whose careers can be ascertained, whose libraries can be studied, whose styles can be critically judged. At first sight they seem a rather diverse lot; but as a group they collectively represent a new degree of maturity typical of the third phase of the classical mind.

Most famous of them, perhaps, is Peter Harrison (1716–1775). He is also in some respects the most *retardataire*. Not alone because, as we have seen, his designs rarely advance beyond Queen Anne concepts of composition; his status, too, is that of the gentleman intellectual like Price, Andrew Hamilton, or John Kearsley who dominated architecture in the second classical phase. Whatever Harrison's reputation with posterity, it was as an English Quaker sea captain who married into the Pelham family of Newport and established himself as a Newport gentleman merchant trading in rum and mahogany, molasses and wines, eventually customs collector of the Port of New Haven in Connecticut, that his contemporaries knew and judged him. His architectural interests they took for granted; a gentleman's avocation at which he was uncommonly skilful but for which, of course, he never asked money. Neither did this "polite accomplishment" have to do with style as such; that was a matter for the woodworkers and bricklayers who carried out the gentleman's plans. What buildings like the Redwood Library (1748–9), Touro Synagogue (1759–63), or the Brick Market (c.1760) in Newport have in common with King's Chapel in Boston (1749–54), Christ Church in Cambridge (1759–61), or St. Michael's in Charleston, South Carolina (1752–61), is essentially little more than the particular library of architectural books from which their motifs were selected. What distinguishes Harrison's work is not so much an artistic personality as a generally recognizable preference for certain Palladian plans and forms; and since other gentlemen in

the period had the same kind of taste, where no documents attach Harrison's name to a building —as at St. Michael's—attribution cannot be even reasonably certain. You could call Harrison, to paraphrase the title of Chippendale's book, a "Gentleman and Artisans' Director, as Being Calculated to assist the one in the Choice, the others in the Execution of the Designs." The respect with which his opinions are treated—for example, the letter in which the vestry of Christ Church, Cambridge, requests him to provide designs for a church "of wood, and covered on the outside with Rough-cast . . . only one tier of Windows and no Galleries," and "*if Mr. Harrison approves of it*, there be no steeple, only a Tower with a Belfry"—implies no recognition of his artistry as such, only the kind of prerogative upper-class gentlemen would normally expect, the kind "King" Carter and the State House Building Committee and Governor Spotswood enjoyed as a matter of course.

With Robert Smith of Philadelphia (c.1722–1777), the situation was quite different. From the time he first receives eight payments for work on the construction of Christ Church steeple between 1752 and 1754, to the Walnut Street prison of 1774–5, "designed and built under the direction of the late Robert Smith" (as Dr. James Mease described it in his 1811 *Picture of Philadelphia*), there is no doubt on what Smith's reputation was based. To his contemporaries, Smith was a "builder": sometimes, too, they called him a "carpenter," or "a house-carpenter," occasionally "architect." He was most famous as the designer of Carpenters' Hall, to which he also contributed as a fund raiser and active early member of the Carpenters' Company, dedicated to raising the status and standards of builders to a professional level. And it was on his professional competence as a builder that his contemporary reputation was based. For he not only commanded the practical skills of a carpenter; he owned a considerable architectural library (three of his books, Campbell's *Vitruvius Britannicus* of 1731, which he bought in 1756; Langley's *City and Country Builder* of 1750, bought in 1751; and a 1738 edition of Palladio's *Four Books,* bought in 1754, are now in the Carpenters' Company Library) which he knew how to use. In Smith we see the functions of master craftsmen like Munday and Woolley, and theoretical designers like Andrew Hamilton and Peter Harrison, beginning to be combined in the same person. When we list the works of Robert Smith: Nassau Hall in Princeton (1753); St. Peter's Church in Philadelphia (1758); the Pennsylvania "New College" (1761); Zion Lutheran Church, Philadelphia (1767); plans for the Hospital for Persons of Disordered Minds in Williamsburg (1769), or the College Edifice for Rhode Island College (Brown University) 1770; and a good many others, we are talking about the *oeuvre* of a professional architect as we have not before but will often again.

In England by this time trained professionals, distinct alike from the gentleman intellectual who turns his hand to designing, and the artisan expanding his activities to cover plans as well, were becoming the rule. James Gibbs was perhaps the first example; by 1749 John Gwyn had written *An Essay on Design,* which urged formal architectural education at English universities (Gibbs had had to train in Italy); by the 1770s it was finally possible for young men who were neither lords nor artisans to choose architecture as a profession, by following a pattern of training with established architects plus lessons in drawing and design at the Royal Academy and (hopefully) a finishing trip to Italy. And in the South, always following close behind English precedent, "professionals" like Robert Smith were becoming more the rule than the exception. John Ariss (c.1725–1799), John Hawks (1731–1790), and William Buckland (1734–1774) are only the best-known examples; probably there were a good many more whom history has forgotten.

All these men still work in collaboration with gentleman patrons who take much more than a passive interest in questions of taste, and to whose wishes they must defer; Buckland works with George Mason, Ariss with George Washington and the Tayloes, Hawks with Governor Tryon, and so on. But they work with them on much more equal terms than artisans ever had before. Ariss, earliest and least well known of them, is also an exception in that he was a native of the country, born in Albany, Virginia. In the late 1740s, however, he goes to England, presumably for architectural training, and when by 1751 he is back and living in Westmoreland County, he advertises in the *Maryland Gazette* that he can undertake "Buildings of all Sorts and Dimensions . . . either of the Ancient or Modern Order of Gibbs' Architect. . . ." He also has "a great Variety and sundry Draughts of Buildings in Miniature, and some buildings near finished after the Modern Taste," which from the records we can infer he employed variously in Richmond and Berkeley counties. In him, then, a new type of trained professional builder-designer appears. Evidently he "specializes" in large country houses on more or less Palladian lines, of the sort represented by Mount Airy; the Carlyle House at Alexandria (1751), Mannsfield (c.1765, now destroyed), Harewood (c.1769), Blandfield (1770), Elmwood (c.1774), are typical of the reasonably sure attributions to him. His "practice" probably also included— again in what is a familiar modern pattern— consultations with gentlemen whose theoretical knowledge of architecture and enthusiasm for it exceeded their practical experience; in this capacity he may well have assisted Washington, with whose family his had close connections, with the remodelings of Mount Vernon in 1757–8 and 1773–9, and the building of Pohick Church in 1771–2. And that from first to last the work attributed to him is drawn so heavily from Gibbs's *Book of Architecture* and William Adam's *Vitruvius Scotticus* of 1750 suggests an explanation for the scarcity of attributions to him after the Revolution; time and changing tastes had made obsolete the personal style he had developed and perfected in his youth. The familiarity of such a story would be all the more evidence of the almost modern status architect-designers like Ariss were beginning to achieve.

John Hawks makes a similarly "modern" appearance in architectural history. It is as a trained professional that he comes to North Carolina from England with Governor Tryon in 1764, specifically to build the Palace at New Bern. It is as an acknowledged authority on all phases of operations, someone capable of formulating the plans and of hiring and supervising workmen recruited in Philadelphia, that he is known in the province. And if he later leaves the profession of architecture to take a succession of public offices, it is because the skills he has learned in the service of Stiff Leadbetter of Eton, designer of gentlemen's country houses and sometime surveyor of St. Paul's Cathedral in London, have also fitted him to work as accountant and assessor.

William Buckland, however, is the figure who best represents the changing status of architectural practitioners in the Chippendale–Georgian age. When we first meet him, at Gunston Hall in the mid-1750s, he is working in much the same capacity as Richard Munday or Edmund Woolley a generation earlier. A master artisan—in this case, a joiner, trained by his uncle in London in the specialized craft of "joining" wood by nails, dovetails, glue, grooves, or however—he works within a general design which, if not decided upon before his arrival, was undoubtedly worked out in collaboration with his employer-patron, George Mason. Furthermore, his tendency to overscale details in relation to given settings, and to draw motifs rather miscellaneously from here, there, and all over, manifests much the same sort of limited concept of design evident in Woolley's work on the Independence Hall tower. But in 1759, his indenture to Mason discharged, Buckland marries, and with Mason's certificate recommending him "as an honest sober diligent man & I think a complete Master of the Carpenter's and Joiner's business both in theory and practice" in his pocket, he

strikes out on his own. Presumably he operated at first as carpenters and joiners habitually did in London (and as he had done at Gunston Hall), undertaking to execute interior woodwork for buildings already standing; there are references to his doing so at various places in Virginia: Falls Church glebe house in Truro parish (1760); Rockledge for John Bellendine (1761); Mount Airy (1762); prison and workhouse for Richmond County (1766–8); Pohick Church, among others. But it also appears that, as had happened ever since the beginnings of architecture in America, circumstances wrought changes in the European pattern. Writing to the Honorable Robert Carter by the middle of the 1760s, he declares, "I have now some of the Best Workmen in Virginia among whom is a London Carver, a masterly Hand"—in other words, he has aspirations to be not merely an artisan-decorator, but to run what in the next century would be called an architectural "office."

It is in this capacity, apparently, that we find Buckland going to Annapolis in 1771. For while in only a few cases is there anything like specific proof that Buckland worked on Annapolis buildings—most notably for the Hammond House (1773–4), whose plan and elevation he holds in a portrait painted by Charles Willson Peale; the Bryce House (presumably built c.1740), for whose woodwork Buckland's estate submitted a bill; and the Chase–Lloyd house (shell completed 1771), about which Buckland corresponded with Edward Lloyd—all around Annapolis buildings can be found dating in the 1760s and 70s whose ornamental woodwork is characterized to a greater or lesser extent by motifs and handling typical of Buckland's work style as we know it from Gunston Hall: the Upton Scott and John Ridout houses in Annapolis; Strawberry Hill, Whitehall, Tulip Hill, Montpelier in adjacent areas and counties; the Ringgold house in Chestertown. That one man executed it all in the three years or so Buckland lived in Annapolis seems incredible. Even assuming he executed some commissions in his Virginia workshop, or was commuting to Annapolis for some years before settling there, one must infer that he operated a professional establishment whose members were more like the junior partners of an architectural office than the old kind of youthful apprentices; that on his establishment he imposed not merely technical but stylistic standards. Or, in other words, in him artisan and designer combined to produce a figure greater in status than either, who at least approximated to the full classical role of the artist moulding his environment to his will, putting his stamp on the community around him. Where the medieval artisan worked in the nature of his materials and according to unquestioned tradition, the classical artist consciously commands both. In Buckland the classical mind seems to be reaching full maturity of expression; the age that follows him will carry this evolution to its logical conclusion in the person of men who, acknowledging classical principles and tradition, will yet take for granted their right and even duty to create a consciously personal style of their own within it.

By the Adamesque–Federal period the majority of "architects" we find in the records follow a pattern of development of the sort set by Buckland. The career of Samuel McIntire (1757–1811), for instance, is thus summarized in an obituary in the *Gazette* of his native Salem, Massachusetts (February 12, 1811): "Mr. M'Intire was originally bred to the occupation of a housewright [his father's trade], but his vigorous mind soon passed the ordinary limits of his profession, and aspired to the highest departments of the interesting and admirable science of architecture. . . . To a delicate native taste in this art, he had united a high degree of that polish which can only be acquired by an assiduous study of the great classical masters; with whose works, notwithstanding their rarity in this country, Mr. M. had a very intimate acquaintance." Like Buckland's, his evolution from artisan-carpenter through master craftsman and professional sculptor to the position of head architect of an "office"

(consisting in this case mainly of family—his son Samuel Field, brothers Joseph and Angiers) can be traced by stylistic analysis of works attributable to him. We can follow a development in architecture from the *retardataire* naïveté of earlier (1782) parts of the Pierce–Nichols house, drawn from the half-century-old *Builder's Treasury* of Batty Langley, through the growing refinement of the later (1801) woodwork in its hall, east parlor, and chamber, to the decorative and spatial subtleties of the Pingree house, wholly designed by McIntire in 1804 under the Adamesque influence of Charles Bulfinch. As much as —perhaps more than—Buckland in Annapolis, McIntire stamped Salem with his personality, in the form of stylistic standards and character established in his shop; even more cogently we may recognize in him the classical artist shaping an environment to his will and principles:

> Salem at the end of his life presented a very different aspect from its appearance when he began his work. The churches and public buildings had been rebuilt or remodelled from his designs. Where a solid gambrel-roofed house had been, with one or two exceptions, the height of domestic pretension, rows of tall stately mansions, a great number from McIntire's hand, lined Essex Street, Federal Street, and Washington Square. That was no idle phrase when the town clerk called Samuel McIntire, on his death, "the architect of Salem." [Fiske Kimball, *Mr. Samuel McIntire, Carver*]

Where McIntire's career differed from Buckland's, and represented a later classical phase, is in the recognition of his achievement not only by later historians but by his contemporaries. "This day," wrote Salem diarist William Bentley on hearing of McIntire's death,

> Salem is deprived of one of the most ingenious men it had in it. He was descended of a family of Carpenters who had no claims on public favor. . . . By attention he soon gained a superiority to all of his occupation and the present Court House, the North and South Meeting houses, and indeed all the improvements of Salem for nearly thirty years past have been

under his eye. . . . Upon the death of Mr. Mc-Intire no man is left to be consulted upon a new plan of execution beyond his bare practice.

All this might have been said of William Buckland; but it is unlikely that any of his patrons, no matter how much they respected his technical skill, would have said or even thought Annapolis similarly deprived. No such tombstone was raised to him as reminded posterity how Samuel McIntire was "distinguished for Genius in Architecture, Sculpture, and Musick."

The difference was not so much in the men as in the age. Partly it was the new democratic and national spirit. That McIntire, who never left his native town, would venture to submit a design for the national capitol in 1792, suggests a new cultural atmosphere, one presaging an end to the long pattern of Southern aristocratic superiority. But even more, it is characteristic of the final phase of the classical mind. Everywhere artists were asserting their individuality, and gaining recognition for their art as such. Though still based and dependent on the traditional framework of classical principles, art is now a means of personal expression, and of fame and fortune, as never before.

McIntire was far from the only man "descended of a family . . . who had no claims on public favor" for whom art was a means of rising above humble origins to success and renown. Such, too, was Robert Cary Long, Sr., of Baltimore (1770–1833), who began life apprenticed to a carpenter, rose by assiduous study to be chief builder of the new Dancing Assembly Rooms by 1797, and ended as the most respected architect of the city, designing such diverse and important works as the College of Medicine (1801), the Union Bank (1807), and the Peale Museum (1813).

Most striking, perhaps, was the case of James Hoban (c.1762–1831). An Irish immigrant who had worked, presumably as a laborer, on Lord Newcomen's bank in Dublin (1781), Hoban studied architectural drawing in Dublin

Society schools. He is called a carpenter when he buys a house in Charleston, South Carolina, early in 1789. In May 1790, he advertises that he will teach architecture to an evening class of young men, and that he and his partner, Purcell, will execute plans and carpentry. But by the end of that year he has designed a statehouse at Columbia, South Carolina; in 1791, when President Washington visits Charleston, Hoban is "introduced to him, as a man of merit and of genius, under the patronage of general Moultrie, Mr. Butler, &c. . . ."; in July 1792, according to a letter published in the *Charleston City Gazette,* "the president of the United States and the commissioners of the federal buildings, examined the plans for a capitol and president's house, to be erected in the city of Washington . . . a gold medal and premium for the best plan of a president's house was adjudged to Mr. James Hoban from Charleston, South Carolina; and he was accordingly appointed architect for the federal buildings. It is remarkable, Mr. Hoban had but 20 days to complete his plan after his arrival here, and that after he explained it to the commissioners, they unanimously agreed that it should be adopted." And Charlestonians feel the same pride in having an artist among them that was expressed by the men of Salem about McIntire: ". . . It is no small matter of universal satisfaction to the citizens of Carolina," says the same paper, "that their fellow-citizen, Hoban, has succeeded in this enterprise." Though henceforth he builds little else of significance, Hoban's reputation is assured; he dies in 1831 a man of fame and wealth.

But art is more even than a means of helping artisans rise in the world; it has stature enough now to enhance the reputation of any man, no matter what his station in life. Gabriel Manigault of Charleston (1758–1809), for instance, came of a family long since risen from humble Huguenot refugee origins to a position of wealth, social prominence, and political leadership; he was educated at the Inns of Court in London; he owned half a dozen rich plantations.

Yet in contrast to, say, Ezra Stiles's account of the opening of Touro Synagogue in Newport, which described both services and architecture in great detail but never mentioned Peter Harrison's name, the *Charleston City Gazette* obituary for Manigault especially emphasized his "talents both useful and ornamental" and asserted that "he was remarkable for his taste in the fine arts: and several public buildings in Charleston testify that his talents were judiciously employed. . . ." As a wealthy planter, Manigault was one among many; as a designer introducing the new Adamesque style to Charleston in houses for himself and his brother (1790–1800) as well as the Orphan House Chapel (1801–2), the South Carolina Society Hall (1801), the Bank of the United States (now City Hall, begun 1800), and presumably some others, he impressed his unique personality on the city.

Clearly, the old distinction between gentleman designer and artisan executor is fast vanishing, and there appears the "architect" who combines something of the functions of both, who shares the gentleman's intellectual pretensions in society and the craftsman's concern for tangible style. Of this development, the age offers two great examples—Charles Bulfinch of Massachusetts (1763–1844) and Thomas Jefferson of Virginia (1743–1825).

Bulfinch's career begins rather like Manigault's. Son of a well-connected and well-to-do Boston merchant family, he takes a European trip as soon after his Harvard graduation as political conditions allow, and on his return [he says in his autobiography], "I . . . passed a season of leisure, pursuing no business but giving gratuitous advice in architecture, and looking forward to an establishment in life." This advice included plans for public buildings (Hollis Street Church, 1788; column on Beacon Hill, 1789; statehouse, Hartford, Connecticut, 1792), as well as houses for his friends (Joseph Coolidge, 1792; Joseph Barrell, 1792). So well received is the introduction of Adamesque features that he undertakes to build Tontine Crescent as

a commercial venture—a unified block of sixteen houses designed as a single unit in the manner originated in Bath and Nancy in the mid-18th century, and elaborated by Adam. His capital is insufficient and his loans are called; though the Crescent soon proves a huge success, he is bankrupt; thenceforth he is a professional architect, living on his fees. It is the kind of switch that would have been impossible earlier in the century. Bulfinch has no training in craftsmanship; his architecture is entirely theoretical, like Harrison's—and could one imagine Harrison making a living providing architectural designs? But now times are different. Bulfinch not only prospers but retains his social standing—indeed, he even complains on occasion that his public responsibilities as selectman and in other offices leave him too little time for architectural work. For Boston he designs theatres (1794–5), the statehouse (1795), an almshouse (1799), churches (Holy Cross, 1803; New North, 1804; Federal Street, 1809; New South, 1814), markets (Faneuil Hall, 1805; Boylston, 1809), five bank buildings (1800–15), a courthouse (1810), a hospital (1818–20), and all sorts of city houses and country mansions (e.g., three for Harrison Gray Otis alone, 1796, 1801, 1805). His fame as a designer spreads; he becomes recognized as a "genius" who has made fashionable Boston over into his own Adamesque–Federal image; he receives diverse commissions all over the region, in Portsmouth, in Lancaster (Christ Church, 1816), in Andover (Pearson Hall, 1817; Phillips Academy, 1818), and elsewhere; he inspires followers and imitators, notably Samuel McIntire, in Salem, and Asher Benjamin, who takes almost exclusively from Bulfinch whatever advanced ideas there are in the early editions of his first American builders' guides. National fame follows; on December 12, 1817, he accepts appointment as architect to the Capitol in Washington. The new prestige of artists in this age has lifted Bulfinch from social and financial failure to success. But now he finds himself in another atmosphere. Cultural standards in Massachusetts were not yet what they are in Washington. When he is given the plans of his predecessor as Capitol architect, B. H. Latrobe, to study,

> at the first view of these drawings, my courage almost failed me—they are beautifully executed, and the design is in the boldest stile— after longer study I feel better satisfied and more confidence in meeting public expectation. . . . There are certainly faults enough in Latrobe's designs to justify the opposition to him. His stile is calculated for display in the greater parts, but I think his staircases in general are crowded and not easy of access, and the passages intricate and dark. . . .

This was a job demanding more than some stock repertoire of plans and details. Here Bulfinch for the first time met the kind of architect, trained not only in general principles and forms but in historical styles and sophisticated means of expression, that would dominate the next generation. Bulfinch's reputation carries him forward to other commissions all over the country—a Unitarian church in Washington (1822); a prison in Alexandria, Virginia (1826); a capitol for the new state of Maine, at Augusta (built 1829, remodeled 1911). But in 1829 he returned to Boston and did no more work. The old collaboration of intellectual and artisan, which he, like the other representatives of the profession in his generation, maintained, was being destroyed by a kind of individuality and specialization, characteristic of the Victorian age, which he could neither understand nor share.

Very different was Thomas Jefferson. In him, representative alike of that older tradition and the transition from it to the intellectual individuality of the new age, the architect's evolving status is summed up and consummated. Like Harrison or the young Bulfinch, Jefferson begins as leisured aristocrat culling plans and motifs from books, exploring the implications of Palladian theory, for the edification of himself and his friends. Unlike them, however, he combines with this theoretical interest the kind of competence in the practical side of building which we might associate with a Robert Cary

Long or a Samuel McIntire. Typical of his whole career are the calculations written on the back of his drawing for the Rotunda of his University of Virginia—calculations concerned at once with the geometric ratios of his proportions, the number of bricks required, and the proper technique for laying them. He is equally capable of analyzing the stylistic distinctions between French and English classicism, the chemistry of mortar, and comparative labor costs in various cities; of exploring the spatial intricacies of Adamesque design, ways of seasoning lumber, and the possibilities of building adobe walls of local clay, waterproofed with buttermilk. Last great representative of the classical mind as it developed in the patrician world of the Old Dominion, he takes so for granted man's command over every aspect of his environment that even as President of the United States he sees no incongruity in turning his mind from affairs of state to consider the design of hen coops on his Pantops farm. In his remodeling of Monticello, it would be difficult to say whether he was the more concerned with the symbolic aspects of its design, as showing forth the dignity of the presidential office, or the practical details of weather-vane and clock mechanisms, double doors that open and close simultaneously, automatic dumb-waiters; whether the plan was influenced more by spatial aesthetics or the practical location of living, sleeping, and service quarters. But just as the Virginia aristocracy by creating the Union also created the conditions of its own inevitable decline, so was Jefferson at once the greatest and the last representative of the kind of architect the classical mind at its best produced.

This paradox is most apparent in the contrast between his domestic and his public buildings. For himself at Monticello (1773–5, 1796–1808) and Poplar Forest (designed before 1804, built c.1812), for his friends at Brandon (c.1766), Edgehill (first house 1799, second from Jefferson's drawings, 1828), Farmington (begun 1803, completed 1850s on Jefferson's plans), Bremo (c.1815), and elsewhere he produces designs in the great 18th-century tradition of free play of decorative, spatial, and structural forms within the authority of the classical canon, balanced compromise of practical considerations and theoretically absolute principles. But in his public buildings there appears a new concern. Jefferson has sometimes been compared to the 18th-century English Lord Burlington in that his art, unlike that of Bulfinch or Manigault or Buckland, transcended local associations; he aspired to create a national taste. And of course it is true; as Secretary of State and later as President, he was in a position to influence national taste in matters aesthetic to a degree even Burlington could never realize.

But with this final maturity of the classical mind, as represented by Jefferson, is mixed up another idea—one as essentially foreign to Burlington as to Bulfinch or Buckland—the idea of style as a vehicle of literary meaning. At the State Capitol and the University of Virginia, in the alterations he suggested for the White House and the Capitol in Washington, and in the remodeling of Monticello—insofar as he conceived of it as a building of public significance—Jefferson employed classical forms neither primarily because their shapes and proportions were self-evidently right, nor because they represented a spontaneous expression of man in general controlling his environment, but because they symbolized the idea of the new nation being a reincarnation of the Roman Republic. In consequence, he handled them with a kind of pedantry and rigid adherence to "correct" imitation of their Graeco-Roman models essentially new in American civilization. These forms represent less a phase of the living, developing classical mind than a deliberate and conscious effort to "revive" some dead architectural style. In them "intellectual" and artisan collaborate no longer, even in the person of one man; intellectual considerations dictate all others. Thus Jefferson is concerned more with shapes as such than with either abstract principles or formal relationships; he is an architect who conceives of architecture as something to be read, and of architects as, above all, men of erudition. This kind of architecture represents not the consummation of the classical mind but the beginning of its disintegration. In what we call neoclassicism in architecture, the Empire style in furniture, outward forms of the classical tradition are preserved, but its spirit is lost. This neoclassicism is the vehicle for a transition from 18th-century, classical America to the new 19th-century civilization we know as Victorian.

NOTES

Quotations from Marcus Whiffen, "Bishop Berkeley" (*Architectural Review*, February 1958, pp. 9–13); quotations and data on Cary, Nicholson, and Spotswood from Whiffen, *The Public Buildings of Williamsburg* (Williamsburg, 1958), p. 32; from S. F. Kimball, *Mr. Samuel McIntire, Carver* (Portland, Me., 1940); reference to diary of Ezra Stiles in C. Bridenbaugh, *Peter Harrison* (Chapel Hill, 1949), pp. 1–2, fn. 1. Quotations from Joseph Moxon, *The Mechanick Exercises applied to the Art of Bricklayers Work* (London, 1700), and the Duchess of Marlborough, from Frank Jenkins, *Architect and Patron* (Oxford, 1961).

Salient facts of Richard Munday's life were first published by Norman M. Isham, *Trinity Church, Newport* (Boston, 1936). For critical analyses of his work, see Hugh Morrison, *Early American Architecture*, pp. 442–5, and A. F. Downing and V. J. Scully, *The Architectural Heritage of Newport* (Cambridge, 1952), pp. 48ff. John H. Green, *The Building of Old Colony House at Newport* (Newport, 1941) published the record of payment to Munday of £25 "for draughting a plan" which for Downing and Scully was proof "beyond doubt" that he designed the structure.

Edmund Woolley's receipted bill was known as early as 1906; in 1910 the *Pennsylvania Magazine of History and Biography* republished it in an article under the title "Who Was the Architect of the State House, Andrew Hamilton or Edmund Woolley?" Joseph Jackson, *Early Philadelphia Architects and Engineers* (Philadelphia, 1923), gave Woolley's dates as 1696–1771. See further C. E. Peterson, "Early Architects of Independence Hall" (*JSAH*, XI, 3, 1952, pp. 23–6), and Edward M. Riley, "The Independence Hall Group," in *Historic Philadelphia* (*Transactions of the American Philosophical Society*, XLIII, 1, 1953, pp. 10–18).

Quotation on Taliaferro from Morrison, *Early American Architecture*, p. 350; references to discussions of him in T. T. Waterman, *Mansions of Virginia*, and Whiffen, *Public Buildings of Williamsburg*.

On Harrison, the standard biography is by Bridenbaugh, *op. cit.* On Robert Smith, see C. E. Peterson, "Carpenters' Hall," *Historic Philadelphia*, and especially the Appendix, "Notes on Robert Smith," pp. 119–23. Quotation from Dr. Mease in "The Walnut Street Prison" (*JSAH*, XII, 4, 1953, pp. 24–5). On Ariss, see T. T. Waterman, *Mansions of Virginia*, pp. 244–5 and *passim*. On Hawks, see Alonzo T. Dill, *Governor Tryon and His Palace* (Chapel Hill, 1955), and T. T. Waterman and F. B. Johnston, *The Early Architecture of North Carolina* (Chapel Hill, 1941), pp. 32–4. On Buckland, see R. R. Beirne and J. H. Scarff, *William Buckland* (Baltimore, 1958). Results of recent research on McIntire (suggesting, among other things, that he may not have been a cabinetmaker as such, but only a supplier of decorative carvings for furniture) were presented in *Samuel McIntire: A Bicentennial Symposium* (Salem, Mass., 1957). On Robert Cary Long, Sr., see R. H. Howland and E. P. Spencer, *The Architecture of Baltimore* (Baltimore, 1953), pp. 54–9. On Hoban and Manigault, see B. St. J. Ravenel, *Architects of Charleston* (Charleston, South Carolina, 1945), wherein is found the "Extract of a letter from a gentleman in Georgetown to his friend in this city dated July 19, 1792" in the *Charleston City Gazette* for August 8, 1792. On Bulfinch see, *inter alia*, Charles Place, *Charles Bulfinch, Architect and Citizen* (Boston, 1925). Bulfinch's work on the Capitol is described by T. F. Hamlin in *Greek Revival Architecture* (1944) and *Benjamin Henry Latrobe* (1955). On Jefferson see, *inter alia*, S. F. Kimball, *Thomas Jefferson, Architect* (Boston, 1916).

VICTORIAN AMERICA: THE 19th CENTURY

I

The "Classical Revivals":

Transition to Victorian America

1. THE CLASSICAL SYMBOL:
Forms and Spirit of Neoclassicism in the New Republic

. . . Bombastic, pedantic, trashy. . . . Many of the objects, being exactly copied from the fine remains of ancient art, are unquestionably beautiful in themselves; but we . . . think them, for the most part, quite unsuitable for articles of household furniture.

SO A WRITER in the *Edinburgh Review* for 1807 greeted the introduction to England of what later came to be called the "neoclassical" or "Empire" style in Thomas Hope's *Household Furniture and Interior Decorations*. Many an American must have felt the same when this fashionable style of the Napoleonic Empire came in its turn to this country. Looking at examples like those illustrated (*84A, B*), he might well have agreed that "the articles are in general too bulky, massive, and ponderous for general use"; wondered why, after "the improving luxury of the age has gone on to make [furniture] lighter and lighter for the greater part of a century, Mr. Hope . . . has produced such an assemblage of square timber and massive brass . . ."; and joined in objecting "to the whole scheme and system of embellishment, as being . . . a chaos of symbols and effigies which no man can interpret who has not the whole Pantheon at his finger ends." And to many modern connoisseurs and historians of furniture, what happened in the early decades of the 19th century still does seem some strange and inexplicable collapse of taste. From delicate ornament and subtle proportion to ponderous exercises in classical sculpture laboriously bolted together; from nice co-ordinations of structure and decoration to glaring contrasts of dark wood, hard white marble, and shiny brass fittings—that such a shift could occur, and so suddenly, seems incredible. Yet it did; and it was irresistible. People like the Edinburgh reviewer may point out that Empire decoration is inconsistent with structure, that Empire furni-

ture is ill proportioned and unfunctional; it will do them no good. They may "venture to predict" that the preoccupation with classical "emblems and symbols" at the expense of every other consideration—which is really what explains the sudden change of form Hope introduced—"will not be much more permanent than those [fashions] which it has supplanted"; they will be disappointed. For this Empire style was not a change in fashion, not a logical sequence in classical development; it represented the first step towards a different concept of art altogether.

Just as a century before, furniture first manifested the coming of the classical mind, so now it provided the first and most dramatic indication that art in the 19th century would be based on very different principles. But precisely what was happening, to what extent symbolism was becoming an obsession not merely with pedantic aesthetes like Thomas Hope but among intellectual leaders of all kinds everywhere, we may realize best by considering the architectural ideas of Thomas Jefferson.

Throughout his lifetime, Thomas Jefferson had a hand in designing all sorts of buildings, from small houses for neighbors to seats of government in the new Federal capital. Most of the houses were designed according to basically Adamesque–Federal principles. But the three major works on which his great place in American architectural history depends—the Capitol in Richmond, Monticello as rebuilt during the years of his public life, and the University of Virginia campus in Charlottesville—were not. In them is evident a very different approach to design, based on a concern for what, failing a better word, can be called classical symbolism. What their forms "say" is more important than the forms or their composition as such. And it is this concern for symbolism that explains an otherwise inexplicable

84. "EMPIRE" FURNITURE IN THE WIN-
TERTHUR MUSEUM

 (A) "Empire Parlor" from an Albany, New
York, house, c.1830.

 (84 B) "Empire" chair, c.1815–20.

 First popularized as a symbolic statement
of Napoleon Bonaparte's pretensions to the Holy
Roman Empire, the Empire style had become
dominant in American furniture by the 1820s.
These pieces illustrate the style's heavy dependence on archaeology, not only in deliberate and
pedantic imitation of Greek and Roman motifs

contradiction in these buildings—comparable to the sudden shift from nicely functional delicacy to ponderous Empire pedantry in furniture—between the eminently practical nature of the details and the extraordinarily unfunctional character of the whole.

In arranging the interior space of the new capitol, Jefferson showed the same deft awareness of functional needs as in his smaller houses or the earlier proposed remodeling of the Palace at Williamsburg. But why choose a Roman temple form in the first place? Anything more impractical and inconvenient for meetings of large numbers of people could hardly be imagined than a box lighted only from the front door, intended

and materials (columns, caryatids, lyres, scrolls; dark mahogany, gilt appliqués, marble), but in direct reproduction of what were thought to be Graeco-Roman types of chairs, doorframes and window frames, lamps, etc. Most of the work was done in New York, center of American cabinetmaking from this time until the Civil War.

to store offerings to some god and never for accommodating people, with a great portico and podium contributing little or no usable space at enormous expense. At Monticello, Jefferson's inventive practicality was demonstrated in dozens of ways, in recessed beds and co-ordinated sliding doors, in an automatic dumb-waiter and indoor weather vane and "chaise-desk," in the location of service buildings under a terrace, in brick arches to provide ventilation under the main floor. But in the basic concept of the enlargement program undertaken while Jefferson was President, functional considerations are everywhere sacrificed. To add the functionally useless dome and portico, he had to destroy his own large and airy second-floor library room, substitute for it cramped and awkward spaces next to his bedroom; he had in effect to split his house into two separate parts connected only by an open balcony, and plunge his drawing room into gloom. Similarly with the University of Virginia campus. Whatever the advantages in Jefferson's mind of an "academical village" over a single large building, certainly practicality was not foremost among them; the cost of building rows of temple-houses separated by colonnades was equaled only by that of heating and servicing them.

In each case, it is clear that symbolic value was the justification of such inconveniences and extravagances. And it is equally clear what that symbolism was. In Jefferson's mind, public buildings in the new United States should be more than things of beauty; above all, they should state a creed. They should declare to the world the full meaning of American independence, that what was created in 1776 was not just another political entity, but a basically new way of life. With this nation, conceived in liberty and dedicated to an equality the Old World never knew, a new era in world history had begun. Its mission and destiny were plain—to be a light to lighten the Gentiles, the inspiration and model by which all peoples might come to freedom. But first that ideal must be realized and perfected at home. All the old pernicious habits of European

85. State Capitol, Richmond, Virginia. When the capital of Virginia was moved in 1780, Thomas Jefferson, as governor, presented a bill providing for the building of three new government offices, one each for legislative, judicial, and executive branches. After his departure as Minister to France in 1784, the legislature decided to house all three offices under one roof, and wrote requesting Jefferson to provide a design. Assisted by archaeological authority Charles-Louis Clérisseau, Jefferson obliged with plans and a model of the Roman temple at Nîmes (1st century A.D.) known as the Maison Carrée; construction was begun in August 1785, and was completed—with brick substituted for the original stone columns and walls, windows and an interior dome introduced, and the structure otherwise adapted for assembly usage—in 1788. Furnishings, including desks and draperies, were also designed by Jefferson; these were mostly destroyed when an upper floor collapsed in 1870, but were replaced by close replicas. Other changes include wings added 1904–6, and restoration of the Hall of Delegates in 1929.

thought must be rooted out so that every department of life might become truly American. It followed that Americans must develop a new and distinctive architecture of their own; and for Jefferson there was no doubt what that should be. The whole cast of his mind, his upbringing in patrician Virginia, predisposed him to see analogies between the new republic in America and the ancient Republic of Rome. Indeed, it was more than analogous; to him and his contemporaries it seemed as if this new nation, living proof of the classical conviction that men could control their destinies and mould worlds to their will, was the very reincarnation of the grandeur that had been Rome. In the heroes and statesmen of the Revolution, the selfless patriotism of Horatii and Cincinnati lived again; in the new Senate on the Potomac, the old Senate on the Tiber would be reborn; just so, in the new courthouses and capitols and official mansions of America the monuments of Rome would be rebuilt. Succeeding to Rome's destiny, America should succeed to Rome's architecture. No truth seemed more self-evident.

And to achieve this symbolism in architecture Jefferson was willing to sacrifice not only practical convenience but personal taste as well. He "stood for whole hours" in uncharacteristic ecstasy "gazing at the Maison Carrée, like a lover at his mistress," not because he felt its proportions were finer or its details more perfect than those of other buildings he had seen, but because for him it was the speaking symbol of all that America could and should stand for, proclaiming the strength of republican virtue, the beauty of discipline, the wisdom of rule by law rather than men, in a language he wanted all the United States to learn. To see this temple from Nîmes reconstructed in Richmond he was prepared to ignore all its functional inadequacies, forget all stylistic preferences of his own. It was not for aesthetic reasons that in remodeling and enlarging his Charlottesville home he substituted simple Roman windows for the subtle receding planes of his model from Morris's *Select Architecture;* that he raised the dome at the expense of low harmonious horizontal lines; that he renounced Adamesque delicacy of detail in favor of interior ornament based on measured drawings of antique friezes in Desgodets's *Edifices anciens de Rome.* The furniture that he imported, and the designs he supplied for friends' country homes much later than this, showed clearly enough what his personal taste was. There was nothing "wrong" with the original Monticello, physically or aesthetically speaking; Jefferson's family was no bigger, his periods of residence were shorter, and as an example of a cultivated Virginia planter's home the 1770s building had been advanced enough in style to be perfectly acceptable still. It was the architectural "language" that was wrong. Now that Jefferson was no longer an English squire in the provincial plantations, but one of the most prominent citizens—and indeed, as President, first citizen—of a republic in which the values and virtues of ancient Rome lived again, Monticello must be made an appropriate architectural symbol of them. By dome and portico men would be reminded of the Pantheon in Rome, and of the virtues that should ever (ideally at least) animate the public servants of a free republic; by the act of making Monticello a symbol Jefferson

would demonstrate how equality and the pursuit of happiness meant not that men should fall or be held to some common low denominator but all be free to use their talents to the full, how men born to means and taste should cultivate the arts and sciences and so through their own pursuit of happiness promote the welfare of all. Or again, if in his plan for the University of Virginia campus Jefferson damaged natural visual unity by making each pavilion demonstrate not merely different orders but particular variants of them— recognizably drawn from Diocletian's Baths, the Temple of Fortuna Virilis, the Theatre of Marcellus, and so on—it was not because he no longer accepted the older precepts of harmony, proportion, or balance. It was because for him all functional or aesthetic disadvantages were outweighed by the symbolism achieved by these rows of temples. Their diverse columns and arches and pediments put the whole range of classical orders before students' eyes, kept the whole panorama of Roman virtues before their minds. In these temples was an architectural exemplification of the "fasces" principle of Federal union—each building preserving individual differences and excellences, but deriving full meaning only in contributing to the common whole. As all these diverse façades took common orientation from the Pantheon-library, so all the diverse peoples settled in the United States might be unified by a common body of law and culture they all inherited from antiquity. Such an environment will do deliberately for the rising generation what the classical mind in art had done spontaneously for their fathers who founded the new republic: form their minds and pattern their actions on the sound Roman principle of freedom within discipline. Here in this academical village, girded round by its serpentine wall, was recreated a small piece of the ancient Roman world. Like those earlier American communities of Ephrata and Plymouth and Philadelphia, this was conceived by its founder as a new and perfect world; like them, too, it was intended to be a cell from which others would spring, even-

86. MONTICELLO, CHARLOTTESVILLE, VIRGINIA
Home of Thomas Jefferson. Originally built c.1773–c.1779, remodeled over the years 1796–1809.

(A) Garden façade, present appearance.
(86 B) Elevation of the central pavilion (left), compared with its probable inspiration, "Elevation of a Garden House," Pl. 43 of Robert Morris, Select Architecture, 1755 (right).

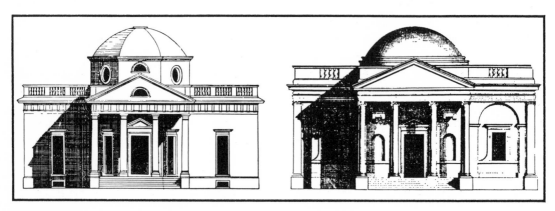

(86 C) Jefferson's bed and sitting room. Characteristic of Jefferson's practical ingenuity is the bed built into the wall and permitting access to two rooms, and the combination lounge and writing table; of his French taste, the drapery of French material arranged from his own sketches, and the Louis Seize chair, one of many he brought from France.

tually to cover the continent. To its students Jefferson might have said, as had Governor Winthrop to those Puritan voyagers on the *Arabella* two centuries before: ". . . Always having before our eyes our commission and community in the work . . . we must consider that we shall be as a city upon a hill, the eyes of all people are upon us." The ends were different, perhaps; the dream was the same.

The Roman forms of which Jefferson thus proposed to make an "American" art were familiar; a century of use had made them commonplace to every educated man. But the use Jefferson made of them was not commonplace. It is not what they are, but what they say, that determined the forms of the Capitol, Monticello, the library and pavilions of his university. What was involved was an altogether new way of looking at architecture. Where and how had it come about?

The idea of a symbolic architecture was hardly new with Jefferson, or to his time. It was in fact at least as old as the pyramids; and in more recent Western tradition, Jefferson had half a dozen sources to draw on. Possibly he learned of it first in his Masonic lodge. In those days Freemasonry was much less a benevolent and fraternal organization, much more a kind of religion and a way of life, than it is now. Men took its teachings very seriously; and for more than a century Freemasonry had been introducing initiates to the mysteries of "speculative architecture," showing them esoteric meanings of columns and capitals and ornamental motifs once revealed by the Supreme Architect to Solomon, Adam, and King Alfred, preserved through dark centuries of barbarism into the Enlightenment of the 18th century. It may well have been Freemasonry that motivated the otherwise rather inexplicable change from the Corinthian order of the

87. The University of Virginia at Charlottesville, originating as Albemarle Academy, in 1816 became, through action of the legislature, the first state university in the new nation. Shortly thereafter Thomas Jefferson, who had inspired the new kind of institution, began designing an equally new kind of campus—"an academical village," with "a small and separate lodge for each professorship, with only a hall below for his class, and two chambers above for himself; joining these lodges by barracks . . . opening into a covered way to give dry communication between all the schools, the whole of these arranged around an open square" at the head of which stood a library, the Rotunda. Construction, begun 1821, was largely completed by the time of Jefferson's death in 1826. Since then—aside from normal additions to the campus in the course of its growth—the principal change has been the replacement of the Rotunda in 1895–6 (it had been destroyed by fire in 1894) by the firm of McKim, Mead & White along what Late Victorian taste considered more "correct" lines. This firm also added the overscaled buildings that close the south end of Jefferson's campus.

Maison Carrée capitals to Ionic in those of the Richmond Capitol. Unlike Jefferson's other departures from his model—the introduction of windows, for instance—this can hardly have been forced by functional considerations. Even if it were true, as is often stated, that American workmen were too unskilled to execute Corinthian acanthus leaves, why not then have elected the more easily executed Doric order? Ionic is almost as difficult to carve as Corinthian. Considering Jefferson's basic sacrifice of practicality to symbolism by choosing such a model in the first place, the essentially needless departure from it in this detail makes real sense only if we assume that here too symbolism was the determinant. Freemasonry taught that each of the classical orders embodied a different and specific moral virtue; could it not have been that Jefferson was thinking here in Masonic terms of the Ionic order as embodying Solomonic wisdom, and hence appropriate for a legislative building as Corinthian, identified with the "beauty of the sanctuary," could never be?

But classical symbolism was hardly an exclusively Masonic idea, of course. In Jefferson's library there were many books that presented it in one form or another. Palladio in the *Four Books*—of which Jefferson was such an admirer that he owned three English and two French editions—made much of a correspondence between the absolute principles of classical architecture and the fundamentals of natural law; we know that Jefferson found the argument impressive. Or there were more explicit expositions, like those by Robert Adam—whose *Spalatro* Jefferson noted in his 1784 inventory as one of the books he wanted to own—urging patriotic Britons to adopt Roman Imperial forms to show forth the might of their even greater empire; here was an idea—that one nation might legitimately express its aspirations in the architectural forms of another—which he would later remember. But undoubtedly it was during Jefferson's stay in France from 1784 to 1789 as first Minister from the United States that all these disparate ideas came to focus in his mind, and his concepts of classical symbolism took mature shape.

Jefferson came to France fresh from the Revolution, detesting everything English, full of gratitude for the French help which had done so much to make Independence secure, predisposed to admire and adopt for American use every possible French idea in arts and science and thought. And everywhere he found them, for France in these last years before its own revolution was seething with "radical" thought on all subjects. Professor Alexander has described how "the public memorial as we know it is essentially a creation of the Revolutionary Age in France,"

and how "the allegorical temper of that age was especially amenable to symbolic architecture." That Jefferson soon became acquainted with the advance-guard theories of a "rational" architecture promulgated by Claude-Nicolas Ledoux and

THE PILLARS OF

WISDOM, STRENGTH AND BEAUTY.

88. MASONIC INFLUENCES ON NEOCLASSICAL SYMBOLISM

(A) The Pillars of Wisdom, Strength, and Beauty. This page from a textbook on Scottish Rite Freemasonry illustrates the symbolic approach to architecture so strongly inculcated by this secret society in the early 19th century; it teaches that the Ionic order, on which stands King Solomon, is the embodiment of wisdom; the Doric (Hiram, King of Tyre), of strength; the Corinthian (with the legendary "Hiram Abiff"), of beauty. In the fifty years before the Morgan scandal and the anti-Masonic movement of the 1830s broke its power, Freemasonry was a force of incalculable influence in American life; it is perhaps no coincidence, then, that so many of the heroes of Revolution and Independence were commemorated by columnar monuments like these.

K ★
Masonic Hall

★ Corner of St Pauls St and Court House Lane ★

Erected by the Gr. Lodge of Maryland. Begun 1813. Finished 1822 Cost $20000.

J. Small Arch.t

(88 B) Masonic Hall, Baltimore, Maryland, as built c.1813–22. Composed of symbolic elements used sculpturally, with virtually no structural relationship to the building behind, this façade represents the direct translation to America of the concept of symbolic classicism developed in Revolutionary France. Its designer, Maximilien Godefroy (c.1765–c.1845), had been personally associated with both Jacques-Louis David, founder of neoclassical painting in France, and Étienne-Louis Boullée, revolutionary innovator in architectural symbolism; this particular façade seems most immediately derived, however, from the Pavillon de Louveciennes of Claude-Nicolas Ledoux, whose 1804 book of symbolic designs, L'Architecture considerée sous le rapport de l'Art des Moeurs et de la Législation, *was widely used by avant-garde architects of the period.*

Étienne-Louis Boullée is evident from his description of Ledoux's new Paris city gates in an early letter home. From such sources he could realize hitherto unsuspected potentialities in using classical forms for expressive purposes; but given his upbringing and early devotion to Pal-

ladio and Robert Morris, it was hardly to be expected that he would accept entirely "radical" ideas of composing classical elements in deliberately unclassical ways, disregarding classical unity to obtain romantic or geometric effects. By temperament he was much more disposed to the rival camp headed by archaeologist Charles-Louis Clérisseau, who had accompanied Robert Adam on the famous expedition to Spalatro, and who advocated stricter, not looser, adherence to Graeco-Roman prototypes. It was to this man, and to his *Monumens de Nismes,* published in 1778 and one of Jefferson's earliest purchases in France, that Jefferson turned when he received the Virginia legislature's definite commission to design the new capitol at Richmond. But in all probability what came as the greatest revelation to Jefferson was not so much the developments in French architecture as the revolution in the concept of art embodied in the neoclassical painting of Jacques-Louis David.

It was in 1784, the year of Jefferson's arrival in France, that David first exhibited his "Oath of the Horatii," which inaugurated the new movement. Jefferson must surely have seen it and heard its sensational new principles discussed; for a time, the whole French intellectual world talked of little else. And the new concept of art it embodied was perfectly calculated to appeal to a man of his temperament. No connoisseur of painting, he found here something that required no special knowledge, for it was hardly painting in the old sense at all; it was more of a literary document, the statement of a political position. And it was a statement made with just the sort of single-minded logic, the impatience with qualifying clauses or concessions to circumstance, that marked his own Declaration of Independence. The forms David used and the rationale with which he justified them were those Jefferson was best qualified to understand. If, as theories of painting since the Renaissance had maintained, of all possible subjects in painting the ideal human form in noble action is the most beautiful; if of all forms Graeco-Roman classical are the most ideal; and if of all actions Graeco-Roman history and mythology provide the most noble ex-

(88 C) "Oath of the Horatii," the painting by Jacques-Louis David, exhibited in 1785, which effectively dramatized the new symbolic concept of classical forms at the moment Thomas Jefferson arrived in Paris searching for a vehicle to express American national aspirations in art. Small version, painted 1786, in the Toledo (Ohio) Museum of Art.

amples, why bother with half-measures and general principles—why not imitate Graeco-Roman art exactly and be done with it? Paint pictures that are truly, totally Roman, with outlines as precise as the drawings on ancient vases; clear decisive primary colors like those the ancient writers ascribed to Polygnotus and the other great masters of antiquity, and which are still to be seen in the Tuscan tombs discovered by modern scholars; composed in large simple forms against plain neutral backgrounds like ancient statues in a gallery, ranged along a foreground plane like friezes on temple pediments. David's new theory of the purpose of painting was equally congenial. Sir Joshua Reynolds in Eng-

land had pronounced in his *Discourses* that the artist's proper goal is "to improve mankind by the grandeur of his ideas"; David, with French logic, went further—the artist, he declared, owes it to mankind to rise above mere aesthetics. More than simply please or elevate, he must instruct. And most congenial of all to Jefferson would have been David's notions of what kind of instruction artists should give. In the "Oath" and the paintings which followed it David pointed out, with the same uncompromising clarity as their uncompromisingly Roman forms, the virtues of republican self-government and the vices of absolute monarchy. The paintings proclaimed by inference precisely those truths which Jeffer-

253

son held most self-evident, which justified the American Revolution for him and gave meaning and purpose to the new United States. How under the hereditary rule of degenerate kings and venal noblemen you could never hope to find citizens with the simple patriotism Horatius's sons learned in their republican home. How only in a republican state could there be a scene like "The Lictors Bringing Brutus the Body of His Son," because only republican government bred officials honest enough to condemn their own sons' crimes. How free men must always guard against that despotism which always lurks ready to pervert their institutions and, as "The Death of Socrates" warns, persecute dissent and destroy the greatest and wisest spirits.

Here in France it seemed that David's new art, which later generations would call "neoclassical," could never be more than a subversive protest. Not so in America. There the ideal had become a reality. There the Roman world and its republican virtues had been reborn. In that sense, David's neoclassicism was already "American"; there remained only to translate it into a suitable medium. Painting was as yet too small a part of American life to move the masses. The development of neoclassical furniture had to await the triumph of David's ideas in Revolutionary and Napoleonic France. At this stage of his nation's development, only "architecture," as Jefferson wrote in 1788, is "worth great attention. . . . In every space of twenty years . . .

houses are to be built for three-fourths of our inhabitants. It is, then, among the important arts; and it is desirable to introduce taste into an art which shows so much." Jefferson returned from France determined to use his influence to propagate neoclassical ideals for official architecture in every way he could. And, of course, no one was in a more strategic position to do it. As Secretary of State, Vice-President, President, and senior statesman, he had all sorts of opportunities to influence choice of suitable designs for public buildings, and of suitable men to carry them out. He made the most of them. If America in the early decades of the 19th century revived Roman, and later Greek, architecture on a scale unequaled anywhere else, it was in no small measure due to Jefferson's tireless promotion. In 1807 B. H. Latrobe, who of all men was in the best position to know, wrote to him: "Your administration, Sir, in respect to public works, has hitherto [had] claims of gratitude and respect from the public and from posterity. It is no flattery to say that you have planted the arts in your country. The works already in this city [Washington] are the monuments of your judgment and of your zeal and of your taste." So it is that the development of neoclassical principles in architecture and furniture during the quarter-century from 1800 to 1825 could be considered in large part as the triumph of "Jeffersonian classical" symbolism.

NOTES

Quotations from Wendell D. Garrett, "The Earliest Known Review of a Furniture Design Book" (*Winterthur Newsletter*, May 29, 1961); of Latrobe's letter, from S. F. Kimball, *Thomas Jefferson, Architect* (Boston, 1916), p. 84; from Robert L. Alexander, "The Public Memorial and Godefroy's Battle Monument [in Baltimore, 1815–25]" (*JSAH*, XVII, 1, pp. 19–24, 1958).

Jefferson's skill at arranging interior spaces was particularly well demonstrated in the rotunda-library at the University of Virginia. While conceiving of the building *in toto* as a half-scale replica of the Pantheon in Rome, he characteristically departed altogether from Roman precedent on the interior, designing a group of three Adamesque–Federal oval rooms around an irregularly curving entrance hall. This concept was destroyed in the academic rebuilding directed by Stanford White in 1895.

For Jefferson's letter describing his visit to Nîmes, and a general account of it, see G. Chinard, *Thomas Jefferson* (Boston, 1929), pp. 169ff. On the relation of Monticello to Morris's *Select Architecture*, see Clay Lancaster, "Jefferson's Architectural Indebtedness to Robert Morris" (*JSAH*, X, 1, 1951, pp. 3–10). On Jefferson's personal French taste, see Marie Kimball, *The Furnishings of Monticello* (Charlottesville, 1954). On Jefferson's Masonic connections, cf. I. T. Frary, *Thomas Jefferson* (Richmond, 1940), pp. 49–50, in which is preserved the record of Jefferson's participation in the laying of the cornerstone of the first building of the University of Virginia (Pavilion VII) "by the Charlottesville Lodge of Masons" on October 6, 1817. There are few details on Jefferson's Masonic affiliation, probably because the records were destroyed; J. Hugo Tatsch, *Freemasonry in the Thirteen Colonies* (1929), especially comments on the obscurity of Masonic records in Virginia. Washington, of course, was very prominent in the Craft.

The State Capitol at Richmond is only one of many monuments wherein possible Masonic influence on design may be detected. For example, William Strickland exhibited at Philadelphia, in May 1813, a design for the Washington Monument in Washington described as "a grand allegorical figure. The characteristic strength of the Doric order represents the firmness of Washington . . . upon which was erected the Temple of Liberty, supported by the Wisdom and Beauty of the Confederation." (A. A. Gilchrist, *William Strickland*, p. 47.) At the same period, DeMontlezun in his *Voyage fait dans les années 1816 et 1817* . . . (Paris 1818) was bewailing the prevalence of what he, as an old Bourbon, called "this mass of childish [Masonic] absurdities" in Baltimore, not only among "workers and artisans" but also among "men of education, who should have had sense. . . . The whole mass of people here is gangrened, and the few individuals enlightened enough to laugh and mock are too far dominated. . . ." In many respects, Freemasonry was the "state religion" of the early republic; and while the Morgan scandal was immediately responsible for its decline, ultimately the cause was that general collapse of the whole rationale of 18th-century thought so well described by D. J. Boorstin, *The Lost World of Thomas Jefferson* (1948).

2. TOWARDS A NATIONAL STYLE:
Experiments in Classical Symbolism, 1800—1825

"GOOD GOD! Who besides a tory could have foreseen, or a Briton predicted . . . such inconsistency and perfidiousness . . . ? We are fast verging to anarchy and confusion!" So George Washington wrote to John Jay of the political situation in 1786. He might well have used the same words to describe the state of architecture in the post-Revolutionary period. For by the 1790s classical art, once the expression and vehicle of unity, was visibly dissolving into a welter of conflicting "styles," helping only to compound a general cultural confusion.

It seemed at times as if the Revolution which had broken off the old common connection with Britain must have the result of splitting the country into irreconcilably different cultural regions and classes, each with a classical expression of its own. True, the old 18th-century tradition was still strong; the Adamesque elegance of its final phase was becoming the chosen expression of the new ruling mercantile class of the young republic, while among conservatives the even earlier principles of its Chippendale phase were being perpetuated in a post-Georgian style, all the more fervently because the standards and way of life it manifested seemed so triumphantly vindicated by the Revolution. But in the more cosmopolitan centers of Baltimore, Philadelphia, and New York, and among the consciously intellectual class, it seemed that the Revolution demanded a complete break with the past; and to give expression to this conviction, all sorts of "foreign" artists and "radical" ideas were coming into the country, introducing what appeared to be hopelessly diverse forms and contradictory theories.

Many of the artists were French, riding in on the great Revolutionary wave of pro-French enthusiasms. Of these, some came for only a few years and left again, leaving a variety of monuments to every shade of French taste. Joseph-

François Mangin, for example, appeared in New York, recommended by Washington, as city surveyor in 1794; in 1802 he collaborated with local artisan-architect John McComb, Jr. (1763–1853), in designing a city hall in Louis Seize style; around 1815 he left, presumably returning to France. Joseph-Jacques Ramée (1764–1842) came to New York in 1811 via Hamburg to assist in developing upper New York State; in 1812 he designed for Eliphalet Nott, inspiration and first president of Union College in Schenectady, a campus whose uniformity of style in all buildings and common orientation to a central library were intended to symbolize the principle of union in accordance with the laws of reason, whose great open court like that of Versailles symbolized the "royal privilege" of education being thrown open to all, and which may well have been an inspiration to Jefferson in designing the campus at Charlottesville. This success was not repeated when he competed for the Washington Monument commission in Baltimore, however, and after some work on a nearby country house (the grounds and possibly the façade of Calverton), Ramée left the country in 1816. Or again there was Maximilien Godefroy (c.1765–c.1845), whose stay in Baltimore from 1805 to 1819 resulted in the first Gothic Revival church in the United States (St. Mary's Seminary chapel, 1806), the first American-made war memorial (the Battle Monument, 1815–25, based on Napoleonic columns of the decade before), and several more or less advanced examples of French "rational" classicism (the Masonic Hall of c.1813, Unitarian Church of c.1817, etc.).

Other Frenchmen, though they stayed, had similarly meteoric careers, rising to sudden fame and relapsing into almost equally sudden obscurity; such were architect Stephen Hallet (d.1825), cabinetmakers Charles-Honoré Lannuier (1779–1819) and his successor Charles

89. UNITED STATES CAPITOL, WASHINGTON

A summary of classical traditions in 19th-century America:

(A) Original plan (1791) by William Thornton. Reflecting the amateur and derivative culture of an earlier, provincial America, Thornton's plan was simple and straightforward. It called for a central rotunda capped by a dome in the manner of fashionable mid-18th-century public buildings in Europe; flanking this somewhat naïve proclamation of grown-upness, a wing devoted to the House of Representatives chamber (left), and a Senate wing, containing the Senate chamber, arranged in a Roman hemicycle, with committee rooms and grand staircase behind.

(89 B) Perspective design for the Capitol by B. H. Latrobe. Under the regime of European-trained Latrobe (1803–17), most of Thornton's naïvetés were eliminated, and the Capitol largely completed (and restored after the 1814 fire) with sophisticated monumentality and refinement typical of the last phase of the 18th-century classical tradition. Charles Bulfinch of Boston completed the Capitol (1817–31) along Latrobe's lines, adding touches of his local Adamesque idiom, particularly in interior décor.

(89 C) The Capitol after addition of new and larger House and Senate wings, and elevation of the dome, by Thomas U. Walter, 1855–65. Nineteenth-century technology made possible a higher, iron-ribbed dome, and High Victorian taste encouraged more picturesque outlines and massing, but the original classical tradition remained dominant.

Gruez, and the engineer-designer Pierre-Charles L'Enfant (1754–1825). Hallet arrived in 1797; though Jefferson's early protégé, and winner of second prize in the competition for the United States Capitol with an advanced neoclassical design, he never really managed to establish himself and died almost forgotten at New Rochelle. Lannuier had much the same experience. After settting up practice in New York in 1803 by advertising, in the *Evening Post* for July 15, that he "makes all kinds of Furniture . . . in the newest and latest French fashion," in 1812 he was commissioned to make a set of twenty-four mahogany armchairs for the Mangin–McComb City Hall (presumably in the neoclassical Empire manner of those owned by the Maryland Historical Society); but when he died after a lingering illness in October 1819 his business had long been languishing too. Charles Gruez,

who in the *Evening Post* for November of that year "has the honor of informing . . . the public . . . that he has taken the establishment of the late Mr. Lannuier . . . where he continues to make all kinds of furniture and fancy work for which said establishment was so well known throughout the United States," soon failed entirely, drifted out of business and out of history.

L'Enfant's was the most spectacular example, however. A major of engineers who had gained a reputation as an architect and become a personal friend of George Washington's while a volunteer in the Continental Army, he was commissioned in 1788 to design what was hoped would be the new seat of the Federal Government, Federal Hall in New York City (demolished 1812, cf. *21A*). When the decision was made to lay out the new Federal capital on the Potomac, L'Enfant wrote to Washington in Sep-

90. UNION COLLEGE, SCHENECTADY, NEW YORK

Designed in 1812 by Joseph-Jacques Ramée, at the request of President Eliphalet Nott.

(A) The original Ramée campus plan, showing the concept of blocks of buildings in uniform style arranged around a great court with central library, the whole symbolizing the concept of union and democratic opportunity to which Nott's new college was dedicated, and possibly providing a precedent for Jefferson's University of Virginia campus.

tember of 1789 offering his services; they were accepted, and it was on his plans, published in 1791, that Washington City was (and is) built. Both designs showed a new kind of conscious symbolism. In Federal Hall it took the rather naïve form, popular in mirrors and other furniture in the time, of using American materials (marble for fireplaces, e.g.) and emblematic motifs such as capitals with stars and rays in foliage, exterior frieze with thirteen metopes each containing a star, pediment crowned by an eagle grasping thirteen arrows, and so on. The symbolism of Washington City was more mature, coherent, and inherent—radiating streets and squares named after the thirteen states, centering on the Capitol and the White House to symbolize union, embellished with

> . . . statues, columns, obelisks, or any other ornaments . . . to perpetuate not only the memory of such individuals whose counsels or military achievements were conspicuous in giving liberty and independence to this country, but also those whose usefulness hath rendered them worthy of general imitation, to invite the youth of succeeding generations to tread in the paths of those sages or heroes whom their country has thought proper to celebrate.

Conceived on a grand scale to symbolize the future greatness of the nation, this plan assured

(90 B) South College, as built c.1813. As executed, the forms are more Adamesque than originally called for; probably local workmen modified to their own traditions the more severely "rational" geometric designs of Ramée.

L'Enfant's place in American history. It did not, however, assure him future success; dismissed in 1792 for insubordination to the Federal commissioners, further frustrated in carrying out grandiose plans for Robert Morris's mansion in Philadelphia, L'Enfant spent the rest of his life in futility, feuds, and interminable recriminations.

Then there were immigrant Britons, likewise bringing with them all sorts of new ideas and variants on old ones. In South Carolina and in his winning design for the White House, James Hoban introduced Palladian forms learned in Ireland. Duncan Phyfe, though arrived in Albany from Scotland by 1784 and presumably trained to cabinetmaking in New York, exhibited such receptivity to every new trend that in the course of his long practice—established in New York by 1792, in 1837 incorporated as a com-

pany with a hundred workmen—he worked through four distinct styles, from a delicate Heppelwhite–Adamesque to a degenerate "Empire" that he himself called "butcher furniture." George Hadfield (c.1764–1826) came from England, where he had been gold medalist at the Royal Academy, to superintend building the Capitol in 1795; unable to resolve the complicated conflict of personalities among himself and the other architects, Hallet and Thornton, he was dismissed in 1798, and thereafter worked intermittently around Washington, producing such novel monuments to new tastes as the Van Ness mausoleum based on the Temple of Vesta and the Custis mansion at Alexandria (Arlington, c.1804–17), which featured a massive portico modeled on Greek Doric temples at Paestum he had seen in 1794.

Finally there were cosmopolitans so diverse in background and skills as William Thornton (1759–1828) and Benjamin Henry Latrobe (1764–1820). Born in the Virgin Islands, educated as a physician in Scotland, traveled in Paris, associated with John Fitch in developing paddle-wheel steamboats, Thornton began his architectural career soon after settling in Philadelphia in 1787, when "I got some books and worked a few days, then gave a plan in the ancient Ionic order which carried the day" in the 1789 competition to design a building for the Library Company of Philadelphia. In 1791 he won the competition for the United States Capitol with a neoclassical design widely believed to have been stolen in essentials from Stephen Hallet, who (ironically enough) had to be engaged to execute it, since Thornton admittedly had at this time no practical architectural knowledge whatsoever. Subsequently Thornton drew designs for such variously Adamesque to Roman Revival works as The Octagon in Washington, Tudor Place, and Pavilion VII of Jefferson's University of Virginia.

In contrast to this very model of an ingratiating dilettante was the even more cosmopolitan Benjamin Henry Latrobe, who appears from the first as a completely trained professional. Born in England of Moravian parents with extraordinarily colorful backgrounds—his father born in Dublin, son of a French count; his mother born in Bethlehem, Pennsylvania, granddaughter of a German baron who had been abbot of a Roman Catholic monastery—Latrobe had been educated to an awareness of all the latest architectural trends in England, France, and Germany, and as head draftsman in the office of the senior S. P. Cockerell had participated in such large projects as the Admiralty Buildings in London. His coming to America at all was something of an accident; his wife died young, architectural commissions were few because of the Napoleonic wars, and he had an inheritance to claim in Pennsylvania through his mother. Once arrived, however (in Norfolk, Virginia, 1796), he was soon recognized by Jefferson, Washington, and other prominent people as by far the ablest architect on the American scene; for the rest of his life commissions followed rapidly, in every part of the country.

In his work an amazing versatility and command of every current idiom was displayed.

Latrobe undertook engineering projects from waterworks in Philadelphia and New Orleans to a dry dock for the first American "mothball fleet." He executed private houses, banks, exchanges, theatres, churches, Masonic halls, Federal commissions—he gave the Capitol and the White House in Washington their polished forms —college buildings, lighthouses, tombstones, statue pedestals, and funiture. And he worked in every style. His houses varied from geometric simplicity at Adena (Chillicothe, Ohio, 1805–6) to Adamesque–Federal elegance in Henry Clay's Ashland (Lexington, Kentucky, c.1812, later altered) and "Gothick" at Sedgeley outside Philadelphia (for William Crammond, c.1800).

On some public buildings—the Virginia Penitentiary at Richmond (1797) or the Center Station Pumping House in Philadelphia (1799), for instance—he worked in broad geometric forms expressive of utilitarian function inspired by Ledoux's rational classicism in France. On others, such as the 1798 Bank of Pennsylvania, where the first Greek Revival portico in America was ingeniously combined with a Pantheon-like Roman dome, or the Custom House at New Orleans (1807–9), he played with subtle spatial combinations of forms in the manner of Sir John Soane, whose English Regency elegance he undoubtedly knew. And he also displayed a precocious command of historical styles used as symbolic images. In 1808 he proposed a library of congress to be built on the model of an Egyptian hypostyle hall, presumably in allusion to the wisdom of the ages kept therein. The furniture that he designed for Dolly Madison in the White House (1809–10), and the close approximation to a Greek Doric façade that he adapted from the Temple of Marcellus for Pavilion X of the University of Virginia (sent at Jefferson's request, c.1817), were appropriate because, as Latrobe explained in an *Anniversary Oration* before the Society of Artists in Philadelphia in 1811, a new Greece was developing "in the woods of America": "Greece was free; in Greece every citizen felt himself an important . . . part of his republic." At the same time, he was introducing Gothic in designs for the Roman Catholic Cathedral in Baltimore (first large-scale Gothic Revival design in the country, 1805), Christ Church in Washington (1808), St. Paul's in Alexandria (Virginia, c. 1816), and the Bank of Philadelphia (1807; later demolished and replaced with a classical building by Strickland). Of these, Latrobe's plans for the Baltimore Cathedral were perhaps the most important historically, for more than usual symbolic significance attached to this building. As seat of what had once been governing Catholic diocese of all the English provinces, it was a reminder that not all Catholics were Spaniards or Frenchmen, that Catholics had played a part in building up English America, and that the new United States was not entirely a "Protestant country." Nothing is more typical of the new approach to art coming in during the early 19th century than the alternate sets of plans Latrobe submitted to the Bishop and his advisors, one in Gothic, the other an adaptation of the Pantheon in Rome. In discussions of their relative merits, hardly any weight was put on aesthetic value; the whole question was whether Gothic, as symbolic of a Church "the same yesterday, today, and forever," was more suitable than Roman. Roman won out simply because Gothic could not match its combination of "patriotic American" and "loyal Roman Catholic" symbolism.

Between the two extremes of provincial conservatives and "foreign stylists" were native "architects" of every description. Gentleman designers like Gabriel Manigault of Charleston, quasi-professionals like Charles Bulfinch of Boston, men growing to architectural pretensions out of provincial artisan traditions like Samuel McIntire of Salem, the younger John McComb in New York, the senior Robert Cary Long in Baltimore, and many more—all were working in provincial versions of later phases of the old classical tradition, adding local Palladian or Adamesque variants to the potpourri that was American architecture in the early Federal period. Typical of the general level of taste among them, their patrons, and the public, was the First Bank of the United States building in Philadelphia, designed by an ex-captain of militia and unsuccessful business entrepreneur from New Hampshire named Samuel Blodget (b. 1757). Over this three-story New England brick house with a Palladian portico in front, the *Gazette of the United States* rhapsodized as follows on December 23, 1797:

> Wednesday morning the workmen at the new Bank of the United States struck their scaffolding, and unfolded the novel and enchanting scene of a truly Grecian edifice, composed of American white marble [i.e., the portico; walls were brick]. The entrance to this building is by a flight of nine steps through a Portico, in its proportions nearly corresponding to the front of the celebrated Roman temple at Nismes; the pediment is supported by six columns of the order of Corinth, with the decorations they bore at Palmyra and Rome when architecture was at its zenith in the Augustan age.... As this is the first finished building of any consequence wherein true taste and knowledge has been displayed in this country [*sic!*], it is a pleasing task to inform its inhabitants that the architect is an American, and was born in the state of Massachusetts [*sic*].

As the figure of Washington stood out over the political confusion of the time, however, so above all this architectural chaos rose the figure of Thomas Jefferson. It was not so much that he was more knowledgeable architecturally than anybody else—obviously he was not—as that he had a consistent idea and vision of what an American architecture ought to be. Jefferson might talk occasionally in a fashionable vein of building as garden temples at Monticello "a specimen of Gothic, model of the Pantheon, model of cubic architecture [Maison Carrée], a specimen of Chinese"; but this was in the 18th-century tradition of "play architecture," of "Gothick" and *chinoiserie*. For serious architecture he never lost sight of the forest for the trees; he knew what would symbolize American ideals and what would not, and he radiated his

91. *Cathedral of the Assumption of the Blessed Virgin Mary, Baltimore, Maryland. First designs for a new cathedral were submitted to Bishop Carroll by B. H. Latrobe in 1804, in the new Gothic Revival style, to symbolize the medieval Catholic heritage. Eventually, however, an alternate set adapted from the Pantheon in Rome was chosen, on the basis of its double allusion to "patriotic Americanism" and "loyalty to Rome." Construction began in 1809; interrupted by the war, it was resumed in 1817, the building enclosed in 1818 and dedicated 1821, but not finally completed until 1863, when John H. B. Latrobe finished the portico his father had designed. In the cathedral's final form Catholic symbolism was accentuated by addition of an extra length of nave and two towers, reminiscent both of St. Peter's and of the 17th-century towers added to the Pantheon itself (and since removed again).*

idealism on everyone connected with architecture —on his own slaves (whom he tried in spite of all discouragements to train as artisans); on workmen employed on the Virginia Capitol, Monticello, and the university; on the aristocratic Virginia families for whom he provided house plans; even on finely trained European architects like Hallet and Latrobe. He tried, though without much success, to have fine arts formally taught at the College of William and Mary, Albemarle Academy, and the University of Virginia; significantly enough, it was the professor of *Ideology,* according to the 1818 report of the Educational Commission written by Jefferson, who was to teach fine arts at the University. He encouraged native painters like Charles Willson Peale and John Trumbull in their attempts to raise standards of taste, by supporting the Pennsylvania Academy of the Fine Arts and by providing the country with distinguished examples of French and Italian art—Houdon's statue of Washington and bust of Lafayette, Andrei and Franzoni's sculpture in the Capitol, Raggi's capitals at the university. The indirect influence of works like the Virginia Capitol, Monticello, and the university campus is literally incalculable, though the later spread of forms reminiscent of theirs throughout the whole country is some measure of it.

Such was the direct power of Jefferson's position, personality, and ideas that even professionals as highly trained as Latrobe found themselves influenced by him. This was apparent in their first collaborative effort, the Richmond penitentiary; here Latrobe, while designing in accordance with Ledoux's modern "rational" theories, was also carrying out Jefferson's insistence on a "plain, decent, appearance" and following the ideal prison plan by Pierre-Gabriel Bugniet of Lyons that Jefferson had found published in the *Mercure de France* for July 1765 and sent to Governor Wood of Virginia in March of 1797. After Jefferson, as President, appointed Latrobe Surveyor of Public Works of the United States in 1803, they worked together to make something more monumental, more symbolically American out of Hoban's White House and Thornton's Capitol. Always Jefferson insisted that in determining forms, associations with Roman prototypes should supersede the kind of aesthetic or functional considerations to which Latrobe's training predisposed him. Thus the two disagreed violently over roofing the House of Representatives. Latrobe on practical grounds wanted a hemispherical dome lighted by a lantern with vertical glass panes which would be easily waterproofed.

Jefferson, however, wanted something like the dome over the new Halle aux Blés that he had seen in Paris, with long ribs springing from a drum to meet an oculus above, the spaces between them glassed to admit floods of light—not merely because he felt "the Halle au bled lights . . . would solely have made it the handsomest room in the world" but because, of course, the room would represent a version of the Pantheon in Rome, dramatized in grand light and shadow as in the drawings of Piranesi. Latrobe wriggled and argued, but in the end Jefferson had his way; the dome was built substantially as he wished, and when it leaked, in fulfilment of Latrobe's doleful predictions, the problem was remedied by a little extra putty. For the same reason, their most successful collaboration was in designing the porticos of the White House (1807). Latrobe in proposing porticos was probably thinking in stylistic terms of perfecting the Adamesque–Federal character of Hoban's design with greater spatial sophistication; Jefferson saw at once how they would give the building more deliberately classical allusions like his own Monticello. One consideration complemented the other, and together they pushed the work forward to the point where Hoban in completing it after 1814 could do nothing but literally build on the foundations Latrobe and Jefferson had laid.

The men of his own generation, however, never entirely understood what Jefferson was trying to do. They associated his concept of a symbolic architectural style, understood by the great masses of the people as embodying American ideals, with the particular political party he headed; they thought of the "Jeffersonian classical" style as opposed to the Adamesque–Federal in the same way Jefferson's "Democratic Republican" party was opposed to the Federalist party in politics—the one envisioning an America ruled by aristocratic, propertied interests and cultivated tastes; the other, an America dominated by lower, commoner, more vulgar classes and tastes. Just as it seemed to more and more people that he failed to realize how very different the consequences of the revolution in France had been from the one in America, that he went on talking of French liberty and English tyranny long after it was clear England was defending civilization and religion against monstrous excesses of anarchy and terror, so it seemed that he failed to realize how Napoleon's adoption of Roman art as the official symbol of his dictatorship weakened the case for Roman forms being the only truly American style. That even a man as close to him as Latrobe never accepted Jefferson's ultimate goals is suggested by certain snide remarks Latrobe made to Dolly Madison about Mr. Jefferson and "his old French books" when they were furnishing the White House together in 1809; furthermore, when Latrobe was called back to rebuild the destroyed House of Representatives dome in 1815, he reverted to his original plan, which Jefferson had characterized during their earlier controversy as "a common thing, exceeded by many, and even by some corporation buildings."

It was the men of the next generation who accepted Jefferson's concepts and in the 1820s and 30s spread a classical "American" architecture all across the country, as he had envisioned. They did it, however, by making a compromise. What happened is dramatically revealed in the competition for designing a Second Bank of the United States building in Philadelphia, held in the summer of 1818. Latrobe was the leading contender; indeed, feeling that his experience in designing the Bank of Pennsylvania building twenty years before, let alone his intervening Federal work, qualified him as the leading authority on bank architecture in the country,

he resented being forced to compete at all, and submitted what was essentially a larger version of his earlier success—a three-part plan, with a large more or less Roman dome over the main banking room flanked on each end by porticoed blocks containing offices. What was his mortification to find the competition won by William Strickland (1788–1854), a native of Navesink, New Jersey, whose father had worked as a carpenter under Latrobe on the Bank of Pennsylvania, and who himself had been Latrobe's appprentice from 1803 to 1805! Angrily charging that Strickland had stolen ideas from him, Latrobe left for New Orleans, dying there two years later. It marked the end of an era. For Strickland had not in fact stolen Latrobe's design; he had only followed more exactly competition specifications that allowed little basic variation. Latrobe's design, half-Roman, half-Greek, a bit Adamesque, had typified the confusions of classical architecture for the last few decades. Strickland's, which won specifically because it was in the judges' view "more classic," represented what was to come. It was unified in form—the banking room a long barrel-vaulted rectangle with low basilica-like aisles extending from one side of the building to the other, the office sections balancing it on either side. More important, it was unified in style. And the style was not Roman; it was, as the specifications precisely called for, "a chaste imitation of Grecian architecture in its purest form." It would be in Greek, not Roman forms, that Jefferson's vision would be realized, that a revived classical architecture, keeping ever before the eyes of its citizens the ideals of life, liberty, and the pursuit of happiness, would sweep across America.

NOTES

Quotations of Washington's letter to John Jay, August 1, 1786, from Marcus Cunliffe, *George Washington*, Sect. IV, Chap. 2; from Lorraine W. Pearce, "Arrival of Charles-Honoré Lannuier in America" (*Winterthur Newsletter*, June 27, 1960) ; from article on Gruez in E. H. Bjerkoe, *Cabinetmakers of America* (1957) p. 118; of letter by L'Enfant, from J. J. Jusserand, "Major L'Enfant and the Federal City," *With Americans of Other Days* (1916), pp. 137–99.

Basic source on the architects referred to here is Talbot Hamlin, *Greek Revival Architecture in America* (1955). Rich Bornemann, "Some Ledoux-inspired Buildings in America" (*JSAH*, XIII, 1, 15–17), has useful material on Godefroy, Latrobe, and Ramée. On Ramée, see further Codman Hislop and Harold J. Larrabee, "Joseph-Jacques Ramée and the Building of North and South Colleges" (*Union Alumni Monthly*, XXVII, 4, pp. 1–16). On Ledoux, see Yves Christ, *Ledoux* (Paris, 1961). On Lannuier, see Lorraine Waxman Pearce, *Charles-Honoré Lannuier* (unpublished M.A. thesis, University of Delaware, 1958). On L'Enfant, see H. Paul Caemmerer, *The Life of Charles L'Enfant, Planner of the City Beautiful* (Washington, 1950). On Hadfield, see Murray Nelligan, "The Building of Arlington House" (*JSAH*, X, 2, 1951, pp. 11–15). On Thornton and Latrobe, see T. F. Hamlin, *Benjamin Henry Latrobe* (1955). Reference to the Washington Dry Dock in "Jefferson's Mothballs," (*JSAH*, X, 2, 1951, p. 23) ; to Latrobe's furniture, R. L. Raley, "Interior Designs by Benjamin Henry Latrobe for the President's House" (*Antiques*, LXXV, 1959, pp. 568–71). Aspects of Jefferson's influence on Latrobe treated in "Virginia Penitentiary" and Howard C. Rice, "A French Source for the Prison at Richmond" (*JSAH*, XII, 4, 1953, pp. 27–30) ; and especially Paul Norton, "Latrobe's Ceiling for the Hall of Representatives" (*JSAH*, X, 2, 1951, pp. 5–10). On Strickland's Second U. S. Bank, see A. A. Gilchrist, *William Strickland* (Philadelphia, 1950).

3. NEOCLASSICAL AMERICA:
The Greek Revival, c.1820–c.1840

"GRECIAN ARCHITECTURE," as the early 19th century called it, had long been known in America. As early as 1770 the Carpenters' Company of Philadelphia owned a copy of *The Antiquities of Athens,* which James Stuart and Nicholas Revett, among the first visitors of serious artistic interests to see actual buildings in ancient Greece, had published in London nine years before. A copy of their book was also in Jefferson's library. But the men of his generation made little use of it. For them Greek was never more than another competing classical variant— Doric columns without bases or capital rings, a somewhat different and generally less showy way of handling Ionic and Corinthian orders. With the men coming to maturity around 1820 it was a different matter, however. For them "the Grecian" had a unique appeal. They came on the scene prepared to accept wholeheartedly the principle of architecture as a symbolic language; they could understand what Jefferson had been talking about as his own contemporaries did not. Only his Roman enthusiasms they found hard to accept. Napoleon Bonaparte had appropriated the Roman Revival and debased its currency; he had demonstrated in fact what fifty years of increasingly painstaking research had made historians generally begin to suspect—that out of a Roman republic empires easily grow. Napoleon's "Empire style," complete with eagles, fasces, temples, and triumphal arches like those of the supposedly "American republican" style, came too late to change the minds of Jefferson's generation, but made younger men decidedly uneasy about the symbolism of Roman forms. About the Grecian there seemed no such difficulty. Here historical research had the opposite effect; where men in Jefferson's youth had believed that Rome was the great mother of classical art, and Greece merely one of her offshoots, it was now clear that the reverse was true; it was in Greece

that classical forms had their origin. It was in Greek city-states, not in the Roman imperium, that liberty flourished. Rome had not created but destroyed the classical spirit, had stamped out the Greek city-states much as resurgent Imperial British power had burnt the Capitol and White House in Washington and almost crushed the struggling republic in 1814. Surely it was of Greece, and not Rome, that America was the reincarnation. Even in modern times the parallel was apt. Rome under papal rule seemed the epitome of the reactionary powers that everywhere dominated Europe after the Napoleonic wars; the Greeks, by contrast, were in rebellion against a degenerate and tyrannical Turkish rule, thrilling romantically minded people everywhere.

Furthermore, Grecian architecture appeared to this new generation free of what might be called "campaign commitments." The Roman Revival was associated with the Democratic Republican Jeffersonian party in politics. It represented an American symbol in the same sense that the Jeffersonian party was the "party of the people." Into a scheme like Jefferson's University of Virginia campus you could read (if you chose) the typical Democratic Republican concept of the Union as a league of sovereign states, each as complete in itself as one of his temple-houses, delegating only the minimum of its inherent and inalienable powers to a Federal authority; you could see the Richmond Capitol —self-contained, independent of its environment—as a kind of symbol of states' rights doctrine. The Roman style was somehow tied up with opposition to the tariff, to moneyed aristocracy, to class privilege. As such, it was anathema to the very people who in the nature of things were most likely to give important architectural commissions. All this put the young American-born architect who might sympathize with Jeffersonian architectural ideals in an unpleasant dilemma indeed. From it, the Greek Revival neatly rescued him. It was no accident that the Directors of the United States Bank in their 1818 competition specified "Grecian architecture in its purest form"; a Roman building, associated as it must have been with the party which proclaimed a national bank the most horrible of threats to free institutions, would have been altogether too paradoxical. Greek architecture, by contrast, stood for liberty in general; it seemed to be above party, universally applicable, by all kinds of people. No wonder, then, that through the 1820s and 30s, and on into the 1840s, Greek Revival forms dominated the American architectural scene as no other "style" before or since.

One by one the leading young architects picked up the new theme. Of them the most outstanding was Robert Mills (1781–1855) of Charleston, South Carolina. Beginning his career under the successive aegises of Hoban, Jefferson, and Latrobe, gaining the reputation of first native-born American "architect," he had become famous through his winning design for the Washington Monument in Baltimore (designed c.1810, accepted 1814, construction begun 1815, completed 1829), which combined Latrobe's sense for monumental mass with a thoroughly Jeffersonian symbolic concept—a mighty Roman Doric column inspired by Trajan's Column in Rome, half sculpture, half architecture, all symbol. But after 1820, when he returned to South Carolina as Civil and Military Engineer of the state, Greek superseded Roman in his work. The Insane Asylum at Columbia (1821–8), though still set on arched basements and approached by curving stairs set off by delicate ironwork in Latrobe's Adamesque manner, now was dominated by a great Greek portico; so was the Record Office at Charleston, famed for its "fireproof" masonry throughout (1822–7, slightly altered in execution). Under Mills's regime as Federal Architect and Engineer in the 1830s, official architecture in the United States became a thing of monumental simplicity—great blocks of

buildings, ornamented with Greek friezes, pilasters, and porticos; such were the Treasury, the Post (now Land) Office, and the Patent Office he built in Washington over the years 1836–42, and his numerous smaller official buildings all over the country (e.g., customhouses at New Bedford and Newburyport, Massachusetts). Twenty years after his Roman monument to Washington in Baltimore, he designed another for the Fed-

92. CLASSICAL SYMBOLS OF AMERICAN PATRIOTISM

(A) Washington Monument, Baltimore, as it was in the 19th century, with surrounding park. Designed c.1814 by Robert Mills, it was the first important architectural monument in the United States and the first important civic monument to the memory of George Washington. Though considerably simplified from his original designs by the time construction was substantially finished in 1829, the shaft of brilliant white marble—inspired by the Nelson Column in London, the Vendôme Column in Paris, and ultimately by Trajan's Column in Rome—was all the more impressive for that. Long considered one of the wonders of America, it gave Baltimore the title of Monumental City.

eral City, which he described as a "grand circular colonnaded building . . . from which springs an obelisk shaft"; the shaft as designed was Egyptian, and the colonnaded building—in Mills's mind evidently at least as important a feature—was uncompromisingly Greek Doric (monument designed c.1833, begun 1848, the shaft not completed until 1884, the colonnade never built at all).

William Strickland's career followed the same pattern. After winning the United States Bank competition with his Grecian design in 1818, he abandoned the experimenting with stylistic variations he had done under Latrobe's influence (e.g., the curious "Gothic" Masonic Hall in Philadelphia, 1808; destroyed 1819), and made Grecian the chosen idiom of his major works, adapting it to such varied uses as a mint (1829), naval asylum (1827–48), and exchange (1833–6) in Philadelphia, and to the increasing mid-19th-century taste for "picturesqueness" in the Tennessee State Capitol (1845–59) and Belle Meade (c.1850) at Nashville. You could see it too in New England; by 1820 the ideologically more acceptable Greek Revival was clearly successful, as the Roman Revival had never been, in superseding Adamesque–Federal forms in the mercantile aristocracy's affections. So Alexander

Parris (1780–1852) abandoned the delicate regional Adamesque style of his architecture in Portland, Maine (e.g., Old Shepley house, for Richard Hunnewell, 1805), for the Greek simplicity of St. Paul's, Boston (1819), and the granite Doric of the Quincy Market (begun 1825). So Solomon Willard (1788–1861) turned from the post-Georgian tradition in which his carpenter and cabinetmaker father had raised him, and which he perpetuated as late as 1820 in the Salem church he executed with Peter Banner (an English Adamesque designer, in Boston 1805–22), to build an almost exaggeratedly solid Greek Doric temple for the Boston branch of the Bank of the United States (1824; he even refused to give the columns entasis). So the Tremont House in Boston (1828–9), which made Isaiah Rogers (1800–1869) famous, was entirely Greek in detail, with no trace of Adamesque or post-Georgian regional forms in it.

The decade 1825–1835 was the great age of the Greek Revival in America. The New York correspondent of *The Architectural Magazine* in London wrote in December 1834:

> The Greek mania here is at its height, as you infer from the fact that everything is a Greek temple from the privies in the back court, through the various grades of prison, theatre, church, custom-house, and state-house.

Thereafter, however, though Greek forms dominated American architecture for another decade and more, it became clear that architects generally were losing their enthusiasm for them, and only popular acceptance of Greek as a symbolically American expression maintained their widespread use. This is suggested in various ways by the careers of John Haviland (1792–1852), Minard Lafever (1797–1854), Thomas U. Walter (1804–1887), and Asher Benjamin (1773–1845). All of them are considered generally as Greek Revival architects; three of them wrote builders' guides which helped spread Greek forms all over the country. Yet in every case their reputations were made with buildings which were, to say the least, far from displaying any passionate attachment to the style.

Asher Benjamin, belonging to an older gen-

93. CLASSICAL SYMBOLS OF AMERICAN BUSINESS ENTERPRISE

(A) Second Bank of the United States (United States Custom House, 1844–1932), Philadelphia. Designed in 1818 by William Strickland, built 1819–24, it marked a triumph of Greek over Roman neoclassicism in the United States. With porticos modeled on the Parthenon in Athens (Cf. 54) at each end, and banking rooms all contained within a building of temple-like shape and proportions, it was a brilliant adaptation of Greek forms to 19th-century commercial functions.

eration, introduced plates of Greek orders as early as the fifth edition of his *American Builder's Companion* (1826), and his later books— *The Practical House Carpenter*, or *The Architect* (first edition 1830), *The Practice of Architecture* (1833), and *The Builder's Guide* (1839)— helped mightily to spread the Greek Revival style through Greater New England; but his presentation of it, affected in turn by Adamesque–Federal fragility and Empire heaviness, suggested that he never fully accepted its premises, never completely broke away from the Bulfinch–McIntire tradition on which his early successes (West Church, Boston, 1806, e.g.) were based.

John Haviland—an exception to the rule in his generation in that he was born in England

and came to Philadelphia in 1816—had his first great success with an 1821 design for the Eastern State Penitentiary (completed 1829) in Philadelphia, in castellated Gothic; his Halls of Justice in New York (1836–8), equally famous, was in Egyptian, hence its nickname "The Tombs"; and his handling of Greek forms, as in the Moody house at Haverhill, Massachusetts (c.1818), the Deaf and Dumb Asylum (begun 1824), and the Walnut Street Theatre (remodeled 1828) in Philadelphia, was almost consistently unorthodox. Yet Haviland's *Builders' Assistant* (1818–21, first American publication to give plates to the Greek orders) and *Young Carpenter's Assistant* (1837) were almost entirely concerned with Greek forms, and provided a great impetus in the early spread of the Greek Revival from cosmopolitan centers into the countryside.

Or, again, Minard Lafever rose from obscure origins as a carpenter in the Finger Lakes region of New York State to national prominence on the strength of three books of Greek Revival design appearing in the early 1830s: *The Young Builder's General Instructor* (1829), *The Modern Builders' Guide* (1833), and *The Beauties of Modern Architecture* (1835), which were soon being used everywhere. But of his own practice in New York during this period (he came to the city in 1828) practically nothing is known; and when Lafever did make a local reputation it was as a designer in Gothic (Holy Trinity and The Saviour churches in Brooklyn, 1844–7, e.g.) and the early picturesque manner (Brooklyn Savings Bank, 1847; Reformed Church of the Heights, 1851).

There is the same curious contradiction in Thomas Ustick Walter's work. In the series of buildings he designed for his native town of West Chester, Pennsylvania, you can trace a steady progress away from Greek forms—from the First

(93 B) Quincy (or Faneuil) Market, Boston, begun 1825 on the plans of Alexander Parris. Faneuil Hall appears in the background of this 1828 engraving. The flanking rows of warehouses have been destroyed, but the Market itself still stands.

94. CLASSICAL SYMBOLS OF FREEDOM FROM AND FREEDOM OF RELIGION

(A) St. Andrew's (Presbyterian) Church, Niagara-on-the-Lake, Ontario (Canada). Built in 1831 from plates in Asher Benjamin's American Builder's Companion, *this church typifies the* spread of American ideals throughout the Mid-west and across the border, and affords an early instance of cultural influences exported from the United States. Greek here symbolizes both demo-cratic political freedom and freedom from an "established" church.

Presbyterian Church (1832–4) and the National Bank of Chester (1836), which are quite correct; through the Chester County Courthouse (1846–8), where the forms are muddy; to the Horticulture Society Building (now Historical Society, 1848), where they are hardly classical at all. As for the three buildings that made Walter most famous, two—the Theseum portico he added to Nicholas Biddle's Andalusia c.1832, and his winning design for Girard College in Philadelphia (1833,

completed 1847)—were dictated by the enthu-siasms engendered in social and financial leader Nicholas Biddle by a trip to Greece many years earlier, while in the wings of the United States Capitol and the new dome he executed in 1850–63, he modified the original Roman prescription not by adding Greek elements, but by drawing inspiration from grandiose Baroque monuments.

Thus by the 1840s a great paradox had de-veloped in American architecture. Superficially, the classical and particularly the Greek Revival reigned supreme; no other style came near challenging it. Yet at this very moment when all over America the great bulk of buildings erected over the last twenty years were Greek, its hold on the intellectual and artistic community was decisively broken. It was becoming fashionable for young and "promising" men to attack classical art as derivative, dead, and—what was more serious—essentially un-American. Leader of this new group was Andrew Jackson Downing (1815–1852). In his *Treatise on the Theory and Practice of Landscape Gardening Adapted to North America* (1841) he noted that while ". . . such is the rage for this style [Grecian] among us just

now, and so completely have our builders the idea of its unrivalled supremacy in their heads, that many submit to the most meagre conveniences . . . without a murmur," if "we consider fitness and expression of purpose, two leading principles of the first importance in Rural Architecture, . . . Grecian architecture in its pure form, viz., the temple, when applied to the purposes of domestic life, makes a sad blow at both these established rules." He will concede that "as a public building, the Greek temple form is perfect . . . ," but when he further remarks that "it has been well observed by modern critics, that there is no reason to believe the temple form was ever, even by the Greeks, used for private

(94 B) *Girard College, Philadelphia, designed 1833 by Thomas U. Walter. Nicholas Biddle, as president of the board of trustees of the college founded by bequest of Stephen Girard, insisted on the "pure Grecian forms" which for him symbolized that right to freedom from interference with private affairs which he championed in business, and which Girard wrote into his will by excluding clergymen from his college campus forever. Completed 1836, the building is remarkable structurally for low segmental groined vaulting which concentrated weight and made it virtually fireproof.*

dwellings," the implications are ominous; soon enough critics will discover that temples were not used for public gatherings either. His *Cottage Residences* (1842) carries on the theme; now, it seems, "if we talk pure Greek, and build a Grecian temple for a dwelling, we shall be little understood, or perhaps only laughed at by our neighbours." At this point the classical revival is effectually dead; it has become the mark of cultural backwardness, gaucherie, an expression of popular culture and country workmen. Yet it was as such that it has the most lasting significance for us. For in it we can see, as we could not when it was still the expression of an intellectual advance-guard, to what extent the Roman and Greek Revivals, better than any other manifestation, embodied the spirit and proclaimed the vision of the United States as they were in the first half of the 19th century.

NOTES

On Mills's Baltimore monument, see J. J. Miller, *Evolution of the Baltimore Monument* (unpublished M.A. thesis, University of Delaware, 1962); on the Patent Office, Louise Hall, "The Design of the Old Patent Office" (*JSAH*, XV, 1, 1956, pp. 27–30). Quotation on the Washington monument from H. M. Pierce Gallagher, *Robert Mills* (1935). On Strickland, see A. A. Gilchrist, *William Strickland* (Philadelphia, 1950). On Walter's work in Chester County, see G. Carroll Lindsay, *Athens on High Street* (unpublished M.A. thesis, University of Delaware, 1955). A significant indication of Walter's personal tastes, as contrasted to those of his patrons, is to be found in his designs for the university at Lewisburg (now Bucknell), Pennsylvania, 1848–51, described by George L. Hersey, "Thomas U. Walter and the University at Lewisburg" (*JSAH*, XVI, 1, 1957, pp. 20–24), as having "plain brick antae and simple white entablatures" so as to "constitute a reaction to the archaeological niceties of Girard College." On Walter's work at the Capitol, see T. C. Bannister, "The Genealogy of the Dome of the U. S. Capitol" (*JSAH*, VII, 1–2, 1948, pp. 1–31).

4. CLASSICAL REVIVAL ARCHITECTURE AS NATIONAL EXPRESSION

IT WAS IN 1842, at the height of the American classical revival, that Charles Dickens visited the United States, and found, all over the country,

> Every little colony of houses has its church and schoolhouse peeping from among the white roofs and shady trees; every house is the whitest of the white; every Venetian blind the greenest of the green; every fine day's sky the bluest of the blue. . . . All the buildings looked as if they had been built and painted that morning, and could be taken down on Monday with very little trouble. In the keen evening air, every sharp outline looked a hundred times sharper than ever.

Many of the buildings were, in fact, new; it was a time of great prosperity throughout the North at least, and even those that were not classical in forms and proportions could be made classical in color. Mrs. Louisa Caroline Higgins Tuthill, writing of American building in the 1840s in her *History of Architecture* (1848), was delighted to see how fast the "wooden enormities" of 17th-century America were disappearing: "Happily, they were all of such perishable materials that they will not much longer remain to annoy travellers in 'search of the picturesque' throughout the beautiful villages of New England."

But the same process of incessant change, growth, and rebuilding that gave Mrs. Tuthill such satisfaction in turn destroyed her America, too. Not much of classical America remains now. It takes some imagination to visualize the world she and Dickens saw in the wilderness of skyscrapers, billboards, diners, motels, Victorian mansions, and 20th-century housing developments that buries most of what remains of that world today. Here and there patches survive in something like an original setting—in the hills of western New England or northern Georgia, in the valleys of the Mohawk or the Wabash or the

Ohio, through the old Mississippi plantation country, along the Ridge Road in western New York. There you can sometimes still come upon a neat pedimented farmhouse or the remains of a pillared mansion, standing out white and gold in the slanting rays of a setting sun, against a background of emerald fields falling away into purple valleys and the ruddy grey haze of wooded slopes—a landscape idyllic in the spirit of Poussin or Claude; then for an instant you catch a glimpse of America when the Republic was new, of that lost nation of "templed hills" and Revolutionary ideals modeled on classical antiquity. And from these fragments you can imagine the whole, and see in them an expression of the first great era of American national civilization.

To wax sentimental about classical revival architecture is easy. It was intended to be romantic, and in retrospect is even more so. It seems to speak of a golden age of economic hope and national glory that moved even so somber a writer as George Orwell to uncharacteristic nostalgia for "the native gaiety, a buoyant, carefree feeling, which was the product, presumably, of the unheard-of freedom and security which nineteenth-century America enjoyed," and which for him was

> the connecting link between books seemingly so far apart as *Little Women* and *Life on the Mississippi*. The society described in the one is subdued, bookish, and home-loving, while the other tells of a crazy world of bandits, gold mines, duels, drunkenness and gambling hells: but in both one can detect an underlying confidence in the future, a sense of freedom and opportunity.

Nineteenth-century America was a rich, empty country which lay outside the main stream of world events, and in which the twin nightmares that beset nearly every modern man, the nightmare of unemployment and the

95. CLASSICAL REVIVAL HOUSE TYPES, NORTH AND SOUTH

(A) Campbell–Whittlesey house, Rochester, New York. A fine example of the famous Greek Revival architecture of Rochester's old Third Ward, built 1835–6 for merchant and miller Benjamin Campbell, later owned by Justice Frederick Whittlesey of the New York State Supreme Court, restored by the Society for the Preservation of Landmarks in Western New York beginning in 1937. Most of the details, inside as well as out, are taken from the Beauties of Modern Architecture *by Minard Lafever, and some think the building was supervised by Lafever himself, who grew up in the Finger Lakes region. The interiors of this house are famous for meticulous authenticity—paints compounded according to formulas current at the time, contemporary wallpapers,* Empire *furnishings matching the Greek exterior.*

nightmare of State interference, had hardly come into being. There were social distinctions, more marked than those of today, and there was poverty . . . but there was not, as there is now, an all-prevailing sense of helplessness. There was room for everybody, and if you worked hard you could be certain of a living— could even be certain of growing rich: this was generally believed, and for the greater part of the population it was even broadly true. In other words, the civilization of nineteenth-century America was capitalist civilization at its best. Soon after the Civil War the inevitable deterioration started. . . .

Politically, socially, culturally, the nation

seemed to be realizing its destiny with a speed and on a scale the Founding Fathers had hardly dared hope for. And of this, Greek and Roman Revival architecture was the great and tangible expression. Neat white pillared houses and churches appearing in Texas and California and Oregon, spilling over the border into Canada, seemed to imply no limit to national expansion; they gave substance to Daniel Webster's turgid thunderings about "the power of this republic . . . spread over a region one of the richest and most fertile on the globe, and of an extent in comparison with which the possessions of the house of Hapsburg are but a patch on the earth's surface." In fifty years a whole vast wilderness between the Appalachians and the Mississippi had been transformed into a region of tidy little towns with wide streets and spacious courthouses, rich farms and rolling plantations. There Jefferson's vision seemed to have come true. There the frustrated religious impulse of the 17th-century founders seemed fulfilled; what had been withheld by inscrutable grace was being brought about by education in the classics. Arcadia had displaced Jerusalem as the American dream, just as Troys, Athenses, Spartas, and Carthages had displaced New Zions, Bethlehems, Salems, and New Arks on maps of the new American states.

Most of all, classical revival architecture seemed a witness to the success of the great American experiment of government "of the people, by the people, for the people." Capitals and pediments and gleaming white walls, embodying in their identical classical forms and proportions common ideals and standards everywhere from Maine to Alabama, seemed visible refutations of old sour predictions that the new republic would fall apart into anarchy like the city-states of antiquity. Concurrently, all sorts of local and regional variants developing within the common classical framework seemed proof that conformity had not been the price of union, that republics need spawn no Napoleons or Caesars to survive.

Indeed, in this society individual craftsmen were free to grow, develop, express their own tastes and community traditions as men had

(95 B) Jabez Finch–Harold C. Brooks house, Marshall, Michigan. Built in 1842, an example of the full-blown temple-house with *porch, which proclaimed the prosperity achieved in the new Western states only a few decades after serious settlement had begun.*

hardly been, it seemed, since the "elder days of art" that reared the great temples and cathedrals of the Old World. It was not so much that telegraph and railroad had not yet developed to the point of imposing uniformity, as that the early republic was to a considerable extent what it claimed to be, not an imitation but a reincarnation of classical conditions of life. Its communities were still small enough that a man could feel something of genuine classical control over his own destinies, could take literally the premise that his new nation was carrying on where the faltering republics of antiquity had left off, and

build on it his personal interpretation of "American classical" architecture. With the more numerous and complete guidebooks of the classical revivals letting them copy where they did not understand, and the buoyant spirit of the age encouraging them to elaborate where they did, local builders flourished in every town and region of the country with an independence unequaled before or since. Some worked onto broader stages, exemplifying in architecture the fact which Lincoln and Douglas, Jackson and Polk proved in politics—that in early America there was still room enough to advance as much on merit as on family or inherited wealth: such, for instance, was Isaiah Rogers, coming to Boston in 1826 from a Massachusetts farm to practice carpentry and rising within ten years to national fame as architect of old Astor House in New York (1832–6) and subsequently hotels all over the country from Charleston to Cincinnati; or the obscure English immigrant Stephen Hills, who won a competition for the Pennsylvania Capitol over the country's most famous native architect, Robert Mills, in 1820 and went on from there to design the State Capitol (1838–45) and first building of the University of Missouri (1840). Most were more limited in their aspirations, working in localities where they were born or had settled as young men, developing regional accents within the national classical revival speech. To name all or most of them would be tedious if not impossible; the list is almost endless. There was the Boston school of Rogers, Parris, and Willard, with their satellite, carpenter Edward Shaw, born 1784 in New Hampshire, come to Boston 1822, publisher of *Civil Architecture* in 1831 and *Rural Architecture* in 1843. There was the Providence school of John Holden Greene (1777–1850), Russell Warren (1783–1860), and James Bucklin (1801–1890). And there were local masters in every New England town; Isaac Damon of Northhampton and Elias Carter (1781–1864) of Worcester in Massachusetts; Thomas Lord (1806–1880) of Bluehill and Ellsworth in Maine; Lavius Fillmore of Bennington and Middlebury in Vermont; David Hoadley (1774–1839) of New Haven in Connecticut. In the West, there was Philip Hooker (1766–1836) of Albany and Hugh Hastings of Rochester in New York; Jonathan Goldsmith of Painesville in Ohio; Sylvanus Grow of Ottawa and Henry J. Stouffer of Galena in Illinois; Francis Costigan (1810–1865) in Indiana. There was the Baltimore school of Robert Cary Long, Jr. (1810–1849), William F. Small, "Architect of the City" (1798–1832), and John Hall, better known as publisher of *The Cabinetmaker's Assistant* (1840), a book of designs for furniture to go in classical revival houses. Farther south, there was John Berry (1798–1870) of Hillsboro in North Carolina and James Hamilton Couper of Georgia; in Kentucky, Gideon Shryock (1802–1880); in New Orleans, James Gallier, Sr. (1798–1868) and Jr. (1829–1870), and Henry Howard (1818–1884). And so on and on. Some of their lives we know, and of some we know nothing; but collectively these men bring to mind what seems to a succeeding century an intoxicating image of some lost idyllic world, sober husbandmen developing the nation's wealth in happy collaboration with kindly small industrialists, contented local craftsmen working with uncorrupted good taste to satisfy the simple civic pride of small communities with their distinctive regional adaptations of classical models to local tastes, needs, and traditions.

Almost as endless is the list of local stylistic variations. In Boston, ruggedly simple forms developed in Quincy granite. In western Pennsylvania, fusions of classical detail with the characteristic brick and stone building traditions originating in the colonial East. In central New York, and sporadically westward into Ontario, Ohio, and Michigan, "cobblestone" architecture: plans and details from classical revival guidebooks picked out by walls set with rows of smooth beach pebbles in herringbone, zigzag, and other distinctive patterns. A distinctive "basilica" type in Michigan—temple-houses with side wings so proportioned as to resemble in effect the aisles of a medieval church. In Ohio a characteristic kind of sprawling farmhouse, all elements spread out on an ingenious one-level plan. In the South generally, two distinctive types: the familiar great plantation house fronted with giant columns which serve both to dramatize the owner's social pretensions and support a second-story piazza, so combining symbol and function; and one-and-a-half-story "classical cottages," proportioned and detailed with variations of infinite subtlety. In Louisiana, a distinctive type produced by fusion of the classical temple-house with vaguely French umbrella roof and

(95 C) The Hermitage, Nashville, Tennessee. This famous façade of Andrew Jackson's home dates from reconstruction of the original house built 1819, following a fire; it was probably designed by Robert Mills, in 1836. The columns are Greek Corinthian, carved in wood (though some Corinthian acanthus leaves in the region were moulded in iron, these were not). Characteristic of Southern plantation building is the second-floor balcony.

galerie. And so on and on again. It does indeed seem as if we are back in that truly classical world where "the boundless variety of things arises from the different proportions of a very few ingredients," where over and above all local variations and peculiarities there are broad principles uniting every section of the country in a common national expression. . . .

Or are there? Only if we look superficially at the forms. Consider more deeply why these forms were used, how their builders understood them, and the idyllic picture suddenly dissolves; in its place appears an architectural expression of that same ominous cleavage between the two great sections of the country which from the 1820s onward increasingly occupied every thoughtful mind, and in the end came close to wrecking the Republic forever. For on the classical revivals, as on politics and economics and society, there was a Northern and a Southern point of view—and they were nearly irreconcilable.

In Northern eyes, classical forms were associated, however vaguely and often contradictorily, with individual freedom. They were the expression of that all-pervading confidence in equality of opportunity which justified the abuses of burgeoning industrialism by faith that its material benefits could and would be one day enjoyed by all.

We do wish the humblest man an equal chance to get rich with everybody else. When one starts poor, as most do in the race of life, free society is such that he knows he can better his condition.

*

Twenty-five years ago I was a hired laborer. The hired laborer of yesterday labors on his own account today, and will hire others to labor for him tomorrow. Advancement—improvement in condition—is the order of things in a society of equals.

*

I happen, temporarily, to occupy this White House. I am a living witness that any one of your children may look to come here as my father's child has.

So in speech after speech throughout his political career Abraham Lincoln expounded the faith of the 1820s and 30s in which he had been raised. And in the North, it was this faith that supported the classical revivals, and to which Greek and Roman architecture was understood as giving witness. Rich and poor alike can live in the shelter of classical forms. Details from the same guidebooks by Shaw or Lafever or Benjamin, appearing on the laborer's row house in the city and the capitalist's country mansion on the hill, proclaim how easy it is to pass from one to the other. Classical forms could be used with quite contradictory symbolism, and by bitter enemies, but in Northern minds they had a common denominator as symbolic statements of the individual's freedom to order his life and better his condition as he chose. So you could find Greek temples used both as churches, to symbolize freedom of religion, and as college buildings, to symbolize freedom from religious authority (spectacular examples were those designed by Thomas U. Walter in 1833–47 for the college founded in Philadelphia by bequest of Stephen Girard with the stipulation that no clergyman might set foot on the grounds). Or you could find classical forms symbolizing civic enterprise in merchants' exchanges and its opposite—retreat from the world—in little tholoi serving as gazebos in private and public parks. Financier Nicholas Biddle was a lifelong admirer of Greek forms, which to him stood for freedom

of the financial community to manage its own affairs; under his regime as leading director and then president of the Bank of the United States, the Bank's buildings in every major American city were specimens of "purest Grecian," modified inevitably, of course, by all-pervasive local traditions: Strickland's 1818 Bank in Philadelphia; that of William Jay (fl.1817–22) in Savannah (c.1820); of Solomon Willard in Boston (1825); of Martin Thompson in New York (c.1822). But when that freedom was challenged, and by President Jackson's veto of recharter in 1832 Biddle was crushed, Greek was the style chosen for the United States Treasury in Washington (by Mills, c.1833–6) to symbolize how, in the words of Jackson's message,

> When the laws undertake to add to . . . natural and just advantages [of wealth and family] artificial distinctions . . . to make the rich richer and the potent more powerful, the humble members of society—the farmers, mechanics, and laborers—who have neither the time nor the means of securing like favors to themselves, have a right to complain of the injustice of their Government.

In sheer size as well as monumental proportions, the new Treasury overwhelmed Biddle's bank buildings in a way ominous to those who remembered the Jeffersonian ideal of a government which undertook little more than to bless the labors of every independent citizen in his own well-ordered corner of Arcadia. If this is what Jeffersonian equality meant, the Northern capitalists wanted none of it. Even less did it appeal to the plantation aristocracy of the South. For them the whole concept of a "free society" where "one starts poor [and] knows he can better his condition" was a dismal perversion, a farcical extension of the classical ideal far beyond its proper bounds:

> Free society! We sicken of the name! What is it but a conglomeration of greasy mechanics, filthy operatives, small-fisted farmers, and moon-struck theorists? All the Northern and especially the New England states are devoid of society fitted for well-bred gentlemen.

The prevailing class one meets is that of mechanics struggling to be genteel, and small farmers who do their own drudgery; and yet are hardly fit for association with a southern gentleman's body servant. This is your free society....

Obviously for people like the writer of this editorial in a Charleston newspaper during the campaign of 1856, classical forms had a very different, almost an opposite, significance from that held in the North. For Southern aristocracy, Greek and Roman architecture was the symbol and assurance that sound society could perfectly well combine ideals of liberty with the institution of slavery—an interpretation early hallowed by Jefferson's University of Virginia plan with its temples for masters of philosophy set side by side with quarters for their slaves. Greek temples were in Southern eyes practically a statement of the Southern way of life, precisely the opposite view held of them in the North.

The Greek Revival was slow, generally speaking, to take hold in the South, not, as in New England, because of any strong mercantile class attachment to Adamesque–Federal or post-Georgian expressions, but because the same decades of the 1820s and 30s that saw such industrial expansion in the North were times of depression for many Southern states. But once established, the Greek Revival spread fast; all over the South, down to the Civil War, it was the chosen style for aristocratic plantation houses. And as such it became the symbol of Southern conservatism, of determination to maintain at whatever cost rigid social patterns inherited from the 18th century. As the small white temple of the Northern farmer, or the neat row house of the Northern mechanic, was taken to symbolize a mobile society with equal opportunity for all, so the Southern planter's columned mansion proclaimed his devotion to the hierarchical mores of an old-fashioned, almost feudal world. It is so to this day. Near Geneva in New York, for instance, stands Rose Hill, an enormous mansion with many outbuildings, quite different from other contemporary houses in the region. Grandiose in scale, too costly to heat, too elegant to be decently pulled down—in short, entirely unsuited to the country—it is a monument to the single-minded futility of wealthy Virginian Robert Kirby Strong, who came here in 1838 with a full complement of slaves and equipment determined to establish a full-blown Southern plantation in the wilderness of central New York. Or think of "old Southern plantation houses" generally; what images come to mind? Ghosts along the Mississippi. Scarlett O'Hara entertaining her beaux, soon to be blown away. Decaying ruins, with Faulkner's and Tennessee Williams's decaying people playing their decadent parts in them. Of the really old South, the 18th-century South that led America towards political liberty and cultural maturity, hardly a trace remains.

For if the classical revivals symbolized democratic progress in the North, in the South they meant aristocratic stagnation. Like the dinosaurs who perfected themselves into extinction, the Southern planters had evolved a way of life so rigidly oriented around great plantations, so entirely dependent on slave-produced cotton, that no other was conceivable—and classical revival architecture became its chosen symbol. While in the North all sorts of new intellectual and artistic currents were stirring—romantic Gothic, Picturesque Eclecticism—the South clung to Greek and Roman forms. While great cities grew and industry matured in the North, the South remained almost as rural as it had been when George Washington was growing up. As it fell behind in the arts and industry, so it lagged in population growth: in 1790, populations in the North and South were nearly equal, but by 1850 the census showed 13,527,000 North to 9,612,000 South. In the middle of the 19th century the South was still holding practically the same outlook and values as it had in 1800, except that whereas then Southerners had been advance-guard and positive, now they were negative and reactionary. As it was with the old French Empire in North America, the South's inevitable defeat in the Civil

War was written in every aspect of its institutions, and in none more plainly than in its classical revival architecture.

All of which makes the reason for the failure of the classical revivals—that is, why there succeeded to Greek simplicity and Roman dignity the bombastic eclecticism of mid- and later-19th-century America—something less than a mystery. It was simply that by the 1840s the whole rationale of the revivals had collapsed. No educated man could take seriously any longer the Jeffersonian view of Greek and Roman architecture as embodying American republican ideals. With such divergence of interpretation North and South, it was obvious that classical forms, far from being the vehicle and expression of unity they had been in the older 18th-century tradition, were in fact almost the opposite; in them you could read plainly how regional antagonisms were ripening towards civil war. Originally conceived as a symbol of political liberty, they had been extended in so many diverse and contradictory ways as to become virtually meaningless as symbol. Freedom of business from government interference, and freedom of government to regulate business; freedom of religion, and freedom from religion; freedom for slaves, and freedom to keep slaves; the rights of free labor, and the privileges of free capital—the wonder is not that forms so heavily freighted with symbolism so diverse should have eventually broken down, but that the Greek and Roman Revivals dominated American architecture as long as they did.

In Jefferson's mind, the mark of American civilization had been a kind of Arcadian simplicity. American superiority to Europe, he thought, lay not in techniques or enterprise or wealth, but in a certain guilelessness and cheerful contentment. "As for France and England," he moralized in old age to John Adams, "with all their preeminence in science, the one is a den of robbers and the other of pirates." Let these decadent sophisticates have their Baroque magnificence; America's architectural expression should be one of classical simplicity, for "if science produces no better fruits than tyranny, murder, rapine, and destitution of national morality, I would rather wish our country to be ignorant, honest, and estimable, as our neighbouring savages are." Alas for this vision! By the 1840s and 50s, with senators urging national expansion on grounds that "it is no more possible for this country to pause in its career than it is for the free and untrammeled eagle to cease to soar," it was obvious that Americans were no longer content to be thought ignorant, honest, and estimable. Industries were flourishing; wealth was accumulating; cities and railroads and arsenals were multiplying—assets much more tangible than republican virtue. Already towards the end of his life Jefferson had noted uneasily that "it cannot be denied that we are a boasting nation"; by mid-century boasting had become a national characteristic, and, more and more, the boasts were of military power and material possessions. More and more obviously, too, they were being made to cover up the great, growing, frightening internal dissension over slavery; Daniel Webster used to admit privately that the real intent of his more bombastic speeches was simply to "touch the national pride, and make a man feel *sheepish* and look *silly* who should speak of disunion." More and more, the old classical symbolism in architecture was coming to have a correspondingly artificial, pompous, and futile quality. The whole pace of American life was speeding up, changing in direction; and as it did, Jeffersonian classicism, whether Roman or Greek in form, seemed ever more naïve and obsolete.

In theory no longer corresponding to the realities of American life, in practice disintegrating like the old Jeffersonian Democratic party itself, so too by the 1840s Jeffersonian classicism seemed to have lost its basis in historical fact. Addison's drama of the selfless Cato that so enthralled Washington, Swift's vision of the Roman Senate as an assemblage of demigods and heroes, Jacques-Louis David's portrayal of the

(95 D) The classic plantation house of Gone with the Wind flavor: D'Evereux, near Natchez, Mississippi. Built on the designs of one *Mr. Hardy for William St. John Elliott, close friend of Henry Clay, 1840. Famous in its day for elaborate Empire furnishings in rosewood.*

noble Horatii and the stoic Brutus, Jefferson's Arcadia, all were exposed by the new, deeper, more critical scholarship of 19th-century historians as idle if not ridiculous myths. There never was such a perfect society; the men of antiquity were of like passions with ourselves—as Shakespeare had seen them. There never was a perfect art; if Greeks were simple and Romans grave, it was only because their limitations in space and time gave them no choice. Classical antiquity was just another period in the past; interesting enough, to be sure, but not necessarily more so than Pharaonic Egypt, or France under Saint Louis, or Imperial China. The same was true of Graeco-Roman art. It was no longer *the* style, it was *a* style—and one, furthermore, whose old pretensions were becoming increasingly tiresome.

Already people were appearing who claimed that Roman and Greek architecture, far from being ideally American, was not suitable in America at all; that the more scholars learned about the ancient world, the more "foreign" it proved to be. Would it not be more "American" to use a "Christian" style like the Gothic? Surely the United States is a Christian, not a pagan, country? Or perhaps combine to create something entirely new, that would be a truly American creation? And to this, defenders of the classical revivals had no real answer. The same arguments that promoted Greek could just as well promote Gothic, or Egyptian, or anything else. Their own case, the standards on which architectural judgment had always rested, they had destroyed. For the moment they assumed classical architecture was something to be read, to be composed in a literary manner, the neoclassicists had in fact changed its nature fundamentally. Just as in founding the new republic the gentlemen of Virginia effectively began the destruction of their own way of life, so Jeffersonian classicism meant the end, not the culmination, of the 18th-century classical cycle—the beginning of a new approach to art, which later generations would call Victorian.

NOTES

Quotations from Dickens, *American Notes*, Chap. V; from George Orwell, "Riding Down from Bangor," *Shooting an Elephant, and Other Essays* (1950), pp. 199–200; of Webster's reply in 1849 to the Austrian minister protesting American sympathy for the Hungarian revolt, from T. A. Bailey, *A Diplomatic History of the American People* (1940), p. 248; from Richard Hofstadter, "Abraham Lincoln and the Self-Made Myth," *The American Political Tradition* (1948).

Besides the basic study and bibliography by Talbot Hamlin, *Greek Revival Architecture in America* (1944), reference is made here to the following articles and books (in addition to others cited elsewhere):

On men: S. M. Green, "Thomas Lord, Joiner and Housewright" (*Magazine of Art*, XL, 1947, p. 230); R. L. Alexander, "William F. Small, 'Architect of the City'" (*JSAH*, XX, 2, 1961, pp. 63–77); Raymond F. and Marguerite W. Yates, *A Guide to Victorian Antiques* (1949), pp. 1–6 (on John Hall); Charles L. Dufour, "Henry Howard, Forgotten Architect" (*JSAH*, XI, 2, 1952); Rexford Newcomb, "Gideon Shryock and the Greek Revival," *Architecture in Old Kentucky* (Urbana, Ill., 1953), Chap. XI; E. I. Gatling, "John Berry of Hillsboro, N.C." (*JSAH*, X, 1, 1951, pp. 18–24).

On regions: Federal Writers' Project *American Guide* series to the several states; Carl F. Schmidt, *Cobblestone Architecture* (Scottsville, N. Y., 1944) and *Greek Revival Architecture in the Rochester Area* (Scottsville, N. Y., 1946); Gerda Peterich, "Cobblestone Architecture of Upstate New York" (*JSAH*, XIV, 2, 1956, pp. 12–18); John Drury, *Historic Midwest Houses* (Minneapolis, 1947); E. H. Rosebloom and F. P. Weisenburger, *A History of Ohio* (Columbus, 1954); F. D. Nichols and F. B. Johnston, *The Early Architecture of Georgia* (Chapel Hill, 1957); Ralph Hammond, *Ante-Bellum Mansions of Alabama* (1951); F. J. Roos, Jr., "Ohio: Architectural Cross-Road," Patricia S. Ingram, "Hudson: Early 19th Century Domestic Architecture," and A. L. Cummings, "The Ohio Capitol Competition" (*JSAH* Ohio Sesquicentennial Issue, XII, 2, 1953). Dorothy and Richard Pratt's guides—*American Homes, North,* and *American Homes, South* (1956)—have many practical uses for people wishing to visit the places they describe.

On Nicholas Biddle the man, see H. D. Eberlein and C. V. D. Hubbard, *Portrait of a Colonial City* (Philadelphia, 1939), pp. 543–52; for his influence on Walter, see C. E. Peterson, E. Newbold Cooper, and A. A. Gilchrist, "The Girard College Competition" (*JSAH*, XII, 2, 1957, pp. 20ff.); for his controversy with Jackson and quotation from the veto message, A. M. Schlesinger, Jr., *The Age of Jackson* (1945).

VICTORIAN AMERICA:
THE 19th CENTURY

II

Style as Language and Symbol:

The Victorian Mind in Art

1. FROM ROMANCE TO ARCHAEOLOGY:
Three Phases of Victorian Art

OUTWARDLY, American architecture in the first two or three decades of the 19th century looked very much the same as it had for the preceding hundred years. Except for somewhat more consistently "correct" forms, and a good deal more conscious imitation of particular Greek or Roman models, much of the familiar vocabulary of later-18th-century classical tradition had been retained, and, certainly among country builders, much of the genuine classical spirit, too. But the change in spirit and attitude was immense. The very idea of deliberately "reviving" the art of some long-dead epoch in history involves a kind of theatricality, an artificial posing, foreign to earlier America. Once conceive of the basic "function" of a "beautiful" building or chair or table or picture as being to make a statement, once admire visual forms for the "literary" associations they call to mind, and a fundamental shift of standards is involved, a whole new framework of reference inevitable. And by the 1840s the forms of architecture were beginning to change, too. Art generally, and furniture and architecture in particular, were becoming a kind of erudite game of immense complication. This game people everywhere—high and low, apt and inept—were eager to play; and they would be long tiring of it. In fact, preoccupation with symbolic values external to forms, taking precedence over beauty and functional convenience, would be the common denominator of most architecture for the next hundred years.

The game will not always have the same rules, however. Over the period from, roughly, the 1820s to the 1930s, three quite well-defined phases can be discerned, each ultimately based on symbolism, but each with distinct characteristics of its own:

(1) *Early Victorian.* This is the phase of the Revivals proper. It is dominant approximately from the 1820s into the 1850s. Of course, as in all historical periods, there are exceptions before—the alternate sets of Gothic and Roman designs Latrobe submitted for the Baltimore Cathedral in 1805 already offer an admirable example—and after. In this phase all sorts of styles from the past are reused. A "good" architect or designer is expected to know the distinguishing characteristics of half a dozen or more, and be able to use them in the proper way and place—Roman to suggest civic virtue, Greek for liberty, Egyptian for permanence, Gothic for Christian ideals, and so on. But he must not mix them in the same building. If he does, he may expect to find his work denounced as "utterly monstrous and barbarous," as was the New York Custom House by the *American Monthly Magazine* in 1835, simply because Town and Davis had dared to combine styles so similar (and not so long before considered practically identical) as Greek in the portico and Roman in the dome. To critical Early Victorian minds, it seems self-evident that just as each style has its own particular forms, so each has a cluster of more or less well-defined ideas peculiarly associated with it alone.

(2) *High Victorian.* By the 1850s this neat and naïve system begins to break down. Mixing styles on the same building soon becomes common, then practically obligatory; it characterizes the second phase of Victorian art, which lasts well into the 1880s. As late as 1884 one John Moser, an Alabama architect, proposed a building for the American Institute of Architects in New York "where every epoch in architectural history shall be represented by details from the best examples now obtainable, following each other in a regular and orderly sequence"; this, he hoped, might produce an "American Style" with "proportions as agreeable and the whole as harmonious as the Greek. As agreeable as the

French. As vigorous as the English. As refined as the Florentine. As systematic as the German. . . ." It sounds like madness, but there was oftener than not method in it. The best architecture and furniture of this period are, in fact, so governed by consistent taste for certain general visual principles of design—especially for what High Victorians called "picturesqueness" of outline, massing, and texture—and so effectively express ideals and ways of life common to the middle and upper classes, as to justify being considered in some degree as a true historical style: "Picturesque Eclecticism."

(3) *Late Victorian.* On lower economic and cultural levels, Picturesque Eclecticism survives well into the 20th century. But among the "taste-makers," reaction against it begins in the 1880s, and by the 1890s a new concern is dominant—"realism." But just as painters' interpretations of "realism" may vary all the way from photographic literalism to "nonobjective verity," so realism means very different things to different architects. To some, like Louis Sullivan, it means incorporating the technological advances that made possible radically new types of structure and ornament, expressing the sociological changes that were transforming the old individualistic society into a world of "organization men." But men like Sullivan were in the minority; in the Late Victorian period generally "realism" takes the form of what seems at first sight a return to the principles of the first phase—for any given building, a single style, with a particular association of ideas. The differences between Early and Late Victorian are considerable and obvious, however. In the intervening fifty years, enormous advances in historical scholarship have been made. Now "styles" involve much more than collections of details from a given period hung indifferently on a structural frame; Late Victorians really know what the principles of Roman or Gothic or any other style historically were, and go about reproducing them with scientific accuracy. Symbolism correspondingly

loses its earlier naïveté; just as the forms are so much more exact—Late Victorians can reproduce not simply "Roman buildings" but a Roman building of the 1st or 2nd or 3rd century A.D.; not simply "Gothic" but 13th-century French Gothic or Tudor English Gothic—so the ideas associated with them are sophisticated, based on careful historical research. The leaders of this last Victorian phase are a different breed of men from the first, too. Most of them still can and do work in a variety of revived historical styles; but they do so more in response to the demands of patrons than by their own inclinations. Much of the old impartial eclecticism is gone; no longer do we have books like Lafever's or Sloan's or Dwyer's, presenting neatly labeled plans and drawings of "Gothic" alongside "Greek" and "Egyptian" from which readers are encouraged to select impartially according to particular needs, circumstances, and moments. Now if architects have a taste for writing books, the result is oftener than not some polemic in favor of one style over all others, on all occasions. A "Gothic" champion like Ralph Adams Cram will want to see "the greatest synthesis of beauty made operative through art that man has ever achieved"—to wit, "a Gothic cathedral of the thirteenth century during a Pontifical High Mass, and somewhere about the middle of the fourteenth century in England, or the fifteenth century in France or Spain"—the standard for everything, from churches to college dormitories to department stores; and why? Because "it is no less than Christian civilization we have to restore . . . every stone that we cut and lay, however clumsily and by inadequate modern methods, is so much added to the new fabric of a restored civilization. It is not the pandering to an ephemeral fashion but the proclamation of a creed." At the same moment, somebody else will be declaiming that only by creating "cities beautiful" in Roman Imperial architectural dress can America reclaim her soul. And so on. This last, more than the first, symbolic phase is the true uncompromising bitter-end "battle of the styles."

By the end of the 19th century wealth has piled up to match the new scholarship; the "revival of the revivals" is on a far larger scale, costs far more, than was dreamt of before; houses, churches, hotels, city plans, everything is absolutely and relatively bigger. More than ever, architecture in this last phase becomes a rich man's game. No wonder, then, that 1929 marks the end of its dominance, and of the whole attitude to art in which it culminates.

What should be the proper name for an epoch like this? "Victorian" is the one that comes first to mind; but the word has some unfortunate associations. It makes us think of aesthetic chaos —of the kind of later-19th- and early-20th-century middle-class art that dumped elements and ornaments from here, there, and all over into one blurred and indistinct stew; of once picturesque but now simply aimless and sprawling plans; of details once meaningful now heaped up in pointless piles; of outlines and shapes once fresh and eye-appealing now stale and monotonous. It is redolent of old senile forms hanging on and on into the 20th century while a host of new materials and new techniques accumulate and demand expression, of a slowly decaying way of life perpetuated without conviction through the inertia of convention and entrenched privilege.

Yet "Victorian" is the only word that will really do. To talk in stylistic terms of successive "romantic," "picturesque eclectic," and "archaeologically realistic" revivals would be more accurate, perhaps; it would also be cumbersome, ambiguous, and jawbreaking. The English associations of "Victorian" are not entirely appropriate in a 19th-century American setting; but American alternatives like "Jacksonian art," "Rutherford B. Hayes Rococo," or "First Roose-velt Mission" are at best inadequate, at worst grotesque. "Victorian" has at least the merit of familiarity and, provided we take it in a descriptive and not an emotional way, is comprehensive enough to cover the whole epoch in question. So "Victorian" it is.

"The Victorian age" as we use the term here does not refer to a chronological period; it begins well before and ends well after the sixty-four years of Queen Victoria's 1837–1901 reign in England. Nor does "Victorian art" refer to any particular forms—the forms of architecture and furniture in this period are legion, drawn from every time and place in history, from Karnak to Versailles. Rather it refers to that characteristic habit of mind permeating the whole period from the 1820s to the 1930s, which sees visual forms in terms of intellectual images, uses them as a kind of symbolic language. That is what all three phases of 19th-century art have in common, and to think of them as Early, High, and Late Victorian helps keep them in proper perspective to one another. "Victorian art" in this sense is not a catchall label for some aimless welter of conflicting details, but refers to a tradition having guiding principles and an inner consistency as essentially coherent as any other. Once understand how throughout this whole epoch visual forms are used like words and phrases, freely and variously as different occasions and the need to say different things demand, and "Victorian art" no longer seems some insane jungle of whimsy and rhetoric; it appears as the Victorians themselves wanted to see it, as part of a historic past, a living expression of the times that produced it, the century that changed the United States from a tiny rural republic into a major world power.

NOTES

Quotations of John Moser's articles in *The American Architect and Building News* from John Burchard and Albert Bush-Brown, *The Architecture of America* (Boston, 1961), p. 178. Professor C. L. V. Meeks has written definitively on Picturesque Eclecticism as a High Victorian characteristic in "Picturesque Eclecticism" (*Art Bulletin*, XXXII, 1950, pp. 226–35), and *The Railroad Station* (New Haven, 1956), Chap. 1, "The Nineteenth-Century Style." See also H.-R. Hitchcock, *Early Victorian Architecture in Britain* (New Haven, 1954), Chap. 1. Quotations from R. A. Cram, "Ordeal by Beauty: Phi Beta Kappa Oration, Harvard University, 1921," in *Convictions and Controversies* (Boston, 1935).

96. Thomas Cole, "The Architect's Dream." Courtesy of The Toledo Museum of Art. Gift of Florence Scott Libbey, 1949.

2. INTRODUCING THE ECLECTIC MIND:
Forms and Spirit of Early Victorian Art, c.1820—c.1850

RISING HIGH over the plain of mundane affairs, a great carved pedestal of polished marble. Piled on the pedestal, great leather-bound tomes heavy with the weight of architectural lore from all the ages past. On the books, a small elegant figure reclining. This is "The Architect's Dream." In his hand a plan unrolls; above his head, curtains part; before him unfolds the whole vast panorama of human history. Temples of Greece and pyramids of Egypt; Gothic cathedrals and Roman aqueducts; Tuscan arches and Byzantine capitals; obelisks and tholoi—all mankind's achievements are there, and they all belong to him, to use as he will. This is Thomas Cole's pictorial allegory of the architect as men by the 1840s had come to conceive him.

What they admire is no longer the man of skill, the artisan whose practiced eye can proportion and whose trained hand can shape forms in wood and stone and brick. Neither is it any more the man of leisured taste, the gentleman patron whose wealth makes possible and whose discrimination inspires what the artisan creates. Now the ideal is the man of erudition, he who has education to know which peoples built what masterpieces long ago, and judgment to tell where and when to reproduce them again. This is the beginning of a fundamentally new concept of the artist, at once product and creator of that changed attitude to art later generations would call Victorian.

The new architect is more a literary figure— an intellectual, even a scholar—than he is artisan or connoisseur. Ranging over all historical time in search of appropriately symbolic models, he is eclectic as artists had never been before. To be sure, eclecticism as such—borrowing "from the best" in the past—was no 19th-century invention. No artist in history ever created in a vacuum; everyone must learn from what others did before him. And, of course, the idea of borrowing forms for symbolic purposes was not new either; it was at least as old as the Renaissance. But the typical architect of this, the Early Victorian period, now goes about it in a different and more systematic way. He borrows forms not primarily to integrate them into a style of his own, or express the spirit of his age, but to compose visual statements. His borrowings from the past are consistently determined on intellectual grounds, by the mind more than the eye. He thinks of art as essentially a system of pictorial symbolism, of the artist's business as matching appropriate images with given ideas. That is the kind of architecture the subject of Thomas Cole's "Dream" is practicing. As his representative figure, the painter chose Ithiel Town of New Haven, Connecticut—and it was an apt choice. For in the year "The Architect's Dream" was painted, Town was literally as well as allegorically on a pedestal. At the height of his career, for fifteen years past he had been, if hardly the one great figure on the American architectural scene, certainly the one who best typified the principles of practice of Early Victorian art in America.

Town typified the new age in his professional background and the kind of social status he had achieved. Although he had begun working as a carpenter in rural New England where he was born—in the hamlet of Thompson, Connecticut, in 1784—and by 1812 had acquired enough local reputation as a builder to be commissioned designer of the important Center Church in New Haven, Town seems never to have been an artisan in the full craft sense. His fundamental métier was what later times would call engineering. It was as inventor of an engineering device, the Town Lattice Truss for bridge building which he patented in 1820, that national fame and fortune came to him, and made him a gentlemen of leisure, practicing architecture by choice. And it may well have been this fundamental bent of mind that made him so typical of the new age in his approach to the art of architecture long before becoming the representative figure for that age of the architect in society. For whereas artisans by nature excel in executing detail, instinctively tend in approaching larger problems of design to take some detail as a module and work out from it, the engineer by nature, begins with general theoretical principles and works back from them to particular cases. A man of Town's temperament would be much better prepared than an artisan to appreciate the symbolic approach to design coming in with the Victorian age, so that it is not entirely surprising to find him displaying so remarkably precocious (for the time and place) a grasp of it as is evident in his two early churches on the New Haven Green—Center (begun 1812) and Trinity (begun 1814). In many ways, they represent the first appearance of thoroughly Victorian concepts of architecture in America.

Town designed Center Church in forms almost as traditional—though, significantly enough, rather more erudite—as those local carpenter-builder David Hoadley was using for its neighbor, the United Church, begun at the same time. Of wood and brick, in style a combination of post-Georgian exterior details, derived from as venerable a source as Gibbs's *Book of Architecture*, with Adamesque–Federal lines and light saucer dome learned from Asher Benjamin on the interior, Center Church was about what you might expect in Connecticut in 1812. But Trinity, two years later, was totally different. Instead of white clapboard, there are walls of tawny sandstone, with woodwork painted to match. Gibbsian cornices and pilasters are replaced by mullions, pointed arches, pinnacles, crockets, and tracery picked from prints of medieval cathedrals. No spacious flow of light in this interior; whatever feeble rays penetrate the heavy colored glass of its windows are swallowed up in the shadows of stuccoed groin vaults, floors darkly varnished, pews and chancel rails and galleries finished in deep mahogany. Why the change? Not because

the physical function is so different; the Episcopal Church in early-19th-century America, even more than in England, was hardly more liturgically inclined than its Congregational neighbors. Nor yet because of a difference in basic structure; actually, both churches are the same kind of stiff boxy meeting houses. Town changed the forms for only one reason; because the two buildings had differing symbolic functions. As a Congregational church, representing the established religion of Connecticut since its foundation, Center was appropriately designed in traditional 18th-century forms. But it seemed clear to Town that the Episcopal Church, only now reviving from the Revolutionary crisis which had tainted its polity with Toryism and made Methodists of one congregation after another, demanded some other expression—a style which quite as emphatically did *not* recall the colonial past. Whatever claims it had—and Town evidently accepted them, for he joined the Episcopal parish soon after Trinity was built—rested on an even older, earlier medieval and Early Christian heritage. And it was this heritage that Town intended Trinity's Gothic dress to proclaim. Thus early did Town work in terms of a consistent and logical association of ideas rather than beauty or physical function; the rest of his career was built on this foundation.

Superficially, Town's idea of Gothic, as displayed at Trinity Church, seems little different from Batty Langley's in *Gothic Architecture Improved by Rules and Proportion* half a century before; indeed, he may very well have drawn some details from that source. Take a New England meeting house of standard proportions, plan, and structure; put pinnacles and crockets on it instead of urns or balusters; make the rectangular windows pointed—and there is your Gothic church! About Gothic architecture as it really was, about medieval constructional principles, about the relationship of ornament to structure, he seems neither to have known nor cared. The result, to us, is a ludicrous parody of real medieval building. These thin buttress strips and wiry details look like nothing so much as a collection of Gothic shapes cut out of cardboard and pasted together; Trinity Church in New Haven could be accepted as Gothic, we imagine, only by people who had never seen the real thing, whose idea of Gothic was in fact composed of paper images. And in one sense we would be right; there is little evidence that Town, or the vestrymen of Trinity, or for that matter most builders of Gothic for the next twenty or thirty years, had any real hope or intention of producing actual Gothic structures. If what they got was a collection of details, that was largely because a collection of details was in fact what they wanted. They wanted forms not to be medieval (or Roman, or Greek) as such, but merely to make visual statements by general allusion to Gothic or whatever other historical period was appropriate. And that is what distinguishes them both from "mediaevalists" half a century later and from "Gothick" builders half a century before. For them these Gothic details were neither primarily ornamental variations and distractions within a controlling classical framework, nor archaeological reconstructions; they were symbols. As symbols, however, they were taken very seriously and used very consistently. If the Early Victorian Gothic Revivalist did not try to reproduce actual medieval building, neither did he try to "improve" the style by rules, proportions, or details originating in some other historical period. Although Trinity was begun only two years after Center Church, its formal details are entirely different; whatever of classical proportions survives is by accident and not intent. And in this refusal to mix styles Town again typified the Early Victorian mind.

By the early 1820s Town's patented lattice truss was beginning to make him wealthy. More important, it made him free to follow his own inclinations in architectural practice. Never basically interested in building operations as such, more and more he grew into what we could call an architectural consultant rather than a contractor-builder. He used his money to acquire a li-brary, which by 1834 had grown to over eleven thousand volumes, contained hundreds of paintings and prints, and was called by Dunlap in his first *History of the . . . Arts . . . in the United States* "truly magnificent and unrivalled by anything of the kind in America; perhaps no private library in Europe is its equal." His approach to architectural styles became increasingly erudite; his Eagle Bank in New Haven (1824) and the Joseph Bowers house in Northampton, Massachusetts (1825, both now demolished) were among the first introductions of pure Greek Revival in New England. He began to make acquaintances in the literary and artistic circles which New England's growing industrial wealth was beginning to foster, particularly in the circle of James Abram Hillhouse, at whose house in New Haven Benjamin Silliman, Noah Webster, Eli Whitney, Samuel Morse, Trumbull, Cole, and Asher B. Durand gathered.

But for a man of Town's type, New England in the 1820s was still too small. All its advances in wealth and culture during the fifty years since independence were nothing compared to what had been happening in New York. Located at the head of the greatest natural waterway into the heart of the continent, New York profited by every advance of settlement into the interior at a rate neither Boston nor New Haven nor Philadelphia, with hinterlands hemmed in by mountain ranges, could hope to match. Early the country's most cosmopolitan city, it had now become the most populous as well, the center for new ideas and developments of every sort. Already New Yorkers were quite aware of this:

We do not measure our steps as they do in Philadelphia [says an editorial in the *New-York Morning Courier and Enquirer* for November 10, 1829]. We do not study fluxions and eat cod for salmon as they do in Boston. . . . There is more life and spirit and variety in New-York in one day, than in all the other cities put together in a fortnight. New-York is Athens revived. . . . Everybody wants to know what's the news? So did they of Ancient Athens. . . . How would the people of Baltimore, or the readers of Philadelphia, or the *classiques* of Boston get along in this world, if they had not a New-York—a great, active, bustling, ever curious New-York to furnish them with topics and news; to show them the way of living and moving, and to tell them what is fashionable in politics or pantaloons—in commerce or in coats and corsets?

New York was, then, as natural a place for a New Englander like Town to go as Philadelphia had been in Benjamin Franklin's day. In 1825 he went there, soon began to move in Dr. David Hosack's "circle," which included such cosmopolitan intellectuals as James Fenimore Cooper, Washington Irving, William Cullen Bryant, and traveled painters like Washington Allston and William Page, and established an architectural firm which is perhaps most typical of the new Early Victorian concept of art.

In his *Autobiography* James H. Dakin noted that in 1832, when he arrived in New York looking for architectural employment, "there was, properly speaking, only one architect's office [of the "modern" sort he had known in England] in New York, kept by Town and Davis." Town had established it in 1827, with Martin Thompson (1787–1875) as his partner; in 1829 Thompson was replaced by Alexander Jackson Davis (1803–1892), who remained with the firm almost until Town's death in 1844, and from time to time other men from various parts of the country and in various capacities (including Dakin himself) were associated with it. But there was never any doubt who dominated and ran the office. Nor was there any doubt that in it Town played an essentially new role, one recognized by his contemporaries as dramatizing a new ideal status for the artist in society.

Town always conceived his firm essentially, as the articles of agreement between him and Davis stated, as "a partnership for the transaction of business." And by the 1830s it had come to be a very businesslike operation indeed. In it little of the old informality of earlier builder-patron relationships, the "Won't-you-build-me-a-house-something-like-Squire-Smith's-down-the-street?" approach, remained. You come to the firm of Town & Davis, as you would to a merchant, or manufacturer, and are given the same kind of direct service. You state your needs, anything from a church to a warehouse to a country cottage. Mr. Town, in the capacity of president and public relations officer, sits you down at a table and discusses them. He shows you the firm's stock in trade—sheets of neat drawings prepared by his partner or assistant draftsmen, something suitable for every occasion. Should you express preference for something unsuitable—say, a Greek temple-house as a country retreat—you are gently corrected. Of course, the firm is always happy to oblige, but, frankly, for a gentleman like yourself, that would not perhaps be entirely proper—let me show you why. . . . He refers to his library—who in America has not heard of it? He speaks of his trip to Europe in 1830, of seeing the originals of the various styles he has to offer, in their original setting. He demonstrates which style is appropriate for what. Surely, for a man of your character, an "American Gothic" villa would be much better? Now here we have some standard designs; we can supply you with one of them for, say, fifty dollars. But perhaps you would prefer something more . . . personal? Mr. Davis, our executive vice-president in charge of production, will be glad to have some plans specially drawn for you. There will be a slight extra charge, of course—say, thirty-five dollars for the working drawings, and ten for a pair of very elegant gateposts and a fence to go with them? And so on. . . . A price list from which such quotations were made still survives from 1848, in Davis's hand. It is all very systematic, very plain. Each style has its particular advantages and disadvantages; there is a place for each, and each belongs in its place.

Town's firm, in short, was typical of the new spirit of commercial enterprise everywhere developing in America during the 1820s, 30s, and 40s. It had a characteristic new organized efficiency. And it was typical, too, in its national scope.

97. *Symbolism on the New Haven Green: "View of Three Houses for Public Worship on the Public Square, New Haven"* (right to left: *United Church by David Hoadley, c.1812; Center [c.1812] and Trinity [c.1814] churches by Ithiel Town*), as they were c.1827. During the Early Victorian period, advance-guard architecture was beginning to manifest the unprecedented accumulation of wealth and leisure through industrialization and flourishing trade that was steadily shifting the cultural center of the United States northwards to the New York–Hudson Valley–New Haven area.

In order to supervise the bridges which were being built on his patent all over the country in this age of tremendous expansion of transportation by road, rail, and water, Town had to travel frequently and far; he used the trips as an opportunity to make contacts for the firm, and solicit business. In Town's office there began the process of imposing metropolitan standards over the whole countryside which culminated in the days of radio and television; it was a remote corner of the United States indeed that had not at least seen designs by Town & Davis. New York City, naturally, had a full gallery of their offerings: Greek in Bleecker Street Church (1831); Gothic for New York University (c.1830); Roman for the New York Custom House (now Subtreasury, completed 1836; its Greek porticos were bitterly criticized for their incongruity); a delicate Ionic design for the French Protestant Église du St.-Esprit, to suggest tasteful French tradition (1832–4); monumental Corinthian in Lafayette Terrace (Colonnade Row, 1836) to dramatize New York's cosmopolitan kinship with the great centers of European wealth and society; warehouses with mighty granite piers to embody ideas of security and strength (e.g., Tappan Store, Ware Street, 1831); and up the Hudson Valley and into Connecticut, one villa after another in suburban "American Gothic" or the new "American Tuscan" style. The firm supplied designs for state capitols in North Carolina, Indiana, Illinois, and Ohio; an alumni hall at Yale and the first buildings for the University of Michigan at Ann Arbor (unexecuted) and Virginia Military Institute at Lexington; a hospital for the insane and a college (Davidson) in

98. *Custom House (Subtreasury Building), New York. Town and Davis secured the commission to build a customhouse on the site of Federal Hall (demolished 1812) in 1833, and work began on their plans in 1834. Objections to their combination of a Roman dome with Greek temple forms was so great on both symbolic and practical grounds that plans were revised, possibly by superintendent of construction Samuel Thomson, to keep the dome entirely inside. John Frazee was appointed "Architect and Superintendent" in July 1835, after Thomson's resignation in April; he completed the interior of the building. Elevation* (above), *section* (right), *and plan of the main floor* (below).

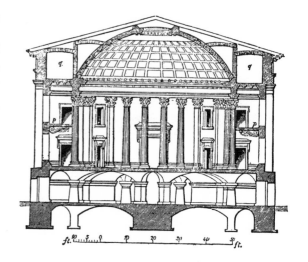

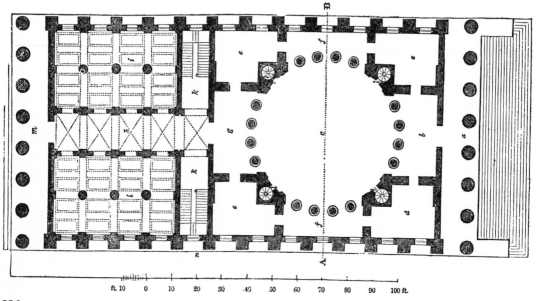

North Carolina; and so on and on.

But it was as he typified the new status of the architect as creative personality that Town made perhaps the greatest impression both on his own times and on the future. Early in the 1830s he is encouraging the formation of a professional association to secure architects public recognition as practitioners of a learned and specialized profession demanding the same sort of training and extensive knowledge as, say, medicine or law or belles-lettres. It is an age when cultural organizations are springing up everywhere—a society of the dilettanti, an antique school, academies of fine arts and sciences, drawing associations, mechanics' institutes, and historical societies. Why not something the same for architects? In 1836 Strickland, Haviland, Walter, Davis, Isaiah Rogers, and Charles Reichard meet in Astor House, New York, to discuss the matter; but the following March we hear only that a "committee" of Davis, Haviland, and Walter are going to "explore the possibilities." Anyone who has ever served on committees will not be surprised, after that ominous phrase, to find nothing further forthcoming; it will be 1857 before the American Institute of Architects becomes a fact. One of the causes of this first failure is perhaps that Town had no formal connection with the project, apparently; he seems to have been inactive for a year or two at this time, even withdrawing temporarily from his firm. And with the possible exception of Davis, only he seems to have really belonged to the new age and understood its full potentialities for the architectural profession. Only he—as Cole recognized in "The Architect's Dream"—fully realized what professional freedom could mean, how it could lift the architect forever out of the ranks of artisans into an intellectual and cultural aristocracy.

Correspondingly, of course, professional elevation of the architect degraded craftsmen. The further architects climb above the ranks of artisans, the more surely furniture makers slip back into them; ever sharper and more final becomes the line between those who make designs and those who execute them. And once again it is Town who introduces and typifies the new age. As in his person he exemplifies the architect's claims to independent creative stature, so in the relationship of cabinetmakers to his firm is foreshadowed the decline of furniture making from a major art to a minor one at best, and ultimately to an assembly-line-laborer's job.

To furniture Town applies the same standards and symbolic values that govern his architectural thinking. Characteristic is his designing the bookcases that housed his famous library in New York to symbolize what they contained—some Egyptian, some Grecian, some Gothic. For him, that is to say, furniture is simply a kind of architectural detail, a form of decoration rather than an art with pretensions to equality. It is the kind of attitude apparent in the first (1828) American edition of Mrs. William Parkes's *Domestic Duties; or Instructions to Young Married Ladies on the Management of Their Households*, wherein furniture, once as much a man's concern as architecture, now falls to women to choose, on loosely symbolic lines:

> . . . Every room should be furnished in a style not inconsistent with the use for which it is set apart. The dining-room, the place of rendezvous for the *important* concerns of the table, should not be furnished in the light and airy style which you may adopt in your drawing-room, in which amusement and ease are the objects desired. . . . The furniture most usual in the dining-room is of a substantial kind; for instance, mahogany chairs, tables, and sideboards. . . . A solid simplicity generally characterizes the style of the dining-room, rendering it less subject to the variation of fashion than in some other parts of the house. . . . The style of the drawing-room furniture is almost as changeable in fashion as female dress; sometimes it is Grecian, then Egyptian, and now Turkish. . . .

It follows that, except for their necessarily rather more specialized skills, men who supply furniture like this will have much the same status as those who lay the bricks for the walls of Town's houses, saw timber for his barge-boards. All alike are hired by the job, work impersonally and anonymously to the firm's specifications. Only occasionally is a name preserved, usually for extraneous reasons, like that of John Frazee (1790–1852), the versatile tombstone cutter turned sculptor and sometime architect who performed the remarkable feat (for that time) of executing classical furniture to Town's order in metal for the New York Custom House. And if we happen to know something about that Joseph (or Richard) Byrnes (c.1810–c.1884) who, according to Mr. Newton, came to the United States from his native Limerick County in Ireland c.1835 and executed Gothic furnishings for Davis's villas from 1838 into the 1860s, it is hardly as a creative personality. It is difficult enough to guess the extent to which partners like Thompson and Davis, hired draftsmen like Dakin or Stirewalt, or protégés like Henry Austin (1804–1891) of New Haven or William P. Elliott of Washington (who assisted the firm in its bid for the old United States Patent Office and Treasury commissions in the mid-1830s), were merely carrying out Town's ideas or inventing their own; separating Byrnes's stylistic personality from Davis's, or even trying to learn something concrete about Byrnes at all, is almost impossible. Whatever he does is only an extension of Davis's mind, a useful tool picked up as occasion demands. And this kind of relationship is increasingly the shape of things Victorian to come.

Now the Chippendales and Heppelwhites, the Goddards and Randolphs and Sandersons, whose work in an earlier time was their own creative expression, disappear; in their place come nameless laborers sawing out reproductions of designs supplied by others. They work from *The Cabinet Maker's Assistant,* published in 1840 by "Architect" John Hall of Baltimore; or from the book of the same name published in 1842 by Robert Connor of nobody knows where —as qualifications he claimed only to have been "engaged as a practical Cabinet Maker in Paris and London for several years"; or from Mrs. Lydia Maria Hale's "Cottage Furniture Department" in *Godey's Lady's Book* (beginning in 1849). And they do more and more of their work in factories. There are dozens of factories now, of all descriptions, operating in every major city and region. Lambert Hitchcock's is one of the most famous of them today; beginning his career making chair parts for Samuel Roberts in Colebrook, Connecticut, in 1804, Hitchcock went on to become proprietor of an establishment whose stenciled trademark, "L. Hitchcock, Hitchcocksville [now Riverton, Connecticut] Warranted," gave a name to a whole class of painted "rush-bottom" chairs. But his was a small operation, compared even with the Union Chair Company of Winsted, Connecticut, whose output from the 1820s until the 1870s was diverse enough to be confused both with Hitchcock and Pennsylvania-German products, and far greater than either; compared with those of big-city factories, it was minuscule. From New York City, for instance, Tweed & Bonnell exported astronomical numbers of chairs all over the country, and as far afield as Casablanca and Constantinople, from the late 1820s to the time when "Boss" Tweed found even more lucrative kinds of work. From Cincinnati, Bird & Burrows's products flooded the Midwest in the 1840s and 50s. From Pittsburgh, Graham & Montgomery was supplying settlers in the new Western territories with factory-made furniture as early as the 1820s and 30s. From their four-story plant with steam-powered machinery, Birge & Brothers turned out chairs by the thousands in the 1840s and 50s at Troy, New York. . . . And now these nameless laborers number in the thousands; whereas from the census of 1810 it appears that something like 1,000 persons were engaged in making cabinets and chairs, by 1850 there were 37,359, with 83,580 in "furniture making and allied trades."

Furniture soon betrays the change. Shoddy construction becomes commoner and commoner, even in "custom-made" work for leading de-

99. *Early Victorian Furniture Styles, as advertised in 1833 by Joseph Meeks & Sons in a color lithograph by Endicott and Sweet. To our eyes, they may seem all very much alike, and equally* *devoid of governing principle; but in their own time they were intended to be quite distinctive, each "historical style" having suitability in different parts of the house.*

signers. That is inevitable. The less furniture makers think of themselves as creators of works of art in their own right and sphere, the faster their old incentive to fine craftsmanship dies. The more their art degenerates into drudgery, the greater their temptation to cut corners, literally as well as figuratively, and the easier it becomes to mass-produce. Equally inevitable, too, is the breakdown of stylistic standards once mass production becomes the rule. Not that "factories" as such were to blame. Furniture factories of a kind were not unheard of in the later 18th century; for example, one George Shipley of New York advertised as early as May of 1792 that he had "in employment a number of excellent workmen . . . at his cabinet manufactory"; and there is no reason to doubt that what was produced there, and in later establishments like Duncan Phyfe's (at least into the 1820s), was in fact "made in the neatest and most fashionable manner," as was claimed. Even Lambert Hitchcock's earlier products, though cheap and simple, were not poorly made. It was when "factories" began to be run by businessmen (whatever their origins) turning out articles supplied by outside artists and architects instead of by trained cabinetmakers, that the collapse came. For cabinetmaking in the proper sense is an art with its own laws like any other. True, it may depend on the same general principles as architectural composition—the classical tradition in the 18th century, eclectic symbolism in the Early Victorian decades—but their application in detail is necessarily different. Once let this art fall into the hands of designers, however sensitive, who lack a basic feel for its peculiar qualities, and degeneration is swift and sure. When even so erudite a master as A. J. Davis could see no inherent incongruity in loading spires and crockets from 15th-century cathedrals onto beds and chairs of basically 18th-century proportions drawn from Chippendale's *Director*, it is only to be expected that what Joseph Meeks & Sons, "oldest and now the largest Manufactory of Cabinet and Upholstry Articles" in New York, advertised in 1833 was already a spectacular parade of gaucheries. These first mass-producers were still Early Victorian enough not to mix styles deliberately. They meant to be "correct" when they called this chair Gothic and that Greek, one Egyptian and another Elizabethan, and they had some idea of an appropriate association for each. But just as they had to ignore the fine points of craftsmanship to reach mass markets, so they could not afford the niceties of erudition. It was inevitable that styles would begin to be muddled earlier and oftener in furniture than in architecture, that vaguely Louis Quinze chairs would have backs pierced with vaguely Gothic pointings and cuspings, that vaguely Empire scrolls would be lightened to create an effect of simplicity vaguely Grecian, and so on. And herein furniture again, as it had so often in the past, intimated future developments even as it expressed the culture of its own age.

In the development of mass production that Early Victorian furniture so well represents we can see a counterpart to the whole pattern of American cultural history from the 1820s through the 1850s—the rise of a nation-wide network of capitalist enterprises centralized in major cities, the emergence of the kind of political machines based on an urban proletariat that Martin van Buren began to build in the 1830s, the spread of urban standards at the expense of old regional distinctiveness. The blurring of sharp style divisions in these mass-produced articles parallels the blurring of the old simple self-evident facts of American life as the Founding Fathers had conceived them. Just as style had to become a thing of conflicting chance and fancy once men began taking their inspiration in libraries instead of shops, creating with books and drawing boards instead of chisels and compasses, so the old tidy categories of Greek liberty, Gothic piety, Roman virtue, and so on could not survive in the ever-increasing complexities of American life. Like the famous drawings in Augustus Welby Pugin's *Gothic Furniture in the Style of the Fifteenth Century* (London, 1835) that required such intricate carving they could not be executed, men found the ideals in the Founders' books coming to have less and less relevance to either life or art. And it is in this mass-produced furniture that the inevitable change begins. Here starts that mixing of styles which will create Picturesque Eclecticism, characteristic expression of the second, High Victorian phase of American art and civilization. How the transition from Early to High Victorian art came about is, however, a chapter in itself.

NOTES

On Ithiel Town and the firm of Town & Davis generally, see R. H. Newton, *Town and Davis* (1942), and T. F. Hamlin, *Greek Revival Architecture in America* (1944). On the Custom House (Subtreasury) and other extant Town & Davis work in New York, see Huson Jackson, *New York Architecture* (1952); also Louis Torres, "Samuel Thomson and the Old Custom House" (*JSAH*, XX, 4, 1961, pp. 185–90).

For a fuller quotation from *Domestic Duties*, see Frank J. Schmidt, "Household Concerns" (*Winterthur Newsletter* VII, 1, 1961, pp. 1–6). On Early Victorian furniture, a most useful reference is the series by Robert C. Smith in *Antiques* (LXXIV, 5, 6, 1958, pp. 429–34, 519–23; and LXXV, 3, 1959, pp. 272–282): "The Classical Style in France and England 1800–1840," "Late Classical Furniture in the United States, 1820–1850," and "Gothic and Elizabethan Revival Furniture, 1800–1850." See also T. H. Ormsbee, *Field Guide to American Victorian Furniture* (Boston, 1952), pp. 15–16, 30–35.

100. EXOTIC REVIVAL STYLES

(A) Egyptian Revival in the Corinthian mode: Whalers' Church, Sag Harbor, Long Island, New York, as it was before 1938. Built 1843–4 by local carpenters and shipbuilders working to the designs of Minard Lafever. The spire, which served as a landmark for sailors, was blown down in the hurricane of 1938; the small and devoted congregation which maintains the church hopes to replace the spire if funds can be raised.

3. THE "BATTLE OF THE STYLES":
Gothic Revival as Anticlassical Expression, 1820—1850

"AMERICAN LOG CABIN, Farm Villa, English Cottage, Collegiate Gothic, Manor House, French Suburban, Switz Chalet, Switz Mansion, Lombard Italian, Tuscan from Pliny's Villa at Ostia, Ancient Etruscan, Suburban Greek, Oriental, Moorish, Round, Castellated . . ." So in the 1850s and 60s Alexander Jackson Davis listed the styles of architecture with which he was prepared to supply his clients—a famous list, often taken as typical of the transformation of a once coherent and meaningful American architectural scene into something more like an arena, where past and present styles of every description battled inconclusively for popular acceptance, at the expense of all principle or purpose. But appearances, especially literary ones, are deceptive. Though any number of exotic new styles were introduced on paper, most of them were represented by relatively few executed examples. And for all the seeming diversity, there were in fact only two styles of real consequence in the Early Victorian period—classical and Gothic. What seems to be a third, the Tuscan or Italianate, is essentially a combination of these two; and all the rest turn out on examination to be basically variants of one or the other.

It is obvious, for instance, that the Egyptian Revival was essentially a variant of the dominant Greek and Roman modes. To all intents and purposes it began with Napoleon's campaign on the Nile, and came into America favored by the general wave of enthusiasm for all things French at the turn of the century. As early as 1808 Latrobe had proposed an Egyptian Library of Congress; Baron Vivant Denon's *Viaggio nel basso ed alto Egitto* was an early acquisition in Town's library; and the symbolic associations of Egyptian forms were widely enough understood so as to be useful in a variety of special situations— gloomy incarceration for prisons (e.g., Haviland's "Tombs" in New York, c.1836; Walter's debtor's

wing at Moyamensing, Philadelphia, c.1836); funereal dignity for cemeteries (gateways to Grove Street in New Haven by Henry Austin, c.1830, and for Greenmount in Baltimore by Robert Cary Long, Jr., c.1845); early medical science (Egyptian Building, Medical College of Virginia in Richmond, by Thomas S. Stewart, 1854); Near Eastern heritage for synagogues (Mikveh Israel by Strickland, c.1824, and Beth Israel, by Walter, c.1849, in Philadelphia); Solomonic wisdom for Old-Testament–oriented churches (First Presbyterian Church in Nashville, Tennessee, by Strickland, c.1849; Whalers' Church at Sag Harbor, New York, by Lafever, 1844; even stability for insurance companies (Pennsylvania Fire Insurance Company, opposite Independence Square, begun by Haviland c.1839) and public works (old Croton Reservoir, New York). But they could hardly be acceptable on any broad or universal scale. Indeed, their general association with death and despotism was so strong that only provincial naïveté would condone Egyptian as a style for public buildings. And even when particular circumstances allowed Egyptian forms and decorative motifs to appear in a "normal" setting, as in the Whalers' Church at Sag Harbor (where they were intended, as the dedicatory sermon emphasizes, to bring the Temple of Solomon to mind), they were carefully combined with other, more familiar ones (e.g., the tower, with its ring of Corinthian columns, Greek key fretwork, and spire vaguely reminiscent of Gibbs), and the whole solidly based on traditional plans and proportions.

Obviously a classical variant, too, was the Renaissance Revival which flourished briefly here and there, as in the Athenaeum building in Philadelphia (by John Notman, 1845–50), where cosmopolitan culture was suggested by the imitation of the architectural style of Sir Charles M. Barry's London clubs, or the façade of the

(100 B) Octagon in the Moorish mode: Longwood, designed for Haller Nutt near Natchez, Mississippi, by Samuel Sloan in 1855, left unfinished in 1861.

old Harper Building in New York (by James Bogardus, 1854), whose Italian arcades connoted equally cosmopolitan literary aspirations. So, again, was the brief flare-up of enthusiasm for octagon houses in the 1850s, fanned by Orson Squire Fowler's *A Home For All* (1854). Whatever claims of greater healthfulness, convenience, and functional efficiency were made for the octagons, their basic appeal depended on the old classical belief in absolute, perfect forms; as Fowler expounded it, "Some forms are constitutionally more beautiful than others. . . . A square house is more beautiful than a triangular one, and an octagon or duodecagon than either . . . the octagon form is more beautiful as well as capacious, and more consonant with the predominant or governing form of Nature—the spherical."

Quite as obviously, other exotic styles were essentially variants of the Gothic mode. Each in its way accentuated one or another characteristic quality of the more comprehensive Gothic Revival. Conspicuous new wealth was displayed by the endless array of "Oriental" domes, towerlets,

and fretwork at Longwood in Natchez, Mississippi (by Samuel Sloan, 1855–6); ostentatious and self-conscious individualism in the "Persian" style of P. T. Barnum's Iranistan near Bridgeport, Connecticut (built 1848 on designs by Leopold Eidlitz, burned 1857); sophisticated, traveled, exotic tastes in Nathan Dunn's "Chinese cottage" at Mount Holly, New Jersey (designed, along with its grounds, by John Notman c.1840, admired and cited by Andrew Jackson Downing). The deliberately extravagant lavishness of Gothic was so exaggerated in "steamboat Gothic" that the latter was essentially a style in itself. No one ever described the effect of its masses of more or less Gothic motifs better than Mark Twain; as he remembered it from the 1840s and 50s, "steamboat Gothic" consisted of

> curving patterns of filigree work touched up with gilding, stretching overhead all down the converging vista; big chandeliers every little way, each an April shower of glittering glass-drops; lovely rainbow-light falling everywhere from the colored glazing of the skylights; the whole a long-drawn, resplendent tunnel, a bewildering and soul-satisfying spectacle.

Yet however far any of these styles departed from medieval forms, they sprang from the same spirit and appealed to the same kind of people as the Gothic Revival—the only style ever accepted on a scale wide enough to be considered any sort of real rival to the dominant Grecian and Roman modes through most of the Early Victorian age.

Not that Gothic ever competed with the classical revivals on anything like even terms. However splintered by internal contradictions, classical forms remained the preponderant choice of most Americans throughout the Early Victorian period, overwhelmingly favored alike by solid middle class home builders and furniture-factory owners catering to a mass market. The Gothic Revival proper (as distinct from 18th-century "Gothick" motifs) began, on the other hand, in eccentric diversions and wilful contrasts from classical norms; and to all intents and purposes retained that character through much of the 19th century. It began uncertainly, as a brief fad—Latrobe's

101. GOTHIC ECCENTRICITIES

(A) Wedding Cake House, Kennebunk, Maine. A provincial Adamesque–Federal house of yellow brick built c.1820, transformed into a bizarre spectacle by an elaborately sawn jacket of Gothic scrollwork, and pinnacles, quite literally added (it has been removed on occasion, e.g., for painting) c.1845, with barn and fence to match.

(101 B) Old State Capitol, Baton Rouge, Louisiana. Completed 1849 on the designs of James H. Dakin. Reconstructed and enlarged in 1882, it served as capitol until 1932.

(101 C) "Great" Temple, Salt Lake City, Utah. Succeeded earlier temples at Kirtland, Ohio (1836), and Nauvoo, Illinois (1846). Its site was designated by President Brigham Young in July 1847, four days after the Latter Day Saints' arrival in Great Salt Lake Valley; cornerstone laid April 1853; completed, with six towers entirely of granite, 1893. Not used for worship services but, like Hebrew temples, for sacred ordinances and ceremonies, it is highly symbolical in plan, proportions, forms, and carved emblems.

Sedgeley outside Philadelphia in 1799, Godefroy's St. Mary's Chapel in Baltimore in 1806, Strickland's Philadelphia Masonic Hall in 1808–11, and a few others constituting a kind of Gothic boomlet—that nearly petered out in the 1820s, and only attained wide popularity later in the 1830s and 40s, under the aegis of Davis and Andrew Jackson Downing. And it was nearly always associated with eccentricity in one form or another. Its most solid credential was its

"Christian," as opposed to "pagan" Greek or Roman or Egyptian, associations, and on this ground it was widely adopted by denominations like the Episcopal or Roman Catholic churches which wanted to display their claims to a historical heritage more substantial (if less "American") than that of their Evangelical rivals. Several architects made reputations in this line: Richard Upjohn (1802–1878) with Trinity Church, New York (1839–46); James Renwick (1818–1895) with Grace (1843–6), Calvary (1846), and St. Patrick's Cathedral (begun 1853) in New York; John Notman (1810–1865) with St. Mark's in Philadelphia (1848–50). But somehow or other the kind of people who came most prominently to mind in connection with Gothic more often than not seemed to be what the age would describe as "somewhat irregular." You thought of odd churchmen like Bishop Doane of Burlington, New Jersey, famed for such exploits as building an elaborate Gothic library in his "Riverside" villa (which he could not pay for) and having himself packaged in a box and shipped to New York by freight train to meet a speaking engagement. Or you read of the celebrated Englishman Augustus Welby North Pugin, forever writing treatises explaining how medieval Catholic England was a heaven on earth which could be revived if only people would use a Gothic style again for town pumps and parish churches, forever threatening to leave the Anglican for the Roman Church and vice versa, forever proclaiming that Gothic architecture and sailboating were the only true joys in life, finally going mad and falling out of his sailboat to drown. Or you heard how the Mormons—they of the gold plates and the many wives—after earlier essays in vaguely Romanesque-cum-Masonic temple designs, had finally settled on an enormous Gothic-pinnacled temple at Salt Lake as the perfect expression of their Church of Jesus Christ of Latter Day Saints in Utah.

Then again, Gothic always seemed to have something vaguely English and un-American about it, something of an undemocratic association with rich men's whimsies. Orson Fowler's great argument against the style, particularly as presented in Andrew Jackson Downing's *Treatise on Landscape Gardening* (1841), was that the kind of plans for country houses and landscaped estates Downing talked about were good only for aesthetes and landed gentlemen, not ordinary people; and certainly Downing's was hardly the best possible presentation during the surging egalitarian democracy of the Age of Jackson. For he was fond of pointing out how "modern landscape gardening owes its existence almost entirely to the English," how it "has been developed and carried to its greatest perfection in the British Isles"; but unfortunately "in the United States, it is highly improbable that we shall ever witness such splendid examples . . . here the rights of man are held to be equal." His observation that "its capabilities may be displayed to their full extent . . . in fifty to five hundred acres devoted to a park or pleasure grounds," but that "most of its beauty and all its charms may, however, be enjoyed in ten or twenty acres, fortunately situated and well treated," was not entirely consoling to most Americans; and the kind of houses he chose to illustrate—Hyde Park, whose grounds are "finely varied . . . including, as they do, the noble Hudson for sixty miles in its course," the Manor of Livingston "commanding prospects for sixty miles around"; Kenwood, near Albany, "a country residence of much picturesque beauty, erected in the Tudor style . . . there are about 1200 acres in the estate, and pleasure grounds . . ." did little to encourage most people to choose Gothic. Still in the 1870s Mark Twain had basically the same objections to it; speaking of the Louisiana State Capitol at Baton Rouge built in Gothic by James H. Dakin in 1849 (and still standing), he summed up—as he so often did so well—what ordinary people had always thought about Gothic generally, from the time it first appeared:

> It is pathetic enough that a whitewashed castle, with turrets and things—materials all ungenuine within and without, pretending to be what they are not—should ever have been built in this otherwise honorable place; but it is much more pathetic to see this architectural falsehood undergoing restoration and perpetuation in our day. . . . By itself the imitation castle is doubtless harmless, and well enough; but as a symbol and breeder and sustainer of maudlin Middle-Age romanticism here in the midst of the plainest and sturdiest and infinitely greatest and worthiest of all the centuries the world has seen, it is necessarily a hurtful thing and a mistake.

For all these reasons, it is easy to see why Gothic never developed anything like the mass following of the classical revivals. Except for country cottages—which, especially as designed by the more practical Davis, had some functional advantages (fewer drafts, more cupboard nooks, etc.) over temple-houses—completely Gothic houses remained comparative rarities. As for Gothic furniture, an atmosphere of "special occasion" clung to it from the 1830s well into the 1880s; it was something you might expect to find in the halls or libraries of people with cultural pretensions, in Masonic lodges or steamboat lounges or the chancels of churches, but not commonly elsewhere.

Socially pretentious, culturally nonconformist, undemocratically eccentric, an intellectual conceit—no wonder the Gothic Revival never spread as widely as classical styles in its own time. But it is precisely this artificiality, this lack of roots in any American craft tradition, that makes the Gothic Revival so much clearer a revelation of the characteristic standards and artistic values of the Early Victorian mind than the classical revivals could ever be. Greek and Roman forms inherently preserved enough of older 18th-century principles so that the real source of their appeal is to some extent disguised. Not so the Gothic. Nobody could look at a building like the "Wedding Cake House" in Kennebunk, for instance, and have any illusions about Early Victorian ornament growing out of structure or the nature of materials; this ornament is too unmistakably and entirely conceived as an extraneous addition, a kind of costume put on or taken off at will, as need for symbolic expression or personal

102. THE "NATURALIZATION" OF GOTHIC IN AMERICA

(A) Trinity Church, New York, built 1839–46 on the designs of Richard Upjohn, as illustrated in Putman's Magazine II, 9, 1853, p. 235. Replacing a vaguely Gothic building of 1788–90, Trinity provided the first great impetus towards making Gothic respectable for churches. So successful was it in this respect that by the time Putnam's Magazine surveyed "New-York Church Architecture" in 1853, fourteen of the seventeen buildings chosen for illustration were Gothic.

show may dictate.

Classical revival builders in the nature of things used their borrowed forms in a more or less genuine way; even the simplest country builder can understand the basic post-and-lintel structural systems of ancient buildings, and in executing dentils, cornices, or capitals in wood instead of stone he was only reverting to the material in which the Greeks of archaic times had originally invented them. But Gothic Revivalists, equally in the nature of things, created obvious shams. Even had they known the principles of Gothic vaulting, executing it in stone would have been far beyond their means; lath and plaster had to be the rule. However uneasily Davis and Downing might warn against foolish attempts to reproduce towering stone castles in painted wood, available materials and skills left their followers little alternative. Classical furniture designers had some reasonable idea, from vases and manuscripts and stelae, what Greek and Roman furniture might actually have been like; the Gothic Revivalist had only chests and cupboards and Coronation chairs to go on, and if he pieced out furniture designs with crockets and colonnets from chimney pieces, trefoils and tendrils from illuminated borders, what else could he do? Under the circumstances, the remarkable thing was not that the Gothic Revival was limited in scope, but that there was a Gothic Revival at all.

If it is true that a good deal of the Gothic Revivalists' claim to have the style for "superior" people was sheer snobbery, it is also true that Gothic was, on the whole, an expression of the more serious "intellectual" class in American society. Its advocates in the 1830s and 40s were, in fact, in much the same position as advocates of abstract expressionism in painting, say, a century or so later. Their ranks included so many assorted crackpots, fanatics, and social climbers that the average person, when he thought about the movement at all (which was not often), tended to assume anybody connected with it was some kind of dissembler or fool. Every advocate of the Gothic Revival found, as Gervase Wheeler complained in *Rural Homes* (1851), that "many persons of pure taste are frightened when the idea of 'Gothic' is presented to them as the style suggested for their home." They did not know, and had little inclination to find out, how many of the

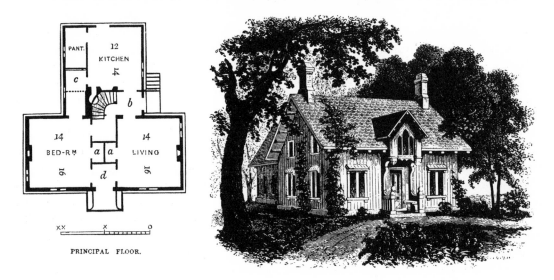

(102 B) Plan and perspective of a "Bracketed Cottage," drawn by A. J. Davis for Andrew Jackson Downing's Country Houses *(1850).*

most sensitive and enlightened spirits of the age were Gothic Revivalists, how often enthusiasm for Gothic was based on a reasoned understanding of it as the truest cultural expression of the times.

The best of the Gothic Revivalists understood consciously what the mass of Americans in the 1840s and 50s were coming to sense only intuitively—that the intellectual and cultural basis of the old classical tradition had crumbled away, leaving Greek and Roman forms with no more real roots in the American past than any others. However inadequately, they realized how surely and how fast the growth of cities, of nation-wide industry and finance, of complexity in every side of life was destroying the old self-sufficiency, that confidence in individuals' abilities to control and mould their world, on which the 18th-century classical tradition depended; and they believed that Gothic, imperfect as it was, was a better expression of and response to the new civilization that was taking shape.

For as the Gothic Revivalists conceived it, the difference between Gothic and classical was more than a matter of forms; it had to do with a whole altered relationship between man and nature. In the crisp outlines, stark white walls

and geometrical self-containment of Greek and Roman Revival buildings, they saw a continuation of what had come to seem the outmoded attitude towards nature as something to be conquered, disciplined, shut out; of the old sharp separation between the reasoned works of man and the chaotic world of nature around him. Their ideal, by contrast, was to have the one complement and lead into the other, to contrive to have elements drawn from the world of nature drawn into the orderly architectural world of men. So the Gothic Revivalists painted houses in "natural" colors—russets and greys and roses (Downing's *Rural Architecture* of 1842 actually has an insert giving samples for painters' guidance). So they covered walls with wisteria and trumpet creepers and ivy nestling into the lines of lacy eaves and bargeboarding. So they reinforced and gave visual meaning to the "naturally" irregular lines of clustered roofs, massy chimneys, steep-pitched gables, turrets, and bay windows by setting them off against clumps of shrubs, great bending trees, and curving hedgerows.

Conversely, they introduced touches of human order throughout the landscape around. Not brutally or conspicuously, of course; on no point

309

was Downing, the great spokesman for the new attitude, more emphatic than on this. The great difference between the "ancient" style of landscape gardening which he abhorred and the "modern" which he advocated was precisely that, whereas the "ancient" or "classical" garden in Egypt and Greece, Holland and Versailles, "tamed and subdued . . . and tortured" nature, the grand principle of "modern" gardens was to co-operate with nature. Don't plant on an arbitrary pattern, he said, but rather plan your landscaping around whatever trees you find standing on your property; except for the most obtrusive boulders or gullies, don't try to level off your terrain, but let your roads curve gracefully around existing contours.

By this introduction of "natural" elements into architecture and "formal" elements into landscape, the Gothic Revivalists contrived to produce the effect of a single co-ordinated whole, in which was expressed a fundamentally new relationship between men and nature. It is not yet the 20th-century concept of a total integration; the Gothic Revivalists, making no systematic attempt to open up solid walls, keep man and nature spatially separate still. But neither is it any more the 18th-century relationship. This is in fact the first clear expression of that attitude to nature which is perhaps the most universal single characteristic of the romantic or anticlassical movement in Western civilization generally throughout the 1820s, 30s, and 40s. If Nature in this Early Victorian age is no longer something to be struggled with and conquered, as it was for the classical mind, neither is it yet a tool for human use, as it will be for the mind of the 20th century. If no longer wild and hostile, neither is it something to be tamely ordered. Nature for the romantic exists in her own right, distinct and different from the world of men. For him her appeal is as something remote, a means of getting away from the humdrum, the complexities, the tensions of everyday life. Set a temple-house in the country, and you are in the world of men still; every line of it reminds

you of civic virtue, of Roman *gravitas* and the duties of Grecian liberty. From this, the Gothic villa can free you; imperceptibly melting into a natural setting, it is not a product of life ordered by reason, but an escape from life into imagination.

It follows that individualism will be the common denominator of the Gothic Revival. That is why the adherents of Gothic seem such a curiously mixed parade of profound philosophers and social snobs, sober churchmen and bigoted fanatics, sensitive poets and conceited visionaries. It follows, too, that the Gothic Revivalist will tend to be apolitical. Unlike the Jeffersonian classicist, he will take little delight at the thought of men moulding the world they live in; all he wants to do is get away. Horrified by the growing cities with their nascent slums he may be, but he is not moved to do anything positive about them: his instinct is to escape to a suburban villa. There, just as he does not want his Gothic house "improved" by the doctrinaire rules and proportions of Batty Langley or anybody else, but only to be "natural," so he will be content to watch nature take its course in the growth of cities as it does in the woods and hills of his suburban grounds. So the Gothic Revival expresses that streak in American society represented in their several ways by Thoreau, by Bryant, by Cole and the Hudson River School of painters, by Washington Irving and his tales of happy primitive life on the Hudson, by the young Walt Whitman.

So too it is no accident that neither of the two leaders of the Gothic Revival in America had any kind of craft background, that both Alexander Jackson Davis and Andrew Jackson Downing began their careers with nonarchitectural interests and instincts, never felt the moulding influence of a training in the classical artisan's tradition of shaping and ordering materials to human rules and proportions.

Davis's inclinations were all in the direction of painting. As a student he supported himself by drawing; in the biographical sketch he sup-

(102 C) Surgeon's Quarters, Fort Dalles, Oregon, remodeled in the 1850s following the design in Downing's Country Houses. Davis claimed to have first introduced to America the "English perpendicular Gothic Villa with Barge Boards, Bracketts, Oriels, Tracery in Windows, etc. . . . in 1832." Whether or not he did in fact, certainly it was only later, as propagated in Downing's books, that Davis's Gothic designs gained wide acceptance throughout the country.

plied for Dunlap's *History* he says it was only because "a friend" (the ambiguous reference may be either to John Trumbull or Rembrandt Peale, or both) "advised him to devote himself to Architecture" that he went to work for Josiah Brady as a draftsman and apprentice designer (1826); and throughout his long and successful practice he always referred to himself as an "architectural composer" rather than an architect proper. Probably it was because his background was so different from Town's in engineering that their partnership worked so well; they were an Early Victorian version of the old collaboration of intellectual and artisan, Town

supplying the structural and stylistic ideology, Davis giving the ideas visual form. Certainly it explains why Davis so early became the firm's authority on nonclassical styles, and why after Town's death in 1844 Davis so naturally gravitated into the orbit of Andrew Jackson Downing and in a sense functioned with him as he had with Town himself, illustrating Downing's books and working out Downing's ideas.

Downing, of course, was never an architect or even an artist at all. He was the son of a poor nurseryman in Newburgh, New York, who by assiduous cultivation of unusual plants and wealthy people had become an authority in the profession of landscape gardening. In the *Treatise on Landscape Gardening* (1841) that made him famous, architecture was a kind of afterthought, only the last one and a half of the book's ten sections being concerned with buildings. And although Downing later wrote two books on architecture alone—*Rural Cottages* in 1842 and *The Architecture of Country Houses* in 1850—it was always obvious that for him architectural style was something to be determined by landscape and vistas rather than by laws of its own, far more a matter of setting than structure.

Downing and Davis were, then, ideal collaborators; their approaches to architecture generally, and to Gothic in particular, were perfectly complementary. And although their joint influence was not enough ever to make the Gothic cottage and its variants real rivals to the Greek and Roman Revivals for popular acceptance, it is essentially to their understanding of the sociological and cultural implications of the Gothic Revival that we owe three of the most lasting Early Victorian contributions to the American scene—the "picturesque estate," the "garden suburb," and the city park.

One of the best and certainly most familiar examples of Downing's principles is Central Park, New York. Although Downing was killed in a steamboat accident before the park was begun, his influence governed Calvert Vaux (1824–1895) and Frederick Law Olmsted (1822–1903), under whom it was completed in the years 1858–61 and 1865–78; Vaux had come to America from England at Downing's invitation and been his collaborator at Newburgh from 1850 to 1852, while Olmsted remained Downing's faithful disciple far enough into the 19th century to become one of the bridges between Downing's picturesque landscape and the organic planning of Frank Lloyd Wright. Here too you can still see what Downing conceived a city park to be. Instinctively aristocratic, Downing's park, like his landscaped grounds, was fundamentally ornamental and only incidentally of practical use, less a place for recreation than a frame and setting for the buildings around its edge. Downing may never have envisaged quite the kind of towering apartments that line Central Park today, certainly, but they would have delighted him, for these jagged and endlessly varied cliffs provide exactly the visual foil and architectural complement he intended his landscapes to have.

If Downing could have had his way, there would have been a second Central Park in Washington, D.C., for such was the fame of his *Treatise* that he had been officially invited to re-

---

103. GOTHIC AS ROMANTIC ESCAPE

(A) Andrew Jackson Downing, "View of a Country Residence, as frequently seen," and "View of the same Residence, improved," Fig- *ures 19 and 20 in* A Treatise on the Theory and Practise of Landscape Gardening with a View to the Improvement of Country Residences *(1841), pp. 99–100.*

(103 B) Llewellyn Park, West Orange, New Jersey. First of the "garden suburbs," a community of Improved Residences designed and built by A. J. Davis, 1852–69.

Of Davis's buildings there remain in original condition only the gatehouse and a cottage built for landscape painter Edward W. Nicholls and later boyhood home of Charles F. McKim; but the winding roads and picturesque landscape have been generally preserved. The illustration, showing "castellated" Castlewood House, was seen by readers of the New York Illustrated News in 1860.

---

design L'Enfant's Mall along its principles. Fortunately, or so it may seem to us, the project was abandoned after Downing's death in 1852. There remains of it only an urn to Downing's memory and that strange collection of medieval spires, arches, buttresses, and turrets (expressing "heritage from the past") that James Renwick assembled in 1846 under Downing's inspiration to house the historical and scientific institute James Smithson had bequeathed the nation. In its present state, the Smithsonian Institution is a paradoxically effective monument to Downing's ideas; nothing, surely, better proves his conviction that Gothic Revival architecture must have its proper landscape setting than the lonely incongruity of this "picturesque pile" amid the cold marble geometry of a republican and Imperial Roman capital. Yet if the Washington project was abortive, others inspired by Downing were not; and in the work of Olmsted particularly, Downing's influence was perpetuated in parks of the 1870s and 80s all over the continent—the reservation at Niagara Falls (1878), Mount Royal Park in Montreal (1874–6), Arnold Arboretum in Boston (1878–9).

Most lasting of Downing's contributions, perhaps, was the "garden suburb," which extended to entire communities the principle of "natural" houses integrated with gently controlled nature. The first of his communities was Llewellyn Park near West Orange, New Jersey, which was financed by chemical manufacturer Llewellyn P. Haskell. Its villas (each, according to the "covenant" signed by prospective purchasers, on not less than an acre of ground) were built, over a period of years, between 1852 and 1869 by A. J. Davis, in a great variety of quasi-medieval styles. Llewellyn Park typified both Downing's aristocratic concept of "democracy" ("a retreat for a man to exercise his own rights and privileges," provided he had enough unearned income to buy and live in a house so far from the city) and the kind of eccentricities popularly associated with the Gothic Revival generally (atheists holding marriage ceremonies under a great tree, public scandals of various sorts). More significantly, it set the pattern for a host of progeny: famous aristocratic parks like Riverside (a "suburban village" planned nine miles outside the business section of Chicago in 1868 by Vaux and Olmsted) in the 1860s; Tuxedo Park (a colony of mansions on farm-size lots occupying a whole range of hills around Suffern, New York, financed by Pierre Lorillard and designed by Bruce Price) in the 1890s; Arden, outside Wilmington, Delaware, in 1900–10; Shaker Heights outside Cleveland in 1910–20; Coral Gables outside Miami in the 1920s; and all sorts of humbler variants, culminating in the endless suburban developments of the post-World-War-II period, through which millions of Americans came to feel, however unwittingly, the century-old power of Andrew Jackson Downing's ideas. Downing's was not the only influence on the modern suburban development, to be sure; but his was the essential one. The building forms may be different— vaguely classical, vaguely modernistic, perhaps— but their split-level plans, overhangs, painted gables and porches are conceived in his picturesque spirit; and it is to Downing more than anybody else that we owe the mid-20th-century suburb, those rows of wooden boxes set on little roads with cute names that wind in and out over gullies (on the promoter's map, called "brooks") and around odd patches of gashed tree trunks (called "choice wooded lots"), each with its little plot where busy gardeners toil away Saturday nights and Sunday mornings setting bur-

lapped saplings into the barren subsoil clay.

By a kind of unpoetic justice, however, it is also to the garden suburb that we owe the general disappearance of what Downing himself considered his greatest achievement, the old "picturesque estates" once to be found on the outskirts of every large population center. Precisely because of their distance outside 19th-century cities, they have been peculiarly attractive to 20th-century "developers," with the result that they have become one of the chief casualties of the exploding metropolis. Every great city now has its ring of subdivisions named after what were once the rural properties of its wealthy class—Blythewood Acres and Boothhurst Farms, Oaklands and Brooksides and Spring Woods. To see the kind of estate conceived by Downing and Davis in anything like its original condition you have to go far afield indeed. Of most of them, only a wraith remains; only if you look closely can you see, in ghostly outline, what was there before the bulldozers moved in. Here and there fragments of Osage–Orange hedges and hawthorns run wild reveal where once, according to Downing's precepts, the old carriage roads used to "break off from the highway at the entrance lodge and proceed in easy curves to the mansion"; sometimes an eager or impoverished gardener will try to get a young tree or two out of them, and strike the old cobblestones a few inches below the present surface. Occasionally, too, some scraggly knot of saplings will spring up from deep-buried roots to betray where once a clump of ash or hickory was planted to screen farm buildings or accentuate the curves of a hillside; some pile of blasted stumps, like a picture of Boileau Wood in 1917, will preserve the memory of some ancient essay in "pomology" following directions in the *Cottage Residences*.

Often, too, the mansion itself still stands— a crumbling ruin or the developer's headquarters, as the case may be—and for all its peeling paint and broken gables, disfiguring wires and signboards, still evokes a ghost of its former grandeur. Wisteria, ivy, trumpet creepers running wild over flaking walls and rotting eaves, still tie it into a picturesque setting long since wrecked. Sometimes the house is Gothic, with blasted fragments of scrollwork still hanging from steep gables and old rust-colored paint peeling off pointed window frames. More often than not, however, while the plan is a rambling collection of porches and bow windows, the forms are classical—columns and cornices and round-headed windows. Even in such a ruin it is evident that Downing's favored Gothic never matched the popularity of his landscapes; and thereby hangs another chapter.

NOTES

Quotations of Davis's "Classification of Styles" and Davis's diary for July 1867, from R. H. Newton, *Town and Davis* (1942), pp. 81, 281; from Samuel Clemens, *Life on the Mississippi* (1874), Chap. 38; from Andrew Jackson Downing's *Treatise on Landscape Gardening* (1841), "Beauties and Principles of the Art."

On octagons, see Walter L. Creese, "Fowler and the Domestic Octagon," (*Art Bulletin*, XXVIII, 2, 1946, pp. 89–102), and Clay Lancaster, "Some Octagonal Forms in Southern Architecture" (*ibid.*, pp. 103–11). On "steamboat Gothic," see Denys P. Myers, "The Architectural Development of the Western Floating Palace" (*JSAH*, XI, 2, 1952, pp. 25–31). On Notman's Gothic, see Jonathan Fairbanks, *John Notman: Church Architect* (unpublished M.A. thesis, University of Delaware, 1961). For a characterization of Downing, see Carl Carmer, "Hudson River Aesthete" (*The Hudson* [1939]). On Olmsted and picturesque parks, see the article on Frederick Law Olmsted by Theodora Kimball Hubbard in *Dictionary of American Biography*, XIV (1934), summarizing F. L. Olmsted, Jr., and T. K. Hubbard, *Frederick Law Olmsted: Landscape Gardener* (1922). On Llewellyn Park and similar projects, see Christopher Tunnard, "The Romantic Suburb in America" (*Magazine of Art*, XL, 1947, pp. 183f.).

4. FROM EARLY TO HIGH VICTORIAN:
Picturesqueness in the Italianate Manner, c.1845−c.1860

ANDREW JACKSON DOWNING in his 1841 *Treatise* introduced the subject of architecture by remarking that "the only styles at present in common use . . . are the Grecian and Gothic. . . ." But even as he wrote, the situation was changing. In the course of the 1830s a new "mode" appeared on the American scene, which was destined in the 1840s to supersede both Greek and Gothic as the leading interest of major designers, and in the 1850s to surpass them in the number of executed examples. In its own time, the new style was variously and loosely called "Round," "Tuscan," or "Italian Villa" (especially when used on houses, with classical details), "Lombard," "Norman," and "Romanesque" (particularly in churches, or when combined with early Italian or German medievalisms like blind arcades and wall strips). In retrospect we can best call it simply "the Italianate manner."

The Italianate manner was not, properly speaking, a "revival" style like Greek or Gothic or Egyptian. Its origins were complex, even contradictory, and so was its American development. As first introduced in England—John Nash had built an "Italian villa" at Cronkhill as early as 1802—it was conceived as a sophisticated variant of the classical style, a composite deriving in part from the kind of architecture seen in "classical landscapes" by Poussin, Claude, Salvator Rosa, or Italian Renaissance painting generally, and in part from actual contemporary buildings in Italy; and it was as a classical variant that it appeared in J. C. Loudon's architectural encyclopaedia, and was widely used by the 1830s in English speculative building. But in America the Italianate appeared in a quite different context. Here it was conceived essentially as a variant of Gothic. In domestic architecture, its characteristic round-headed windows and arched entranceway under a tower were first seen in Sunnyside, the "snuggery" Washington Irving

built for himself at Tarrytown-on-the-Hudson in 1832, in a style described accurately enough by Downing as "quaint . . . partaking somewhat of the English cottage mode"; it was Alexander Jackson Davis, just making his name as a Gothic Revival specialist, who introduced the Italian villa proper to America, in a drawing exhibited in 1835; and the first such villa actually built, Riverside at Burlington, New Jersey (1836–7), was designed for Gothic enthusiast Bishop Doane by Gothic expert John Notman, largely furnished in Gothic (the library is a famous example), and singled out for praise by Downing himself. In church and public architecture, too, the Italianate manner was first introduced by men famed as Gothic Revivalists—Richard Upjohn, whose "Norman" or "Lombard" Church of the Pilgrims (Brooklyn, New York) and frescoed "Romanesque" chapel at Bowdoin College (Brunswick, Maine) appeared in 1844–5; and James Renwick, whose 1846 design for the Smithsonian Institution dramatized "Norman" forms in one of the nation's most conspicuous places.

This difference in development is easily explained. As long as it was merely a variant of the classical style, Italianate had no particular place in America, where the roots of the classical tradition proper were so deep, the symbolical associations of Greek and Roman almost a cult. But considered as a variant of Gothic, it took on another aspect entirely. In this capacity Italianate was a very welcome and extremely useful means of realizing the aesthetic qualities and aspirations of the Gothic Revival in a manner acceptable to masses of people who could never accept what seemed to be the eccentric and foreign character of medieval forms as such. The very looseness of association and vagueness of form that made Italianate uninteresting in the earlier part of the century gave it a peculiar and overwhelming appeal in the 1840s and 50s. De-

104. THE ITALIANATE MANNER, EARLY AND LATE

(A) "Sunnyside," Tarrytown, New York. Washington Irving's famous "snuggery" on the Hudson, restored as a historic and literary shrine. A 17th-century rural New Netherlands farmstead, it was bought by Irving and remodeled from 1832 on as a rustic retreat, designed by himself with the collaboration of Boston miniaturist George Harvey. The stepped gables make allusion to the "Dutch" regime romanticized in Irving's writings but in the arched entranceway and round-headed windows we can recognize one of the earliest appearances of the taste for "Round" or "Italianate" styles which swept the country a decade or two later.

fending Renwick's design for the Smithsonian in his *Hints on Public Architecture* (1849), Robert Dale Owen declared that besides being more moral, economical, and convenient, "Norman has the same variety as Gothic . . . but its entire expression is less ostentatious, and if political character may be ascribed to Architecture, more republican." Four years later, in *Plans for Churches* published by the Congregational Church, it was pointed out that

> a true Gothic structure would be as inappropriate on a wide and level prairie as Grecian Doric would be in the wildest and most abrupt regions of New England. The modifications of

these styles, however, known as the Rural English and the Norman and the Romanesque are adapted to a great diversity of situations, and they are almost any of them a great improvement upon the miniature temples and cathedrals which have been so much in vogue in our country for years past.

So it was that as developed in the middle years of the 19th century, the Italianate manner was far and away the most flexible in conception and freest in execution of all Early Victorian styles.

If you wanted to think of Italianate columns and gables and pediments as symbolic of classical Italy and the great civic ideals of the Re-

*(104 B) Victoria Mansion, Portland, Maine.
Built for R. S. Morse by Henry Austin in 1859,*
*it is an example of the Italianate villa in mature
elegance and full Renaissance dress.*

public, you could. But if you wanted to find in its towers and arches and asymmetrical plans evocations of the Early Christian and Romanesque Middle Ages, they were there, too. A "Tuscan villa," for instance, might be anything from a classical cube with low pyramidal roof, simply adorned with a few brackets and a nicely proportioned "cupola" (called variously "observatory" or "belvedere") on top, to a sprawling pile of assorted living units, towers, porches, columns, arches, gables and flat roofs, embodying all the picturesque irregularity of a Tudor manor house. Its walls might be bargeboarded, stuccoed, brick plain or patterned, or stone. Its ornament might vary from meticulously correct copies of Italian Renaissance columns, balustrades, cornices, and rusticated quoins, to Palladian motifs or balconies and brackets of vaguely medieval inspiration. And it was suitable in almost any situation. On city streets, it fitted well with older colonial or classical row houses; New York's famous "brownstones" are mostly Italianate, for instance. Treated more expansively and set on a spacious lot, it made an equally good "suburban" house; in his late *Architecture of Country Houses* Downing used comparative streets of Italianate suburban villas to illustrate how "suspicion and selfishness" (as well as a bad, i.e., classical, taste for precise definition) were manifested by people who fenced in their yards, and "co-operation, kindness, and regard for all," as well as due regard for proper picturesque vistas, by those who left them open. And though Downing only reluctantly admitted it—for him, Italianate was pre-eminently suited to "plain" and "cultivated" rather than "wild" landscapes—plenty of people by the 1850s were using Italianate for true country houses as well, particularly after the introduction of lawn mowers in the 1840s made it easy to effect nice transitions from rugged nature to smooth stuccoed walls by means of rolling lawns of "velvety turf."

So conceived and executed, the Italianate manner offered something freely to everyone. To civic leaders of conservative mind, it offered the means of having a town hall or a railroad station, church or post office, at once related to the official classical tradition but agreeably up-to-date in appearance. To all but High Church Episcopalians and dogmatic Roman Catholics it offered a perfect compromise between the "patriotic" but also "pagan" forms of the Greek or Roman Revivals, and the "Romanist," "English," or otherwise unacceptable connotations of Gothic proper. Everywhere rural artisans, trained in classical traditions and unwilling or unable to tackle Gothic intricacies, found it easy to adapt their skills to Italianate arches or brackets; local builders, uneducated in historical associations and relying on pattern books, found in Italianate a longed-for means of escape from the tyranny of fixed prototypes and fanatic protagonists that dogged them in the Greek and Gothic modes. No pedant could complain their bracketed villas were barbarous because they lacked a proper moulding, or mixed a Roman with a Greek detail. No shrill Pugin or fierce ecclesiologist denounced departures from pure 14th- or 13th- or whatever-century Gothic when they chose to build a "Norman" or "Lombard" or "Romanesque" church.

But most of all the Italianate manner was significant and useful to the leading theorists and tastemakers of the 1840s and 50s—Downing, Upjohn, Davis, and their followers. For Italianate offered them, as none of the other more rigidly categorized Early Victorian styles could, the chance to develop and experiment with what by this time was increasingly coming to be their main concern—the theory and practice of "the picturesque."

"Picturesqueness" was far from a new concept. Downing, its first great advocate in the United States, who devoted many pages of his *Treatise on Landscape Gardening* to defining it, frankly drew his ideas from late-18th-century English sources, chiefly the *Three Essays: On Picturesque Beauty, etc.* of 1792 by William Gilpin (1724–1804) and the *Essay on the Picturesque* of 1794 by Uvedale Price (1747–1829):

105. ITALIANATE IN THE UPJOHN MAN-NER

(A) St. Paul's (Episcopal) Church, Balti-more, as designed by Richard Upjohn, 1852. Completed 1856, except for the upper four stories of the campanile.

wild and irregular branches tell of the storm and tempest. . . .

Architecture borrows . . . the same expression. We find the Beautiful in the most symmetrical edifices, built in the finest proportions, and of the purest materials. It is on the other hand in some irregular castle . . . , some rude mill nearly as wild as the glen where it is placed, some thatched cottage, weather stained and moss covered, that we find the Picturesque. The Temple of Jupiter Olympus in all its perfect proportion was prized by the Greeks as a model of beauty; we, who see only a few columns and broken architraves standing, with all their exquisite mouldings obliterated by the violence of time and the elements, find them Picturesque.

Like his sources, Downing conceived picturesqueness as supremely embodied in Gothic, especially ruinous Gothic. Unlike them, however, he lived in a country where Gothic ruins were in very short supply, and where all sorts of social and intellectual prejudices frustrated his attempts to gain any wide acceptance of Gothic Revival building as a national expression. In this situation, he came more and more to think of what he had described in the *Treatise* merely as that "intermediate kind of architecture, originally a variation of the classical style, . . . which, in becoming adapted to different and more pictur-

Gilpin defines Picturesque objects to be "those which please from some quality capable of being illustrated in painting." Nothing can well be more vague than such a definition. We have already described the difference between the *beautiful* landscapes of Claude and the *picturesque* scenes painted by Salvator. . . . The Beautiful is an idea of beauty calmly and harmoniously expressed; the Picturesque an idea of beauty or power strongly and irregularly expressed. As an example of the Beautiful in other arts we refer to the Apollo of the Vatican; as an example of the Picturesque, to the Laocoön or the Dying Gladiator. In nature, we would place before the reader a finely formed elm or chestnut, whose well balanced head is supported on a trunk full of symmetry and dignity . . . ; as a picturesque contrast, some pine or larch, whose gnarled roots grasp the rocky crag on which it grows, and whose

(105 B) King Villa, Newport. Designed by Richard Upjohn for Edward King, 1845, it was an early manifestation both of the coming vogue for Italianate villas, and of the renaissance, this time as a vacation resort, of once-bustling colonial Newport after half a century's decline.

esque situations, has . . . become quite picturesque in its outlines and effects . . ." as the answer to American circumstances and needs. More and more it seemed to him that "the Swiss and *bracketed cottage,* and the different highly irregular forms of the *Italian villa*" were the best vehicle for expressing American aspirations, and by the later 1840s he was referring to the "Tuscan, or American" style.

Many others were coming to the same conclusion. In fact, appearance of the Italianate style marks the beginning of a distinct second phase within the Early Victorian period, a pattern apparent in the career of almost every leading builder of the time. Davis, Upjohn, Austin, Ammi Young—all of them, beginning with a doctrinaire adherence to well-defined Revival styles chosen on considerations of function, structure, or commonly accepted symbolism, have developed by the 1840s an increasingly obvious preoccupation with over-all picturesqueness of effect. And to achieve it, they turn increasingly to freer and freer versions of the Italianate manner.

Alexander Jackson Davis began his career under Ithiel Town's influence, with neatly circumscribed essays in Greek or Gothic, Egyptian or Roman, and although in the course of the 1830s he designed several villas that might be called Tuscan (e.g., Codwise villa in New Rochelle, to have been published in the abortive project for *Rural Residences* in 1837; W. W. T. Mali villa, Manhattanville, New York, 1839; possibly the Alsop house in Middletown, Connecticut, c.1840), they remained classical in spirit, basically symmetrical in concept and correct in detail. From 1840 on, however, Davis's Gothic became more and more variegated and picturesque, his Greek simpler, plainer, and looser; by 1845 he had worked into a kind of Graeco-Italianate style, featuring an abundance of square and octagonal towers and sprawling composition. And in the 1850s his designs became looser and more picturesque still. Using Italianate as a framework, he began to experiment with tentative mixtures of styles, as in the Edwin Litchfield house on Greenwood Heights (now Prospect Park) in Brooklyn of 1854, which added a round conical-roofed tower and cornices of Gothic inspiration to a basically Tuscan body, and the abortive plans for Mount Wollaston Hall drawn over a period of years from 1845 on, for John Quincy and Charles Francis Adams at Quincy, Massachusetts—its Italianate walls and wide roof crowned by a mansard of Second French Empire inspiration presaging the emergence of High Victorian Picturesque Eclecticism out of the Italianate manner in the 1860s and 70s.

Richard Upjohn made his reputation as a Gothic Revivalist so doctrinaire that he even refused the commission for a Unitarian church on the grounds his strict Episcopal convictions would make him too unsympathetic towards the required symbolism; and when called on in 1840 to remodel the 18th-century house of Stephen van Rensselaer in Albany (now Sigma Phi fraternity in Williamstown, Massachusetts), this same insistence on separation of styles led him to design Palladian detail to approximate the original, thus creating one of the first (if not remarkably successful) historical restorations in the country. Yet by 1845, when he began a villa for Edward King in Newport, Rhode Island, he was already coming under the picturesque spell, so that instead of a "regular" Gothic house (like the Thomas Taylor villa he had designed on Staten Island, 1839–40), he chose irregularly composed Italianate forms. At the end of the decade, when by coincidence he had to remodel another 18th-century mansion, Martin van Buren's ancestral Lindenwald at Kinderhook, New York, he unhesitatingly buried it under a picturesque array of Italianate towers, bay windows, porches, and bracketed cornices. Correspondingly, his treatment of Gothic altered. In place of the severe boxlike basic form of Trinity, his early (1839–46) masterpiece, come picturesquely asymmetrical compositions with massed chapels and irregular turrets, as in St. Paul's, Buffalo (1849–50, restored 1888); St. James's, New London, Connecticut (1847–50); or the "country church" published in his *Rural Architecture* (1852). By the 1850s Upjohn even begins to use Italianate for Episcopal churches (e.g., St. Paul's, Baltimore, 1852–6), justifying it ideologically by Early Christian allusions, and visually by the picturesqueness of its campanile, arcades, and patterned wall surfaces; he designs city halls, office buildings, and banks in it (e.g., City Hall, Utica, New York, 1852–3; Trinity Building, New York, 1851–2; Corn Exchange Bank, New York, 1854); and in his handling of Italianate villas created real masterpieces of spatial composition (Wyman villa, Baltimore, c.1855, destroyed 1959; John Stoddard house, Brattleboro, Vermont, 1853–6, etc.).

The same two phases appear in the career of Henry Austin. As Town's protégé and follower in New Haven, he used Greek and Gothic alternatively and dogmatically (Yale College Library, c.1842, recalling King's College Chapel in Cambridge, is perhaps his best-known work; he also executed the Egyptian gateway to Grove Street Cemetery). But from c.1845 to c.1860 he concentrated on developing the monumental possibilities of picturesqueness in the Italianate vein. From rather naïve essays in the early manner of Davis (e.g., Dana house on Hillhouse Avenue c.1849, with "Mohammedan" fringe detail; Wallis Bristol house, c.1847, with cresting and cast-iron detail of Gothic inspiration) he began to develop a solider, heavier manner of his own. It appears first, perhaps, in the Congregational church he designed at Kent, Connecticut, in 1848, and the pronounced relief of the detail in his Norton house (c.1850) as compared with its model published in Downing's *Cottage Residences* eight years before; it is climaxed in the R. S. Morse house (Victoria Mansion) in Portland, Maine (1859), with its dignified brownstone columns, rusticated quoins, and lavish stone brackets.

All over the country the same thing was going on. Ammi B. Young (1798–1874) began professional life as a carpenter building churches in rural Vermont from Asher Benjamin's guide

books (e.g., Congregational Church, Norwich, c.1825), then worked with a strict Early Victorian separation of styles in the 1830s (e.g., St. Paul's, Burlington, 1831, much like Trinity, New Haven; a classical capitol at Montpelier in 1836; and a customhouse in Boston, Massachusetts, in knowledgeable Greek Revival, 1837). By 1848, however, he was building in "Romanesque" for Bromfield Church in Boston, and as United States Supervising Architect in Washington (1853–60), worked in a free Italianate manner that departed from the official classical idiom in picturesque fusions of Tuscan, Greek, and Roman forms, and in the novelty of its materials (metal beams, girders, window sashes, doorframes; the Custom House at Wilmington, Delaware, is a good example of his work).

In the Delaware Valley John Notman was simultaneously developing more and more picturesque Gothic churches (compare the archaeological correctness of St. Mark's in Philadelphia—for which he relied on English plans by R. C. Carpenter sent over by the Ecclesiological Society—with Holy Trinity in 1857 or St. Clement's in 1859, e.g.), more and more picturesque Italianate villas (compare the tight stiffness of Riverside at Burlington in 1837 with the luxuriant spread of Prospect at Princeton, New Jersey, in 1849). In 1848 Notman designed the first hospital with Italianate villa towers, the State Asylum in Trenton, New Jersey; it had all sorts of imitators. So popular had the style become a decade later that even the Wren Building of the College of William and Mary in Virginia was unhesitatingly rebuilt in Italianate forms after the fire of 1859.

There was, in fact, no doubt about it; during the 1850s the Italianate manner became the closest thing to a national style the United States had had since the early days of the classical revivals. But of all this efflorescence comparatively little, unfortunately, remains in anything like original condition today. Lacking the sentimental and prestigious associations of Greek or Gothic, easily executed by local builders and for that reason often employed on structures for which no long life was expected, and often, too, located in districts which demographic changes have turned from fashionable suburbs into inner-belt slums, Italianate buildings have been dealt with very roughly by time. Nowadays, with their lofty towers blown down, their walls spalled, and their darkly frescoed walls and timbered ceilings painted in tasteful pastel shades, Norman or Lombard or Romanesque churches of the 1850s make a poor show. And with most surviving Italianate villas decayed into rooming houses, remodeled as orphanages and lodge halls, making melancholy backdrops to yardfuls of weeds and junk and old cars, it takes even more imagination to see them as they were when Currier & Ives took them as the most elegant examples of "The American Home," when the hedges were clipped and flowerbeds tended, when the creamy walls and dark trim were freshly painted, and the old rotting stumps were young blossoming trees. Only occasionally do you find some villa restored as a period house, like Fountain Elms at Utica, New York, or Victoria Mansion in Portland, Maine. But when you do, it is easy to see why so many Americans in the 1840s and 50s found Italianate irresistible, and proclaimed it the "truly American" style; why in so many ways Italianate was indeed the great creation and consummation of Early Victorian culture in America.

Elegant and yet informal, simple in line yet lavish in decoration, classical in derivation and picturesque in execution, the exteriors of Italianate villas embody at once something of the old aristocratic dignity of 18th-century American civilization preserved in the person of a Daniel Webster or a Henry Clay, something of the earthy luxuriance welling up from the frontier that is Mark Twain's most enduring appeal, and something too of the subtle sophistication and erudition we think of in connection with Emerson or the elder Oliver Wendell Holmes. This is the expression of a society growing ever richer, but not yet vulgarly aware of it; of wealth still thought of, as it was in earlier times, as something to be spent and enjoyed rather than speculated with. This is the expression of people sure enough of their own taste to eschew eclectic imitations with neither fear nor ostentation; confident they can use the past freely to create a stylistic expression of their own.

Interiors like those at Fountain Elms complete the picture in fullness and depth. As the least derivative, the most indigenous of all Early Victorian styles, Italianate architecture provides a setting which brings out the basic character of Early Victorian furniture as nowhere else; conversely, the furniture complements and confirms the cultural expression of the architecture.

Just as there is no "Italianate style" in the same well-defined sense as Greek or Gothic, so there is no "Italianate" furniture as such. In its own day, the furniture appropriate to villas like Fountain Elms might have been called variously "antique" in the case of vaguely Empire-style pieces, "old French taste" or "Louis Quatorze" in others. In ours, we might think of it generally as "Victorian Rococo Revival," or in the case of more elaborate examples, "Belter"—itself a generic name for combinations of Rococo curves with lavish masses of fruit and flower ornament intricately moulded in rosewood produced more or less indiscriminately by John Henry Belter (1804–1863), Charles Baudouine and Alexander Roux in New York, George Henkels and Daniel Pabst in Philadelphia, A. Eliaers in Boston, Seibrecht and Mallard in New Orleans, and many others. No matter; in basic concept and general effect, the closest parallels of advanced furniture design in the 1840s and 50s, however labeled, are with the Italianate manner in architecture.

All these furniture substyles show the same general "Italianate" combination of rather ponderous geometric shapes with light and intricate decoration; a resemblance even more obvious when Italianate villas were complete with their original elaborate cast-iron balconies, urns, gateposts, brackets, finials, and so on, and when Italianate churches had their original lofty spires

106. ITALIANATE INTERIORS, NORTH AND SOUTH

(A) Bedroom, Fountain Elms, Utica, New York. Built 1850 by Philip Thomas of Utica on the designs of William J. Woollett, Jr., of Albany, as the gift of Alfred Munson to his daughter Mrs. James Watson Williams. Maintained as a period museum by the Munson–Williams–Proctor Institute, Utica.

(106 B) Parlor, Wickham–Valentine house, Richmond, Virginia. Built for jurist John Wickham in 1812 by Robert Mills, the house is maintained as a museum, with parlor furnishings as redone in the 1850s. Though going under a variety of names—"Belter," "French Rococo," "Late Empire," such furniture basically belongs to the same Italianate manner as villas like Fountain Elms and Edward King's at Newport.

107. ITALIANATE FOR HOME AND OFFICE
  (A) View of Fifth Avenue, New York, looking south from 36th Street, in 1857. The "round styles," easily executed, demanding no great scholarly erudition, dominated American architecture during the 1850s. As the view here makes evident, New York by the 1850s already had rows of brownstone Italianate houses, many of which still survive today. Less fortunate have been the commercial store fronts and office fronts (usually more decidedly Renaissance, to emphasize "civic enterprise") prefabricated in iron by firms like those of Daniel Badger and James Bogardus; of the many famous examples built all over the country, only a few now remain.

and frescoed interior walls, than it usually is now. All of them display forms of the same vaguely Italian and classical inspiration—details and proportions reminiscent of the Empire style, marble fittings in fireplaces and table tops actually coming from Italy or chosen (like the favored white marble from Tennessee or carnelian from California) to approximate Italian imports. Indeed, the so-called "French Rococo Revival" style as a whole was not French, but ultimately based on 18th-century Italian furniture designs. And in all of them these forms are handled with the picturesque variety, irregularity, and vagueness of historical allusion typical of Italianate architecture. Like Italianate architectural designers, these cabinetmakers conceive their work in relationship to surrounding space. As the Tuscan villa is designed without a formal façade in order to achieve picturesque irregularity from all points of view, so "Belter" furniture is remarkable for visual interest from the back as well as from the front. Or again, as the "natural" landscape around Tuscan villas was only gently directed by the gardener's hand, so roses and garlands and grapes seem to spring spontaneously from chair frames and table legs, more arranged by art than made with tools. Most of all, cabinetmaker and architect alike seem to revel in their freedom from rigid archaeological prototypes to invent new variations and combinations of old motifs in the interests of more and more picturesque effects. And this is significant, for it was by its incipient mixing of styles that the Italianate manner most creatively anticipated the future.

By the later 1840s and 50s the rationale of all Revival styles was clearly collapsing. The farther scholarship developed and sophistication spread, the fewer educated people there were who could seriously believe in Roman pediments as embodiments of pure civic virtue, pointed arches as symbols of unsullied fervent Christian faith, or Greek capitals as imbued with dedication to liberty; and the less reason there was to maintain the old strict distinction of styles. Gradually, subtly, inevitably, the controlling standards of artistic excellence began to change.

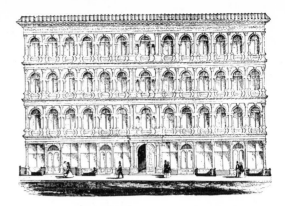

(107 B) Prefabricated façade for a store or office building, advertised by the Badger Architectural Iron Works, c.1855.

Symbolism became increasingly a matter of evoking moods, of suggesting pastness in general rather than any specific historical associations. It followed that picturesqueness—of which deliberately vague historical allusion was an essence —came to be not (as originally for Downing's generation) only one among several varying possibilities of artistic expression, but a basic and primary necessity in all design. And it followed further that the Italianate style, which until then had seemed no more than the most practical of several means to make a transition from older classical traditions to Early Victorian romantic ideals, now appeared as the only avenue for further growth and development. For only Italianate allowed real freedom to experiment with various and irregular combinations of forms. Only Italianate with its loose prototypes offered legitimate escape from the rigid categories of Early Victorian styles. Only by building on the principles of the Italianate style could artists hope to respond to the spirit of the new and maturer American civilization taking shape in their time. So it was that the Italianate style became the vehicle by which American art expressed the change from a still rural, individualistic, and naïvely romantic world in the early 19th century to the harder, brittler, more complex mid-19th-century world of high finance and heavy industry that the Civil War brought to maturity.

NOTES

Quotations of *Plans for Churches,* from Carroll
L. V. Meeks, "Romanesque before Richardson in the
United States" (*Art Bulletin,* XXXV, 1953, pp. 17–
33). With this article, and its predecessor, "Henry
Austin and the Italian Villa" (*Art Bulletin,* XXX,
1948, pp. 148f.), Professor Meeks opened up and
defined a major field of research in American architecture.

On Sunnyside, see Harold Dean Cater, "Washington Irving and Sunnyside" (*New York History,*
XXXVIII, 2, 1957, pp. 123–66; republished by Sleepy
Hollow Restorations, Tarrytown, N. Y., 1957). On
Upjohn, see E. M. Upjohn, *Richard Upjohn: Architect and Churchman* (1939). On Fountain Elms, see
Richard B. McLanathan, "History in Houses: Fountain Elms in Utica, N. Y." (*Antiques,* LXXIX, 4,
1961, pp. 356–64). Calvert Vaux's *Villas and Cottages* (1857) affords another example of the change
from Downingesque Gothic cottages (in earlier
plates) to Italianate picturesqueness (in the later
ones).

5. END OF INNOCENCE:
Picturesque Eclecticism and Postwar Civilization in the High Victorian Age, c.1860—c.1885

IN HIS LATER YEARS Alexander Jackson Davis used to walk the streets of New York, commenting in his diary on the new buildings that were going up. To him they seemed inexplicable. Suddenly, mysteriously, all taste and sense of fitness had collapsed. A new generation had arisen, one that spoke another architectural language, held different standards, and was creating a new world in which the old principles of Early Victorian building were all being modified, transformed, and, as he saw it, perverted:

> 1872. Apr. Walk up Madison Avenue noticing *Monstrosities* at corner of 34th. Church of Messiah for feeding lambs at 32 Park Avenue *barbarous*. The Jews' Synagogue seems no more Christian than the Church of the Messiah, of Heavenly Rest, and others. . . . Lenox Library on Fifth Avenue indicates a *depraved architecture*.
>
> Oct. 17. New York Post Office—*a costly, diseased courtesan; a broken heap of littleness.* . . .

Precisely what was his complaint? Not that the new architecture was totally different from his; in fact, its basic principles—symbolism, additive ornament, eclectic borrowings from the past—were the same. Rather it was that these principles had been "depraved." In Early Victorian terms, the succeeding period represented not so much error as heresy, the concentration on and exaggeration of a few elements at the expense of the whole.

The new architects were still very much interested in the past; they still talked of "Gothic" and "Renaissance" and "Greek" styles, and they still borrowed from them. But where Early Victorians had believed that each style had an appropriate set of associations which should not be confused, their High Victorian successors heaped up details from any and every historical style on the same building, so that "the Jews' synagogue seems no more Christian than the Church of the Messiah." Early Victorians had made a fairly rigid distinction between styles which allowed a spread-out plan, like the Tuscan, and those, like Grecian, which denied it; now all buildings seemed to sprawl indiscriminately—sometimes upwards, in tortuous towers and shelves five, seven, ten stories high; sometimes horizontally, spreading over whole blocks in "broken heaps of littleness." However additively the ornament of Early Victorian buildings was conceived, however unrelated to structure it may have been, it at least had the clearly understood purpose of making buildings meaningful in symbolic terms. But the new architects seemed to consider lavish masses of decoration as an end in itself. They designed as fashionable mid-Victorian authors were writing. Just as Nathaniel Hawthorne, say, introducing the *Scarlet Letter* (1850) with a reference to some document found in the old Salem Custom House, rambles on for paragraphs and pages, tacking together long strips of dependent clauses and fragments of phrases to create a general image of quaint antiquity but never quite getting to the point, so High Victorian designers assembled mighty heaps of niches, pinnacles, railings, staircases, brightly painted lattices and shutters, green and purple tiled roofs, porches, oriels in stained glass and finials in cast iron, balconies, brackets, that in the end buried structure, plan, and proportion alike beneath one great, incoherent, "massy pile."

Most of all, where "picturesqueness" for Early Victorians had been only one possibility among many, appropriate to some styles and occasions—Gothic, or landscaped estates, for ex-

108. SETTING FOR A NEW AGE

(A) State, War, and Navy Building, Washington, D.C. Fit symbol of the sprawling bureaucratic growth of the Federal Government during the Civil War was this first major postwar governmental building, completed 1871 on the designs of A. B. Mullett. The abandonment of the simple and severe Greek Revival of older official architecture for mansarded floridity modeled on the Tuileries in Paris symbolized the end of a simpler, isolated epoch in American civilization and the nation's first long step towards international power status. As the trend here begun continued, even this twelve-million-dollar structure was soon too small; first the War, then the Navy, finally (after World War II) the State Department moved out to buildings of their own, leaving for "Old State" only the President's executive offices.

---

ample—but not others, now it dominated everything. Beds and tables in the Louis Quatorze style, chairs in the Gothic manner of Charles Eastlake's "Hints on Household Taste," offices in the Italian Renaissance manner, or villas in the ornamental mode—no matter what they were called or where found, all alike had to be "picturesque." All had to display the same jagged silhouettes, endlessly varied shapes and angles, eye-catching contrasts of texture, decorative patterns, projections, deliberate asymmetry. All rejected the old principle of specific copyings from earlier historical styles as somehow naïve and unimaginative. Instead, combinations of forms appear, drawn more or less vaguely and indiscriminately from many ages past, intended to set before mind and eye a tangible expression of the continuity of all human culture, past and present.

To create an image like this, each form must have a recognizable function. There was a reason why High Victorian buildings so often rested on such rugged foundations, and High Victorian furniture on bases and legs of bulbous ponderosity; in this way High Victorians suggested that quality of triumph over time which for them was one of the greatest attractions of picturesqueness. As Downing admired "some pine or larch whose wild and irregular branches tell of the storm and tempest it has so often struggled against . . . ," so Samuel Sloan will argue that Louis Quatorze furniture was "very grand and imposing, and will endure the ravages of time," and John Ruskin declare that the finest new buildings were those that looked a century old the day they first stood complete. Nor was it accidental that High Victorian buildings had roof lines so lavishly edged in cast-iron "gingerbread," and High Victorian furniture such an array of little knobs, tassels, antimacassars in lace, and fringed upholstery; with all sharp outlines so deliberately broken, the outlines were made to trail off into infinite space in the same way their eclectic forms trailed back into indefinite time. In short, this is a new style, with consistent principles, predictable effects, and a name of its own—Picturesque Eclecticism, the characteristic art of the new, High Victorian age in America.

As a genuine historical style, the product and expression of a distinct cultural period, Picturesque Eclecticism could only be appreciated fully by those who understood that period, were spiritually a part of it. Nothing demonstrates the fact better than the failure of almost all of the older generation, men born in the early 1800s, to continue their careers after the War. No matter how much their own picturesque and eclectic experiments in the Italianate manner of the later 1840s and 50s may have contributed to and prepared the way for Picturesque Eclecticism, the men of this generation seemed unable to understand or appreciate it when it came. One by one they dropped from professional prominence.

Alexander Jackson Davis, perhaps the most famous of living architects at the time, made one attempt to adjust to the new era with a design

(108 B) "Library furniture," Pl. 197 from Samuel Sloan, Homestead Architecture (Philadelphia, 1867). "The style," wrote Sloan, "is what is called 'Renaissance' in France, and 'Antique' in this country." Elsewhere, he defines "Antique" as "a style not distinctly its own, . . . but borrowed from most of the other decorative styles." Here is the mixing of styles so characteristically High Victorian; and it is appropriate to use "library" furniture as illustration, for it was the ever-increasing accumulation of historical knowledge through study that broke down the old rigid Early Victorian categories of style.

for a new New York Post Office, submitted in 1867. It was a hybrid of classical motifs drawn from sources as varied as the Roman Colosseum and Gibbs's Radcliffe Camera, combined with structural ideas drawn from 19th-century glass-and-iron arcades, Paxton's 1851 Crystal Palace in London, and Walter's new iron-ribbed dome of the United States Capitol, which to Davis's mind represented great concessions to the new eclectic taste. But the very clarity of structural expression and creative use of new materials that makes it to us as attractive as anything Davis ever did, made it hopelessly unacceptable in the 1860s. In that atmosphere it seemed merely old-fashioned, a dressed-up version of the old Italianate style, hardly "picturesque" in the new sense at all. Davis's design was ignominiously rejected in favor of what he in disgust called a "costly diseased courtesan," a tremendous pile of miscellaneous motifs assembled by a group of younger men. Davis suddenly found himself a forgotten man, his career abruptly terminated, with nothing ahead of him but thirty futile years of retirement, recriminations, and attempts to restore "sanity" to art:

1881. Jan. Engaged upon my paper entitled "Abuses in Architecture"
1883. July 5. Adding verses to Poem on "Abuses in Society," a moral invective. . . .

Henry Austin attempted to move with the times; his New Haven City Hall of 1860 abandoned Italianate in favor of a French "Second Empire" style with mansarded roofs, ruggedly grouped columns, and other accoutrements of the new obsessive picturesqueness. But he was no more able than Davis to develop any real feeling for the full rich mixture of forms demanded by the spirit of the new age; his practice soon dwindled and failed. Similarly Richard Upjohn found it impossible, with his doctrinaire convictions, to treat Gothic with the requisite eclectic freedom; from 1860 on his practice was more and more in the hands of his son, who knew better how to handle it in terms the High Victorian age could

appreciate and understand. The career of Thomas U. Walter effectually ended with the completion of the wings and great dome of the United States Capitol. So little use had the postwar era for classical talents, even those of the second president of the American Institute of Architects (1867–87), that when the massive new picturesque City Hall of Philadelphia was building (1876), all Walter could do was serve as consultant—presumably on classical detail—to its designer, John McArthur (1823–1900). Even a man with the adaptability Ammi B. Young had shown in rising from humble beginnings as a Vermont carpenter in Asher Benjamin's tradition to be supervising architect in Washington found that the new age demanded something more ("we always find," as an authoritative writer put it in 1861, "that the architects who are most successful in practice are those who have studied the history of their art the most carefully"), and when Young's term (1851–60) expired, he too fell into obscurity.

The generation born around 1820, growing up to take picturesqueness for granted as a dominant factor in art, understood much better, because more instinctively, what expression the new age demanded. However inferior in talents, however indebted for ideas to Downing, Davis,

---

109. CITY HALL, PHILADELPHIA

(A) The "new" City Hall of the 1870s, as High Victorians saw it. Designed 1869 by John McArthur, Jr., largely built 1871–81, completed 1907, sculpture by Alexander Calder (1846–1923). In the hundred years since 1776 Philadelphia had lost its former supremacy among American cities; but nothing of that was evident here. Intended to be the largest building on the continent, its tower the highest artificial structure in the world, its ornament heaped on from every land and culture, past and present, City Hall dramatized the new ideal of American destiny—no longer so much to be independent from Europe, as to consummate and embody the whole of the historical achievement of Western civilization.

THE
CITY HALL,
PHILADELPHIA.

L.H.Everts Phila.

P.F.Goist Del.

or Upjohn, men like Gervase Wheeler (from England, fl.1840–60) or Samuel Sloan (1815–1884) may have been, Wheeler's *Rural Homes* (1851) and Sloan's *Model Architect* (1852) demonstrate a grasp of the essential High Victorian concept of ornament as a picturesque device these older men never realized. They see ornament less as a symbolic language than as a means to a visual end. For them, the most important consideration in choosing a style is eye-catching pattern, textural contrasts, picturesque massing, rather than any consistent association of ideas. It follows that they see nothing inherently wrong with mixing styles. If the various styles are still more or less distinct in Sloan's *Model Architect*, it is simply by convention; anyone who divorces structure and ornament as completely as he, who can cheerfully demonstrate how sets of Norman or Tuscan or Gothic or ornamental decorative detail may be applied to the very same building in the same place and serving the same purpose, as if changing architectural styles were like shifting stage scenery, can have no reason for keeping them distinct. And by 1866, indeed, he is already aware of and making a virtue of mixed styles in his *Homestead Architecture:*

> Look for a moment at the Church of St. Mark [in Venice]. . . . Lo! we see a structure arise bearing the impress of Roman and Gothic art harmoniously blended, and yet developing a character so clearly and decidedly its own, that none have ventured to gainsay or question its nationality. . . . Without condemning what has been done . . . we pass sentence on servile imitation as being unworthy of the genius and spirit of the American people.

In this, Sloan speaks the language of the High Victorian age. Calvert Vaux, the English landscape architect Downing brought to Newburgh in 1850 as his assistant and architectural partner, spoke the same language in his *Villas and Cottages* (1857):

> Webster and Clay were orators of originality, but their words were all old. . . . All previous experience in architecture is the inherited property of America; each beautiful thought,

form, and mode not unsuited to the climate and the people ought to be studied, sifted, tested. The past should be looked on as the servant and not the master; individual sentiment and education should be encouraged, and by degrees a genuine public taste will be unfolded. . . .

And it was from men like these that the new age learned. While the older builders' guides of Minard Lafever, Asher Benjamin, and the rest sank into oblivion after 1860, the books of Sloan and Wheeler and Vaux went on to printing after printing, influencing popular building through the 1870s and on into the 80s.

The great majority of leaders in this new architectural generation were either, like Vaux and Wheeler, immigrants trained abroad, or men who had early come under European influence, or had European connections. This was particularly true in New York City, whose position of financial dominance the Civil War had confirmed, and whose intellectual and cultural leadership was challenged only by Boston. There flourished Leopold Eidlitz (1823–1896) from Austria, Dietlef Lienau (1818–1887) from Germany, and Frederick Diaper (1810–1905) from England. Richard Morris Hunt (1828–1895), though born in Vermont, had been entirely trained at the École des Beaux-Arts in Paris, and showed it in the easy eclecticism of his Stuyvesant Apartments—first in the United States (1869)—and the Tribune Building (1873–5). Similarly Richard Mitchell Upjohn (1828–1903), though raised in New York, had always been surrounded by English influences, and renewed them by a stay in his English birthplace before taking up active partnership in his father's firm in the 1850s; in his hands, his father's austere and naïve Gothic became a many-splendored High Victorian thing, bristling with pinnacles and parapets, rich in polychromy (e.g., Greenwood Cemetery entrance, Brooklyn, 1861; St. Thomas's Church, 1868–70), and it was he who provided Connecticut with its unique High Victorian capitol at Hartford (1878–85), a glorious conglomeration of Gothic and Roman, Lom-

(109 B) The "old" City Hall of the 1960s. Where High Victorians saw their City Hall standing in unrivaled majesty, dwarfing everything around it, we see it hemmed in by tall department stores and office buildings, of Late Victorian form and scale. Comparison of its scale with theirs makes evident how much of the older, humanistic scale High Victorians preserved; this is the characteristic which gives them at once that appearance of incoherent assemblages of detail so much disliked by succeeding generations, and that quality of picturesque massing which both High Victorians and we can enjoy.

bard and Palladian, capped by a parade of gables and turrets, fluttering flags, and kaleidoscopic colors.

To a lesser extent the same was true elsewhere. To be sure, postwar architecture in Boston—as might be expected—was dominated by old American families and Harvard graduates, most notably the partnership (1863–81) of William R. Ware (1832–1915) and Henry Van Brunt (1832–1903). But so completely were they —as well as patrons like President Norton of Harvard—under the influence of John Ruskin* that their Memorial Hall, for instance (1865–78), might as well have been built to illustrate passages in the *Stones of Venice* praising "daring interruptions of the formal plan" and explaining how "in the best times of Gothic, a useless window would rather have been opened in an unexpected place for the sake of surprise, than a useful one forbidden for the sake of "symmetry." The designer of the Philadelphia City Hall in 1869, second largest public building in the United States and one of the great cultural monuments of the age, was John McArthur, an immigrant from Scotland, trained by an uncle. So, too, the precocious Alfred B. Mullett (1834–1893), who as supervising architect for the Treasury from 1866 on was responsible more than anyone else for the sudden and dramatic overthrow of the old classical tradition in public buildings, had come to America from his native England in 1845. Mullett's earliest work, the Mint in San Francisco (begun 1870, designed earlier as the last "official" Greek Revival building), betrayed an American training received in Isaiah Rogers's Cincinnati office in the late 1850s; but "continental" influences dictated the sprawling piles of the late 1860s and 70s that made him famous—the State, War, and Navy Building in Washington (1871), the New York Post Office, the United States Marine Hospital in Chicago.

As for furniture making, it had been increasingly the province of immigrant artisans ever since the introduction of factory methods,

two or three decades before; and when in the 1870s it was becoming to all intents and purposes a matter of designing patterns to set for machines, Europeans dominated furniture design as well. Sometimes such men were immigrant artisans who by luck or initiative had managed to acquire capital enough to buy machines and establish factories of their own. One such was Charles Buschor (1823–1885) of Philadelphia. Emigrating from Germany in the 1840s, he had begun his career as an ornamental carver, but was forced out of business by machine-made competition in the 1860s. Working successively as a farmer, superintendent of a steamship company office, then supervisor of the Smith & Campion furniture manufacturing company, he was able to save enough to open a factory himself, about 1875. But in this new capacity he operated not so much as an artisan or designer proper as a businessman, manufacturing exhibition equipment for the 1876 Centennial, then branching out after 1878 to supply interior fittings and furniture for ships.

Even more typical of the age was the "Eastlake furniture" which poured from American factories in endless variations during the 1870s and into the 80s. Inspired immediately by the *Hints on Household Taste in Furniture, Upholstery, and Other Details* of English architect Charles Eastlake (1836–1906)—which appeared first in England in 1868, in the United States in 1872, and by 1881 had gone through six American editions—and ultimately by French Gothic theorist Viollet-le-Duc, it was "American" only insofar as American factories popularized, vulgarized, and emphasized its High Victorian character. For all that Eastlake's text spoke of the "functionalism" of Gothic, it was the irregular, eye-catching, picturesquely lavish character of Gothic decoration that appealed to the manufacturers, and they made it the bombastic expression of an untrammeled era.

In fact, almost the only "native" American to practice successfully both before and after the war was James Renwick.* Renwick's career is a

* See notes following this chapter.

kind of summation of the whole age. It begins in the old "American" tradition of the self-made artist, the engineer who learns Gothic and wins a competition for famous and fashionable Grace Church in New York (1843–60). In the Early Victorian Gothic Revival manner he continues with Calvary (1846) and St. Patrick's (1858–79, spires 1887) churches, typical compositions of naïvely symbolic ornament applied to basically simple cubical shapes, plaster vaults, and wooden crockets. But he early comes under Downing's influence, and moves into the picturesque phase or Early Victorian with his design for the Smithsonian Institution in Washington (1846–55). Thence he adopts—as did Henry Austin—what furniture catalogues called "Louis Quatorze," and architects "Second Empire," forms, vaguely French Baroque and vaguely Italian Renaissance, but all controlled by picturesque principles of receding and advancing planes in elevation (e.g., Charity Hospital, 1858–61, New York; Vassar College at Poughkeepsie, 1860–61). But at this point, where Austin faded, Renwick moves on. He travels to Europe, becomes a collector of all sorts of eclectic art (his house is described as a museum in itself) and consequently is able to build up an enormous and successful practice to the day he dies (New York Post Office, collaborating with Mullett, Hunt, and Sands; Booth's Theatre, New York, 1869, with Sands, etc., etc.).

The reason for this sudden influx of European artists and principles is not hard to understand. What has been called variously the Golden Day, the Age of Innocence, the great years of liberal capitalist culture, when the promise of the Republic for a new kind of human life on earth seemed so near fulfilment, came to an abrupt end with the slaughter of the idealistic and the rise of the crafty to power and fortune in the Civil War. All of a sudden the mood of American civilization changed, became harder and soberer; if not necessarily wiser at least more cynical and sophisticated; certainly more cosmopolitan. All at once the United States was no longer a Young Country, a Great Experiment. Symbolically, the theme of the 1876 Centennial in Philadelphia was not so much the new beginning and break from European patterns that had been made in Independence Hall, as it was American progress towards emulating Europe in arts and manufactures, culture and commerce. It followed that the old naïveté would do no longer. Early Victorian American art seemed suddenly simple, absurdly unworthy of a nation that aspired to rank among great world powers. The vogue for French mansard roofs that blossomed on villas and post offices and town halls all over the country in the 1860s and 70s, and that more than any other innovation marks the appearance of High Victorian architecture, was no accident; its associations with the Louvre and the Tuileries made it representative of precisely that cosmopolitan and courtier elegance which, however scorned by old Jeffersonians, now seemed the very epitome of American aspirations. Men of Davis's generation recognized the change, consciously or unconsciously realized that in the 1860s a new architectural world was being created. What they failed to admit was that it was not some sort of whim, some inexplicable collective aberration, but the product of deep forces making for inexorable social and cultural changes. That is why, with the exception of men like Renwick or early skyscraper-builder George B. Post, whose engineering experience helped them handle the far bigger and far more complex kinds of buildings the new age required, this generation was at such a disadvantage. But by the same token, that is why it was not in the end the European-influenced generation of the 1820s, but Americans born in the later 1830s and 40s, growing up to understand the peculiarly American as well as the international spirit of High Victorian art, who created its greatest monuments. And that is why, finally, if we want fully to understand Picturesque Eclecticism in America, we need to begin by considering it as the distinctive and spontaneous expression of its particular time in the history of civilization in the United States.

NOTES

Quotations of Davis's diary, from R. H. Newton, *Town and Davis* (1942), pp. 109–10; from the introduction to the 1861 edition of John Henry Parker, *An Introduction to the Study of Gothic Architecture* (originally published 1849); from 1868 New York edition of *The Stones of Venice* (John Wiley & Son), pp. 230–31; from Samuel Sloan, *Homestead Architecture* (Philadelphia, 1867), appendix on "Furniture," pp. 311ff. Sloan admirably represents basic Victorian attitudes in many ways. Speaking of materials, e.g.:

Oak . . . will grow dark with age if left unvarnished so that the atmosphere may operate on it; when dark and old it is most valued in Europe. But what is the use of waiting for oak to grow dark when we can produce the same effect and better furniture with walnut?

The emulation of Europe; imitating in one medium the qualities of another; love of age for its own sake —it is all there in these two sentences (p. 316). On Eidlitz, and his period generally, see W. H. Jordy and Ralph Coe (eds.), *American Architecture, and Other Writings by Montgomery Schuyler* (Cambridge, 1961), Introduction, and pp. 136–91. On Buschor, see H. H. Hawley, *Charles Buschor* (unpublished M.A. thesis, *University of Delaware*, 1960).

On Renwick's later career, see Rosalie Thorne McKenna, "James Renwick, Jr., and the Second Empire Style in the United States" (*Magazine of Art*, XLIV, 1951, 4, pp. 97–101). That architects rarely worked successfully both before and after the Civil War is a generalization to which there are specific exceptions, of course. One such was Arthur Gilman of Boston (1821–1882), perhaps. Gilman made his early reputation with a violent attack on Greek Revival architecture in the *North American Review* for 1844, went on to effect what he called "a return to those solid and classical principles which . . . have not been put in practice among us . . . since . . . the Revolution" in the Arlington Street Church (1859–61), and after the war continued practice successfully in New York. (Cf. G. L. Wrenn, ". . . Arthur Gilman . . ." [*JSAH*, XX, 4, 1961, pp. 191–3], and Winston Weisman, "New York and the Problem of the First Skyscraper" [*JSAH*, XII, 1, 1953, p. 15]; Professor Weisman felt Gilman's Equitable Life Assurance Building of 1868–70 "ushered in a new era of commercial architecture in New York.")

Mid-19th-century Ruskinian Gothic played much the same role in English architectural evolution as Italianate in American—its looser forms and freer associations making it a comparable vehicle of transition from Early Victorian styles to High Victorian eclecticism.

6. POWER AND PLENTY:
Picturesque Eclecticism as Cultural Expression

PICTURESQUE ECLECTICISM was as infinitely varied a style as the High Victorian was an infinitely varied era. That era marked the moment in history when 18th-century social constraints had all melted away without the new moneyed power of 19th-century industry having yet matured enough to be widely felt, when the old apprenticeship system had collapsed without either the new corporate technology or the new scholarship being yet developed enough to give the artist any firm direction. The result was an individualism in life rampant as never before, an individualism in art so untrammeled that different people may see High Victorian art in completely different ways.

To some, it means no more than an absence of all taste, all direction, all sense, comparable to the social scene peopled with the "dreadful caricatures" of the postwar period. Any art, to be meaningful, needs some clearly defined rationale and guiding principles, so the argument runs; this age seemed to have none. Therefore any question of "good" or "bad" High Victorian art is idle; picturesque eclectic architecture, furniture of the 1860s and 70s, are a wasteland of meaningless excrescences and empty elaboration; the sooner torn down and thrown away, the better.

Others, while taking no higher view of High Victorian art as such, still see it with affectionate nostalgia as part of a general image of bygone "good old days," when life was somehow fresher, more interesting, more fun than now. To them, the picturesque parade of gables and mansards and gingerbread edgings drawn with such gay abandon from anywhere and everywhere appeals primarily because its fantasy conjures up such diverse images and moods: the fiends of Charles Addams's cartoons, the reverie of Edward Hopper's canvases, the carefree corruption of a simpler economic era, and the playful pranks of college life (bulls in the belfry, cannon balls in the dean's office) in the days before education got somehow mixed up with national survival and the Gross National Product. And certainly there is an element of truth in this image. For while the High Victorian age's concept of history was wider than before, it was still far from consistently based on scientific scholarship. Ignatius Donnelly's *Atlantis* was as characteristic of this age as Francis Parkman's works; and if it is fair to say of the Early Victorian age that men could then believe so much—all Romans virtuous, all the Middle Ages Christian—because they knew so little, we can quite as justly say of the High Victorians that they could speculate so freely because they knew not too much more. Not until the 1880s, in fact, did foreign travel become commonplace enough to kill altogether the old naïvely romantic concept of the past.

Others again, more seriously, see Picturesque Eclecticism as the historic expression of a uniquely attractive period in American economic life and theory. For them, it is a monument to the glorious progress of untrammeled free enterprise, to a great age of rugged individualism, when everything was somehow brighter, louder, freer than ours—when clothes were fancier, flowers bigger and brighter, meals heavier and richer, drinks stronger, music brassier, speeches more pompous; when all life seemed pervaded by the contagious confidence, the enviable *joie de vivre*, the optimistic expansiveness of America's greatest age of material growth. And while it is suspicious that an age beginning with a murderous civil war, punctuated by the great depression of 1873–9, and featured throughout by expanding slums and sundry assorted miseries, should shine with such an aura, in some ways this image too is fair enough. For in this time before the era of total wars, public calamities cast a lighter shadow than now over private

affairs. People not directly touched by poverty, disease, or marauding armies led what today seem to us lives of unbelievable personal liberty and varied opportunity. Great armies might be bleeding to death in the swamps and creeks of northern Virginia or the mountains of Tennessee, but back in the East huge new industries were coming to birth, new fortunes being made and new families founded on them. Precisely during the years 1863–5 the National Academy's costly new home in New York was financed and erected by public subscription; farms and cities were springing up everywhere from the Midwest to California; railroads, mines, steelyards, all began their mushroom growth in this period when, as Judge Thomas Mellon sagely reminded his sons, "a man may be a patriot without risking his own life or sacrificing his health." And this liberty was enjoyed with public approbation. That is the point, and the real attraction of High Victorian America. In retrospect, it seems another

110. COSMOPOLITAN AMBITIONS
(A) "Old Main," University of Arkansas, Fayetteville.

FACING PAGE: (110 B) Hotel Cambridge, Cambridge, New York.

Far to the west, or in the remote upper Hudson Valley, cosmopolitan grandeurs of Washington, Philadelphia, and New York could hardly be equaled; but they could be emulated, on an appropriate scale. So during the late 1860s and 70s one college after another—particularly the new land-grant institutions created during the war—erected those fine new towered, mansarded, gingerbreaded buildings beloved as the "Old Mains" of later alumni reunions, dramatizing the new kind of American education, comprehensive in subject matter and democratically available to all. And even remote railroad junctions could provide travelers with accommodations whose graceful and eye-catching porches were at least faintly reminiscent of the splendors of postwar hotels in Saratoga Springs and Cape May.

fabulous and glorious lost Age of Faith, rooted in an unshakable acceptance of the doctrine of inevitable progress.

It was Lord Macaulay who perhaps best phrased the creed that supported this era. Writing in 1848, a year of turmoil, famine, and uncertainty everywhere, he declared in his *History of England*, as a general proposition needing neither defense nor elaboration, that

> In every experimental science there is a tendency towards perfection. In every human being there is a wish to ameliorate his own condition. These two great principles have often sufficed, even when counteracted by great public calamities and by bad institutions, to carry civilization rapidly forward. No ordinary misfortune, no ordinary misgovernment, will do so much to make a nation wretched, as the constant progress of physical knowledge and the constant effort of every man to better himself will do to make a nation prosperous.

This was a truth most Americans of the 1860s and 70s still held to be self-evident, and many in the mid-20th century believe still. Was economic life clouded by vicious speculation and incipient monopolies? Only leave men alone, and technological progress will go on so fast that be-fore any great industry is monopolized, inventions will make it obsolete, and a host of new, small competitors arise. Was municipal disgrace abounding? Men of good will can always overcome it; reform is sure; Evangelical Christianity has never been more active, more confident, more respected. Was it true that there was less and less room at the top in the older States—that (as Cleveland Amory wrote in *The Proper Bostonians*) "the death in 1878 of John Lowell Gardner, last East India merchant, is a sort of generally recognized curfew . . . all of a sudden, as it were, the Golden Gates to Boston's First Familyland clanged shut and, generally speaking, they have remained shut ever since"? The West was still open; High Victorian America still had frontiers, where men could go, as in the 17th century they crossed the Atlantic, to recoup lost fortunes and build new reputations. Was the very proposition that all men are created equal being challenged? Surely the outcome of the Civil War proved history to be on the side of democracy. This is the superb confidence proclaimed in all the greatest works of High Victorian architecture in America. Such a monument as the Philadelphia City Hall, carrying skyward in limitless exuber-

ance its loads of treasure from Periclean Greece and Bourbon France, Caesar's Rome and Dante's Florence, was the tangible counterpart (albeit not quite what he had in mind, perhaps) of Whitman's exhortation to

> Sail, sail thy best, ship of Democracy
> Of value is thy freight, 'tis not the Present only,
> The Past is also stored in thee,
> Thou holdest not the venture of thyself alone,
>   not of the Western continent alone,
> Earth's résumé entire floats on thy keel . . .
> With thee Time voyages in trust, the ante-
>   cedent nations sink or swim with thee,
> With all their ancient struggles, martyrs,
>   heroes, epics, wars,
> Thou bear'st the other continents.

It was in this confidence that High Victorians felt free, as did no one before or after, to appropriate the whole heritage of the past, mix and mould it to suit their own taste and express their own aspirations. As the musicians of the High Victorian age "interpreted" Mozart and Bach, its philosophers drew with equal assurance on contemporary scientific theory, ancient religion, and historical research to construct systems of their own, and its editors adapted Shakespeare and Milton, so its architects felt Gothic, Roman, Baroque, Mohammedan all alike were theirs to use, play with, transform. For the first time men felt they understood history fully enough to try and rise out of its stream, use its laws to mould their own future, become its movers instead of its manifestation.

There was a sense of elation about the study of history then. No longer the concern of a few scholarly clergymen or gentlemen of independent mind and means, as it had been a century before, history was now the consuming interest of most educated people. Historical novels, biographies, works of sweeping imagination and intensive period studies, all became "best sellers." Even more than scientific invention, in fact, the advancement and wide dissemination of historical knowledge was the High Victorian age's most outstanding and characteristic achievement. For men felt, in the 1860s, 70s, and 80s, as if they had

been suddenly set on firm ground after ages of floating in outer space, with no way of knowing up from down. For ages men had lived among monuments and institutions vaguely supposed to be "very old"—but exactly how old, or which came before what, they had no way of knowing. Now they knew. Now they had the technique of correlating diverse historical evidence, of extracting, from chronicles, letters, earlier histories, and—far from least—archaeological study, coherent patterns of cause and effect. Now at last they felt they understood precisely how things came to be the way they found them, how the present was related to the past. Knowing the laws of history, they could look at the past with new tolerance, and to the future with brave anticipation. And that was a wonderful feeling. The new enthusiasm for history permeated all the upper levels of Victorian society; no aspect of High Victorian culture—least of all the lavish and brash richness of High Victorian decoration—can really be understood without taking it into account. No won-

FACING PAGE:

111. THE HIGH VICTORIAN VILLA AS SYMBOL OF AN ERA; THEN AND NOW

(A) Page 172, Volume IX, National Cyclopædia of American Biography (1899). The "residence" here serves in lieu of the portrait usually accompanying biographical entries.

(111 B) Drawing by Saul Steinberg, c.1955. Detroit Institute of Arts.

As cultural expression, text and pictures speak for themselves. In such houses a vestige of the old Tuscan villa persists, like some ghost in residence; the old simple cubical shapes of towers and porches and balconies are blurred and blanketed in seemingly endless masses of niches, pinnacles, polychromatic tiles and shingles, verandahs great and small, stairways, turrets—all combining to create what later generations would call the "General Grant" house, and so infinitely various that the precise moment of its appearance in the 1860s is as uncertain as that of its disappearance sometime in the 1890s.

BURKE, Stevenson, railroad president, was born in St. Lawrence county, N. Y., Nov. 26, 1824, son of David and Isabella Burke. His early education was received in the district schools, and at the age of seventeen he became a teacher, conducting successfully various schools through several terms. In 1846 he became a student in the Ohio Wesleyan University at Delaware, where he began the study of law, which he had determined to adopt as his profession. He read law with Powell & Buck, of Delaware, and Hon. H. D. Clark, of Elyria, and was admitted to the bar Aug. 11, 1848; a few months later forming a partnership with his former preceptor, Mr. Clark. At twenty-seven he controlled the most extensive law business in Lorain county, and in 1861 was elected to the common pleas bench. In October, 1866, he was re-elected for a term of five years; he retained his position two years, when, de-

Residence of Stevenson Burke

siring a wider field for his efforts, he removed to Cleveland, O., (1869) and entered into partnership with Hon. F. T. Backus and E. J. Estep. [...] widely known as a most able corporation law[yer] his connection with important railway affairs ha[s] brought him into much prominence. The mos[t] [no]table case with which he had to do in Lorain co[unty] (known as the Oberlin rescue case) touched cl[osely] the question which led to the civil war, [and] served to greatly strengthen the abolition senti[ment] already so strong in northern Ohio. As if his [pro]fession were not sufficiently absorbing, Judge B[urke] has for years been one of the most energetic and [suc]cessful railway men in the country. For a [long] time he was general counsel for the Cleveland, [Co]lumbus, Cincinnati and Indianapolis Railway C[o.,] director, vice-president during four or five y[ears] and subsequently president; he has also been c[hair]man of its financial and executive committees, [and] represented, as attorney, a large amount of [stock] owned abroad. Among other important cases [are] that of Butzman and Mueller, in the supreme [court] of Ohio, involving the constitutionality of the [new] liquor law, in which Judge Burke opposed th[e law] and won; that of Kimberly vs. Arms, involv[ing a] large sum; tried in the U. S. circuit court of n[orth]ern Ohio; and a series of cases tried at Indiana[polis] and Chicago and in the supreme court at Was[hing]ton, connected with the foreclosure of the mort[gage] upon the Indianapolis and St. Louis railroad [and] the obligations of that road to other rai[lway] companies. For a dozen years he was ge[neral] counsel and attorney of the Cleveland and M[a]ning Valley Railway Co., has been its president [since] 1880, and for the last decade has represented, [as at]torney, all its stockholders. He has been vice-[presi]dent and president of the Indianapolis and St. [Louis] Railway Co. In June, 1881, Judge Burke [made] his first great venture in railroading. He poss[essed] large interests in the coal lands of Hocking v[alley] and decided that it would be advantageous to c[ontrol] the railroads carrying coal from that region. [Ac]cordingly, he, with others, bought the capital [stock]

for about $7,000,000. He was at that time president of the Snow Fork and Cleveland Coal Co., which owned a very large tract in the Hocking valley; he and his associates promptly purchased an additional tract, aggregating about 11,000 acres, and organized what is now known as the prosperous Hocking Coal and Railway Co. In 1885, after the re-organization of the Ohio Central railway, a line running from Toledo to Corning, O., the centre of the Hocking coal field, with a branch to Columbus, O., Judge Burke negotiated an exchange of a small percentage of the stock of the Columbus, Hocking Valley and Toledo Railway Co. for three-fourths of the stock of the new Toledo and Ohio Central Railway Co.; he and his associates thus became the owners of a controlling interest in both corporations, the two greatest coal carrying roads in the West. Railway men of experience pronounced this last move of Judge Burke the most important of all. The difficulties of the undertaking may be more easily appreciated when it is known that there are nearly 800 stockholders in the Toledo and Ohio Central Co., with whom contracts had to be made before control of the railway could be secured. Judge Burke also negotiated the purchase of the New York, Chicago and St. Louis railway—the "Nickel Plate"—for William H. Vanderbilt, Oct. 26, 1882. For years he represented as attorney three-fourths of the stock of the Shenango and Allegheny Railway Co. in Pennsylvania; he was also a director in each. For more than two years (until 1885) he was a director of the Cincinnati, Hamilton and Dayton, and of the Cincinnati, Hamilton and Indianapolis Railway Co. He has long been a director of the Central Ontario Rail-

der that in our soberer, harder, cleverer, and more bitterly experienced times, High Victorian art has come to seem at once infinitely remote and full of nostalgic appeal.

That something like this might happen was foreseen long ago. In the same chapter of his *History of England* that stated the creed of his age so unequivocally, Macaulay also warned against unduly idolizing it. "In truth," he wrote,

> we are under a deception similar to that which misleads the traveller in the Arabian desert. Beneath the caravan all is dry and bare; but far in advance, and far in the rear, is the semblance of refreshing waters. The pilgrims hasten forward and find nothing but sand where, an hour before, they had seen a lake. They turn their eyes and see a lake where, an hour before, they were toiling through sand. A similar illusion seems to haunt nations through every stage of the long progress from poverty and barbarism to the highest degrees of opulence and civilization. But, if we resolutely chase the mirage backward, we shall find it recede before us into the regions of fabulous antiquity.... We too shall, in our turn, be outstripped, and in our turn be envied. It may well be, in the twentieth century, that . . . labouring men may be as little used to dine without meat as they now are to eat rye bread; that sanitary police and medical discoveries may have added several more years to the average length of human life; that numerous comforts and luxuries which are now unknown, or confined to a few, may be within the reach of every diligent and thrifty working man. And it may then be the mode to assert that the increase of wealth and the progress of science have benefited the few at the expense of the many, and to talk of the reign of Queen Victoria as the time when England was truly merry England. . . .

All of which, of course, has come true even more in the United States. High Victorian America has another side; we need to see that, too, if we are going to understand the full significance of Picturesque Eclecticism as cultural expression.

We need to see the High Victorian mansion not only as the expression of engagingly naïve individuality, but also, as Sinclair Lewis saw it

in *Babbitt*, as the symbol of a new and exceedingly unpleasant breed of men:

> . . . The residence of William Washington Eathorne, president of the First State Bank . . . preserves the memory of the "nice parts" of Zenith as they appeared from 1860 to 1900. It is a red brick immensity with gray sandstone lintels and a roof of slate in courses of red, green, and dyspeptic yellow. There are two anemic towers, one roofed with copper, the other crowned with castiron ferns. The porch is like an open tomb; it is supported by squat granite pillars above which hang frozen cascades of brick. At one side of the house is a huge stained-glass window in the shape of a keyhole.

> But the house has an effect not at all humorous. It embodies the heavy dignity of those Victorian financiers who ruled the generation between the pioneers and the brisk "sales engineers" [in the Midwest] and created a somber oligarchy by gaining control of banks, mills, land, railroads, mines. Out of the dozen contradictory Zeniths which together make up the true and complete Zenith, none is so powerful and enduring yet none so unfamiliar to the citizens as the small, still, dry, polite, cruel Zenith of the William Eathornes; and for that tiny hierarchy the other Zeniths unwittingly labor and insignificantly die.

We need to remember that besides being a place of buoyant gaiety, bustling growth, and irresistible progress, the High Victorian city was all too often a place of what seems in retrospect incredible corruption—physical, aesthetic, political. Consider, for example, the implications of such an editorial as this from the Cleveland *Leader* for March 5, 1861:

> A petition is now before the City Council praying for the repeal of an ordinance, which was passed four years ago, making it unlawful to pour any slops, filth, &c., into the Cuyahoga River within the city limits, and which in effect shuts off manufactories and refineries from being established upon the river banks. This petition should be granted.

> [We look again—surely there is a "not" left out, or something. But no! he means it:] To refuse to do it is to pursue the same policy toward manufactures that has diverted trade

112. HIGH VICTORIAN EXUBERANCE IN THE FAR WEST

(A) "Portland, Oregon"; (B) "Residence of Charles Crocker [San Francisco]."

Two plates from Marvels of the New West *by W. M. Thayer (Norwich, Connecticut, 1887), one of the typical books that give the full rich flavor of High Victorian optimism reaching an apogee as the West rose to wealth and greatness* in the 1860s, 70s, and 80s. Bursting with an enthusiasm that finds everything "astounding," "imposing," and "amazing," bristling with italicized and capitalized statistics, the Marvels *are climaxed by Crocker's house, "large enough and good enough for a king . . . one of the kings found among the sovereign people of America, where all are sovereigns. Outside, inside, and surroundings are as complete and near perfection as money could assure . . ."*

and business to other more favorable points, and has greatly retarded the legitimate growth of our city.

And we need to see High Victorian furnishings, too, not only as a great buoyant individual expression, but as a triumph of the impersonal machine. These endless arrays of amusing curlicues and brackets and plaster foliage that so delight people of antiquarian mind in this day of polished glass and enameled steel had a very different significance for the men who lived at the time of their appearance.

In the Downs Library of the Winterthur Museum is a notebook entitled *Personal Experiences of an Old New York Cabinet Maker*. It was written in 1908 by a seventy-eight-year-old craftsman named Ernest Hagen, who came to New York from Hamburg in 1844, and for twenty years practiced cabinetmaking around Rivington, Norfolk, and Suffolk streets. Hagen was never prosperous; even in his youth men without capital found it hard to compete with the bigger establishments that used machinery, and they had to eke out livings making one standard type of chair, or even a single standard part—Hagen was no Chippendale. But he got along, and by working for Charles A. Baudouine, Belter's rival, who had "200 hands all told" in his establishment, built up some capital, and after the Civil War set up a shop of his own. The result was disaster:

> In the fall of 1867 we bought the property #213 East 26th Street and built a shop on it, and all went well for the next 2 or 3 years, when the great change came over the cabinet making trade of New York. . . . The factory work, and especially the Western factory work, drove everything else out of the market. All the smaller cabinet makers were simply wiped out. There are very few left now which make a scanty living by repairing; and even the larger establishments have a hard time in competing with the Western concerns of Grand Rapids in Michigan and other out of town concerns . . .

To simple artisans like Hagen it seemed that machines were the villains; and so, often, it

seems to us. But that is only a half-truth. It was not machines as such, or alone, that caused the collapse of old craft traditions in the High Victorian age. Rather the cause was a change in basic social structure of which machines and declining craftmanship were symptoms.

The traditional craftsman who worked directly with his material, personally carrying out each operation from raw wood to polished table or painted cornice, was part and expression of a society which from the beginnings of American civilization almost until the Civil War had always been distinguished by a close and direct relationship between men and the work they did. In every department of life it had been the same. Pioneers on their homesteads, seeding between the stumps they had girdled; merchants in their countinghouses, watching their own ships come into their own wharves; politicians representing communities small enough for them to know and be known by almost everyone; aristocratic Virginians riding over their plantations, supervising spring planting and fall harvest; volunteer militiamen, breaking ranks to fight Indian-style; early factory owners setting up machinery in Rhode Island and laying out mill towns on the Merrimac and the Brandywine; even the first canal and railroad promoters, all in their several ways could feel they knew what they were doing, personally understood how it was done. But as the 19th century progressed and the country grew bigger, its communications better and faster, its working capital larger, a subtle change set in, which the Civil War brought to a dramatic head. All at once, it seemed, the men who worked on farms and in factories, in banks and on railroads, were losing control of them. Others, who as often as not knew nothing of their actual operation, were taking over. Men who made money in shipping began putting it in railroad stock, whether or not they knew anything about trains. A bank president who had never lived on a farm might "take over" mortgages on a dozen plantations, and begin running them through agents. Land speculators might buy controlling

113. *Parlor, Henry Ford Homestead, Dearborn, Michigan. A typical High Victorian farmhouse, restored in Greenfield Village. The familiar surroundings of one of the great representatives of High Victorian individualism, "The Last Billionaire." In the fierce independence of each piece in this parlor—stove, organ, chairs, curtains, lamp—from each other and from the whole, we may recognize a counterpart to the fierce resentment against "interference" by anybody—government, unions, or competitors—displayed by the man who, born here in 1863, went on to create almost single-handed one of the greatest of all American corporations.*

interests and preside over textile mills of whose workings they had not the faintest comprehension. Rocky Mountain mines might come under the direction of stock manipulators who never left the floor of the exchange.

In politics the same thing was going on; by means of political "machines" a man might come to office knowing nothing of his constituents, nor they of him. And it was no different in the arts. There the instrument happened to be a tangible thing, a creation of wheels and cogs and levers—lathes that could produce dozens of finely turned chair legs or cornice brackets while the old-time craftsman was still sharpening his chisels; cameras that could accomplish in seconds what took the old-time portrait painter weeks of sittings; sawmills turning out in hours as much standard-size lumber as old-time housewrights shaped in a year; foundries producing beams and girders and window frames mechanics could bolt together. But in every case the effect was the same. These new "machines"—whether consisting of stock certificates and bonds, political organizations, or wheels and wire—made it possible as never before in history for goods, services, and art to be produced impersonally, by men not directly or ultimately involved in the actual work; they were symptoms of a fundamental change in the nature of human labor itself.

Once upon a time Americans had lived in a world where they felt in control of themselves and their destinies, in which the things that happened to them—even disease and accident—proceeded from reasonably discernible causes. In that world it had seemed self-evidently right that the details of their furniture should be precise and commensurable, the forms of their buildings co-ordinate and articulated. But now, just as surely, men felt themselves losing control of their lives and fortunes, pulled about by unseen strings and hidden forces. "They" are going to pass laws to do thus and so. "A depression" has come and we are out of work, knowing neither how nor why. "The company" hands us clerks and stonemasons and woodcarvers bits and pieces "its" machines have made, and we assemble them, ignorant of both the beginning and the end of what we do.

And to a greater or lesser degree people everywhere were quite aware of what was happening. When Cyrus Hall McCormick died in 1884, for instance, one of the workmen in the great Chicago factory he had built declared quite sincerely that

> ". . . he was one of us, understand? . . . He knew machines like his own mother. While he was livin' we had one boss—and if anything went wrong, you could go right to him and get it fixed up. In these new days of big companies, you have a dozen bosses—and where are you? With Old Cy we knew. When he died there were mourners in our crowd, for now we had lost him, and we knew we'd never have a boss like him again."

In such circumstances, the old classical precision and self-containment and order seemed quite pointless and meaningless; it was Picturesque Eclecticism that spoke to this age.

By definition a style indefinable, fleeting, and fluid, Picturesque Eclecticism gave the High Victorian artist his vehicle for expressing all the malaise and insecurity provoked by a world whose foundations seemed dissolving in vagueness, shift, and flux. Conceived as it was in libraries and on drawing boards, isolated at once from craftsmen's skills and engineering principles, Picturesque Eclecticism seemed instinctively right in a world where separation from direct contact with their work was the increasingly common lot of men everywhere. Consciously or not, men recognized in the contrast between the measured order of Mills's Treasury or Latrobe's Capitol and sprawling piles like the Washington War and Navy Building or the Philadelphia City Hall all the difference between ages when men could generally know how and by whom they were ruled, and an age when, in an ever-thickening fog of bureaucratic machinery, they generally could not. And through the freedom Picturesque Eclecticism allowed them to pile on masses of additive ornament without rule or measure, these men could compensate outwardly at least for the inner uneasiness they felt, whistle loud and gaudy in an ever-gathering, ever more brittle dark.

That is how artists born around 1840, coming to maturity with the picturesque eclectic style, saw it; this generation, accepting its forms and principles without reservation as a self-evident part of the spirit of their age, made it a personal as well as a cultural expression, and created its greatest monuments. This was the generation, and this the motivation, of Henry Hobson Richardson (1838–1886).

NOTES

Of the disgust that High Victorian art of the 1860s and 70s as a whole engendered in a sensitive critic, the early chapters of Lewis Mumford's *Brown Decades* (1931) are an eloquent example; it was perhaps for this reason that Dr. Mumford tended to emphasize those elements in Richardson's work that made him a pioneer of modern architecture, rather than those in which Richardson so effectively manifested the High Victorian spirit of his own age. Perhaps the best picture of the gay and fantastic side of High Victorian is presented by John Maass, *The Gingerbread Age* (1957). "When I first came to this country," Maass wrote in the Foreword,

> I was startled by American nineteenth century buildings; though widely traveled I had never seen more fanciful houses. . . . There was little in print on the subject then and most of that was derogatory. Some books warned the reader to shut his eyes to one and all of these Victorian "monstrosities." . . . I hope this book will serve as an antidote to long-entrenched clichés.

In this respect *The Gingerbread Age* has indeed been successful, as I know from the many students whose eyes have been opened by it. Wayne Andrews, *Architecture, Ambition, and Americans* (1947) gives a sympathetic picture of High Victorian architecture as the expression of laissez-faire capitalism.

Quotations from Harvey O'Connor, *Mellon's Millions* (1933); from Cleveland Amory, *The Proper Bostonians* (1947) and *Who Killed Society?* (1960); from Macaulay, *History of England*, I, Chap. 3; of Hagen's diary, from Elizabeth A. Ingerham, "Personal Experiences of an Old New York Cabinet Maker" (*Winterthur Newsletter*, VIII, 1, 1962, pp. 1–7).

7. "RICHARDSONIAN ROMANESQUE":
High Victorian Art as Personal Expression

HENRY HOBSON RICHARDSON made his first designs for Trinity Church, Boston, in 1872. By 1877, when the church stood ready for use, Trinity had made him; the young Southerner who had opened his first office on Staten Island only eleven years before had become the most famous architect in the United States. In 1870 Richardson was known mainly to a few well-connected friends, and to them best for his social success as a student at Harvard (1854–9); in 1880, when a symposium was held to determine the ten greatest buildings in America, five of those named were his. And the United States, where only a decade before all native traditions seemed to have foundered under conflicting and confused waves of imported ideas and immigrant architects, now had an internationally recognized style of its own—"Richardsonian Romanesque."

What was it that made Trinity such a triumph? Not the style itself, certainly; Romanesque was not new in America, and the climate for its acceptance had long been prepared by qualities and characteristics inherent in the Italianate manner of the 1850s and Second Empire in the 1860s. Nor was Richardson any great rebel, making a revolutionary break with the past. Quite the opposite, in fact. Although his years of study in Paris (1859–65) gave Richardson close familiarity with Henri Labrouste's experiments in new structural materials and Viollet-le-Duc's theories of functionalism derived from Gothic example, his work never showed much evidence of it, from the first house he built for himself—Arrochar on Staten Island in 1868, a design which, were it not for Richardson's name being connected with it, would be dismissed with hardly a second glance as little more than "General Grant"—to his last major work, the Marshall Field Warehouse in Chicago, whose construction, almost wholly of masonry, still ignored the obvious advantages of metal frame.

What appealed to his generation was precisely that Richardsonian Romanesque was so perfectly High Victorian, so entirely a result of the conditions of American life in the 1870s and 80s.

Of this fact, Trinity Church is the great example. In essence it represented not a different but a fuller and more mature realization of the visual and intellectual implications of Picturesque Eclecticism. To the eye, this mighty pile of heavy porches, arches, and buttresses building up to its massive central tower, sprayed with pinnacles and turrets, presented a rich complex of ever-shifting shapes and unexpected sequences of pattern in color and texture that carried High Victorian picturesqueness to a point where all earlier buildings seemed somehow dry, tinny, unsubstantial, and gauche. And in the mind these forms, eclectically reminiscent of diverse medieval epochs but distinctive of none, evoked more consummately than ever before that sense of vague and formless pastness in general which was the High Victorian symbolic ideal. Neither archaeology nor symbolism motivated Richardson's predilection for Romanesque here and later. So little interest had he in the style for its own sake that it is doubtful if in all his years in Paris he ever visited the Romanesque country of southern France; all his life he was content to pick details from his collection of books and photographs, and whatever direct suggestions of Arles or Salamanca are evident in Trinity today apparently came mainly from his draftsman Stanford White (1853–1906), who here anticipated the preoccupations of the succeeding Late Victorian era in which he played so large a part. Neither did Richardson read into Romanesque any particular symbolism. If he made his reputation with churches, that was accidental; Romanesque was not necessarily a "churchy" style for him, and he had no hesitation in using the same eclectic forms for churches, libraries, jails,

114. *Trinity Church, Boston. Designed in 1872 by H. H. Richardson; somewhat altered in effect by the addition in the 1890s of porch and capping of towers on the facade by Richardson's successor firm of Shepley, Rutan & Coolidge. When Trinity was first completed in 1877, its dramatic presentation of a new architectural idiom made Richardson nationally famous. Now dated ("engulfed in the Brown Decades," Professor Hitchcock described it in 1936), and not even the best representative of "Richardsonian Romanesque," it remains one of the great creations of Pic-*

turesque Eclecticism in America, and a monument to the cultural supremacy that New England generally, and Boston in particular, attained in the 1870s as a result of the Civil War. In the background, the John Hancock Life Insurance Building, built 1945–9 by the successor firm of Cram & Ferguson; one of the last of Late Victorian skyscrapers, it is still largely sheathed in masonry, though the elimination of ornament foreshadows the starker steel-and-glass skyscrapers that were to dominate American architecture in the 1950s.

---

town halls, private homes, and railroad stations. In Richardsonian Romanesque there was no lingering Early Victorian flavor or attempts to find neat correlations between specific forms and spe-

cific ideologies. For Richardson, Romanesque was a means to an end—and that end was the High Victorian one of creating an emotional mood, an intellectual attitude, a visual impression. This heavy stonework that seemed to rise from roots sunk deep in the subsoil, these ponderous forms that seemed to stand for and from eternity, these details that were old before ever the ecclesiologists' Gothic had been imagined, brought to mind and eye an impression of solidity, an attitude of stability, a mood of security—or what Richardson himself called "quiet." And it was for this reason that the Richardson Romanesque which later came to seem so ponderous, gloomy, and grotesque spoke to its own generation with infinite satisfaction and power.

The High Victorian age in America was, more than most, an era of paradox. It was at once a time of confident, exuberant creation and growth, and a time of frantic change, upheaval, destruction, and demoralization. All its arts, all of its representative figures show this. On the one hand there is infatuation with human progress, the extension of human powers generally that science and the machine are so visibly providing. Never was man's command over his material environment better manifested than in the works of High Victorian designers—furniture manufacturers with steam-driven presses and saws forcing their will impartially on wood, papier-mâché, metal, marble, bending and twisting and beating them into ponderous knobs and lacy carving and sinuous mouldings; landscape architects with fountains and fireworks violating the natural uses of fire and water; builders delighting to imitate one material in another, treating stone like wood and wood like stone; piling up forms to dizzy heights and unexpected projections. Never were the glories of locomotive steam power so feelingly portrayed as by that greatest of all High Victorians, John Ruskin. But for all their satisfaction at the "advancement of the generality of mankind," men of this age were disturbed by it, deeply afraid of the effects on themselves personally. They eagerly looked for anything, however symbolic and on whatever scale, that might recall the old lost sense of permanence and belonging that their fantastic material progress had taken away. They burst with

pride in describing their bustling new cities; but the more people moved into them and left the stable round of rural life behind, the more popular became paintings of barefoot boys with cheeks of tan (Winslow Homer made a reputation with them in the 1860s and 70s), songs about the Little Brown Church in the pristine Vale of Nashua, Iowa, John Rogers's little groups of village dalliances and checker playing down on the farm, and Currier & Ives's idyllic series of "American Home Life" in earlier, simpler days. The more commonplace and efficient became the marvels of indoor plumbing, the more fondly people loved to sing about "The Old Oaken Bucket." The farther evolutionary theories and historical criticism permeated society to shake the old fundamentals of religion, the higher church spires sprouted on the American skyline, as if to reassure faith by force of numbers, size, and antiquity. The thicker cities spread over the prairies and suburbs ringed every old Eastern center, the more people wanted to surround themselves with buildings that looked old and seemed to stand above the tumult of frantic progress. It is in this setting that Richardson's stone fastnesses had their great appeal.

And it was in this setting, too, that the old houses which only a quarter-century earlier Mrs. Tuthill had described as "happily . . . all of such perishable materials that they will not much longer remain to annoy travellers in 'search of the picturesque' through the beautiful villages of New England" suddenly became eminently "picturesque" themselves, ideal evocations of a wistfully remembered past. By the 1870s architects were visiting the "beautiful villages of New England" precisely to search them out, and create from their inspiration a characteristically nostalgic High Victorian "shingle style." Of this shingle style Richardson was himself a master, using it throughout his career—for the Sherman house at Newport in 1874, the Bryant house at Cohasset in 1880, the Potter house in St. Louis, 1886–7. But it was the stone Richardsonian Romanesque, rather than the wooden shingle-

115. VARIETIES OF RICHARDSONIAN ROMANESQUE

(A) Exterior, Watts Sherman house, Newport, Rhode Island, as originally designed by H. H. Richardson in 1874 and drawn by Stanford White for The New York Sketch Book of Architecture, *1875. Manifesting at once the post-Civil War "cult of New England" and the new "realism" in expressing materials, the "shingle style" in Richardson's hands had the same undefined medieval quality as his masonry work, the "woodiness" of wood being given a sophisticated emphasis comparable to his "stony" treatment of stone.*

style variant, to which the pervasive malaise of the 1870s and 80s most readily responded; only the exaggerated and overwhelming bulk of stone could adequately compensate for an insecurity so deep and inexpressible. Well into the 1890s it remained (often combined with various shingle elements) the chosen expression of the upper middle class, an architectural counterpart to the cult of "manly" and "masterful" action epitomized so well by Theodore Roosevelt; as in Roosevelt an entire generation found vicarious compensation for uneasiness, fear, and depression, so Roosevelt's Sagamore Hill on Long Island, with its combination of features from the shingle style and Richardsonian Romanesque, was the consummate expression of those architectural qualities which the generation coming to maturity in the 1870s and 80s most instinctively appreciated and understood.

As Professor Hitchcock was perhaps first to point out, Richardsonian Romanesque was neither particularly Romanesque nor peculiarly Richardson's. "Richardsonian" is in fact as much a generic title like "Chippendale," as a personal style. With his specific borrowings from French and Spanish Romanesque models, Richardson also combined at various times, in the typical manner of High Victorian Picturesque Eclecticism, details drawn (among other sources) from Late Gothic in France, Victorian Gothic of Italian inspiration, the vaguely English Renaissance style his age called "Queen Anne," the 16th-century castles of Francis I on the Loire, French Second Empire Norman, and published remains of early Christian monuments in Syria. And he was by no means the only architect of his age to exhibit the characteristic ponderous massiveness and play on textures of Richardsonian Romanesque. Frank Furness (1839–1912) interpreted these qualities in Ruskinian Gothic terms for Philadelphia in his Pennsylvania Academy of the Fine Arts (1872–6); the Provident Life &

(115 B) J. J. Glessner house, Chicago, Ill., 1885–7, as illustrated in Harper's Magazine, *LXXXIII, 1891. In the accompanying commentary, Montgomery Schuyler wrote that "Richardson's domestic architecture in Chicago . . . arrests attention and prevents apathy. . . . A granite wall over 150 feet long, as in the side of this building, almost unbroken, and with its structure clearly exhibited, is sure enough to arrest and strike the beholder . . . but . . . the merits of the building as a building . . . are much effaced when it is considered as a dwelling, and the structure ceases to be defensible, except, indeed, in a military sense."*

Trust Company Building (1879)—the best example, perhaps; even in the later Broad Street Station (1892–4). Bruce Price (1845–1905) played variants on them in his "château style" Windsor Station in Montreal (1888) and Château Frontenac in Quebec (1890), his fashionable New York City Queen Anne houses, and his shingle-style hotels like the West End (1878–9) and Craigs (1879–80) at Mount Desert in Maine. The same qualities were emulated by a host of local figures for fashionable houses and office buildings in Chicago and Minneapolis, Kansas City and San Francisco; they could be seen in the sprawling homes of the well-to-do in all the fashionable places by all the fashionable architects: the Pierre Lorillard house at Newport (1878) and Kragsyde for G. Nixon Black at Manchester-by-the-Sea (Massachusetts, c.1882) by Peabody and Sterns; Lamb and Rich's work in New Jersey (A. B. Rich house, Short Hills, 1881–2) and Long Island (S. P. Hinkley house, Lawrence, 1883; Sagamore Hill, Oyster Bay, 1884–5); Shingleside at Swampscott, Massachusetts (1880–81), by Arthur Little; and so on and on. The famous comment about Richardson: "My God, how he looks like his own buildings!" sums up the whole situation. The man was a symbol, in his person and in his architecture.

He is a symbol first of the triumph of industrial capitalism in America after the Civil War. No artisan come up in the world, no gentleman amateur, the mature Richardson of the later 1870s and 80s is fundamentally an executive, efficiently organizing and running an office in the spirit of industrialists directing the operations of their factories, or political bosses their electoral machines. Some men in this age are building corporations in meat or sugar or steel; Richardson is building an architectural corporation. As orders come in he analyzes how best to handle them, then assigns to each "staff department" an appointed job. An engineer works out structural problems, draftsmen draw up the details, an accountant figures costs, subcontractors take over stone chipping and mortar laying and

sawing, and off this assembly line there rolls a product as distinctive and efficiently standardized as that of any other new industry—a Crane Library in Quincy, Massachusetts (1880–83), or a Billings Library in Burlington, Vermont (1883–6); a city hall for Albany, New York (1880–82), or a courthouse for Allegheny County in Pittsburgh, Pennsylvania (1884–8). Richardsonian Romanesque has a local trademark—the Civil War has made Boston an ideal distribution center for cultural products—but its market is nation-wide, especially suited for use in the new industrial cities. And from such an office, too, roll out the leaders of the next architectural generation, men trained not as apprentices learning the master's skills, but in the arts of running an architectural business; the systematic habit of mind they learn in these surroundings goes far to explain the insistent emphasis on archaeological correctness and polish characteristic of the succeeding Late Victorian age.

Businessman among businessmen, tycoon among tycoons, Richardson symbolizes too the architect's attainment of a new social status. Materially, he prospers as artists rarely have before. He is no starving genius in an attic sacrificing present prospects for future fame. Member of the Harvard Porcellian Club, friend and associate of every sort of industrial, social, and political magnate, Richardson takes his full

_____

(115 C) Allegheny County Court House, Pittsburgh, exterior and plan. Built on the designs of H. H. Richardson, 1884–8. The essential qualities of stone are combined with eclectic Romanesque detail: "Pittsburgh's Allegheny County Court House and Jail are conceded on every hand to be among the preeminent monuments of American architecture—national treasures of the first magnitude. . . . Not only are both buildings venerable facets of Richardson's genius, they are part of the very bone and flesh of Pittsburgh—in short, they are Pittsburgh." [James D. Van Trump, "Project H. H. Richardson," The Charette, April 1962.]

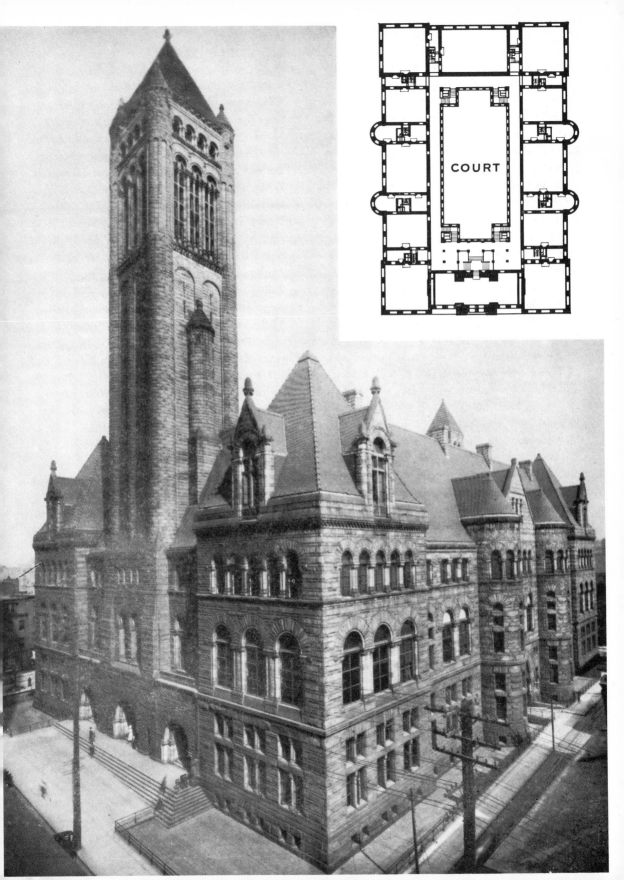

COURT

share both of the values and of the new wealth of this gilded age. For this, he and the art he represents have often been condemned; but that is hardly fair. Just as the new industrialists in amassing their great profits also created new sources of real wealth for the country, so in achieving a new professional and social standing High Victorian artists found unsuspected possibilities for new kinds of creativity opening up for them.

In the High Victorian age artists become aware of themselves as independent creative personalities as never before. The awareness is manifest in their outward appearance and behavior. We think of Richardson with his great bulk, booming voice, extravagant habits; or Frank Furness as Sullivan remembered him: ". . . a curious character. He affected the English in fashion. He wore loud plaids, and a scowl, and from his face depended fan-like a marvellous red beard, beautiful in tone, with each separate hair delicately wrinkled from beginning to end. Moreover his face was snarled and homely as an English bulldog." Or Bruce Price, "that elegant gentleman and erratic genius," father of Mrs. Emily Post. But most of all the awareness is manifest in the artists' attitude to and conception of their own work. They conceive of themselves now as something more than ordinary men, not so much in skills, as in perception, sensitivity, erudition, and intuition. No longer content to be mechanics, adorners and adornments of society, they aspire to lead men towards fuller life in every sense. More than mere discoverers and purveyors of something called "beauty," they think of themselves as cultural and intellectual leaders, as interpreters and creators of whatever is to be thought real. It is on these grounds that they begin to claim equality with the social and political leaders of society. It is on these grounds that they begin to conceive of art as a kind of activity altogether different from what it had been in the past. And it is at this point that American architecture, in the person of Henry Hobson Richardson, first American of

really international reputation, re-enters the mainstream of development in Western art.

The artist's new claims were first explicitly made by painters, in Paris, during the 1850s and 60s. That Richardson knew and understood what was going on is entirely probable, if not certain. He arrived in Paris only four years after Courbet's "Encounter" and "Studio" had been exhibited in the then-notorious "Pavilion of Realism," which presented the artist as one whom the richest bourgeois might meet hat in hand, the center of a world peopled by creations of his own mind and directed by his own will and insight. The years Richardson was there—1859 to 1865—saw the appearance of Manet's early Spanish pictures of toreadors and the "Old Musician," his scandalous "Luncheon on the Grass" and "Olympia," Degas's "Bellelli Family," Whistler's "White Girl," in which were demonstrated how artists could emulate the camera in directness of technical statement, yet interpret the world in terms of personal reactions and experience. And when Richardson returned to America, he created an architecture based on the same principles as this new painting.

All of this generation born in the 1830s— French painters and American architect alike— were raised to take eclecticism for granted; the artists had no more compunction about borrowing ideas and motifs from Old Masters than Richardson had about borrowing from earlier architecture. But they were none of them imitators of the past, as the artists of the preceding generation had been. As these painters did not aspire to be either "classicists" or "romantics," but to create from a variety of elements styles of their own, so Richardson used Syrian arches and dormers from the Loire as well as Auvergnat stonework in creating his "Romanesque." Both Richardson and the painters put new insistence on the intrinsic qualities of their art as such. As in paintings by Manet or Whistler or Degas you are aware of the painting itself—the texture of brushwork or pastel, elements of composition in the abstract, independently of what these may "represent"—so in Richardsonian Romanesque you are always aware of the essential "stoniness" of stone, the "woodiness" of shingle, formal and spatial organization, regardless of "what" the building may be in use or as symbol. And most significant of all, painters and architect alike in their several ways were working out more and more fully the implications of Courbet's concept of the artist as a commanding personality, shaping and moulding reality, determining how it shall be presented to the world. For the new painters, this concept meant rejecting literal counterfeits of natural appearance, insisting on their right to define what reality is and how it shall be interpreted. For Richardson, the concept meant a corresponding rejection of exercises in precise literary symbolism and archaeological copyings, an insistence on his right to give his work whatever character he personally felt appropriate: "I cannot, however, guarantee" —so he writes in a promotional circular from his office in the early 1880s—"that the building shall conform to [a client's] ideas of beauty or taste, or indeed to those of any person or school." And for him and the painters, it meant a new sense of comprehensive responsibility. As the painters' concern with reality demanded of them both an objective definition and a subjective interpretation, so the idea of a personal architectural style required of the architect equal attention to both exterior elevations and interior design—which is the significance of Richardson's place in the history of furniture.

That Richardson was as intensely concerned with the interiors of his buildings as with their exteriors is often overlooked. Yet from the beginning to the end of his career this was so. In his first important commission, Unity Church in Springfield, Massachusetts (1866–9), he was already designing hammerbeam roof and cathedra in golden oak, stenciled border on the plaster wall, and colonnette capitals to complement the exterior effect. Trinity in Boston was as remarkable for its coherence inside as out—the contrasts in color and texture of the exterior

walls repeated in the play of dark-brown varnished roof beams against reddish-orange and buff walls, the sculptured ranges of figures and the Spanish-inspired tendency to bunch decoration in lush patches outside finding visual correspondence in painted figural panels and clusters of complex forms in colonnette capitals and chandeliers within. Coming into the hall of the Sherman house at Newport (1874–5), you found a counterpart to the subtle play of spatial planes and surface patterns in stone and shingle outside created by the balanced tension of monumental fireplace and stair landing, and the various patternings of paneling, tilework, rugs, and stained-glass windows. And so on. It followed that for buildings so conceived in totality, no detail was too small for the architect to consider. Ironwork, grilles, benches, clocks, armchairs, side chairs, cathedras, and balustrades, all were subject to Richardson's supervision, because all contributed to a new total unity of design. And at this point a new concept of furniture develops, to match the expanded concept of the artist in society.

In 18th-century America builders and cabinetmakers had worked, generally speaking, as substantially independent equals. The one erected buildings, the other furnished them; together, they composed unified wholes. That could be so, because there existed a common body of classical principles to which each subscribed, ensuring that whatever furniture went into a house would have the same general proportions and detail as the architectural setting. But early-19th-century eclectic symbolism destroyed this natural rapport. Rising to the status of architects on the basis of pretensions to literary erudition, builders came to think of furniture as utilitarian and beneath their serious attention; by and large they were content to have furniture supplied from catalogues, made by artisans and eventually mere machine operators, working from whatever designs factory owners or pattern-book writers condescended to provide. By the 1850s and 60s conformity of architecture and furniture

116. *RICHARDSONIAN INTERIOR DESIGN* (A) *Entrance Hall of the Watts Sherman house, Newport, Rhode Island, designed by Richardson in 1874 and drawn by Stanford White for* The New York Sketch Book of Architecture. *Exposed ceiling beams, paneling, and other features representing a revival of 17th-century New England folk building are combined with "Romanesque" eclecticism.*

(116 B) *Furniture designed by Richardson for the Public Library of Woburn, Massachusetts, 1878. In keeping with the nonarchaeological character of "Richardsonian Romanesque," Richardson's furniture combined elements of William and Mary, 17th-century "Pilgrim," 18th-century Queen Anne, and other historic furniture styles with basically medieval forms and materials (golden oak, velvet, etc.), and was designed as an integral element in larger compositions, to complement the exposed ceiling beams, rich textiles, and massive structural forms of Richardsonian interiors.*

was rarely more than a happy accident. Now, in Richardsonian Romanesque, the old unity of architectural and furniture design was restored, but this time on a different basis, and with a different rationale. Now masons, carpenters, woodworkers found themselves equals again; not in independence, however, but in common dependence on a single controlling and directing mind. For now, like the capitalist manipulating the assets of unseen corporations, like the executive organizing businesses by telegraph, like Courbet in his "Studio," the architect sits at his desk conceiving on pieces of paper designs that will impose form and meaning on the world. Everything and everybody else he uses as impersonal instruments for his purpose—carpenters framing panels, masons setting foundation walls, cabinetmakers carving chairs and tables. Even as outstanding a landscape architect in his own right as Frederick Law Olmsted was merely an instrument, when he designed the picturesque setting for Richardson's North Easton Town Hall (1879).

Possibly because it was conceived and executed as a subdivision of his architecture, Richardson's furniture has rarely been sufficiently appreciated. We conventionally tend to think of furniture as a separate and independent art; and, as it happens, whenever Richardsonian furniture is seen today (which is not very often) it generally is in fact so presented, either in actual isolation (on a pedestal or in a photograph by itself) or in some architectural setting quite different from its original one. Misconception is inevitable. Properly to appreciate the kind of benches, chairs, clocks, or fireplaces Richardson designed, we need not only to see them complete with original appointments—thick velvet cushions with fringes and tassels to soften their stark frames, deep red and green leather to enrich their golden oak, perhaps a large potted plant in some robust bowl to heighten textural contrasts—but even more to see them in the original setting of a Richardsonian library or church in-

terior or parlor. There it is at once obvious how the structural lines and ornamental detail are designed in conjunction with hammerbeams and carved bookstalls and balustrades; and how similar to Richardsonian architecture in stylistic conception is the admixture within a generally medievalizing framework of vaguely Jacobean spindles, Queen Anne chair backs, William and Mary stretchers, and sweeping curves suggestive of the contemporary English Arts and Crafts movement. We need to see the furniture, that is to say, as an integral and inseparable part of a larger whole, no more to be understood apart from its total setting than are figures on the façade of a medieval cathedral, and just as inappropriately judged by classical standards.

In fact, Richardson's furniture reveals even better than his architecture how essentially new was the concept of art developing in his work. As a completely integral part of its surroundings, with no real existence of its own, it represents the very antithesis of the classical ideal of self-contained forms; it is fundamentally alien to the Renaissance tradition. Nor does Richardsonian furniture revive medieval tradition, either. In form, it is, if anything, less "Romanesque," more eclectic, than Richardsonian architecture; its spirit is thoroughly picturesque, in the High Victorian manner. In a word, it is itself; it belongs to a "tradition" of its own. Like Richardson's architecture, his furniture is ultimately distinguished by insistence on the intrinsic qualities of materials, on forthright expression of load and support. This is "functional" furniture in the same sense, and to the same extent, that Richardsonian Romanesque is "organic" architecture. In both is evident and embodied an instinctive preoccupation with "reality" that leads directly to the next, Late Victorian phase of art in America.

It was because Richardson was first to realize, however intuitively, the new architectural ideal of "reality" that Richardsonian Romanesque came as such a revelation to younger architects

117. RICHARDSON'S DIVERSE LEGACY
(A) Marshall Field Warehouse, Chicago, 1885–7. For a straightforward utilitarian purpose, Richardson made his most mature statement of direct expression of construction in stone. Of all his works, this was the greatest influence on the development of Louis Sullivan, Frank Lloyd Wright, and the Chicago school of "organic architecture."

like Ralph Adams Cram (1863–1942). Recalling his early years in *My Life in Architecture,* Cram described how

> ... for fifty years architecture in America fell to a lower level than history had ever before recorded ... vulgar, self-satisfied and pretentious, instinct with frontier ideology, and as rampantly individualistic as the society it so admirably expressed. In this maelstrom of horrid revelations and hesitant hopes, Richardson burst upon an astonished world as a sort of savior from on high. ... For a space of time we were all Richardsonians ... here was a real *man* at last.

But this was precisely why the Richardsonian

spell was so soon broken. For there was, as Richardson apparently did not recognize, an inherent and inescapable contradiction between the new concept of "reality" as the proper goal of art, and the forms and principles of Picturesque Eclecticism in which Richardsonian Romanesque tried to embody this concept.

By the time of Richardson's death in 1886 that contradiction was already plain. Over the preceding dozen years he had been steadily developing along two ultimately quite divergent lines, with the result that the twenty or thirty projects left at varying stages of completion in his office fell into two distinct categories. Largest and most important representative of the one was the Marshall Field Warehouse in Chicago, begun in 1885 and completed in 1887; of the other, the Chamber of Commerce Building in Cincinnati, commissioned in 1885 and executed 1886–8.

Connoisseurs have long considered the Marshall Field Building Richardson's best—in the sense of his most creative and progressive work. Certainly, with the exception of monuments as such, like the rough stone pyramid he designed to commemorate completion of the Union Pacific Railroad at Sherman, Wyoming, in 1879, or the so-called Town Hall at North Easton in Massachusetts—which never in fact functioned as a town hall but rather as a large three-dimensional memorial to Oliver Ames—the warehouse is Richardson's great demonstration of "pure" architecture. It is to his work what paintings like the "Rue de Berne" or "On the Beach" were to Manet's, or the various "nocturnes" to Whistler's—an exposition on the essential nature of his art, of what architecture "really" is. The Cincinnati building, however, is usually consigned a place alongside productions like his early high school in Worcester, Massachusetts (1869–71), in the category of unfortunate aberrations defying rational explanation. Yet essentially both proceeded from the same impulse and premises.

Richardson's Marshall Field Warehouse was in fact no more and no less "real" than the Cincinnati Chamber of Commerce Building; it is only the concept of "reality" that varies. In the one case "reality" is conceived in architectural terms—as an expression of the intrinsic qualities of stone: its texture, its capacity to bear weight, the constructional techniques appropriate in such a medium. Of this kind of "reality" the warehouse is the culminating statement in a long series that in retrospect can be seen stretching back to the first years of Richardson's maturity—to include the Glessner house in Chicago (1885–7), the Paine house in Waltham (1884–6), the Crane Memorial Library in Quincy (1880–83), the F. L. Ames Gate Lodge in North Easton (1880–81), the Brattle Square Church in

(117 B) Chamber of Commerce Building, Cincinnati, 1886–7. For a more pretentious urban monument, Richardson designed an ambitious assemblage of French medieval forms, with an effect quite different from the strong simplicity of his Field Building in Chicago. Yet it was equally the consummation of precedents in his earlier work; if Sullivan could point to the one as justification for his development, his Beaux-Arts rivals could quite as legitimately point to this and its antecedents as justification for theirs.

Boston (1870–72) and Grace Church in Medford with its glacial-bouldered walls (1867–9). In the case of the Cincinnati building, however, "reality" means archaeological accuracy, the demonstration of how forms of a past style may be adapted to modern uses with minimum sacrifice of historical reference. And this example of an early-16th-century château on the Loire serving functions of a late-19th-century chamber of commerce has its chain of antecedents, too—works like the Warder house in Washington (1885–7), the Higginson house in Boston, contiguous to McKim, Mead & White's Whittier house (1881–3), the American Merchants' Union Express Company Building in Chicago (1872) and the Hampden County Courthouse in Springfield, Massachusetts (1871–2).

In Richardson's mind there was evidently little incongruity between these two concepts. Many of his buildings (including most of those he and his generation particularly admired) embody elements of both—the Gratwick house in Buffalo (1886–9), for instance, or the Allegheny County Courthouse in Pittsburgh (1884–8), the Albany City Hall (1880–82), Sever Hall at Harvard (1878–80), the Cheney Block in Hartford, Connecticut (1875–6), and the State Hospital in Buffalo (1872–8). Trinity itself is one of the best examples. But on Richardson's death, the divergence of these two lines of development became very apparent. Within a dozen years two distinct and practically irreconcilable schools of American architecture were beginning to take shape. One, led by Sullivan and taking inspiration from the Marshall Field Warehouse, was working towards the concept of "organic architecture" later perfected by Frank Lloyd Wright. The other, represented by Charles F. McKim, Stanford White, and their followers, developed out of precedents set in Richardson's own office a monumental style based on academic reproduction of archaeological prototypes. In spirit these schools were antithetical, in practice hostile to each other; yet both could drape themselves with equal justice in Richardson's mantle and claim legitimate descent from his inspiration.

It seems a strange development. But it is neither unique nor mysterious. In retrospect we can see that precisely the same thing happened in the case of Richardson's contemporary in painting, Manet. By the 1890s, what had been for Manet no more than variant directions within his brush-stroke style had on the one hand developed into the facile academic impressionism of John Singer Sargent, Zorn, Sorolla, and their progeny of magazine illustrators, and on the other provided a technical vehicle for such entirely different, subjective, expressionist painters as Van Gogh and Edvard Munch. And the reason

for this is plain. Picturesque Eclecticism was losing its hold as a controlling principle: at the same time, artists were realizing that the concept of "reality" as a goal could be interpreted in quite as many diverse ways as the "beauty" it had displaced, and had even more complex implications. Consequently, these divergent trends within Richardsonian Romanesque (or impressionist theory) came to seem not variants but definite alternatives, compelling Richardson's successors in architecture (like the postimpressionists) to choose between them. How and why these choices were made is the theme of art history in Late Victorian America.

NOTES

The standard biography and scholarly study of Richardson's work long has been Henry-Russell Hitchcock, *The Architecture of H. H. Richardson and His Times* (1936, 2nd ed., Hamden, Conn., 1961). For good photographs of Furness's work, see "Fearless Frank Furness" (*Architectural Forum*, CXII, 1960, pp. 109–15). Sullivan's description of Furness quoted from Hugh Morrison, *Louis Sullivan* (1935), pp. 35–6. Characterization of Price by V. J. Scully, *The Shingle Style* (New Haven, 1955), p. 77.

Quotations of Richardson's office circular, from Lewis Mumford, *Brown Decades* (1931), p. 121; from R. A. Cram, *My Life in Architecture* (Boston, 1936), pp. 29, 31.

Some idea of the vogue for Richardsonian Romanesque may be gained from the various articles by Montgomery Schuyler reprinted as "The Richardsonian Interlude" by W. Jordy and R. Coe, *American Architecture and Other Writings by Montgomery Schuyler* (Cambridge, 1961), Sect. III, pp. 191–292. Richardson's furniture was described by Marianna Griswold Van Rensselaer, *Henry Hobson Richardson* (Boston, 1888), but largely forgotten afterwards. In January 1962 the Boston Museum of Fine Arts had an admirable exhibition of his furniture, for which Richard H. Randall, Jr., provided a short but illuminating catalogue note.

8. VARIETIES OF REALISTIC EXPERIENCE:
The Late Victorian Mind, c.1885—c.1930

WHAT WE CALL HERE the Late Victorian phase of art in America lasted from the 1880s into the 1920s. At first sight it seems that, in contrast to the preceding Early and High Victorian phases, it is governed by no single common denominator; that in it there are two distinct trends —one "conservative" or "academic," the other "progressive" or "modern"—which are basically incompatible, indeed antithetic. And Late Victorian art often is considered as if it consisted of two quite separate histories, the one representing a concluding chapter to Victorian art history, the other an introduction to the modern age. But if we analyze the period per se, rather than in terms of any relationship to what went before or came after it, we find that these two trends, while definite enough, are far from being so mutually exclusive as they might seem. Not only do they manifest much the same attitude and outlook in many respects, but, even more, they have the same psychological origin. For both represent reactions to, and developments out of, the Picturesque Eclecticism of the 1870s, particularly as represented by Richardsonian Romanesque and the shingle style.

We have seen how both massive Richardsonian stonework and the earthy textures of shingle-style mansions were a response to the pervasive sense of insecurity generated by the vast social and economic changes going on in the High Victorian age. But this response, given as it was in the High Victorian language of "picturesqueness," and depending as it did on artists personally creating images of solidity and moods of stability through more direct and original handling of bulky, old-fashioned materials, could not satisfy for long. For while such originality did offer some compensation for the increasingly mechanical quality of life in general, and the dehumanized relationship between men and their

work, it alone was no cure for the basic malaise of the age. Indeed, in some ways the cure was worse than the disease. For far from checking the erosion of old standards, such an extravagant emphasis on originality could only accelerate it; precisely this sense of being adrift on a chartless sea of untested principles, indeterminate values, and shifting social order was what essentially produced the uneasiness in the first place. And so, beginning in the late 1870s and increasingly through the 1880s, artists, scientists, politicians, all began to feel a new imperative to find some solid fundamentals on which to build for the future.

That such fundamentals could be found they never doubted. For along with the malaise of the High Victorian spirit, they had inherited its optimism: though the present be difficult, progress is somewhat inevitable; we cannot fail. The only question is, which way is "progress"? In what do the real fundamentals of art, of politics, of life consist? Do you return to the past and rediscover old fundamentals there? Or do you abandon the past and go forward to discover new fundamentals, or at least formulations of the old ones in terms meaningful to the new situation? Late Victorian art is the tangible record of these divergent approaches to the same basic problem. And if this art seems split into two separate histories, that is only because two equally basic and essentially equally legitimate kinds of answer were possible. That the resulting forms will be different is inevitable and obvious; but that both answers are representative expressions of their age should be obvious, too.

In political, social, and economic life, for instance, this is the great age of "reformers." All reformers start out on the premise that things are not what they have been or should be, and invoke fundamental principles as the means of bettering them. But as to what these fundamental principles are, or where one finds them, there is no agreement. The majority of reformers want to "go back" to what they conceive of as the "good old days." The temperance advocate and his successor the prohibitionist want a return to what they think of as a time of plain living and high thinking and sober acting. The social reformer and his successor the isolationist preach a return to village folkways on a national scale. As for the political reformer, Professor Hofstadter has pointed out, in *The American Political Tradition,* how "beginning with the time of Bryan" (and on into the era of "normalcy" in the 1920s)

> the dominant American ideal has been steadily fixed on bygone institutions and conditions. In early twentieth-century progressivism this backward-looking vision reached the dimensions of a major paradox. Such heroes of the progressive revival as Bryan, LaFollette, and Wilson proclaimed that they were trying to undo the mischief of the past forty years and re-create the old nation of limited and decentralized power, genuine competition, democratic opportunity, and enterprise.

But there is a minority which looks for salvation in the opposite direction, towards the future. Such are the "improper Bohemians" of Greenwich Village, with their "revolutionary" ideas on freedom of speech, love, and marriage; such are the social critics of many shades, from the "Ash Can" school of painters, and cartoonists like Art Young, to socialists and Communists, who see the problem of poverty and misery as solvable only by the replacement of established institutions with those founded on newer, juster, more "realistic" principles. The means may differ, so that the ends seem poles apart; yet both groups of reformers start with an identical impulse, and both are typical manifestations of their age. And it was the same in art. There were those—a majority—who felt somehow that the solution was to return to precedents and im-

prove on them; this meant in effect reproducing past styles as the Early Victorians had done, but with all the greater accuracy now allowed, and all the greater size and scale demanded, by half a century's accumulated wealth and scholarship. Then there were the "rebels"—or, depending on the point of view, "pioneers"—who started with the proposition that the past is gone and will never return; they see their job as creating a new architecture, with forms and principles suitable to what they recognize as a new society and a new technology.

Representative of the first group were "academicians" like Richard Morris Hunt; Richardson's successor firm of Shepley, Rutan & Coolidge; his pupils Charles Follen McKim and Stanford White; Ralph Adams Cram and Bertram Goodhue; the firm of Carrère & Hastings; John Russell Pope; Henry Bacon—men whose work was based on scholarly reproductions of Roman, Gothic, Georgian, and other specific historical styles. To this group also belong the colonial revivalists: William R. Ware (1832–1915), whose question in the *American Architect* for October 1877 whether "with our centennial year we have not discovered that we too have a past worthy of study" was motivated by his realization that "the old Fairbanks house at Dedham . . . forms a most picturesque pile"; Arthur Little (1852–1925) and William Ralph Emerson (1833–1918), who, by contrast, made the New England house type into a vehicle for functional planning and direct expression of materials; and the dozens of figures, highly trained architects and mere speculative builders alike, who splattered Dutch colonial and "Cape Cod" developments on the outskirts of every great city from Eugene to Baltimore and Spanish colonial retreats from Coral Gables to Beverly Hills. Their inspiration went back to the picturesque shingle style of the 1870s, but what they created was not so much picturesqueness as an evocation of past security and simplicity to soothe America in its transition into the tense status and anxious responsibilities of a major world power. Collectively and loosely we could call all these the "Beaux-Arts" men.

In the same way, we could call their rivals the "progressives" or "pioneers." Among them are included such members of the "Chicago school" as Louis Sullivan, John Root, and the young Frank Lloyd Wright, and the "California school" of Bernard Maybeck, Irving Gill, Charles S. and Henry M. Greene, and others. But merely to name them is to recognize at once how various were the approaches possible within their common framework of principles, and how many are the similarities between them and the Beaux-Arts men. All are primarily concerned in achieving what Sullivan in an article in the *Interstate Architect* for 1900 called "Reality in the Architectural Art," only secondarily with "beauty." And it is with this pervasive search for reality in mind that we can approach the age as a whole, and trace a unifying theme through all the complex confusions and contradictions of Late Victorian architecture and furniture in America.

9. "REVIVAL OF THE REVIVALS":
Late Victorian Academic Realism

TO SEVENTEEN-YEAR-OLD Ralph Adams Cram, coming to Boston in 1881 to begin an architectural apprenticeship, it seemed that American architecture was in a "general condition . . . of confusion worse counfounded." Looking back in 1936 on those early days, in *My Life in Architecture,* Cram wrote that "prior to 1830 nothing really bad had been done . . . hitherto, the Republic had been explicitly aristocratic, selective, even fastidious in the choices it made . . . from then on nothing good, except sporadically, came into existence, and for fifty years architecture in America fell to a lower level than history had ever before recorded." Even Richardson, as Cram saw him in retrospect, was not the "saviour" he had seemed, but had only added one more confused and illogical eclectic style to the heap. "It was evident that, compared even with contemporary Europe, we were artistic barbarians, and that for our own national credit that condition of things would have to be changed." Then came what seemed to him the miraculous transformation. "The American Institute of Architects . . . took on a new life; schools of architecture, notably those of Massachusetts Institute of Technology and Columbia University, began systems of consistent training, and more and more students began going over to the French Ecole des Beaux Arts, at that time the one great and effective centre of architectural training. The 'American Renaissance' had begun." Already by 1890 it was apparent that the Early Victorian concept of consistent stylistic symbolism was not the buried and forgotten thing it had seemed only a decade before, but was on the way to being vigorously and successfully brought back to life. Archaeological correctness was returning; all the old styles—Roman, Gothic, Italianate—had their new young adherents and protagonists, and a new "American" style, reviving colonial Georgian forms, had

emerged. History, it seemed, was about to repeat itself. By 1890 the Early Victorian revival styles—only "improved," like Batty Langley's "Gothick," by "rules and proportions"—were themselves having a revival. An "academic realism" characteristic of the third, Late Victorian phase in American art was well established.

"Elder statesman" of the movement was Richard Morris Hunt. Born in Brattleboro, Vermont, Hunt spent 1843–55, the most formative years of his life, in Paris, not only as a student, but in actual professional practice, and according to the memoirs of his wife "was constantly taken for a Frenchman [even as late as his return trip to Paris in 1889], which, considering . . . his foreign way of gesticulating and his perfect French, is not extraordinary; indeed, when he first came back to America, and for years afterward, it was difficult for him to write in English." And although, as she says, "he was always indignant at the supposition that he could be anything else but an American," it was Hunt's Frenchness that made his reputation and professional success; that put him in a position to compete on equal terms with the foreign-born architects who dominated the fashionable architectural world of New York in the 1860s and 70s as the ordinary American-trained architect never could. At the same time, the disciplined consistency of his French training made him a natural leader of the reaction against Picturesque Eclecticism that set in during the 1880s. From the first, Hunt had important and lucrative New York commissions in which he followed to some extent the prevailing picturesque eclectic canons of asymmetry, polychromy, variegated outline, and mixed motifs. But in retrospect it is evident that his Picturesque Eclecticism never had the freedom—or as he would have put it, license—of American contemporaries, or even pupils of his like George Post (1837–1913) or Frank

Furness. Throughout the 1860s and 70s he manifested a concern for consistency of function and, if not precisely of style, certainly of stylistic effect essentially foreign to the others and clearly anticipating his own later development. It is no accident that Hunt was the architect of the first building specifically designed to suit the needs of artists and to be co-operatively owned by them (Studio Building on West 10th Street, 1857); of the first building specifically designed as an apartment house in the modern sense, with self-contained living units on each floor reached by elevators (Stuyvesant Apartment, East 18th Street, 1869–70); and of what Professor Weisman has called the first building specifically designed as a skyscraper (the old Tribune Building at Printing House Square, 1873–5). It is no coincidence, either, that all of these buildings, in contrast to similar types (compare the Tribune Building with its rival for first-skyscraper honors, George B. Post's Western Union Telegraph Building, also 1873–5), show the same tendency to simplification—within the limits possible in such an age, of course—and, more significantly, to drawing details more or less from a single period; or that Hunt's own house at Newport (1870–71, later sold to George Waring) seemed to Professor Scully possibly the "first built evidence of colonial revivalism to exist anywhere." And so it comes as no surprise, finally, that it was Hunt who in 1879 signaled the revival of the Revivals by designing for William Kissam Vanderbilt a house on Fifth Avenue at 52nd Street (completed 1883) which displayed for the

118. BEAUX-ARTS ELEGANCE AND LATE VICTORIAN LITERACY
(A) The Breakers, built by Richard Morris Hunt for Cornelius Vanderbilt at Newport, Rhode Island, 1892–5. A 16th-century Genoese merchant's palace—three centuries out of time.

first time a real and scholarly consistency of period style—plan, elevation, and details all drawn from early-16th-century French prototypes in Francis I's châteaux on the Loire.

To other architects Hunt was the first great inspiration of their attempt to restore archaeological correctness and order to American architecture on a grand scale. Charles McKim, for instance, used to walk up Fifth Avenue late at night to admire Hunt's Vanderbilt mansion; he "always," he said, "slept better for enjoying the sight." And for the American new-rich it was an inspiration, too. For the first time they realized how wealth and social position might be visibly manifested not merely in the size and lavishness of one's house, but in the degree of accuracy with which the architect had copied acceptable European models. Thenceforth to the day of his death Hunt was kept busy with commissions for similar great mansions. Most of them were in a similar late-Gothic-to-early-Renaissance manner—Ochre Court at Newport 1885–9), the Elbridge T. Gerry château on Fifth Avenue at 61st Street (1891), Mrs. William Astor's double house on Fifth Avenue at 65th Street (1891), and, climaxing them all, George Washington Vanderbilt's Biltmore near Asheville, North Carolina (1890–95), largest country estate in America. But when variety or a specific symbolism seemed to demand it, Hunt could switch styles quite as easily as any Early Victorian; to that extent he betrayed how early in the century he had been born. So he might design Ellerslie at Rhinecliff, New York, in Tudor "half-timber" (1886), a marble house at Newport for William Kissam Vanderbilt in Imperial Roman tinged with Louis Seize (1892–5), or Belcourt for Oliver H. P. Belmont in the Louis Treize manner of the earliest buildings at Versailles (Newport, 1892). But for Hunt there were really only two proper styles—the Gothic and the classical; all others were variants of them. And as in his Fifth Avenue châteaux Hunt brought the old Gothic Revival villas of Davis and Downing back to new, bombastic, and pedantic life, so

he revived the old "classical American" idiom on a comparably stupendous scale. It was Hunt who decided on Imperial Roman as the style best suited to express the spirit of American civilization in the Columbian Exposition at Chicago in 1893; his Administration Building and general plan there set the pattern for a grandiose official return to what was alleged to be the Jeffersonian ideal of white Roman architecture as the symbolic manifestation of American greatness. But of all his buildings, The Breakers for Cornelius Vanderbilt at Newport (1892–5) was perhaps the most famous; and what is this but a colossal version of the Italianate villas under construction in America during Hunt's youth? Here is the same vaguely "Italian" exterior, with its arcades and recessed piazzas, this time, of course, specifically modeled on 16th-century Genoese merchants' palaces. And here is the same concept of interior design; as in Notman's Riverside with its Italianate exterior and Gothic library, neither impinging on the other, or Fountain Elms, each room, however different in style from its neighbor it may be, is complete in itself—Louis Quatorze, Louis Quinze, Louis Seize, or whatever.

This, then, is the Early Victorian age revived; and however errant the whole thing might later seem to some, in the 1880s and 90s it looked to most—as Cram expressed it so well—like an "American Renaissance." Even such a supporter of the "Chicago school" as Montgomery Schuyler saw no incongruity in praising Hunt as well: "What have our modern times to show more noteworthy than this [Biltmore] as an example of a free and romantic domestic architecture, or how is it less noteworthy than the châteaux of the Loire, except that it has been preceded by them?" he asked in a commemorative essay (1895). The direction Hunt pointed seemed not only the plainest avenue out of High Victorian confusion into a new era of rule and order, but the way to achieve a demonstrable "reality" of style as well, one securely based on tested traditions. What is more—and this is by no means least important—it was a path down which clients of established wealth but unestablished social position could easily be led; like Town before them, Hunt and his compeers had only to turn to well-stocked libraries to overwhelm waverers with documented proof of scholarly correctness and social acceptability. No wonder that for the next few decades the biggest commissions and the greatest prestige went to whichever architects best exemplified, refined, and elaborated the precedent Hunt had set. No wonder, either, that the number of architects working this vein on a greater or smaller scale seemed to be legion. To attempt mentioning even a majority, let alone all of them, would be tedious and superfluous. Let us here consider three typical firms, each of them distinguished for a particular "speciality" of style.

Representative of a firm specializing in "American symbolism" was McKim, Mead & White. For Charles Follen McKim (1847–1908) and Stanford White, the preoccupation with such symbolism began early; at the time both were working in Richardson's offices, they toured New England to study the detail of colonial houses in New England following the great stir created by the "early American log cabin" exhibited at the Philadelphia Centennial of 1876. When they joined with William Rutherford Mead (1846–1928) to found a firm of their own in 1879, their "American style" at first meant little more than vague elements of folk building—stained shingles, weather-beaten clapboard, and walls of fieldstone—handled in a spirit of Richardsonian Picturesque Eclecticism, as in the casinos at Newport (1879–81) and Narragansett Pier (1884–6) and the Low house at Bristol, Rhode Island (1887), or the First Methodist (Lovely Lane) church in Baltimore (1882–6). It preserved and even developed Richardson's feeling for the "real" texture and quality of materials. But both designing partners had inherent archaeological leanings—McKim had studied at the École des Beaux-Arts from 1867 to 1870, and White's greatest achievement in Richardson's

office had been to model the tower of Trinity, Boston, on Salamanca Cathedral—so that by the mid-1880s they began increasingly to see "Americanism" as better exemplified in the more strictly classical forms of the early republic, and moved steadily out of Richardson's orbit into Hunt's, leaving the further development of a colonial style to local architects like John Calvin Stevens (1856–1940) or William Ralph Emerson. In the Henry Villard houses (New York, 1885) and the Boston Public Library (1888), McKim, Mead, and White worked in a revived Italianate manner; in the house for E. D. Morgan at Newport (1890–91), colonialisms were submerged in a formality of planning and classical detail claimed to be of Jeffersonian inspiration; finally, as chief architects of the World's Columbian Exposition in Chicago, they found in the Imperial Roman pattern (originally fixed by Hunt) the perfect American symbol, and made it and themselves famous. The Roman grandeur of their Fair, of their Rhode Island capitol in Providence (1895–1901); their University Club (1899), Morgan Library (1902), and Pennsylvania Station (1906–10) in New York; their remodelings of the White House undertaken for Theodore Roosevelt (1902)—all combined to set a taste that swept the country. Until well into the 1920s Imperial Roman architecture and Louis Seize furniture remained the expression of official American ideals and upper-class American aspirations, promulgated alike by McKim, Mead, and White's countless imitators and emulators—men like Paul Cret (1876–1945), John Russell Pope (1874–1937, architect of the National Gallery in Washington), or Henry Bacon (1866–1924, architect of the Lincoln Memorial, 1914–22), and, of course, their own successor firm, responsible for so many Imperial Roman and "Georgian" campus buildings all over the country.

Outstanding representative of the revived Gothic Revival was the firm of Ralph Adams Cram, Bertram Grosvenor Goodhue (1869–1924), and Frank W. Ferguson (1861–1926). Cram and Goodhue could and would use other styles if need be, of course—Georgian for Protestant Evangelicals (Second Unitarian, Boston); Spanish Renaissance for Texans (Lovett Hall, Rice University, Houston, 1910–13); Spanish Baroque Colonial for Californians (California Building, Panama–California International Exposition, San Diego, 1915); and Goodhue's Nebraska State Capitol at Lincoln was a famous example of "modernistic" architecture in the 1920s. But for Cram especially, all other styles were but pale reflections of Gothic. Gothic was for him, as it had been for Pugin, Upjohn, and other Early Victorians, not so much a kind of architecture as a means of moral and social reform. His writings, his speeches, his buildings were all part of a crusade to restore "truth" and "beauty" to the world. For him, as for Plato and Palladio, these qualities were identical; Cram differed from them, and from Early Victorians too, however, in subsuming both under a concept of "reality" which he believed was best embodied in the kind of honest structure and direct expression of materials to be found in High Gothic architecture. In this spirit he and his followers often turned their backs on other kinds of reality—social, technological, even financial—characteristic of their own age, to design monuments that in construction and function were intended to carry 13th-century realism into the early 1900s: collegiate buildings (e.g., additions and chapel at the United States Military Academy, West Point, 1903–4; Graduate College, Princeton University, 1913) presuming to evoke and revive the cloistered atmosphere of education in medieval Oxford and Cambridge; the Episcopal cathedrals of St. John the Divine in New York (begun in Romanesque, transformed by Cram into a High Gothic cathedral to be built over generations to come) and in Washington, D.C.; and Gothic churches for any denomination tending to return to medieval sacramental or liturgical order—the Episcopal church of St. Thomas in New York (1908), the First Baptist in Pittsburgh (1909), the Fourth Presbyterian in Chicago (1912), the Swedenborgian at Bryn

Athyn, Pennsylvania (1913–14), and so on.

Less polemically inclined than Cram, Goodhue & Ferguson or McKim, Mead & White, and so more representative of the tides of academic taste in the Late Victorian period, was the firm formed to carry on Richardson's practice after his sudden death in the spring of 1886, by his associates George F. Shepley (1858–1903), Charles H. Rutan (1851–1914), and Charles Allerton Coolidge (1858–1936). Nowhere is Late Victorian architectural history better summarized, perhaps, than in Professor Forbes's study of this firm and its successors in the *Journal of the Society of Architectural Historians* (XVII, 3, 1958). The firm began, in a spirit of fidelity to the Master's memory, to carry out the backlog of some two dozen projects left in his office; but, except for continuing a few (e.g., Allegheny County Courthouse in Pittsburgh, Chamber of Commerce Building, Cincinnati) practically completed already, they almost immediately began to depart from his principles and precedent in the direction being set by Hunt, McKim, and White. First came the appearance of Italianate mannerisms mixed in the Richardsonian Romanesque, and a general smoothing of texture and simplification of ornament (e.g., Ames Building, Boston, 1889–92). Then when the firm struck out on its own, "there was almost a historical reenacting of the transition from medieval to Renaissance ideals and forms." The campus they designed for Leland Stanford Junior University at Palo Alto, California, in 1888 called for buildings in a smooth, almost Byzantine kind of Romanesque, laid out on a severely classical axial plan like Union College and the University of Virginia nearly three-quarters of a century before; the Montreal Board of Trade Building (1893) was half Italian and half Romanesque in style; and when in 1894–5 Shepley, Rutan, and Coolidge added a Romanesque west porch to Trinity Church in Boston, it was less out of belief in Richardsonian principles than in pure academic conformity to an existing structure. Already in 1891 they had competed for the state capitol

(118 B) Thirteenth-century cathedral nave of the Cathedral Church of St. John the Divine in New York City, built on the designs of Ralph Adams Cram, who was appointed consulting architect in 1907 and replaced the original designer, Grant LaFarge (1862–1938), in 1911.

commission in Providence with an Italianate design almost as Roman as the winning one by McKim, Mead & White; a few years more, and the Imperial Roman style was equally their favorite. In this style they built the Public Library (1895) and Art Institute (1897) in Chicago; thenceforth they and their successor firms used Imperial Roman for courthouses, banks, office buildings, and hospitals all over the country, well into the 1920s. At the same time, however, they manifested the influence of Cram's type of medieval idealism in turning to Gothic to suggest appropriate symbolism for higher education in the campuses of Chicago (c.1900–c.1930), Oklahoma (Norman, 1910), Southern Methodist (Dallas, 1910), Nebraska (Lincoln, 1920), and Vanderbilt (Nashville, hospital and medical school, 1925). And for Harvard, where they were entrenched for decades as the favored designers, they designed one building after another in the Wrennish-colonial manner called "Georgian" which schools without medieval leanings tended to adopt in the interests of creating a sense of campus tradition (e.g., Perkins and Conant halls, 1895; Fogg Art Museum, 1927; Dunster House, c.1930).

Versatile, thoroughly eclectic, often pretentious but always careful to imitate past styles with ingenious correctness no matter how unprecedented the occasion for their revival might be, Shepley, Rutan & Coolidge was but one of dozens of similar firms typifying the academic concept of "realism" in the Late Victorian age, all working on the same general principles. These principles, rather than redundant names and dates, are of lasting significance, for in them was expressed the fundamental character and outlook of this period in American civilization. I think at least six can be defined, roughly as follows:

(1) *Literacy*. First and most obvious, perhaps, is the intense self-consciousness of this academic copying from the past. These neorevivalists are even more literate than their Early Victorian prototypes. They collect great libraries

of books and photographs—"during the years that Richard passed in Paris," Hunt's wife remembered typically, "in fact from the very commencement of his architectural career, he accumulated architectural books, denying himself almost anything that he might add to his collection." And they write voluminously themselves. This was a great period for founding new architectural magazines and journals; publishing articles in them is one of the main ways (besides choosing ancestors with care) that Late Victorian academic architects build careers. Many become authors of note; Ralph Adams Cram, for instance, wrote every bit as stylishly and dogmatically as he designed, while even in his lifetime a man like Russell Sturgis (1836–1909) was much better known as the author of prolific articles and books on art and architectural history than as architect of four picturesque Gothic buildings at Yale (1870–85) or the Farmers' & Mechanics' Bank in Albany. And books are written about them; sumptuous productions, often enough, like the *Monograph of the Work of McKim, Mead and White* (1915). But it is not the late Victorians' reliance on books alone that makes them so self-conscious about style, or even their inheritance of the High Victorian passion for history as such. Basically it is that they know their models at first hand as their Early Victorian predecessors never could or did.

In the decades since the Civil War, sea travel became steadily faster, safer, and commoner; the boats that brought immigrants over to make gilded-age fortunes began to take more and more Americans back to see European architecture for themselves—not merely architectural students for the École des Beaux-Arts, but tourists, off to compare the wonders of the Old World with those of the New. At first these Americans "abroad" were often enough the kind of "innocents" Mark Twain took off so well, aglow with the excitement of their one great and never-to-be-repeated adventure, eagerly looking at everything, seeing nothing. But during the last

(118 C) A court in "Vizcaya," near Miami, built for James Deering by F. Burrall Hoffman, Jr., and Paul Chalfin, 1913–16. Now Dade County Art Museum.

two decades of the century a new kind of tourist appeared. People born to wealth, accustomed to luxury, began taking regular travels to Europe as an accepted right, anticipated privilege, even obligation of their class. And it is from them that the demand for a new, more "realistic" kind of imitation of European models comes. Little Greek Revival houses of the 1830s or Gothic Revival churches of the 1850s seem merely laughable to people familiar with Athens and Westminster Abbey; after Flanders and Provence, bits and pieces of medieval monuments piled together in the Richardsonian manner appear provincial and naïve. Just as the "gentleman" is now—or at least claims to be—a cosmopolitan, equally at home in New York, London, Paris, and Boston, so now he expects his art to be the "real thing." Ideally, that would mean transporting European art to America wholesale. And it is at the end of the 19th century, indeed, that the eccentric American "millionaire collector" makes his appearance, trotting about the world with a crowd of dealer-agent-experts like pack mules strung out behind him, buying ancestral busts and tapestries, paintings and furniture by the boatload for shipment to Newport or Los Angeles or Miami. Sometimes, too, he buys a Spanish monastery or a Chinese temple or an English town hall to put his acquisitions in. But on the whole this is not a very satisfactory arrangement; it is easier to construct some replica at home, and architectural replicas of Loire châteaux or Genoese palaces are still socially acceptable, as copies of Titian or Raphael no longer are. To the building of such replicas, then, some of the best-trained architects of the age give their time and talents; and in them, the characteristic "literacy" of Late Victorian art finds its most dramatic expression.

Here the object is quite literally to counterfeit the real thing. These Louis Quatorze dining halls or Rococo bedrooms or Italian Renaissance courts are imitations as exact as several generations of accumulated scholarship can make them; indeed, in many cases what is involved is not so much imitation as simply the assembling and co-ordination of authentic details—tapestries, chairs, sculpture, cornices, doorways—which have been stripped from the floors and walls of European palaces and transported bodily over the ocean. These architects are not so much designers as arrangers of period-room displays:

On Christmas Day, 1916, when the late James Deering opened the doors of Vizcaya in Miami, Florida, he saw a dream come true. For 25 years he had collected in Europe architectural backgrounds, rare period furniture, textiles, sculpture, and ceramics. To enshrine them he built Vizcaya. . . . The architects, F. Burrall Hoffman, Jr., and Paul Chalfin, designed the building to accommodate the remarkable collection. . . . Mr. Deering leased large warehouses in which he and the architects, over and over again, experimentally laid out and furnished room after room. The height of the second floor was determined by the size of a tall entranceway . . . from the palace built for Niccolo Pisani and his son, Vettor, daring Venetian admirals of the 14th century when Venice was a great sea power. . . .

The tall, graceful doors at either end of the loggia once stood in the vestibule of the Hotel Beauharnais in Paris, . . . occupied by Napoleon's stepson Eugène. . . . The library shows . . . a fine Corinthian mantel, over which an ancient Roman mosaic has been set into the wall. . . . The style of Vizcaya's 18th-century salon is Louis XV . . . [the] size of the room determined by the plaster ceiling, which once graced the Palazzo Rossi in Venice. . . . In the music room . . . ornate ceiling and paneled, painted canvas walls came out of a Milanese palace. . . .

Obviously in such circumstances there can be no question of any High Victorian freedoms of invention; each room must be "correct" in itself. "Originality" in the High Victorian sense of mixing styles from many periods, or even in the Richardsonian sense of mixing details from different styles within a single period, can never be reconciled with the ultimate object of creating a monument to a patron's cultured taste. Far better to be correct at the risk of being timid and conventional than to be original at the risk of being vulgar—for any suggestion of vulgarity is what the average Late Victorian patron, so recently risen from lower-class ranks, above all passionately wants to avoid.

Of all this there can be only one outcome—the creation of a kind of "instant museum." Vizcaya, now the Dade County Museum, is only one of dozens of such mansions which later became museums in fact, more or less simply by being made available to the public. All over the country you can find them still. Sometimes only a room or two has been preserved, like the "Moorish Room" from John D. Rockefeller's 54th Street residence, in the Brooklyn Museum; or the "Indian Room" from Henry LeGrand Cannon's mansion in remote Burlington, Vermont, whose exotic potpourri of Burmese sofas and Tibetan prayer rugs and Persian lamps and suits of Turkish mail was bequeathed to be forever on display untouched in the Robert Hull Fleming Museum. Oftener it is the whole house itself; Hunt's Breakers at Newport, for instance, or Henry Clay Frick's palace at Fifth Avenue and 70th Street in New York, built in the Imperial Roman–Louis Seize manner by John M. Carrère (1858–1911) and Thomas Hastings (1860–1929) in 1914, displaying its owner's collection of paintings, sculptures, enamels, and porcelains. Greatest of all, qualitatively in a class by itself, is Winterthur near Wilmington, Delaware. So authentically did Mr. Henry Francis du Pont and his scholarly collaborators, Joseph Downs and architect-historian Thomas T. Waterman, furnish his rambling ancestral mansion (built at various times during the 19th century) with American antiquities and interiors taken bodily from old American houses that he needed only to open Winterthur's doors to the public in 1952 to make it one of the world's great museums of decorative arts. Late Victorian archaeological realism and literacy could hardly go further.

(2) *"Honesty."* Going along with this realistic copying of past styles is a new awareness of the "real nature" of architectural structure and materials. This too is a High Victorian inheritance from Richardson; but the extent to which academic architects could indulge it depended, of course, entirely on the character of the style they were using. In American colonial styles, where natural expression of materials was an inherent quality, architects effectively and fully exploited the texture and pattern of New England shingle, clapboard, and fieldstone; Georgian brick and marble trim; Spanish colonial tile and stucco. If it was not entirely true that William Ralph Emerson was, as his obituary in the *AIA Journal* for 1918 declared, "the creator of the shingle country house of the New England coast," still he, along with his academic contemporaries, had indeed "taught his generation how to use local materials without apology, but rather with pride in their rough homespun character." Similarly, the concurrent vogue for reproducing "colonial" furniture, as inaugurated by Gustav Stickley (1858–1942) in the 1880s, was originally inspired by the same Ruskinian "honest craftmanship" that later led to Stickley's "mission" style. Equally inherent, of course, was a frank expression of construction in Gothic; Cram's archaeologically perfect Gothic vaulting, and Goodhue's free renditions of Gothic furniture, contributed rivulets at least to the stream of "functionalist" theory in the period. Even in the classical styles you can recognize a kind of "realism" in the treatment of materials. As in his earliest "stick style" houses he showed a competent awareness of the expressive possibilities of wood, so in an Imperial Roman mansion like The Breakers Hunt went out of his way to express what he could of the smoothness of marble, and create subtle contrasts in color and texture with interior combinations of blue marble, tawny alabaster, gilt, and velvet. To this extent Hunt, McKim, White, and Cram clearly belong in the same age as Sullivan, Maybeck, and Wright. Where they differ from the latter is, of course, that the same archaeological realism which restricted their freedom of individual invention in style restricted personal expres-

sion of structure or materials even more. If materials and structure were expressed in the style they were using, they could express them; if not (and in the favored styles it was usually not), they remained bound fast to their prototypes, and nothing new could grow.

(3) *Generalized symbolism.* This same precise awareness of the nature of the styles being used accounts for yet another characteristic of Late Victorian art—the abstractness of its symbolism, in contrast to the specific associations of Early Victorian styles. Pugin or Upjohn could never have written, as did Cram in *My Life in Architecture,* that "after all,"

> Gothic is no isolated style with its own individual laws wrought out of nothing for its own original ends. The *forms* of beauty vary from age to age; the creative and controlling laws are ever the same, and it is because these were recognized and obeyed in Trinity [i.e., by Richardson], in the McKim Library [i.e., Boston Public] and in St. Augustine [i.e., Ponce de Leon Hotel, by Carrère & Hastings, 1887] that they are all good. . . .

because for all his love of the Middle Ages Cram knew, as those predecessors of his could not, to what extent Gothic was the product of economic and social conditions as well as religious impulse. It was impossible for him to accept the

119. LATE VICTORIAN "AMERICAN" SYMBOLISM

Three buildings of the years between the wars illustrating how Late Victorian architects, though too knowledgeable now to read specific meanings into particular styles or to mix them, remain Victorian enough to associate ideas with historical forms.

(A) Post Office, Middlesboro, Kentucky, a revival of the old official Greek Revival style of public buildings, typical of Federal architecture; "colonial" styles were a frequent variant.

naïve notions of Gothic being specifically and exclusively devised to express Christian ideas. When he called Gothic Christian and Catholic, he meant not that it made specific and dogmatic statements in symbolic language, but rather that in Gothic architecture, as in Catholic Christianity, was to be found the highest embodiment of those universal principles of truth and beauty which constituted the good life generally. Similarly, whereas for Early Victorians the "American" connotations of classical architecture were precise and specific—Roman Republican virtue, Greek democratic liberty, and so on—Late Victorians understood the "American" implications of Imperial Roman railroad stations or Louis Seize mansions in a far more general way, as

ABOVE:

(119 B) Greenbrier Hotel, White Sulphur Springs, West Virginia. Built to replace the Old White Hotel which stood at this famous resort from 1858 to 1922, in an appropriately "colonial" style. Even as late as this, the typical Victorian attitude to architecture remains strong: the central portico (vaguely reminiscent of the White House) and the five-story colonnade (vaguely reminiscent of "old Southern man-sions"), are quite obviously extraneous ornament, added to give "meaning" to an otherwise undistinguished set of blocklike shapes.

BELOW:

(119 C) New Mexico State Supreme Court building, part of the capitol group in Santa Fe, in what is officially called "a modified form of territorial style architecture . . . decorated with the Zia Indian sun symbol."

manifestations of the wealth, power, and cultural achievements possible under the American system of government. Late Victorians could see "Americanism" embodied impartially in such diverse forms as rough, rambling, shingled Cape Cod cottages, the plain brick walls and chaste rows of dormers on "Georgian" college dormitories, or grandiose Roman porticoes and marble walls, because fifty years of intervening scholarship enabled them to see each of these styles in the perspective of given times and conditions in American history, understand them as general manifestations of the American past rather than specific statements about the American character.

(4) *"Bigness."* Where Late Victorian differs most obviously from the Early Victorian it superficially resembles is in scale. Everything about it is big. The country is big now; that earlier America of small towns and tidy courthouses and simple citizen-farmers seems very, very far away, and architecture shows it. Individually, buildings of every kind are bigger than comparable types fifty years before. Just as Andalusia or Montebello at the beginning of the century might have served as outbuildings for the mansions of Newport and Fifth Avenue, so in place of the neat residences illustrated by Downing or Lafever, or Mark Twain's little house in Hannibal, come those spacious high-ceilinged many-roomed wide-porched houses in which the Penrod Schofields of prosperous middle-class small towns grew up around 1900—hard to heat, costly to paint, with cramped kitchens and minuscule chambers for the hired help, but pretentious parlors for entertaining the rector, the literary circle, or dinner guests. Theodore Roosevelt, archetypal image and ideal of the early 1900s in his temperament, symbolized the era too in the size both of his person and of his house at Oyster Bay. He planned Sagamore Hill, according to Hermann Hagedorn, as

> . . . a home . . . with elbow room. . . . The architects gave it to him. The agglomeration . . . that they designed was nothing if not spacious. The ten bedrooms on the second

floor and two on the third, besides maids' rooms, suggested a program of family increase which might well have frightened a young wife about to have her first baby. . . . "I wished [Roosevelt instructed Lamb and Rich, his architects] a big piazza . . . big fireplaces for logs. . . ." The architects gave him . . . foundations twenty feet thick; joists, rafters, and roofboards . . . in proportion. . . . Theodore's desires regarding fireplaces were fully covered, moreover, with four on the first floor, four on the second, and a dumb-waiter for firewood rising from the cellar to feed them. Apart from the satisfaction of crackling logs and dancing flames, Theodore was assuming—quite correctly, as the event proved—that even two hot-air furnaces in the cellar might need supplementing.

This age, too, built factories of a complexity, and office buildings on a scale, unimaginable earlier. Compared to the gargantuan complex of plants the Ford Motor Company spread around Detroit in the early decades of the 20th century, for instance, the little New England factories of a century before appeared as ridiculously primitive as the bicycle shed in which Henry Ford built his first car. Nor could the men of the 1830s who hailed Isaiah Rogers's Tremont House in Boston as the wonder of an age have dreamt of something like the Traymore Hotel, which William L. Price (1861–1916) and M. Hawley McLanahan (1865–1916) built at Atlantic City only seventy years later (1906), let alone imagined that by the 1930s such miniature cities contained in a single shell would be commonplace in every metropolis.

And these buildings were put into settings of comparable grandeur. "Make no little plans!" wrote Daniel H. Burnham (1846–1912), greatest city planner of his generation, in 1912. "They have no magic to stir men's blood. . . . Make big plans. . . . Remember that our sons and grandsons are going to do things that would stagger us." In some ways he was right; but it was rather men like Burnham who staggered his successors. Burnham was the very embodiment of the Late Victorian mania for bigness; he had, Louis Sul-

120. LATE VICTORIAN "BIGNESS"

(A) World's Columbian Exhibition, Chicago, 1893. It was Richard Morris Hunt who determined the prevailing Imperial Roman style of the Fair; but Daniel Burnham set the great scale, which more than anything else impressed its visitors. For most people it was the sheer "bigness" of the Fair that best expressed the theme of four hundred years' growth since Columbus. Certainly that was what impressed the correspondents of the London Graphic in a long article published May 6, 1893; this panorama is typical of the way they illustrated it.

livan said scornfully, an "unconscious stupor in bigness," which was for him a dream, "a fixed irrevocable purpose in life, for the sake of which he would bend or sacrifice all else." It was Burnham who set the colossal scale of the 1893 Chicago Fair. In his offices was designed (probably by Charles G. Atwood, 1849–1895) the first Fair building, the temporary railroad station behind the Administration Building site which ultimately begot a mighty progeny of vaulted and columned Roman baths serving passengers from Vancouver to Philadelphia, and which was so immediately popular that, as Professor Meeks has remarked in The Railroad Station, "a scale nearly that of Michelangelo at St. Peter's was considered normal for public buildings in the early part of this century." Burnham had a large

part, too, in the evolution of skyscraper design in Chicago. What appealed to him about the ever more complex multistoried office buildings and warehouses developing from the 1880s on was primarily the opportunities they afforded to revel in elephantine scale. This he expressed at first, when the skilful engineer and sensitive artist John W. Root (1850–1891) was his partner, in terms of basic structure and materials. In a sequence of buildings beginning with the Montauk of 1882 and climaxed by the Monadnock of 1889–91, Burnham and Root demonstrated how impressive in itself the simple unadorned bulk of masonry required to carry ten or sixteen stories could be. Beginning with the Masonic Temple undertaken in the years of Root's death, however, and increasingly after his work on the

379

(120 B) A lagoon in Coral Gables, Florida, c.1925. Planned by founder George E. Merrick (1886–1942) in collaboration with architect H. George Fink, Coral Gables remains a monument to the great Florida boom of the 1920s and the Late Victorian taste of that decade. Calling for a series of villages in various styles—"Mediterranean," "Chinese compound," "American colonial," among others—Merrick's plans evidenced the characteristic bigness and literacy; their use of rough coral rock, tile, and brick, how the Beaux-Arts manner allowed honest expression of materials within limits of a chosen style. Even more typically Late Victorian was Merrick's loose and vague symbolism; Coral Gables architecture stood, he said, for "(1) Romance (2) Beauty (3) Inspiration, and (4) Home."

Chicago Fair, Burnham began expressing bigness in terms of contrasting scale. This principle was seen most strikingly, perhaps, in his Flatiron Building in New York (1901). Executed in classical detail on a consistently colossal scale intended to dwarf the "ordinary" buildings around, the Flatiron Building looked, originally at least, like something Gulliver might have built in Lilliput, an enormous toy, proportioned to itself but not at all to its environment, built by and for giants.

Burnham's most grandiose feats, however, were in the realm of city planning. This was the age when architects designed not merely little Places d'Armes or single parks, but took whole cities for their province. Burnham gave the lead with his spacious "Great White City" in Chicago;

only eight years later he, McKim, the sculptor Saint-Gaudens, and old Frederick Law Olmsted were appointed by the McMillan Commission to revive L'Enfant's original plan for Washington, realization of which has been going on ever since. Subsequently Burnham worked out grand-scale plans for Cleveland, for San Francisco, for Manila in the Philippines, and, most notable of all, an entire regional plan for Chicago (1906–9) so comprehensive that as simplified in the Wacker Manual it was used to teach local history in Chicago schools. At the same time, college campuses were being laid out in a comparably expansive manner.

It was typical of the age that when Jefferson's Rotunda at the University of Virginia burned in 1895, McKim, Mead & White should not only rebuild it as a more archaeologically correct imitation of the Pantheon, but make the interior "more spacious," and that they should then proceed to finish off the campus as if they understood the Sage of Monticello to mean he had wanted an "academical city" rather than a "village." In 1902 a formally classical campus was designed for the University of California by Émile Bénard, a French Beaux-Arts architect who won a competition for it, though he never carried out his design, and John Galen Howard of New York; it was the signal for a rush and rash of such designs, from Minnesota to Delaware. Big art galleries, big libraries, big concert halls blossomed in every city. Every proper parlor had its big sumptuous books. Every ambitious young man had to have "big ideas."

Late Victorian academicians justified their passion for bigness not only on grounds that they were building for the ages, but also because their buildings were "functional" and "realistic." They thought of a grand Imperial Roman portico as functional, that is, in precisely the same way an Early Victorian would have called Gothic a "functional" style for churches, or Roman Temples a "functional" form for courthouses. Function for them, as for all Victorians, was essentially psychological or symbolic rather than a matter of physical convenience. To build all of Pennsylvania Station in New York, say, with the same frankly exposed frame of steel and glass that could be seen in the train shed would in these terms have been to destroy one of the main functions of the building, which would no longer have "functioned" as a great public monument, an ornament to the city. It would have been simply a utilitarian structure, a mechanical contrivance hardly fit to be called architecture at all. Mighty Roman vaults and cornices were absolutely essential to a public building like this, if it were to have any meaningful function in the 20th century at all.

If Late Victorian design seems unfunctional to us because of its size, the reason is not that these academicians had no concept of function, but that their concept was different from ours. They rejected as unrealistic the "progressive" idea of "going back to fundamentals" and conceiving of great metropolitan stations in terms of shelter, or of skyscrapers as essentially problems of structural expression. A world of great corporations and huge metropolises, they argued, above all demanded "bigness" of its architects.

(5) "Richness." Architecture has never been a poor man's game, but seldom has the fact been so obvious as in the Late Victorian period. It was an age dominated by rich men. "There never was in the history of the world a time," George Orwell once wrote, "when the sheer vulgar fatness of wealth . . . was so obtrusive as in those years before 1914 . . ."; and Late Victorian architecture and furniture shows it. The favored materials were rich—heavy oak and walnut, polished marble, gilt fittings, velvet draperies, tiled flooring. The favored effects were lavishness and conspicuous waste. The dominant architects were rich; if not born to wealth, they soon acquired gelt by association. It was because McKim and White, Hunt, Burnham, Price, and the rest were able to meet moneyed aristocracy on their own terms that they were able to get and carry out commissions on such grand scales. When McKim and Burnham, for example, began trying to restore L'Enfant's original plan for Washington, they found a Pennsylvania Railroad station standing where the Mall should be. No matter; they not only persuaded Pennsylvania president Alexander J. Cassatt to move his station at enormous expense, but so impressed him with their ideas that he negotiated with the Baltimore & Ohio to build a union station far to the north, and soon after gave McKim a commission to build a new Pennsylvania station in New York.

That is not to say these academic architects dominated their wealthy clients. Far from it. In this Late Victorian age money not only talked, it planned and built as well. Never before, and never again, were the wealthy so prominent or had they so much influence in shaping the tastes of society at large. People of wealth were for the middle and lower classes what Hollywood stars became in the 1930s and 40s—remote, unattainable figures of glamor, yet irresistibly desirable models of dress, of manners, of conversation. Still in the 1920s they determined the kind of house George F. Babbitt lived in, the kind of music Myra Babbitt thought "cultured," the kind of unread books shelved in the Babbitts' living room, and the kind of unlooked-at reproductions that hung on their walls. As late as 1924 there was a genuine popular movement to make Henry Ford President of the United States on the basis of his wealth alone. Only after the development of radio and the perfecting of motion pictures did the influence of wealth on taste begin to abate. Needless to say, those architects and designers closest to it were even more affected.

Late in life Richard Morris Hunt was heard to say that he hoped to be remembered not simply as the "Vanderbilt architect" but also as the originator of the stick-style houses he had built long ago at the very beginning of his career. He hoped, that is, that people would think of him as having a few ideas of his own. It was a sentiment most of these academicians had at one time or another. Feebly, intermittently, or vainly, they all recognized how completely their art was dictated by upper-class taste and convention. They knew quite as well as Sullivan or Maybeck or Wright that no great art was ever based on servile copyings from the past. They were much too intelligent not to realize the real rationale of what they were doing—that these classical palaces and Gothic castles represented little self-contained worlds insulated against the present, in whose remote fastnesses the owners could escape all reminders of how, when, and by whom their fortunes had been gained. Quite as well as any modern satirist, they could see the incongruity of coke kings and lumber barons posing as Renaissance princes and Baroque potentates. And if for us they created a great cultural expression of a vanished age, that was no comfort

to them. They knew that just as their patrons had not really achieved the status of Medicis and Valois, so as artists they were not really walking in the footsteps of Michelangelo or Sanmicheli.

(6) *"Mechanization."* Finally, Late Victorian academic art was distinguished by what we can best call the mechanization of the creative process. In perfection of organization was summed up all the other qualities, and indeed the whole century-long development of the Victorian mind in art. What we see beginning in an Early Victorian firm like Town & Davis with the designs of its cabinetmakers directed from above, and developing further in the businesslike atmosphere of Richardson's prolific office, is consummated in such establishments as McKim, Mead & White; Shepley, Rutan & Coolidge; Cram, Goodhue & Ferguson; Daniel Burnham & Company. On a big job, such firms may employ hundreds of assistants, from lowliest bricklayers to entire subcontracting firms of interior decorators or furniture manufacturers. Under their direction work armies of sculptors, stonecutters, carpenters, like the thousand Italians James Deering imported to decorate Vizcaya, or the even greater numbers who worked on the Chicago Fair:

> In the early days of its existence the Forestry Building was peopled by a crowd of statues, for the most part of heroic size, destined for the adornment of the Administration and other buildings. They were cast and rested here.... It was one of the sensations of the time to drop in among the Italians, who were shredding car-loads of flax into huge caldrons, which soon afterward bubbled and boiled with plaster; to see them oiling moulds as large as horse-troughs in which to receive the steaming mixtures; or afterward chipping away the mould to let some imprisoned creature through to the sunlight. One of the first delightful surprises of the fair is the immense population of inhabitants whose flesh is plaster, whose sinews are flax, and whose bones are iron, a population as varied as the history, traditions, arts, virtues and passions of mankind. It recalls the days of Greece, when men thought in marble....

Well, not exactly.

Similarly, the Early Victorian principle of using historical styles for symbolic effect, and the High Victorian concept of Picturesque Eclecticism, are both comprehended by and subsumed under the full Late Victorian command of history. Past, present, future—this age aspires to control and direct them all. In earlier times, there had been some attempt at preservation of buildings with special historical associations— Independence Hall in 1828, for instance, or Old South Church in Boston in 1876. Now people are not merely content to preserve relics of the past, they intend to bring the past back to life, physically and literally, with every resource modern technology can command; it is to this Late Victorian impulse that we owe Williamsburg and Winterthur, Old Sturbridge and Greenfield Village. And they lay their hand on the future with equal confidence, organization, and technological power. When they lay out a city plan, or fix the style of a college campus, they intend it be forever; when they bequeath a collection, as often as not they specify where and how it shall be seen for all the ages to come. They have no doubt that theirs is a "golden age," knowing all about the past that needs to be known, entirely competent to dictate the future. "I count these years between 1880 and 1900," wrote Cram in his 1936 autobiography, "as the most remarkable in American architectural history, for in so brief a space of time it was given a wholly new direction. Ten years before the beginning of this era it was, as I have said, the most degraded in human history; at the close, it stood in the front of all the work of the Western world, with new possibilities opening before it in the thirty years to follow on—possibilities that were to be taken advantage of to the full."

Not too many would agree today, perhaps. Or if they did, they would not likely be thinking of the men and buildings Cram had in mind, but of those who worked at actual or implicit cross purposes to them. For most people today McKim, Hunt, Burnham, and himself are interesting chiefly insofar as their work expresses a kind of culture largely vanished—a world of the fabulously rich and fabulously wasteful; that curious epoch of jingoism when the United States indulged, in the Philippines and Cuba, a strange imperialist mania for empire building in the old 19th-century style which fortunately enough evaporated; when great wealth was its own reward and justification as it only covertly can be now.

And as for the theory of academic art itself, that is studied chiefly for its historical interest; as an example of a paradoxical determinism. For the one thing most striking about the theory today is precisely that in their very act of consummating, refining, and perfecting the Victorian attitude to art, Late Victorian designers destroyed its foundations forever.

The process by which this happened was both simple and inevitable. If you compare Cram's Gothic with Upjohn's or Davis's, or Jefferson's kind of reproduction of Roman prototypes in the Richmond Capitol and the University of Virginia library, with McKim, Mead, & White's reconstruction of the Baths of Caracalla for Pennsylvania Station in New York, you will see at once that the later builders plainly and demonstrably *know* more about the historical style they are using. Not only do they copy the details more accurately, from specific prototypes known and studied thoroughly, but they understand the basic character of these historic styles—their structural principles, their proportions, their "feel." To all appearances (forgetting for the moment hidden steel-and-concrete frames or contemporary plumbing), these *are* Gothic or Roman buildings. And that was emphatically not true of most Early Victorian buildings, let alone those of the High Victorian period. Nobody would mistake Richard Mitchell Upjohn's capitol at Hartford for real Gothic, or Richardson's Trinity for real Romanesque, or John McArthur's city hall in Philadelphia for anything but a product of the Picturesque Eclecticism of its time; furthermore, nobody was expected to. The

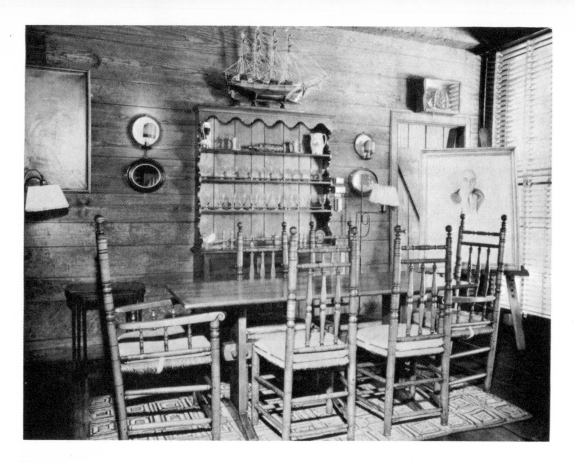

High Victorians called themselves eclectics, and were proud of it. When Mr. McGuffey titled his most famous work *The Eclectic Reader*, for instance, he meant it as an advertisement; he meant that he had "drawn from the best"—literature, in this case—of the past, and made something modern, something recognizably belonging to his own time, out of it. So Richardson or McArthur or Mullett would have quite honestly called himself an "eclectic" architect. None had any intention of trying to revive the architecture of specific historical epochs as such; the goal was to create from selected historical elements new combinations expressive of the age. But the Late Victorian academic designers were different. If we should ask ourselves, what is Hunt's style? there is no good answer; a creature of circumstances, producing to flatter his patrons, following, not leading, the times, he has no style at all. Cram is the same; he knows Gothic as few understood it before, but you could hardly speak of

121. SIMPLICITY, HONESTY, AND "AMERICAN HERITAGE" IN LATE VICTORIAN DRESS

(A) Dining room of the "Little White House," Warm Springs, Georgia. Preserved as it was when President Franklin D. Roosevelt died here, in April 1945. Besides symbolizing "Old American" in a typically Late Victorian generalized way, these revived "Pilgrim" furnishings express the nature of materials and structure directly, like their medieval prototypes.

"Cram Gothic" as you might of "Richardsonian Romanesque." And because these men were *not* creating a style of their own, because they were quite deliberately making recognizable versions of Gothic manor houses or collegiate residences or Roman baths and atriums, they squarely raised a basic problem which High Victorians by originality and Early Victorians through ignorance had always been able to avoid. For if you

(121 B) Eisenhower home, Abilene, Kansas. The original square house was built c.1884, with some later alterations and additions; the Eisenhower family occupied it in 1899. It is typically Late Victorian in its "bigness" of scale and in the concept of "sturdy Americanism" attaching to its plain construction and generous proportions.

know so much about the past that you can no longer believe in any simple interpretation of its forms as being "Christian" or "virtuous" or anything else; if what you build has no particular reference to your own times but is simply a reproduction of some earlier building type, sooner or later you must ask—why? What is all this about? Why use historical styles at all? And there is no good answer.

Once you come to the point of seriously beginning to wonder if a 13th-century cathedral really is the best house of worship that 20th-century congregations can find; if a great Georgian mansion really can accommodate the functions of a collegiate gymnasium or dining hall; if an Imperial Roman bath really is the best atmosphere for conducting modern railroad or banking operations—then the whole eclectic game is over. You will recognize in this sort of thing—to use clichés appropriate to it—not a wave of the future, but the dead hand of the past. You will realize that thirty years of intensive, disciplined study of architectural history have had the same result as, say, Frazer's enormous labors amassing folklore in the *Golden Bough*, or Freud's or Ellis's relentless collecting of data on behavior; that is to say, to cast doubt on the ultimate value of the whole proceeding as far as practical application is concerned. Now the excitement of the chase is over and the past has been firmly and finally captured, you can look objectively at the result—at the dullness of historical buildings, exactly reproduced—and wonder if it was all worth while. What has been gained?

Something, surely; but hardly what you expected. Seeing these historical forms perfectly reproduced at last, you realize that what is significant about them is *not* their forms at all, but the universal principles of proportion, balance, organic plan, and expressive use of materials that are common to all great architecture. As for the forms themselves, they at last stand out starkly for what they are—nothing but shells whose only value was to encase living principles, and which now can have at best no more than the dead and frigid beauty of flowers preserved in wax long past their time. All that Late Victorian academic architecture illustrates, in the end, is

the principle that nothing fails like success.

To this realization men were coming, here and there, throughout the Late Victorian period. Sometimes consciously, sometimes by instinct, they began to see that the ideal of "realism" might lead in other directions. Sometimes independently, occasionally in more or less organized groups, they began to work out implications of the idea that "reality" might mean something other than archaeological accuracy, might make men not less but more masters of their own artistic destinies. In confused, hesitant steps, they began to explore these possibilities. And, exploring them, they gradually found themselves taking a new attitude towards art altogether, breaking with the Victorian age, creating the new and distinctive art and architecture we like to call modern.

NOTES

Quotations of Mrs. Hunt's memoirs, from Alan Burnham, "The New York Architecture of Richard Morris Hunt," (*JSAH*, XI, 2, 1952); from Winston Weisman, "New York and the Problem of the First Skyscraper" (*JSAH*, XII, 1, 1953); from A. Downing and V. J. Scully, *The Architectural Heritage of Newport* (Cambridge, 1952), p. 138; of Montgomery Schuyler's "The Works of the late R. M. Hunt," from Jordy and Coe, *op. cit.*; from W. H. Nicholas, "Vizcaya: An Italian Palazzo in Miami" (*National Geographic Magazine*, XCVIII, 1950, pp. 595–604); from Hermann Hagedorn, *The Roosevelt Family of Sagamore Hill* (1954), pp. 6ff.; from Sullivan's *Autobiography of an Idea*; from George Orwell, *Such, Such Were the Joys* (1953), p. 47; from Candace Wheeler, "A Dream City" (*Harper's New Monthly Magazine*, LXXXVI, 1893, p. 839).

On Late Victorian bigness, see particularly Frederick Gutheim, *One Hundred Years of Architecture in America, 1857–1957* (1957), pp. 64–74, "The Increase in Scale." On Burnham's city planning, and Beaux-Arts design generally, see Christopher Tunnard and H. H. Reed, *American Skyline* (1953), Part VI: "The City Beautiful . . . 1880–1910."

20th-CENTURY MAN AND 20th-CENTURY ART IN THE UNITED STATES

I

"Organic Reality":
The Late Victorian "Modern Generation,"
c. 1885–c. 1920

1. THE "REBELS":
Radicals versus Conservatives before World War I

TO THE OVERWHELMING MAJORITY of American people over the two generations between the 1880s and the 1920s, "good architecture," "advanced architecture," "American architecture" meant the work of Beaux-Arts academicians, the revival of the Revivals. When they talked of the great and leading American designers, they were referring to McKim and White, to Daniel Burnham, to Bertram Goodhue, to Cram and Cret and Pope. Of other American architects with differing views they heard only occasionally, if at all. In Chicago, Louis Henri Sullivan had acquired something of a regional, even national, reputation by the early 1890s, and local people at least were aware of a group of his admirers working on what they called "progressive" principles in the early 1900s, a group including George W. Maher, Robert C. Spencer, Jr., Dwight Heald Perkins, Frank Lloyd Wright, Claude Bragdon, Myron C. Hunt, Walter Burley Griffin, and others. In California, Bernard Maybeck, the brothers Charles and Henry Greene, and Irving Gill had local reputations for more or less "novel" approaches to their art, as did Gustav Stickley with his "mission style" in New York and New Jersey, and Frank Miles Day and Wilson Eyre with tentative ventures into "frank" expressions of material and construction in the Philadelphia area. But that such men could ever be considered as equals or rivals to the big, well-established, prolific academic Eastern firms, with their branch offices everywhere, would have seemed incredible. And by 1920, when most of these "radicals" had either fallen into deep obscurity or conformed to eclectic standards, it would have seemed not merely incredible but ludicrous to suggest that within fifteen years people would begin to call them the really great architectural figures of the Late Victorian age. For, of course, it was true; these "modern pioneers" never did compete with the established firms on anything like equal terms.

Writing his *Genius and the Mobocracy* in the 1940s, Frank Lloyd Wright recalled how twenty years earlier Sullivan, in bitter obscurity, "had taken great pride in the performance of the Imperial Hotel, volunteered to write articles concerning it. . . . 'At last, Frank,' he said, 'something they can't take away from you.' I wonder why he thought 'they' couldn't take it away from me? 'They' can take anything away from anybody." He spoke from hard experience. It had happened to him, when the greatest of all his "Prairie House" commissions, the Harold McCormick mansion in Lake Forest, had been completely designed, then suddenly taken away from him and given to New York academician Charles Augustus Platt, in 1908. It had happened to Sullivan even earlier, when in 1890 the World's Columbian Exposition was first being organized in Chicago. First the local firm of Burnham & Root had been put in charge; but when Root died in January 1891, a consulting board of ten other architects had been appointed, five of them Easterners led by Hunt, McKim, and White. Almost at once they had taken command of the whole, determined it should be Imperial Roman on the most grandiose scale, converted Burnham completely, overrode Sullivan. The critics had been delighted: "The trumpet note of his [Hunt's] voice has sounded from East to West, and finds its first loud echo in the exposition. . . . It means the dawn of a real art in this country." As for "the crowds," they, Sullivan wrote later, "were astonished. They beheld what was for them an amazing revelation of the architectural art . . . unaware that what they saw was . . . an imposition of the spurious upon their eyesight, a naked exhibitionism of charlatanry. . . . The damage wrought by the World's Fair will last for

389

half a century from its date. . . ." Wright's estimate was more succinct: "They killed Sullivan, and they nearly killed me." And twenty years later the same thing happened again, when the appointment of chief architect for the Panama-California Exposition in San Diego, which opened in 1915, was being considered in December 1910. It had been almost a certainty that Irving Gill, whose creation of a new kind of concrete architecture particularly well suited to the climate and related to the local adobe tradition had earned him a great local reputation, would be given the post. Yet a few days before Gill's confirmation was due, Bertram Goodhue had written from New York that this was "a position I want very much indeed . . . a perfectly lovely problem, and one . . . I am better fitted to deal with than any other architect, thanks to my studies of, and book on, Spanish Colonial architecture in Mexico . . ."; three weeks later Goodhue was appointed instead, and the Spanish colonial he designed for that fair killed Gill as the Chicago Fair had killed Sullivan. And so on; it happened all the time.

And it was true also that by 1920 the old "radicals" were scattered and to all appearances demoralized and forgotten. If for no other reason than that individual creativity was one of their distinguishing characteristics, there never was anything like a formally organized "Chicago" or "California" school. It was largely coincidence that in 1907 Wright, Spencer, Dwight Perkins, and Myron Hunt were all working in the same Chicago building; whatever Maybeck, Gill, the Greenes, and Polk knew of one another was in the same way more through common interests and aspirations than effected by any systematic communication. And during the 1920s most of them had largely faded from public sight, into obscurity or conformity. In this respect, their careers are remarkably similar.

Leader and outstanding personality of the "radicals" was Louis Henri Sullivan (1856–1924). By now his career had become a kind of legend, on the plane of high tragedy; most people at all acquainted with American architectural history know the general outlines of it. Sullivan's birth in Boston to an itinerant Irish dancing master and a French mother. His rebellious youth, and peripatetic education—in Cambridge, at the Massachusetts Institute of Technology (1872); in Philadelphia, working with Frank Furness (1873); in Chicago, working with William LeBaron Jenney (1832–1907), a French-trained engineer and veteran of Sherman's campaigns who had set up architectural practice in 1868 and pioneered in using metal-cage construction for tall buildings (1873); in Paris, at the École des Beaux-Arts (1874–6), where he was inspired by mathematics professor Clopet's "demonstration" of "rules so broad as to admit no exceptions." How he returned to Chicago, and after several tries found a congenial partner in Dankmar Adler (1844–1900), an architect who was virtually self-educated, like Jenney a military engineer in the Civil War, with whom he formed the firm of Adler & Sullivan in 1880. How one early success followed another, climaxed by the Auditorium Building (1886–9), largest architectural undertaking in Chicago to that time, extraordinary for Adler's feats of engineering in balancing the load of the tower and perfecting the theatre acoustics, and for Sullivan's ornament, so well described in Professor Morrison's *Louis Sullivan*. How in the Wainwright Building in St. Louis (1890–91) and the Guaranty Building in Buffalo (now Prudential Building, 1894–5), Sullivan approached the first definitive solution to the problem of designing tall buildings as organic wholes, fully utilizing metal-frame construction. How his Transportation Building was the only work of architecture in the Chicago Fair (1893) to win international acclaim, and how critic Montgomery Schuyler hailed him, when he was only thirty-seven, as "one of the most striking and interesting individualities among living architects." But how after 1895 a combination of factors—dissolution of his partnership with Adler, a business depression, the triumph of academic eclecticism at the Fair—brought about a sudden and, as it proved, permanent decline in his fortunes, so that in the thirty years thereafter he built only twenty commissions, more than half of them small banks in out-of-the-way Midwestern towns. And thereafter the climactic scenes—frustration and neglect taking their toll of him, his subsisting in a poor Chicago hotel, begging money from Frank Lloyd Wright, imposing on friends to find a publisher for his manuscripts. A few days before his death from a heart condition caused by "overuse of stimulants," completed copies of his *Autobiography of an Idea* and plates of his *System of Architectural Ornament* were placed in his failing hands, making "his last days . . . among the most pleasant he had experienced for many years, as he felt that his life's work had been splendidly consummated." And then he died, seemingly forgotten by all but a few friends; the *National Cyclopaedia of American Biography,* for instance, never mentioned him, attributing all his work to Adler. Finally, triumph: within ten years Sullivan was being hailed as one of the greatest of all figures in American architecture, and in 1946 the American Institute of Architects met to "render to Louis Sullivan this grateful tribute, highest honor of our profession, the Gold Medal of the American Institute of Architects."

No other architect's story was quite as tragic in the classic sense, perhaps; but most of them were similar. That of Frank Lloyd Wright (1869–1959), a generation later, provides a particularly striking parallel. Born at Richland Center, Wisconsin, of the same sort of parentage—his father an itinerant teacher of music who abandoned the family when Wright was sixteen; his mother Welsh in origin, strong-minded, mystical. The same turbulent youth—taken at five to Weymouth, Massachusetts, where his mother introduces him to the then-revolutionary Froebel kindergarten concept of creative play with geometric blocks; return to Madison, Wisconsin, around 1880; by 1885 already working as a draftsman for local builder and Dean of Engineering at the University of Wisconsin Allen D. Conover, at the same time taking civil engineering courses at the university; in 1887 flight to Chicago, to work in the office of J. Lyman Silsbee, early Western exponent of a Richardsonian shingle style, in whose manner Wright designs his first works, most notably plans of a building for his aunts' Hillside Home School in Spring Green, Wisconsin (1887); then the famous six years' apprenticeship in the offices of Adler & Sullivan (1887–93), during which he takes over much of the firm's domestic practice and begins to evolve his own distinctive house style, of which the Charnley house of 1891 is the best-known example. The same early successes. From the still essentially closed classical form of the Charnley house he progresses in steady stages towards the mature "prairie" house of centrifugal plan and freely interpenetrating exterior and interior space—the Winslow house in River Forest (1893); the Helen Husser house in Chicago (1899); the model "home in a prairie town" published in the *Ladies Home Journal* (1901); the Bradley and Hickox houses in Kankakee, Illinois (1900); the Ward Willits house in Highland Park, Illinois (1902); the Dana house in Springfield, Illinois (1902–4); the Darwin D. Martin house in Buffalo, New York (1903–4); the Isabel Roberts house in River Forest, the Avery Coonley house in Riverside, the Frederick Robie house in Chicago, Illinois (1907–9). Larger commissions begin to come to him, and he proves himself to have, in Grant Manson's neat phrase, "a double-faceted mind": the Francis Apartments in Chicago (1895); the unexecuted Luxfer Prism office building in Chicago (1894), the Larkin Building in Buffalo (1904); Unity Church in Oak Park, Illinois (1906). He achieves some international reputation; German professor Kuno Francke visits him, returns to encourage Ernst Wasmuth of Berlin to publish *Frank Lloyd Wright: Ausgeführte Bauen und Entwürfe,* which appears in 1910 and has tremendous influence on the Continent. . . .

But then, the same sudden decline in popularity, as the full weight of academic convention and eclectic revival hits him. Wright loses his biggest commission, the Harold McCormick house in Lake Forest. "Had it been executed," this 1907 design "would" as Professor Manson has said, "have placed Wright in the vanguard of successful American architects, and . . . have placed the stamp of social approval on the whole progressive movement in Chicago . . . extended its scope immeasurably . . . turned the tide of eclecticism." But it was not; an archaeologically correct Italian villa went up in its stead. By 1909 Wright was "weary, I was losing my grip on my work and even interest in it." In the fall of that year he abandons his family and goes to Europe with the wife of one of his clients; when he returns, it is almost to repeat Sullivan's story. He builds a new home and studio at Spring Green, Wisconsin—Taliesin East, it came to be called —and starts rebuilding his practice with the great Midway Gardens Restaurant in Chicago (1913–14); but his new home and family both are destroyed in a terrible disaster (1914). He spends most of the next five years in Japan (1915–20), working on the great Imperial Hotel in Tokyo; its survival of the 1922 earthquake is a glorious triumph, but by now the United States is in full reaction back to "normalcy," and few commissions are available for so "eccentric" a man and architect. He designs a few houses in California—the Barnsdall house in Hollywood (1920), the Millard house in Pasadena (1923), the Freeman house in Los Angeles (1924). But debts pile up, so that like Sullivan before him he is forced to sell many prized possessions, saves himself from bankruptcy only by incorporating himself and selling shares on his potential earning power to a few wealthy friends. In 1929 the Depression aborts his major work of the decade, the St. Mark's Tower in New York, and brings him close to destitution. True, Wright never starved; his ebullience saved him from falling as far as Sullivan. Yet had he died in 1930, the parallel between their two careers would have been nearly complete.

This is the pattern, too, of the life of Ber-nard Maybeck (1862–1957). Like Sullivan and Wright, he is born of migrant and artistic parentage—German, in his case, his father being a woodcarver and later manufacturer of furniture in New York. Like them again, his education is peripatetic: a brief spell with his father, then six years (1880–86) studying at the École des Beaux-Arts in Paris but with much traveling about; a couple of years in the office of Carrère & Hastings, working on the Ponce de Leon Hotel in St. Augustine; a year of unsuccessful practice in Kansas City; then to California (1889), working successively for Ernest Coxhead, an English practitioner of the fashionable Queen Anne style, A. Page Brown in San Francisco on the Crocker Building (1891), and a Swedenborgian church (1894). In 1894 he takes a position teaching descriptive geometry at the University of California, expands the course into a department of architecture, and becomes administrator of an international competition to design a new campus endowed by Phoebe Appleton Hearst. This is his moment of fame; he travels about Europe organizing the competition, while the "Women's Student Union" Mrs. Hearst commissioned him to build in 1899 is everywhere talked of for its revolutionary introduction of laminated arches, its originality of plan and fenestration, and ingenious decorative uses of wood. But when in 1900 the competition winner, Émile Bénard of the École des Beaux-Arts, refuses to supervise execution of his plans and New York academician John Galen Howard of New York is invited to take over, Maybeck soon discovers, like all the others, how fast " 'they' can take anything away from anybody." Howard treats Maybeck's departures from archaeological correctness with undisguised contempt and ridicule; Maybeck loses first his commission for the Mining Building, then his job at the university.

Enough local reputation survives, however, to provide Maybeck a decade or so more of opportunities for maturing his highly original expressions of the structural and decorative potentialities of diverse materials; of wood in the

Hopps house in Ross Valley (1906), the Tufts house at San Anselmo (1906), the Goslinsky house in San Francisco (1909); of stone in Mrs. Hearst's McCloud River mansion, Wyntoon (1902); of stucco in the adobe tradition (Men's Faculty Club, University of California, Berkeley, 1900); of concrete (Lawson house, Berkeley, 1907); and above all, of creative eclecticism in the Leon L. Roos house in San Francisco (1909) and the Christian Science Church of Berkeley (1910). Then comes—from parallel careers—the predictable decline. His perfectionism seems too expensive; his eccentricity too "vulgar" (certainly the habit of designing his own clothes is no help to him here); soon he nears bankruptcy. Already by 1912 he was counting himself lucky to be hired as draftsman in the office of one of his former students, Willis Polk (1867–1924), then head of the architectural committee for the Panama Pacific International Exposition in San Francisco. Here his imaginative sketch for a Piranesi-like Imperial Roman Palace of Fine Arts caught the eye of classical academician Henry Bacon (1866–1924), designer of the Lincoln Memorial in Washington (1914–22); on Bacon's recommendation, it is approved for execution. Thenceforth, though flashes of the old radical inventiveness continued to appear in the few smaller commissions Maybeck executed, in larger ones he tended to conform more and more to the prevailing simplified Revival styles of the 1920s. For the University of California at Berkeley he designed a more or less classical Hearst Memorial Gymnasium (1927); for the Packard Agency in Oakland, a more or less Romanesque showroom (1928). The mansion he built for Earle C. Anthony in Los Angeles (1927) combined a variety of styles so bizarre that one "section seems the work of some wandering Spanish mason, while only a Tudor craftsman would have designed these leaded windows"—in addition to which there was a thirty-five-foot high living room, walls of Caen stone five feet thick, a solid walnut door weighing fifteen hundred pounds, an authentic Gothic chapel, a Norman tower, and a

seven-Packard garage. For Principia College in Elsah, Illinois (planned 1923, executed 1938), he provided a feebly Tudor campus. Unlike Sullivan, then, Maybeck lived on, but only in body; in spirit, as Esther McCoy sums it up, he showed "little of the vigor of the man who had once . . . 'travelled in common darkness to shed uncommon light.'" Though Maybeck continued to go to his office until 1942, his effective career had ended long before; there remained only again the belated recognition of his early genius, the Gold Medal of the American Institute of Architects (1951), and his death at the age of ninety-five.

It was the same with the brothers Charles S. (1868–1957) and Henry M. (1870–1954) Greene. First a period of experimentation in various styles, culminating in the formulation of a distinctive "California bungalow" developing logically out of the "shingle style" (e.g., James Culbertson house, Pasadena, 1902). Then a few years of fame and highly creative expressions of the natural character and structure of wood (R. R. Blacker house, Pasadena, 1907; David B. Gamble house, Pasadena, 1908; Pratt house, Ojai, 1909). Next, from 1914 on, a sudden decline in popularity as Beaux-Arts academicism spreads; a few half-hearted attempts to conform, mainly in the direction of the "California mission" style (D. L. James house at Carmel, by Charles Greene, 1917–21; William Thum house by Henry Greene, Pasadena, 1925). Thenceforth virtual inactivity. And again, finally, citation from the American Institute of Architects in 1952 as "formulators of a new and native architecture"; and death a few years later.

So, too, it was with Irving Gill (1870–1936). Early eclectic searchings, in directions suggested by work as a youth in the drafting rooms of Adler & Sullivan. Maturing discovery of the expressive and structural possibilities of concrete, and a series of great houses exploiting it: the Laughlin house, Los Angeles, 1907; Scripps Building, Water Tower, and Wilson Acton Hotel in La Jolla, 1908; Bishop's Day School, San Diego, 1909; the Miltimore house, South Pasadena, 1911; the Banning house, Los Angeles, 1912; Women's Club and Community House in La Jolla (1913, 1914); the Dodge house, Los Angeles, 1914–16; the Ellen Scripps house, La Jolla, 1915–16. Considerable fame; he is one of the first architects to make a success of practice in a small city, making San Diego the center of a lively and creative regional movement. Then decline. Goodhue takes the Panama Pacific Exposition commission away from him; a vogue for Spanish colonial sweeps over the area; it is thirteen years before Gill receives another major commission, and when he does—for the Christian Science Church at Coronado, and the Oceanside City Hall, Fire Station, and Police Station

(1929)—the flaccid quality of his work betrays the dulling effects of his long inactivity. No medal or citation for him; he dies too early, quite forgotten.

The similarity of the "radical" careers of all these men is no accident. It was the inevitable result of their principles' reacting against the changing intellectual and cultural climate of their generation. And it is as we see them collectively, rather than in terms of their individual careers, that we can best understand precisely what their principles were, and how these men, quite as fully as the academic Beaux-Arts Revivalists, expressed American culture in the Late Victorian age.

NOTES

On the comparatively minor members of the Wright–Sullivan circle at the turn of the 20th century, see *inter alia* H. Allen Brooks, Jr., "The Early Work of the Prairie Architects" (*JSAH*, XIX, 1, 1960, pp. 2–10), and David S. Gebhard, "Purcell & Elmslie, Architects," a catalogue of exhibition in the Walker Art Center (Minneapolis, 1953), with introduction by Donald R. Torbert.

Quotations from Frank Lloyd Wright, *Genius and the Mobocracy* (1949), pp. 72–3; on the Columbian Exposition, from F. D. Millet, "The Designers of the Fair" (*Harper's New Monthly Magazine*, LXXXV, 1892, p. 883); of Sullivan, from Hugh Morrison's standard biography, *Louis Sullivan* (1935), pp. 183–4; of Goodhue's letter, from Esther McCoy, *Five California Architects* (1960), p. 87; from Grant Manson, *Frank Lloyd Wright to 1910* (1958), p. 30.

2. NEW REALITY IN OLD FORMS:
Late Victorian Principles in Early Modern Architecture, c.1885—c.1920

AS WE LOOK BACK ON IT, the history of American art between 1885 and 1920 has more and more come to seem a story of bitter, stark, romantic struggle. On the one hand, "academics," Beaux-Arts men—entrenched in public favor and rich commissions, complacent fatteners off dead men's minds. On the other, "rebels"—a dedicated few, fighting the battle of the future, their only champions a small band of far-sighted clear-eyed visionary critics led by the indomitable Montgomery Schuyler, who, as Lewis Mumford once dramatized it, "never hauled down the flag." Beaten over and over, by the 1920s the "rebels" have been driven to their Valley Forge. But they never give up; slowly the tide turns; Yorktown is in sight, and their ideas sweep grandly to final victory. It is indeed an appealing picture.

But at the time, things rarely seemed quite so black and white. As the editors of *American Architecture and Other Writings* by Montgomery Schuyler have so ably pointed out, this same Schuyler who in revered retrospect seemed such a sterling defender of Richardson, Sullivan, and Wright was by no means so single-minded in fact. Not only did he criticize the mighty Richardson, on occasion calling Richardson's houses "defensible only in a military sense"; not only did he deplore the "gauntness," the "attenuation," the ugliness that resulted from "true and logical exposition of the structure" by Sullivan the Seer; but he also had extraordinarily kind words for wicked pillars of the Beaux-Arts order like Richard Morris Hunt. Nor is it difficult to see why even so perceptive a critic could be so "confused." Then as always, purely artistic judgments were colored by considerations of personality and family that time has made insignificant. Just as Rembrandt's being a miller's son meant much more to his contemporaries than to critics

looking at his pictures long after everyone connected with them was dead, so it once seemed much more significant than now that Hunt, Burnham, McKim, and White had such impeccable 17th-century ancestry and educational backgrounds, while their "progressive" rivals were so often sons of immigrants and in many cases—notably Wright's and Sullivan's—ne'er-do-wells at that. But what was even more significant was that both "radicals" and "academics" shared a great body of common assumptions about the nature and direction of artistic development in the Late Victorian era.

At the time, the theoretical differences between "rebels" and conventional "Beaux-Arts" men seemed quite minor. A slightly different angle of vision; slightly different conclusions drawn from similar basic premises—little more. Only with the passage of decades has it become apparent how fundamental was the nature of these deviations, how totally divergent was the development inherent in them, how inevitably by the 1930s academic eclecticism would be left at a dead end while an essentially new architecture was being built on the achievements of the "rebels." Only much later would the variations of emphasis and interpretation in the work of the "rebels" assume the major proportions that so impress us today. At the time, their work seemed to be based on essentially the same six basic principles as those that motivated the Beaux-Arts men:

(1) *Literacy.* Intensely self-conscious literacy is by no means an exclusive perquisite of Beaux-Arts men. Quite as much, perhaps even more, the "rebels" are aware of what they are doing, talk and write voluminously about it, have people writing and talking about them. We think of Sullivan on his deathbed counting "his

life's work . . . splendidly consummated" less by his buildings than by publications in book form of his *Kindergarten Chats* and *Autobiography of an Idea*; of Wright from beginning to end of his career attracting attention to himself with torrents of talk, articles, books; of Maybeck with his articles, letters to editors, *Planning of a University* (1910) and *The Palace of Fine Arts and Lagoon* (1915); conversely, of Gill writing only locally in *The Craftsman* and so losing to the verbose Adolf Loos credit for innovating simplification in concrete; and so on.

Where Beaux-Arts men differ from rebels is in the relationship of their written to their architectural creations. For academicians, the written word comes first. Their buildings are confirmations of research, practical demonstrations of literary symbolism. For the "rebels," it is the other way around. Their writing essentially represents attempts to rationalize what they have done, to explain the new kind of purely architectural "realism" they have created. That is the reason it so often seemed (and still seems) disjointed, repetitive, stumblingly polemic, in contrast to Cram's polished expositions of Gothic, say, or the grand clarity and logic of Burnham's treatises on city planning. Rationalizing the intuitive is always hard and rarely satisfactory, if only because the intuitive creator never precisely understands himself what it is he is really trying to do. So it is not surprising to find long passages by Sullivan and Wright that are chaotic at best, and at worst simply unreadable; as one reviewer put it (this is a complete review of *Genius and the Mobocracy*):

"—push bottom power," plush bottom power could be push button power. Why not? All gagism (ours). Bewildered, the reader flounders along with his Boswell, looking in vain for Johnson. Wonders sometimes whether Boswell is Johnson, or Johnson is Boswell. Assive of reader. It will appear strange to posterity as to mobocracy (ours) that so lucid a mind (his), the master of so organic an approach to modern building, could produce so unorganic a discourse, or is it that he who, in construction, is so conscious of wood is, in writing, mesmerized by the trees. Lieber Meister deserved better treatment. Sad, resurrected (not really, Giedion did a good job) only to be reinterred in morass of pseudo quasi philosophy Can't help lovin' that man. Which? Why?

So it was that as long as the Victorian literary approach continued to dominate the cultural climate, as it did throughout this age, the academicians were bound to seem more successful.

(2) *"Honesty."* Writing to a friend about Irving Gill, his defeated rival for the Panama Pacific Exposition commission, Bertram Goodhue said in 1914, "I do think he has produced some of the most thoughtful work done in the California of today, and that for the average architect his theories are far safer to follow than mine." It was a perceptive remark, if something less than a wholehearted compliment. Nowadays we tend to think of men like Gill as leading the reaction against Victorian eclecticism, while their

---

122. LATE VICTORIAN LITERACY IN EARLY MODERN ARCHITECTURE

(A) "Studies of Different Exterior Treatments of the Same Plan," Pl. 46 in H. V. Von Holst, Modern American Homes *(American Technical Society, Chicago, 1914). "These pen and ink sketches by Lawrence Buck, Architect, Chicago, Illinois, show the possibilities of variation in the exterior style of the house after the plan has been decided upon."*

Except that the proposed variations are rather vaguer in historical association ("an Italian feeling"; "the feeling of an English country house"; "Colonial Type of House"), they seem at first sight little more than typical examples of Late Victorian rejection of mixed styles in favor of a single "revival" per building. Yet in this book by Von Holst—the same man to whom Wright turned over his Oak Park practice when he left the country in 1909—are illustrated works by such famous names as Greene & Greene, Griffin, and Frank Lloyd Wright, alongside those by architects largely forgotten, like Buck; and in many cases it would be hard, without the identifications, to distinguish among them.

Colonial Type of House with Hip-Roof. This May Be Executed in Wood, Plaster, or Brick

This Design Has the Feeling of an English Country House of Brick or Plaster, with Small Windows

A Plaster or Brick Design. The Hip-Roof Combined with the Arches Gives It an Italian Feeling

First Floor Plan

A Colonial Design with Gable Ends—Brick Material

Studies of Different Exterior Treatments of the Same Plan

THESE pen and ink sketches by Lawrence Buck, Architect, Chicago, Illinois, show the possibilities of variation in the exterior style of the house after the plan has been decided upon. The rough studies enable the architect to find out for himself what type of exterior design will best suit the location and also to ascertain the preference of the client for different types of houses.

An English Type of House. Plaster or Brick Would Be Suitable Materials for This Design

(122 B) Christian Science Church, Berkeley, California. Interior of the sanctuary. Designed and built by Bernard Maybeck, 1909–10. Quite as sophisticated as its expression of the nature of materials and structure (hinged timber trusses, supported by columns of cast concrete, etc.) was Maybeck's adaptation of Romanesque and Gothic forms to suggest a generalized atmosphere of "churchiness" in this, probably his most famous work.

academic contemporaries were perpetuating it. But to these academics themselves it seemed quite the opposite. They considered it was Gill, Sullivan, Wright, Maybeck, and the rest who were perpetuating—however "thoughtfully"—the kind of High Victorian Picturesque Eclecticism that had been endemic on the American architectural scene since the 1870s. To them it seemed obvious that the concept of skyscraper design Sullivan demonstrated in his Wainwright Building of 1890 in St. Louis was little more than a free adaptation of Renaissance principles of contrived articulation, based on the same broad prototype of a classical column with base, shaft, and capital as Alberti's Rucellai Palace in Florence. Even had they not known of the young Frank Lloyd Wright's early flights into straight eclectic fancy—the Palladian Blossom house in Chicago (1892), the Dutch colonial Bagley house in Hinsdale, Illinois (1894), the Tudor house for Nathan G. Moore in Oak Park (1895), and others—they could easily see how his "prairie houses" of the 1900s developed out of eclectic precedents going back from the shingle style through General Grant mansions to the Tuscan villa of the 1850s. Maybeck's bizarre wanderings in worlds of Romanesque pilasters, Japanese timbering, columns from Baalbek, and stencilings from Byzantium were notorious. It was obvious how the Greenes' furniture was freely adapted from Chippendale, their redwood houses from colonial shingle-style prototypes; how Gill's architecture could be understood as attempts to suggest in new materials the effects of adobe and tile characteristic of what was then considered to be the "native style of California." The difference, as the academics saw it, was that whereas through academic discipline they were bringing rules and order out of the chaos of High Victorian individualism, these "rebels" were in effect simply prolonging the chaos, by their unwillingness—or inability—to follow the rules recent scholarship had discovered. To the academics it seemed plain: one did not create a "medieval type of church" by "trying to put

himself [as Maybeck expressed it] in the boots of a fellow in the 12th century"; you got a book and found out exactly what rules a fellow in the 12th century followed. In this sense, the Beaux Arts men thought of themselves as progressive, and their rivals as perverse, if not indeed reactionary—"safer" for ordinary builders whose education was not great enough to follow academic rules correctly, but hardly in the same class with truly and thoroughly trained men.

In one important respect at least this academic point of view is still valid and useful. It recognized what later criticism all too often ignored: that High Victorian Picturesque Eclecticism was not the antithesis of modern architecture but rather its starting point. In an earlier chapter we noted how the romantic planning of buildings in picturesque relation to landscape led by logical steps to the kind of interpenetration of exterior and interior space that characterized the work of Wright, the Greenes, Maybeck, and Gill. More significantly in this context, if these architects were able to develop distinctive expressions of the nature of new materials like metal, glass, and concrete, it was because Early Victorians had introduced these materials and High Victorians had made them commercially practicable. In each case the pattern was the same.

Large-scale architectural use of iron was first introduced, apparently, by John Haviland in a façade designed for the Miners' Bank of Pottsville, Pennsylvania, in 1830. By the 1850s cast-iron façades were becoming common. Philadelphia had a famous example in the Jayne Building (1849–50), designed by William L. Johnston (1811–1849) and completed by Thomas U. Walter, where iron columns supported the wooden floor joists; while in New York a number of competing manufacturers of architectural iron were well established before the Civil War. Among them were Daniel D. Badger, whose 1865 catalog listed 604 projects executed in cast iron, beginning with an 1842 store front on Washington Street in Boston that he claimed was the

"first Iron Front in the United States"; John B. Cornell (1821–1887), whose firm built the famous A. T. Stewart store on Broadway (1859–60, later Wanamaker's; destroyed 1956) designed by John Kellum (1807–1871); Janes, Beebe & Company, who supplied the metal for the Library of Congress and dome of the Capitol in Washington as built by Thomas U. Walter (1852–65); and, most famous of all, James Bogardus (1800–1874). By contemporaries, Bogardus was regarded as the leader in the movement. A fertile inventor whose patents included clocks, cotton spinners, sugar mills, gas meters, and an engraving machine used to produce the first British postage stamps (1839), Bogardus

---

Unity Church), Oak Park, Illinois, built by Frank Lloyd Wright, 1906. The geometric simplicity of its moulded forms was dictated by the monolithic poured-concrete structure; both technique and forms carried typically Late Victorian vague implications of unity and simplicity appropriate to the religious tenets of its builders.

123. IN THE NATURE OF NEW MATERIALS

(A) Steel and glass in the "Chicago School": Louis Sullivan's Wainwright Building, St. Louis, Missouri, 1890. First great mature statement of Sullivan's "realism," largely achieved through treatment of ornament. By the confinement of decorative luxuriance to non-bearing parts of the outer masonry envelope, the true nature of the steel-cage structure beneath the envelope is revealed. By the contrast of light and elaborate cornice to heavy and plain ground stories, a tripartite division of each elevation is effected, roughly corresponding to the base, shaft, and capital of a classical pilaster, and functioning in the same way to articulate the wall, unify the design as a whole, and dramatize the architect's command over his medium. To achieve this effect, Sullivan was willing to sacrifice complete expression of structure, thickening the corners of his base (though in fact the corners of a steel cage carry no weight) and breaking the vertical pattern of his middle zone.

(123 B) Detail of entrance to the auditorium of the Universalist Church (originally

wrote the treatise *Cast Iron Buildings: Their Construction and Advantages*. His advertised claim to be the "originator of iron buildings" on the strength of his factory in New York (1847–8) was accepted to the extent of his appearing among the nineteen "Men of Progress" in Christian Schussele's painting of 1857, now in the White House, along with such worthies as Samuel Morse, Cyrus McCormick, Peter Cooper, Charles Goodyear, and President Eliphalet Nott of Union. How true that may be is beside the present point, which is that the High Victorians' widespread acceptance of metal made building with it architecturally feasible. They used metal for façades everywhere from New York to St. Louis to San Francisco. Gradually they learned how it could replace wooden beams altogether, first in bridges like John and Washington Roebling's Brooklyn Bridge of 1869–83 and James B. Eads's bridge over the Mississippi at St. Louis in 1868–74; then in tall buildings, beginning with columns of cast iron within masonry frames, culminating in complete metal frames, of which William LeBaron Jenney's Home Insurance Building in Chicago (1883–5) is generally considered to have been the first. Without this background Sullivan's concept of the high building, however admirable in theory, could never have been realized in practice.

New ways of using glass in walls and roofs were introduced first, too, in the Early Victorian period, in arcades like the one built 1827–9 in Providence by Russell Warren (1783–1860), in the New York Crystal Palace of 1853, and particularly (as might be expected) by Gothic Revivalists working from medieval precedent—A. J. Davis's projects for the New York City Post Office in 1867 and various commercial buildings of the 1860s were the culmination of a long development. But it was the proliferation of windows in High Victorian offices and warehouses that made such creations as the Chicago "strip window" and the glass façade of the Hallidie Building in San Francisco (by Willis Polk, 1918) practicable.

It was the same with concrete. Natural cement rock was discovered at several points in upper New York State early in the 19th century, and the builders of the Erie Canal made extensive use of concrete. In 1835 the first known structure of poured concrete was erected—a small building in New York described by the *Mechanics' Magazine and Register of Inventions and Improvements* for August of that year; by 1844 Joseph Goodrich was building poured-concrete structures in Wisconsin. Such classical revival stalwarts as Mills, Strickland, and Walter all experimented with concrete for fireproofing, while by the 1850s the vivid white line of lime mortar was beginning to be replaced in brickwork everywhere by the grey of concrete. But it was, again, the High Victorian builders who made large-scale concrete building practical. The technological ancestry of Gill's poured-concrete houses and Wright's Unity Temple is to be sought in such buildings as the large monolithic Ward house at Port Chester, New York (c.1871–6); in the poured retaining walls of Fort Snelling, Minnesota (1882); in the development of concrete block in the 1870s (e.g., in Dwight Place Church, New Haven, Connecticut, by David R. Brown, c.1872); in San Francisco, where the Pacific Stone & Concrete Company was organized in 1768 and concrete statuary designed for the new California State Capitol in 1872; in Hawaii, where lack of other materials induced a concrete "boom" sparked by the English builder J. G. Osborne, who built the Honolulu Post Office in 1870 and the Hawaiian Hotel in 1871 entirely of this new material. And, of course, it was the combination of iron with concrete effected during the High Victorian age which more than any other single factor distinguished what later generations came to think of as "modern" architecture.

The achievement of the Late Victorian "pioneers" was not, then, to discover new materials. Nor was it to make more extensive use of the materials they had; as a matter of fact, most of them achieved their effects largely with conventional materials—Maybeck with wood, Sullivan with terra cotta and brick, and so on. What they did was to realize more fully the implications of using new materials for structural and decorative expression. Their predecessors saw in new materials little more than cheaper or more fire-resistant substitutes for conventional ones. As they used moulded terra cotta to produce effects of stone sculpture, imitated mahogany chairs in papier-mâché, metal tubing with "Thonet's patented bentwood" and rustic stick construction in iron, so they used iron as if it were wood, and concrete as if it were brick or stone. Iron façades were cast in the form of wooden columns, roughed and painted to look like sandstone. Concrete usually imitated stone, but as late as 1917 Dr. Henry Chapman Mercer built a fireproof museum for his collection of tools at Doylestown, Pennsylvania, which reproduced not only masonry vaults but summer beams and even dormer windows complete with mullions entirely in concrete. In the 1830s the new "balloon frame" system of wood construction was introduced; by the 1850s it was being popularized by such influential guide-writers as Gervase Wheeler, and by the 1870s it had almost completely displaced traditional wood framing; yet it did little to introduce a new architecture. Likewise, metal-cage construction was hidden behind curtain walls of masonry shaped like Gothic buttresses or Renaissance arcades. Even the New York Crystal Palace of 1853, like its London prototype three years earlier, was detailed in vaguely "Saracenic" forms. What the "progressives" wanted to do was to bring out the "real" character of these materials, to design shapes and plans "natural" to them, whether it was the structural character of the steel cage as in Sullivan's tall buildings, the smooth whiteness and sculptural possibilities of poured concrete in Gill's houses, the roughness of stucco as Maybeck used it, or the infinite variety of oiled, roughed, jointed effects achieved by the Greenes in redwood.

But this kind of treatment was precisely what academic critics—and with them, the public generally—found so objectionable. The difference between Goodhue and Gill, or McKim and Sullivan, was not that one appreciated the idea of expressing the nature of materials and the other did not; it was a question of degree. As the eclectics saw it, this excessive and exaggerated emphasis on texture and frank expression of construction merely perpetuated the chaotic and vulgar formlessness of High Victorian Picturesque Eclecticism, from which they were trying to rescue architectural design. Of course they appreciated the effects achieved; it was Ralph Adams Cram who wrote of the Greenes' buildings that

> one must see the real and revolutionary thing in its native haunts of Berkeley and Pasadena to appreciate it in all its varied charm and its striking beauty. Where it comes from heaven alone knows, but we are glad it arrived, for it gives a new zest to life, a new object for admiration. There are things in it Japanese; things that are Scandinavian; things that hint at Sikkim, Bhutan, and the fastness of Tibet, and yet it all hangs together, it is beautiful, it is contemporary, and for some reason or other it seems to fit California. Structurally it is a blessing; only too often the exigences of our assumed precedents lead us into the wide and easy road of structural duplicity, but in this sort of thing there is only an honesty. . . .

But, he adds, "an honesty that is sometimes almost brazen." Precisely. Far better, said the academicians, to express materials in moderation, in conformity with older traditions, in ways and forms tested by the approbation of generations past. And only in retrospect did it become plain how wrong they were, how crippling this dependence on precedent must be. In the early 20th century, academic arguments seemed largely unanswerable; the triumphs of expression in the nature of the new materials had to wait for some more favorable climate than the Late Victorian years.

(3) *Generalized Symbolism.* Academicians and "rebels" both shared, again, the penchant

of their age for generalized and abstract rather than specific symbolic meanings read into architectural forms; again, the difference between them is one of degree. "Colonial" as interpreted by McKim, Mead & White, say, involved no nice distinction of the four phases in 18th-century classicism, and indeed distinguished little between 17th-century "colonial" and 18th-century "Georgian"—as so many of their college buildings so painfully show. But they did have very definite ideas about the difference between "Dutch," "New England," and "Palladian" styles, and were very ready to criticize those who ignored them. And the "progressives" by and large certainly did ignore them. Not only did they often take "colonial" as merely a synonym for "simple" or "unornamented," but they often went so far as to ignore historical styles altogether, and read meanings into purely abstract architectural qualities. They talked, in the language of Arts and Crafts Societies (of which an active body was established in Chicago in 1895 and chartered in 1897), of buildings expressing such things as "honesty" in ornament and "truth" in construction; indeed, of creating a new architecture free of historical reminiscence altogether in the "unspoiled" and "new" regions of the United States. "The West," as Irving Gill once put it,

> has an opportunity unparalleled in the history of the world, for it is the newest white page turned for registration . . . to hold the record of this generation's history, ideals, imagination, sense of romance, and honesty. . . .

Admirable, indeed, the sober academician might say; but what can it possibly mean in practical terms? Sullivan in particular presented a puzzle. He often seemed to talk less like a practicing architect than some kind of Old Testament prophet preaching moral revolution in occult allusions. He called bad buildings obscenities; he equated good building with moral virtue. It is all very well, and very moving, to ask rhetorically, "What is the chief characteristic of the tall office building?" and to answer oneself,

> It is lofty. This loftiness is to the artist-nature its most thrilling aspect. It is the very open organ-tone of its appeal. It must be in turn the dominant chord in his expression of it, the true excitant of his imagination. It must be tall. The force and power of altitude must be in it, the glory and pride of exaltation must be in it. It must be every inch a proud and soaring thing, rising in sheer exaltation that from bottom to top it is a unit without a single dissenting line. . . .

But such an answer is not really very helpful. The most disturbing thing, to the academic mind, is that these people seem to have no system. Truth and honesty are infinitely flexible; they vary according to circumstance. "Honest" expression of materials may mean emphasizing painted plaster in Sullivan's Transportation Building, ponderous stone in his Auditorium, steel cage in his Wainwright Building, glass in his Carson–Pirie–Scott Building. Ornament has no "meaning" any more; its purpose is only to articulate the total design and make the structure somehow more "honest." "True" construction means bringing out verticality in the Wainwright Building, horizontality in the Carson–Pirie–Scott. It is all a matter of individual decision, apparently.

Furthermore, Sullivan particularly seemed ready to carry his theories to such extremes that architecture in the old sense of an "educated" art seems on the point of disappearing altogether. He admires engineering for its own sake, to the extent that he seems to consider the Eads Bridge a work of architecture. He lavishes care on tombs, which by academic definition are not "living space" at all; the Ryerson and Getty tombs in Chicago (1889, 1890) and the Wainwright Tomb in St. Louis are among his finest designs.

"Functionalism" in the sense of utility and convenience the academicians could have perfectly well understood. But Sullivan meant at once more and less by the word than that. His

124. INHERENT SYMBOLISM IN EARLY MODERN ARCHITECTURE

Three examples of the "nature of American life and potentialities" expressed by generous proportions, free plan, frank use of materials:

ABOVE:

(A) David B. Gamble house, Pasadena, California, designed by Greene & Greene, 1908.

(124 B) Frederick Robie house, 5757 South Woodlawn Avenue, Chicago, Illinois, designed by Frank Lloyd Wright, 1909. Generally considered the quintessence of the "Prairie House." Commenting in his 1954 Exhibition catalogue on a predecessor, the "House in a Prairie Town" published in the Ladies' Home Journal for February 1901, Wright called his creation "the first truly democratic expression of our democracy."

*(124 C) Walter L. Dodge house, West Hol-
lywood, California, designed and built by Irving
Gill, 1914–16, in Gill's typical concrete medium
and on his characteristic luxuriously sprawling
plan.*

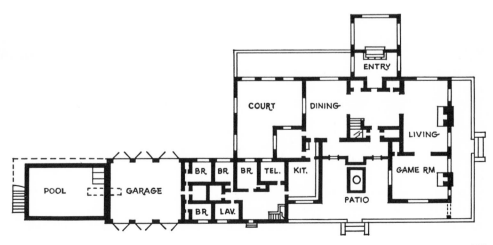

kind of "function" was—not so incidentally, like the Early and High Victorian concept—composed of emotional and spiritual as well as physical realities; and in this Wright, Maybeck, Gill, and the rest followed him. Indeed, these men seem to be aspiring to something far beyond the status of builders or educated gentlemen. They are becoming inspired seers and mystics, people who, like Humpty Dumpty, make forms mean what they choose; people who create worlds for themselves. How much more easily understood, how much more modest, the pose of eclectics who promise nothing more than faithfulness to inherited tradition! Or so it seemed to the public at large. In the personal world these self-styled "creative spirits" were building, most of their own generation was content to let them languish.

(4) *"Bigness."* It is common to contrast the work of men like Hunt, Burnham, and White, with their mania for "bigness," and the smaller-scaled production of Wright, Maybeck, and Gill, and of such architects, essentially residence builders, as George W. Maher (1864–1926) and Robert C. Spencer, Jr. (1864–1953). And certainly it is true that we hardly think of Pennsylvania Stations or Breakers or World's Fairs in connection with the California School or the Prairie Architects. Yet once again it is a question of degree; to imagine that "progressives" were exempt from the characteristic Late Victorian fondness for grand scale would be mistaken.

"Progressives" were not opposed to size as such. Sullivan had his greatest successes with big buildings like the Auditorium and the Wainwright. Wright handled with the same consummate skill as his smaller houses such grandiloquent ventures as the Wolf Lake Resort project of 1895, the Larkin Building in Buffalo, the McCormick mansion in Lake Forest, Midway Gardens in Chicago, and the Imperial Hotel in Tokyo. Maybeck's conceptions, as exhibited in Wyntoon, the Palace of Fine Arts, or the Anthony house were, to say the least, not petty; neither were the Greene brothers' ideas for com-

pany towns like Torrance. And certainly there is nothing small about the forms or spirit of the sprawling plans for Wright's or the Greenes' great houses, about the sense of great spaciousness common to all this new architecture (what one of his carpenters said of Maybeck could have been said of all these men: "He liked plenty of room up there"), about its characteristic large beams, broad windows, and grand fireplaces. The difference was not in size but in scale.

Common to all the "new architects" was their insistence on maintaining human scale. Where the eclectic academicians tended simply to blow up forms indiscriminately—to build Doric columns eighty feet high, mammoth vaults, reception rooms the size of convention halls—their rivals tried to keep forms in meaningful relation to human needs and comprehension. This concern informs the Wainwright Building; like a Renaissance palace, it has a unity immediately comprehensible to the mind. The "human scale" explains the decorative system Sullivan employed on the Carson–Pirie–Scott Building; all this lavish ironwork is placed down on a normal eye-level, where passers-by can see and appreciate it. Where Burnham in his Flatiron Building takes a pigeon's-eye view, Sullivan designs for men. His ornament serves to put the building into meaningful human proportion. Wright's prairie houses, the Greenes' rambling mansions, Gill's Dodge house, all have the same rationale—however big, sprawling, or complex they may be, they never lose human scale; they never become overwhelming or intellectually stultifying. With details, plans, and setting all designed in relation to one another, to human eyes, and the human mind, these houses are "classical" in the best and basic sense. That French critic who called Sullivan's Transportation Building a truer embodiment of the Beaux-Arts spirit than any of the "classical" buildings at the Chicago Fair could have made the same comparison between Wright's Taliesin East and the pompous academic villas at Newport; these "progressives" knew the difference between true bigness and mere inflated forms as the academic revivalists never could.

From this concern for human scale, too, grows the characteristic interest of all these men in "human engineering." It is no accident that Adler and Sullivan were famous for the acoustics of their auditorium, for the ballroom that could be emptied of 8,000 people in four and a half minutes, for the ingenious devices that contracted or enlarged the capacity of the theatre as necessary. Nor is it an accident that Wright's Larkin Building introduced such conveniences as an early air-conditioning system, new designs in metal office furniture and lighting fixtures. Or that Gill was famous for developing colored and waxed concrete, garbage disposals, vacuum-cleaner outlets, automatic car-washing devices in his garages, and what he described generally as "the idea of producing a perfectly sanitary, labor-saving house, one where the maximum of comfort may be had with the minimum of drudgery." Or that Maybeck should invent burlap sacking coated with foamy "bubble stone" concrete for fireproofing houses in areas prone to brush fires, built-in ovens, techniques for splattering and shooting paint onto walls. Nor is it hard to explain, in consequence, why despite the fall from favor of the Prairie architects and the California school generally after 1910, their work continued to have such a hidden, but for all that the more profound, influence on the evolution of the suburban "period house" in the following two decades.

It is this human scaling more than any other single characteristic, perhaps, that distinguishes the "rebels" of the early modern period both from their eclectic contemporaries and from the "Internationalists"—as Wright later called them —who followed them in the 1930s on the American scene. And it was on this scaling that their claim to be the most "American" of all architects was most securely based. For if you walk from one of the great halls of the Breakers or even from a shingle-style or colonial mansion into the parlor of an 18th-century house, you experience

at once the enormous gulf that separates Late Victorian academic creations from their supposed models; the one is on what is essentially a superhuman scale, the other is scaled to human living. Nothing like the same gulf exists between 18th-century building and comparable houses by the Prairie architects or the California school. Even though these later houses share the bigness of their age, they retain the old human scale— they belong in the humanist tradition—that the others, for all their pretensions to culture, dramatically lack.

(5) *"Richness."* Wealthy clients were by no means the exclusive perquisite of eclectic academicians. What Walter Curt Behrendt said of Wright in *Modern Building* applies in fact to all the "rebels" of that generation:

> Jacob Burckhardt . . . used to say that one must have money as well as luck and humor for the pleasure . . . of creating an unsymmetric building. This pious prescription has been fulfilled for Wright insofar as he has almost always been able to build for the more affluent, who have placed at his command large, and even unusual means.

Think of Wright's Dana Mansion in Springfield, Illinois, intended from the first to be a showplace where economy was no object; his Darwin Martin house in Buffalo; his palace for Harold McCormick at Lake Forest; his prairie houses generally. Or Maybeck's fairy-tale castle Wyntoon, and his half-million-dollar Anthony house in Los Angeles. Or Sullivan with Wainwrights and Ryersons for clients, Gill with the Mason sisters (patrons of Tuskegee), Walter L. Dodge, and George Marston; or the Greenes' $100,000—in pre-World War I money—Blacker house. These are hardly what you would call poor men's architects. Quite as much as Late Victorian eclecticism, early modern architecture developed in an age dominated by rich men, and shows it.

But this common ideal of "richness" is expressed here in a different way—not by ostentatious heapings-up of imported marbles and gilded furnishings, but by untrammeled expanses

125. "DEMOCRATIC RICHNESS"

(A) Exterior, and (B) interior of the Banking Room, of the National Farmers' Bank (now Security Bank and Trust Company), Owatonna, Minnesota, as designed 1906–8 by Louis Sullivan and George Elmslie. On this small commission Sullivan lavished a luxuriant richness of material and fertility of decorative invention characteristic of the great commissions of his heyday twenty years before.

of native materials: rugged redwood, smooth tile, rough stucco, massive boulders; not by conspicuous waste, but by judicious selection from abundance. It grows naturally out of the character of a society which is reaching unheard-of prosperity through fuller and fuller utilization of its lavish natural resources. That is why there is nothing hypocritical about these early modern architects at once building for men of great wealth and treasuring the philosophy of Walt Whitman. When they called their new architecture truly democratic, they did not mean it was or should be pitched to some lowest common denominator of taste, or that it was intended for poor men as contrasted to wealthy capitalists. There was no "leveling" involved in it. Rather, it was democratic in the sense that it demonstrated how in this new country men could aspire to something grander than mere blown-up copies of Renaissance palaces or medieval chapter houses; how they could create a new architecture, in every way finer, freer, more human, more beautiful, than anything history had yet seen. In this new architecture the old vision of a new Zion, of a reborn republic, lived in a form appropriate to the new age. To what Danas and Blackers and Dodges had, every citizen might one day aspire. For every citizen, industrialization meant that more and more of the old chores —baking, washing, sewing—could be done outside the home, that what had once been the work areas of kitchens and cellars could be turned into spaces for living. The development of central heating allowed plans to be spread out as never before; the development of rolled and plate glass meant that windows could be enlarged and the old separation of exterior and interior space broken down at will; the development of electricity meant that no room need be dark. These things their freedom let the "progressives" realize in practice far faster and far more fully than academic designers. And as they did, they witnessed to the potentialities of a society conceived in freedom and dedicated to equality of opportunity. Theirs was an architecture truly American,

deeply democratic, rich in the best sense.

(6) *"Mechanization."* "Mechanization" we defined earlier as that tendency for architectural offices to grow huge and impersonal, to become machines in which craftsmen, laborers, draftsmen alike had their individuality subordinated to the personality of the architect-director, while he in turn was bound by impersonal and arbitrary rules of styles long past and dead. Surely, here at last is one clear difference between academicians and "rebels." For is not the very foundation of the "rebel" position the idea of uncompromised personal integrity? Was not one of the main reasons that academicians flourished while the "rebel" cause faltered the fact that academic designers so slavishly followed earlier styles? Anybody could understand the "religious" character of a Gothic cathedral, appreciate the patriotic associations of Cape Cod bungalows or the appropriateness of Spanish churrigueresque for a California fair; but who except for the rare initiate of perception could imagine what kind of architecture might result from such a dictum as Sullivan's

> All life is organic. It manifests itself through organs, through structures, through functions. That which is alive acts, organizes, grows, develops, unfolds, expands, differentiates, organ after organ, structure after structure, form after form, function after function. That which does not do these things is in decay! This is a *law*, not a word!

Since Sullivan himself complained, according to Wright, that "Frank . . . , you are the only one who ever worked with me who understood," who could blame the masses, who had rarely seen "organic architecture" demonstrated in practice, for finding his theories unintelligible? Does this not prove that however else the "rebels" were part of their age, they shared nothing of its increasingly mechanical, organized spirit?

Not entirely. For the fact is, that although men like Sullivan and Wright did indeed demand for themselves complete freedom from obedience to outside rules and dicta, they showed little evi-

126. *"Mechanization in the Oak Park manner":* *Dining room of the Robie house, Chicago, Illinois, as originally designed by Frank Lloyd Wright, 1909. Everything—furniture, mantelpiece, lamps, window glass—is under the control of a single dominant mind: the architect's. Furnishings like these were not only designed as* integral *but also as* inseparable parts of the house; they were intended to go with it forever —when one owner sold a "prairie house," he was supposed to sell the furniture* in situ, *leaving it exactly as arranged by the architect. The architect's clients, in short, have no more individual freedom of choice and expression than the cabinetmakers or bricklayers who work for him.*

dence of wanting to extend the privilege to the men who worked for them. To the outsider, there seemed little difference between the lot of a draftsman or subcontractor associated with them, and one of the cogs in a Beaux-Arts machine.

Sullivan's chief designer, George Elmslie (1871–1952), is one example. Elmslie is now believed to have designed and supervised the execution of most of the decoration on the Carson–Pirie–Scott Building (1897–1903) and the Owatonna Bank (1906), for which Sullivan is famous; to have largely designed the Babson house in Riverside, Illinois (1907); to deserve at least equal credit for the Bradley house in Madison (1909). Yet until recent scholarship unearthed his part in Sullivan's work, his later

career in Minnesota, and his independent creations (e.g., Bradley house, Woods Hole, Massachusetts, 1911), Elmslie was no more than "faithful George," a stage property in the "Dear Master" legend of Sullivan's greatness.

Or consider the fate of Wright's early collaborators. Concerning them, Grant Manson said:

> In all truth, Wright, despite the power and originality of his ideas about the role of the minor arts in his houses, could not stand alone in executing them. The debt which he owed to clever craftsmen who, to their eternal credit, understood in those unsubtle days of house-furnishing what he was driving toward must be acknowledged. Chief of these, per-

127. ARTS & CRAFTS INTERIORS

(A) *Two typical interior designs by Gustav Stickley, published in* The Craftsman. *Founded by Stickley in 1901,* The Craftsman *was a great organ of the early 20th-century "progressives." In it were published the works of the Greenes, Irving Gill, Purcell, and Elmslie, to name only a few; and they in turn wrote for it. A regular feature was Stickley's complete "Craftsman Homes." As a chair manufacturer in Binghamton, New York, in the 1880s, Stickley (1858–1942) had conceived the idea of fusing Ruskin's and William Morris's cult of handicraft with the Late Victorian "Revival of Revivals," and making reproductions by hand of 18th-century models. But competitors soon began mass-producing reproductions and priced Stickley out of his market. Moving his operation to Eastwood,* New York, and renaming it The Craftsman Workshops, Stickley began designing "packages" of house and furnishings for mass production that would still retain the quality of handicraftsmanship. For the purpose he drew heavily on "primitive" precedent—wickerwork, and folk furniture generally, especially that of the Spanish colonial missions. The resultant simple, heavy, geometric forms were so easy to imitate that "mission" and "wicker" furniture soon degenerated into vulgarity, and by the 1920s was already being relegated to summer cottages and sun porches. Yet to appreciate how many forms and ideas the great figures of early modern American architecture took from the contemporary pool of "craft" ideas, one need only compare designs like these with those of the "Old Pioneers" of the modern movement, like the preceding plate, or with the next.

(127 B) Detail of the dining room in the James A. Culbertson house, Pasadena, California, built by Greene & Greene 1902, remodeled 1907. Tiled and hooded fireplace, wood carving by Charles Greene, redwood paneled walls, wood-work assembled with pegs, all represent an emphasis on handicraft and direct expression of materials less an invention of Wright or the Greenes than simply something "in the air" at the turn of the 20th century.

---

haps, was the Milwaukee cabinetmaker and decorator, George Niedecken. Wright relied upon Niedecken through the entire Oak Park period and well past it for the actual fabrication of everything that went into the custom-built Prairie House or club or public building. In the sense that what they contributed became physically integrated with the architecture, certain glassmakers, too, were of immense importance to Wright's early success. The leaded casements and interior doors, without which Wright's structures of the time would have had a blank, unfinished look, were usually the work of Orlando Giannini of the firm of Giannini and Hilgart—more rarely, of the Linden Glass Company. It is no exaggeration to say that Giannini was indispensable to Wright in bringing to completion his famous, personal vision of architecture.

But who, again, ever heard of Niedecken, or Giannini, or the sculptor Richard Bock (who executed the figures atop the Larkin Building buttresses, e.g.), or potter-muralist Blanche Ostertag, when they worked in the Oak Park studio, except as ancillaries to the master? Or of Paul Mueller, who directed construction of the Auditorium and Schiller buildings in Chicago for Sullivan and the Imperial Hotel in Tokyo for Wright? Such people were completely dominated—"he [Sullivan] had no respect whatever for a draughtsman," Wright once wrote admiringly—just as later the Taliesin apprentices were dominated, denied the very freedom of personal expression their Master so passionately arrogated to himself.

In the same way, the California school leaders buried the men who worked for them. Typical of them all was the Greenes' practice. Of their Gamble house in Pasadena, for instance, Esther McCoy notes that

> furniture, carpets, lighting fixtures, silverware, picture frames, linen, etc. were all designed for the house by the brothers, and no detail was left to the discretion of the carpenter; every peg, oak wedge, downspout, air vent, opening and fixture was designed into the whole. . . . The elaborate stained glass detail in the lighting fixtures was designed by Charles Greene and executed by Judson Studios. Instead of the usual leaded joint, the brothers developed their own method. . . .

In short, every one of the famous "rebels" exhibited to the full the characteristic tendency of the age to treat sculpture, engineering, carpentry, painting, and furniture as fundamentally minor arts, entirely and properly subordinate to the dominant personality of the architect. Where they differed from the academicians, of course, was in the freedom they demanded for themselves. And this was an enormous difference indeed. It was perhaps the one thing about them that most impressed the public—not always very favorably. For in the persons of men like Sullivan and Wright, even more than in their works, people sensed something indefinably, disturbingly, fundamentally new—a changed concept of the art of architecture, and of the status and function of artists in society.

NOTES

Quotations from Lewis Mumford, *Roots of Contemporary American Architecture* (1952), perhaps the most eloquent presentation of the *Sturm und Drang* motif in early modern architectural history; from review by Eric R. Arthur in the *Journal of the Royal Architectural Institute of Canada* (XXVI, 1949, p. 314); of R. A. Cram's *American Country Houses of Today* (1913) and article by Irving Gill in *The Craftsman* for 1907, from Esther McCoy, *Five California Architects;* from Sullivan's "The Tall Office Building Artistically Considered" (*Lippincott's Magazine*, LVII, 1896, pp. 403–8)—probably the most lucid statement of his creed Sullivan ever wrote; from W. C. Behrendt, *Modern Building* (1937), p. 41; from Wright's *Genius and the Mobocracy*, p. 91; from Manson, *Frank Lloyd Wright to 1910*, pp. 118f.; from McCoy, *Five California Architects*, pp. 112–3.

A standard account of the early uses of iron, glass, and concrete is found in S. Giedion, *Space, Time, and Architecture* (Cambridge, 1949). On skyscraper development in Chicago, see Carl Condit, *The Rise of the Skyscraper* (Chicago, 1951); in New York, Winston Weisman, "New York and the Problem of the First Skyscraper" (*JSAH*, XII, 1, pp. 13–21, 1953). On iron, see particularly T. C. Bannister, "Bogardus Revisited I: The Iron Fronts" (*JSAH*, XV, 4, 1956, pp. 12–22) and "II: The Iron Towers" (*JSAH*, XVI, 1, 1957, pp. 11–19). On the Jayne building, see G. B. Tatum, *Penn's Great Town* (Philadelphia, 1961), p. 181, Pl. 84; on the Providence Arcade, R. L. Alexander, "The Arcade in Providence" (*JSAH*, XII, 3, 1953, pp. 13–16).

On concrete generally, see the introductory section of A. A. Raafat, *Reinforced Concrete* (1958). Specifically on early examples, see C. E. Peterson, "Poured Concrete Building" (*JSAH*, XI, 2, 1952, pp. 23–4) and "Concrete Blocks, Honolulu, 1870s" (*JSAH*, XI, 3, 1952, pp. 27–9); also Louise Hall, "Mills, Strickland, and Walter: Their Adventures in the World of Science" (*Magazine of Art*, XL, 7, 1947, pp. 266–72). On early modern architecture as democratic expression, see James Marston Fitch, "Architects of Democracy: Jefferson and Wright," in *Architecture and the Esthetics of Plenty* (1961).

3. TOWARDS A NEW TRADITION:
The "Rebel" Rationale

WHAT WAS IT that "killed" Sullivan, Gill, and the Greenes, made Maybeck a conformist, crippled Wright for so long, and generally spoiled the flourishing early prospects of a new, modern American architecture in the early 20th century? The Beaux-Arts resurgence and entrenched power, certainly; American cultural immaturity, perhaps; "the sheer vulgar fatness of wealth," to some extent. But at least as much, possibly more, it was the intransigent arrogance of the leaders of the movement themselves.

To most people, their attitude and behavior seemed entirely inexplicable. That Sullivan at the age of thirty, already designer of the greatest structures ever built in America, should have "wandered about in a haughty sort of way," that "the Master's very walk at this time [as Wright remembered it in his *Autobiography*] bore a dangerous resemblance to a strut," was perhaps understandable if not endearing. But that the old Sullivan, poor, broken in body, neglected, should go on in the same way was absurd. J. R. Wheeler, president of the Farmers' & Merchants' Union Bank in Columbus, Wisconsin, recalled how "shockingly egotistical" seemed Sullivan's boast that his building "won't be copied, it can't be copied"; how very incongruous, considering the impoverished state of his affairs and reputation in that year of 1919 was Sullivan's reassuring admonition to his uneasy client to "just remember . . . you will have the only Louis Sullivan bank in the State of Wisconsin." It was almost as astonishing for Irving Gill, with his reputation still local at best, to walk out on jobs like the Christian Science Church in San Diego (1909) or the Duplex in Coronado for Louis Wilde (1919) because these clients insisted on telling him what features they wanted. Or that Bernard Maybeck, with all the academic hostility towards him, should continue his cavalier experimentations with materials at his client's expense,

should go on wearing his bizarre self-designed clothes and ignoring all the "rules" he learned in his years at the Beaux-Arts.

But most striking of all was the case of Frank Lloyd Wright. Even as a youth in Sullivan's office he affected patrician airs, long hair, flowing ties, and loose shirts *à la* Walt Whitman. You might think it was some grandfather reminiscing about the "good old days" who wrote,

> I well remember how "the message" burned within me, and how I longed for comradeship until I began to know the younger men and how welcome was Robert Spencer, and then Myron Hunt, and Dwight Perkins, Arthur Heun, George Dean, and Hugh Garden. Inspiring days they were, I am sure, for us all. . . .

But at the time Wright was thirty-nine, and a good many of the "younger men" he mentions were in fact older than he. Nowadays, when most of them have been forgotten by all but architectural historians, we tend to take for granted the assumption implicit in this article, that Wright towered over all his contemporaries; but that was hardly the case in 1908, when it was written. In the *Architectural Record* for those years, or the *Inland Architect,* or books like Von Holst's *Modern American Homes,* Wright's name figures as one among many, and by no means the most prominent. Few then could have guessed that the day would come when Hugh Garden would be remembered chiefly for his "Wrightian" lighting fixtures in Humboldt Park, or Dwight Perkins for his "Wrightian" Carl Schurz High School (Chicago, 1910); or that landscape architect Jens Jensen (1860–1951), whose work with the Chicago Park Service (1886–1900; 1906–20) changed the face of the city, would come to seem important chiefly as a counterpoint influence on Wright's development.

In short, considering the contemporary

reputations of early modern architects generally, their arrogance seemed to most people at the time not merely inexplicable but, when not patently ridiculous, unforgivable. And if we see them differently today, that is not so much because we are more charitable, perhaps, as that time has sifted genuine creativity from simple pretentiousness and—what is more important—given a historical understanding of what motivated their arrogance.

In the best of these men, arrogance was born of honest conviction, proceeding logically from given premises. Sullivan was their most articulate early spokesman. "One does not learn how to create beauty," he declared; "one becomes the kind of person who can and does create it." Artists, that is, were a different breed from ordinary mortals. Where carpenters or engineers or cabinetmakers or businessmen were people who had learned a trade or a technique or a skill, the architect was a person who could not be made by education, who was born with his superior perception. Sullivan sincerely believed himself to be that kind of person. Through no fault or presumption of his own, he happened to be superior to those around him. Wright believed the same. So, to a lesser extent, did Gill, Maybeck, the Greenes.

These men were hardly the first to take such an attitude. Long ago—four hundred years before, in fact—Leonardo da Vinci had made the same kind of claim. In an age when painters were generally considered as no more than skilled artisans, apprentice-trained craftsmen, he had dared to proclaim, in the *Paragone*, that "painting is philosophy . . . truly . . . a science and the legitimate issue of nature." He had declared that painting comprehended and surpassed all the other arts, that it was the painter's destiny to have a great and peculiar power:

If the painter wishes to see beauties that charm him, it lies in his power to create them, and if he wishes to see monstrosities that are frightful, he can be lord and god (Creator) thereof. . . . In fact, whatever exists in the universe, in essence, in appearance, in the imagination, the painter has first in his mind and then in his hands.

Thence the ideal of the artist as a superior being can be traced through later centuries; but only in the free-ranging individualistic world of the later 19th century could artists begin to think of this ideal as a reality. Only in the 19th century could a poet proclaim to the artist, as Schiller did, that "the dignity of mankind is laid in thy hands," and assert that he is "a king, living on the summits of mankind." And not until 1855, in Gustave Courbet's Pavilion of Realism in Paris, was the new creed explicitly set forth. There, in "The Studio" and the manifesto accompanying it, the traditional concern of artists with beauty was repudiated, and a new goal proclaimed: henceforth, the artist's function was to be discovery, definition, and revelation of reality. Henceforth, the artist was to be no longer a humble learner from nature, no longer a caterer to the whims and pleasures of patrons or public. Henceforth, he was to be a leader and not a follower, an intrepid seer, whose vision penetrated ever deeper mysteries of being, whose mission it was to lead mankind to ever higher perceptions of truth. Steadily during the next two generations the new concept spread, gained adherents; by the early 1900s it dominated advance-guard painting completely. Picasso and his emulators; Der Blaue Reiter; De Stijl; the Bauhaus—all in their several ways were dedicated to the proposition that artists could and should "save" society by creating a new realism, revitalize the meaning of life through artistic acts of creation and redemption.

And consciously or not, it was towards a parallel concept of the architect as a social leader and rejuvenator of society that the American "progressives" at the turn of the 20th century were moving. And in this context the penchant for sociological moralizing, which all the "rebels" without exception share, becomes not merely explicable but inevitable. It is no hobby, no yearn for publicity that motivates it; they feel it to be their plain and simple duty. They are not ordinary mortals, bound by the conventions of past and present, but form-givers who shape their own and all mankind's environment. They are godlike creators, with the right and duty of imposing form on the world not because they know the rules, or even because they make the laws, but because they themselves constitute the rules, on them "hang all the law and the Prophets."

Nor is it accident that such an ideal should have achieved the public expression of architecture—as distinct from the essentially private expression of easel painting—so early in America. Sometimes it has seemed incredible, mere chauvinistic boasting, to claim that Sullivan influenced Berlage, that Gropius and Behrens developed their architecture on the basis of Wright's early ideas, that Gill's experiments in concrete building antedated and surpassed Adolf Loos's. But in a sense it would be incredible had they not, for the United States was of all countries the one best suited to nurture what is essentially this new concept of Man the Creator. Except for the disaster of the Civil War, the concept might have developed even sooner. For what is involved here is nothing less than a reinterpretation of the traditional hope of Eternity, that translation of salvation from Heaven to Earth which had become an essential part of the American heritage and tradition. It was to the United States that men came in the 17th and 18th centuries to found new godly societies where Heaven on earth might be realized—communities of Peace, Brotherly Love, Hope, Charity. It was here too that the Christian communal ideal had been translated into the mundane terms of the Declaration of Independence, whereby the vision denied on a spiritual plane was to be realized in a new kind of free society, built by a new kind of free men. And it was in this direction, towards such a goal, that the "rebel" architects were setting out again at the end of the 19th century.

In a very real sense, this new concept involves the artist's becoming a god himself, the kind of rival creator to the Almighty that Mohammed condemned in the Koran and Moses in the Second Commandment. When Sullivan wrote,

> Every infant born in what is generally called normal health, is gifted by Nature with a normal receptivity, which if cherished and allowed to be nourished will unfailingly develop those normal, natural and sane qualities of mind to which today we give the name Genius. . . . The potentialities of the human mind are almost unlimited. . . . It is almost folly to talk of the limitations of the mind. . . . The so-called average mind has vastly greater powers, immeasurably greater possibilities of development than is generally supposed. . . .

it was more than the normal optimistic view of human evolution at the end of the 19th century, more than the fantasy of earthly paradises of supermen controlling wind and weather that we associate with H. G. Wells. Sullivan and his admirers are serious. They think of themselves as disciples of Herbert Spencer—nowhere in the world was Spencer more admired than in America—and through him of Darwin; it was no accident that one of the first things Sullivan did for the young Wright was to give him Spencer's *Synthetic Philosophy* to read. From such men they absorb the doctrine of inevitable upward evolution; and in American history, they think they see its best demonstration. But American history is not over; it is just beginning. The new society that the Founding Fathers brought forth on this continent will go on developing; it must and will go on, until it produces the new type of man this new environment predetermines, with capacities infinitely beyond anything now imagined.

That men can, must, and will develop these capacities they have no doubt. What is more, they believe they know the tool that can do it. That tool is art. Not so much the finished product —though that can influence environment and so predispose men to intellectual growth—as the act of creating itself. Through the act of designing, of painting, above all through the total experience of creating three-dimensional architectural concepts, men exercise and move towards fullest realization of their innate capacities. The result will be a new species of man, supermen, gods— of whom Sullivan, Wright, and the rest are harbingers and prophets. Sullivan expressed these aspirations with passion and prolixity in the *Kindergarten Chats:*

> If it happens that a given man be gifted, as is said, with stronger brain, more resolute will, a more fluid imagination, let him pause to reflect that these powers are not truly speaking his alone, that he did not make these original powers [here we might expect him to say God made them, but no——] but that they make him, and that they came to him out of the long birth-and-death struggle of the people of all times, and that he is answerable to all people—to the world—for their prolific democratic use.

Wright was more matter-of-fact. "Not only do I intend to be the greatest architect who has yet lived," he said in his fifties, "but the greatest who ever will live. Yes, I intend to be the greatest architect of all time." And still at the age of eighty-eight he was lamenting, "If I had another fifteen years to work I could rebuild this entire country. I could change the nation."

No wonder the "rebels" found acceptance of their views slow and difficult. Who wanted to be associated with such conceited visionaries? Who, certainly in the early days, could sort out the genuine creators from the mere romantics—who could distinguish between Wright and Elbert Hubbard, for instance? Both were outwardly eccentric in dress, both contemptuous of lesser breeds; who but the most recondite could see that "Fra Elberto" looked back to a fuzzy romantic past, Wright forward to a new world of promise? Surely it must have seemed to many that the attitude of the "rebels" towards the "reactionary" and "un-American" East represented the

same sort of chauvinistic Midwestern provincialism as did Ignatius Donnelly or William Jennings Bryan.

But there was an even more deep-seated opposition to the new ideas, which sprang from their very nature. This was no mere change of "style." This was a change of tradition, comparable to the shift from medieval to classical at the beginning of the 18th century, from classical to Victorian a century after that. As such, it involved something more than educated taste. It demanded acceptance of a whole new set of basic premises about art, a re-evaluation of the bases and direction of American life. And such a re-evaluation American people generally were not prepared to make in the first three decades of the 20th century. Associated as it was with an age in which the country had grown to national greatness, the Victorian tradition was not so easily shaken.

Even had the Victorian tradition been weaker, acceptance of the ideas of the "rebels" would have been hampered by the fact that so many "rebels" had so little specific or conscious understanding of what they were ultimately doing, and in consequence presented their ideas with such confusion and inconsistency. So it was that when the Victorian rationale was finally shaken by the Great Depression to the point where new ideas were broadly welcomed, it was not, by and large, from the native pioneers of the modern movement that Americans took them. They turned instead to the more systematically formulated architecture emanating from Europe. And with this development, beginning about 1930, the story of modern architecture proper—as a new tradition resting on a broad basis of popular acceptance—commences.

NOTES

Sullivan's attitude at the end of his life is well described by John Szarkowski, *The Idea of Louis Sullivan* (Minneapolis, 1956), "Prologue," pp. 2–17. Quotation from "In the Cause of Architecture" (*Architectural Record*, XXIII, 1908, pp. 155–221). On Jensen, see Leonard Eaton, "Jens Jensen and the Chicago School," (*Progressive Architecture*, XLI, 1960, pp. 144–50).

20th-CENTURY MAN
AND 20th-CENTURY ART
IN THE UNITED STATES

II

Modern Architecture between the Wars:

From Cult to Cultural Expression,

c. 1920-1940

1. "MODERNISM" AND THE "PERIOD HOUSE":
"Normalcy" in the 1920s

The armistice was signed this morning. Everything for which America fought has been accomplished. It will now be our fortunate duty to assist by example, by sober, friendly counsel and by material aid in the establishment of a just democracy throughout the world.

SO PRESIDENT WILSON expressed, on November 11, 1918, the generally held view of what American entry into the Great War a year and a half before had meant. Like most people, he believed that it marked the end of one era in American history and the beginning of another. In this he was right. But as to what the change involved he was, like most people, mistaken. He assumed that breaking with the traditional policy of avoiding "European entanglements," entering the "war to end war" and saving the faltering Allies, meant that in years to come American ideals would be spread over Europe, that what had begun on this continent in 1776 was now to be consummated on a world-wide scale, that people everywhere were about to fall under the spell of American ideas, and be taught the blessings of life, liberty, and the pursuit of happiness as practiced in the United States.

But, of course, what actually happened was very different. The American people as a whole did not rush forward to "assist . . . throughout the world." Instead, they rushed back into their past, tried desperately to pretend that nothing had changed at all, that there had been no entanglement, that the world was just as wide and Europe just as far away as ever. And since in fact it was not, since travel to and from Europe and interchange of ideas were in fact proceeding on a scale unprecedented in history, the result was first a decade in which "the American heritage," so far from being exported, was jealously guarded against any possible contamination from "sick" and "corrupt" Europe; and next, a decade

in which European ideas flooded into the United States as they never had since the 1860s. All of which was faithfully manifested in American architecture between the wars.

By the time the United States entered it, the Great War had long been beyond winning. For those who had been in from the start—England, France, Germany, Russia—it had gone on so long and cost so much that everything about it, the whole social and intellectual and political system that made such a catastrophe possible, had come to seem senseless and ridiculous. By 1917 Lloyd George, stumping England on a "We Shall Win" campaign, was greeted with derisive calls of "Win what?" On the other side of the trenches Paul Bäumer, hero of *All Quiet on the Western Front*, mused that "for us lads of eighteen they [his teachers, i.e., the whole older generation] ought to have been mediators and guides to the world of maturity, the world of work, of duty, of culture. . . . But the first death we saw shattered this belief. . . . The first bombardment showed us our mistake, and under it the world as they had taught it to us broke in pieces." And when at last "what was left of the war generation had crept out of the massacre to find their elders still bellowing the slogans of 1914," the result, as George Orwell remembered it, was that "the old-young antagonism took on a quality of real hatred," and "so far as the younger generation was concerned, the official beliefs were dissolving like sandcastles."

Nowhere was this more evident than in postwar European art. What once was considered as peevish and eccentric criticism of Victorian aesthetics appeared to the new generation as a body of revealed truth, condemning the whole Victorian approach to art forever. What the Victorians had considered idle or visionary speculation about the possibilities of expression in "modern" materials and techniques now became the basis of a new and fervent faith. That brave new world which the young had lost all confidence in their elders' ability to bring about, they came to believe could be achieved through the medium of art, by new godlike artists who could and would "make all things new." As yet, this younger generation in Europe actually built little. In the nature of things, architectural taste on any large scale is usually dictated by older, richer, socially powerful men; tangible expressions of the "new spirit" had to be confined largely to painting and crafts. But though building comparatively little, the young architects planned big. In small groups—the German Bauhaus in Dessau; the Stijl group in Holland, Le Corbusier and his circle in Paris—they laid plans, devised formulas, to rebuild society on new, "realistic" foundations over the ruins of the old sham; to sweep away those petty nationalisms which had nurtured the farces of Victorian art and world war, bring in a truly New Tradition, a universal "International Style."

In the United States, the immediate effects of the war were quite different. Proportionately far fewer of its population had been casualties; economically, the nation came out of the war richer, not poorer. Furthermore, this first immersion in European affairs after a century and a half—in the horrors of trench warfare, in the inane wranglings of what was curiously called the Peace Conference—served largely to confirm American convictions that Europe was, after all, just as Jefferson had described it: a nest of pirates and robbers, hopelessly degenerate, corrupt in craftiness, full of crazy ideas. A violent reaction back to the "good old days," to 100 per cent Americanism, was inevitable. In the social sphere, the result was prohibition. In foreign affairs, high tariffs and anti-immigration laws. In politics, the cult of "normalcy." And in art, what seemed the final defeat and collapse of the turn-of-the-century "rebels" and the lasting triumph of a Late Victorian eclectic concept of "Americanism."

Superficially, American architecture during the 1920s generally seems considerably more "modern" than its antecedents of the 1890s and 1900s. Buildings big and small, skyscrapers and suburban homes, all generally appear to be simpler in form, more obviously related to natural environments. Best representative of the age, perhaps, was the upper-middle-class suburban residence that has been called the "period house." Its allusions to historical styles are much less specific and literary than those of the Victorian villas from which they derive. To be sure, period houses are usually recognizable as "Tudor" or "Spanish" or (most often) "colonial," and they preserve a general "picturesqueness" of irregular outline. But they have much less detail and ornament; they suggest historic styles in massing, by a few obviously borrowed details, in general proportions and materials, rather than by exact imitation. And they characteristically establish a much closer relationship between exterior and interior space. The typical suburban house plan of the 1920s is looser and more sprawling, the rooms generally fewer in number, but larger and

---

FACING PAGE:

128. The House of Dr. F. W. Pratt, Bronxville, New York, Penrose V. Stout, Architect, from House Beautiful *for 1926. From the advertisements of magazines like this the full rich scent of the 1920s rises—its lingering Victorianisms in symbolism ("The oldest houses in America are built of wood and none are so homelike as those of wood. . . .") and taste for additive decoration ("Elsie de Wolfe says, 'Plain walls are the refuge of the artistically destitute!' Send for booklet, 'Wallpaper, Room by Room'"); its adulation of science ("Every housekeeper knows how ordinary wood toilet seats soon become hard to clean. . . . Now science has changed all this—a marvellous substance called Whale-Bone-Ite . . ."). And despite superficial modernities, the "period houses" promoted in such magazines were full of lingering Victorian symbolism and picturesqueness, too.*

THIS HOUSE HAS BEEN PLACED IN SUCH A WAY AS TO PRESERVE AS MANY AS POSSIBLE OF
THE TREES AND THE NATURAL SLOPE OF THE LAND. IT HAS A NARROW TERRACE AT THE
FOUNDATIONS TO GIVE IT AN APPEARANCE OF STABILITY. THE EXTERIOR WALLS ARE OF
STUCCO, COLORED A LIGHT SALMON-PINK, WITH A BROOMED SURFACE, AND THE ROOF
SHINGLES, LAID WITH AN UNUSUALLY NARROW EXPOSURE, ARE GRADUATED IN COLOR
FROM BLACK AT THE EAVES, THROUGH VARIOUS SHADES OF BROWN, TO A GOLD AT THE
RIDGE. THE TRIM IS VERY DARK BROWN, AND THE SASHES A DEEP RED

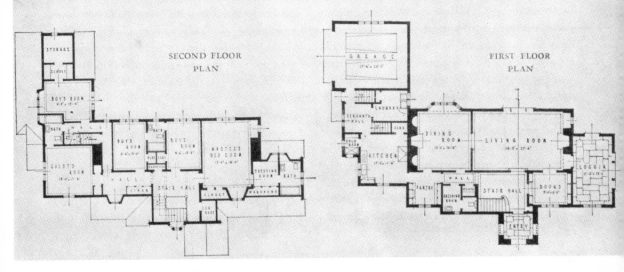

SECOND FLOOR
PLAN

FIRST FLOOR
PLAN

more irregular in size, so that exterior space is incorporated in corners and angles. Verandahs and porches tend to be reduced to small stoops or disappear entirely; their place is taken by terraces and carports at the back or side of the house, which demand lots on the average considerably larger than before. But the same qualities characterize large-scale work as well. Great housing speculations like Coral Gables near Miami (from 1922 on), Shaker Heights outside Cleveland (1916 on), the "garden suburb" of Radburn, New Jersey (throughout the 1920s); public monuments like Magonigle's Liberty Memorial in Kansas City (1925) or Goodhue's Nebraska State Capitol (completed 1932); famous skyscrapers like the Tribune Building in Chicago (designed by Raymond Hood, 1922) and the Empire State Building in New York (Shreve, Lamb & Harmon, 1928–31)—all show the same tendencies to over-all simplification, reduction of eclectic detail to suggestions of Gothic or Renaissance or colonial, and integration of exterior and interior space (in skyscrapers, by stepping back stories; in housing speculations, by landscaping, curved roads, open plans, etc.).

"Modernism" like this, obviously enough, is as superficial as the "progress" represented by prohibition or normalcy, and for the same reasons—essentially, its rationale derives not from present or future, but from the past. It represents no attempt to create a new architecture on fundamentals, derives from no new convictions about "realism" in life or art. As much as anything else, perhaps, the cleaner lines and plainer ornament of skyscrapers in the 1920s result from the disappearance of craftsmen and the consequent prohibitive expense of ornament on the old lavish scale. As for the period house and its surburban-development cousins, their "simplicity" represents less aesthetic conviction than a perpetuation of typically Late Victorian vagueness of symbolism; simpler or not, their forms are still used to symbolize an essentially literary idea, the concept of American life as somehow distinctively plainer and purer than that of

degenerate Europeans. Similarly, their emphasis on natural settings and integration of space indoors and out is not so much a conscious expression of technology altering the existing relationship between men and nature as a nostalgic attempt to recapture the old American "pioneer heritage," to recover by force of imagination the old confident feeling that the United States is a free, empty country where the sky is still the limit; it is no accident, perhaps, that the "Western" movie which embodies this same "American dream" also achieved its definitive form in the 1920s.

Such an atmosphere made the 1920s the dark decade of modern architecture in America. To most people, it seemed that "modernistic" architecture had incorporated the best creative ideas of the "rebel" generation of the 1890s and early 1900s; with the exception of Frank Lloyd Wright, its leaders withered and froze, and Wright only survived the decade by means of a few commissions in California (Barnsdall house, Hollywood, 1920; Millard house, Pasadena, 1923, e.g.) and elsewhere, and publicity-catching designs like the St. Mark's Tower in New York (1929), which, though unexecuted, still kept him from vegetating as Gill and Sullivan had, or conforming as Maybeck and most of his old Chicago associates seemed forced to do. As for the new ideas developing in Europe, Babbitt summed up the judgment of "normalcy" upon them; Americans had nothing to learn from "a lot of shabby bums living on booze and spaghetti." Only a trickle from the ferment going on across the ocean reached the United States, and that chiefly through the agency of occasional Europeans settled in the country and keeping up contacts abroad, such as Raymond Schindler and Richard Neutra from Austria, William Lescaze from Switzerland, and Eliel Saarinen from Finland. At the time none of them cut what could be described as imposing figures. Only in the long run did it become apparent how significant their work in the 1920s had been, as a preparation for the great influx of European ideas which transformed the American architectural scene in the decade following.

Earliest to come was Raymond Schindler (1887–1953); he arrived in 1914, attracted by the European fame of Frank Lloyd Wright. Schindler was the draftsman in charge of the Taliesin office during Wright's absences in Japan (1917–21), and his work in California during the 1920s showed in open planning, interpenetrations of exterior and interior space, and relation of planning to site (his own Kings Road house in Hollywood, 1921–2; Packard house, Pasadena, 1924; Lovell beach house, 1926; Wolfe house, Catalina Island, 1928). But Schindler could never quite forget his education and early work in Vienna; even when he was most under Wright's spell, his work had a kind of doctrinaire emphasis on simplicity of texture and construction foreign to Wright's poetic approach, and owing a good deal to Adolf Loos's example. He used great expanses of plain concrete, canvas, insulating board; he invented undercut grooves to replace drawer handles; and so on. And when in 1931 he and Wright had a violent quarrel over Schindler's claim to a major share in the work of the Taliesin office while Wright was away, Schindler's European background at once came to the fore. His work in the early 1930s implicitly manifested the "Internationalist" theme of the house as a "machine for living"; his smaller houses particularly (the William Oliver house, Los Angeles, 1933, e.g.) were stark in their simplicity, almost mechanical in their insistence on efficient planning—bathrooms with Pullman basins, furniture designed as simple units combinable in a variety of ways, designed to fit into walls to conserve maximum floor space as if in a ship or train; tiny and compact kitchens more like laboratories than living spaces— while his larger houses (Buck house, Los Angeles, 1934; Rodakiewicz house, Beverly Hills, 1937) were composed as interlocking geometric blocks in the spirit of Le Corbusier and the cubist painters.

Richard Neutra, trained in the same Vienna Academy as Schindler, had remained in Europe throughout the war and come to the United States (with Schindler's assistance) only in 1923, at the age of thirty-one. In consequence, he was always closer in sympathy to the developing "modern" architecture of Europe than Schindler, and it was perhaps inevitable that their early collaboration soon ended. The town house that Neutra designed for Dr. Phillip Lovell in Los Angeles in 1928 represented one of the first full-blown appearances of the new European architectural ideas anywhere in the United States; there was nothing "modernistic" about its advance-guard structural and ornamental severity, and it is hardly surprising to find Neutra in the 1930s one of the foremost exponents, in precept and example, of the concept of "human survival through design" propagated by the German Bauhaus.

William Lescaze came to the United States in 1920, when he was twenty-four, and established an office in New York three years later. He lacked connections, however, and his first works were mostly minor (e.g., Capitol Bus Terminal, New York City, 1927). Only in 1929, when he was fortunate enough to find a sympathetic partner in George Howe (1886–1955), did he have an opportunity to introduce to America the ideas he had learned from Karl Moser in the Zürich Technische Hochschule; but then he introduced them on a grand scale. Howe had been commissioned as early as 1926 to prepare designs for the main office of the Philadelphia Savings Fund Society, and in them had been steadily working away from what he described as the "Jumbo, Anti-economy Romantic Country House package"—i.e., period houses—on which his earlier practice had been built, towards bolder expressions of material and structure. Lescaze provided the direct connection with European developments and experience that could give Howe's ideas mature form; together, Howe and Lescaze created what Professor Jordy has called "the most important tall building erected between the Chicago School of the 80s and 90s and the metal

425

and glass revival beginning around 1950," and a major impetus in the "International Style" wave of the 1930s.

Most famous of all these Europeans, and in the public mind at least considered the leading representative of "modern" as compared with "modernistic" architecture (whenever such a distinction was made) in the United States during the 1920s, was Eliel Saarinen (1887–1950). His arrival in 1922 and subsequent appointment as professor at the University of Michigan in Ann Arbor were motivated by his competition

design for the Chicago Tribune Building (1922), which was widely admired in all sorts of diverse quarters, and imitated in many covert ways. That design seemed, at the time, to be quite free of historic precedents, a challenge to the domination of Late Victorian eclecticism all the more welcome because so well mannered and unimportunate. In retrospect, we can see that this was hardly the case. Professor Creese has demonstrated convincingly how much Saarinen's Tribune design, as well as his later Chicago Lake Front (1923) and Detroit River Front (1924)

129. EUROPEAN INFLUENCES IN THE 1920s
   (A) Phillip Lovell (Health) house, Los Angeles, built and furnished on the designs of Richard J. Neutra, 1928. Architecture and furniture were conceived totally in terms of 20th-century technology, completely free of historical reminiscence—one two-story wall of glass, the rest of thin concrete shot against expanded metal; balconies suspended by slender steel cables from the roof frame; chair seats suspended from metal tubing; an ostentatiously dramatic site, proclaiming technological mastery of environment.

(129 B) *Philadelphia Savings Fund Society Building, Philadelphia. Built 1929–32 on the plans of George Howe and William Lescaze. The same kind of dramatic statement of the new* "*pure architecture*" *as the Lovell house, but this time in the most conservative center of the conservative East, it served notice that the decade of* "*normalcy*" *was over, and with it the hold of Victorian tradition on American architecture.*

projects, owed to medieval and folk precedent in Finland, to the vaguely medieval side of the work done by Otto Wagner and Joesph Olbrich in the Vienna Workshop and by Sullivan in Chicago, and to Viennese city planner Camillo Sitte's idea of a return to "organic" medieval principles. In retrospect, too, it is apparent that Saarinen's famous "modern" buildings at Bloomfield Hills in Michigan (Kingswood School, 1929; Institute of Science, 1930–33; master plan for Cranbrook Academy of Art, 1931) represented essentially the same sort of simplification of historical precedent, rather than anything truly new.

And it was precisely because Saarinen was so far from a radical, because his kind of modern architecture was so close in spirit to the period house, that he could achieve the reputation he did in the 1920s. Only because "Howe was no wildly revolutionary modernist, but, like [PSFS President James M.]

Willcox, saturated in the great tradition," could he have been entrusted with the commission for the Philadelphia Savings Fund Society Building; only because Beaux-Arts principles could be demonstrated in them were his "modern" plans approved. For the fact was that the United States in the 1920s simply was not the kind of place where direct challenges to Victorian traditions, of the sort being made in Europe, could succeed. If Americans wanted to know what was going on in Europe, they had to go there to see; if they wanted to practice the new ideas, they had to stay. During the Coolidge era, it seemed as if the Victorian age were going to be indefinitely prolonged in the United States. But then, abruptly, everything changed. The Crash of 1929, and the Great Depression that followed, shook American confidence in the old system as the war never had. American culture was gripped by an anti-Victorian mood; the old order ended and a new one began.

NOTES

Quotations from E. M. Remarque, *All Quiet on the Western Front* (1929), Chap. 1, and George Orwell, "Inside the Whale," *Inside the Whale and Other Essays* (1952). On period houses, see Jonathan Lane, "The Period House in the 1920s" (*JSAH*, XX, 4, 1961, pp. 169–78). On Neutra, see Esther McCoy, *Richard Neutra* (1960). On Howe and Lescaze, see W. H. Jordy, "PSFS: Its Development and its Significance in Modern Architecture" (*JSAH*, XXI, 2, 1962, pp. 47–83). On Saarinen, see A. Christ-Janer, *Eliel Saarinen* (Chicago, 1948), and the perceptive article by Walter L. Creese, "Saarinen's Tribune Design" (*JSAH*, VI, 3–4, 1947).

2. FROM EUROPE TO AMERICA:
Anti-Victorian Reaction in the "International Style"

. . . The entire generation of businessmen of which he [Hoover] was a part was under singular disadvantages in understanding the twentieth century. They had been brought up by the masterful post-Civil War generation of business magnates and had inherited their ideas. The success of the earlier generation had been impressive, and the prestige of its ideas . . . ran correspondingly high wherever the old promises of American individualism still warmed the spirits of men. That life is a race which goes to the swift was still plausible to many people in 1891 when Hoover entered Stanford, and classic spokesmen of the *status quo* like William Graham Sumner at Yale were still thundering at undergraduates the truth that millionaires are the bloom of a competitive civilization. Although the heated criticisms of the Progressive era slightly tarnished these notions, they were refurbished and repolished in the New Era of the twenties. The terrible and sudden collapse of 1929 left the inheritors of the old tradition without a matured and intelligible body of ideas to draw upon and without the flexibility or morale to conceive new ones. Driven to reiterate with growing futility the outworn creed on which they had been suckled, the very men who had made such a fetish of being up to date, pragmatic, and hardheaded in their business activities now displayed in politics the sort of archaic, impractical, and flighty minds that made the Liberty League possible.

SO RICHARD HOFSTADTER described the suddenness of the reaction against the old order in business and economics that begin with the 1930s. It was the same in art. All at once the older academic ideas seemed "archaic, impractical, and flighty"; the persons and principles of the old "progressives" of Chicago and California took on new and widespread appeal. No longer did they seem isolated eccentrics, but noble figures who had cried truth in a wilderness. All at once people everywhere wanted to find out what they had to say. Unfortunately, few of them were saying much any more. Gill was inactive. The Greenes had retired to potter in philosophy. Sullivan was dead. Griffin was in Australia. Purcell was ill, Elmslie was old, Maybeck was tired. Only Frank Lloyd Wright was as vigorous as ever, and this was the decade in which he stepped forward into really wide acceptance and national prominence.

People were ready to listen now to Wright's ideas of an "American" art, tempered as they were by the trials of the 1920s. He found patrons ready to build what he envisaged, began to realize his ideals on a bigger and better scale than ever before. In his Johnson Wax Company Building in Racine, Wisconsin (built 1937–9), Wright perfected, elaborated, and refined the principles inherent in the Larkin Building twenty years before; and for every one who knew his earlier work, a thousand acclaimed what he built now—the concept of the factory as a shelter, a "home away from home," closed to the outside world but fully opened up within; the rich technical inventiveness displayed in "golf tee" supports and glass tubing; the principle of humanizing the industrial process, anticipating what a still later generation would call the "other-directed" and "people-oriented" corporation, all one big happy "family" dedicated to group adjustment and the proposition that business is a joyful way of life. In Falling Water, the Kaufmann house at Bear Run (Pennsylvania, 1937), Wright presented the basic principle of the "Prairie House"—total integration of architecture with total environment—in a new, more mature, more dramatic form: the core of the house literally growing out of the living rock, its "arms" swinging free in space like a windmill, a man-made tree of steel and glass and concrete taking some natural and predestined place in the rugged forest. The "Usonian House" that he demonstrated first at Madison, Wisconsin (Her-

130. "OLD" AND "NEW PIONEERS" IN THE 1930s

(A) Lobby of the Administration Building at S. C. Johnson & Son, Inc., Administration and Research Center in Racine, Wisconsin, built on the plans of Frank Lloyd Wright, 1936–9. Imbued with but never dominated by 20th-century technology, this building carried on ideas Wright had first given form in the Larkin Building in Buffalo (1904): richness of texture, humanization of scale and ornament, the factory conceived as a shelter built by, for, and around man. But whereas in 1904 Wright's achievement was known only to a few people, in the changed atmosphere of the 1930s this design made him nationally famous.

FACING PAGE:

(130 B) Interior view of Siegel Hall, physics and electrical engineering building of the Illinois Institute of Technology, Chicago. Built 1956–7 on a master plan devised by Miës van der Rohe, 1939. Though an educational institution,

this building resembles a factory far more than Wright's Johnson Wax Building (indeed, it has an almost "assembly line" duplicate in the I.I.T. chemistry building). Here technology is in command—stark steel framework, plate glass, concrete dictate their own terms to designer and user alike. However unattractive the view of sheds and parking lot outside, the nonbearing outside wall must be opened; however uninteresting the pattern of buff brick or plywood or ceiling panels, they must be left alone. In the comparison between the "purity" of Miës's expression of structure and materials and Wright's dramatization of their inherent warmth, color, and decorative patterning is all the difference between the "Old Pioneers" of the turn of the century and the International Style generation of the 1920s.

bert Jacobs house, 1937), later in the Suntop Apartments at Ardmore, Pennsylvania (1939), if it failed to materialize Wright's Jeffersonian dream of independent citizens each freely and happily living in and with their own bits of American soil, still made millions aware of the idea who had never heard of it before. And to all of them the concept of an "American art" created not by allusions to past styles, but out of American conditions, needs, materials, and technology, spoke with new clarity and persuasiveness.

Relatively few acted on the concept, however. In scattered parts of the country regional "schools" did appear, based on generally "organic" principles. One example is the Pacific Northwest architecture of Pietro Belluschi (b.1899); Harwell Hamilton Harris's development of Maybeck's principles in California is another. But in the United States as a whole, the voices of the old native prophets were drowned out by those speaking in louder and more bewitching foreign accents of the accomplishments of the generation of the 1920s in Europe. While new ideas were being paralyzed by normalcy in the United States, the Europeans had been able to go on working, establishing schools, publishing prolifically. The result—or so it seemed —was the doctrine of a new art and architecture more "scientific" than Wright's, more coherent than Sullivan's, more consistent than Gill's or Maybeck's. And it was to these voices and this doctrine that the bulk of the younger spirits turned.

The new gospel came first in books—as always. One of the earliest was Henry-Russell Hitchcock's *Modern Architecture* of 1929, by which title he meant essentially "the architecture of the New Pioneers, the international style of Le Corbusier, Oud and Gropius, of Lurçat, Rietveld, and Miës van der Rohe." Others followed, in floods; however great their reticence in matters ornamental, the New Pioneers had little when it came to publicizing themselves and their works. Architectural opinion in the United States responded spectacularly. Raymond Schindler, for instance, had once called the International Style "an expression of the minds of a people who had lived through the World War, clad in uniforms, housed in dugouts, forced into utmost efficiency and meagre sustenance, with no thought for joy, charm, warmth"; now he began to build something very like it himself. So did Eliel Saarinen, as comparison of the earlier with the later units of his Cranbrook Academy buildings shows clearly enough. Neutra and Lescaze, of course, needed no incentive to work in the new manner (California Military Academy, West Los Angeles, 1936; CBS Building, Hollywood, 1936, e.g.). By the mid-1930s the United States was ready for the New Pioneers in person; and thanks to Hitler's follies, they soon began to arrive. Walter Gropius (b. 1883), director of the seminal Bauhaus in Dessau during the 1920s, came to Harvard in 1937 at Dean Hudnut's invitation to be professor in the School of Architecture (he soon became head of the school); he brought with him Marcel Breuer (b. 1902), a sometime pupil of his from the Bauhaus, famous for "functional" furniture composed of bent steel tubes (rather like Thonet's bentwood furniture, and Peter Cooper's famous chair of the 1860s and 70s). The next year Gropius's successor at the Bauhaus, Ludwig Miës van der Rohe (b. 1886), arrived in Chicago as Director of Architecture at the Armour Institute (now Illinois Institute of Technology). And these were only the best-known figures in a great wave of European intellectuals, chiefly Germans or German-educated, streaming into the country—designers like László Moholy-Nagy at the Art Institute of Chicago, and Joseph Albers, who taught at Black Mountain College in North Carolina and later at Yale; art historians of all descriptions, headed by Erwin Panofsky; such painters as George Grosz, Piet Mondriaan, and Wassily Kandinsky; all at least sympathetic to and most of them actively propagating the general ideal of an international style in contemporary art. By the end of the 1930s and through the 1940s they made their International Style the dominant vehicle of American artistic expression, steadily but surely overriding the opposition of native eclectics and radicals alike.

This success was not so much due to anything actually built by the New Pioneers in America—Gropius and Breuer in fact built little in the 1930s beyond a few small houses, while Miës was largely preoccupied with his master plan and first buildings for his Illinois Institute of Technology campus (begun 1939); it was simply a case of their being better attuned to the "climate of the times." If they so soon held such strategic positions in the American educational world, it was simply because their European experience in the 1920s gave them the same kind of advantage over native architects in satisfying the new demands of suddenly shifted currents in American life that had been enjoyed by the comparable wave of immigrant architects in the 1860s. But most of all, their success was determined by the nature of the International Style itself.

Like all major cultural movements, modern architecture took form less in response to reasoned argument than to an intuitive and emotional sense of "rightness." Before 1914 it was a positive moral appeal that had most weight; indeed, when the early Chicago and California school architects argued for "honest" expression of materials, "clean" lines, or "natural" and "organic" structure, they often seemed to be doing little more than restating, in different terms, the time-honored pleas of classical and Gothic revivalists for "good" and "virtuous" building. After the Great War it was different. The appeal was still to a sense of morality—but in a reverse, negative way. As we look back on the 1920s now, it seems obvious that the really driving incentive behind the International Style as it developed in Europe during those years was simply revulsion against all things and ideas Victorian. Architects take the High Victorian age as their horrible example, and create a kind of negative image of it. Were Victorian buildings composed of complex shapes, intricately organized? They will take the simplest shapes, assemble them without fuss. Did Victorians like to texture walls in colorful patterns? They will keep theirs smooth and plain. Victorian surfaces were loaded with ornament; theirs were iconoclastically blank. Victorians enjoyed manipulating materials in bizarre ways; they insist on leaving them alone—largely unpainted, unmoulded, unadorned, as nearly as possible in their natural state. Victorians disguised the structure of buildings; they go out of their way to expose it, deliberately use stone and wood as nonstructural, ornamental sheaths, even if this involves denying the primary nature of the material. Where Victorians loved picturesque, bulgy outlines, they are infatuated with severe flat planes. Where Victorians deliberately emphasized the roughness and solidity of materials to create an effect of monumental bulk, they equally deliberately emphasize reflective surfaces—glass and polished stone and steel—which dissolve the solid mass of the building and make it melt into its surroundings.

Of course advocates of the "New Tradition" could point to plenty of positive qualities, too. They claimed it was more economical, more functional, more healthful, than Victorian architecture; and so, more often than not, it was. But these were at best relative and not absolute merits. If people complained that great expanses of plain concrete or glass left their souls unthrilled, that factories ought by some means to be distinguished from churches or office buildings or schools, that an upended box of steel and glass did not quite represent Sullivan's ideal of the tall building as a "soaring thing," that free-flowing interior space was something less than a perfect solution to the problems of life in a family with three or four children, that glass walls were one thing in city apartments and quite another in lonely countrysides—to such complaints there was no absolutely convincing answer. The best you could say was that "architecture ought to be created in the spirit of its own times."

Which of course was both irrefutable and meaningless—who decides what is the spirit of the times one lives in? The criteria of the "New Tradition" were in fact (and as always) ultimately subjective; the secret of its appeal was precisely that it did so sensitively answer a prevailing mood in the 1920s and 30s. And it is as a cultural expression that the International Style is still most meaningful today.

NOTES

Quotation from R. Hofstadter, *American Political Tradition* (1948), pp. 298–9. On Wright in the 1920s and 30s, see Henry-Russell Hitchcock, *In the Nature of Materials* (1942). Perhaps the best introduction to the International Style as contemporaries in America saw it in the early 1930s is Henry-Russell Hitchcock and Philip Johnson, *The International Style: Architecture since 1922* (1932). On individuals, see *inter alia* Peter Blake, *The Master Builders* (1960, on Wright, Le Corbusier, Miës); J. M. Fitch, *Walter Gropius* (1960); Jo Stubblebine, *The Northwest Architecture of Pietro Belluschi* (1953); E. B. Mock (ed.), *Built in USA*, 1932–1944 (1944).

3. NEW DEAL, NEW ORDER, NEW ARCHITECTURE:

The "International Style" as American Cultural Expression

WHAT WAS THERE about the International Style that made Americans in the 1930s turn to it and its European New Pioneers instead of to their own "Old Pioneers" of Chicago and California at the beginning of the century? In part, of course, no more than the old ambivalent American attitude towards Europe: on the one hand taking for granted American superiority in wealth, in political stability, in "vigor" and "free enterprise"; on the other still feeling inferior in sophistication, historical experience, intellectual savoir-faire. But what was more significant, the anti-Victorian emphasis of the International Style suited the dominant mood of the 1930s so very much better. That same Whitmanesque optimism and Darwinian sort of faith in progress which made the turn-of-the-century "progressives" typically American now made them seem merely embarrassingly naïve. Rather than these lingering Victorianisms, the New Pioneers seemed to offer precisely what they claimed —a really New Tradition. And the International Style represented a tradition, furthermore, whose premises seemed to correspond so perfectly to the spirit of its times that all reasoned justifications were unnecessary. To rationalize its principles seemed as superfluous to the intelligentsia of the 1930s and 40s as questioning the self-evident "rightness" of classical principles had seemed to the 18th-century mind, or the desirability of "picturesqueness" to High Victorians. In the International Style's basic premises the fundamental spirit of these decades was expressed to complete satisfaction. We could summarize these premises roughly as follows:

(1) *Negative Morality.* The New Tradition took for granted that "good art" was primarily achieved by avoiding what was "bad." In nothing was it closer to the spirit of its age than in this; many of the most characteristic phenomena of life in the 1920s and 30s rested on the same premise. Flourishing religious cults based on the general principle that evil is the absence of good, and vice versa. "Progressive Education"— keeping children from unpleasantness makes them pleasing. Prohibition—society made moral by default. Disarmament and pacifism—get rid of armies and munition makers, and peace must descend. Socialism—eliminate wicked capitalist institutions, and a golden age of virtuous abundance is ensured. This premise so infected the thought of the times, was so taken for granted, that it was often left unspoken; yet we can always recognize it. Consider, for example, the following presentations of the idea that "happiness begins at home," as typical expressions of their respective centuries:

> The main of life is, indeed, composed of small incidents and petty occurrences; of wishes for objects not remote, and grief for disappointments of no fatal consequence; of insect vexations which sting us and fly away, impertinences which buzz awhile around us, and are heard no more. . . . For very few are involved in great events, or have their thread of life entwisted with the chain of causes on which armies or nations are suspended; and even those who seem wholly busied in public affairs, and elevated above low cares or trivial pleasures, pass the chief part of their time in familiar and domestic scenes . . . to be happy at home is the ultimate result of all ambition, the end to which every enterprise and labour tends, and of which every desire prompts the execution. [Samuel Johnson, *The Rambler*, No. 68, Saturday, November 10, 1750]

> The first act of Nicholas, when he became a rich and prosperous merchant, was to buy his father's old house. As time crept on, and there

came gradually about him a group of lovely children, it was altered and enlarged; but none of the old rooms were ever pulled down, no old tree was ever rooted up, nothing with which there was any association of bygone times was ever removed or changed. Within a stone's-throw was another retreat enlivened by children's pleasant voices, too; and here was Kate . . . the same true, gentle creature, the same fond sister, the same in the love of all about her, as in her girlish days. [Dickens, *Nicholas Nickleby,* 1839]

The thought flitted through Winston's mind that it would probably be quite easy to rent this room for a few dollars a week, if he dared to take the risk. It was a wild, impossible notion, to be abandoned as soon as thought of, but the room had awakened in him a sort of nostalgia, a sort of ancestral memory. It seemed to him that he knew exactly what it felt like to sit in a room like this, in an armchair beside an open fire with your feet in the fender and a kettle on the hob, utterly alone, utterly secure, with nobody watching you, no voice pursuing you, no sound except the singing of the kettle and the friendly ticking of the clock. [George Orwell, *Nineteen Eighty-Four,* 1948]

All three writers make the same point; but whereas Johnson and Dickens make it positively, Orwell puts it in negative terms. Johnson describes a "minimum good" attested by the experience of ages in the measured, balanced phrases of 18th-century classicism, like those stating inalienable rights to "life, liberty, and the pursuit of happiness" in the Declaration of Independence. Dickens wraps an ideal of material and marital security in a series of images as rich and specifically detailed as the decoration on a General Grant villa. But Orwell, using the terse "realistic" prose of the 1920s and 30s, envisions the good life as those few moments when unhappiness is absent—when one can be free from unpleasantness, pain, and fear. His is the same unspoken assumption that motivates the anti-Victorian emphasis of the International Style, as we have seen it. And on this assumption, too, Le Corbusier and his followers devise their ideal city plans; the way to make people content is to eliminate by scientific analysis all the foul air,

131. THE POSTWAR TRIUMPH OF INTERNATIONAL STYLE PRINCIPLES

(A) Meditation Room, United Nations Building, New York: "a room of quiet, devoted to peace and those working for it. A fresco by the Swedish artist Bo Beskow and a six-ton polished block of Swedish iron ore are the main features." The United Nations complex as designed by Wallace K. Harrison and an international board of design was the great monument at once to the new international role of the United States in world affairs, and the triumph of International Style principles in architecture at home during the later 1940s. In this room the basic anti-Victorian negative morality of the International Style finds microcosmic expression: as peace is to be attained by eliminating positive elements of discord, so the ultimate in religious expression is to be achieved by ignoring everything suggestive of dogmatic controversy. Whatever the consequences of this premise in international diplomacy, the architectural result is four walls enclosing two cult objects—one a block of iron, the expression of a variety of religious experience last enjoyed by the tribesmen of Mecca before Islam; the other, a painting of the "New Reality" created by a 20th-century man to provide a religious experience of his own.

poor light, crowded conditions of their Victorian urban environment, then package what is left into multistory boxes of steel and glass. In the disillusioned atmosphere of the 1930s, the superiority of such planning to Wright's positive ideal of enriching individual environment seemed self-evident. Every family on its own free acres seemed an archaic, Utopian, Victorian notion to a generation that considered the anti-Victorian premise of the International Style not so much negative as simply natural and right.

(2) *Salvation through System.* Those who embraced the New Tradition took for granted, again, that artistic salvation—the creation of a new and vital art—lay in some simple system or creed. Of course they were far from alone in assuming that such systems did exist and could be found, in every aspect of life. Theirs was the same trust that inspired admiration for Jay Hambidge's discovery that the secret of artistic success lay in the "dynamic symmetry" ascertainable in Greek vases and Gothic temples; or, at the other end of the social scale, magazine readers who clipped coupons and sent away for ten easy lessons that would make them painters or pianists of genius, accomplished raconteurs or well-paid writers. But of all these "systems," the International Style offered the greatest prestige, the least Victorian associations, the most cosmopolitan satisfactions. To men confused and disturbed by an age of upheaval and dissolution, when, as Fitzgerald's famous cliché had it, all wars were fought and all gods dead and all faiths in man shaken, the New Pioneers offered the same simple means of escape from baffling problems of individual choice, the same welcome relief at belonging finally to some coherent, organized, disciplined body of belief that led other men variously to embrace Fascism, Communism, or the Catholic Church. As some found in Marx-

(131 B) Wire-frame chairs by Charles Eames (b.1907) of California, typical of the furniture for which Eames became famous in the 1940s. Their ultimate inspiration derives from the structural theories of Bauhaus design generally, and in particular from the tubular chairs developed in the mid-1920s by Marcel Breuer and Miës van der Rohè. By the 1950s such furniture was found everywhere, taken for granted as a normal appointment of life in a society based on mass consumption, mass production, and common International Style tastes.

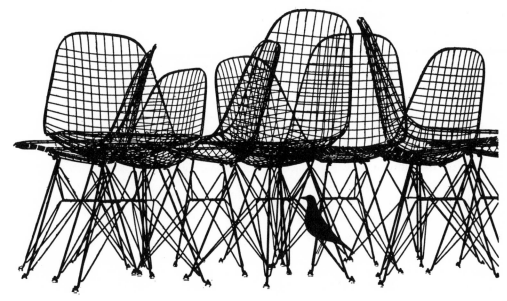

ism an infallible key to understanding all the perplexing contradictions of capitalism and nationalism, as others let themselves be persuaded all their troubles were the fault of wicked Jews and "November criminals," and still others that the ugliness of 20th-century mechanization could all be traced to 16th-century Protestant Reformers, so the young American artist, harassed by the conflicting claims af academic Goths and Romans, "radical" designers and Art-Nouveauists, machine worshipers and handicrafters, found irresistible appeal in the simplicity of the regenerating formulas preached in Gropius's Bauhaus, in Neutra's doctrine of "survival through design," in Le Corbusier's Modulor, in the kind of simple basic unit employed by Miës to unify the complexities of the Illinois Institute of Technology buildings.

Of course the basic principles of the International Style system were hardly new. Emphasis on simplicity, textural values, free interpretation of exterior and interior space, incorporation of new technological achievements in planning and design—all these were characteristic of Wright or Gill or Maybeck twenty years before, as well as of the period houses still being built. The difference was one of degree. International Stylists made these tenets a fervent creed, carrying them to their relentless conclusions with *furor Teutonicus* and remorseless Gallic logic. And this kind of fervor was precisely what Americans in the 1930s were looking for. "The only thing we have to fear is fear itself," Franklin Delano Roosevelt had said in 1933; and the cause of fear was lack of leadership, the feeling that American culture had somehow been left "without a matured and intelligible body of ideas to draw upon and without the flexibility or morale to conceive new ones." Very well; the International Style offers leadership. To be sure the New Pioneers, like President Roosevelt, often seem a bit unsure of their direction; like him, they have a markedly tentative and experimental streak. For all their talk about good art they tend, if you pin them down and ask on what grounds one judges

between good and bad, to give equivocal answers; they admit, in fact, to having nothing like the absolute rules and principles that governed art in the classical tradition, nor even the kind of general consensus that determined what was or was not "picturesque." In their positive opinions they show what the sociologists would call "other-directedness"; they rely for validation on the shifting values of their own "peer group." That they do so does not matter. On one question they are positive, and that is what counts: they know what "bad" art is. Whether or not they are sure what they like, they emphatically know what they do not like. The do not like "Victorian"; and they can provide you with unequivocal rules and formulas to keep you from being Victorian —or, as Le Corbusier once put it, a way to make "good" art easy and "bad" art hard. Nothing could be simpler, and, in the climate of the times, more instantly convincing.

(3) *Democratic Equality*. "Democracy" in the American tradition has always meant liberty more than equality. Whenever the two conflicted in the past, Americans had preferred to be free rather than equal, and they would make the same choice in the future again. But not in the 1930s; nothing better reveals the depths to which American traditions had been momentarily shaken than the acceptance by so many intellectuals at that time of the European concept of democracy as demanding equality above all else, however maintained. And when the New Pioneers spoke of democracy, this, of course, was the kind they meant. Their simple rules and formulas were "democratic" because they were binding on all men everywhere and reduced them to a lowest common denominator of cubic, regular, bare building. This, as they saw it, was the great

breach between Wright and the younger architects who created the contemporary style after the War. Ever since the days when he was Sullivan's disciple, Wright has remained an individualist. A rebel by temperament, he has refused even the disciplines of his own theories. . . . The case against individualism in

(131 C) Lobby of the Hotel Americana, built on the plans of Morris Lapidus in Miami, Florida, 1950. In the lavishness and indiscriminate agglomeration of its decoration, this hotel is clearly Victorian in spirit, irresistibly reminiscent of nearby Vizcaya: "ceramic door escutcheons, enamel elevator panels, handmade Cuban lamps, handmade Peruvian and Panamanian tile and other objets d'art . . . a huge terrarium [seen here] 35′ in diameter and 40′ high . . . containing a miniature volcano-type mountain and one of the most complete collections of subtropical rain-forest flora in existence." But, in forms, it belongs to the New Tradition.

architecture lies in the fact that Wright has been almost alone in America in achieving a distinguished architecture; while in Europe, and indeed in other parts of the world as well, an increasingly large group of architects work successfully within the disciplines of the new style. There is a basic cleavage between the international style and the half-modern architecture of the beginning of the present century. . . . While the innovations of the half-moderns were individual and independent to the point of divergence, the innovations of their juniors were parallel and complementary, already informed by the coherent spirit of a style in the making. [Hitchcock and Johnson, *The International Style*, 1932, pp. 26–8]

It was an attractive premise. Surely a uniform art based on elementary principles derived from the obvious nature of things, and universally applicable, was more truly democratic than one based on academic scholarship, or the jostling caprice of "half-modern" Old Pioneers. Surely a reduction of artistic complexities and mysteries to a lowest common denominator most truly gave expression to the "Age of the Common Man," even if the "common man" was hardly yet aware of it. Even Wright briefly succumbed to the mood of the moment, and in the first edition of his 1930 lectures at Princeton published some "Nine Principles of Design," a kind of short course in "organic architecture made easy." He recovered quickly, however, and in the second edition left them out. For most of his contemporaries it was different. It took them decades more to realize how many layers of esoteric implications lay beneath the superficial simplicities of International Style doctrine; how many of the International Style leaders were in fact intellectual aristocrats ("What," Le Corbusier was to write later at Chandigarh, "can grocers and peasants know of the work I am doing?"); in short, how foreign to American traditions was International Style democracy. In the egalitarian atmosphere of the 1930s, all these things seemed not merely minor and unimportant, but a positive asset—another of the International Style's expressions of the spirit of the times.

(4) *Economic Determinism.* International Style theorists shared with Bolsheviks and businessmen alike the pet premise of the 1920s and 30s that economic causes can explain almost everything. Underlying and motivating all overt differences of political opinion, the struggles of nations and classes, philanthropy, marriage customs, and religious creeds are basic economic facts; he who understands this principle and works in accordance with it is wise in his generation. And in their generation, the leaders of the "International Style" were indeed the wise men. They taught that good architecture must above all be "functional," by which they meant (among other things) that the architect must never forget he is part of the community—or conversely, that his art grows out of "community forces and resources." What he does is conditioned by economic forces, which in turn are determined by technology. As a typical apologist put it:

Roman architecture . . . developed so far from the Greek model on which it was based because the Romans discovered the use of the round arch and vault, whereas the Greeks built only with columns and beams; and Gothic church architecture blossomed out of the simple solidity of the Norman period into more and more daring feats of construction, chiefly as the medieval architect-engineers learned the science of mechanics and discovered thereby exactly how small a pier could safely carry the load of a roof, and how it was possible to transfer some of the downward thrust on to a series of flying buttresses. . . .

Modern architecture is conditioned by the same sort of factors. We know more exactly than our ancestors how materials behave in different circumstances, and we have invented or discovered a number of new materials. For both these reasons our range of vocabulary is greater, and for the former reason we have no excuse for building unscientifically. We cannot avoid the obligation to build scientifically. In no past age did men build less skilfully than they knew how. [J. N. Richards, *An Introduction to Modern Architecture,* 1940, Chap. III]

That this is hardly so—that things happen, and always have happened, the other way round, is beside the point. Never mind if there is no law that says the nature of materials *must* be expressed, their structural potentialities *must* always be fully exploited; or that there is no evidence people always built to the limit of their technological capacities and plenty of evidence that they did not. What if the Greeks did know about round arches and vaults, if Romanesque builders knew about pointed rib vaults, if Theophilus knew about oil painting long before Jan van Eyck, and Victorians about iron-and-glass construction half a century before "modern" architects? What if it was only as the impulse and necessity to use these innovations later developed that their implications were worked out? Or that if you take for your criterion the complete expression of the technological resources of your age, you must conclude (as many did) that practically all architecture before 1920 was "bad"? It does not matter. For the International style was not dependent on any theory of functionalism for justification; rather, theories of functionalism were propounded to justify modern architecture in terms to suit the temper of the times. Functionalism helped present the New Pioneers in a "democratic" light; where an Old Pioneer like Sullivan had declared creativity to depend on individual genius, the New Pioneers modestly implied that what they built was inherent in the economics of their age—had they not done it, community forces and resources would have generated other builders like them. And the correspondence of International Style principles with economic determinism had still further advantages; it made the New Pioneers seem "scientific" and (since it was in fact they and not others who had been perceptive and responded to the economic forces of their times) let them appear coleaders in the march of science towards a brave new 20th-century world.

(5) *The Scientific Attitude as a Way of Life.* Science, as Frederick Lewis Allen observed in *Only Yesterday,* was one of the few human activities to survive the Great War unshaken in people's minds:

> The prestige of science [in the 1920s] was colossal. The man in the street and the woman in the kitchen, confronted on every hand with new machines and devices which they owed to the laboratory, were ready to believe that science could accomplish almost anything; and they were being deluged with scientific information and theory. . . . The word science had become a shibboleth. To preface a statement with "science teaches us" was enough to silence argument. If a sales manager wanted to put over a promotion scheme or a clergyman to recommend a charity, they both hastened to say it was scientific. . . .

And, needless to say, architectural writers did the same. Eclectics like Cram claimed their reproductions of older styles were "scientific"—which, compared to preceding efforts, they certainly were; apologists for Wright's "organic" architecture could claim that to study and observe nature's structural principles in trees and

birds and butterflies was the essence of science. But theirs was nothing like the "scientific attitude" embodied in the International Style. For the New Pioneers, science was more than a technique; it was a religion.

You could sense it in their writings:

> The reality of our century is technology: the invention, construction, and maintenance of the machine. To be a user of the machine is to be of the spirit of this century. It has replaced the transcendent spiritualism of past eras,

as Moholy-Nagy once put it. You saw it embodied in their stark exposures of structure. In the New Pioneers' envisaging of such wholesale rebuilding of cities on "scientific lines" as Le Corbusier's plans for Paris and Algiers, you recognized the visible expression of science's claim to remake the world. You felt it implicit in the idea of putting art education on new "scientific" foundations promulgated by Bauhaus theoreticians; in talk of controlling temperature with buildings that revolved in the sun, of manipulating climates with gigantic domes arching over whole countrysides. But most of all you found the scientific attitude consummated in the New Pioneers' attitude towards ornament.

Perhaps the most striking distinction between the New Tradition and all older ones was in the aversion to ornament as such. Any and every kind of applied ornament was rejected on principle—Sullivan's or Wright's quite as much as Georgian pilasters or Victorian gingerbread. This aversion went beyond mere anti-Victorianism; it sprang from an approach to ornament fundamentally new in history. The Victorian age, for all its scientific advances (and science, after all, was no 20th-century invention), still revered the past; and the classical mind, for all that it rejected medievalisms, similarly revered antiquity. But the typical New Pioneer despised "the old" in general. Victorians liked to think of themselves in historical perspective; when they learned the facts and laws of history (which were, of course, "scientific"), they believed they were learning about themselves, and they liked to express their oneness with the past in their architecture. But the new, self-consciously "modern" men felt no such tie with the past. They used their knowledge of the past to free themselves from it. They felt they were not part of history; they *made* history. You can see this most obviously in the new totalitarian states of the 1930s, like Nazi Germany or Communist Russia, whose rulers busied themselves rewriting history to suit their own purposes, re-creating the past so as to control the present and the future; but a similar attitude to history appeared everywhere to a greater or lesser degree. The past as an objective fact with any real influence or claim on them ceased to exist for large numbers of people in the 1920s and 30s, particularly in "intellectual" circles. Scorn for an architecture that borrowed from the past or was in any way dependent on it, followed as a matter of course.

In this relationship with the past the New Pioneers parted company both with the eclectics and the Old Pioneers, with the Beaux-Arts men and with the generation of Sullivan, Wright, and Maybeck in America, and McIntosh, Otto Wagner, and Berlage in Europe. They had only scorn for the idea that ornament humanized art, contempt for people who complained about schools looking like factories and churches looking like department stores:

> Wright belongs to the international style no more than Behrens or Perret or Van de Velde. . . . Their individualism and their relation to the past, for all its tenuousness, makes of them not so much the creators of a new style as the last representatives of Romanticism. They are more akin to the men of a hundred years ago than to the generation which has come to the fore since the War. [Hitchcock and Johnson, *The International Style*, 1932, p. 27]

The starkness of the New Tradition, its mechanical qualities, the New Pioneers felt to be positive merits. For if they held one principle more firmly than any other, it was this: that anyone who wanted to be part of the 20th century had to understand that this was an Organization Society, dependent on scientific machines not only for goods but for its whole way of life, and that all art and all living must, to be successful, be conceived and governed accordingly.

(6) *"Totalitarian Order."*

> . . . We are now but on the threshold of the coming era of true cooperation. The time is fast going by for the great personal or individual achievement of any one man standing alone and without the help of those around him. And the time is coming when all the great things will be done by the cooperation of many men in which each man performs that function for which he is best suited, each man preserves his individuality and is supreme in his particular function, and each man at the same time loses none of his originality and proper personal initiative, and yet is controlled by and must work harmoniously with, many other men.

Who could have written a passage like this? It sounds like something that might have come out of the Bauhaus—an expression of the "cathedral" philosophy of all artists submerging themselves in the discipline of a great Whole. Or possibly some Marxist of the 1920s, developing the to-each-according-to-his-need-from-each-according-to-his-ability line. But it was neither; far from being a Marxist, the author was one of the great formulators of late-19th-century industrial capitalism; far from being an artist, he was an efficiency expert. The writer was in fact that Frederick Winslow Taylor whose efficiency studies for the Bethlehem Steel Company in the 1890s earned him the title of "father of scientific management" in American industry. But the passage could quite as well have been written by or of any of the New Pioneers of the 1920s and 30s, for it perfectly expresses their basic conception of the proper relationship of artists to their work. As they saw matters, the architect controls everything, using "scientific" principles. Like the efficiency expert, he designs chairs and tables, flagpoles and fountains, factories and city squares, not as entities in themselves but always as units within a larger whole. Climaxing a process begun in High Victorian times, he brings about the extinction of furniture design as such. Once take it for granted that there is absolutely no difference in basic principle between a complex of skyscrapers and the humblest chair in a reception room, and furniture becomes nothing more than a contributing element to a new kind of Total Architecture. It is thus no accident that most of the New Pioneers—as distinguished from Old Pioneers like Sullivan, Wright, Gill, Schindler—began their careers in some other field than architecture: Miës and Breuer in furniture design, Rietveld as a jewelry draftsman, Le Corbusier in painting, for example. In their careers they symbolize the subsumption of all other arts under the Master Art of architecture.

But the moment this happens, the architect in the old sense ceases to exist, too. He becomes a kind of efficiency expert. He sees furniture as part of buildings, buildings as parts of cities, cities as parts of landscape, landscape in relation to the universe, on all of which he feels compelled to impose some kind of "order." His "scientific" mind is horrified at the panorama of heterogeneous individuals—buildings, people, plants—all unorganized, all going their own ways, just as it is horrified by the idea of designers, craftsmen, engineers, builders, each with *their* little sphere of supremacy. As the fearful consequence of such freedom, he points to the chaos of the Victorian streetscape, with its buildings of every size and shape and style jostling in furious competition like the bourgeois merchants who built them. The solution, clearly, is to stand outside the whole process, analyze it objectively, then devise a master order into which all the disparate units best fit—to act, in other words, like the scientist running a laboratory team, a Frederick Winslow Taylor called in to study a corporation program, a Mussolini making locomotives and marsh drains and political enemies all run on his schedule.

And this, in effect, is just what the New Pioneers try to do. But when it comes to stepping back into the plan themselves, to guide and direct it, they find something quite unexpected has happened. The analogy with efficiency experts breaks down. It is one thing to put plans for reorganizing office routine or yard work into operation; quite another to rebuild a city. The difference is that the expert does not expect to enforce the plan himself. He takes his pay and departs, leaving the corporation to put it into effect or not—and the corporation has full power to do either. With the architect it is different. He wants to direct the execution of his plans himself; without his supervision and leadership, he feels, they will be manhandled. Yet this he cannot manage. Physically, the kinds of plans the New Pioneers make are not those that architects can execute alone. Even a sizable house requires many subcontractors and official permits; as for skyscrapers and city plans, they require the services of big loan companies, real estate operators on a corporation scale, politicians on every level. And the architect soon finds that they who pay the piper call his tune; he is shouldered aside while politicians, corporations, financiers decide among themselves what form architecture shall take in practice. Psychologically, too, he loses control of the situation he has created. Once abandon the principle of natural, organic growth, once begin imposing "scientific plans" on society or architecture, and you are doing something "radically new" in a sense the New Pioneers never quite envisaged. They never really intended to leave man out of the picture; they always intended to bring the individual back into their building sooner or later. But in fact, what happened is well summarized by analogy in Professor J. W. Ward's analysis of the significance of Frederick Winslow Taylor's innovations in "scientific management":

What Taylor has done is stand outside the work process, consider all its parts, and put it together again in its most logical order, which is what we mean by saying that he has rationalized the work process. But Taylor never questions the unstated premise that work is in and of itself its own measure of value. Quite the contrary, testifying before a Congressional Committee that was inquiring into his system, he explicitly accepted that criterion: "In my judgment," Taylor said, "the best possible measure of the height in the scale of civilization to which any people has risen is its productivity."

Now this is a curious remark; only in modern western civilization could it have been made. In the East—in India and China at least until they too decide to "modernize"—in ancient Greece and in Christian Europe until the end of the middle ages, it was the most obvious and axiomatic piece of orthodoxy that action was a means to the end of life which was contemplation. In Taylor's world, and in the world of modern industrialism, this is utterly reversed: thought is a means to further action. Action, Work, Productivity—choose what word you will—these become ends in themselves.

. . . In a book setting forth the principles of his system, Taylor said bluntly, "In the past the man has been first; in the future the system must be first." Taylor had the great virtue of seeing clearly what he was doing. . . .

This virtue was one New Pioneers rarely possessed in the same measure. Yet the "primacy of the system" was at bottom the rationale of International Style architecture in the 1920s and 30s; and it is no accident that this principle triumphed in American architecture when it did. For just as the blank walls and steel columns and glass curtains of the great new plants American corporations were constructing in the late 1940s and 50s marked the disappearance of Victorian traditions in American art, so the transformation of the ideal executive from rugged individualist to bland blender-with-the-group marked the final collapse of the Victorian spirit in American business and social life. Whether the New Tradition meant a permanent transformation of the nature of art or was merely a catalyst, unimportant in itself but serving to set the stage for possibilities of new expression, would be the central problem in architectural practice and theory in the years that followed.

NOTES

Reference to Jay Hambidge (1867–1924), *Dynamic Symmetry in Composition as used by the Artists* (1923), *The Parthenon and Other Greek Temples: Their Dynamic Symmetry* (New Haven, 1924), etc. On International Style systems, cf. the three principles enunciated by Hitchcock and Johnson, *The International Style*, 1932 ("A First Principle: Architecture as Volume; A Second Principle: Concerning Regularity; A Third Principle: The Avoidance of Applied Decoration"); preamble (2nd edition, Cambridge, Mass., 1954) to C. É. Jeanneret [Le Corbusier], *The Modulor: A Harmonious Measure to the Human Scale Universally Applicable to Architecture and Mechanics;* on Bauhaus theories H. Bayer, (ed.), *Bauhaus* (1938), P. Klee (introd. Sibyl Moholy-Nagy), *Pedagogical Sketchbook* (1953), etc. Relevant here is the discussion in P. H. Scholfield, *The Theory of Proportion in Architecture* (Cambridge, Eng., 1961), Chap. VI, pp. 105–26. Reference to Frank Lloyd Wright, *Modern Architecture: Being the Kahn Lectures for 1930* (Princeton, 1931). Quotation from Frederick Lewis Allen, *Only Yesterday* (1931), Chap. 8, Sect. 4. Quotation from J. W. Ward, "The Organization Society" (*University*, V, 1960, pp. 8–11). For architectural analogies, cf. C. É. Jeanneret [Le Corbusier], *Towards a New Architecture* (London, 1931), W. Gropius, *Scope of Total Architecture* (1955).

20th-CENTURY MAN
AND 20th-CENTURY ART
IN THE UNITED STATES

III

Since 1945:

Architecture, Civilization, and Man
in Modern America

WHEN HENRY-RUSSELL HITCHCOCK wrote *Modern Architecture* in 1929 and *The International Style* in 1932, it was as a young critic working in the spirit of a Peacecorpsman helping bring the blessings of enlightened civilization to some underdeveloped land. Thirty years later he could describe "The Rise to World Prominence of American Architecture" in a very different mood. Then, as acknowledged dean of architectural historians throughout the world, he could say without hesitation that "for good or ill, modern architecture has come to seem almost synonymous with American architecture."

Generally speaking, the forms of this new American architecture as they crystallized in the 1950s were derived from International Style precedent and formulas. That was inevitable, perhaps. Though Wright's prestige in these years had grown to enormous proportions—never had he been more prolific than in the decade before his death in 1959—his style was always too personal for successful mass emulation. It was on the teachings of the New Pioneers, radiating from a dozen key points in the American educational system since the late 1930s—Gropius alone trained at Harvard a dozen and more of the most outstanding architects coming to maturity in the late 1940s and 50s—that the bulk of "modern architecture" in the United States was based. What had once been their revolutionary emphasis on flat roofs, horizontal window strips, wide plain expanses of wall, exposed steel and concrete and glass, and general lack of ornament was now commonplace for offices and apartments in every city, schools and churches and drugstores in every town, diners and motels and gas stations along every highway. In these circumstances the style often enough consisted of clichés, bits of formal vocabulary tacked together in the manner of some journalistic hack. But there were plenty of examples, too, of the New Tradition used imaginatively and on a superb scale by the old masters of the movement themselves—Miës's Farnsworth house at Plano, Illinois (1950), his Lake Shore Drive apartments in Chicago (1951), and the Seagram Building in New York (with Philip Johnson, 1958) finally achieving the suave glass towers proposed by New Pioneers back in the early 20s; Gropius's Harvard University Graduate Center in Cambridge (with Architects' Collaborative, 1949–50); Neutra's Kaufmann house in Palm Springs, California (1947); and so on. And the diverse work of the direct followers of the masters made an equally splendid show— Lever House in New York (1952) and the Connecticut Life Insurance Company Building at Bloomfield, Connecticut (1957), by William S. Brown and Gordon Bunshaft of Skidmore, Owings & Merrill; the Mile-High Center in Denver, Colorado, by I. M. Pei (1955); the United Nations complex in New York by Wallace K. Harrison and an international board; the Alcoa Building in Pittsburgh by Harrison & Abramovitz (1949–51); Philip Johnson's twin houses of glass and brick in New Canaan, Connecticut (1949); the General Motors Technical Center at Warren, Michigan, by Eero Saarinen (1951–7), and so on through an endless list.

So complete was the triumph of the International Style that already in the 1950s the question was not whether America had a new architecture, but whether there was in this new architecture anything specifically "American." Surely with skyscrapers in Tokyo and Buenos Aires and Milan looking so much like those in Indianapolis or Los Angeles or Houston, with design so universally derived from the basic human physical needs of people everywhere, is it not idle to speculate on whatever minor variations might be identified as more typical of the United States than elsewhere? Is it not obvious

447

what is happening—that just as the great 19th-century improvements in transportation and technology all but obliterated old "regional" traditions from earlier times, so the much greater improvements of the 20th century are wiping out national distinctions, creating an International Style in fact as well as name, that what America's new architecture expresses is simply the shape of "One World" to come? And in any event, was not Walter Gropius right when he said that "styles . . . should be named and outlined by the historian only for past periods. In the present we lack the dispassionate attitude necessary for impersonal judgment of what is going on. . . . Why don't we leave it, then, to the future historian to settle the history of today's growth in architecture, and get to work and let it grow?" Of course; for an art "historian" to attempt an analysis of recent architecture is something of a contradiction; such analysis is at best a business for critics, for connoisseurs, above all for the artists concerned. But if we cannot properly make judgments, still it is true that just as architecture has always been the product and mirror of societies past, so it must be now. And while we cannot hope completely to understand contemporary architecture as cultural expression, yet it does still speak to us, as architecture always has, of men's hopes and aspirations and relationship to their world; and a few observations intended to set contemporary developments in a perspective of past architectural history may perhaps not be entirely out of order.

One of the minor intellectual parlor sports of the years following the war was the invention of apt titles for the age. At no time in history were people ever more historically self-conscious; nor, it would seem, less agreed on the kind of era they were living in. The Aspirin Age, the Space Age; the Age of Conformity and the Age of the Man in the Grey Flannel Suit, the Scientific Age; the Bland Age, the Fabulous Fifties; the Age of Anxiety, the Atomic Age: given such an array, the only title that really fits would seem to be the Age of Paradox. And in many senses that title may be history's ultimate choice. For all the other titles are not really as diverse as they might appear; which you chose depended simply on one of two points of view. If you looked at the collective power amassed by human society as a whole, these seemed years of triumphant achievement—in science, in space, in economic productivity. But if you looked at the individual's place in this scheme—in the West as well (of course) as east of the Iron Curtain—they seemed years of compounding futility, of little men ground smaller and smaller by pressures of organization, of bureaucracy, of international crisis, of regulation in every department of life. And this Age of Paradox was nowhere better expressed than in that postwar "modern architecture . . . synonymous with American architecture." Modern architecture as cultural expression may be summarized best under three heads: the paradoxes of Power, of Space, and of Genius.

132. *"City–County Building, Indianapolis, Indiana: Allied Architects & Engineers, Huber, Hunt & Nichols, Inc., General Contractors."* Under construction, June 1961. This picture was duplicated all over the United States in the 1950s and 60s; it shows, on the one hand, what the Union Title Insurance News for July 1961 described as "an embarrassed interloper from a Victorian scrapbook"—the old courthouse, due soon to be "emptied . . . its statues and relics auctioned off, the gingerbread and fretwork, the balconies and towers all torn down. . . ." On the other, "a new structure of glass and steel [that] will stand alone . . . a shining monument of progress." In their contrast is a monument, too, to the transformation of American civilization over eighty-odd years. As International Style stark steel and glass and concrete has displaced the ponderous whimsy of High Victorian Picturesque Eclecticism, so the old ideal of rugged individualism that this picturesque variety expressed has been swallowed up in the suave, bland, group-adjusted world of Organization Men and other-directed corporations that these featureless expanses of machined materials contain.

PARADOX I:
Aspirins in the Age of Science

IN THE PERIOD after World War II and well into the 1950s the United States was unquestionably the greatest national power in the world. American wealth, American resources, American technology seemed unlimited, and American architecture showed it. Big buildings were bigger than anything comparable before; small buildings were more numerous; in the mid-1950s 6,000 office buildings, 35,000-odd stores, more than 70,000 multiple dwellings, some 100 urban hotels were going up every year, not to mention whole cities of development houses. And builders had a wealth of resources equally unheard of in earlier generations: besides traditional materials, they had cinder and glass blocks; imitation stone and brick; cork, rubber, asphalt, acoustical tiles; aluminum for wall panels and insulation; Fiberglas, tempered glass, lucite, corrugated and striated glass; laminates, plastics, insulation board. Besides traditional structural techniques, they had prefabricated aluminum and steel windows, steel and plywood trusses, concrete slab construction of all kinds, sandwich walls and curtain walls, T beams and lally columns. Of the Public Auditorium in Pittsburgh (1961), 417 feet in diameter with six retractable panels opened or closed in two and a half minutes by means of movable segments running on rails, structural engineer Edward Cohen remarked laconically that while it is the first such roof anywhere, "it was unnecessary to evolve any new structural principles." Builders had prefabricated bathroom and kitchen and heating units at their command; and they could transport all these things almost at will.

Modern architecture makes a dramatic display of these great new powers. It puts up enormous buildings, the composite product of hundreds of different operations and full of the most elaborate equipment, that look as simple as a child's tower of blocks. It specializes in complicated multifunctional structures, characteristic and product of sprawling urban environments. Churches in which the sanctuary is lost in a maze of subsidiary units, Sunday-school rooms that are elaborate educational plants in themselves, kitchens and banquet halls and theatres and boardrooms. Hotels, theatres, shopping arcades all combined. Housing by the acre. Shopping centers sprawling over scores of blocks, offering goods and service for every sort of man and beast. And most dramatically of all it displays these new powers in the way it almost literally plays with materials. Here are glass towers, heavy as pyramids, looking fluid as water. Here are great domes hung in space like children's toys (e.g., Kresge Auditorium, Cambridge, by Eero Saarinen, 1955; State Fair Arena, Raleigh, North Carolina, 1952–3, by Matthew Nowicki [1910–1949] and William Henley Dietrick). Here are all kinds of materials moulded into every kind of sculptural form, on every conceivable scale and for any conceivable social purpose. Sensitive critics deplore roadside diners in the shape of pigs or wieners or coffeepots (there is one at Plymouth in the shape of a Pilgrim's hat, even), but these proceed from the same impulse and express the same delight in technology in their way as the famous works of leading architects in theirs; all we need do is name examples at random. Charles Eames's chairs of moulded plywood and wire. Philip Johnson's rippling shingled Rappite Shrine at New Harmony, Indiana (1960). Eero Saarinen's flowing brick chapel at M.I.T. in Cambridge (1955). The soaring Lambert–St. Louis airport by Yamasaki, Hellmuth & Leinweber (1954). The great megalithic shapes of Breuer's St. John's Abbey buildings at Collegeville, Minnesota (1953–60). Wallace K. Harrison's First Presbyterian Church at Stamford, Connecticut (1958). Alvar Aalto's Baker House Dormitory in Cambridge (1947–8), with brick walls undulating like plywood. Louis Kahn's Medical Research Building at the University of Pennsylvania (1960), with brick "shafts" resembling great steel beams driven into the ground. And, above all, the characteristic later works of Frank Lloyd Wright, a gift shop giving one the sensation of having stepped into a piece of jewelry (Morris Gift Shop, San Francisco, 1948), a synagogue shaped like a huge aluminum tent (Beth Shalom, Elkins Park, Pennsylvania, 1958–9), a museum of nonobjective art itself resembling an enormous piece of abstract concrete sculpture (Guggenheim, New York, completed 1959). Here, in short, is a seemingly endless panorama of seemingly unlimited power, a display of human technological achievement never remotely approximated in human history.

In this respect there appeared to be a marked difference between the New Tradition in architecture and its counterparts in other mid-20th-century arts. Where architecture seemed to celebrate the cumulating triumphs of three generations' growing skill in structure and command over materials, the great themes of drama, music, literature, and painting seemed to be individual frailty and futility—"psychological" plays about little lost people, novels of bestial behavior, music that tormented and disturbed, paintings of a world that individuals were finding meaningless, empty, evil, and wretched. But the difference was more apparent than real. Once penetrate the superficial subjects, and it became evident that the expression of human powers obvious in architecture was inherent in all the other arts: never had playwrights been more in command of stagecraft or writers of language, never were musicians more competent or painters more knowing. Conversely, the expression of individual futility obvious in paintings and plays and novels was everywhere expressed inherently in modern architecture. It can be recognized most clearly, perhaps, in the environment in which the bulk of the new architecture was set—the sprawling, inchoate supermetropolis that by the mid-20th century had become one of the great inescapable facts of American life.

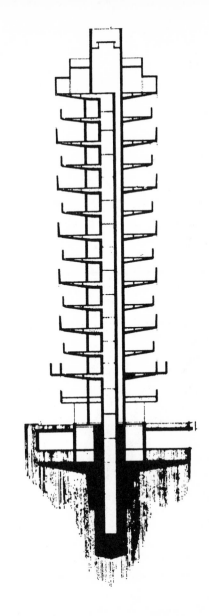

133. THE STRUCTURE OF POWER IN MID-20th-CENTURY ARCHITECTURE

(A) Section, Laboratory Tower for Johnson Wax Company, Racine, Wisconsin, built on the designs of Frank Lloyd Wright, 1949. One of Wright's greatest postwar expressions of "organic" structure, the fifteen-story, 156-foot high Johnson Tower with its alternating cantilevered square and circular floors is supported on a central shaft (containing elevator, stairs, and plumbing), only 13 feet in diameter at its narrowest point, whose "roots" strike treelike deep into the ground.

OPPOSITE:

(133 B) Interior perspective, proposed chapel (first unit of new master plan) for Tuskegee Institute, Tuskegee, Alabama, designed by Paul Rudolph in association with Fry & Welch. The roof is to be a hyperbolic paraboloid of open-web steel joists with long skylights of heat-resistant glass springing from massive supporting piers, the whole designed with special attention to acoustics, to accommodate Tuskegee's famous choir.

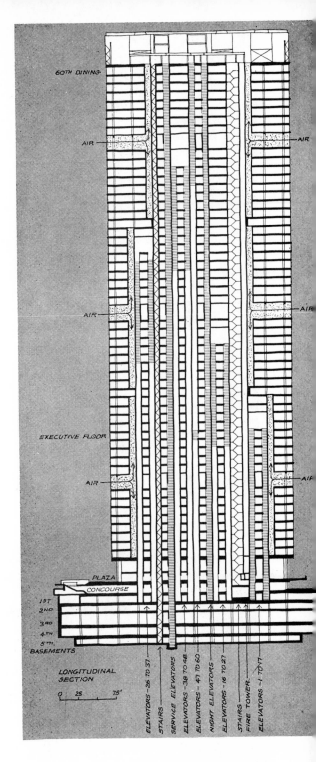

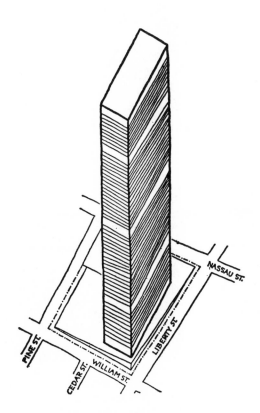

(133 C) Site plan, and section showing elevator banks ("bank A serves floors 1–17; B, C, and D, floors 17–47 in ten-floor increments; E, 47–60; F, not shown, serves the five basements"), Chase Manhattan Bank Building, New York, completed 1961 on the plans of Skidmore, Owings & Merrill; Gordon Bunshaft, chief designer.

134. FORMS OF POWER IN MID-20TH-CENTURY ARCHITECTURE

(A) Complete freedom of wall treatment: installation of first aluminum wall panel and column cover on Alcoa Building, Pittsburgh, *1951—a thirty-story tower entirely sheathed in a curtain of 6- by 12-foot prefabricated aluminum sheet panels "stamped out like cookies" complete with built-in reversible windows. Harrison and Abramowitz, architects.*

(134 B) Sculptured concrete: cantilevered bell banner of reinforced concrete resting on parabolic supports, completed 1960 on the designs (begun 1953) of Marcel Breuer for the church at St. John's Abbey, Collegeville, Minnesota.

The census of 1960 revealed—or more exactly, confirmed—the existence of a continuous urban belt composed of some thirty-five big cities and their suburbs, stretching through ten northeastern states. You can now drive from Lawrence–Haverhill in the north through Boston, New York, Philadelphia, and Baltimore to Washington in the south, without ever leaving thickly populated areas. In this one belt alone live 31,469,000 people, accounting for 17 per cent of the total population, 19 per cent of all retail store business, and 23 per cent of all manufacturing done in the United States. And there are in addition nine other similar, somewhat smaller clusters, including Chicago, Los Angeles, and Houston. In these ten supermetropolises live

135. NEW TECHNOLOGY, OLD ENVIRONMENT

(A) Las Vegas, Nevada, at night.

FACING PAGE:

(135 B) Central Artery, Boston, Massachusetts, looking north towards Custom House tower.

In scenes like these we recognize dramatic symbols of the immensely powerful new tools modern technology has put at the architect-planner's command; but in their chaotic backgrounds is revealed, too, the immense complexity of the problems modern technology has at the same time created.

the overwhelming majority of the population of the United States; by them the character of most new American architecture has been ultimately determined. Consequently, where in earlier times city planning was something of a specialized branch of architecture with its own peculiar problems, now city planning has become a major problem for everyone seriously concerned with the art of architecture.

Since the beginning of the 20th century all sorts of schemes for replanning cities had been projected, and many put at least partly into practice. There was the "City Beautiful" concept of the early century, identified with Daniel Burnham, based on Baroque precedent, and exemplified in the return to L'Enfant's plan for Washington and Burnham's plan for remodeling Chicago in a manner reminiscent of Baron Haussmann's Paris. There was the "Green City" concept represented ideally by Frank Lloyd Wright's Broadacres, and more prosaically in many local suburban developments—essentially an attempt to modernize the old Jeffersonian ideal of free and happy citizens living the good life each on his own plot under his own fig tree, within easy reach of decentralized industry. And there was the opposite International Style ideal of the 1920s, associated with Le Corbusier, and at least partially exemplified by Rockefeller Center in New York and Gateway Center in Pittsburgh: abolish individual building units, concentrate population in skyscrapers, and dedicate the land so saved to parks. And there were all sorts of projects in between. But by the end of World War II practically all of them were academic; the problem had clearly gotten out of hand.

Even while architects talked of city planning more than ever before, cities in the old sense were vanishing, melting away into the surrounding landscape (for example, the thirty-five cities proper of the East Coast urban belt collectively lost 2.8 per cent in population during the 1950s, while their surrounding suburbs gained 44.2 per cent). Even while the doctors were conferring as

to whether they should best advise a diet of attrition by decentralization, the radical surgery of urban renewal, or a psychological drugging to promote love of city life, their patient was dissolving like a jellyfish stranded in the sun; when they turned to give treatment, all they found remaining of the old compact 18th-century and Victorian city were damp patches of concentrated stores and office buildings and warehouses, amid endless stretches of suburbs sprawling off in all directions. The city was indeed changing under the pressures of 20th-century life, as the planners had said it must; but hardly in the way they envisioned. Indeed, they often seemed to be merely observers of what was going on, spectators and commentators like everyone else. The city was assuming new forms, not because but in spite of them. And in this was an enormous paradox. The city was disintegrating as never before, at the precise moment in history when for the first time controlled planning of urban growth had in fact been technologically possible.

Through most of human history—indeed, roughly up to the middle of the 20th century—where and how people lived were largely determined by elementary natural forces. Farmers lived where there was soil and rainfall; cities grew up by rivers or seacoast harbors, on defensible hilltops or convenient crossroads. When soils were exhausted or eroded, farmers moved away; when patterns of trade or transportation shifted, cities died. It happened in every century up to the present. So Jamestown and St. Mary's City, located off what developed into the main arteries of plantation trade, failed in the 17th century; so Hopewell Village, a Pennsylvania iron manufacturing center while Pittsburgh was still forest, had to be abandoned in the 1850s because it had no rivers to bring charcoal and iron ore to its furnaces once local supplies were exhausted; so Cairo in 19th-century Illinois was ruined when the Mississippi changed course; so the Rocky Mountain country is full of settlements become ghost towns when veins gave out;

so Buffalo on the "right" side of the Niagara grew into a metropolis while Fort Erie, on the "wrong" side, remained a hamlet.

But this is so no longer. The same command over nature manifested in the structure and materials of modern buildings is available to city planners, making dense clusters of population unnecessary. Just as chemistry can cure sick soil and agrotechny check erosion, so the conditions no longer exist that made it seem easier to fill in the coves of Shawmut Peninsula, say, and crowd more and more people onto it instead of occupying empty mainland two or three miles away from Boston. Once upon a time, perhaps, business offices had to be crammed onto the narrow tip of Manhattan Island, because the problems of communication even a few miles away from the harbor seemed so insuperable; and for the same reason, all the surrounding land had to be thickly built up in apartments and suburbs. But now with telephones and automobiles and rapid transit of all sorts the need for such enormous city concentrations is gone. One of the wonders of the world is the superhighway system built in the United States during the 1940s and 50s; this system—not to mention the vast improvements of rail and airways—is in form and function a symbol of the new powers that make it easier to bring materials to a site than to transport people. Theoretically, cities could now be located anywhere but in the middle of the ocean; they do not need rivers or crossroads or mines to thrive. Theoretically, there is no need to crowd thirty-two million people into one narrow coastal strip; it is now possible as it never was in Jefferson's time to realize his American dream of every man on his own pleasant and spacious bit of land, within easy reach of his work; for that matter, the International Style ideal of glittering orderly planned cities is now feasible as it never was in the 1920s. The power to provide individuals with any sort of richer, fuller, happier lives, insofar as improved environment can do it, is available; but it is being used mainly to produce aspirins.

Like the 20th-century painter who has all the techniques in the world and no place to exercise them, like the 20th-century playwright whose consummate stagecraft is expended on minuscule probings of petty psyches, the 20th-century architect, literally competent to change the face of America any way he chooses, is forced to stand by and watch historic buildings ground into dust for parking lots, bulldozers chewing up hills and valleys and spewing out "split-level traps" on barren plains; he must put more and more buildings in the same stale places, wrestle with problems of water shortage and river pollution, traffic congestion and juvenile delinquency, the by-products of an entirely unnecessary overpopulation.

Glittering new buildings set in urban sprawl, unlimited technological powers manifested in surroundings of mushrooming confusion—this is the first great paradox of 20th-century architectural expression.

PARADOX II:
Grey Flannel Suits in Space

THE CONCEPT of free-flowing space, uniting exterior and interior, has been the common bond of "modern" architecture from the California and prairie houses early this century through the glass-walled and stilted International Style buildings of the 1920s down to the present; it is what the late Wright most obviously shares with Miës, Le Corbusier, and Gropius. And ostensibly there is no doubt what it expresses—a tremendous change in man's relationship to nature. No longer is nature, as in 18th-century America, something whose conquest is to be celebrated by the precisely outlined and self-contained art of a classical tradition, making sharp distinction between the ordered works of man and the chaotic, hostile world around him. No longer even is it to be thought of as an exotic place of retreat from industrialized society, as by romantic Victorians. Now man's control of nature is complete; applied science has made it a tool for him to use,

*136. NEW WORLD OF DISCIPLINED SPACE
(A) Styling Administration* (left) *and Styling Auditorium* (right, background), *two units* in the General Motors Technical Center complex at Warren, Michigan, built on the designs of Eero Saarinen, 1951–5.

(136 B) Interior, State Fair Building, Ra-   leigh, North Carolina, built 1952–3 by Matthew
Nowicki and William Henley Dietrick.

an extension of himself. In that spirit, he opens buildings out to embrace nature, using glass walls, deep insets, patios, balconies, stilts, so that all division between exterior and interior, between the building and its surroundings, is virtually obliterated (sometimes, indeed, to the extent that people are so unaware of walls—of where interior space ends and exterior space begins—that they try to walk through glass, making it necessary to distinguish doorways from walls by stickers or etched designs). Conversely, he brings nature into the house, sets large indoor plants where they will form a continuous visual unit with foliage outside. Where even the Victorians—to say nothing of 18th-century classical designers—took care in composing interiors to

provide pictures, doorways, and windows with heavy frames of gilt or wooden mouldings or curtains, modern "interior decoration" is conceived in the spirit of a painting by Cézanne, as a series of receding planes, those inside—furniture units and walls—complemented and completed by the fore-, middle-, and background planes in the view through the "picture window" outside. Even paintings lose frames proper in favor of thin lath edging, or even, as in the Guggenheim Museum, float entirely frameless in a surrounding void.

In one sense it is obvious what this new architectural space expresses. Surely here is the manifestation of man rising triumphant over all natural limitations, the consummation of generations of struggles *per ardua ad astra,* the most fitting of all creations and symbols of the Space Age. That, of course, it is. But it has another, deeper, more pessimistic side, too.

Through most of history men have thought of themselves as a special creation, different from the rest of nature. Even the Victorian theory of evolution conformed to this age-old assumption, with its picture of the "tree of life" supported by a mass of amoebae at the bottom and bearing on its topmost bough a high-domed, bearded, Caucasian professor. But in the course of the 20th century evolution gradually took on other interpretations. Instead of confirming men the judges and crown of nature, it seemed more and more to prove them mere products of her workings, essentially no different from others. Instead of the "tree of life," it provided the image of parallel roads whereon each species perfects itself according to its kind, elms and eels being as perfect triumphs of the evolutionary process in their ways as man in his. Of such a world man is both master and creature; and if in handling interior and exterior space as indivisible he architecturally shows himself master, in his conception of space as a positive thing he architecturally manifests his creaturely self.

For space in 20th-century architecture involves much more than infinity, nothingness, or the absence of mass; characteristically, it is itself handled as a tangible thing. Roofs—for example, the arcades of Wright's Florida Southern campus—are not so much "opened up" with holes or skylights, as built around voids. Windows become elements in design quite as positive as the walls between them. Empty spaces are as vital a part of city planning as the buildings on and in them. The same is true of furniture design, and of its arrangement in rooms. In every aspect of contemporary art, awareness of the void as a dominant force is a controlling force.

In this concept of space lies the association, so often noted, of modern with 17th-century Baroque design. And it is a most significant one. It is no accident that Baroque designers like Bernini, Borromini, and Guarini were the first consistently to design walls as a kind of skin shaped by the forces of void pressing on them from without, or conversely, as envelopes around freely moulded interior space. It was in the Baroque era that men first forcefully created architectural counterparts to a world ordered by intangible forces, collective powers: authoritarian churches and states, things you cannot touch, see, or personally control, but which instead control nature and through nature individual men as well.

Enlightenment and the new attitude of confident command over nature through pure science, through discovery and exploration, through successful nation building, temporarily stemmed the appeal of Baroque space in countries outside the control of authoritarian states and churches; as we have seen in American William and Mary and Queen Anne art, whatever outward forms 18th-century Anglo-American architecture borrowed from Baroque Italy, it largely ignored Baroque spatial implications. But as the Jeffersonian world gradually broke down, space began to reappear as a tangible force in American architecture—first in Gothic Revival landscaping as preached by Downing, then in High Victorian Picturesque Eclecticism, reaching mature expression in the sweeping eaves and deep balconies of the Prairie House. At this point, however, it was still an uncertain expression of the mixed blessings conveyed by adolescent industrialism, partly satisfying feelings of delight at the new collective power over nature so recently established, partly manifesting uneasy awareness of the strong and more intangible forces curtailing individual freedoms. Only in the infinitely greater spatial triumphs of mid-20th-century American architecture was the full paradox expressed: as the spatial fantasies of modern architects reached heights unimagined in the Baroque age, so did the sense of being hemmed in on every side by uncontrollable and impersonal forces—political, technological, electronic, atomic.

Free-flowing space, space moulded by forces

(136 C) Interior of the gallery building of the Solomon R. Guggenheim Museum in New York City, built on the plans of Frank Lloyd Wright and officially opened October 21, 1959.

In the combination of intricate spatial organization, disciplined order, and daring structure that characterizes typical major works of mid-20th-century architecture like these, critics have long recognized a resemblance to the palaces, churches, and landscaped parks of 17th-century Baroque Europe. But whereas Baroque power was personified in kings and popes, and consequently humanized by applied sculpture and painting, these modern structures express the impersonal powers of technology embodied in industrial corporations and political entities.

inexorable and intangible; individuals crushed into featureless conformity by the very degree of social organization that enables them collectively to reach for the stars—that is the second great paradox expressed in American architecture of the mid-20th century.

PARADOX III:
Supermen in the Age of Anxiety

IT IS AGAINST THIS BACKGROUND of malaise amid omnipotence, personal futilities adding up to collective might, that we can best appreciate the appearance of the Comprehensive Designer, the Universal Architect. For just as infallibility was claimed for popes at the very moment when their temporal powers were least, when all their old political authority in Italy had been lost and the whole drift of civilization appeared to be towards ever more liberal and agnostic modes of thought, so now, at the very moment when the old individualistic kind of architectural creation seemed to be more and more impossible to maintain, when more and more important buildings were being done without the services of any architect as such, architects appeared making claims for themselves and their profession of a breadth and scope unimagined before.

Buckminster Fuller is one famous and flamboyant example of this tendency. His Comprehensive Designer is the "integral of the sum of the product of all specializations," whose delight it is to be "preoccupied with anticipation of all men's needs by translation of the ever-latest inventory of their potentials," so that he may "provide new and advanced standards of living for all people of the world. . . ." He is a new Moses, leading mankind forward to a Promised Land of mass production, where all property will be "ephemeralized" so that men may concentrate on the pure life intellectual. This the Comprehensive Designer will do by first ephemeralizing himself, working with the detachment from material things of angels—or, alternatively, of dedicated Organization Men, of electronic computers, of an efficiency expert like Frederick Winslow Taylor. In this mystic state he proclaims the use of light tensile-structured geodesic domes as a ritual act of salvation, an emergence from the "darkness of complete and awful weight to eternal light which has no weight"—not symbolically only, but in practical terms as well, for the Dymaxion house, built on geodesic principles, becomes a prime instrument for freeing men from the tyranny of matter. Suspended from a central mast within which is contained its own septic tank, diesel engine, and "sun-machine" for electricity (as yet uninvented), the Dymaxion house is "free as a ship of public utilities, sewerage, water, and other systems of the political hangnail variety," and, like a ship, too, can be moved freely about, carried by airplanes. In it men attain something of the same independence from material environment as blessed spirits; but, like angels, they will use their freedom wisely, and live by choice in colonies where they can enjoy the delights of pure brotherhood among free spirits. And here again the Comprehensive Designer will be at hand to guide them to this higher level of spiritual life; he will devise town plans that provide "geodesic environment control"; he can help them avoid the dangers of subtropical climates, which predispose the ecological pattern to "semi-fasicism"; he can also assist the transition from present misery to future bliss by establishing a world-wide monetary system based on a kind of Social Credit plus speculative investment in industrial stocks, by preaching a new social ethic dedicated to releasing the "residuary mental or time-consciousness, eliminating the fallacial autosuggestive phenomena of past and future, to the infinity of delight in the Eternal Now"—he is the Prophet bringing from Sinai a new heaven on a new earth.

Another exponent of the same principle, albeit a rather different sort of prophet, is Louis Kahn. Here and there along the base of Kahn's designs—his proposed Philadelphia City Hall is typical—stand little figures, overwhelmed (curiously enough, rather as in the present City Hall) by the grandiosity of their architectural setting. They are reminiscent, and with good reason, of the little boy who stands looking up at the great canvas on which the master is working in Gustave Courbet's "Studio" a century ago. The boy symbolizes not so much admiration for the artist's technical skill, as the younger generation being taught by the painter how and what to see; just so, Kahn's public is not so much awed by his structures as taught through them how to live. The architect gives meaning and purpose to life, commanding with equal assurance a cosmic plan or a fragment of typography:

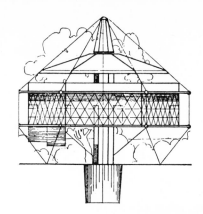

The nature of space reflects what it wants to be
  Is the auditorium a Stradivarius
    or is it an ear
  Is the auditorium a creative instrument
                keyed to Bach or Bartók
                played by the conductor
  or is it a convention hall
In the nature of space is the spirit and will to exist a certain way
                    [from *Perspecta*, No. 3]

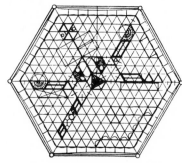

That is at least in part, perhaps, what Professor Hitchcock meant by calling Kahn's University of Pennsylvania Medical Research Center in Philadelphia ". . . the finest statement, perhaps, of mid-nineteenth century 'Realism.'" It is indeed "realism" of the sort proclaimed in Courbet's manifesto and perfected in 20th-century painting. Like Courbet, Kahn explicitly rejects beauty as an artistic goal: "Order does not imply Beauty: the same order created the dwarf and Adonis. Design is not making Beauty, Beauty emerges . . . etc." Like "modern" painters, he draws empathetic analogies between his art and music. For him "realism" involves the creation of private worlds into which the public enters by invitation of the creator only. Spaces take on mystic meanings of their—and the architect's—own. A city plan becomes an ideal vision to be pursued for its own sake regardless of practical difficulties. The architect architects as the painter paints, in a self-satisfying act of pure creativity that is its own justification. Since architecture is not painting, practical considerations can never be quite avoided—but they are distinctly secondary in importance. It was radical enough

when Miës van der Rohe rejected Sullivan's dictum, "Form Follows Function" and declared of his generation, "We do the opposite. We reverse this, and make a practical and satisfying shape, and then fit the functions into it. This is the only practical way to build today, because the functions of most buildings are continually changing, but economically the buildings cannot change." But men like Kahn go further. They would defy all practical dependence; in their mystique, form not only does not follow function, it determines function. Function springs from form—and the architect defines both.

Visions of the architect as a mystic godlike figure transcending limitations of space and time likewise inspire Paolo Soleri's City on a Mesa. That no such city exists or ever did exist, neither is there any such mesa or any such buildings as those put on it, are obscurantist objections. The 55,000-acre site, the two million people, the self-sufficient economy are the stuff of dreams, free of all niggling practicality, needing no other substance of reality than the continuous sheets of butcher paper hundreds of feet long onto which they come spinning out of the plan-

137. *PROPHETS OF A NEW AGE: Four projects essentially conceived, as in the mind of God,* ex nihilo, *rising above all practical temporal exigencies:*

OPPOSITE:

(A) Buckminster Fuller's "Dymaxion house," first proposed, 1929—that man may emerge "from the darkness of complete and awful weight to eternal light which has no end."

(137 B) Project for Philadelphia City Hall, part of a larger city study by Louis I. Kahn, 1956–60: "Those like Kahn, who show a marked individualism in a world in which team-work is becoming widely accepted, who aim to build for eternity in a world of the economy of consumption, find themselves in a certain sense beyond the contingencies of time. . . ." (Enzo Frateili, "Louis Kahn," Zodiac, 8.)

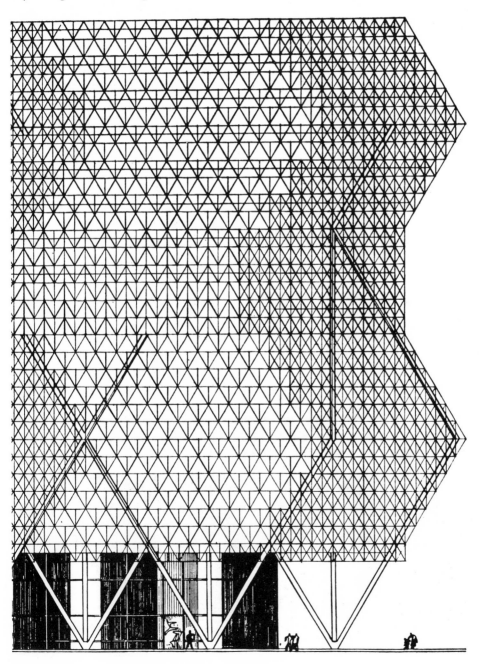

ner's fertile brain. Stuff of dreams, too, is Frederick Kiesler's "Endless House" model in the Museum of Modern Art in New York. Its pure tensile egglike forms floating on stilts in space, the continuous curves of its floors and walls flowing together, the location of its shelf-seats and balconies and windows simply wherever structure dictates—all represent solutions to no problem in any traditional sense. Like the "public" of modern painting, its inhabitants are expected to adjust to the architect's visions, not he to their needs. They must prove themselves worthy of him, not he of them. As Adam and Eve had only to obey to experience Paradise, so in the Endless House are many mansions prepared for them that believe going barefoot and chairless and whatsoever else its maker commands to be small price for the bliss of "living inside a sculpture that is changing every second with the light."

Summarizing the law and the prophets, of course, was Frank Lloyd Wright. The 1940s and 50s were his finest hour, the moment when he, as

the great if not the sole living link with those generations who knew Richardson and Sullivan, stood forth as the embodiment of American architectural history and heritage, the patriarch of modern American architecture. Long ago when he, whose major projects were mostly lying rolled up in drawers, had said that he intended to be the greatest architect who ever lived or ever would live, it had seemed an idle boast; now he had lived long enough to see most of these projects realized in one form or another. At Florida Southern College (Lakeland, begun 1938, built through the 1940s and 50s), he gave a microcosmic demonstration of the architect remaking the face of the earth—a campus in which men and nature were perfectly integrated, in which social relationships were moulded and defined, the differing psychological and physical functions of administration building, chapel, and library being expressed in varying architectural forms. His Price Tower in Bartlesville, Oklahoma (1953–6) brought to mature expression the concept of an organic skyscraper aborted in the St. Mark's

(137 C) "Endless House," model of a shell house first proposed by Frederick Kiesler in 1929, commissioned by the Museum of Modern Art for exhibition in 1959: "The artist must learn only one thing in order to be creative: not to resist himself, but to resist without exception every human, technical, social, economical factor that prevents him from being himself." (Frederick Kiesler in the College Art Journal.)

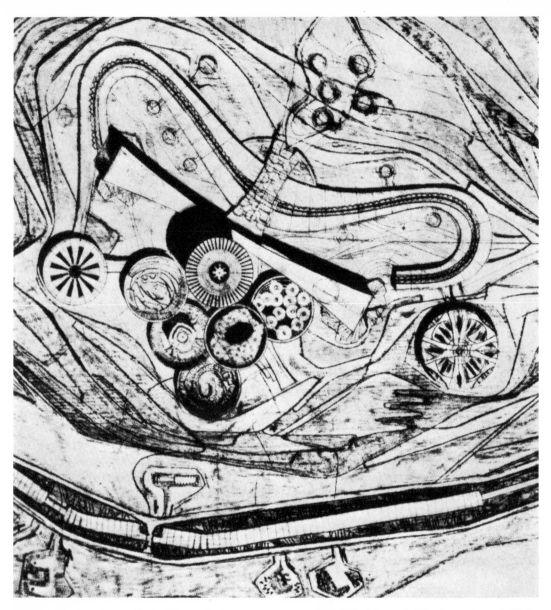

project of 1929—a tall building with floors cantilevered freely into surrounding space from a central spine, like branches from a tree. His Mile-High Building (1956) would have involved redesigning the entire center of Chicago. And so on. Tolerated before, he now heard the doctrines he had preached so early and so long made official: the president of the American Institute of Architects, in a 1961 advertisement published by the Inland Steel Products Company, proclaimed: "I hold that the architectural profession should assume responsibility for noth-

(137 D) Plan of Theological and Philosophical Center of Paolo Soleri's "City on a Mesa," project envisioned c.1960. The hypnotic effect of such endless rolls of plans and drawing is remarkable, and comparable to the effect of abstract expressionist paintings. Like the mesmerist's swinging watch or the pilgrim's relic gazed at for hours, or the mystic's endless repetition of set prayers, they create hypnotic patterns which serve to put the conscious part of the brain to rest and allow the unconscious—seat of inspiration and extrasensory perception—to take over.

ing less than the nation's MAN-MADE ENVIRON-MENT, including the use of land, water, and air, AN ENVIRONMENT IN HARMONY WITH THE AS-PIRATIONS OF MAN." Success confirmed his patri-archate: "Le Corbusier and Miës van der Rohe might be 'Corbu' and 'Miës' to every architect the world over but," writes Peter Blake in *The Master Builders*, "Wright was always 'Mr. Wright.' He was the King, unchallenged, unchallenge-able." But he was never satiated; the more spec-tacular his triumphs, the higher soared his ambi-tious visions. For of course his vision was insatiable. Wright was still only beginning to realize and demonstrate the implications of 19th-century architectural theories of the artist as [in Schiller's words] "a King, sitting on the sum-mits of mankind," when he—somewhat incon-gruously—died.

Even more significant than the making of such claims was the acceptance that the public, however desultorily and reservedly, was begin-ning to give to them. Not so much the painters' claims, though these were louder; in keeping with a national tradition three centuries old, most Americans tended to think of painting as a less serious business than architecture, and treat painters' claims more lightly. But architec-ture they intuitively understood better, and while not accepting all the specific claims of Universal Architects or Comprehensive Designers, perhaps, they at least had some sympathy with them. However dimly, they recognized in the allusive language of these claims one of the fundamental premises of 20th-century thought, and they re-sponded to it.

In many other ages men have behaved as if this life were all there is, as if after death came nothing. But the society of the mid-20th century was possibly the first in history a large propor-tion of whose members explicitly acted on this assumption, for whom "Make the most of this world, for it is the only one we know" was no longer a cliché but an earnest imperative. It was in this setting, and on this premise, that the claims of Universal Architects or Comprehen-

sive Designers, or whatever else they called themselves, became historically understandable. In effect, consciously or unconsciously, what they were saying was that God is dead, therefore long live Man; there is no god but man, let us there-fore fit ourselves to play the part; let us become Creators ourselves, for there is none other work-eth for us. And they could point out that in so saying they were hardly unique; that their works, like architecture always, were no more than expressions of a spirit of the times. In every walk of life they could point to people talking and acting and working along the same lines towards the same end.

There were medicine men whose conquest over disease was reaching the point where it was foreseeable when nothing would be left to die of; immortality of a Struldbrug sort was already in view, and presumably a fountain of youth not far behind it. There were physicists whose suc-cess in sending men orbiting the earth encour-aged hope that the time was coming when what used to be called the Heavens would be peopled by an earthly host. There were biologists who anticipated nature's blind evolutionary workings being brought under scientific light, and made to breed up an ever more superhuman race. Con-versely there were psychologists probing inwards to reassemble men's motivations and so achieve by reason that peace of "Soul" once sought by mystics in prayer. There were psychic research-ers who hoped to discover and develop extra-sensory powers of perception, to provide infal-libly by telepathy and mental control those powers of command over environment once feebly attempted by rites of magic in palaeolithic eras. And there were sociologists who claimed to have discovered something like this already in a "lonely crowd" of "other-directed" people, and for whom manipulating people and judging per-sonalities rather than performance were goals as natural and normal as control over things had been for their "inner-directed" Victorian predecessors—sociologists, furthermore, who themselves took so for granted the premise that this world is all there is, as hardly to consider the possibility that this change from "inner" to "other" direction might be explained in terms of declining religious faith, in ultimate judgments of meaning and value being determined outside this life. Most of all there were science-fiction writers who were able to express in their peculiar species of fantasy and allegory, so native to the 20th century, those hopes and dreams their age was otherwise often afraid or ashamed to put into soberer words—dreams no longer of mere mechanical marvels (so many having come true that they were hardly fiction any longer) as of new kinds of men, men who have "discovered the secrets of their nervous system," men who have "mental control of nucleonic, nuclear, and gravitonic energies," men who "can travel through space at will" without machines (by nucleonically reassembling their molecular structures), and who, needless to say, have achieved not only "personal immortality" but the ability to bring the dead from past ages back to life by reconstructing bodies as they choose. Collectively, what these people represented was an aspiration entirely new in human history. Though we know from the old stories of Icarus and Ptah, the Garden of Eden and Faust, that men in all ages have aspired to godlike powers, this time they hope to achieve them not in moments of ecstatic revelation, but in a sober, methodical, materialistic way; they intend to become gods in an actual, literal sense.

Put baldly, the whole idea sounds such nonsense that those holding it fall back on allusion, on poetic language, on implicit embodiment, on allegory. That in itself is no argument against it, however; the deepest premises of civilization have always been those that men either felt unnecessary to mention ("the self-evident is not discussed"), or lacked proper language to describe. What does seem difficult to understand is the timing. To put forth intimations of immortality at a moment in history when mankind stands in imminent peril of extermination seems the grossest paradox. And, of course, it is—the great-

est of all the great paradoxes of mid-20th-century life. Of this, architecture is perhaps the most obvious expression.

It was odd enough, to begin with, for architects to be claiming "responsibility for nothing less than the nation's MAN-MADE ENVIRONMENT" at the very moment when their practical influence seemed most ineffective, when speculative housing developments were proliferating everywhere while being deplored by almost every leading architectural planner as the worst kind of urban growth economically, sociologically, and aesthetically. Even more discouraging and paradoxical, it was at this same moment that big buildings, as well as little ones, were slipping out of the planners' control. Cities were getting so complex, the tax laws so encouraged mass speculative building in stereotyped forms, the number of people and institutions involved in erecting an office building was getting so enormous, that no one individual, not even a single profession, could manage them. In the 1930s Rockefeller Center "had promised," according to an editorial in the July 1961 *Architectural Forum*,

> the beginning of a new urban world . . . an idea in the use of city land—the superblock. This lets the towers be pulled back, many of them, from the street line . . . it leaves pleasant open ground space, and terrace space, for people to enjoy. . . . It has been sound economically all the way. All this is so well known that repetition should be superfluous—as it is not. For Rockefeller Center remains distressingly unique. . . .

Rockefeller Center had had so many different architects working on it (Reinhard & Hofmeister, Corbett, Harrison & MacMurray, Hood & Fouilhoux) that only twenty years after it was built scholars were writing articles on "Who Built Rockefeller Center?" as if it were some cathedral out of the misty medieval past. Elsewhere as in New York, everybody gets into the building act—real estate boards and planning boards, loan companies and preservation societies, school boards and zoning commissions, labor unions and manufacturers' associations—and into the architect's way. The result is that skyscrapers and $6,000 development "homes" ("no down payment for veterans") alike take architectural form less in accordance with the will and vision of creative architects (or any architects at all) than as compromise solutions to myriads of problems, among myriads or more or less co-operating individuals and agencies. No matter what the claims of Universal Architecture in theory, in practice what is built is less and less determined by architects and more and more by simple force of circumstance.

To this generalization there would seem to be plenty of particular exceptions. We might think, for example, of the work of George Nelson, or Charles Eames, or Victor Gruen Associates' huge shopping centers at Northland near Detroit and Southdale near Minneapolis, and the masterly replanning of downtown Fort Worth in Texas. But exceptions like these in a sense prove the rule. For what most distinguishes men like these architects from Comprehensive Designers like Buckminster Fuller or Louis Kahn, say, is precisely that the former work so deliberately within the inherent limitations of a problem—locating "centers" outside city limits, accepting existing freeways and other facilities wherever possible, and so on—rather than insisting on the architect's right to impose perfection on an imperfect society.

And beyond all these immediate paradoxes, of course, is the ultimate one of Architectural Immortals building in an Atomic Age. Every age in history has taken for granted that nothing human can be entirely permanent; men have always known that sooner or later time must have a stop. But surely was there ever a time when the transience of human life and works was so inescapably obvious? Why, then, should this be the moment for Universal Architects and Comprehensive Designers to appear?

There are several reasons, perhaps. One is simply that at all times and places men have had to live under the shadow of death, push on with work whose end they probably will never see. In this sense those who choose this moment to proclaim the ultimate triumph of mankind work in the same great human tradition as those Spartans combing their hair before Thermopylae, as Wolfe discussing poetry on his way to the Plains of Abraham, as Boëthius in prison composing the *Consolations of Philosophy*, as cavemen planting corn. Furthermore, they work in what is perhaps a peculiarly American tradition of idealism. Apparently ludicrous visions have been consummated all too often in this country for any to be taken too lightly. Once upon a time the idea that a great nation, or any kind of nation, could be planted in North America seemed nonsense; the greatest European savants were firmly convinced that "everything degenerates in the American continent." Once upon a time, too, it seemed nonsense to imagine that any state could be governed without divinely appointed kings and a caste born to rule. To be sure, precedents establish no historical laws; because some fantastic visions come true is no reason to suppose that all will; this vision may really be nonsense. One thing we can say, however—that it should be in American architecture that the great dream of the 20th century has been best expressed is no accident. For it is precisely this spirit of experimentation with ideas and free minds, this search for utopias, that from the beginning has been the peculiar promise of American civilization.

Ever since Jefferson's time, there has been much to-do about the question of an "American" art. Do we have one, and if not, what should it be? Each generation in turn has propounded its theories; no satisfactory answer has ever been found. And certainly, as far as forms are concerned, there is none today. With architects and painters and furniture designers all over the world doing very much the same things, with nonobjective design in India and Japan looking much like nonobjective design in New York, with office buildings in Marseilles and government offices in Brasilia looking much like office buildings in San Francisco and government offices in New Zealand, it is obvious that modern architecture and furniture in the United States are even more the product of international cultural intercourse than they were when Wright was drawing inspiration from Japan and young Germans drawing inspiration from him fifty years ago. Nor is there any prospect of the process slowing down. But perhaps the answer is, as was suggested a good many years ago, that an "American style," if there is one, must be sought not in the realm of forms but in spirit. What is American about architecture in the United States is in fact precisely that spirit of eager experimentation which we see at its best in the mid-20th century—the conscious, continuous, restless search for new ideas and new expressions that proceed from life, liberty, and the pursuit of happiness in a free society. Paul Rudolph may yet prove to have been right when he wrote that

> modern architecture is still a gangling, awkward, ungracious, often inarticulate, precocious, adolescent thing, which has not yet even begun to reach full flower. . . . We are incredibly lucky, for we have yet to see a Golden Age.

NOTES

Quotations from Henry-Russell Hitchcock, "Notes of a Traveller: Wright and Kahn" (*Zodiac*, 6, 1959, pp. 5–18) and "America" (*Zodiac*, 8, 1961, pp. 65–73); of Louis Kahn, from Enzo Frateili, "Louis Kahn" (*Zodiac*, 8, 1961, pp. 14–26). Quotation of Miës van der Rohe, from Illinois Institute of Technology news release July 6, 1954, "Biographical Information on Ludwig Miës van der Rohe, Director, Department of Architecture, I.I.T., p. 3; of AIA President Philip Will, Jr., from *Architectural Forum*, (CXIV, 1961, 3, inside front cover); of Gropius from Peter Blake, *The Master Builders* (1960), p. 38; from "Pittsburgh's Dome Gets Ready" (*Architectural Forum*, CXIV, 1961, 3, p. 123); of Buckminster Fuller, from Paul and Percival Goodman, *Communitas* (2nd ed., 1960), pp. 76–82; from Paul Rudolph, "Architectural Education in the U.S.A." (*Zodiac*, 8, 1961, p. 164).

Statistics from *Building, USA*, by the editors of *Architectural Forum* (1957); and from *The New York Times*, August 13, 1961.

On Soleri, see Peter Blake, "The Fantastic World of Paolo Soleri" (*Architectural Forum*, CXIV, 1961, 3, pp. 104–10), and "Paolo Soleri's Visionary City" (*Architectural Forum*, 3, pp. 111–19); on Kiesler's "Endless House," see "Tough Prophet" (*Time*, May 25, 1959, pp. 78–81).

References made to the following: J. B. Rhine, *New Frontiers of the Mind* (1937); *New World of the Mind* (1953). A. L. Huxley, *Brave New World* (1932); *Ape and Essence* (1948); *Brave New World Revisited* (London, 1959). D. Riesman, R. Denney, and N. Glazer, *The Lonely Crowd* (New Haven, 1950), whose index lists under "religion" only "Catholic" (one reference, to the "immense veto-group power of the American Catholic Church") and "Puritan Ethic" (under which we find, in a book otherwise remarkably free from clichés, a number of stock clichés à la Tawney); typical is p. 237: ". . . as the old-time religion depended on a clear image of heaven and hell and clear judgments of good and evil"—one might have thought it put better the other way round, i.e., the clarity of "inner-directed" judgments of good and evil being dependent on the "old-time-religion." John Langdon-Davies, *The Nature of Man* (1960). Science-fiction quotations from "The Monster"—one of the most perfect summations of the new vision I know—by A. E. van Vogt, originally written in 1948 for *Astounding Science Fiction*, and republished in *Destination Universe* (Signet, 1952).

On skepticism regarding American potentialities, cf. K. Umbreit, *Founding Fathers* (1941), pp. 37ff.:

The attitude of Europe toward the Americas has always been peculiar. . . . The purpose of the western hemisphere was to produce riches for Europe, not to make homes for men. It was impossible for any culture to exist there save as a pale reflection of European culture. [I have often run across this same attitude in discussing this present book with Europeans: "*Is* there an American architecture?" they ask, in polite, skeptical surprise.] That was one reason why Europe took so to Franklin. To wrest lightning from the heavens was marvelous enough, but that an American should do it . . . it was like a talking dog. In the 18th century Europe even had a scientific law to justify its attitude. Buffon was regarded as Europe's greatest biological authority, and Buffon had laid it down as a law of nature that all forms of animal life tended to degenerate in America. . . .

Picture Credits

The following abbreviations are used: HABS for *Historical American Buildings Survey*, and *JSAH* for *Journal of the Society of Architectural Historians*.

p. xvi: Photo by the author.

p. xvii: Public Relations Office of Rockefeller Center, Inc.

1A: Rexford Newcomb, *Architecture of the Old North-West Territory*, University of Chicago Press, 1950.

1B: Sketch by Sidney E. King, from J. C. Cotter and J. P. Hudson, *New Discoveries at Jamestown*, Washington, 1957.

2A: Kentucky Publicity Department.

2B: Montana Historical Commission.

3: Essex Institute of Salem, Massachusetts.

4: Herbert Georg; Publix Pictorial Service.

5: Kansas State Historical Society, Topeka.

6: Photo by Eric M. Sanford, New Hampshire State Planning and Development Commission.

7: Photo by the author.

8: Photo by Laura Gilpin, Museum of International Folk Art, Santa Fe, New Mexico.

9: San Xavier Mission, Tucson, Arizona.

10: Texas Highway Department.

11A: National Park Service.

11B: Florida State News Bureau, Tallahassee.

12: New Mexico State Tourist Bureau.

13A: Historical Collection, Union Title Insurance Company, San Diego, California.

13B: Bancroft Collection, University of California.

14A: Inventaire des Oeuvres d'Art de la Province de Québec.

14B: From Ramsay Traquair, *The Old Architecture of Quebec*, Toronto, Macmillan, 1947, by permission of Mrs. Hilda Napier.

15A: Inventaire des Oeuvres d'Art de la Province de Québec.

15B: The Montreal Museum of Fine Arts.

16A: Courtesy Ernest Allen Connally.

16B: HABS.

16C: Photo by Richard Koch, HABS.

17A: Photo by the author.

17B: Michigan Historical Commission.

18A: Redpath Library, McGill University, Montreal.

18B: Inventaire des Oeuvres d'Art de la Province de Québec.

19A: Inventaire des Oeuvres d'Art de la Province de Québec.

19B: Louisiana Department of Commerce and Industry.

19C: Bibliothèque Nationale, Paris.

20: Photo by Donald A. Webster.

21A: Museum of the City of New York.

21B: Delaware State Archives, Hall of Records, Dover.

22: Historic Sites, New York State Education Department, Albany.

23A: Kingston, New York, Chamber of Commerce.

23B: *Winterthur Newsletter*.

24A: Photo by Louis H. Frohman, Architectural and Industrial Photographer, Sleepy Hollow Restorations, Inc.

24B: New Jersey Department of Conservation and Economic Development.

25: Henry Francis du Pont Winterthur Museum.

26A: Commonwealth of Pennsylvania.

26B: Photo by the author.

27A: Museum of the City of New York.

27B: From C. H. Winfield, *History of the County of Hudson*, 1874.

28A: Henry Francis du Pont Winterthur Museum.

28B: Photo by André Snow, courtesy the congregation of First Unitarian Church, Hingham, Massachusetts.

29A: From C. A. Place, "From Meeting House to Church in New England," *Old-Time New England*, 1922, courtesy The Society for the Preservation of New England Antiquities, Inc.

30: American Iron and Steel Institute.

31: State of Connecticut Development Commission.

32: Courtesy Yale University Press.

33A: From Walter M. Whitehill, *Boston, a Topographical History*, Cambridge, The Belknap Press of Harvard University Press, map prepared by Samuel C. Clough to illustrate his 'Remarks on the Compilation of the Boston Book of Possessions,' *Publications of the Colonial Society of Massachusetts*, XXVII, 1927-1930, 6-21.

33B: Courtesy The Bostonian Society, Old State House, Boston.

34: Courtesy George E. Haynes, Commonwealth of Pennsylvania.

35: Historical Society of Pennsylvania.

36A: From Thompson Westcott, *The Historic Mansions and Buildings of Philadelphia*, Philadelphia, 1877.

36B: Letitia Street house from T. T. Waterman, *Dwellings of Colonial America*, Chapel Hill, University of North Carolina Press, 1948; others from W. J. Murtagh, "The Philadelphia Row House," *JSAH*, 1961.

37A: New Jersey Department of Conservation and Economic Development.

37B: Photo by Ned Goode for HABS.

38: Philadelphia Museum of Art, photograph by A. J. Wyatt, Staff Photographer.

39A: Historical Society of Pennsylvania.

39B: Photo by Paul Galbreath, HABS.

39C: Commonwealth of Pennsylvania.

40A: Virginia Department of Conservation and Development.

40B: Photo by Nina Tracy Mann.

41: From Henry Chandlee Forman, *The Architecture of the Old South*, Cambridge, Harvard University Press, Copyright 1948 by The President and Fellows of Harvard College, reprinted by permission of the publishers.

42A: Photo by Frances Benjamin Johnston, HABS.

42B: Virginia Department of Conservation and Development.

43A: Painting by Sidney King, National Park Service.

44: Reconstruction by Henry Chandlee Forman, *The Architecture of the Old South*, Cambridge, Harvard University Press, Copyright 1948 by The President and Fellows of Harvard College, reprinted by permission of the publishers; plan from T. T. Waterman, *The Mansions of Virginia*, Chapel Hill, University of North Carolina Press, 1948.

45A: Colonial Williamsburg.

45B: Commonwealth of Pennsylvania.

45C: Photo by M. E. Warren, Maryland Department of Information.

45D: Massachusetts Department of Commerce.

46B: Art Reference Bureau, Inc., for Fratelli Alinari.

47: Courtesy Henry Francis du Pont Winterthur Museum.

48A: Courtesy of the Massachusetts Historical Society.

48B: Virginia Department of Conservation and Development.

49A: From J. Kip, *Britannia Illustrata*, 1707.

49B: From J. S. Ackerman, *The Architecture of Michelangelo*, London, A. Zwemmer Ltd., 1959.

50A: From Curtius-Adler, *Olympia*.

50B: Courtesy of The Walters Art Gallery, Baltimore.

50C: Louvre.

51: Courtesy, Henry Francis du Pont Winterthur Museum.

52A: Plan from T. T. Waterman, *The Mansions of Virginia*, Chapel Hill, University of North Carolina Press, 1948; north front from T. T. Waterman and J. A. Barrows, *Domestic Colonial Architecture of Tidewater Virginia*, New York, 1942.

52B: Virginia Department of Conservation and Development.

53: From James Gibbs, *Book of Architecture*, 1728.

54: Chamber of Commerce, Nashville, Tennessee.

55A: The Board of Regents, Gunston Hall, Lorton, Virginia.

55B: *White Pine Series*, XVI, 3.

56: From Thomas Chippendale's *Gentleman and Cabinet-Maker's Director*.

57A: The Board of Regents, Gunston Hall, Lorton, Virginia, and Virginia Chamber of Commerce, photo by Flournoy.

57B: Henry Francis du Pont Winterthur Museum.

58: The Mount Vernon Ladies' Association.

59B: Photo by R. L. Knudsen, courtesy Mrs. John N. Pearce.

60: From Robert Adam, *The Ruins of the Palace of Diocletian at Spalatro*, 1764.

61: Drawings from Moreton Marsh, *The Easy Expert in Collecting and Restoring American Antiques*, Philadelphia, J. B. Lippincott Company, 1959.

62: Courtesy of The Henry Ford Museum, Dearborn, Michigan.

63: Courtesy of The Henry Ford Museum, Dearborn, Michigan.

64A: State of Connecticut Development Commission.

64B: Massachusetts Department of Commerce.

Western New York.

95B: Michigan Historical Commission.

95C: Photo by Paul A. Moore, Tennessee Conservation Department.

95D: Mississippi Agricultural and Industrial Board, Jackson.

96: Courtesy of the Toledo Museum of Art, gift of Florence Scott Libbey, 1949.

97: Courtesy of Yale University Art Gallery, Mabel Brady Garvan Collection.

98: From *The Architectural Magazine*, 1835, reproduced in Louis Torres, "Samuel Thomson and the Old Custom House," *JSAH*, 1961.

99: The Metropolitan Museum of Art, gift of Mrs. R. W. Hyde, 1943.

100A: Courtesy K. W. Anderson, Old Whalers' Church.

100B: From Samuel Sloan, *Homestead Architecture*, 1867.

101A: Maine Department of Economic Development.

101B: Louisiana Development Commission.

101C: Information Service, Church of Jesus Christ of Latter-Day Saints.

102A: From *Putnam's Magazine*, 1853.

102B: From A. J. Downing, *Country Houses*, 1850.

102C: Photo by Marion D. Ross.

103A: From A. J. Downing, *A Treatise on . . . Landscape Gardening*, 1841.

103B: From *New York Illustrated News*, 1860.

104A: Sleepy Hollow Restorations, Inc.

104B: Maine Department of Economic Development.

105A: From Howard, *The Monumental City*, 1873.

105B: Courtesy of John Maass.

106A: Munson-Williams-Proctor Institute, Utica.

106B: Photo by H. Bagby, Virginia Department of Conservation and Development.

107: Courtesy John Maass, from *The Gingerbread Age*.

108A: Courtesy John Maass.

108B: From Samuel Sloan, *Homestead Architecture*, 1867.

109B: Photographic Unit, Philadelphia Department of Public Works.

110A: Photo by Phelps, Arkansas Publicity and Parks Commission.

111A: Page from *National Cyclopaedia of American Biography*, 1899.

111B: From the collection of the Detroit Institute of Arts, by permission.

112A and B: From W. M. Thayer, *Marvels of the New West*, 1887.

113: Courtesy of The Henry Ford Museum, Dearborn, Michigan.

114: Photo by the author.

115A: Drawing by Stanford White from *The New York Sketch Book of Architecture*, 1875.

115B: From *Harper's Magazine*, 1891.

115C: Carnegie Prints.

116A: Drawing by Stanford White from *The New York Sketch Book of Architecture*, 1875.

116B: Woburn Public Library, from R. H. Randall, Jr., *The Furniture of H. H. Richardson*, Museum of Fine Arts, Boston.

117A: Chicago Architectural Photo Co.

117B: From H. R. Hitchcock, *The Architecture of H. H. Richardson*, 2nd ed., New York, The Museum of Modern Art, 1961, by permission of Arthur Drexler, Director of Architecture and Design, The Museum of Modern Art.

118A: Rhode Island Development Council.

118B: The Cathedral Church of St. John the Divine.

118C: Vizcaya, Dade County Art Museum.

119B: West Virginia Industrial and Publicity Commission.

119C: New Mexico State Tourist Bureau.

120A: From the London *Graphic*, 1893.

120B: Coral Gables Chamber of Commerce.

121A: Photo by Carolyn Carter, Georgia Department of Commerce.

121B: KIDC (Kansas) Photo. (Kansas Industrial Development Commission)

122A: "Studies of Different Exterior Treatments . . . by Lawrence Buck," from H. V. Von Holst, *Modern American Homes*, Chicago, American Technical Society, 1914.

122B: Photo by Roy Flamm, from *Architectural Forum*.

123A: Carnegie Prints.

123B: Chicago Heritage Committee.

124A: From Esther McCoy, *Five California Architects*, New York, Reinhold, 1960, photographed by Marvin Rand.

124B: Chicago Heritage Committee.

124C: From Esther McCoy, *Five California Architects*, New York, Reinhold, 1960, photographed by Marvin Rand.

125A and B: Courtesy Security Bank & Trust Company of Owatonna, Minnesota.

126: Chicago Architectural Photo Co.

127A: From *The Craftsman*.

Indices

The following abbreviations are used as occasion warrants: hs, hss: house, houses; ch: church; bldg: building; cstxn: construction; cy: century; *qu*: quoted; vic: vicinity.

Figures in italics refer to illustrations.

INDEX A: PERSONAL NAMES

Aalto, Alvar, 450-1
Abramovitz, Max, 447, 454
Adam, Robert, 169f., *qu* 170; 251
Adam, William, 184, 232
Adams, Charles Francis, 321
Adams, Pres. John, *qu* 163; 282
Adams, Pres. John Quincy, *qu* 207; 321
Adams, Nehemiah, 208
Adler, Dankmar, 390, 391, 407
Affleck, Thomas, 198
Albers, Joseph, 432
Alden, John, 13
Alexander, Robert, *qu* 251
Allen, Frederick Lewis, *qu* 441
Allston, Washington, 294
Alsop, George, *qu* 76; 78
Ames, Oliver, 361
Amory, Cleveland, *qu* 341
Anderson, Joseph Horatio, 118, 181
Ariss, John, 181, 184, 226, 231, 232-3, 239
Armstrong, John, 191
Ash, Gilbert, 206
Ash, Thomas, 216
Astor family, 206
Astor, John Jacob, 35
Astor, Mrs. William, 368
Atwood, Charles G., 379
Austin, Henry, 298, 303, 318, 322, 328, later career, 332; 337

Bacon, Henry, 364, 369, 393
Badger, Daniel, 326, 327, 399, 400
Badlam, Stephen, 208
Baily, Rosalie F., *qu* 54
Banner, Peter, 270
Barnum, P. T., 304
Barry, Sir Charles, 303
Baudouine, Charles, 323, 346

Bayliss, Richard, 186
Beaumont, Dr. William, 35
Behrendt, Walter Curt, *qu* 407
Behrens, Peter, 416
Beissel, Johann Conrad, 86, 89
Bellendine, John, 233
Belluschi, Pietro, 432
Belmont, Oliver H. P., 368
Belter, John Henry, 323, 325
Bénard, Emile, 381, 392
Benjamin, Asher, 220, 236, career & books, 270; 272, 292, 322, 334
Bentley, William, *qu* 234
Berkeley, Bishop, *qu* 224-5
Berlage, Hendrik Petrus, 416, 442
Bernad, Bartholemew, 77
Berry, John, 278, 284
Biddle family, 206
Biddle, Nicholas, 272, 273, 280, 284
Bidermann, James, 211
Birch, William, 211
Bjerkoe, Ethel Hall, 223
Bjork, Pastor Erik, 17, 226
Black, G. Nixon, 354
Blake, Peter, *qu* 470
Blanchard, Joshua, 201
Blodget, Samuel, 262
Bock, Richard, 412
Bogardus, James, 304, 326, career, 400-401; 413
Boorstin, Daniel J., 13, *qu* 104-6; *qu* 171; 255
Booth, Elijah, 208
Boullée, Étienne-Louis, 252
Boyer, John, 48
Bradstreet, Mistress Anne, *qu* 90
Brady, Josiah, 311
Bragdon, Claude, 389
Braun, Hugh, *qu* 78

Breuer, Marcel, 432-3, 437, 443, 450, 455
Bridenbaugh, Carl, *qu* 107; 163
Briggs, Martin, *qu* 64
Broek, Wessel Wesselse ten, 50
Bronck, Leendert and Peter, 46f.
Brooks, H. Allen, 394
Brown family (R.I.), 207
Brown, A. Page, 392
Brown, David R., 401
Brown, Joseph, 192, 206-7
Brown, William S., 447
Bruyn, John Hendricks de, 47
Bryant, William Cullen, 294, 310
Bryant, William Jennings, 364, 417
Buck, Lawrence, 396, 397
Buckland, William, 153, 181, 184, 202, 231, 232-4, 239
Bucklin, James, 278
Buffon, George-Louis, Comte de, 474
Bulfinch, Charles, 119, 208, 212, 234, 236-7, 239, 257, 262, 270
Burnaby, Andrew, *qu* 13
Burnham, Daniel H., 378-380, 381, 382, 386, 389, 395, 396, 406, 458
Bunshaft, Gordon, 447, 453
Bunyan, John, *qu* 65-6
Burlington, Lord (Robt. Boyle), 148, 156
Burroughs, P. H., 181, 223
Buschor, Charles, 336, 338
Burwell, Carter, 187
Byrd, William, II, 142, 145, 148, 190
Byrnes, Joseph (?), 298

Cady, J. Cleveland, *qu* 48
Calder, Alexander, 333
Campbell, Colin, *qu* 156; 231

INDEX B: ARCHITECTURE

BY STATE (OR FOREIGN COUNTRY) AND TOWN

NORTH CAROLINA

OHIO

OKLAHOMA

OREGON

INDEX C: GENERAL

494

Icon Editions